CONTENTS

CW00494298

Legend for Club Stadium Plans

 Covered seating

Covered standing

Uncovered seating

Uncovered standing

 Disabled Facilities, wheelchairs access and viewing areas

Main entrances

Main exits

Legend for Clubs' 10-year League Record

 Premier Division/S.P.L.

 First Division

 Second Division

Third Division

 Hatched area indicates where the number of teams in the division has been fewer than 12 or 14 (see right).

Footnote to Each Club's 10-year Playing Record

The number of teams playing in each division of The Scottish Football League and The Scottish Premier League has altered on several occasions during the past ten seasons and in order to assist the reader, the following information explains the various formats in operation during the following period:-

SEASON	PREMIER DIVISION	FIRST DIVISION	SECOND DIVISION	THIRD DIVISION
1990/91	10	14	14	N/A
1991/92	12	12	14	N/A
1992/93	12	12	14	N/A
1993/94	12	12	14	N/A
1994/95	10	10	10	10
1995/96	10	10	10	10
1996/97	10	10	10	10
1997/98	10	10	10	10
	S.P.L.	S.F.L. FD	S.F.L. SD	S.F.L. TD
1998/99	10	10	10	10
1999/2000	10	10	10	10

A VERY WARM WELCOME

I am once again delighted to introduce all football fans to the 21st edition of The Scottish Football League Review.

As both my predecessors in office and myself have intimated in previous editions of the Review, this publication has acted as an extremely important vehicle of communication between the League, the media and supporters during the past two decades as well as being regarded as the most authoritative and comprehensive reference book published on Scottish football. Given the changes in The Scottish Football League since the formation of The Scottish Premier League, it has become more difficult to produce this book, however, the League Management Committee recognised the important contribution that this publication has played in not only promoting The Scottish Football League but also in providing an historical record of Scottish football and was unanimous in its view that this season's publication should go ahead as normal.

I am delighted that we have been able to attract a new sponsor for this season's Review in the form of the Nationwide Building Society. As followers of our national team will probably be aware, Nationwide have been associated with the Scotland squad for the past couple of seasons in its capacity as an official partner of The Scottish Football Association and during that period, they have enjoyed an excellent working relationship with our colleagues at the Association. I do hope that their decision to sponsor this prestigious publication will further strengthen their links with Scottish football and I would take this opportunity in extending our sincere thanks for their support. Unfortunately, the uncertainty that I mentioned earlier has slightly delayed the publication of this season's Review but hopefully, the end product is to your satisfaction and maintains the high standards set in previous editions.

We are also indebted to the support given by Bell's and you will note that we have included an article on the company that should provide an informative insight into the tremendous work and activities that have been undertaken by our League Championship sponsor during the past season. Indeed, I think that it would be appropriate at this juncture to reflect on the events that shaped and ultimately decided the various divisions of the Bell's Scottish Football League Championship during season 1999/2000. With The Scottish Premier League increasing its membership to twelve clubs this season, St. Mirren set out their stall in the First Division right at the outset maintaining their top position for most of the season and returned to the top flight of Scottish football after an absence of eight seasons. Dunfermline Athletic finished in second place and with Falkirk's ground not meeting the Membership Criteria of the SPL, there was no requirement for a "round robin" series of play-off matches resulting in the Pars also being automatically promoted to the SPL. With three automatic promotion places up for grabs in both the Second and Third Divisions to compensate for the loss of the aforementioned two clubs, Clyde, Alloa Athletic & Ross County dominated proceedings in the Second Division with the Bully Wee securing the Championship on the penultimate Saturday of the season. The final day drama was left to the Third Division with Queen's Park and Berwick Rangers contesting the Championship whilst Forfar Athletic and East Fife were the remaining contenders for the third promotion spot. On a day of ever changing fortune, drama and tension, the Spiders won their first Championship trophy since season 1980/81 whilst the Station Park club leap-frogged the men from Fife to return to the Second Division after a one year absence.

Last season saw the League Cup sponsored for the first time by CIS Insurance and the competition once again provided plenty of goals and excitement with Celtic securing their second success in the competition in three seasons, defeating Aberdeen 2-0 at The National Stadium, Hampden Park. The Dons also reached the Final of the Tennents Scottish Cup, but once again, had to act as bridesmaids, this time losing out to the other half of the Old Firm, Rangers, at the same venue by four goals to nil thereby securing the Ibrox club with the domestic "Double", having already won The Scottish Premier League title by an impressive 21 point margin. In the Bell's Challenge Cup Final, we witnessed one of the best matches of the season with Alloa Athletic and Inverness Caledonian Thistle serving up an eight goal thriller with the Wasps clinching their first ever major domestic cup trophy following a dramatic penalty shoot-out.

On the International front, the national team narrowly lost out in the Euro 2000 Play-Off matches to the "Auld Enemy" in two titanic matches and it certainly

was unusual for Scottish supporters to leave Wembley disappointed after recording a fine victory there. Everyone watching the action from Holland and Belgium during Euro 2000 could not help but have been impressed by the high level of skill shown by most of the countries competing not to mention the tremendous entertainment provided throughout. Hopefully, that tournament left an indelible mark on our managers, coaches and players as there is no doubt that we still trail behind a number of countries not only in Europe but elsewhere in the world with regard to the level of skill and technique shown by foreign players. Whilst The Scottish Football Association, The Scottish Football League and The Scottish Premier League are all working hard to provide a platform for the future well-being of our game, much of the responsibility lies with the clubs themselves, especially their attitude and commitment towards youth development.

The World Cup is without doubt the showpiece event of our sport and, of course, as I write this article, we have already started our qualifying campaign with a welcome away victory over Latvia. Qualification to the Finals of any major competition provides our game with a much needed boost not only for our national prestige but also financially as much of the profits gained from participating are reinvested in youth development by The Scottish Football Association. Accordingly, I am sure that I speak on behalf of all football fans in wishing Craig Brown and the players best wishes in their attempts to reach the Finals in 2002.

One of the most important issues facing football at the present time is the threat by the European Commission to abolish the transfer system that has been in place since football became organised over 100 years ago. As all supporters are aware, the Bosman decision back in 1995 altered the fabric of football not only in Scotland but throughout most of Europe and whilst the game has had to adapt during the past five years, the repercussions and dire consequences of "Bosman 2", as it has now been called, do not bear thinking about. At the time of going to print, FIFA, UEFA and all of the national associations and leagues are making representations to the European Commission on the importance of maintaining the current transfer system and it is still hoped that the Commission will recognise the arguments put forward by football with regard to the financial implications that abolishing the system would have on the football industry throughout Europe.

This season has seen two new clubs become members of The Scottish Football League, namely Elgin City and Peterhead, and I am certain that given time, they will prove to be major assets to this organisation

both on the field of play as well as the facilities that both clubs currently have at their respective stadiums. I have no doubts that they will both be trying to emulate the achievements of the previous "new boys" of this organisation, Inverness Caledonian Thistle and Ross County, who are this season both playing in the First Division and have excellent playing and spectator facilities, and I would take this opportunity in wishing both of our new clubs every success in their endeavours.

Of course, during the past few years, The Scottish Football League have received applications from a number of clubs in membership of not only The Highland Football League, but also the East of Scotland and South of Scotland Leagues. With that in mind, we felt that it would be prudent to incorporate in this publication some information on all of the clubs in membership of these Leagues particularly as they all have an important role to play in the overall development of our game. We do hope that this information, whilst not comprehensive, is helpful and useful to you during the course of the season and should you have any constructive comments, please let us know.

The preparation of the Review involves a tremendous amount of time and effort and I would like to thank the following:-

David C. Thomson (Editor); all of the staff at The Scottish Football League especially Jan Murdoch, Anton Fagan and Brian Jamieson; our member clubs; Alan Elliott; our contributors; the various sectors of the media for their assistance and co-operation; our sponsors, Nationwide Building Society; Creative Services and in particular, Dave Kelly and Emma Robinson; Programme Publications, especially Bill Cotton, Ron Vallance and Christine Green.

Finally, I do hope that the 2000/01 season provides Scottish football with plenty of excitement, entertainment and drama for all football fans.

ENJOY THE SEASON.

James Oliver,
President, The Scottish Football League

COVER PHOTOGRAPHS
Ross Caven and Paul Martin (Queen's Park) with the Bell's Third Division Trophy • Tommy Turner (St. Mirren) with the Bell's First Division Trophy • Craig Valentine (Alloa Athletic) with the Bell's Challenge Cup • Clyde F.C. players with the Bell's Second Division Trophy

Relishing the Challenge

At a time when most of the football talk concerns European Leagues and big name players with big name clubs and salaries to match, thousands of us are just happy to be involved in watching, and in my case, reporting on the action from The Scottish Football League and the other so called lower-Leagues. The menu may be *a la carte* at football's top table, but the bread and butter is still going down a treat in the Bell's Scottish Football League First, Second and Third Divisions.

Everyone involved there knows that the eventual medal winners will not be there for all to see almost from the kick-off. The drama tends rather to run all the way to the closing episodes and this term in the First Division it's going to be tougher still for those who want to join The Scottish Premier League with only one available promotion place. However, all of the 30 clubs have their own level of aspiration to success and will go through tests on wintry nights at the game's various outposts, and it is likely that the majority of the promotion and relegation issues will not be decided until the final Saturday of the season. No-one seems to mind. In fact, some relish the challenge, daunting though it can be for clubs limited in the buyers market and looking increasingly unlikely to be able to reap the benefits of "sell-on" transfers either if the European Commission has its way.

Terry Christie has been in the game as a player and manager for 40 years. He remains first and foremost a fan, though he has made the duffle coat his own trademark, steering Alloa Athletic, a part-time club playing out of a ground with the sort of Ochil Hills backdrop so beloved by Hollywood film folk, to the First Division.

He says: "I am just in love with the game of football, so I am happy to believe that our game is alive and well in general."

Nonetheless, although he wishes others would feel the same about the

patient, he does have one concern and that is the growing threat of part-time operations becoming more common and the continual drain of our talented players if not to totally foreign fields, then to areas outwith Scotland.

He said: "Nothing much has changed there. Sometimes it seems that because players are in the "lower Leagues" they won't be able to do a job at the highest level in their own country.

"I was manager of Meadowbank Thistle when we had a young lad called Darren Jackson. He didn't seem to be rated at the time, though he did enough for Newcastle United. And, of course, he went on to win more than 20 Scotland caps and has played for Dundee United, Hibernian, Celtic and Heart of Midlothian."

Darren Jackson

Terry Christie

Under Christie more recently, Martin Cameron was banging in the goals at Alloa. He was transferred to Bristol Rovers at the end of last season for a six figure sum, which was a welcome boost for the club's finances.

Other players plying their trade in England since last season include Alex Neil, a real prospect when thrown into the Airdrieonians team, and Brian Carrigan, a prolific goalscorer with Clyde who has become a regular in the Scotland Under-21 squad.

"The fact that they slipped through here and moved to England is, to my mind, ridiculous, a shocking indictment," Christie said.

It's not just the players who have enjoyed The Scottish Football League entrance to opportunity. Jim Jefferies has taken Heart of Midlothian into Europe, not to mention their Tennents Scottish Cup triumph in 1998, but learned his trade managing firstly Berwick Rangers and then Falkirk. Tom Hendrie was at Berwick Rangers and Alloa Athletic before giving up his full-time teaching post to be manager of St. Mirren, taking them out of the First Division into The Scottish Premier League as Champions. George Fairley, sparking a revival at East Stirlingshire, came through Junior football's managerial school and would surely settle for the same game fortune that was to come to another ex-Shire boss, Sir Alex Ferguson.

Christie, still a schoolmaster away from the Alloa set-up, said: "The skills that are there have to be nourished and that means we have to have more full-time football. That costs money and although we have two of the biggest clubs in Europe playing in Scotland, the cash they generate is not going into our game."

The Scottish Football League suits one player who, some would say, stepped down by joining First Division Falkirk from Kilmarnock. However, midfielder John Henry feels he is at least now playing in a more open arena.

"There are a lot of teams who are just scared to lose at the highest level," he said. "In the First Division and, I would imagine, in the Second and Third to some extent, you will see more open play.

"We just don't have the situation where, before the season's started, you know that two, maybe three, clubs are definitely not going to be relegated.

"That leaves the rest of them worrying about how their season's going to go. That same fear does not exist in The Scottish Football League, except perhaps where a club facing financial restraints might have to consider cutting back. But that scenario only arises because you have at least four or five clubs going all out for promotion from the first whistle. There are not four or five clubs going all out to win the SPL, at least not thinking they have a real chance of upsetting the odds.

"Don't get me wrong. I'm not criticising the clubs in that division and not saying First Division football is necessarily of a higher quality, just that if you want to see good, open games with attractive attacking football, it's the place to go.

"It's also the place for a youngster hoping to break through as a player. At Falkirk, we have a tight squad and don't have much choice when injuries pile up.

Tom Hendrie

But we have brought in youngsters, maybe earlier than any of us including them would have thought, but they are doing well and they are learning at the same time. You cannot say that always goes on at the top division clubs."

It is a valid point - Alan Combe of Dundee United was a learner firstly with Cowdenbeath in the Third Division and then with St. Mirren at First Division level, Aston Villa's Neil Tarrant at Ross County and Nottingham Forest's Chris Doig at Queen of the South - both Under-21 caps - have also been there. Further up the age scale, First Division football was good enough for Franck Sauzee, who arrived with a European Cup winners' medal in his luggage and has stayed on at Hibernian and is now skipper at Easter Road.

John Henry

Back at managerial level, Allan Maitland is proving to be a star pupil at Clyde. He describes The Scottish Football League as "a land of opportunity for guys like me." Formerly in charge of Maryhill Juniors on Glasgow's north side, Maitland and players from the Junior ranks were such good learners that within a couple of seasons, they had won the Second Division Championship and are hoping to not only consolidate their position but also aim for promotion to The Scottish Premier League.

Maitland says: "Both of these divisions are very competitive. But they also give people like me the chance to

Allan Maitland

see just how well we could manage at a level somewhere between the Juniors and the very top in Scotland."

He is quick to point out: "The players are not the only ones to have come through and learned, putting their lessons to good use. This has been a major opening for me, I just don't know where else I would have had the chance.

"Our lower divisions might not have the quality of some of the top twelve clubs. But where else are people going to go to see open, attacking play that is there virtually all the time?

"Even the three divisions within The Scottish Football League are different in their own ways.

"In the Second and Third Divisions, I believe you have to add a new quality to your portfolio and that is the ability to work hard and dig in.

"If and when your team reach the First Division, some of those attributes have to be remembered, while the skill level has to be increased too.

"It is all part of a learning process for us leading, I hope, to entertainment for the paying customers, the supporters."

As you can see therefore, the First, Second and Third Divisions have proved to be an extremely productive breeding ground for many skilful young players and aspiring managers to progress to the top level of our game. The entertainment level and drama on show is not too bad either.

GRAHAM SCOTT
(Evening Times)

5

Excelsior Stadium, Broomfield Park, Craigneuk Avenue, Airdrie, ML6 8QZ

CHAIRMAN

VICE-CHAIRMAN

DIRECTORS

ACTING SECRETARY
Mrs. Ethel Tappenden

MANAGER

ASSISTANT MANAGER

FIRST TEAM COACH

COACHES

RESERVE TEAM COACH

YOUTH TEAM COACHES

COMMERCIAL MANAGER
Morna Watkins (01236) 622000

CLUB DOCTOR
Brian Dunn, M.B.,CLB.,M.R.C.P.(UK)

STADIUM MANAGER
Alistair Cameron

GROUNDSMAN
John McGuire

FOOTBALL SAFETY OFFICERS' ASSOCIATION REPRESENTATIVE
Alistair Cameron (01236) 622000

MATCHDAY PROGRAMME EDITOR
John O'Brien (01236) 441017

TELEPHONES
Ground/Ticket Office/Information Service (01236) 622000
Fax (01236) 626002

E-MAIL & INTERNET ADDRESS
ac@airdrieonians.com

CLUB SHOP
The club shop is situated at the stadium.

OFFICIAL SUPPORTERS CLUB
c/o David Johnstone,
16 Deveron Street, Coatbridge
Tel (01236) 423812

TEAM CAPTAIN
Fabrice Moreau

SHIRT SPONSOR

KIT SUPPLIER
Printing Dimensions

Airdrieonians

LIST OF PLAYERS 2000-2001

SURNAME	FIRST NAME	MIDDLE NAME	DATE OF BIRTH	PLACE OF BIRTH	DATE OF SIGNING	HEIGHT FT INS	WEIGHT ST LBS	POS. ON PITCH	PREVIOUS CLUB
Aguilar	Mariano		13/04/71	Madrid	04/08/00	6 1.0	12 6	Def	C.D. Manchego
Alfonsolobez	Miguel		09/09/76	Zaragoza	04/08/00	6 0.0	11 2	Def	Zaragoza B
Armstrong	Paul	George	05/10/78	Dublin	15/08/00	5 11.0	11 0	Mid	Brighton & Hove Albion
Boyce	Scott	William	20/01/82	Glasgow	04/08/00	5 9.0	11 2	Def	Airdrieonians B.C.
Brady	Darren		04/11/81	Glasgow	04/08/00	5 10.0	11 0	Mid	Airdrieonians B.C.
Broto	Francisco	Javier S.	25/08/71	Barcelona	04/08/00	6 1.0	12 6	Gk	Malaga
Calderon	Antonio		02/06/67	Cadiz	04/08/00	6 0.0	11 8	Mid	Unio Esportiva Lleida
Capin Martino	Salvador		10/09/75	Gijon	04/08/00	5 9.0	11 0	Mid	Real Sporting De Gijon
Clark	Paul		09/03/80	Dundee	15/08/00	5 10.0	10 7	Mid	Dundee
Coulter	Robert	James	25/05/82	Rutherglen	08/08/00	6 3.0	12 0	Def	Airdrieonians B.C.
Easton	Stewart		10/10/81	Coatbridge	04/08/00	5 9.0	10 10	Mid	Airdrieonians B.C.
Elliott	John		04/07/80	Edinburgh	18/08/00	5 9.0	10 8	Fwd	Dundee
Evans	Gareth	John	14/01/67	Coventry	04/08/00	5 7.5	11 6	Fwd	Partick Thistle
Fernandez	David		20/01/76	Corvina	04/08/00	5 9.0	11 2	Fwd	Deportivo
Forrest	Edward	Alexander	17/12/78	Edinburgh	08/07/99	6 0.0	10 10	Def	Stirling Albion
McAlpine	Joseph		12/09/81	Glasgow	04/08/00	5 9.5	11 9	Mid	Airdrieonians B.C.
McCann	Henry	Austin	21/01/80	Clydebank	31/07/97	5 9.5	11 13	Def	Wolves B.C.
McGoogan	Christopher		03/04/82	Bellshill	29/08/00	5 7.0	9 11	Mid	Airdrieonians B.C.
McGovern	Steven		20/02/82	Glasgow	08/08/00	6 2.0	12 0	Gk	Campsie Black Watch U'21s
McKeown	Stephen	James	17/07/81	Rutherglen	11/09/00	5 9.0	11 0	Fwd	Airdrieonians B.C.
Moreau	Fabrice		07/10/67	Paris	04/08/00	5 9.0	11 0	Mid	C.D. Numancia
Pacifico	Matias	Daniel	25/10/74	Buenos Aires	01/09/00	6 4.0	14 7	Fwd	Deportivo Espanol
Prest	Martin	Hugo	30/11/78	Mar Del Plata	04/08/00	6 1.0	12 6	Fwd	Dundee
Sanjuan	Jesus	Garcia	22/08/71	Zaragoza	04/08/00	6 0.0	11 6	Mid	Cordoba
Struthers	William		04/12/81	Bellshill	29/08/00	6 1.0	11 7	Fwd	Airdrieonians B.C.
Taylor	Stuart		26/11/74	Glasgow	04/08/00	6 1.0	11 4	Mid	St. Mirren
Wilson	Stephen		28/01/82	Bellshill	04/08/00	6 1.0	12 10	Gk	Airdrieonians B.C.

Milestones

YEAR OF FORMATION: 1878
MOST CAPPED PLAYER: Jimmy Crapnell
NO. OF CAPS: 9
MOST LEAGUE POINTS IN A SEASON: 60 (Division 2 - Season 1973/74) (2 Points for a Win)
61 (First Division - Season 1994/95) (3 Points for a Win)
MOST LEAGUE GOALS SCORED BY A PLAYER IN A SEASON: Bert Yarnell (Season 1916/17)
NO. OF GOALS SCORED: 39
RECORD ATTENDANCE: 24,000 (-v- Heart of Midlothian - 8.3.1952 at Broomfield Park)
8,762 (-v- Celtic – 19.8.1998 at Excelsior Stadium)
RECORD VICTORY: 15-1 (-v- Dundee Wanderers – Division 2, 1.12.1894)
RECORD DEFEAT: 1-11 (-v- Hibernian - Division 1, 24.10.1959)

The Diamonds' ten year record

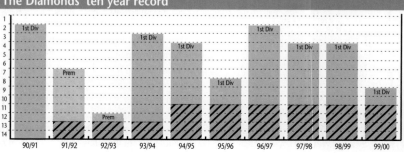

THE DIAMONDS' CLUB FACTFILE 1999/2000
RESULTS... APPEARANCES... SCORERS... ATTENDANCES...

Date	Venue	Opponents	Att.	Res	Thomson S.	Farrell G.	Jack P.	Conway F.	Forrest E.	Sandison J.	Johnston F.	Dick J.	Evans C.	McCormick S.	Moore A.	Stewart A.	Taylor S.	McGuire D.	Farrell D.	McCann H.A.	Ingram S.	McCleland J.	Easton S.	McKeown S.	Wallace R.	Thompson N.	McGinty B.	Gallacher P.	Holsgrove P.	Boyce S.	Neil A.	Wilson S.	Brady D.	Struthers W.	Creachen S.
Aug 7	A	Clydebank	425	2-0	1	2	3	4	5	6	7	8	9[1]	10[1]	11	12	14	15																	
14	H	Dunfermline Athletic	2,930	2-2	1	2	3	15	5	6	11	8	9	10[1]	7[1]				4	12															
21	A	Livingston	2,837	0-3	1	2	5	14		12	6	8		10	7	11			15	4	3	9													
28	H	Raith Rovers	1,493	1-4	1	2	3[1]	4	5		11	8	9	10	7	6	12	15		14															
Sep 4	A	St. Mirren	3,117	0-5	1	12	3	4	5	6	7	8			2	10	15		11	9	14														
11	A	Ayr United	1,888	0-2	1	2	6	4	5			8	11	9	7	3			12				10	15											
18	H	Falkirk	2,868	0-0	1	2	5		6	4	7	12	9		10	3			11				8		15										
25	A	Morton	1,126	2-0	1	2	5	12	6	4			7[1]	10	14	3	15		11[1]				8		9										
Oct 2	A	Inverness Cal. Th.	2,097	1-1	1	2		12		4	6	14	7[1]	10	15	3			5	11			8		9										
16	A	Dunfermline Athletic	3,964	0-0	1	2	4	14	6		8	7	10		3		15	5	12			9	11												
23	H	Clydebank	1,390	1-0	1	2	4		6			7	10		3		5	11	15			9[1]	8												
30	H	Ayr United	1,568	2-1	1	2	4		6	12		7[1]	10[1]	14	3			5	11			15	9	8											
Nov 6	A	Falkirk	2,644	0-2	1	2	4		6	12		7	10		3	15	5	11				14	9	8											
12	H	St. Mirren	3,209	0-2	1	2	4		6	8		7	15	11	3		5	10				14	9												
20	A	Raith Rovers	2,353	1-1		2	4		6	8	10	7	15	11[1]			5	3				14	9	1											
27	A	Inverness Cal. Th.	2,022	0-2		2	4	5		6	10	14	7		11			12	3			15	9	1	8										
Dec 7	H	Morton	1,135	1-0		2	4		6	3	8	9	7			14[1]		5	12			15	11	1	10										
14	A	Livingston	1,492	2-3			4		6	2	10	9	7[1]			14	15[1]	5	3				11	1	8										
18	A	Clydebank	307	1-1			3		4	6	10		9			11	7	5				12	14[1]			1	8	2							
27	A	Ayr United	2,004	0-5		2	3		4	6	12		7				11	5		14		8	9	15	1		10								
Jan 3	A	Falkirk	2,418	0-2			4		5	8			7			6	10	15		3	9		11	1		2	14								
8	A	St. Mirren	3,636	1-3	1		4		5	8			15	7	6	10			3	9		12	14			2	11[1]								
15	H	Raith Rovers	2,098	0-2		8	4		5				7	6	10	15			3	9			14			2	11								
22	A	Morton	1,201	0-4		7	4		5		8			14	6	11		12	3	15			10			2	9								
Feb 5	H	Inverness Cal. Th.	1,597	1-4	1				5		2	8	9		7	6			11	3		4	14[1]		15			10							
26	H	Dunfermline Athletic	2,304	1-2	1	2	5		12	6		8	7		10	4	9		3				14[1]				11								
Mar 4	A	Ayr United	1,038	0-0	1		4		5	6			8		7	2	10	15	3	14					9		11								
18	A	Falkirk	2,927	0-8	1		4		5	2		7		15	11	6	10		3			12	14		9		8								
25	A	Raith Rovers	2,056	0-2	1		6		5			8		11	4	3	10	14				2	15		9			12	7						
Apr 1	H	St. Mirren	2,909	0-1	1				6	12		10	8		11	4	9		5	3		2	15		14				7						
4	A	Livingston	1,473	2-3	1		12		5			4	8		11	6	10	15	3			2[1]	9		14				7[1]						
8	H	Morton	866	3-0					6		4	8		11	5	10	15		3			2	9		14[1]				7[2]	1	12				
15	A	Inverness Cal. Th.	1,404	5-1		5			6		10	8		7	4	15	12		3[1]			2	14		9[3]				11[1]	1					
22	H	Clydebank	797	0-0		5			12	6		8		7	4	10			3			2			9					11	1	14	15		
29	A	Dunfermline Athletic	4,378	0-1					3	6			7	4	10				8			2			9					11	1	12	15	5	
May 6	H	Livingston	1,493	0-2					15	6		9		3	4	10	7		8			2								11	1	12	14	5	
TOTAL FULL APPEARANCES					22	20	29	5	20	25	16	19	25	17	23	28	16	4	14	25	7		14	3	19	4	9	4	6	15	5				2
TOTAL SUB APPEARANCES						(1)	(1)	(5)	(3)	(2)	(3)	(3)		(4)	(4)	(1)	(6)	(14)	(2)	(4)	(5)	(1)	(3)	(15)	(1)	(6)			(1)	(1)		(4)	(3)	
TOTAL GOALS SCORED							1						4	4	2			1	1		2		1	3	5				5				

Small bold figures denote goalscorers.   † denotes opponent's own goal.

Excelsior Stadium

CAR PARK — CAR PARK

EAST STAND

CRAIGNEUK AVENUE

NORTH STAND — SOUTH STAND

PETERSBURN ROAD

CAR PARK

JACK DALZIEL STAND

CAR PARK — CAR PARK

CUMBERNAULD — A73 — NEWHOUSE

CAPACITY: 10,170 (All Seated)

PITCH DIMENSIONS: 115 yds x 74 yds

FACILITIES FOR DISABLED SUPPORTERS: Disabled facilities are provided in the North, East & South Stands

---

Team playing kits

How to get there

Excelsior Stadium can be reached by the following routes:

BUSES: Nos 260 or 15 from Airdrie Town Centre.

TRAINS: From Glasgow Queen Street to Airdrie there is a train every 30 minutes. From the Station beyond Airdrie, Drumgelloch, there is a train every 30 minutes, then a 10 minute walk to the stadium.

CARS: From Glasgow or Edinburgh leave the M8 at Newhouse junction (A73) and the stadium is 2 1/2 miles north of Newhouse. From Cumbernauld, the stadium is 6 miles south on the A73.

The Diamonds

email: info@sfl.scottishfootball.com • website: www.scottishfootball.com

Alloa Athletic

Recreation Park,
Clackmannan Road,
Alloa, FK10 1RY

CHAIRMAN
William J. McKie

VICE-CHAIRMAN
Ewen G. Cameron

DIRECTORS
Robert F. Hopkins,
Patrick Lawlor,
Ian Henderson &
David R. Murray

HONORARY DIRECTOR
Ronald J. Todd

HONORARY PRESIDENT
George Ormiston

SECRETARY
Ewen G. Cameron

MANAGER
Terry Christie

ASSISTANT MANAGER
Graeme Armstrong

YOUTH TEAM COACHES
Billy Morrison (U18)
Fred Stone (U14)
Ronnie McMillan (U13)

CLUB DOCTOR
Dr. Clarke Mullen

PHYSIOTHERAPIST
Jim Law

**FOOTBALL SAFETY OFFICERS'
ASSOCIATION REPRESENTATIVE**
Ian Love (01259) 722695

GROUNDSMAN
John Robertson

KIT MAN
Nicol Campbell

COMMERCIAL DIRECTOR
William J. McKie 01259 722695

MEDIA LIAISON OFFICER
Ewen G. Cameron
Bus. (01324) 612472
Home (01259) 722696

MATCHDAY PROGRAMME EDITOR
John Glencross
Bus. (01324) 622061
Home (01786) 817362

TELEPHONES
Ground (01259) 722695
Fax (01259) 210886
Sec. Bus. (01324) 612472
Sec. Home (01259) 722696

E-MAIL & INTERNET ADDRESS
fcadmin@alloaathletic.co.uk
www.alloaathletic.co.uk

CLUB SHOP
Situated adjacent to
Refreshment Kiosk

OFFICIAL SUPPORTERS CLUB
c/o Recreation Park,
Clackmannan Road,
Alloa, FK10 1RY

TEAM CAPTAIN
Craig Valentine

SHIRT SPONSOR
Alloa Advertiser

KIT SUPPLIER
Pendle

LIST OF PLAYERS 2000-2001

SURNAME	FIRST NAME	MIDDLE NAME	DATE OF BIRTH	PLACE OF BIRTH	DATE OF SIGNING	HEIGHT FT INS	WEIGHT ST LBS	POS. ON PITCH	PREVIOUS CLUB
Armstrong	Graeme	John	23/06/56	Edinburgh	15/07/00	5 9.0	10 12	Def	Stenhousemuir
Baird	James		25/05/83	Bangour	17/08/99	5 9.0	10 0	Gk	Tynecastle B.C.
Barnes	Steven		11/05/82	Glasgow	17/08/99	5 11.0	12 0	Def	Bo'ness, Linlithgow B.C.
Beaton	David	Robert	08/08/67	Bridge Of Allan	30/03/99	5 11.0	11 4	Def	Berwick Rangers
Brigain	Charles	Donald	15/10/80	Edinburgh	05/08/00	5 11.0	11 0	Fwd	Musselburgh Juniors
Brown	Scott		15/10/82	Broxburn	05/08/00	5 10.0	11 4	Mid	Broxburn Rangers
Cairns	Mark	Henry	25/09/69	Edinburgh	05/07/97	6 0.0	12 7	Gk	Partick Thistle
Cassidy	Neil		16/11/82	Glasgow	05/08/00	5 9.0	9 7	Def	Broxburn Rangers
Christie	Martin	Peter	07/11/71	Edinburgh	14/09/99	5 6.0	10 4	Mid	Spartans
Clark	Derek	Grant	24/08/76	Stirling	15/07/98	5 6.0	10 0	Mid	China Fortune
Conway	Francis	Joseph	29/12/69	Dundee	17/12/99	6 0.0	12 7	Def	Airdrieonians
Cowan	Mark		16/01/71	Edinburgh	17/06/96	6 0.0	12 7	Def	Berwick Rangers
Duncan	Ross		19/07/82	Kirkcaldy	13/07/99	5 10.0	10 8	Mid	Glenrothes Strollers U'21
Farrell	Gerard	James	14/06/75	Glasgow	10/03/00	5 8.0	10 10	Mid	Airdrieonians
Gardiner	Steven		06/04/82	Broxburn	24/08/00	6 2.0	12 0	Def	Broxburn Ibrox U'18
Gardner	Robert	Lee	11/07/70	Ayr	03/07/00	5 8.0	11 0	Mid	Clydebank
Hamilton	Ross		17/06/80	Falkirk	31/07/00	5 10.0	11 0	Fwd	Stenhousemuir
Huxford	Richard	John	25/07/69	Scunthorpe	04/08/00	6 0.0	12 2	Mid	Dunfermline Athletic
Irvine	William		28/12/63	Stirling	31/05/96	5 10.0	11 3	Mid/Fwd	Berwick Rangers
Jarvis	Craig		18/05/83	Stirling	13/07/99	5 9.0	9 0	Mid	Riverside Athletic
Kennedy	Andrew		12/05/81	Paisley	24/08/00	6 2.0	12 2	Gk	Clyde
Little	Ian	James	10/12/73	Edinburgh	03/02/00	5 8.0	10 7	Mid/Fwd	Livingston
McArthur	Stuart		06/02/82	Falkirk	28/08/99	5 11.0	11 0	Fwd	I.C.I. Grangemouth
McGarvie	Craig		19/05/83	Stirling	26/08/00	5 6.0	9 0	Mid	Dunfermline Athletic
McQueen	James		10/06/61	Edinburgh	21/08/00	6 3.0	13 10	Gk	Newtongrange Star
Rankin	Billy		06/04/84	Falkirk	24/08/00	5 8.0	10 0	Mid	Falkirk
Thomson	Steven	William	19/04/73	Glasgow	21/06/00	6 2.0	12 7	Def	Hamilton Academical
Todd	Jamie	Alexander	16/07/82	Stirling	17/08/99	5 10.0	11 5	Def	Sauchie B.C.
Valentine	Craig		16/07/70	Edinburgh	20/07/96	5 8.0	11 0	Def	Berwick Rangers
Watson	Gregg		21/09/70	Glasgow	25/07/00	5 9.5	10 9	Def	Stenhousemuir
Wilkinson	Kieran		30/05/83	Falkirk	24/08/00	5 11.0	10 0	Def	Raith Rovers
Wilson	Mark		31/07/74	Dechmont	04/01/97	5 11.0	10 8	Mid	Berwick Rangers
Wood	Christopher Alan		29/09/79	Stirling	05/07/00	5 10.0	12 6	Mid	Stirling Albion

Milestones

YEAR OF FORMATION: 1883
MOST CAPPED PLAYER: Jock Hepburn
NO. OF CAPS: 1
MOST LEAGUE POINTS IN A SEASON: 60 (Division 2 – Season 1921/22)(2 Points for a Win)
  76 (Third Division – Season 1997/98)(3 Points for a Win)
MOST LEAGUE GOALS SCORED BY A PLAYER IN A SEASON: William Crilley (Season 1921/22)
NO. OF GOALS SCORED: 49
RECORD ATTENDANCE: 13,000 (-v- Dunfermline Athletic – 26.2.1939)
RECORD VICTORY: 9-2 (-v- Forfar Athletic – Division 2, 18.3.1933)
RECORD DEFEAT: 0-10 (-v- Dundee – Division 2 and Third Lanark – League Cup)

The Wasps' ten year league record

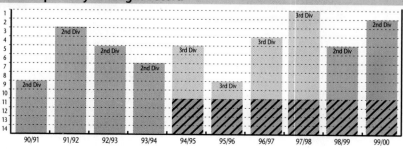

THE WASPS' CLUB FACTFILE 1999/2000
RESULTS... APPEARANCES... SCORERS... ATTENDANCES...

Nationwide

Date	Venue	Opponents	Att.	Res	Cairns M.	Boyle J.	Clark D.	McAenry P.	Beaton D.	Valentine C.	Wilson M.	McKechnie G.	Cameron M.	Irvine W.	Donaghy M.	Nelson M.	Menelaws D.	Clark G.	Sharp R.	Little I.	Christie M.	Bannerman S.	Cowan M.	Conway F.	Walker A.	Stewart C.	Farrell G.	Nish C.
Aug 7	A	Clyde	782	1-0	1	2	3	4	5	6	7	8	9	10¹	11	14												
14	H	Partick Thistle	1,178	1-0	1	2	3	4	5	6		8	9¹	10	11	7	12	14										
21	A	Queen of the South	1,204	1-1	1	2	3	4	5	6			12	9¹	10	11		8	14	7								
28	H	Hamilton Academical	689	1-1	1	2	12		5	6		8¹	9	10	11	4		14	3	7								
Sep 4	A	Arbroath	851	2-2	1	2¹	3		5	6			12	9¹	10	11	4	8		7								
11	H	Ross County	694	2-0	1	2	3		5	6			12	9	10¹	11	4	8	14	7¹								
18	A	Stirling Albion	1,196	1-0	1	2	3		5	6			9	10	11	4	14	8¹		7	15							
25	H	Stenhousemuir	675	1-4	1	2	3		5	6	8		9¹	10	4	11	15			7	14							
Oct 2	A	Stranraer	463	0-0	1	2			5	6	8		9	10		4			3	11	7							
16	A	Partick Thistle	1,801	2-2	1	14	3	4	5	6	2		9¹	10¹	8			15		7	11	12						
23	H	Clyde	814	1-0	1	2	3	4	5	6	12		9	10	8					7¹	11							
30	A	Ross County	2,415	0-1	1	2	3	4	5	6	11		9	10	14		15	8		7	12							
Nov 6	H	Stirling Albion	909	4-4			3	4	5	6	2		9¹	10¹	11		12¹	8¹		7	15				14			
9	H	Arbroath	637	0-0			3	4	5	6	2		9	10	14	11		8		7					4			
16	A	Hamilton Academical	401	2-1	1	2	3	4	5	6			9	10¹			12	8		7¹	11							
27	H	Stranraer	569	1-1	1	2	11		5	6	8		9¹	10	14		12	4	3	7								
Dec 4	H	Stenhousemuir	574	3-1	1		11		5	6	2		9²	10¹		4		3		7	8							
18	A	Clyde	1,071	0-0	1		3		5	6	2	7	9	10	15			8	12	11				4				
Jan 3	A	Stirling Albion	1,398	1-1	1	2	3		5	6	12	14	9	10	15					7¹	11			4	8			
Feb 26	H	Partick Thistle	1,847	1-1			3		5	6	15		9	10¹	11	2	8	12		7				4		1		
Mar 4	A	Queen of the South	1,018	1-2			3		5	6			9	10	14	2	15	12		11	7			4¹	8	1		
7	H	Stenhousemuir	492	3-1			3		5	6			9¹	10¹	11	2		8		7				4	14¹	1		
11	A	Ross County	2,331	4-3			3		5	6	11		9¹	10²	14		15	12¹		8	7			4		1	2	
14	H	Ross County	613	1-2		15			5	6	2		9	10	12		14	3		11¹				4		1		8
18	H	Stirling Albion	939	1-0			3		5	6	2		9¹	10	7		12	8		11				4		1		14
21	A	Stranraer	388	2-2			3¹		5	6	8		9	10¹	14		15	7		11				4		1	2	12
25	A	Hamilton Academical	508	0-0			3	5		6			9	10	7	2	15	12		11				4		1		8
28	A	Arbroath	567	0-2				2	5	6			9	10	7			8		11				4		1	3	12
Apr 1	A	Arbroath	631	2-1			3	5		6	2		9	10¹						11	7			4	8			12¹
4	H	Hamilton Academical	482	1-1			3	15	5	6			9¹	10	2	14				11	7			4	12	1		8¹
8	A	Stenhousemuir	495	1-2				4	5	6	2		9	10	3					11¹					12	1		8
11	H	Queen of the South	620	3-1			3	4	5	6	2		9¹	10	15			14		11	7					1		8²
15	H	Stranraer	605	4-0			3¹	4	5¹	6	2		9	10	14			11¹		7					12	1		8¹
22	H	Clyde	1,739	2-1			3	4	5	6			9¹	10¹	2					11	7					1	15	8
29	A	Partick Thistle	1,803	1-0			3	4	5	6			9¹	10			12			11	7					1	2	8
May 6		Queen of the South	714	†6-1	1								9²	10		14	15	12		11	7¹							8
TOTAL FULL APPEARANCES					20	14	31	17	34	36	19	4	35	36	15	9	6	18	5	29	20	1	1	13	4	16	4	9
TOTAL SUB APPEARANCES						(2)	(1)	(1)			(2)	(5)		(11)	(2)	(12)	(14)		(3)		(4)	(1)	(1)		(4)		(1)	(4)
TOTAL GOALS SCORED					1	2	2				1		16	13				1		4	7			1	1		3	5

Small bold figures denote goalscorers.   † denotes opponent's own goal.

Recreation Park

CLACKMANNAN ROAD

HILTON ROAD

CAPACITY: 3,100; Seated 400, Standing 2,700
PITCH DIMENSIONS: 110 yds x 75 yds
FACILITIES FOR DISABLED SUPPORTERS:
Accommodation for wheelchairs and invalid carriages in front of Stand. Disabled toilets are also available.

Team playing kits

How to get there

Recreation Park can be reached by the following routes:

TRAINS: The nearest railway station is Stirling, which is seven miles away. Fans would have to connect with an inter-linking bus service to reach the ground from here.

BUSES: There are three main services which stop outside the ground. These are the Dunfermline-Stirling, Stirling-Clackmannan and Falkirk-Alloa buses.

CARS: Car Parking is available in the car park adjacent to the ground and this can hold 175 vehicles.

The Wasps

email: info@sfl.scottishfootball.com • website: www.scottishfootball.com

Somerset Park, Tryfield Place, Ayr, KA8 9NB

CHAIRMAN
William J. Barr, O.B.E.,
C. Eng., F.I.C.E., F.C.I.O.B., F.I.Mgt

VICE-CHAIRMAN
Donald R. Cameron B.Sc.

DIRECTORS
George H. Smith,
John E. Eyley, B.A., ACMA,
Kenneth W. MacLeod, M.A.S.I. &
Roy G. Kennedy A.R.I.C.S.

COMPANY SECRETARY
John E. Eyley, B.A., ACMA

ADMINISTRATOR
Brian Caldwell

MANAGER
Gordon Dalziel

COACH
Iain Munro

YOUTH COACHES
I. Campbell Money,
Eric Morris (U18),
Sammy Conn (U15),
Peter Leonard (U14),
Lawrie Dinwoodie (U13),

CLUB DOCTOR
Dr. John A.M. Hannah, B.Sc (Hons)
M.B.Ch.B., M.R.C.G.P., D.R.C.O.G.

PHYSIOTHERAPIST
John Kerr, L.V.M.C. Inst. of H.T.

**FOOTBALL SAFETY OFFICERS'
ASSOCIATION REPRESENTATIVES**
Roy Kennedy & Jim Crombie

GROUNDSMAN
David Harkness

LOTTERY MANAGER
Andrew Downie

MATCHDAY PROGRAMME EDITOR
Brian Caldwell (01292) 263435

TELEPHONES
Ground/Ticket Office
(01292) 263435/6
Fax (01292) 281314
Information Line (09068) 121552

E-MAIL & INTERNET ADDRESS
info@ayr-united.co.uk
www.aufc.co.uk

CLUB SHOP
Ayr United Club Shop, Tryfield Place,
Ayr, KA8 9NB. (01292) 263435.
Open 8.30 a.m.-5.30 p.m. Mon-Fri
and 10.00 a.m.-3.00 p.m.
on all first team home matchdays.

OFFICIAL SUPPORTERS CLUB
c/o Ayr United F.C., Somerset Park,
Ayr, KA8 9NB

TEAM CAPTAIN
John Hughes

SHIRT SPONSOR
First Choice Playing Kit: Ayrshire Leader
Second Choice Playing Kit: Barr Steel

KIT SUPPLIER
TFG

LIST OF PLAYERS 2000-2001

SURNAME	FIRST NAME	MIDDLE NAME	DATE OF BIRTH	PLACE OF BIRTH	DATE OF SIGNING	HEIGHT FT INS	WEIGHT ST LBS	POS. ON PITCH	PREVIOUS CLUB
Annand	Edward		24/03/73	Glasgow	01/06/00	5 11.0	11 1	Fwd	Dundee
Armstrong	Gareth	James	31/08/80	Irvine	10/12/99	5 11.0	11 0	Fwd	Troon Juniors
Black	Aaron		19/12/83	Larne	06/09/00	6 0.0	11 10	Mid	Larne Youth
Bradford	John		15/12/79	Irvine	13/01/98	5 11.0	11 0	Fwd	Dalry Thistle
Bruce	Robert		20/02/82	Dumfries	09/05/00	5 9.0	10 7	Mid	Wigtown & Bladnoch
Burns	Gordon		02/12/78	Glasgow	19/01/00	6 1.0	13 10	Def/Mid	Troon Juniors
Campbell	Mark	Thomas	04/02/78	Irvine	26/02/99	6 0.0	10 12	Def	Stranraer
Chaplain	Scott		09/10/83	Bellshill	27/07/00	5 9.0	10 0	Mid	Rangers
Craig	David	William	11/06/69	Glasgow	16/06/98	6 2.0	13 0	Def	Hamilton Academical
Crilly	Mark		23/05/80	Glasgow	26/09/97	5 10.0	11 0	Mid	Gleniffer Thistle
Dodds	John		16/12/81	Edinburgh	01/10/99	6 3.0	12 11	Gk	Maybole Juniors
Duffy	Cornelius		05/06/67	Glasgow	01/07/99	6 1.0	13 5	Def/Mid	Dundee United
Duncan	Lee		23/01/83	Irvine	22/03/00	5 10.0	11 0	Mid	Maybole Juniors
Dunlop	Michael		05/11/82	Glasgow	13/09/00	6 1.0	11 8	Def	Kilmarnock
Ferry	Martin	Neil	18/04/83	Glasgow	30/06/00	6 0.0	12 0	Def	Ayr United Youth
Grady	James		14/03/71	Paisley	01/06/00	5 7.0	10 0	Fwd	Dundee
Hamilton	Brian		06/02/84	Glasgow	04/08/00	6 0.0	10 4	Gk	Ayr United B.C.
Hughes	John		09/09/64	Edinburgh	01/07/00	6 0.0	13 7	Def	Hibernian
Hurst	Glynn		17/01/76	Barnsley	23/03/98	5 9.0	11 0	Mid	Emley
Kean	Stewart		04/03/83	Irvine	15/01/00	5 9.0	10 0	Fwd	Craigmark J.F.C.
Love	Alan	Kenneth	01/04/83	Omagh	06/09/00	5 10.0	10 2	Mid	Dungannon Swifts
Lovering	Paul	James	25/11/75	Glasgow	24/05/00	5 10.0	11 1	Def	Hibernian
Lyle	William		14/04/84	Irvine	27/07/00	5 10.0	10 1	Def	S Form
McGinlay	Patrick	David	30/05/67	Glasgow	01/07/00	5 10.0	11 1	Mid	Hibernian
McKeown	John		21/04/81	Glasgow	23/10/99	6 2.0	12 5	Def	Maybole Juniors
McVeigh	Aidan		24/06/83	Portadown	26/05/00	5 11.0	11 7	Fwd	Glenavon
Nelson	Craig	Robert	28/05/71	Coatbridge	13/07/98	6 1.0	12 3	Gk	Falkirk
Pettigrew	Craig		08/04/84	Ayr	13/09/00	5 10.0	11 0	Fwd	S Form
Potter	Craig		18/09/84	Irvine	27/07/00	5 9.0	9 6	Def	S Form
Renwick	Michael		29/02/76	Edinburgh	01/06/00	5 9.0	11 6	Def	Hibernian
Reynolds	Michael		19/06/74	Huddersfield	11/12/98	5 5.0	10 7	Mid/Fwd	Emley
Rogers	David		25/08/75	Liverpool	23/06/99	6 2.0	10 7	Def	Dundee
Rovde	Marius		26/06/72	Trondheim	31/03/00	6 3.0	13 10	Gk	L.F. Honefoss
Scally	Neil		14/08/78	Paisley	16/02/98	5 11.0	12 0	Mid	Glenafton
Spence	John	David	04/06/84	Kilmarnock	15/08/00	5 9.0	10 8	Mid/Fwd	Ayr United B.C.
Stevenson	Craig		16/02/82	Dumfries	29/08/00	6 0.0	12 0	Def	Morton
Teale	Gary		21/07/78	Glasgow	02/10/98	6 0.0	11 4	Fwd	Clydebank
Wilson	Marvyn		01/12/73	Bellshill	06/07/99	5 7.5	10 0	Mid	Airdrieonians

Milestones

YEAR OF FORMATION: 1910
MOST CAPPED PLAYER: Jim Nisbett
NO. OF CAPS: 3
MOST LEAGUE POINTS IN A SEASON: 61 (Second Division – Season 1987/88)(2 Points for a Win)
77 (Second Division – Season 1996/97)(3 Points for a Win)
MOST LEAGUE GOALS SCORED BY A PLAYER IN A SEASON: Jimmy Smith (Season 1927/28)
NO. OF GOALS SCORED: 66
RECORD ATTENDANCE: 25,225 (-v- Rangers – 13.9.1969)
RECORD VICTORY: 11-1 (-v- Dumbarton – League Cup, 13.8.1952)
RECORD DEFEAT: 0-9 (-v- Rangers, Heart of Midlothian, Third Lanark – Division 1)

The Honest Men's ten year league record

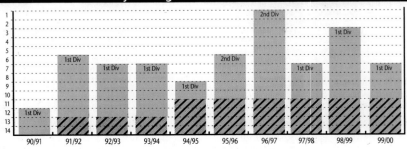

THE HONEST MEN'S CLUB FACTFILE 1999/2000
RESULTS... APPEARANCES... SCORERS... ATTENDANCES...

Date	Venue	Opponents	Att.	Res	Gill T.	Prenderville B.	Rogers D.	Duffy C.	Traynor J.	Lennon D.	Reynolds M.	Davies J.	Bradford J.	Bone A.	Lindau P.	Kelly R.	Bowman G.	Scally N.	Hurst G.	Teale G.	Robertson J.	Craig D.	Lyons A.	Wilson M.	Campbell M.	Jemson N.	Nelson C.	Shepherd P.	McMillan A.	Adams D.	Nolan J.	Knudsen J.	Grant R.	Hogg K.	Crilly M.	Tarrant N.	Hansen J.	McNally M.	Armstrong G.	Burns G.	Rowde M.	Dodds J.	Kean S.	McKeown J.	Duncan L.
Aug 7	A	St. Mirren	3,671	1-1	1	2	3	4	5	6	7	8	9	10¹	11	12	14	15																												
14	H	Livingston	2,533	1-2	1	2	5	4			6¹		14	8	9	12	11		3		7	10	15																							
21	A	Falkirk	2,938	1-2	1	2	3	4			14	10	8		9	15			7¹	12	5	6	11																							
28	H	Inverness Cal. Th.	2,157	1-0	1	15		4			14	8			9	12		3	7¹	10	2	6	11	5																							
Sep 4	A	Raith Rovers	2,368	1-5	1	12		4			8	14			9¹	15		3	7	10	2		11	6	5																						
11	H	Airdrieonians	1,888	2-0	1		3	4			12	14		9		15		8		7	2		11	6	5	10²																					
18	A	Clydebank	476	2-0	1		3	4			14	7		12		9		8		15	2		11	6	5¹	10¹																					
25	A	Dunfermline Athletic	4,044	1-2	1		3	4				14	8					11	7¹	9	2		12	6	5	10																					
Oct 2	H	Morton	2,186	3-0			3					12	8			15		11	7¹	9	4		6	5	10²	1	2																				
16	A	Livingston	2,332	1-4				4				8				15	3	7	12	2	6¹	14	11	5	10	1	9																				
23	A	St. Mirren	3,467	0-3				4				8	9				14	7	12	15	6	3	11	5	10	1	2																				
30	A	Airdrieonians	1,568	1-2	12								14				15	7	11	3	6		4	5¹	10	1	9	2	8																		
Nov 6	H	Clydebank	1,727	0-0	14	6					7						4		11	15		12		5	10	1	3	2	8	9																
14	H	Raith Rovers	1,769	0-1		3	4				14						6	7	9			11		5	10	1		2	8																		
27	A	Morton	1,168	0-0		3	5						12	9			4	8	7	15	6	11				14	2	10		1																
30	A	Inverness Cal. Th.	1,073	1-1		5					8	3				10	7	6		11					1	4	2			9¹																	
Dec 4	H	Dunfermline Athletic	2,113	0-3			8					14	3			10	7	6		11		12		1	4	2			9	5	15															
11	H	Falkirk	1,729	1-1		6					12						7	3	14	8	5	15		1	4	2			9			10	11¹													
18	A	St. Mirren	3,607	2-1		6					14	12					7	3	5	15	8			1	4	2			9¹			10¹	11													
27	H	Airdrieonians	2,004	5-0	15	6					12					9²	7	3	5	11	8¹		14	1	2							10¹	4¹													
Jan 3	A	Clydebank	901	2-0	3¹	6					15					9¹	7		5	12	8			1	4	2			12			10	11													
8	H	Raith Rovers	2,583	0-2	3	6										9	7	15	5	14	8			1	4	2			12			10	11													
22	A	Dunfermline Athletic	3,684	0-2	3	6					14					9	7	11	5		8			1	4	2			12			15	10													
Feb 5	H	Morton	1,985	3-2	3	6					11					9²	7	2	5		8			1	4	14			12			15	10¹													
12	A	Falkirk	2,729	0-1		6					7					9	12	3	5		8			1	15	2			10			14		11	4											
29	H	Livingston	1,765	0-1												7	3	5		8	6			1	9	12	11	10	4	2																
Mar 4	A	Airdrieonians	1,038	0-0		6					7					4		2	3		8	5			12					1	9		14	10	11		15									
7	A	Inverness Cal. Th.	1,274	1-3							11					8			6		14	5		10¹	2			1	9	3	7			4	12	15										
18	H	Clydebank	1,661	4-0		6					11			10		4	9³		7	3	5¹	12	8		1	2					14			15												
25	H	Inverness Cal. Th.	1,790	1-1		6								15		9	7	3		11	8¹	5		4	2					14	10		12			1										
Apr 1	A	Raith Rovers	1,841	0-1							11					14	4	9	7	3	6	12	8	5		1	2	15			10															
11	H	Dunfermline Athletic	1,798	0-2							11					7	9	12		6	3	8	5			2					14	10		4		1										
15	A	Morton	656	2-1							12					14	4	9²	7	2	6	11		5							15	8	10	3			1									
22	H	St. Mirren	4,678	1-2				5			12					8	9	7	3	6¹	11				4	2						10			1												
29	A	Livingston	5,729	1-3				6				10				4	7	3	5	11				2							9	8				12	14		1	15¹						
May 6	H	Falkirk	2,667	3-3				6			7		9¹			8			2	3		5									4¹	10¹				11			1	15	12	14				
TOTAL FULL APPEARANCES					8	3	13	28	1	3	14	7	6	5	2	5	15	25	26	26	23	16	23	19	9	18	20	16	4	1	4	9	2	5	15	8	5	1	4	2					
TOTAL SUB APPEARANCES						(2)	(3)				(4)		(13)	(1)	(3)	(11)	(1)	(1)	(3)				(6)	(5)		(9)	(1)			(3)	(2)	(3)		(4)	(2)	(8)		(3)	(2)	(2)		(2)	(1)	(1)
TOTAL GOALS SCORED							1				1		1	2					14				3		2	2	5		1					2	1	4		2						1

Small bold figures denote goalscorers. † denotes opponent's own goal.

Somerset Park

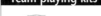

Team playing kits

CAPACITY: 10,243; Seated 1,549, Standing 8,694
PITCH DIMENSIONS: 110 yds x 72 yds
FACILITIES FOR DISABLED SUPPORTERS: Enclosure and toilet facilities for wheelchairs. Match commentary available for blind persons at all first team matches.

How to get there

Somerset Park can be reached by the following routes:

TRAINS: There is a half hourly train service from Glasgow to either Ayr or Newton-on-Ayr. The ground is a ten minute walk from both stations.

BUSES: There are several buses from the town centre with a frequency approximately every five minutes. Fans should board buses bound for Dalmilling, Whitletts or any bus passing Ayr Racecourse. The ground is only a ten minute walk from the town centre.

CARS: A77 to Ayr and at Whitletts Roundabout, take third exit (A719) and follow until after Ayr Racecourse. Take first right at traffic lights then left and right into Somerset Road. Car parking facilities are available at Craigie Road, Ayr Racecourse and also at Somerset Road car parks.

email: info@sfl.scottishfootball.com • website: www.scottishfootball.com

Clyde

LIST OF PLAYERS 2000-2001

SURNAME	FIRST NAME	MIDDLE NAME	DATE OF BIRTH	PLACE OF BIRTH	DATE OF SIGNING	HEIGHT FT INS	WEIGHT ST LBS	POS. ON PITCH	PREVIOUS CLUB
Aitken	Christopher	Ian	31/03/81	Glasgow	06/06/00	5 9.0	10 8	Mid	Morton
Barrett	John	Patrick	18/04/71	Glasgow	31/07/98	6 1.0	11 12	Fwd	Pollok
Bingham	Craig		22/12/79	Irvine	06/07/00	6 0.0	11 4	Mid	Irvine Meadow
Budinauckas	Kevin		16/09/74	Bellshill	17/05/00	5 10.0	11 0	Gk	Partick Thistle
Cannie	Philip		12/11/77	Greenock	28/06/00	6 0.0	12 0	Fwd	Port Glasgow
Convery	Steven		27/10/72	Glasgow	31/07/98	5 11.0	11 6	Fwd	Arthurlie
Cranmer	Craig	Hamilton	21/02/68	Johnstone	31/07/98	6 2.0	12 12	Def	Pollok
Dunn	David	Hugh	01/11/81	Bellshill	19/10/99	5 11.0	12 3	Mid	Motherwell
Grant	Allan		01/07/73	Glasgow	31/07/98	5 10.0	11 0	Fwd	Maryhill
Greer	Gordon		14/12/80	Glasgow	28/06/00	6 2.0	12 5	Def	Port Glasgow
Halliwell	Bryn	Steven	01/10/80	Epsom	12/06/00	6 1.0	12 10	Gk	Wimbledon
Hanley	Daniel		07/04/74	Blackpool	04/08/00	5 11.0	12 2	Gk	Pollok
Hay	Paul		14/11/80	Glasgow	16/07/97	5 8.0	10 4	Def/Mid	West Park B.C.
Henderson	Nicholas	Sinclair	08/02/69	Edinburgh	17/03/00	6 0.0	11 11	Mid	Hamilton Academical
Henry	James		07/07/75	Dundee	06/07/00	5 10.0	11 5	Mid	Lochee United
Kane	Andrew		07/12/76	Paisley	28/06/00	6 0.0	12 8	Fwd	Rutherglen Glencairn
Keogh	Patrick	Sebastian	07/05/76	Redlands	04/08/98	6 2.0	12 10	Def	Maryhill
McAuley	Sean		27/02/80	Edinburgh	03/08/00	5 9.0	10 0	Mid	Links United
McClay	Andrew		26/11/72	Glasgow	31/07/98	5 6.0	9 12	Mid	Maryhill
McCusker	Richard		24/08/70	Glasgow	31/07/98	6 0.0	12 0	Mid	Maryhill
McGhee	Graham	Henry	24/09/81	Coatbridge	02/10/97	6 1.0	12 6	Def	Albion Rovers B.C.
McIntyre	Gordon		15/11/74	Alexandria	31/07/98	6 2.0	12 4	Gk	Maryhill
McLaughlin	Mark		02/12/75	Greenock	28/07/99	6 2.0	13 5	Def	Arthurlie
McPherson	Craig		27/03/71	Greenock	06/07/00	5 9.0	11 3	Mid	Morton
Mitchell	Jamie		06/01/76	Glasgow	05/03/99	5 7.0	10 0	Mid	Scarborough
Murray	Darren	Thomas	25/01/74	Glasgow	31/07/98	6 1.0	11 10	Def	Maryhill
Ross	John	James	05/06/76	Falkirk	02/07/99	6 1.0	11 5	Mid	Camelon
Sellars	Barry	Michael	06/12/75	Arbroath	25/05/00	6 1.0	12 10	Mid	Arbroath
Sherry	Mark		11/01/82	Glasgow	22/05/00	5 10.0	11 6	Def	Morton
Smith	Bryan	James	21/08/70	Clydebank	31/07/98	5 10.0	11 0	Def	Petershill

Milestones

YEAR OF FORMATION: 1878
MOST CAPPED PLAYER: Tommy Ring
NO. OF CAPS: 12
MOST LEAGUE POINTS IN A SEASON: 64 (Division 2 – Season 1956/57) (2 Points for a Win)
65 (Second Division – Season 1999/2000) (3 Points for a Win)
MOST LEAGUE GOALS SCORED BY A PLAYER IN A SEASON: Bill Boyd (Season 1932/33)
NO. OF GOALS SCORED: 32
RECORD ATTENDANCE: 52,000 (-v- Rangers – 21.11.1908 - at Shawfield Stadium)
7,382 (-v- Celtic – 14.8.1996 (Coca-Cola Cup) - at Broadwood Stadium)
RECORD VICTORY: 11-1 (-v- Cowdenbeath – Division 2, 6.10.1951)
RECORD DEFEAT: 0-11 (-v- Dumbarton and Rangers, Scottish Cup)

The Bully Wee's ten year league record

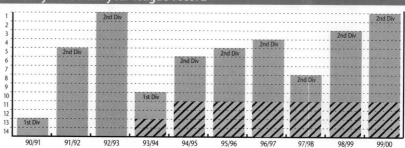

THE BULLY WEE'S CLUB FACTFILE 1999/2000
RESULTS... APPEARANCES... SCORERS... ATTENDANCES...

Date	Venue	Opponents	Att.	Res	Wylie D.	Farrell T.	Cranmer C.	Murray D.	Smith B.	Ross J.	Convery S.	McClay A.	McLauchlan M.	McCusker R.	McLaughlin M.	Carrigan B.	Keogh P.	Craib S.	Woods T.	Mitchell J.	Spittal J.I.	Grant A.	Barrett J.	McDonald I.	McIntyre G.	McGraw M.	Hay P.	Mols T.	Quinn C.	McGhee G.	Dunn C.	Henderson N.	Vickers S.
Aug 7	H	Alloa Athletic	782	0-1	1	2	3	4	5	6	7	8	9	10	11	12	14	15															
14	A	Arbroath	812	1-2	1		3	2	5	6	7		15	10	8	11^1	4	12	9	14													
21	H	Stranraer	722	0-0	1		3	2	5	8		7		12	10	6			9	14	4	11	15										
28	H	Stirling Albion	1,003	3-0	1			2	5	6		8	14^1		7^1	10^1			9	12	4	11	15	3									
Sep 4	A	Queen of the South	1,186	1-1	1	14	3	2	5	6		8	11		7	7	10^1		9	12	4	15											
11	H	Partick Thistle	2,356	2-0	1		12		5			8^1	11^1	14	3	7	10		9	6	4	15			1								
18	A	Ross County	2,840	0-2		12	3	2	5			8	11	10		7			9	6	4	15	14		1								
25	H	Hamilton Academical	865	2-1				2	5	12		8	14	10		7			9^1	6	4^1	11	15	3	1								
Oct 2	A	Stenhousemuir	715	3-1		12	3^1	2	5			8	11	10	6	7^1			9		4	15^1	14		1								
16	H	Arbroath	887	0-0				5	2	4		8	11	12	3	7	10		9	6			14		1								
23	A	Alloa Athletic	814	0-1				5	2	4		8	12	10	3	14	7			6		11					9	15					
30	H	Partick Thistle	2,617	0-0				5	2	4		8	14	10	3	7			15	11						6	9						
Nov 6	H	Ross County	894	3-1				5	2	4	6	8	7	10	3^1	9^2			14			11	12	15									
9	H	Queen of the South	640	3-0				5	2	4	6	8^1	7	10	3	9^1	14^1					11	12	15									
20	A	Stirling Albion	949	2-1				5	2	4	6	12	8	10	3^1	7^1	15		14			11	9										
27	H	Stenhousemuir	882	1-0				5	2	4	6	7	8	10	3^1				14	15	12	11	9										
Dec 4	A	Hamilton Academical	731	3-2				5	2	4	6	8		10	3	7	14^1		15			11^1	9^1				12						
18	A	Alloa Athletic	1,071	0-0				5	2	4	6			3	7	10			15	12		11											
27	A	Stranraer	649	2-2				5	2		8	15	14	10	3	7	4		9^1			11^1	12				6						
Jan 22	H	Hamilton Academical	975	1-0				5	2	4	6	7	8	15	12	9	10^1			14		11											
Feb 5	A	Stenhousemuir	690	4-3				5	4	2	15		14	8	3	7^1	10^1		9	6^1		11^1							12					
12	H	Stirling Albion	1,027	4-1					5				14^1	8	5	7^1	10^2		9	3		11	15						12					
26	A	Arbroath	880	1-1					2	4	6		8^1	3		10			9	7		11	14				15			5			
29	A	Partick Thistle	2,781	1-0					2	4	6	8			3	5^1	10		15	7		11	14				9	12					
Mar 7	A	Ross County	2,002	2-2					2	4	6	8		3	5	7	10^1		9			11					15^1	12					
14	A	Queen of the South	830	0-3					4	6	9		12		3	7	10		15	8		11						2		5	14		
18	H	Ross County	1,107	0-0				5	2	4	6	8	14		3	7	10					11					9					12	15
21	A	Partick Thistle	3,012	2-1				5		4	6	8			3^1	7^1	2					11	12									9	
25	H	Stirling Albion	1,102	6-3				5		4	6^1	8		10	3	7^1	2		11^3			15^1	12						12			9	
28	H	Stranraer	785	1-1				5		4	6	8		10	3	7^1	2		11	12							15					9	14
Apr 1	H	Queen of the South	1,101	3-1					2	4	6	8		10	3	7^2	5			11		9^1					14			12	15		
8	A	Hamilton Academical	851	1-1					2	4	6	8		10	3	7^1	5		15	11		9					14			12			
15	H	Stenhousemuir	1,033	7-0			5^1	2	4	6			10	3^1	7^2	8^1			11^2	14		12					9					15	
22	A	Alloa Athletic	1,739	1-2			5	2	4	6		10	3	7^1	5	11	14		12								9					15	
29	H	Arbroath	1,798	4-1			5^2	2	4	6	15	10^1	3	7	8^1	14	11		12								9						
May 6	A	Stranraer	471	1-2				2	4	6	15	10		7^1	8	3			11	9		12					5	14					
TOTAL FULL APPEARANCES				31	1	24	32	35	29	5	25	9	27	30	31	26		13	15	7	24	9	2	5	4	2	1	1	2		6	
TOTAL SUB APPEARANCES					(3)	(1)		(1)	(5)		(11)	(3)	(1)	(2)	(4)	(2)	(8)	(9)	(5)	(17)	(3)		(2)	(11)		(2)	(2)	(3)	(1)		(4)
TOTAL GOALS SCORED						4		1			2	3	2	6	18	11		3	4	1	7	2			1						

Small bold figures denote goalscorers. † denotes opponent's own goal.

Broadwood Stadium

CAR PARK CAR PARK
CAR PARK
CAR PARK CAR PARK

To A80 & A73

CAPACITY: 8,029 (All Seated)
PITCH DIMENSIONS: 112 yds x 76 yds
FACILITIES FOR DISABLED SUPPORTERS:
Facilities available in Home, Away and New Stands.

Team playing kits

How to get there

The following routes may be used to reach Broadwood Stadium:

BUSES: From Buchanan Street Bus Station in Glasgow, fans should board Bus No. 36A (Glasgow to Westfield).

TRAINS: There are regular trains from Queen Street Station, Glasgow to Croy Station. The Stadium is a 15 minute walk from here.

CARS: From Glasgow City Centre, fans should take the Stepps By-Pass joining the A80 towards Stirling. Take Broadwood turn-off to Stadium.

The Bully Wee

email: sfl@sfl.scottishfootball.co.uk • website: www.scottishfootball.com

FALKIRK

Brockville Park, Hope Street,
Falkirk, FK1 5AX

CHAIRMAN
W. Martin Ritchie

VICE-CHAIRMAN
Colin Liddell

DIRECTORS
Douglas J. McIntyre, Ann M. Joyce,
E. William Moffat, Colin McLachlan
& Campbell Christie, C.B.E.

SECRETARY
Alexander Blackwood

GENERAL MANAGER
Crawford B. Baptie

MANAGER
Alexander Totten

PLAYER/ASSISTANT MANAGER
Kevin McAllister

RESERVE TEAM COACH
Tony Docherty

U-18 YOUTH TEAM COACH
Ian McIntyre

U-16 YOUTH TEAM COACH
Bryan Purdie, Andy Dunleavie

U-15 YOUTH TEAM COACH
Joe McBride, Jim Clark

U-14 YOUTH TEAM COACH
Fraser Davidson, John Darian

U-13 YOUTH TEAM COACH
Larry Haggart, Gerard McCafferty

CLUB DOCTORS
Dr. R. Gillies Sinclair &
Dr. Ivan Brenkel F.R.C.S.

PHYSIOTHERAPIST
Alexander MacQueen

**COMMUNITY/YOUTH
DEVELOPMENT OFFICERS**
Tony Docherty, Ian McIntyre
& Fraser Cooper

COMMERCIAL MANAGER
Sarah Scott

**FOOTBALL SAFETY OFFICERS'
ASSOCIATION REPRESENTATIVE**
Willie Rankine (01764) 655017

CHIEF SCOUT
Bill Parker

GROUNDSMAN
James Dawson

MEDIA LIAISON OFFICER
Crawford Baptie (01324) 624121

MATCHDAY PROGRAMME EDITOR
Keith Hogg (01324) 554790

TELEPHONES
Ground/Commercial/
Ticket Office/Information Service
(01324) 624121 Fax (01324) 612418

E-MAIL & INTERNET ADDRESS
post@falkirkfc.co.uk
www.falkirkfc.co.uk
falkirk@lineone.net

CLUB SHOP
47 Glebe Street, Falkirk, FK1 1HX
Tel (01324) 639366
Open Mon. – Sat. 9.30 a.m. – 12 Noon
and 1.00 p.m. – 5.00 p.m.

OFFICIAL SUPPORTERS CLUB
Association of Falkirk F.C. Supporters
Clubs–Chairman: Gordon McFarlane
Tel (01324) 638104

TEAM CAPTAIN
David Nicholls

SHIRT SPONSOR
John R. Weir - Mercedes-Benz Dealer

KIT SUPPLIER
XARA

Falkirk

LIST OF PLAYERS 2000-2001

SURNAME	FIRST NAME	MIDDLE NAME	DATE OF BIRTH	PLACE OF BIRTH	DATE OF SIGNING	HEIGHT FT INS	WEIGHT ST LBS	POS. ON PITCH	PREVIOUS CLUB
Adams	Neil		22/07/83	Falkirk	07/07/00	5 10.0	11 4	Def	S Form
Boyle	Joseph		16/05/83	Glasgow	11/08/99	6 0.0	11 8	Mid	Westfield B.C.
Carswell	Allan		26/04/82	Falkirk	13/07/99	5 9.0	12 2	Def	S Form
Christie	Kevin		01/04/76	Aberdeen	28/04/99	6 1.0	12 3	Def	Motherwell
Creaney	Philip		12/02/83	Bellshill	09/06/00	5 11.5	11 5	Mid	S Form
Denham	Greig	Paterson	05/10/76	Glasgow	09/06/00	6 2.0	13 6	Def	Motherwell
Deuchar	Kenneth	Robert J.	06/07/80	Stirling	26/08/99	6 3.0	13 0	Fwd	Camelon Juniors
Gray	Alan		14/01/82	Glasgow	03/07/98	6 1.0	10 7	Def	Falkirk B.C.
Henry	John		31/12/71	Vale of Leven	09/09/99	5 10.0	11 0	Mid	Kilmarnock
Hill	Darren		03/12/81	Falkirk	07/07/98	6 1.0	10 6	Gk	Falkirk B.C.
Hogarth	Myles		30/03/75	Falkirk	31/03/99	6 2.5	11 11	Gk	Heart of Midlothian
Hutchison	Gareth	William McK.	04/06/72	Edinburgh	19/08/98	5 10.0	12 0	Fwd	Stenhousemuir
Kerr	Mark		02/03/82	Bellshill	03/07/98	5 11.5	10 11	Mid	Falkirk B.C.
Lawrie	Andrew		24/11/78	Galashiels	18/06/96	6 0.0	12 1	Def	Falkirk U'16s
McAllister	Kevin		08/11/62	Falkirk	08/01/97	5 5.0	11 0	Fwd	Hibernian
McDonald	Colin		10/04/74	Edinburgh	05/06/99	5 7.0	10 8	Fwd	Clydebank
McHendry	Mark		13/03/83	Glasgow	09/06/00	5 9.0	10 7	Def	S Form
McLean	Scott	Thomas	27/10/81	Glasgow	07/07/98	5 8.0	9 12	Def	Denny B.C.
McQuilken	James	Charles	03/10/74	Glasgow	14/07/98	5 9.0	10 7	Def	Hibernian
McStay	Garry		21/11/79	Bellshill	06/11/98	5 10.5	11 2	Mid	Bonnybridge Juniors
Miller	Lee		18/05/83	Lanark	09/06/00	6 2.0	11 7	Mid	S Form
Morris	Ian		28/08/81	Edinburgh	01/07/98	6 0.5	11 11	Fwd	Rangers B.C.
Nicholls	David	Clarkson	05/04/72	Bellshill	25/05/99	5 8.0	12 6	Mid	Clydebank
Nimmo	Scott		07/04/82	Falkirk	13/07/99	5 10.0	11 9	Mid	S Form
Pearson	Charles		21/04/82	Falkirk	03/07/98	5 7.5	10 5	Fwd	Falkirk B.C.
Porteous	Fraser		26/01/83	Edinburgh	22/08/00	6 0.0	10 6	Mid	Hibernian
Rennie	Steven		03/08/81	Stirling	19/07/97	6 2.0	10 12	Def	Hutchison Vale U'15s
Richardson	Grant		15/03/82	Glasgow	26/01/99	5 11.0	10 9	Mid	S Form
Roberts	Mark	Kingsley	29/10/75	Irvine	07/07/00	5 11.0	12 0	Fwd	Kilmarnock
Rodgers	Andrew		18/10/83	Falkirk	07/07/00	5 10.0	9 10	Fwd	S Form
Seaton	Andrew	Murray	16/09/77	Edinburgh	18/04/96	5 10.0	11 6	Def	Stoneyburn Juniors
Thomson	Mark		19/03/83	Glasgow	26/08/99	6 1.0	11 2	Def	Zeneca
Waddell	Richard		04/02/81	Falkirk	14/11/97	5 9.0	10 12	Fwd	Stenhousemuir

Milestones

YEAR OF FORMATION: 1876
MOST CAPPED PLAYER: Alex H. Parker
NO. OF CAPS: 14
MOST LEAGUE POINTS IN A SEASON: 66 (First Division – Season 1993/94)(2 Points for a Win) and 68 (First Division – Season 1999/2000)(3 Points for a Win)
MOST LEAGUE GOALS SCORED BY A PLAYER IN A SEASON: Evelyn Morrison (Season 1928/29)
NO. OF GOALS SCORED: 43
RECORD ATTENDANCE: 23,100 (-v- Celtic – 21.2.1953)
RECORD VICTORY: 12-1 (-v- Laurieston – Scottish Cup, 23.3.1893)
RECORD DEFEAT: 1-11 (-v- Airdrieonians – Division 1, 28.4.1951)

The Bairns' ten year league record

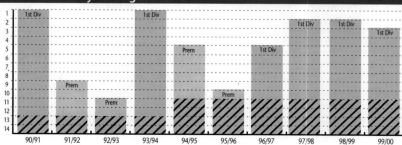

THE BAIRNS' CLUB FACTFILE 1999/2000
RESULTS... APPEARANCES... SCORERS... ATTENDANCES...

Date	Venue	Opponents	Att.	Res	Hogarth M.	Rennie S.	McQuillen J.	Lawrie A.	Sinclair D.	McKenzie S.	Hagen D.	McStay G.	Crabbe S.	McDonald C.	Hutchison G.	Kerr M.	Coyne T.	Moss D.	Nicholls D.	Seaton A.	Henry J.	McAllister K.	Morris I.	Pearson C.	Innes C.	Den Bieman I.	Christie K.	Waddell R.
Aug 7	H	Morton	2,945	2-4	1	2	3	4	5¹	6	7	8¹	9	10	11	14												
14	A	Inverness Cal. Th.	3,022	3-2	1	2	3	4	5	6	11		9¹	8¹	7¹		10	15										
21	H	Ayr United	2,938	2-1	1	2	3	4	5	8	11		9¹		15		7	10¹	6	12								
28	A	Dunfermline Athletic	6,520	1-1	1	12	3	4	5	2	11		9	15	7		8	10¹	6									
Sep 4	H	Clydebank	2,496	3-2	1	2	3	4	5		15		9	8²	7		11	10¹	6									
11	H	Livingston	3,326	0-2	1	2	3	4	5	6	11	14	9	7			15		10	12	8							
18	A	Airdrieonians	2,868	0-0	1		3	4	5	2	11		9	10	7		15		6		8							
25	H	St. Mirren	4,505	3-1	1		3	4	5	2	11		9	15	7	10¹			6	12	8²							
Oct 2	H	Raith Rovers	3,182	1-2	1	12		4	5	2			9¹	8	11	14	10		3	6	7	15						
16	A	Inverness Cal. Th.	2,403	0-2	1	14	3	4	5	2	11		9	8	10				6	12		7	15					
23	A	Morton	1,409	3-2	1			4	5	2	11	14	9¹	8²	7				6	3		10						
30	A	Livingston	3,482	1-1	1			4	5	2	15		9	10	11				6	3	8	7¹						
Nov 6	H	Airdrieonians	2,644	2-0	1		4	12	5	2	11¹		9¹	10	15				6	3	8	7						
14	A	Clydebank	500	3-0	1		4	14	5	2	11¹		9¹	10	15				6¹	3	8	7						
20	A	Dunfermline Athletic	4,263	1-3	1		4	12	5	2	11		9	10	7				6¹	3	8							
27	H	Raith Rovers	2,611	2-1	1		4	3		2	11¹		9¹	10	15				6	14	8	7				5		
Dec 4	H	St. Mirren	4,980	1-2	1		3	4		2	11		9	10	7	14			6¹	12	8					5		
11	H	Ayr United	1,729	1-1	1		3	4	5	2	11		9	10					6¹	12	8	7						
18	H	Morton	2,015	2-1	1		10	4	5	2	11¹	15¹	9	7					6	3	8	14						
27	H	Livingston	3,109	2-3	1		3	4	5	2	11	14	9	10	15				6²	12	8	7						
Jan 3	A	Airdrieonians	2,418	2-0	1		3	2¹		7	11		9	8	15				6¹			10				14	4	5
8	H	Clydebank	2,119	4-0	1		3	2	14	7	11¹		9¹	8¹	15				6¹	12		10					4	5
15	A	Dunfermline Athletic	7,233	2-2	1		3	2		7¹	11		9	8	15				6			10					4¹	5
22	H	St. Mirren	4,746	2-0	1		3	2		7	11			8	9				6			10¹					4	5¹
Feb 5	A	Raith Rovers	4,140	1-0	1		3	2		7	11		8	9¹	15				6			10					4	5
12	A	Ayr United	2,729	1-0	1		3	2¹		7	11		9	8					6			10					4	5
26	A	Inverness Cal. Th.	2,727	3-0	1		3	2		7	11		9²	15	10¹				6	8							4	5
Mar 4	A	Livingston	4,055	1-0	1		3	2	14	7	11		9	15	10				6¹	8							4	5
18	A	Airdrieonians	2,927	8-0	1		3	2¹	14	8	11		9²	10¹					6²	12		7¹	15¹				4	5
25	H	Dunfermline Athletic	5,242	1-1	1		3	2		8	11		9	10					6			7	15				4	5¹
Apr 2	A	Clydebank	727	1-0	1		3	2		8	11¹		9	10					6			7	15				4	5
8	H	St. Mirren	6,742	0-1	1		3	2		8	11		9	10					6			7	15				4	5
15	H	Raith Rovers	4,686	1-0	1		3	2¹		8	11		9	10	7				6				15				4	5
22	A	Morton	1,037	2-0	1		3	2	5	8	11		9	10	7¹				6				15¹				4	
29	H	Inverness Cal. Th.	4,449	2-2	1	12¹	2	5		8	11		9¹	10					6	14	3	7	15				4	
May 6	A	Ayr United	2,667	3-3	1	5	12	2		8	11		9¹	10	14		7¹		6¹	3		15					4	
TOTAL FULL APPEARANCES					36	10	28	33	19	34	33	2	34	26	23	2	6	3	32	9	21	6	8			2	15	14
TOTAL SUB APPEARANCES						(3)	(3)	(2)	(3)	(2)		(4)		(4)	(10)	(5)	(2)	(1)	(1)	(10)		(3)	(7)	(1)				(1)
TOTAL GOALS SCORED							1	4	1	1	6	2	14	6	5	1	1	3	12		3	2	2				1	2

Small bold figures denote goalscorers.   † denotes opponent's own goal.

Brockville Park

WATSON STREET — HOPE STREET — COOPERAGE LANE

CAPACITY: 7,576; Seated 1,700 Standing 5,876
PITCH DIMENSIONS: 110 yds x 71 yds
FACILITIES FOR DISABLED SUPPORTERS:
Disabled Enclosure opposite Main Stand – takes seven disabled fans in wheelchairs plus one helper each.

Team playing kits

How to get there

Brockville Park can be reached by the following routes:

TRAINS: The main Edinburgh-Glasgow railway line passes by the ground and passengers can alight at Grahamston Station. They will then have a walk of 100 yards to the ground.

BUSES: All buses departing from the city centre pass by Brockville.

CARS: Car parking facilities are available in the Meeks Road car park for coaches and cars and also in a local shopping car park which can hold 500 cars. Supporters coaches and cars will be directed to the appropriate parking area by the police on duty.

Inverness Caledonian Thistle

Caledonian Stadium, East Longman,
Inverness, IV1 1FF
CHAIRMAN
David Sutherland
VICE-CHAIRMAN
Kenneth A. Thomson
DIRECTORS
Roy McLennan, Kenneth Mackie,
Ian MacDonald, Graham Bennett
& Alistair MacKenzie
DIRECTOR OF MANAGEMENT COMMITTEE
Alistair MacKenzie
HON. LIFE PRESIDENT
John S. McDonald
HON. LIFE VICE-PRESIDENT
Norman H. Miller
SECRETARY
James Falconer
CHIEF EXECUTIVE
Catrina Bisset
(01463) 222880
MANAGER
Steven W. Paterson
ASSISTANT MANAGER
Duncan Shearer
RESERVE TEAM COACH
John Docherty
DIRECTOR OF YOUTH DEVELOPMENT
James Jarvie
YOUTH DEVELOPMENT CO-ORDINATOR
Jack Sutherland
YOUTH DEVELOPMENT COACHES
John Beaton, Roddie Davidson,
Alan Johnstone, Gary Davidson,
Joe MacMillan & Graeme Thomson
U-16 YOUTH TEAM COACH
John Beaton
U-14 YOUTH TEAM COACH
Roddie Davidson
COMMUNITY COACH
Michael Teasdale
CLUB DOCTOR
Dr. John N. MacAskill
PHYSIOTHERAPIST
Emily Goodlad
ASSISTANT PHYSIOTHERAPIST
Ian Manning
COMMERCIAL MANAGER
Gary Thompson
CLUB CHAPLAIN
Rev. Arthur Fraser
**FOOTBALL SAFETY OFFICERS'
ASSOCIATION REPRESENTATIVE**
John Sutherland, M.B.E.
GROUNDSMAN/KIT MAN
Tommy Cumming
MEDIA LIAISON OFFICER
Ken Thomson (01343) 220550
MATCHDAY PROGRAME EDITOR
Bryan Munro (01463) 230721
TELEPHONES
Ground (01463) 222880
Fax (01463) 715816
Sec. Home (01463) 792358
Sec. Bus. (01463) 724484
Sec. Mobile (07881) 770207
E-MAIL & INTERNET ADDRESS
caley-thistle.freeserve.co.uk
CLUB SHOP
Situated at Stadium. Open Mon-Fri
9.00 a.m. to 5.00 p.m. and Sat on
home match days only
OFFICIAL SUPPORTERS CLUB
Secretary, Caledonian Stadium,
East Longman, Inverness, IV1 1FF
TEAM CAPTAIN
Bobby Mann
SHIRT SPONSOR
SCOTRAIL
KIT SUPPLIER
ERREA

LIST OF PLAYERS 2000-2001

SURNAME	FIRST NAME	MIDDLE NAME	DATE OF BIRTH	PLACE OF BIRTH	DATE OF SIGNING	HEIGHT FT INS	WEIGHT ST LBS	POS. ON PITCH	PREVIOUS CLUB
Allan	Andrew	Joseph	05/11/80	Inverness	03/12/97	6 1.0	12 7	Def/Mid	S Form
Bagan	David		26/04/77	Irvine	20/06/00	5 8.0	10 7	Mid	Kilmarnock
Bavidge	Martin		30/04/80	Aberdeen	24/07/99	6 1.0	13 0	Fwd	Forres Mechanics
Byers	Kevin		23/08/79	Kirkcaldy	09/08/99	5 10.0	9 2	Mid	Raith Rovers
Calder	James	Evan	29/07/60	Grantown-on-Spey	29/06/94	5 11.0	13 4	Gk	Inverness Thistle
Calder	Niall		03/09/84	Inverness	13/09/00	5 8.0	10 0	Mid	S Form
Christie	Charles		30/03/66	Inverness	05/08/94	5 8.5	11 4	Mid/Fwd	Caledonian
Craig	David	Alexander MacL.	22/01/80	Inverness	03/02/00	5 10.0	11 7	Fwd	Inv. Caledonian Th. Youth
Farquhar	Gary	Robert	23/02/71	Wick	26/03/99	5 7.0	11 4	Mid	St. Johnstone
Fridge	Leslie	Francis	27/08/68	Inverness	23/05/97	5 11.0	12 0	Gk	Dundalk
Glancy	Martin	Paul	24/03/76	Glasgow	18/02/99	5 8.0	10 0	Fwd	Dumbarton
Golabek	Stuart	William	05/11/74	Inverness	27/05/99	5 10.0	11 0	Def	Ross County
Hastings	Richard	Corey	18/05/77	Prince George, B.C.	19/07/95	6 0.0	11 8	Def	S Form
Hind	David	Scott	15/02/82	Inverness	24/08/98	6 0.0	11 0	Def/Mid	S Form
Low	Anthony	Kevin	18/08/83	Glasgow	13/09/00	5 8.0	10 4	Mid/Fwd	Form D U-16
MacDonald	Neil		08/01/83	Isle of Lewis	03/02/00	5 8.0	10 5	Fwd	Fort William
Mann	Robert	Alexander	11/01/74	Dundee	05/02/99	6 3.0	14 7	Def	Forfar Athletic
McBain	Roy	Adam	07/11/74	Aberdeen	04/08/00	5 11.0	11 5	Fwd	Ross County
Munro	Grant	John	15/09/80	Inverness	21/02/00	6 0.0	12 7	Def	S Form
Robson	Barry	Gordon G.	07/11/78	Aberdeen	15/10/97	5 11.0	12 0	Mid/Fwd	Rangers
Sheerin	Paul	George	28/08/74	Edinburgh	27/01/98	5 10.0	12 4	Mid	Alloa Athletic
Stewart	Graeme		02/04/82	Aberdeen	21/02/00	6 0.0	10 5	Mid	Lewis United
Stewart	Iain	Angus	23/10/69	Dundee	09/06/95	5 7.0	10 0	Fwd	Lossiemouth
Teasdale	Michael	Joseph	28/07/69	Elgin	08/12/95	6 0.0	13 0	Def	Dundee
Tokely	Ross	Norman	08/03/79	Aberdeen	03/06/96	6 3.0	13 6	Def/Mid	Huntly
Wyness	Dennis	Middleton	22/03/77	Aberdeen	14/01/00	5 10.5	12 7	Mid/Fwd	Aberdeen
Xausa	Davide	Antonio	10/03/76	Vancouver	10/09/99	6 0.0	12 10	Fwd	Dordrecht 90

Milestones

YEAR OF FORMATION: 1994
MOST LEAGUE POINTS IN A SEASON: 76 (Third Division – Season 1996/97) (3 Points for a Win)
MOST LEAGUE GOALS SCORED BY A PLAYER IN A SEASON: Iain Stewart (Season 1996/97)
NO. OF GOALS SCORED: 27
RECORD ATTENDANCE: 4,931 (-v- Ross County – 23.1.1996 - at Telford Street Park)
  6,290 (-v- Aberdeen – 20.2.2000 - Scottish Cup - at Caledonian Stadium)
RECORD VICTORY: 8-1 (-v- Annan Athletic – Scottish Cup, 24.1.1998)
RECORD DEFEAT: 1-5 (-v- Morton – First Division, 12.11.1999)
  (-v- Airdrieonians – First Division, 15.4.2000)

Caley Thistle's ten year league record

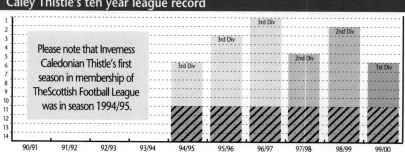

Please note that Inverness Caledonian Thistle's first season in membership of The Scottish Football League was in season 1994/95.

Nationwide

Date	Venue	Opponents	Att.	Res	Fridge L.	Tokely R.	Golabek S.	Teasdale M.	Mann R.	McCulloch M.	Wilson B.	Stewart I.	McLean S.	Christie C.	Sheerin P.	Glancy M.	Robson B.	Allan A.	Hastings R.	Shearer D.	Bavidge M.	Byers K.	Xausa D.	Wyness D.	Calder J.	Hind D.	Munro G.	Craig D.	MacDonald N.	Stewart G.
Aug 7	A	Dunfermline Athletic	4,677	0-4	1	2	3	4	5	6	7	8	9	10	11	12	14	15												
14	H	Falkirk	3,022	2-3	1	2[1]	3	7	5	6		8	9	10	11[1]	14				4	15									
21	A	St. Mirren	3,040	2-3	1	2	3	7[1]	5	6				12	10	11[1]			9	4	8	14								
28	A	Ayr United	2,157	0-1	1		11	4	5	2	14	9	8	10	6				3	12	7									
Sep 4	H	Morton	2,414	1-1	1	2		4	5	6				10	11	8[1]			3	9	7									
11	H	Clydebank	1,697	1-0	1	2		4	5	6	15			10	11[1]	12			3	9	7	8								
18	A	Livingston	2,584	2-2	1	2	15	4	5	6	7			10	11[1]	8			3	9[1]	14									
25	H	Raith Rovers	2,961	0-2	1	2		4	5	6	7	15		10	8	12	11		3	9	14									
Oct 2	H	Airdrieonians	2,097	1-1	1	2	15	4	5		7	8		10	11	12[1]			3	14	6		9							
16	A	Falkirk	2,403	2-0	1	2	11	4	5		7		14[1]	6	8				3	12	10		9[1]							
23	H	Dunfermline Athletic	3,006	1-1	1	2	11	4	5		7	12	14	6	8				3	15[1]	10		9							
30	A	Clydebank	184	3-0	1	2	11	4[1]	5		7[1]	12	14	6[1]	8				3	15	10		9							
Nov 6	H	Livingston	2,474	2-0	1	2	11[1]	4	5		7	12[1]	10	6	8				3		14		9							
12	A	Morton	812	1-5	1	2[1]	11	4	5		7	15	10	6	8				3	14	12		9							
27	H	Airdrieonians	2,022	2-0	1	2	11	12	4	5	7[1]			10	6				3	9	15	8[1]	14							
30	H	Ayr United	1,073	1-1	1	2	11	12	4	5	7			10[1]	6				3	9	15	8	14							
Dec 4	A	Raith Rovers	1,971	2-4	1	2	11	12	4	5	7			15	6[1]				3	9[1]	10	8	14							
11	H	St. Mirren	2,893	1-1		11		2	4	5	7[1]			10	6	14			3		8	9			1					
18	A	Dunfermline Athletic	3,775	0-1		11	3	2	4	7				10	6	12			5	15	8	9			1					
27	H	Clydebank	1,640	4-1		11	3	2	4	7	9[2]			10	6[2]	15			5	14	12	8			1					
Jan 3	A	Livingston	2,656	1-1		11	3	2	4	7	9[1]			10	6				5	14	8				1					
8	H	Morton	1,524	6-2		11[1]	3	2	4	5	9[2]			10	6[1]					8[1]	7[1]				1	14				
22	H	Raith Rovers	2,302	1-1		2	3	4			9			10	6	14[1]			5	11	7	8	12		1					
Feb 5	A	Airdrieonians	1,597	4-1		7	3	2	4		9[1]			10	6[1]	15			5	14	12	8[1]	11[1]		1					
12	A	St. Mirren	3,742	0-2		7	3	2	4		9			6	12				5	8	10		11		1	14	5			
26	H	Falkirk	2,727	0-3		7	3	2	4	8	9			12	6	15			5	14	10		11		1		5			
Mar 4	A	Clydebank	168	1-0	1	2	3	4	8		7				6				5	11	10	9	12[1]					15		
7	A	Ayr United	1,274	3-1	1	2	3	4	8		7[1]				6[1]				5	14	9[1]	10					15	11		
18	H	Livingston	2,206	4-1	1	2	3	5	4		7				6					14	10	9[3]	8[1]					11		
25	H	Ayr United	1,790	1-1	1	2	3	5	4		7[1]				6					12	10	9	8					11		
Apr 1	A	Morton	567	2-0	1	2	3	5	4		7			11	6					10	9[1]	8[1]						14		
8	A	Raith Rovers	2,538	0-2	1			12	4	2	7			6	5					10	9	8					3	11		
15	H	Airdrieonians	1,404	1-5	1		3	4	2	7				12	6				5	10	9	8[1]				14		11	15	
22	H	Dunfermline Athletic	2,677	1-2	1		3	4	5	7				12	6					14	10	9[1]	8				2	11		
29	A	Falkirk	4,449	2-2	1		3	4	5	7[1]				10	6					11	9[1]	8					2			
May 6	H	St. Mirren	3,218	5-0	1		3	4	2[2]	7[1]				10	6				5	15[1]	11	9[1]	8						12	14
TOTAL FULL APPEARANCES					27	30	29	23	27	35	30	3	4	22	32	6	3	4	28	12	21	19	21	9	2	3	6			
TOTAL SUB APPEARANCES						(2)		(4)			(2)	(7)	(6)		(12)	(1)	(1)		(1)	(15)	(10)		(5)		(3)	(1)	(3)	(1)	(1)
TOTAL GOALS SCORED						3	1	2		2	13			2	1	11	3			5	1	10	6							

Small bold figures denote goalscorers. † denotes opponent's own goal.

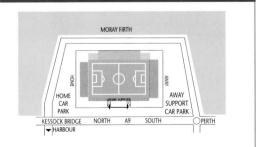

Caledonian Stadium

MORAY FIRTH

HOME | AWAY

HOME CAR PARK | AWAY SUPPORT CAR PARK

KESSOCK BRIDGE — NORTH — A9 — SOUTH — PERTH
HARBOUR

CAPACITY: 6,080; Seated 2,280, Standing 3,800
PITCH DIMENSIONS: 114 yds x 75 yds
FACILITIES FOR DISABLED SUPPORTERS:
By prior arrangement with the Secretary

Team playing kits

How to get there

The following routes can be used to reach Caledonian Stadium:
TRAINS: Nearest Railway Station is Inverness which is approximately one mile from the ground.
BUSES: Local services available from Union Street situated in Inverness Town Centre opposite the Railway Station.
CARS: The Ground is located on the North side of the A9 Perth/Inverness trunk road and fans should access off the roundabout (first after Perth) before Kessock Bridge. Parking available at stadium.

Caley Thistle

email: info@sfl.scottishfootball.com • website: www.scottishfootball.com

West Lothian Courier Stadium,
Almondvale Stadium Road, Livingston,
West Lothian, EH54 7DN
CHAIRMAN
Dominic W. Keane
VICE-CHAIRMAN
John McGuiness
DIRECTORS
Anthony K. Kinder, James Leishman
& Derek J. Milne
HON PRESIDENT
John P. Blacklaw, C.Eng, M.I.E.E.
HON VICE–PRESIDENTS
William L. Mill &
John L. Bain, B.E.M.
SECRETARY
James R. S. Renton
FOOTBALL ADMINISTRATOR
Fiona Thorpe
CHIEF EXECUTIVE/TEAM MANAGER
James Leishman
HEAD COACH
David Hay
FIRST TEAM COACH
John Robertson
**DIRECTOR OF YOUTH
DEVELOPMENT/RESERVE TEAM COACH**
Tony Taylor
YOUTH TEAM COACHES
John McLaughlin (U18)
Gerry Britton (U16)
Alan Morgan (U15)
John McLaughlin (U14)
Alex Gordon (U13)
CLUB DOCTORS
Dr. Stuart Box & Dr. Andrew Malloch
FULL-TIME PHYSIOTHERAPIST
Michael P. McBride
PART-TIME PHYSIOTHERAPIST
Arthur Duncan
COMMERCIAL MANAGER
Charles Burnett (01506) 417000
HEAD SCOUT
James McArthur
**GROUNDSMAN/
STADIUM MANAGER**
William Blair
**FOOTBALL SAFETY OFFICERS'
ASSOCIATION REPRESENTATIVE**
John O'Lone (01506) 432142
BACKROOM STAFF
John Donnelly & Peter Reynolds
MEDIA LIAISON OFFICER
Jim Leishman (01506) 417000
MATCHDAY PROGRAMME EDITOR
Duncan Bennett (01506) 417000
TELEPHONES
Ground (01506) 417000
Sec. Home (0802) 933263
Fax (01506) 418888
Football Dept. Fax (01506) 202598
E-MAIL & INTERNET ADDRESS
livingstonfc@btinternet.com
www.livingstonfc.co.uk
Football Dept: fionathorpe@lvstfc.co.uk
jimrenton@lvstfc.co.uk
CLUB SHOP
Contact Stadium (01506) 417000
OFFICIAL SUPPORTERS CLUB
Duncan Bennett, 63 Granby Avenue,
Howden, Livingston, EH54 6LD
(01506) 495113
CLUB CAPTAIN
Jim Sherry
TEAM CAPTAIN
Graham Coughlan
SHIRT SPONSOR
Motorola
KIT SUPPLIER
Russell Athletic

Livingston

LIST OF PLAYERS 2000-2001

SURNAME	FIRST NAME	MIDDLE NAME	DATE OF BIRTH	PLACE OF BIRTH	DATE OF SIGNING	HEIGHT FT INS	WEIGHT ST LBS	POS. ON PITCH	PREVIOUS CLUB
Alexander	Neil		10/03/78	Edinburgh	22/08/98	6 1.0	11 7	Gk	Stenhousemuir
Allison	Colin	James	01/07/81	Falkirk	10/08/98	5 7.0	10 7	Fwd	I.C.I. Juveniles
Anderson	John	Patton	02/10/72	Greenock	03/06/00	6 2.0	13 2	Def	Morton
Bingham	David	Thomas	03/09/70	Dunfermline	06/07/98	5 10.0	10 7	Fwd	Dunfermline Athletic
Brittain	Richard		24/09/83	Bangour	03/08/00	5 9.0	10 7	Fwd	S Form
Britton	Gerard	Joseph	20/10/70	Glasgow	14/07/99	6 0.0	11 0	Fwd	Dunfermline Athletic
Connolly	David		19/08/84	Glasgow	03/08/00	5 6.0	10 0	Mid	S Form
Coughlan	Graham		18/11/74	Dublin	29/03/99	6 2.0	13 5	Fwd	Blackburn Rovers
Crabbe	Scott		12/08/68	Edinburgh	04/07/00	5 8.0	11 5	Fwd	Falkirk
Deas	Paul	Andrew	22/02/72	Perth	25/06/98	5 11.0	11 7	Def	Stirling Albion
Dolan	James		22/02/69	Salsburgh	08/07/00	5 8.0	11 10	Mid	Dunfermline Athletic
Fairbairn	Brian		07/04/83	Broxburn	24/08/99	5 8.0	9 9	Fwd	S Form
Fairgrieve	Brydon	Gordon	29/07/83	Edinburgh	24/08/99	5 6.0	9 1	Def	Livingston B.C.
Fisher	John	George	19/01/84	Glasgow	29/01/00	5 11.0	11 9	Def	S Form
Fleming	Derek	Adam	05/12/73	Falkirk	20/11/98	5 7.0	10 2	Def/Mid	Dundee
Greacen	Stewart		31/03/82	Lanark	24/06/00	6 2.0	13 4	Def	Airdrieonians
Hagen	David		05/05/73	Edinburgh	04/07/00	5 11.0	13 0	Fwd	Falkirk
Haggart	Denis	Mochan	14/08/83	Falkirk	24/08/99	5 9.0	11 11	Fwd	Gairdoch B.C.
Keith	Marino		16/12/74	Peterhead	30/07/99	5 10.0	12 12	Fwd	Falkirk
Kelly	Patrick		04/02/68	Paisley	05/07/99	5 7.0	11 0	Def	Newcastle United
King	Charles	Alexander	15/11/79	Edinburgh	07/12/98	5 7.0	10 2	Fwd	St. Johnstone
King	Christopher		09/11/83	Edinburgh	29/01/00	5 8.0	10 7	Fwd	East Fife
Love	Christopher		04/01/83	Edinburgh	22/01/99	5 10.0	12 4	Mid	S Form
McCaldon	Ian		14/09/74	Liverpool	21/12/96	6 3.0	12 4	Gk	Glenafton Athletic
McCormick	Mark	Thomas	11/07/79	Bellshill	24/09/97	6 1.0	10 7	Fwd	Harthill Juniors
McCulloch	Mark	Ross	19/05/75	Inverness	04/07/00	5 11.0	13 0	Mid	Inverness Caledonian Th.
McEwan	David		26/02/82	Lanark	28/07/98	6 0.0	12 0	Gk	Shotts Bon Accord
McManus	Allan	William	17/11/74	Paisley	23/10/98	6 0.0	12 0	Def	Heart of Midlothian
McPhee	Brian		23/10/70	Glasgow	06/07/98	5 10.0	11 4	Fwd	Airdrieonians
Moffat	Adam		07/05/83	Kirkcaldy	24/08/99	5 10.0	11 0	Mid	S Form
Morrison	Ross		22/08/84	Dunfermline	03/08/00	5 6.0	10 10	Mid	S Form
Ormiston	David	William	28/11/83	Edinburgh	29/01/00	5 8.0	10 12	Fwd	Hutchison Vale B.C.
Rollo	Andrew	William	27/06/83	Dunfermline	20/09/99	5 10.0	12 0	Def	Cowdenbeath B.C.
Santi	Carlo	Eric	28/01/84	Glasgow	20/04/00	5 7.0	10 2	Fwd	Celtic South B.C.
Sharp	Alan		16/01/83	Falkirk	24/08/99	5 5.0	8 8	Def	S Form
Sherry	James	Cunningham	09/09/73	Glasgow	26/06/98	5 8.0	12 6	Mid	Hamilton Academical
Smith	Gordon		18/12/80	Glasgow	24/07/00	6 3.0	14 13	Fwd	Bolton Wanderers
Smith	Grant	Gordon	05/05/80	Irvine	04/07/00	6 1.0	12 7	Mid	Heart of Midlothian
Sweeney	Sean	Brian	17/08/69	Glasgow	06/07/98	6 0.0	11 0	Def	Airdrieonians
Wilson	Barry	John	16/02/72	Kirkcaldy	23/05/00	5 11.0	13 0	Fwd	Inverness Caledonian Th.
Wilson	Peter	Edward K.	06/03/83	Stirling	24/08/99	5 8.0	9 13	Mid	Gairdoch B.C.

Milestones

YEAR OF FORMATION: 1974 (From Seasons 1974/75 to 1994/95 known as Meadowbank Thistle F.C.)
MOST LEAGUE POINTS IN A SEASON: 55 (Second Division – Season 1986/87)(2 Points for a Win)
77 (Third Division – Season 1998/99)(3 Points for a Win)
MOST LEAGUE GOALS SCORED BY A PLAYER IN A SEASON: John McGachie (Season 1986/87)
NO. OF GOALS SCORED: 21
RECORD ATTENDANCE: 2,818 (-v- Albion Rovers, 10.8.1974 at Meadowbank Stadium)
5,729 (-v- Ayr United, 29.4.2000 at West Lothian Courier Stadium)
RECORD VICTORY: 6-0 (-v- Raith Rovers – Second Division, 9.11.1985)
RECORD DEFEAT: 0-8 (-v- Hamilton Academical – Division 2, 14.12.1974)

Livi Lions' ten year league record

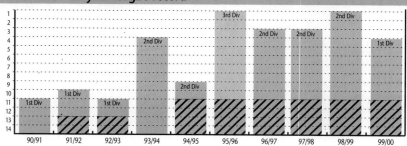

LIVI LIONS' CLUB FACTFILE 1999/2000
RESULTS... APPEARANCES... SCORERS... ATTENDANCES...

Nationwide

Date	Venue	Opponents	Att.	Res	McCaldon I.	Kelly P.	Deas P.	Watson G.	Coughlan G.	Millar J.	King C.	Millar M.	Britton G.	Bingham D.	Keith M.	Little I.	McCormick M.	Macdonald W.	McManus A.	Robertson J.	McPhee B.	Fleming D.	Sweeney S.	McCann G.	Feroz C.	McKinnon R.	McLaren A.	Bennett J.N.	Courts T.	Alexander N.	Richardson L.	Hart M.	Smith J.	Rowson D.	Clark S.	Moffat A.
Aug 7	H	Raith Rovers	3,116	1-1	1	2	3	4	5	6	7	8	9	10	11^1	12	14	15																		
14	A	Ayr United	2,533	2-1	1	2	3		5	6	7	8	9^1	10^1	11				4	12	14	15															
21	H	Airdrieonians	2,837	3-0	1	2	3			6	7	8	9	10					4	12	15^2	11	5^1														
28	A	Morton	1,257	2-2	1	2	3		15	6^1	7	8	9	10	11^1				4	12			5	14													
Sep 4	H	Dunfermline Athletic	5,302	0-1	1		3		5	6	7	8	9	10	11				2	12			4	15	14												
11	A	Falkirk	3,326	2-0	1	2	3			6	7	8	12	10^1	11					9^1			5	15													
18	H	Inverness Cal. Th.	2,584	2-2	1	2	3		15	6	7	8	9	10			12		4		11^2	14	5														
25	H	Clydebank	3,290	2-1	1	2			5	6	7	8	9	10^2					4	14	11	3		15	12												
Oct 2	A	St. Mirren	4,520	1-1	1	2	3		5	6	7	8	9^1					14	4		11	12		15	10												
16	H	Ayr United	2,332	4-1	1	2	3		5	6	14	8	9^1			11^2					15	4				10^1	7	12									
23	A	Raith Rovers	2,942	1-3	1	2	3		5	6	14	8^1	9			11					15	4				10	7	12									
30	H	Falkirk	3,482	1-1		2	3		5	6	14	8^1	15			11					9	12	4			10	7				1					
Nov 6	A	Inverness Cal. Th.	2,474	0-2	1		3		5	6	12	8	14	11					2		15		4			10	7									
14	A	Dunfermline Athletic	4,163	0-3	1	2	3		5	6	7			10					8		9	14	11	4	15												
20	H	Morton	2,490	2-1		2	3		5	6	7		9^1	10^1			14		4		8	11				6	12				1					
27	H	St. Mirren	4,239	1-2		2	3^1		5	6	7		9	10			14		4		8	11	15				12				1					
Dec 4	H	Clydebank	346	5-1		2	3		5	6	7^1	8		10^2			9^1		4		11^1	14					15				1					
14	A	Airdrieonians	1,492	3-2		2	3			6	7	8		10^2			9^1	14	4		12	11	5				15				1					
27	A	Falkirk	3,109	3-2		2	3		5	6	7^1	8		10			9	14	4		12^2						11				1					
Jan 3	H	Inverness Cal. Th.	2,656	1-1		2	3		5	6	7	8		10	14	11	9		4		12^1										1					
8	H	Dunfermline Athletic	3,800	1-0		2	3		5	14	6	7	8	10^1		9	12		4		11					6					1					
22	H	Clydebank	3,064	3-0		2	3		5	6	7	8	9^2	10		11			4		12^1					14					1					
Feb 5	H	St. Mirren	5,015	2-0	1	2	3		5		12	8	9	10^1				14	4		7^1					6							11			
29	A	Ayr United	1,765	1-0	1	2	3^1		5			8		10			12		4		9	6				7							11			
Mar 4	H	Falkirk	4,055	0-1	1	2	3		5		12	8		10			7		4		9	14				6							11			
11	H	Raith Rovers	2,683	0-0	1	12	3		5		14	8		10			7		4		9	15				6							11	2		
14	A	Morton	684	0-1	1	14	3		5	15	7	8		10			9		4		12	11				6								2		
18	A	Inverness Cal. Th.	2,206	1-4	1	2	3		5	6	14			11			10		4		9^1	12	15			8								7		
25	H	Morton	3,252	1-0	1	2	3							10			12^1		4		9	11	5	14		6								7	8	
Apr 1	A	Dunfermline Athletic	4,337	†1-4		2			14	15	12			11			10		4		9	3	5			6			1					7	8	
4	H	Airdrieonians	1,473	3-2	1	2				6	15			11					4		9^1	3	5	14		10^1								7^1	8	
8	A	Clydebank	316	2-1	1	2	3			6^1				10^2			12		4		9	11	5				4							7	8	
15	H	St. Mirren	4,531	1-2	1	2	3		5	10			9^1						4		7	14	6						15				11	12	8	
22	A	Raith Rovers	2,129	3-1		2	3		5			12^1		10					15		9^2	11		14		4			6	1				7	8	
29	H	Ayr United	5,729	3-1						6		5	10	7		15	11^1		14^1		9^1	3		8	4				12	1				2		
May 6	A	Airdrieonians	1,493	2-0			3			5	12		10	11^1			8		15		9^1	4		7		6				1					2	14
TOTAL FULL APPEARANCES					23	30	33	1	26	27	20	24	13	32	8	1	16		28	1	20	17	15		2	17	5		2	13	6	3	5	6	2	
TOTAL SUB APPEARANCES					(2)				(3)	(3)	(11)		(5)		(1)	(3)	(12)	(1)		(4)	(13)	(8)	(3)	(4)	(7)	(2)	(4)		(1)	(2)				(1)		(1)
TOTAL GOALS SCORED							2			2	2	2	5	15	4		6			1	15		1		1	2								1		

Small bold figures denote goalscorers. † denotes opponent's own goal.

West Lothian Courier Stadium

EAST STAND
WEST STAND
SOUTH STAND
NORTH STAND
CAR PARK (AWAY SUPPORTERS)
CAR PARK (HOME SUPPORTERS)
ALMONDVALE BOULEVARD
ALMONDVALE SHOPPING CENTRE
POLICE STATION
BUS STATION
ALDERSTON ROAD
RAILWAY 2 MILES

CAPACITY: 10,004 (All Seated)
PITCH DIMENSIONS: 105yds x 72yds
FACILITIES FOR DISABLED SUPPORTERS: By prior arrangement with Secretary.

Team playing kits

How to get there

West Lothian Courier Stadium can be reached by the following routes:
BUSES: By bus to terminus at Almondvale Shopping Centre. Follow direction signs for St. John's Hospital or West Lothian Courier Stadium and it is a short 5 minute walk.
TRAINS: To either Livingston North or South Stations, and by taxi to stadium. Approximate cost is £2.00.
CARS: Leave M8 at Livingston Junction (East). Follow signs for St. John's Hospital or West Lothian Courier Stadium.

Livi Lions

email: info@sfl.scottishfootball.com • website: www.scottishfootball.com

Morton

LIST OF PLAYERS 2000-2001

SURNAME	FIRST NAME	MIDDLE NAME	DATE OF BIRTH	PLACE OF BIRTH	DATE OF SIGNING	HEIGHT FT INS	WEIGHT ST LBS	POS. ON PITCH	PREVIOUS CLUB
Aitken	Stephen	Smith	25/09/76	Glasgow	04/08/00	5 8.0	11 0	Mid	Beith Juniors
Anderson	Derek	Christopher	15/05/72	Paisley	24/12/98	6 0.0	11 0	Def	Hartlepool United
Boswell	Matthew		19/08/77	Shrewsbury	04/08/00	6 3.0	14 6	Gk	Kendal
Boukraa	Karim		07/03/73	Le Harve	04/08/00	6 0.0	12 0	Fwd	US Fecamp
Carlin	Andrew		06/01/81	Glasgow	23/02/99	6 1.0	13 4	Gk	Ayr Boswell
Curran	Henry		09/10/66	Glasgow	13/03/98	5 9.5	12 0	Mid	Dunfermline Athletic
Davies	Darran		13/08/78	Port Talbot	04/08/00	5 8.0	10 11	Def	Barry Town
Kerr	Brian		30/10/81	Ayr	23/02/99	5 10.0	11 11	Mid/Fwd	Ayr Boswell
MacDonald	Stuart		15/05/81	Glasgow	03/08/99	5 11.0	10 7	Def	Erskine B.C.
Matheson	Ross		15/11/77	Greenock	02/07/96	5 6.0	9 10	Mid	Rangers
McDonald	Paul	Thomas	20/04/68	Motherwell	14/07/00	5 6.5	10 2	Fwd	Partick Thistle
McGregor	David	George	09/06/81	Greenock	04/08/00	5 11.0	11 7	Def	S Form
Medou-Otye	Parfait		29/11/76	Cameroon	04/08/00	5 10.0	12 0	Def	Le Mans UC 72
Millen	Andrew	Frank	10/06/65	Glasgow	01/06/99	5 11.0	11 2	Def	Ayr United
Murie	David		02/08/76	Edinburgh	29/03/99	5 8.0	10 4	Def	Heart of Midlothian
Naylor	Martyn		02/08/77	Walsall	04/08/00	5 10.0	10 3	Def	Telford United
Raeside	Robert		07/07/72	South Africa	04/08/00	6 2.0	13 7	Def	Shelbourne
Robb	Ross		09/03/81	Glasgow	21/08/00	6 1.0	12 0	Def	Hillington B.C.
Tweedie	Garry		02/01/81	Ayr	23/02/99	5 11.0	12 0	Def/Mid	Ayr Boswell
Whalen	Stephen		03/05/82	Irvine	23/02/99	5 8.0	11 7	Fwd	Ayr Boswell

Milestones

YEAR OF FORMATION: 1874
MOST CAPPED PLAYER: Jimmy Cowan
NO. OF CAPS: 25
MOST LEAGUE POINTS IN A SEASON: 69 (Division 2 – Season 1966/67)
MOST LEAGUE GOALS SCORED BY A PLAYER IN A SEASON: Allan McGraw (Season 1963/64)
NO. OF GOALS SCORED: 58
RECORD ATTENDANCE: 23,500 (-v- Celtic – 1922)
RECORD VICTORY: 11-0 (-v- Carfin Shamrock – Scottish Cup, 13.11.1886)
RECORD DEFEAT: 1-10 (-v- Port Glasgow Athletic, 5.5.1884)

The Ton's ten year league record

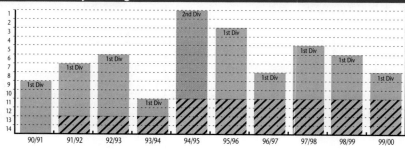

Date	Venue	Opponents	Att.	Res	Maxwell A.	Murie D.	Archdeacon O.	Millen A.	Anderson D.	Fenwick P.	Curran H.	Anderson J.	Wright K.	Thomas K.	Matheson R.	Hawke W.	Aitken S.	McDonald P.	Ferguson I.	McPherson C.	Connolly P.	Slavin B.	Tweedie G.	Carlin A.	Morrison G.	Whalen S.	Hartley P.	Kerr B.	Hart M.	Earnshaw R.	Pluck C.	Ross M.	Walker J.	MacDonald S.	Rice B.	Steverston C.	Aitken C.	Robb R.
Aug 7	A	Falkirk	2,945	4-2	1	2	3¹	4	5	6	7	8¹	9	10²	11	12	14	15																				
14	H	Clydebank	1,433	0-0	1	2		3	4	5		7	6	9	10	8	11			14	16																	
21	A	Dunfermline Athletic	4,030	1-2	1	2		3	4	5		7	6	14¹	11	10	8		9	16																		
28	H	Livingston	1,257	2-2	1	2	2¹	3	4	5		6	9	7	8	16	14	14	11	10¹	12																	
Sep 4	A	Inverness Cal. Th.	2,414	1-1	1	2		4	5		7	6	8	12	14	16	9		10¹	3	11																	
11	H	Raith Rovers	970	2-0	1	2		4	5	6		8	9¹	7	12	11	14	10¹		3	16																	
18	A	St. Mirren	6,773	2-3	1	2		4	5	6		8	9	7	11	3	12	14	10²		16																	
25	H	Airdrieonians	1,126	0-2	1	2		4	5	6		8		7	12	3	11	9	10		16																	
Oct 2	A	Ayr United	2,186	0-3	1	2		4	5		8	12	9	7	10	3	11	14		6																		
16	A	Clydebank	758	3-1	1	2		4	5		8	12	9¹	7	10	14	11¹			6¹	1	3	16															
23	H	Falkirk	1,409	2-3	1	2			5	8¹	4	9		7	10¹		11	14		6		3	16															
30	A	Raith Rovers	2,664	1-3	1	2		4	5	6	8¹		9	7	10	14				11		3	16															
Nov 6	H	St. Mirren	3,733	1-4	1	2		4	3	6	8¹	12	14	7	10					11		5	9															
12	H	Inverness Cal. Th.	812	5-1	1	2			3	6	8¹	4	9¹	7¹	12	16¹		14		11		5¹	10															
20	A	Livingston	2,490	1-2	1	2	2¹		3		8	4	9	7	12	6		14		16	11	5	10															
27	H	Ayr United	1,168	0-0	1	2			3		8		12	7	9	6	16	11		4	14	5	10															
Dec 7	A	Airdrieonians	1,135	0-1	1	2		4	3	6	8	10		7	14	16				11	12	5	9															
11	H	Dunfermline Athletic	1,289	0-3	1	2			3	6	8	10		7	14	16				11	12	4	5	9														
18	A	Falkirk	2,015	1-2	1	2		4	3	6			9	7		8	11¹			10		5	14															
27	H	Raith Rovers	1,056	1-0	1			4		6	8¹	5	9	7		12	11			3	14	2	16	10														
Jan 3	A	St. Mirren	7,266	1-1	1	2		4		6	8	5	9	7		3	11					14	10¹	16														
8	A	Inverness Cal. Th.	1,524	2-6	1	2		4			8¹	5		7	6		11¹			3	12	9	10	16														
22	H	Airdrieonians	1,201	4-0	1	2		4	3	6	10	8¹			14	11²				16		5	9		12	7¹												
Feb 5	A	Ayr United	1,985	2-3	1	2		4	3¹	6	10¹	8		9		11				16		5			12	7	14											
12	A	Dunfermline Athletic	4,289	1-1	1	2		4	3		10			9	14	11				6	16	5			12	7¹	8											
26	H	Clydebank	1,052	1-0	1			4	3		10	8¹	7	9	12	11				16	2	5						6	14									
Mar 4	A	Raith Rovers	2,026	0-3	1	2		4			10	8	7	9	11	16	14					5						6	12									
14	H	Livingston	684	1-0	1	2		4			10¹	8		9	11	6	3			5			7															
18	H	St. Mirren	3,768	0-2	1	2		4			10	8	12	9	11	6	3			5			7								16							
25	A	Livingston	3,252	0-1		2		4			10	8	12	9	11	6				5	1		7	16							14	3						
Apr 1	H	Inverness Cal. Th.	567	0-2		2								9	11	10	6	1		7	16							8	4	3	5	12	14					
8	A	Airdrieonians	866	0-3		2								7	11	3	6			5	9		12	16				8	4			10	14					
15	H	Ayr United	656	1-2	1	2				6				7	8	11	3			10		5	9¹		12			16	4			14						
22	H	Falkirk	1,037	0-2	1	14		4	6		10	5		7			3			8		16	9		11				2									
29	A	Clydebank	339	3-0	1	2		4	6		10¹	8¹		7¹	9		3					5		16	12			14	11									
May 6	H	Dunfermline Athletic	1,039	2-0	1	2		4	6		10	8¹		7	9	14	3¹			12		5		16					11									
TOTAL FULL APPEARANCES			33	33	4	28	28	14	28	26	17	2	33	9	19	16	3	14	5	14	10	3	20	15	3		1	3	3		2	7	1	1	1	
TOTAL SUB APPEARANCES			(1)			(3)	(5)		(1)	(6)	(10)	(8)	(4)	(9)		(6)	(8)		(1)	(6)		(4)	(9)		(1)	(2)	(4)				(1)	(1)	(2)	
TOTAL GOALS SCORED			2	1		1			9	5	4	2	2	1	1	3		3	5		1			1	1	1			2						

Small bold figures denote goalscorers. † denotes opponent's own goal.

Cappielow Park

Limited space - Application only

SINCLAIR STREET

CAPACITY: 7,890; Seating 5,890, Standing 2,000
PITCH DIMENSIONS: 110 yds x 71 yds
FACILITIES FOR DISABLED SUPPORTERS:
Seating facilities below Grandstand.

Team playing kits

How to get there

Cappielow Park may be reached by the following routes:
BUSES: Services from Glasgow stop just outside the park. There are also services from Port Glasgow and Gourock.
TRAINS: The nearest local station is Cartsdyke and it is a five minute walk from here to the ground. There are two to three trains every hour from Glasgow and from Gourock.
CARS: There is no official car park and fans should park in Sinclair Street beyond the railway station.

The Ton

email: info@sfl.scottishfootball.com • website: www.scottishfootball.com

RAITH ROVERS FOOTBALL CLUB

Stark's Park, Pratt Street,
Kirkcaldy, Fife, KY1 1SA

CHAIRMAN
William H. Gray

MANAGING DIRECTOR
Daniel Smith

DIRECTORS
Colin McGowan, Eric W. Drysdale,
Mario Caira, James Whyte
& Archibald O. Smith

HON. PRESIDENT
John Urquhart

COMPANY SECRETARY
Eric W. Drysdale

OFFICE MANAGER
William McPhee

MANAGER
Peter Hetherston

ASSISTANT MANAGER
Kenny Black

YOUTH COACH
David Kirkwood

YOUTH TEAM COACHES
David Kirkwood (U18)
Jim Dempsey (U15)
Sandy McBain (U13)

CLUB DOCTOR
Dr. R. Robertson/
North Glen Medical Practice

PHYSIOTHERAPIST
Paul Greene

**FOOTBALL SAFETY OFFICERS'
ASSOCIATION REPRESENTATIVE**
Bill Brown (01592) 263514

GROUNDSMAN
John Murray

KIT MANAGER
Tam Healy

COMMERCIAL MANAGER
Lana Wood

MATCHDAY PROGRAMME EDITOR
John Litster (01592) 268718

TELEPHONES
Ground (01592) 263514
Fax (01592) 642833
Office Manager's Home
(01333) 422394

E-MAIL & INTERNET ADDRESS
www.raithrovers.com

CLUB SHOP
South Stand Shop situated within stand.
Open during Office hours 9.00 a.m. to
5.00 p.m. and on home match days
2.00 p.m. to 5.00 p.m.

OFFICIAL SUPPORTERS CLUB
c/o Fraser Hamilton,
22 Tower Terrace, Kirkcaldy, Fife

TEAM CAPTAIN
Alex Burns

SHIRT SPONSOR
Fife Fabrications Ltd

KIT SUPPLIER
TFG

LIST OF PLAYERS 2000-2001

SURNAME	FIRST NAME	MIDDLE NAME	DATE OF BIRTH	PLACE OF BIRTH	DATE OF SIGNING	HEIGHT FT INS	WEIGHT ST LBS	POS. ON PITCH	PREVIOUS CLUB
Agnew	Paul		28/06/72	Coatbridge	08/07/99	5 7.0	10 10	Mid	Ayr United
Andrews	Marvin	Anthony	22/12/75	Trinidad & Tobago	04/08/00	6 3.0	13 0	Def	Carib
Black	Kenneth	George	29/11/63	Stenhousemuir	02/07/99	5 9.0	11 10	Mid	Airdrieonians
Blackadder	Ryan	Robert	11/10/83	Kirkcaldy	10/07/00	5 6.0	10 12	Mid	Form D Under 16
Brown	Ian		16/03/84	Kirkcaldy	10/07/00	6 2.0	11 6	Def	Greig Park Rangers
Browne	Paul	Gerard	17/02/75	Glasgow	03/07/96	6 2.0	12 6	Def	Aston Villa
Burns	Alexander		04/08/73	Bellshill	06/07/99	5 8.0	10 6	Mid	Southend United
Caullay	Craig	Grant	04/01/84	Bellshill	10/07/00	5 7.5	12 1	Mid	Coatbridge Amateurs
Clark	Andrew	Alexander	21/04/80	Stirling	01/07/00	5 10.0	10 12	Fwd	Hutchison Vale B.C.
Coyle	Craig	Robert	06/09/80	Edinburgh	01/07/98	5 10.0	10 7	Gk	Salvesen B.C.
Creaney	Gerard	Thomas	13/04/70	Coatbridge	05/08/00	6 0.0	13 10	Fwd	Notts County
Ellis	Laurence		07/11/79	Edinburgh	02/07/98	5 11.0	10 7	Def	Links United
Fennessey	Bryan		02/03/84	Bellshill	10/07/00	5 7.0	9 8	Mid	Coatbridge Amateurs
Gaughan	Kevin		06/03/78	Glasgow	02/07/99	6 1.0	12 2	Def	Partick Thistle
Hamilton	Steven	James	19/03/75	Baillieston	13/07/99	5 9.0	12 10	Def	Kilmarnock
Hampshire	Paul	Christopher	20/09/81	Edinburgh	02/07/98	5 11.0	10 7	Mid	Hutchison Vale
Hetherston	Brian		23/11/76	Bellshill	03/08/00	5 10.0	11 10	Mid	Sligo Rovers
Kirkwood	David	Stewart	27/08/67	St. Andrews	18/07/97	6 0.0	12 7	Mid	Airdrieonians
Maughan	Roderick	Edward A.	18/12/80	Edinburgh	01/07/98	5 10.0	10 8	Mid	Granton B.C.
Mballa	Ivan		26/09/74	Amiens	04/08/00	5 10.0	11 7	Fwd	A.S.F.C. Vindelle
McCulloch	Greig		18/04/76	Girvan	24/02/96	5 8.0	10 7	Def	Aberdeen
McInally	David		03/03/81	Glasgow	01/07/98	5 6.0	9 7	Def	Cathkin United
McKinnon	Raymond		05/08/70	Dundee	21/08/00	5 10.0	11 10	Mid	Livingston
Nicol	Kevin	Andrew	19/01/82	Kirkcaldy	01/07/98	5 8.0	11 2	Mid	Hill O' Beath
Niven	Derek		12/12/83	Falkirk	10/07/00	6 1.0	11 2	Mid	Stenhousemuir
Opinel	Sacha		09/04/77	Bourg, Saint Maurice	06/01/00	5 9.0	12 0	Def	Stockport County
Rushford	John		09/02/82	Dunfermline	13/07/99	5 11.0	10 7	Mid	Rosyth Recreation
Scarborough	Charles	Philip	03/11/83	Kirkcaldy	10/07/00	5 10.0	11 6	Fwd	Buckhaven Colts
Shields	Dene		16/09/82	Edinburgh	14/07/99	5 9.0	12 0	Fwd	Granton B.C.
Slavin	Kevin		05/08/84	Bellshill	10/07/00	5 7.0	8 11	Def	Coatbridge Amateurs
Smith	Christopher		04/04/84	Bellshill	10/07/00	5 8.5	10 2	Mid	S Form
Stein	Jay		13/01/79	Dunfermline	11/10/95	5 7.5	10 7	Fwd	Inverkeithing United
Tosh	Paul	James	18/10/73	Arbroath	02/07/99	6 0.0	11 1	Fwd	Hibernian
Tosh	Steven	William	27/04/73	Kirkcaldy	31/03/98	5 11.0	11 7	Mid	St. Johnstone
Van De Kamp	Guido		08/02/64	's Hertogenbosch	01/07/97	6 2.5	12 12	Gk	Dunfermline Athletic
Wheelwright	Mark	George	06/02/83	Dunfermline	10/07/00	6 2.0	11 11	Fwd	Glenrothes Strollers

Milestones

YEAR OF FORMATION: 1883
MOST CAPPED PLAYER: David Morris
NO. OF CAPS: 6
MOST LEAGUE POINTS IN A SEASON: 65 (First Division - Season 1992/93)(2 Points for a Win)
69 (First Division - Season 1994/95)(3 Points for a Win)
MOST LEAGUE GOALS SCORED BY A PLAYER IN A SEASON: Norman Heywood (Season 1937/38)
NO. OF GOALS SCORED: 42
RECORD ATTENDANCE: 31,306 (-v- Heart of Midlothian – Scottish Cup, 7.2.1953)
RECORD VICTORY: 10-1 (-v- Coldstream – Scottish Cup, 13.2.1954)
RECORD DEFEAT: 2-11 (-v- Morton – Division 2, 18.3.1936)

The Rovers' ten year league record

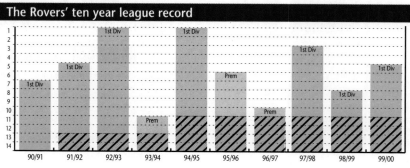

THE ROVERS' CLUB FACTFILE 1999/2000
RESULTS... APPEARANCES... SCORERS... ATTENDANCES...

Date	Venue	Opponents	Att.	Res	Van De Kamp G.	Hamilton S.	McCulloch G.	Andrews M.	Gaughan K.	Black K.	McEwan C.	Tosh S.	Tosh P.	Burns A.	Stein J.	Agnew P.	Hetherston B.	Shields P.	Kirkwood D.	Clark A.	McCondichie A.	Ellis L.	Browne P.	Dargo C.	Coyle C.	Agathe D.	Berthe M.	Stewart A.	Preget A.	Craig S.	Roberts M.	Begue Y.	Opinel S.	Javary J-P.	Owusu A.	Fenwick P.	Nicol K.	Shields D.
Aug 7	A	Livingston	3,116	1-1	1	2	3	4	5	6	7	8	9¹	10	11	12	14	15																				
14	H	St. Mirren	2,787	0-6	1	2	3	4	5	6	12	7	9	10	11	8			14	15																		
21	A	Clydebank	232	1-1		7	14	4		12	2	6		10	11	8			15		1	3	5	9¹														
28	A	Airdrieonians	1,493	4-1			12	4		6¹	2	8		10	11	14			3	15			5	9	1	7³												
Sep 4	H	Ayr United	2,368	5-1				4		6	2	8	14	10¹	11				3	15¹			5	9²	1	7¹												
11	A	Morton	970	0-2			12	4		6	2	8		10	11		16		3	15			5	9	1	7												
18	H	Dunfermline Athletic	6,087	2-2	1			4		6	2	14		10	11								3	5	9²	7	8											
25	H	Inverness Cal. Th.	2,961	2-0	1		12	4¹		6	2	8		10	11								3	5	9	7¹		15										
Oct 2	H	Falkirk	3,182	2-1	1			4		6	2	8	14	10	11								3	5	9²	7												
16	A	St. Mirren	3,815	2-3	1	9		4		6¹	2	8		10	11¹	12	14						5			7					3	15						
23	A	Livingston	2,942	3-1	1			4		6¹	2		8	10	11		14¹						5¹	9		7		3										
30	H	Morton	2,664	3-1	1	3	14	4		6	2	8		10¹	11¹				9	15			5			7¹												
Nov 6	A	Dunfermline Athletic	6,953	1-1	1	3		4		6	2	8	14	10	11¹				9				5			7												
14	A	Ayr United	1,769	1-0	1	3	12	4		6	2		8	10	11	14¹			9				5			7												
20	H	Airdrieonians	2,353	1-1	1	3		4		6	2		8	10	11	14¹			15				5			7						9						
27	A	Falkirk	2,611	1-2	1	3	14	4		6	2	8		10	12	11							5			7¹						9	15					
Dec 4	H	Inverness Cal. Th.	1,971	4-2	1	3	12	4		6	2	8		10²	14	11							5¹			7						9¹	15					
27	A	Morton	1,056	0-1	1	7		4		6	2	8		10	11				15				5	9								3						
Jan 3	H	Dunfermline Athletic	7,464	3-0	1		12	4		6	2	8¹		10¹	11				15				5¹	9		7						3						
8	H	Ayr United	2,583	2-0	1		12	4		6	2	8¹		10	11				15	14			5	9¹		7						3						
15	A	Airdrieonians	2,098	2-0	1		12	4		6	2	8		10¹	11¹					14			5	9		7						3						
18	A	Clydebank	2,754	1-0	1			4		6	2	8¹		10	11	14	15		9				5			7						3						
22	A	Inverness Cal. Th.	2,302	1-1	1			4		6	2	8		10	11								5	9¹		7						3	14					
Feb 5	H	Falkirk	4,140	0-1	1		3	4			2	8		10	11	14			15				5	9		7							6					
26	H	St. Mirren	4,662	1-2	1	12	2		4			8¹		10	11	14	15						5	9		7						3	6					
Mar 4	H	Morton	2,026	3-0	1		2		4	12	6¹	8¹		10	11¹	14							5	9		7						3		15					
7	A	Clydebank	256	1-2	1		2		4		7	8¹		10	11	14							5	9								3	6	15					
11	A	Livingston	2,683	0-0	1		2	4		6	12	10			11	14	15						5			7						3		9					
18	H	Dunfermline Athletic	6,694	2-0	1			4			2	14	15	10	11								5¹	9¹		7						3	6	8					
25	H	Airdrieonians	2,056	2-0	1		3	4			2	14	15	10	11								5	9¹		7							6	8¹					
Apr 1	A	Ayr United	1,841	1-0	1			4	12	15	2	10	14		11								5	9		7						3	6	8¹					
8	H	Inverness Cal. Th.	2,538	2-0	1		2	4		12	14¹	15	10	11									5	9¹		7						3	6	8					
15	A	Falkirk	4,686	0-1	1			4			2	14	15	10	11								5	9		7						3	6	8	4				
22	H	Livingston	2,129	1-3	1			4			2	14		10	15								5	9		7						3	11	8¹	6				
29	A	St. Mirren	8,386	0-3	1		3	4			2	7		10	14	11			15				5	9									6	8					
May 6	H	Clydebank	1,510	0-0	1		3		4		2			8	10	11				12			5	9		7				14			6						15
TOTAL FULL APPEARANCES					32	11	13	29	6	23	30	25	10	34	32	2	3	1	3	3	1	4	34	25	3	30	1		2	3	15	10	8	2	1			
TOTAL SUB APPEARANCES						(4)	(9)		(1)	(2)	(4)	(6)	(8)			(3)	(2)	(11)	(7)	(1)	(15)							(1)		(2)		(2)		(1)	(2)			(1)
TOTAL GOALS SCORED							1	3		5	4	6	5	2	1				1				4	12		7				1		3					

Small bold figures denote goalscorers. † denotes opponent's own goal.

Stark's Park

- RAILWAY STAND
- (HOME) (AWAY)
- FORTH ROAD BRIDGE ROAD
- SOUTH STAND (HOME)
- NORTH STAND (AWAY)
- MAIN KINCARDINE BRIDGE ROAD
- MAIN STAND
- → To Esplanade Parking   PRATT STREET   To Railway Station

CAPACITY: 10,101 (All Seated)

PITCH DIMENSIONS: 113 yds x 70 yds

FACILITIES FOR DISABLED SUPPORTERS:
By prior arrangement with the Secretary.
North Stand – Away Supporters. South Stand – Home Supporters.

Team playing kits

How to get there

The following routes may be used to reach Stark's Park:
TRAINS: Kirkcaldy railway station is served by trains from Dundee, Edinburgh and Glasgow (via Edinburgh) and the ground is within walking distance of the station.
BUSES: The main bus station in Kirkcaldy is also within 15 minutes walking distance of the ground, but the Edinburgh, Dunfermline and Leven services pass close by the park.
CARS: Car parking is available in the Esplanade, which is on the south side of the ground, in Beveridge Park, which is on the north side of Stark's Road, and in ground adjacent to the railway station.

The Rovers

email: info@sfl.scottishfootball.com • website: www.scottishfootball.com

Ross County

LIST OF PLAYERS 2000-2001

SURNAME	FIRST NAME	MIDDLE NAME	DATE OF BIRTH	PLACE OF BIRTH	DATE OF SIGNING	HEIGHT FT INS	WEIGHT ST LBS	POS. ON PITCH	PREVIOUS CLUB
Blackley	Douglas	Michael	30/09/83	Edinburgh	23/08/00	5 7.0	9 4	Mid	Stirling Albion
Bone	Alexander	Syme F.	26/12/71	Stirling	02/08/00	5 9.0	11 2	Fwd	Ayr United
Campbell	Craig		10/12/83	Dingwall	24/08/00	5 8.0	10 5	Fwd	S Form
Canning	Martin		03/12/81	Glasgow	28/07/99	6 2.0	11 11	Mid	Clydebank
Cooper	Neale	James	24/11/63	Darjeeling	02/08/96	6 0.0	12 7	Def	Dunfermline Athletic
Cowie	Don		15/02/83	Inverness	23/08/00	5 5.0	8 5	Mid	S Form
Cunnington	Edward		12/11/69	Bellshill	02/08/00	5 8.5	12 0	Def	Hamilton Academical
Dlugonski	Bryan		18/10/82	Banff	13/09/99	6 0.0	11 0	Mid	Ross County B.C.
Edwards	Steven		09/03/81	Inverness	23/08/00	6 0.0	11 2	Mid	Ross County B.C.
Escalon	Franck		27/07/73	Paris	23/12/97	5 10.0	10 9	Mid/Fwd	Berwick Rangers
Ewing	Garry		10/01/82	Inverness	19/02/99	5 9.0	9 3	Def	Nairn County
Ferguson	Steven		18/05/77	Edinburgh	22/11/96	5 8.0	11 6	Mid	Dunfermline Athletic
Fraser	John		17/01/78	Dunfermline	29/07/99	5 10.0	11 4	Mid/Fwd	Dunfermline Athletic
Gilbert	Kenneth	Robert	08/03/75	Aberdeen	11/02/97	5 6.5	11 4	Mid	Hull City
Gonet	Stefan		11/11/81	Paisley	24/11/99	6 2.0	12 5	Gk	Ross County B.C.
Hamilton	Garry		28/01/81	Tullibody	29/07/99	5 11.0	10 10	Gk	St. Mirren
Henderson	Darren	Ronald	12/10/66	Kilmarnock	02/08/00	5 11.0	12 10	Mid	Hamilton Academical
Holmes	Derek		18/10/78	Lanark	15/10/99	6 0.0	13 0	Fwd	Heart of Midlothian
Irvine	Brian	Alexander	24/05/65	Bellshill	27/07/99	6 2.5	13 7	Def	Dundee
Jack	Darren		09/08/83	Norwich	01/09/00	6 1.5	12 8	Mid/Fwd	S Form
Kenny	Martin	George	14/01/83	Inverness	24/08/00	5 8.0	10 6	Fwd	Inverness Caledonian Th.
Kinnaird	Paul		11/11/66	Glasgow	27/07/99	5 8.0	11 11	Mid	Stranraer
Lamb	Hamish	Alexander	22/01/84	Thurso	24/08/00	5 11.0	10 7	Def	Ross County B.C.
Lees	Allan		03/05/81	Alexandria	24/08/00	6 0.0	10 0	Mid	Ross County B.C.
Mackay	David		17/09/75	Dingwall	16/09/94	5 11.0	12 1	Def	Ross County B.C.
Mackay	Steven		26/06/81	Invergordon	10/03/00	5 11.0	10 5	Mid/Fwd	Nairn County
MacKenzie	Gordon		21/06/83	Inverness	24/08/00	5 10.0	10 2	Def	Inverness Caledonian Th.
Maxwell	Ian		02/05/75	Glasgow	12/06/98	6 3.0	12 5	Def	Queen's Park
McQuade	John		08/07/70	Glasgow	02/08/00	5 10.0	11 10	Fwd	Stirling Albion
Millar	Marc		10/04/69	Dundee	05/08/00	5 9.0	10 12	Mid	St. Johnstone
Ross	David	William	30/06/70	Inverness	12/06/98	6 2.0	12 7	Fwd	Inverness Caledonian Th.
Shaw	George		10/02/69	Glasgow	29/07/99	5 7.0	11 0	Fwd	Dunfermline Athletic
Shearer	Andrew		19/10/83	Aberdeen	23/08/00	6 2.0	12 5	Gk	Brechin City
Taggart	Craig		17/01/73	Glasgow	21/03/00	5 9.0	12 2	Mid	Stirling Albion
Walker	Joseph	Nicol	29/09/62	Aberdeen	19/12/97	6 2.0	12 12	Gk	Aberdeen
Wilde	Scott		23/06/83	Irvine	24/08/00	5 9.0	10 0	Fwd	S Form
Witkowski	Ryan	Thomas	08/02/82	Elgin	19/08/00	5 8.0	10 4	Def/Mid	St. Johnstone
Young	Craig		10/08/84	Edinburgh	24/08/00	5 6.0	9 8	Fwd	Stirling Albion

Milestones

YEAR OF FORMATION: 1929
MOST LEAGUE POINTS IN A SEASON: 77 (Third Division – Season 1998/99) (3 Points for a Win)
MOST LEAGUE GOALS SCORED BY A PLAYER IN A SEASON: Derek Adams (Season 1996/97)
NO. OF GOALS SCORED: 22
RECORD ATTENDANCE: 8,000 (-v- Rangers – Scottish Cup, 28.2.66)
RECORD VICTORY: 13-2 (-v- Fraserburgh – Highland League, 1965)
RECORD DEFEAT: 1-10 (-v- Inverness Thistle – Highland League)

The County's ten year league record

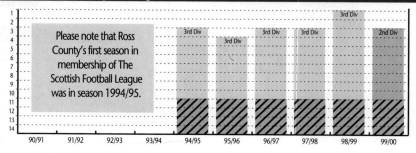

Please note that Ross County's first season in membership of The Scottish Football League was in season 1994/95.

THE COUNTY'S CLUB FACTFILE 1999/2000
RESULTS... APPEARANCES... SCORERS... ATTENDANCES...

Date	Venue	Opponents	Att.	Res	Walker J.N.	Escalon F.	McBain R.	Maxwell I.	Irvine B.	Gilbert K.	Shaw G.	McClashan J.	Geraghty M.	Finlayson K.	Kinnaird P.	Wood G.	Fraser J.	Tully C.	Ferguson S.	Mackay S.	Ross D.	Campbell C.	Hateley M.	Canning M.	Mackay D.	Nicol G.	Lennon D.	Holmes D.	Duthie M.	Mols T.	Hamilton G.	Cormack P.	Ferguson D.	Thompson B.	Roddie A.	Feroz C.	Taggart C.	Boyle S.	Bone A.
Aug 7	H	Hamilton Academical	2,312	2-1	1	2	3	4	5[1]	6	7	8[1]	9	10	11	12	14																							
14	A	Stranraer	475	0-0	1	10	3	4	5	14	7	8	9	12	11	15	6	2																						
21	H	Stenhousemuir	2,612	0-0	1		3	4	5	6	7	8	14	11		9	12	2	10	15																			
28	H	Arbroath	2,303	2-0	1	8	3	4	5	6	7[1]		14		9	12	2	10[1]		11	15																		
Sep 4	A	Stirling Albion	1,015	1-2	1	8	3	4	†5	6	7	12[1]	15			2	9		11	10																			
11	A	Alloa Athletic	694	0-2	1	8	3	4	5	6	7		14	15		11	2	9		12	10																		
18	H	Clyde	2,840	2-0	1	8	3	4	5		7		10	11[1]	9	6[1]			12		2	14	15																
25	A	Partick Thistle	2,171	2-0	1	8	12	4[1]	5	6	7	3		11	9[1]			15		2		10																
Oct 2	H	Queen of the South	2,293	1-1	1		8	4	5	6	7	3	14	11	9[1]	12				2	15	10																
9	A	Hamilton Academical	392	0-1	1		3	4	5	6	7	8	15		9	11	2		14			10																
16	H	Stranraer	2,168	1-1	1	8	3	4	5	6	7[1]		15	12		11	2		14			10	9															
30	H	Alloa Athletic	2,415	1-0	1	8	3	4	5		7			12			2	15			6	10	9[1]	11														
Nov 6	A	Clyde	894	1-3	1		12	4	5		7		15		11[1]	2		8			6	10	9	3														
12	H	Stirling Albion	2,693	1-3	1		3	4	5				14	11	10	7			12			6	9[1]	2	8													
20	A	Arbroath	972	1-0	1		3	4		6	7		11		8		10	14			5		9[1]	2														
27	A	Queen of the South	862	2-0	1		3	4		6	7		11[2]		8		10				5		9	2														
Dec 4	H	Partick Thistle	2,392	2-1	1		3[1]	4		6	7[1]	8	11	12		10				5		9	2															
Jan 22	A	Partick Thistle	2,698	2-4			11	4	5		7[1]		15	12		6	8					9[1]	2		1	3	10											
29	H	Hamilton Academical	1,860	0-1				4	5	6	7		12			10	14					9	2		3		1	11										
Feb 5	H	Queen of the South	2,018	2-0			8	14	4	5[1]	6		11[1]			8	7					9	2		3	10	1											
12	A	Arbroath	2,059	1-1	1			7	4	5	6		11		12	8[1]						9	2		3	10												
19	H	Stirling Albion	661	1-3	1	12	7		5[1]	6	14		15		11	4	2	8				9			3	10												
26	A	Stranraer	472	2-0	1	2[1]	14	4	5	6	7		11		8	9[1]			12			3			10													
Mar 7	H	Clyde	2,002	2-2	1	2	12	4	5	6	7[1]		8		9[1]							14	3			10		11										
11	A	Alloa Athletic	2,331	3-4			12	4	5	6	7		2		9[1]							10[2]	3		8	1	11											
14	H	Alloa Athletic	613	2-1			14	4	5	6[1]	7		12		9[1]		2	8				10	3		1		11											
18	A	Clyde	1,107	0-0			14	4	5	6	7		12		15	9	2	8				10	3		1		11											
21	A	Stenhousemuir	358	2-0				4	5	6	7	15[1]	11[1]		2	9		14				10	3	1				8	12									
25	H	Arbroath	804	2-1				4	5		7[1]	12	11		8	2		6				9[1]	3	1				10	14									
28	H	Stenhousemuir	1,771	2-0			12	4	5		7[1]	2	15	11[1]	8			6				9	3	1				10	14									
Apr 1	H	Stirling Albion	2,148	5-1			15	4	5[1]		7[2]	2[1]	11		14			6				9[1]	3	1			8	10	12									
8	A	Partick Thistle	3,511	1-3				4	5[1]		7	2	15	11	14			6				9	3	1			8	10	12									
15	A	Queen of the South	1,010	3-0	1			4	5[1]	6	7	2	11[1]	15				8				12	3						10	9[1]								
22	H	Hamilton Academical	693	3-0	1			4		6	7[2]	2	11	8				5				12	3						10	9[1]								
29	H	Stranraer	2,812	3-1	1			4	5	6	7[1]	2	11	15				14				12	3					8	10[1]	9[1]								
May 6	A	Stenhousemuir	600	2-2	1			4	5	6	7[1]	2	11	15				14				12	3					8	10	9[1]								
TOTAL FULL APPEARANCES					25	12	18	35	32	26	32	13	3	3	22	8	16	12	18	4		2	5	13	7	20	24	1	8	6	10	3	1	4	9	4
TOTAL SUB APPEARANCES					(1)	(10)		(1)	(1)	(3)	(6)	(8)	(6)	(4)	(10)	(1)	(1)	(7)	(2)		(1)	(5)	(1)		(5)							(3)	(2)			
TOTAL GOALS SCORED							1	1	6	1	13	4		7	3	1				6							8							1	4

Small bold figures denote goalscorers. † denotes opponent's own goal.

Victoria Park Stadium

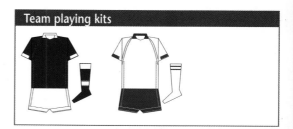

JUBILEE ROAD

CAPACITY: 5,800, Seated 2,800, Standing 3,000
PITCH DIMENSIONS: 110 yds x 75 yds
FACILITIES FOR DISABLED SUPPORTERS:
Areas in Main Stand and Terracing. Toilet facilities are also available.

Team playing kits

How to get there

The following routes may be used to reach Victoria Park Stadium:
TRAINS: The nearest mainline station is Inverness and fans travelling from the south should alight and board a train that takes them direct to Dingwall Station.
BUSES: Regular buses on a daily basis from Glasgow, Edinburgh and Perth.
CARS: The major trunk roads, A9 and A96, connect Dingwall with the North, the South and the East.

email: info@sfl.scottishfootball.com • website: www.scottishfootball.com

AIRDRIEONIANS
SEASON TICKET INFORMATION - SEATED

NO SEASON TICKETS BEING SOLD

LEAGUE ADMISSION PRICES -SEATED

ADULT	£12
JUVENILE/OAP	£7
PARENT & JUVENILE	£18

ALLOA ATHLETIC
SEASON TICKET INFORMATION

SEATED	ADULT	£150
	JUVENILE/OAP	£80
STANDING	ADULT	£140
	JUVENILE/OAP	£70

LEAGUE ADMISSION PRICES

SEATED	ADULT	£10
	JUVENILE/OAP	£6
STANDING	ADULT	£9
	JUVENILE/OAP	£5

AYR UNITED
SEASON TICKET INFORMATION
SEATED

CENTRE STAND	ADULT	£205
	OAP	£105
WING STAND	ADULT	£180
	JUVENILE/OAP	£90
FAMILY STAND	ADULT/JUVENILE	£180
	ADDITIONAL JUVENILE	£45

STANDING

GROUND/ENCLOSURE	ADULT	£140
	JUVENILE/OAP	£70
	ADULT & JUVENILE	£180

LEAGUE ADMISSION PRICES
SEATED

MAIN STAND (Centre)	ADULT	£14
MAIN STAND (Wing)	ADULT	£13
	CONCESSION	£11
FAMILY STAND	ADULT/JUVENILE	£12

(Plus £5.00 for each additional Juvenile)

STANDING

ENCLOSURE	ADULT	£10.50
GROUND	ADULT	£10
	JUVENILE/OAP	£5

CLYDE
SEASON TICKET INFORMATION

SEATED	ADULT	£200
	OAP	£100
	JUVENILE	£50

LEAGUE ADMISSION PRICES

SEATED	ADULT	£11
	OAP	£5
	JUVENILE	£3

FALKIRK
SEASON TICKET INFORMATION
SEATED

ADULT	£220/£205
JUVENILE/OAP (Wing Stand)	£145/£105
HUSBAND & WIFE	£380

STANDING

SOUTH ENCLOSURE	
ADULT	£190
JUVENILE/OAP	£100
GROUND	
ADULT	£175
JUVENILE/OAP	£90

LEAGUE ADMISSION PRICES
SEATED

ADULT	£15/£13.50
JUVENILE/OAP (Wing Stand)	£6.50

STANDING

ENCLOSURE	
ADULT	£11.50
JUVENILE/OAP	£5.50
GROUND	
ADULT	£10
JUVENILE/OAP	£5

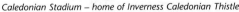

Caledonian Stadium – home of Inverness Caledonian Thistle

INVERNESS CALEDONIAN THISTLE

SEASON TICKET INFORMATION

SEATED	ADULT	£165
	JUVENILE/OAP	£100
STANDING	ADULT	£120
	JUVENILE/OAP	£50

LEAGUE ADMISSION PRICES

SEATED	ADULT	£11
	JUVENILE/OAP	£6
STANDING	ADULT	£9
	JUVENILE/OAP	£5

RAITH ROVERS
SEASON TICKET INFORMATION - SEATED

MAIN STAND/RAILWAY STAND/SOUTH STAND

ADULT	£190
JUVENILE/OAP	£90
PARENT & JUVENILE	£260
PARENT & 2 JUVENILES	£330

LEAGUE ADMISSION PRICES - SEATED
MAIN STAND/ RAILWAY STAND/SOUTH STAND/NORTH STAND

ADULT	£12
JUVENILE/OAP	£5

LIVINGSTON

SEASON TICKET INFORMATION - SEATED

ADULT	£185
PARENT & JUVENILE	£220
PARENT & 2 JUVENILES	£260
2 PARENTS & 2 JUVENILES	£420
OAP & JUVENILE	£85

LEAGUE ADMISSION PRICES - SEATED

ADULT	£11
JUVENILE/OAP	£6

Livingston's West Lothian Courier Stadium

MORTON
SEASON TICKET INFORMATION
CENTRE STAND – SEATED

ADULT	£200
OAP	£150
JUVENILE	£50

ROVING TICKET

ADULT	£150
OAP	£75
JUVENILES 12 to U18	£50
JUVENILES 12 & UNDER	£20

LEAGUE ADMISSION PRICES
SEATED

ADULT	£11
JUVENILE/OAP	£6
PARENT & JUVENILE	£15

ROVING TICKET

ADULT	£10
JUVENILE/OAP	£5
PARENT & JUVENILE	£14

ROSS COUNTY
SEASON TICKET INFORMATION – SEATED

ADULT	£150
OAP/U-18	£80
U-12	£70

STANDING

ADULT	£120
OAP	£60
U-18	£30
U-12	£20

FAMILY SECTION

ADULT	£130
OAP	£70
U-18	£40
U-12	£25

LEAGUE ADMISSION PRICES – SEATED

ADULT	£11
JUVENILE	£5

STANDING

ADULT	£9
JUVENILE/OAP	£4

The Spirit of Scottish Football

Lord Macfarlane of Bearsden does not look as if he even owns an anorak. Nor does he seem the type to have spent his childhood trainspotting. And yet he showed every sign of an obsessive personality as, last season, he and his wife visited all the grounds at which the 30 clubs of the Bell's Scottish Football League are based.

Enthusiam and a pleasure at what he found at those venues carried him down those many roads, but so too, did his awareness of the responsibilities that come with sponsorship. Lord Macfarlane is Honorary Life President of United Distillers and Vintners, the huge company that makes Bell's Scotch Whisky, as well as several more of the most famous brands in the drinks industry.

UDV, in fact, is the biggest alcoholic beverage company in the world. Instead of being an aloof corporate body that communicates only through billboards or slick adverts at the cinema, it has made its way into every corner of Scottish football. When senior football still existed as a single structure, they sponsored all four divisions from seasons 1994/95 to 1997/98. With the formation of The Scottish Premier League, however, UDV had to re-evaluate the situation. They concluded that it would be best to sponsor The Scottish Football League and the current deal, which started in season 1999/2000, is worth £2m over three years.

David Longmuir, Director of Trade Relations for UDV in Scotland, is the person who handles the sponsorship. "We are delighted with the reaction to Bell's from the clubs and the fans throughout Scotland," he said. "We believe Bell's is the spirit of Scottish football. We look forward to maintaining a relationship with clubs at all levels."

There was a clear appeal in the fact that UDV would be reaching a large number of people across a broad geographical spread. Lord Macfarlane felt the mileage in his bones. "The first game I went to was at Ross County," he said, "and the next week I was at Berwick. That's a huge distance, but you just have to get on with it." He radiates the enthusiasm of a man who has enjoyed his travels, but UDV can only pour its money into football for sound commercial reasons and Lord Macfarlane is sure of the sponsorship's impact.

"UDV rather like football," he said, "have establishments everywhere in Scotland. We have 52 distilleries, bottling plants or offices and they cover the same sort of area that football does. We had nothing against The Scottish

Lord Macfarlane with the Bell's trophies

Lord Macfarlane welcomes new Scottish Football League members, Elgin City F.C. and Peterhead F.C.

Premier League, but when you are a company on our scale you have to think things through.

"We decided that supporting clubs in their communities would have a great effect. It would, in fact, almost keep some of them alive. It's been good for us, too, and that is what sponsorship is all about."

Lord Macfarlane's jaunts were also a demonstration that UDV was not content simply to pass over the occasional cheque. "If you decide that something is important enough to sponsor then you have a responsibility to get involved," he said. Nonetheless, he did not take to the road only to carry out his duties.

He admits, guardedly, that there might have been some emotional rewards for himself. As a youth he played for Queen's Park Strollers. An accident while in the Army ended his

football days and, as he puts it, meant that he is "always entitled to think that I might have been an up-and-coming star."

The other small legacy of those days is an interest in the fortunes of Queen's Park. Therefore, he was overjoyed to be at Hampden Park at the start of the season when they raised the Third Division Championship flag. "I have a soft spot for Queen's Park," Lord Macfarlane conceded, "and I told them I very much hoped to be coming back next year."

He is happy to join the celebrations at any venue and treasures, in particular, the memory of his first trip, which carried him to Dingwall in 1999 when they were marking their success in taking the Third Division title. Lord Macfarlane, like any other visitor to the Victoria Park Stadium, knows how dynamic a club Ross County is.

"There were 2,500 people at the game and the population of Dingwall is only 6,000, so that is a remarkable turnout. The Chairman, Roy MacGregor, is a nice person and a very bright businessman too," Lord Macfarlane said.

The presentation of honours took on a variety of forms when it came to St. Mirren. Of course, they became Champions of the First Division last season, but the prizes do not end there. In addition, they were also judged to have the best pies of any club in The Scottish Football League. St. Mirren, in other words, did the "Double" last season.

Lord Macfarlane took a decidely personal interest in the matter and came across Chairmen who seemed more interested in their standing in the culinary table than in their League position. "We had promised a gallon bottle of whisky to the club with the

29

best pies," he said, "and I had one at every single club. My wife thought it was disgusting!"

There appears to have been little else that was not to her taste. Lord Macfarlane notes that the "off-side rule still perplexes her" but exactly the same could be said about supporters who, unlike her, have been watching football for decades. No copy of the Laws of the Game is required for a person to appreciate the charms of the sport.

Lady Macfarlane likes the company of the people she meets, the scornful shouts from the crowd and the inherent excitements of the game. Her husband gets a little concerned that she may respond too strongly.

"She has difficulty being neutral," Lord Macfarlane said, "and because we sit with the hosts, who, of course, are the Board of the home team, I have

asked her not to smile or clap. She points out that it is hard not to and when she tells me that she was reacting to an especially good goal I find it hard to disagree."

He may be forbidden to take sides, but Lord Macfarlane is eager, where possible, to be a champion of football as a whole. No-one can roam from match to match without sensing how football is woven through Scottish life and how, in the process, it holds towns together and forms part of their character.

"On a Board of Directors at a football club," Lord Macfarlane said, "you could find a local publican, a hotelier, an accountant, a garage owner and so on. They are a very good representation of the community from which they come. I try to explain to politicians what a contribution these little clubs make to communities and

how terrible it would be if they disappeared."

Although he has befriended football, Lord Macfarlane does not forget, either, the duties that those clubs have to UDV. While he does not promise to visit every ground this season, he will certainly go to Elgin City and Peterhead and welcome those newcomers into The Scottish Football League.

If they are wise, each of them will prepare for his arrival. Lord Macfarlane is sure to check that his company's advertising boards are in place as they should be and that the UDV brands are stocked in the bar. It would be a mistake to suppose that the examination ends there.

The employees of UDV have also been turned into an informal army of inspectors. "We send a minibus, normally of ladies from our bottling

Gary Clark of Alloa Athletic celebrates his goal in last season's Bell's Challenge Cup Final

plants, to various games and they have to come back and tell us whether they were well received, what the toilets were like and whether they would go back with their children or their husbands," Lord Macfarlane said.

"If we feel things are not as they should be, we tell the Chairman. We can't influence what happens on the field, but if there were a lot of problems we would stop the sponsorship. We are not in the business of doing something that gives us a bad reputation."

These words bring a solemn note to his conversation, but while Lord Macfarlane has encountered an ugly atmosphere at clubs where there have been specific tensions and problems, his view of Scottish football is generally a sunny one.

The welcome that he and his wife receive is, as one might expect, warm, but he has also found that his visit is considered important. "People like it when they see someone who represents the company at a high level coming to share the problems of football with them," Lord Macfarlane said. "There's no way we could send the office boy."

At Ross County, he and his wife were brought onto the pitch and presented to the crowd. The following week, Berwick Rangers went a stage further and rolled out a red carpet to lead them onto the field.

It was that day, too, that a disgruntled fan cried out during the game, "Bring on Lord Macfarlane." An even more dissatisfied supporter then modified the demand - "Bring on Lady Macfarlane." Only companies who sponsor football can ever hope for quite so direct a reaction from their customers!

KEVIN McCARRA
(The Times)

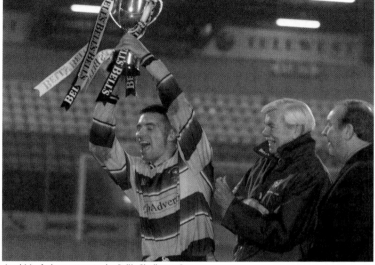

Lord Macfarlane presents the Bell's Challenge Cup

Martin Cameron receives his Bell's Man of the Match award for last season's Final

Arbroath

Gayfield Park,
Arbroath, Angus, DD11 1QB

PRESIDENT
John D. Christison

VICE-PRESIDENT
Charles W. Kinnear

COMMITTEE
R. Alan Ripley (Treasurer),
William J. Thomson, George Johnson,
Michael Caird, David G. Hodgens
Michael J. Leonard & Brian W. Lumgair

SECRETARY
Charles W. Kinnear

MANAGER

ASSISTANT MANAGER

**FIRST TEAM COACH/RESERVE
COACH/CHIEF SCOUT**
Jake Ferrier

YOUTH CO-ORDINATOR
Eddie Wolecki

FITNESS COACH
Jim Stewart

YOUTH TEAM COACHES
Ray McWalter (U18)
Derek Carr (U16)

YOUTH COACHES
Ray McWalter, Derek Carr,
Graham Donald & John Welsh

CLUB DOCTOR
Dr. Dick Spiers

PHYSIOTHERAPIST
Ian Cardle

GROUNDSMAN
Charles Lamb

COMMERCIAL MANAGER
Bruce McLean
Bus. (01382) 907111

MATCHDAY PROGRAMME EDITOR
George Cant (Herald Press)

TELEPHONES
Ground/Fax/Ticket Office/Club Shop
(01241) 872157
Telefax (01241) 431125
Sec. Home (01241) 876640
Sec. Bus. (01382) 424336

E-MAIL & INTERNET ADDRESS
www.arbroathfc.co.uk

CLUB SHOP
Gayfield Park, Arbroath, DD11 1QB.
Open on home matchdays.
Premier Sports, West Port, Arbroath,
DD11 1RF. Open Mon. to Sat.

TEAM CAPTAIN
John McAulay

SHIRT SPONSOR
Abbey Fruits

KIT SUPPLIER
XARA

LIST OF PLAYERS 2000-2001

SURNAME	FIRST NAME	MIDDLE NAME	DATE OF BIRTH	PLACE OF BIRTH	DATE OF SIGNING	HEIGHT FT INS	WEIGHT ST LBS	POS. ON PITCH	PREVIOUS CLUB
Arbuckle	David		12/08/73	Bellshill	21/05/98	5 10.0	11 5	Mid	Queen's Park
Beattie	Derek	Calvin	09/04/84	Arbroath	07/06/00	5 8.0	10 6	Fwd	S Form
Borland	James	David	10/09/83	London	07/06/00	5 9.0	10 0	Mid	S Form
Brownlie	Paul	Jack	30/08/77	Falkirk	31/07/99	5 9.0	10 8	Fwd	Raith Rovers
Campbell	Stephen		11/03/82	Perth	11/02/00	5 6.0	10 9	Def	Dundee
Crawford	Jonathan		14/10/69	Johnstone	31/03/95	6 1.0	12 7	Def	Arthurlie Juniors
Cusick	John	James	16/01/75	Kirkcaldy	14/06/00	5 8.0	12 8	Def/Mid	East Fife
Durno	Paul		19/06/84	Arbroath	07/06/00	5 10.0	10 0	Mid	S Form
Florence	Steven		28/10/71	Dundee	20/05/88	5 6.0	11 5	Mid	Arbroath Lads Club
Fotheringham	Kevin	George	13/08/75	Dunfermline	08/07/00	5 10.0	12 4	Def/Mid	Hill of Beath Hawthorne
Gairns	Stephen		18/10/83	Aberdeen	18/08/00	5 8.0	11 0	Mid	St. Johnstone
Good	Iain	David	09/08/77	Glasgow	08/08/00	6 1.0	11 9	Def	Aberdeen
Graham	Ewan	Douglas	11/01/83	Arbroath	07/06/00	5 11.0	11 0	Def	St. Johnstone
Heenan	Kevin	Alexander	07/03/82	Dundee	30/07/99	5 9.0	10 8	Fwd	S Form
Henderson	Christopher		20/01/84	Perth	17/06/00	6 0.0	10 0	Mid	St. Johnstone
Henslee	Greig		13/01/83	Dundee	16/02/00	5 10.0	11 10	Mid	S Form
Hinchcliffe	Craig	Peter	05/05/72	Glasgow	04/08/95	5 11.0	13 0	Gk	Elgin City
Houston	Steven	James	15/03/82	Dundee	07/02/00	5 8.0	11 4	Fwd	S Form
King	Thomas	Richard	07/03/76	St. Albans	31/03/00	5 11.0	11 7	Mid	Dundee North End
Laverick	Scott		02/03/84	Arbroath	07/06/00	5 8.0	10 0	Mid	S Form
MacMillan	Kenneth		26/01/83	Dundee	07/06/00	6 2.0	11 4	Def	S Form
Mallan	Stephen	Patrick	30/08/67	Glasgow	26/07/00	5 11.0	12 4	Fwd	Queen of the South
McAulay	John		28/04/72	Glasgow	04/07/95	5 9.0	11 7	Def	Clyde
McGlashan	Colin	James	17/03/64	Perth	10/10/98	5 7.0	10 12	Fwd	Montrose
McGlashan	John		03/06/67	Dundee	15/08/00	6 1.0	12 0	Mid	Ross County
Mercer	James		30/07/74	Glasgow	18/07/98	6 5.0	13 7	Fwd	Queen's Park
Peters	Scott		09/12/72	Dundee	29/07/97	5 11.0	11 7	Mid	Hill O'Beath
Peters	Scott	John	01/08/81	Dundee	08/09/00	5 10.0	11 7	Def/Mid	Broughty Athletic
Rowe	John	George	23/08/68	Glasgow	14/07/00	6 0.0	12 10	Def	Queen of the South
Smith	Daryl		29/04/83	Arbroath	07/06/00	6 1.0	11 10	Def	Arbroath Lads Club
Spink	Darren		08/01/81	Arbroath	08/09/00	5 11.0	12 0	Def	Broughty Athletic
Steele	Kevin		11/10/81	Dundee	02/09/00	5 11.0	10 7	Fwd	Broughty Ferry J.F.C.
Stubbs	Ryan	Lee	28/06/83	Germany	18/08/00	6 0.0	10 9	Gk	Brechin City
Swankie	Gavin		22/11/83	Arbroath	07/02/00	5 8.5	9 0	Mid	S Form
Thomson	James		15/05/71	Stirling	05/06/99	6 1.0	12 7	Def	Queen of the South
Thomson	Neil		21/10/69	East Kilbride	09/08/97	5 6.0	10 10	Mid	Montrose
Wares	Colin	Scott	05/02/81	Dundee	16/09/00	5 11.0	10 10	Mid	Broughty Athletic
Webster	Andrew	Neil	23/04/82	Dundee	02/09/00	6 0.0	10 0	Def	S Form
Wight	Craig	MacDonald	24/07/78	Glasgow	09/10/97	6 2.0	12 10	Gk	Hibernian

Milestones

YEAR OF FORMATION: 1878
MOST CAPPED PLAYER: Ned Doig
NO. OF CAPS: 2
MOST LEAGUE POINTS IN A SEASON: 57 (Division 2 – Season 1966/67)(2 Points for a Win)
68 (Third Division – Season 1997/98)(3 Points for a Win)
MOST LEAGUE GOALS SCORED BY A PLAYER IN A SEASON: David Easson (Season 1958/59)
NO. OF GOALS SCORED: 45
RECORD ATTENDANCE: 13,510 (-v- Rangers – Scottish Cup, 23.2.1952)
RECORD VICTORY: 36-0 (-v- Bon Accord – Scottish Cup, 12.9.1885)
RECORD DEFEAT: 1-9 (-v- Celtic – League Cup, 25.8.1993)

The Red Lichties' ten year league record

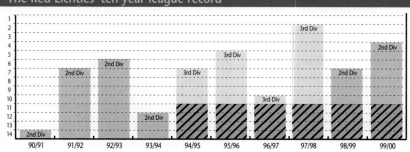

THE RED LICHTIES' CLUB FACTFILE 1999/2000
RESULTS... APPEARANCES... SCORERS... ATTENDANCES...

Date	Venue	Opponents	Att.	Res	Hinchcliffe C.	Florence S.	Gallagher J.	McMulay J.	Arbuckle D.	Crawford J.	Sellars B.	Bryce T.	McClashan C.	Devine C.	Mercer J.	Peters S.	Brownlie P.	Thomson N.	Thomson J.	Cooper C.	Webster A.	Deswarte F.	Raeside R.	Mols T.	Tindall K.	Steele K.	Wight C.	Tosh P.	King T.
Aug 7	A	Queen of the South	1,118	3-2	1	2	3	4	5	6[1]	7	8	9[1]	10[1]	11	12	14	15											
14	H	Clyde	812	2-1	1	2	3	4		6	7[1]	8	9[1]		11	14	10		5	15									
21	A	Partick Thistle	1,915	3-1	1	2	3	4	11	6	7	8[1]	9		14	15[1]	10[1]		5	12									
28	A	Ross County	2,303	0-2	1	2	3		11	6		8	9		12					15			5	7	10	14			
Sep 4	H	Alloa Athletic	851	2-2	1	2	3[1]	4		6	7	8	9[1]		11	15							5						
11	H	Stirling Albion	805	2-1	1		3[1]	4	2	6	7	8	9		11		10[1]		15				5						
18	A	Stenhousemuir	596	3-1	1	12	3	4	2	6	7[1]	8[1]	9[1]		11	15	10	14					5						
25	H	Stranraer	811	1-2	1		3	4	2	6	7	8	9		11[1]		10	14		12			5						
Oct 2	A	Hamilton Academical	489	2-2	1	15	3	4	2	6	7	8[1]	9		11[1]		10	14					5						
16	A	Clyde	887	0-0	1	2	3	4	10	14	7	8	9		11	6	12						5						
23	H	Queen of the South	851	5-2	1	2		4	7[2]	6		8	9[3]	14	11	12	10		5	15			3						
30	A	Stirling Albion	856	4-3	1	15	3	4	2	6	7	8[2]	9[1]	12	11[1]		10						5						
Nov 6	H	Stenhousemuir	866	0-3	1	14	3	4	2	15	7	8	9	12	11		10						5	6					
9	A	Alloa Athletic	637	0-0	1	2	3	4	11	6	14	8	9			5	10							7					
20	H	Ross County	972	1-1	1	2	3	4	10	6	7	8	9	12	11	5		14											
27	H	Hamilton Academical	764	1-1	1		3	4	2	6	7	8	9		11	5									14[1]	15			
Dec 4	A	Stranraer	384	2-2			3	4	5	6	7	12	9[1]	10	11[1]	2									8	15	1		
18	A	Queen of the South	837	0-1		14	3	4	2	6	7	8	9	10	11					5					12	15	1		
27	H	Partick Thistle	1,509	0-0			3	11	2	4	6	8	9				10			5	7						1		
Jan 3	A	Stenhousemuir	381	0-3			3	11	2	4	6	8	9		10					5						12	1		
22	A	Stranraer	720	1-1			3	4	2	6	10	8	9	12	11				5	7					15		1	9[1]	
Feb 5	A	Hamilton Academical	407	2-2		2		4		6	7		9[1]	14	3				5[1]	15					8		1	10	
12	A	Ross County	2,059	1-1		2		4		6		8	9		12				3	5	7						1	10[1]	
26	H	Clyde	880	1-1		14	3	4	2	6	7	8	9[1]		11	5									15	10	1		
29	H	Stirling Albion	580	3-2			3	4	2	6	7[1]	8	9[2]	10	11	5				15					12		1		
Mar 4	A	Partick Thistle	2,210	0-2		14	3	4	2	6	7	8	9	10	11	5			15								1		
11	A	Stirling Albion	681	1-1			3	4	2	6	7	8	9		11		10		5	15									
18	H	Stenhousemuir	730	2-2			3	4		6[1]		10	8	9	12	11			5[1]	7	2				14				
25	H	Ross County	804	1-2	1	12		4				10	8	9[1]	15	11	14		5	7	2		6	3					
28	H	Alloa Athletic	567	2-0	1		3	4	2	6	7	8	9		11[1]		10[1]								5				
Apr 1	A	Alloa Athletic	631	1-2	1		3	4	2	6	7	8	9[1]	12	11		10			15					5		14		
8	A	Stranraer	412	1-0	1		3	4	2	6	7	8	9	14	11		10								5		15		
15	H	Hamilton Academical	604	1-1	1		3	4	2	6	7	8[1]	9	12	11		10								5		14		
22	H	Queen of the South	589	1-2	1		3	4	2	6	14	12	9	8	7		10								5[1]		11		
29	A	Clyde	1,798	1-4	1		3	4		7	11	8	9[1]				10			6					5		12		2
May 6	H	Partick Thistle	889	3-2	1		3			6	7[1]	8	9	14	11	5[1]	10[1]										12		2
TOTAL FULL APPEARANCES					26	31	14	35	31	29	33	32	34	7	31	11	19	1	15	6	4		14	3	4	1	10	3	2
TOTAL SUB APPEARANCES						(3)	(5)		(2)	(2)	(3)		(14)		(5)	(5)	(3)		(10)		(2)				(11)	(4)			
TOTAL GOALS SCORED							2	3	1	4	6		16	1	6	2	5						2		1			1	2

Small bold figures denote goalscorers. † denotes opponent's own goal.

Gayfield Park

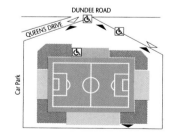

DUNDEE ROAD · QUEENS DRIVE · Car Park

CAPACITY: 6,488; Seated 715, Standing 5,773
PITCH DIMENSIONS: 115 yds x 71 yds
FACILITIES FOR DISABLED SUPPORTERS:
Enclosure at west end of Stand with wide steps to take a wheelchair. Toilet facilities are also available.

Team playing kits

How to get there

The following routes may be used to reach Gayfield Park:
BUSES: Arbroath is on the main route from both Glasgow and Edinburgh to Aberdeen. Buses from these three cities, plus Stirling, Dundee and Perth all stop at Arbroath Bus Station at hourly intervals. There is also a local service between Dundee-Arbroath and Montrose and this service is half hourly until 7.00 p.m. Between 7.00 p.m. and 10.45 p.m. the service is hourly. The bus station is 10 minutes walk from the ground.
TRAINS: Arbroath is on the Inter-City 125 route from London to Aberdeen and there are frequent local services between Arbroath, Dundee and Edinburgh. Trains also travel north from Glasgow, Stirling and Perth. The station is a 15 minute walk from the ground.
CARS: There is free parking for 500 cars just next to the ground in Queen's Drive.

email: info@sfl.scottishfootball.com • website: www.scottishfootball.com

BERWICK RANGERS FOOTBALL CLUB

Berwick Rangers

LIST OF PLAYERS 2000-2001

SURNAME	FIRST NAME	MIDDLE NAME	DATE OF BIRTH	PLACE OF BIRTH	DATE OF SIGNING	HEIGHT FT INS	WEIGHT ST LBS	POS. ON PITCH	PREVIOUS CLUB
Alexander	Ross		05/08/82	Edinburgh	17/08/00	5 8.0	11 2	Mid	S Form
Anthony	Marc		28/03/78	Edinburgh	24/07/99	5 7.0	11 0	Fwd	Celtic
Black	Sean		24/12/82	Edinburgh	17/08/00	5 5.0	9 12	Fwd	S Form
Catlow	Neil		05/06/83	Alnwick	15/09/00	6 2.0	10 10	Def	Berwick Rangers Youth
Duthie	Mark	James	19/08/72	Edinburgh	01/06/00	5 9.0	10 7	Mid	Ross County
Findlay	Craig		22/09/80	Bangour	10/06/00	6 1.0	12 3	Fwd	Heart of Midlothian
Forrest	Gordon	Iain	14/01/77	Dunfermline	12/06/00	5 9.0	10 10	Def	East Fife
Fusco	Gary		01/06/82	Edinburgh	17/08/00	6 0.0	10 0	Mid	S Form
Gordon	Christopher		24/06/82	Edinburgh	17/08/00	5 10.0	10 7	Def	S Form
Grant	Rory		06/07/82	Broxburn	12/08/00	6 2.0	11 0	Fwd	Broxburn Ibrox
Haddow	Lloyd	Simon	21/01/71	Lanark	07/06/99	6 1.0	11 6	Mid	Alloa Athletic
Harvey	Johnny		15/09/82	Glasgow	30/07/00	6 0.0	10 12	Fwd	Whitehill Welfare U'18
Laidlaw	Steven	James	17/06/73	Edinburgh	01/02/00	6 0.0	12 0	Fwd	East Stirlingshire
Magee	Kevin		10/04/71	Livingston	21/06/99	5 10.0	11 1	Mid	Montrose
McIntosh	Chris		01/11/82	Edinburgh	12/08/00	6 0.0	13 0	Def	Musselburgh Windsor
McLean	Mark	Andrew	30/03/72	Paisley	26/07/00	6 1.0	12 10	Gk	Albion Rovers
McMartin	Grant	Thomas	31/12/70	Linlithgow	26/07/00	5 11.0	11 0	Mid	Stranraer
McNicoll	Grant		07/09/77	Edinburgh	30/07/97	5 11.0	11 1	Def	Heart of Midlothian
Murray	Kevin		07/04/82	Edinburgh	12/08/00	6 1.0	11 0	Def	Musselburgh Windsor
Neil	Martin		16/04/70	Ashington	17/11/94	5 8.0	11 7	Mid	Bolton Wanderers
Neill	Alan	John	13/12/70	Baillieston	25/06/98	6 1.0	12 7	Def	East Stirlingshire
O'Connor	Gary		07/04/74	Newtongrange	12/09/97	6 3.0	13 7	Gk	Partick Thistle
Oliver	Neil		11/04/67	Berwick-U-Tweed	26/06/00	5 11.0	12 3	Def	Clydebank
Patterson	Paul	Joseph	30/07/75	Glasgow	30/07/99	5 10.0	9 1	Fwd	East Stirlingshire
Pucko	Craig		30/07/82	Edinburgh	12/08/00	5 10.0	10 7	Gk	Musselburgh Windsor
Ritchie	Innes		24/08/73	Edinburgh	25/06/99	6 0.0	12 7	Def	Clydebank
Ronald	Paul		19/07/71	Glasgow	08/06/00	6 2.0	12 7	Fwd	Stranraer
Scott	Dean		22/09/82	Edinburgh	12/08/00	5 6.0	9 7	Fwd	Granton Sports B.C.
Scott	Robbie		19/03/82	Paisley	17/08/00	5 6.0	9 0	Fwd	S Form
Shankland	Kris		18/04/82	Irvine	12/08/00	5 8.0	10 0	Mid	Dunfermline Athletic Colts
Sinclair	Craig		19/07/72	Edinburgh	03/03/99	5 11.0	12 0	Mid	Edinburgh City
Small	Gary		17/12/82	Edinburgh	12/08/00	5 10.0	11 0	Mid	Musselburgh Windsor
Smith	Darren		04/06/80	Edinburgh	16/10/98	5 7.0	10 2	Mid	Berwick Rangers Colts
Watt	David		05/03/67	Edinburgh	25/06/98	5 7.0	11 4	Mid	East Stirlingshire
Whelan	Jonathan		10/10/72	Liverpool	17/05/00	6 0.0	12 3	Mid	Queen's Park
Wood	Garry	Pringle G.	18/09/76	Edinburgh	18/01/00	5 11.0	12 7	Fwd	Ross County
Yeadon	Paul		09/04/83	Newcastle-u-Tyne	15/09/00	5 8.0	10 0	Fwd	Berwick Rangers Youth

Milestones

YEAR OF FORMATION: 1881
MOST LEAGUE POINTS IN A SEASON: 54 (Second Division – Season 1978/79) (2 Points for a Win)
66 (Third Division – Season 1999/2000) (3 Points for a Win)
MOST LEAGUE GOALS SCORED BY A PLAYER IN A SEASON: Ken Bowron (Season 1963/64)
NO. OF GOALS SCORED: 38
RECORD ATTENDANCE: 13,365 (-v- Rangers – 28.1.1967)
RECORD VICTORY: 8-1 (-v- Forfar Athletic (H) – Division 2, 25.12.1965)
8-1 (-v- Vale of Leithen – Scottish Cup at Innerleithen 17.12.1966)
RECORD DEFEAT: 1-9 (-v- Hamilton Academical – First Division, 9.8.1980)

The Borderers' ten year league record

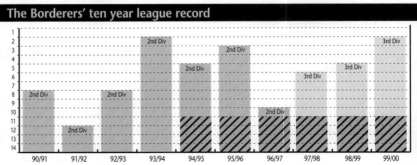

THE BORDERERS' CLUB FACTFILE 1999/2000
RESULTS... APPEARANCES... SCORERS... ATTENDANCES...

Date	Venue	Opponents	Att.	Res	O'Connor G.	Watt D.	Haddow L.	McNicoll G.	Neill A.	Ritchie I.	Neil M.	Patterson P.	Leask M.	Anthony M.	Magee K.	Campbell C.	Forrester P.	Smith D.	Rafferty K.	Humphreys M.	Hunter M.	Porteous A.	Findlay C.	Carr-Lawton C.	McPherson D.	Wood G.	Laidlaw S.	Ramsay S.	Oliver N.	Scrimgour D.	Harvey J.	Moonie D.
Aug 7	A	East Fife	549	2-1	1	2^1	3	4	5	6	7	8	9^1	10	11	12		14	15													
14	H	Albion Rovers	366	1-1	1		3	2	5	6	9	8^1	11	7	4		14	15	10	12												
21	A	Montrose	313	2-1	1	12	3		5	6	4	8	9	7^1	11			15	10	2^1	14											
28	H	Queen's Park	710	1-2	1		3		5	6	7	9		8	11	14		10^1	2			4	15									
Sep 4	A	Dumbarton	324	1-2	1	14	3	2	5	6^1	7	9	12	8	11			10	4													
11	H	Cowdenbeath	457	0-2	1	4	3	2	5	6	7	11	9	8				10	15		12											
18	A	Forfar Athletic	375	1-1	1	6	3^1		5	2	7	9	15	8	11	4	10	12		14												
25	H	Brechin City	407	2-0	1	6	3		5	2^1	7	8	14	10	11	4	9	12		15												
Oct 2	A	East Stirlingshire	266	3-0	1	6	3		5	2^2	7	9		8	11	4	15	12				10^1										
16	A	Albion Rovers	360	3-0	1	6	3	2	4		10	7	14	8^1	11	5		12	15			9^2										
23	H	East Fife	506	0-1	1	6	3		5	2	7	8	15	10	11	4		12				9										
30	A	Cowdenbeath	313	1-1	1	6	3^1	15	5	2	10	7	14	8	12	4		11				9										
Nov 6	A	Forfar Athletic	328	2-2	1		3^1	5		2	7	12		8	11	4		10	14			9^1	6	15								
14	H	Dumbarton	415	0-1	1		3	5		2	6	14		7	11	4		10	15			9	8									
20	A	Queen's Park	678	4-1	1	7^1	3	2		5	6	14		10^2	11	4		8^1				9	12									
27	H	East Stirlingshire	318	1-0	1	7	3	2^1	12	5	6	14		10	11	4		8		15		9										
Dec 7	A	Brechin City	356	3-0	1	6	3	2	12	5	8	7		10^1		4		11^2	15	14		9										
27	H	Montrose	472	0-0	1	6	3	2	12	5	8	7	14	10	15	4		11				9										
Jan 15	H	Cowdenbeath	413	0-0	1	8	3	2	5			7		10	15	4		11				9	6									
22	H	Brechin City	344	3-1	1	6^1	3	2	5	12		7^1		8	11	4		10^1							9							
Feb 5	A	East Stirlingshire	255	1-0	1		3	2	5	12		7			11	4		6	8			14			9^1	10						
12	H	Queen's Park	525	1-1	1		2	5	3			7		14	11	4		6	8			12			9	10^1	15					
26	H	Albion Rovers	756	2-1	1	6		2	5				8^1	11	4			12	7			14	15		10	9^1	3					
Mar 4	A	Montrose	302	3-2	1	6		2	5		15			8	14	4		11				12	7		10^2	9^1		3				
7	A	Forfar Athletic	482	0-2	1	6		2	5		15	7		8	11	4						12			10	9		3				
11	H	Cowdenbeath	402	3-1	1	6		2	5	4	8			10	11			3	7			12	15		9^2		14^1					
14	A	Dumbarton	330	2-0	1	6		5	4	8			10^1	12				3^1	7			14			9	15	2					
18	H	Forfar Athletic	614	2-0	1	6		5	4	8			10^1	14				3	7			15			9^1	12	2					
21	A	East Fife	551	1-3	1	6		5	4	8			10	14				3	7			15			9	12	2^1					
25	A	Queen's Park	964	1-0		8	3	2	5^1	4	7			12	14			11	15						10	9			6	1		
Apr 1	H	Dumbarton	560	0-0		8	3	2	5	4	7			10				11	12			14				9			6	1		
8	A	Brechin City	267	2-1		8	3^1	2	5	4			12	10				11	7			15			9^1				6	1		
15	H	East Stirlingshire	486	3-0		8	3	2	5	4^1			12	10	14			11^1	7			15			9^1				6	1		
22	H	East Fife	942	0-1		8	3	2	5	4				10				11	7			15			9				6	1		
29	A	Albion Rovers	443	0-0			3	2	5	4		7		8				11	12			14			10	9			6	1		
May 6	H	Montrose	1,224	2-1			3^1	2	5	4	8							11	7			10^1				9			6	1	12	14
TOTAL FULL APPEARANCES					29	26	31	26	30	29	25	20	4	32	20	19	2	28	14	1		12	4		15	9	4	9	7		
TOTAL SUB APPEARANCES					(2)		(1)	(3)	(2)	(1)	(7)	(7)	(2)	(9)	(3)	(4)	(7)	(9)	(2)	(4)	(1)	(14)	(3)	(1)		(3)	(2)			(1)	(1)
TOTAL GOALS SCORED						3	5	1	1	5		2	1	9				7	1			5				8	3	2			

Small bold figures denote goalscorers. † denotes opponent's own goal.

Shielfield Park

To Berwick by-pass (North and South)

Offices

Turnstiles B
(ALSO ACCESS TO STANDS)

SHIELFIELD TERRACE

Turnstiles A
Town Centre and Edinburgh North ▶

CAPACITY: 4,131; Seated 1,366, Standing 2,765
PITCH DIMENSIONS: 110 yds x 70 yds
FACILITIES FOR DISABLED SUPPORTERS:
Supporters should enter via gate adjacent to ground turnstiles (see ground plan above) or via official entrance.

Team playing kits

How to get there

Shielfield Park can be reached by the following routes:
The ground is approximately $1^{1}/_{2}$ miles south of Berwick town centre and is situated in Shielfield Terrace, Tweedmouth. (Signposted).
BUSES: The local bus route from the town centre is the Prior Park service and the nearest stop to the ground is in Shielfield Terrace. The bus stop is only yards away from the ground.
TRAINS: The railway station is Berwick, which is situated on the East Coast line and a frequent service operates at various stages during the day. The ground is approximately $1^{1}/_{2}$ miles from the station and a taxi service operates from there or alternatively, fans can take the local bus service as detailed above.
CARS: There is a large car park at the rear of the ground. (Nominal charge).

---

email: info@sfl.scottishfootball.com • website: www.scottishfootball.com

Clydebank

Cappielow Park, Sinclair Street,
Greenock, PA15 2TY

**ALL CORRESPONDENCE
SHOULD BE ADDRESSED TO:**
S. Morrison Esq.,
Administrator,
Burnbrae, Milngavie,
Glasgow, G62 6HX

CHAIRMAN
Dr. John McK. Hall

MANAGEMENT CONSULTANTS
Low & Co.

SECRETARY
Ms. Marie McCaffrey

PLAYER/COACH
Thomas Coyne

FIRST TEAM COACH
Fraser Wishart

CLUB DOCTORS
David Pugh, Andrew Renwick
& Daniel McBryan

PHYSIOTHERAPIST
Kevan McLlenan

GROUNDSMAN
Ian Lyle

TELEPHONES
Ground (01475) 723571
(Match Days Only)
Office/Commercial (0141) 955 9048
Fax (0141) 955 9049

INTERNET ADDRESS
clydebankfc@amazone.com

OFFICIAL SUPPORTERS CLUB
c/o Gordon Robertson,
Clydebank Post,
88 Dumbarton Road, Clydebank

TEAM CAPTAIN
Kenneth Brannigan

SHIRT SPONSOR
RCI

KIT SUPPLIER
Pro Star

LIST OF PLAYERS 2000-2001

SURNAME	FIRST NAME	MIDDLE NAME	DATE OF BIRTH	PLACE OF BIRTH	DATE OF SIGNING	HEIGHT FT INS	WEIGHT ST LBS	POS. ON PITCH	PREVIOUS CLUB
Brannigan	Kenneth		08/06/65	Glasgow	04/11/99	6 2.0	13 7	Def	Partick Thistle
Conway	Christopher		01/03/82	Paisley	08/09/00	5 7.0	9 3	Fwd	Dundee
Coyne	Thomas		14/11/62	Glasgow	04/08/00	6 0.0	12 0	Fwd	Dundee
Fal	Lamine		20/12/77	Paris	08/08/00	6 2.0	12 0	Fwd	FC Atlas Molenbeek
Ferguson	Derek		31/07/67	Glasgow	03/08/00	5 8.5	11 9	Mid	Ross County
Hamilton	Brian		05/08/67	Paisley	05/08/00	5 11.0	12 10	Mid	Canberra Cosmos
Hutchison	Stephen		18/09/70	Glasgow	23/03/00	5 11.5	15 0	Gk	Cowdenbeath
Jacquel	Raphael		22/04/73	Sarrebourg	02/09/00	5 10.0	12 0	Fwd	Martigues
Johnson	Ian	Grant	24/03/72	Dundee	07/08/00	5 11.0	12 3	Mid	Huddersfield
Mackay	Jamie	Andrew	02/09/81	Glasgow	30/08/00	6 0.0	12 6	Def	Petershill
McCormick	Stephen		14/08/69	Dumbarton	25/08/00	6 4.0	12 7	Fwd	East Fife
McKelvie	Daniel		06/06/80	Paisley	25/09/98	5 7.0	10 7	Fwd	Beith Juniors
McKinnon	Robert		31/07/66	Glasgow	03/08/00	5 11.5	13 7	Def	Heart of Midlothian
McKinstrey	James		03/07/79	Glasgow	30/10/97	5 9.0	9 10	Def/Mid	Irvine Meadow
Milne	David		25/10/79	Glasgow	03/08/00	5 11.0	11 7	Mid	St. Mirren
Morrison	Stephen		15/08/61	St. Andrews	01/09/00	6 0.0	12 4	Mid	Largs Thistle
Murdoch	Scott	McKenzie	27/02/69	Glasgow	22/10/92	5 7.0	10 7	Mid	St. Rochs
Murray	Stephen		24/08/80	Irvine	03/12/99	5 9.5	11 2	Def	Celtic
Paton	Eric	John	01/08/78	Glasgow	03/08/00	5 10.0	12 7	Mid	Partick Thistle
Racon	Andy		20/09/80	Strasbourg	12/09/00	5 10.0	12 2	Mid	Le Mans
Rodden	Paul	Andrew	12/08/82	Glasgow	04/08/00	5 4.0	11 0	Fwd	Partick Thistle
Sutherland	Colin		15/03/75	Glasgow	05/02/00	6 0.0	11 7	Def	Scarborough
Walker	John		12/12/73	Glasgow	10/08/00	5 7.0	11 6	Mid	Morton
Welsh	Brian		23/02/69	Edinburgh	01/09/00	6 3.0	13 8	Def	Cowdenbeath
Wishart	Fraser		01/03/65	Johnstone	04/08/97	5 8.0	10 7	Def	Motherwell
Wylie	David		04/04/66	Johnstone	04/08/00	6 0.0	14 2	Gk	Clyde

Milestones

YEAR OF FORMATION: 1965
MOST LEAGUE POINTS IN A SEASON: 58 (Division 1 – Season 1976/77)(2 Points for a Win)
60 (Second Division – Season 1997/98)(3 Points for a Win)
MOST LEAGUE GOALS SCORED BY A PLAYER IN A SEASON: Ken Eadie (Season 1990/91)
NO. OF GOALS SCORED: 29
RECORD ATTENDANCE: 14,900 (-v- Hibernian – 10.2.1965)
RECORD VICTORY: 8-1 (-v- Arbroath – Division 1, 3.1.1977)
RECORD DEFEAT: 1-9 (-v- Gala Fairydean – Scottish Cup, 15.9.1965)

The Bankies' ten year league record

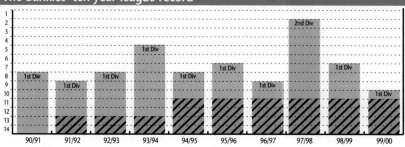

THE BANKIES' CLUB FACTFILE 1999/2000
RESULTS... APPEARANCES... SCORERS... ATTENDANCES...

Date	Venue	Opponents	Att.	Res	Scott C.	Wishart F.	Stewart D.	Murdoch S.	McLaughlin J.	Oliver N.	McInstrey J.	McIntyre P.	Miller G.	Gardner R.L.	McWilliams D.	McKelvie D.	Ewing C.	Cormack P.	Cameron I.	McDonald P.	Macdonald W.	Roddie A.	O'Neill M.	Beach K.	McCondichie A.	O'Neil N.	Geraghty M.	Brannigan K.	Jackson C.	Morrison S.	Stewart C.	McCutcheon G.	Murray S.	Hunter M.	Sutherland C.	Albeche H.	Mackay J.	O'Sullivan L.	Plevey B.	Beggs J.	Stewart A.	Hutchison S.
Aug 7	H	Airdrieonians	425	0-2	1	2	3	4	5	6	7	8	9	10	11	12	14	15																							
14	A	Morton	1,433	0-0	1	2	6	4	5		7	8	9	10		14	11	3	12	15																						
21	H	Raith Rovers	232	1-1	1	2	6	4	5		7	8	9 10[1]	15		12	3	11																								
29	H	St. Mirren	1,513	2-3	1	2	12	4	5	6	7		15[1]	10	11	14	9	3[1]	8																							
Sep 4	A	Falkirk	2,496	2-3	1	2	12	4	5	6		14[1]	9[1]	10	11		15	3			7	8																				
11	A	Inverness Cal. Th.	1,697	0-1	1		6	4	5	2	7	14	9	10	11		15	3			12	8																				
18	H	Ayr United	476	0-2	1	2	3	14	5	6	7	15	9	10		12		11			4	8																				
25	A	Livingston	3,290	1-2	1	2	6	4	5		7	14	12 10[1]		9	3	11				8	15																				
Oct 9	H	Dunfermline Athletic	475	1-4	1	2		4	5		7		9	10	11	15	3[1]	8			14	6																				
16	H	Morton	758	1-3		2	14	4	5		7		9	10	11	15	3	12	6			1	8[1]																			
23	H	Airdrieonians	1,390	0-1	1	2	5		4	7		15	10	11	14		3	9		6		8																				
30	A	Inverness Cal. Th.	184	0-3	1	2	5	4		6	7	14	10		15		3	12			8	11																				
Nov 6	H	Ayr United	1,727	0-0	1	2			5	7		14	10	11	12		3	4		15	8	9	6																			
14	H	Falkirk	500	0-3	1	2		4	5		7		15	10		12	3	11			8	9	6																			
20	A	St. Mirren	4,434	1-2	1	2			5	7		14	10		4		3	11[1]		15	8	9	6																			
27	H	Dunfermline Athletic	4,224	1-2	1	2		14	5	7		15	10		12[1]		3	11			8	9	6	4																		
Dec 4	H	Livingston	346	1-5	1	2		14	5	7		15	10[1]	12	9		3	11			8		6	4																		
18	H	Airdrieonians	307	1-1	1	2			5	7		15	10[1]	9	12		3	11			8		6	4																		
27	A	Inverness Cal. Th.	1,640	1-4		2		4	5	15		7	10	14	9		3	11[1]			12		6	8	1																	
Jan 3	H	Ayr United	901	0-2		2		4	5	15		7		14	9		3	11			12		6	8		1	10														
8	A	Falkirk	2,119	0-4		2		4	5	14		9		7	10		3	15			12		6		1	8	11														
18	A	Raith Rovers	2,754	0-1		6		4	3	2		7	10	11	12		8			15			5			1	9														
22	A	Livingston	3,064	0-3		6		4	3	2		7	10	11	12		8			15			5			1	9		14												
Feb 5	A	Dunfermline Athletic	601	†1-3	1	6			12			7	8	15	9		11			14			5			2			3	10											
26	A	Morton	1,052	0-1	1	6				4		7	12	11	14		10			8			5			2	9	3		15											
Mar 4	H	Inverness Cal. Th.	168	0-1	1	6		4				12	8	7	9		11			14			5			2	10	3		15	5										
7	H	Raith Rovers	256	2-1	1	6			15			7	8	12	14		10[2]			11						2	9	4		3	5										
11	A	St. Mirren	3,388	0-8	6		15		14			7	8		12		10			11						2	9	4		3	5	1									
18	A	Ayr United	1,661	0-4	6				3			8	9		11		7						15			14	10	4		2	5		1	12							
25	H	St. Mirren	2,244	0-0	4			11			7	8		12		6									2	9			3	5		10	1							
Apr 2	H	Falkirk	727	0-1	4			7			11	8		12		10			6				5			2	14			3			9	1						
8	H	Livingston	316	1-2	4			7			12	8	9		11[1]		6						5			2	14	10		3			15	1						
15	A	Dunfermline Athletic	4,969	0-6	4			7			11	8	9		10								5	15		2	12	6		3			14	1						
22	A	Airdrieonians	797	0-0	4			6			7	8		11		10							5			2	9			3			12	1						
29	H	Morton	339	0-3	4			2			7	8		11		10							5	14		6	9			3			1	12						
May 6	A	Raith Rovers	1,510	0-0	4			2			7	8	9				6						5				12			3			11	1						
TOTAL FULL APPEARANCES					21	35	8	18	12	18	26	3	24	33	14	13	3	19	28	3	4	9	1	1	9	5	19	5	1	4	4	12	8	8	1	10	5	1	2	3	6
TOTAL SUB APPEARANCES						(3)	(4)				(6)	(5)	(11)		(1)	(6)	(16)	(7)		(1)	(4)	(1)	(1)		(8)			(3)				(3)			(1)	(5)		(2)		(5)
TOTAL GOALS SCORED												1	2	4		1		2	5								1												

Small bold figures denote goalscorers.   † denotes opponent's own goal.

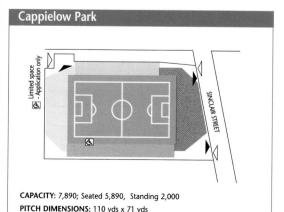

Cappielow Park

SINCLAIR STREET

Limited space – Application only

CAPACITY: 7,890; Seated 5,890, Standing 2,000
PITCH DIMENSIONS: 110 yds x 71 yds
FACILITIES FOR DISABLED SUPPORTERS:
Seating facilities below Grandstand.

Team playing kits

How to get there

Cappielow Park can be reached by the following routes:

BUSES: Services from Glasgow stop just outside the park. There are also services from Port Glasgow and Gourock.

TRAINS: The nearest local station is Cartsdyke and it is a five minute walk from here to the ground. There are two to three trains every hour from Glasgow and from Gourock.

CARS: There is no official car park and fans should park in Sinclair Street beyond the railway station.

The Bankies

email: info@sfl.scottishfootball.com • website: www.scottishfootball.com

Forfar Athletic

Station Park, Carseview Road, Forfar, DD8 3BT

CHAIRMAN
David McGregor

VICE-CHAIRMAN
Neill McK. Wilson

DIRECTORS
Alastair S. Nicoll,
Michael S. McEwan,
Gordon Menmuir (Treasurer)
& Ronald Blair

HONORARY PATRON
Rt. Hon. Lord Lyell of Kinnordy

SECRETARY
David McGregor

MANAGER
Ian McPhee

ASSISTANT MANAGER
Billy Bennett

COACHING STAFF
Jim Moffat, Gordon Wallace,
Donald Ritchie, Eric Fleming,
Ally Taylor & Peter Castle

RESERVE TEAM COACH
Jim Moffat

YOUTH TEAM COACHES
Gordon Wallace (U18)
Ally Taylor (U16)
Peter Castle

PHYSIOTHERAPIST
Diane Cheyne

**FOOTBALL SAFETY OFFICERS'
ASSOCIATION REPRESENTATIVE**

GROUNDSMAN/KIT SUPERVISOR
Martin Gray

**MEDIA LIAISON OFFICER/
MATCHDAY PROGRAMME EDITOR**
David McGregor

TELEPHONES
Ground (01307) 463576/462259
Sec. Home (01307) 464924
Sec. Bus. (01307) 475519
Sec. Bus. Fax (01307) 466956

INTERNET ADDRESS
www.forfarathletic.co.uk

OFFICIAL SUPPORTERS CLUB
c/o Mrs. Yvonne Nicoll,
15 Fyfe Jamieson, Forfar

TEAM CAPTAIN
Craig Tully

SHIRT SPONSOR
Webster Contracts Ltd.

KIT SUPPLIER
Spall

LIST OF PLAYERS 2000-2001

SURNAME	FIRST NAME	MIDDLE NAME	DATE OF BIRTH	PLACE OF BIRTH	DATE OF SIGNING	HEIGHT FT INS	WEIGHT ST LBS	POS. ON PITCH	PREVIOUS CLUB
Bannon	Mark	Steven	22/08/83	Dundee	12/08/00	5 10.0	10 0	Mid	S Form
Bennett	Scott	Henry	30/12/82	Sydney	12/08/00	6 0.0	11 0	Gk	S Form
Bowman	David		10/03/64	Tunbridge Wells	18/07/00	5 10.0	11 4	Mid	Yee Hote Hong Kong
Brand	Ralph		17/07/70	Dundee	14/07/98	5 9.0	12 0	Fwd	Brechin City
Cargill	Andrew		02/09/75	Dundee	11/01/97	5 6.5	10 8	Mid	Dundee
Christie	Sean		15/07/80	Dundee	31/08/98	5 9.0	10 7	Fwd	Carnoustie Panmure
Craig	Douglas	Ewing	30/01/71	London	05/11/94	5 10.0	12 9	Def	Forfar Albion
Donaldson	Euan	Gordon	20/08/75	Falkirk	30/07/99	5 10.0	10 7	Def	Albion Rovers
Duncan	George		26/08/83	Dundee	15/08/00	5 11.0	10 9	Def	S Form
Farnan	Craig		07/04/71	Dundee	05/11/99	5 10.0	13 3	Mid	Montrose
Ferguson	Graeme	William	03/03/71	Stirling	28/08/97	5 10.0	11 10	Def	Clyde
Ferguson	Ian		05/08/68	Dunfermline	20/06/00	6 1.0	13 2	Fwd	Hamilton Academical
Ferrie	James		23/09/83	Dundee	02/09/00	5 8.0	10 0	Mid	Dundee Violet
Ferrie	Neal		23/11/81	Dundee	07/06/00	6 0.0	11 4	Gk	Dundee United
Ferrie	Ryan		02/10/83	Dundee	12/08/00	5 10.0	9 10	Mid	Monifieth B.C.
Galazzi	Alan		26/01/84	Dundee	02/09/00	6 0.0	11 10	Fwd	Dundee Social Club U'15
Garden	Stuart	Robertson	10/02/72	Dundee	04/08/99	5 11.5	12 3	Gk	Brechin City
Harrow	Andrew	John	26/01/81	Kirkcaldy	07/06/00	5 11.0	11 5	Mid	Rangers
Horn	Robert	David	03/08/77	Edinburgh	28/06/00	5 9.0	11 0	Def	Heart of Midlothian
Lammie	Scott	Thomas	12/06/83	Uphall	15/08/00	5 8.0	10 0	Mid	Comrie Colts
McCheyne	Graeme		21/12/73	Bellshill	18/07/97	6 1.0	11 3	Def	Clyde
McPhee	Gary		01/10/79	Glasgow	17/07/99	5 9.0	10 0	Mid	Clyde
Moffat	James		27/01/60	Dunfermline	04/09/98	6 0.0	12 0	Gk	Cowdenbeath
Morris	Roberto		11/02/80	Dundee	30/07/99	6 1.0	10 0	Def	Dundee United Social Club
O'Rourke	Christopher		20/09/83	Dundee	02/09/00	5 9.0	10 0	Mid	Dundee Violet
Rattray	Alan	Raymond	08/06/79	Dundee	16/11/96	5 10.0	11 0	Def	Dundee Violet
Sinclair	David		06/10/69	Dunfermline	18/08/00	5 11.0	12 0	Def	Falkirk
Sorbie	Stuart	Graham	07/09/63	Glasgow	20/06/00	5 9.5	10 10	Mid	Brechin City
Stewart	William	Paul	16/04/77	Glasgow	11/08/00	5 10.0	10 2	Fwd	Cowdenbeath
Stirling	Jered		13/10/76	Stirling	07/09/00	5 11.0	12 4	Def	Partick Thistle
Taylor	Alexander		13/06/62	Baillieston	30/07/99	5 9.5	11 10	Mid	Ross County
Taylor	Scott	Andrew	23/01/77	Forfar	19/05/00	5 9.0	11 0	Fwd	Montrose
Tomlinson	Daniel		30/07/82	Dundee	15/08/00	5 10.0	10 4	Mid	S Form
Tully	Craig		07/01/76	Stirling	28/06/00	6 0.0	12 0	Def	Ross County

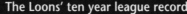

Milestones

YEAR OF FORMATION: 1885
MOST LEAGUE POINTS IN A SEASON: 63 (Second Division – Season 1983/84) (2 Points for a Win)
80 (Third Division – Season 1994/95) (3 Points for a Win)
MOST LEAGUE GOALS SCORED BY A PLAYER IN A SEASON: Dave Kilgour (Season 1929/30)
NO. OF GOALS SCORED: 45
RECORD ATTENDANCE: 10,800 (-v- Rangers – 7.2.1970)
RECORD VICTORY: 14-1 (-v- Lindertis – Scottish Cup, 1.9.1888)
RECORD DEFEAT: 2-12 (-v- King's Park – Division 2, 2.1.1930)

The Loons' ten year league record

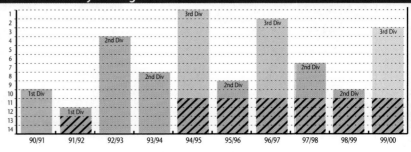

Nationwide

Date	Venue	Opponents	Att	Res	Garden S.	Rattray A.	Donaldson E.	McCheyne G.	Johnston G.	McPhee C.	McLean B.	Taylor A.	Brand R.	Milne S.	Cargill A.	McIlravey P.	MacDonald I.	Ferguson G.	Craig D.	Nairn J.	Christie S.	Robson B.	Morris R.	McKellar J.	Farnan C.	Horn R.
Aug 7	H	Brechin City	620	0-0	1	2	3	4	5	6	7	8	9	10	11	14	15									
14	A	Cowdenbeath	256	3-0	1	2	3	4	5	6	12[1]	8	9[1]	10[1]	11	14		7								
21	H	East Stirlingshire	416	1-1	1	2	3	4	5	6	11	8	9[1]	10			12	7								
28	H	Albion Rovers	421	2-0	1	2	3	4			7	8	9[1]	10[1]	11				15	5	6	14				
Sep 4	A	Queen's Park	764	1-1	1	2	3	4	5	7	15	8[1]	9	10				10	6							
11	A	East Fife	586	0-2	1	5	3	2	15	7	4	8	9	10	11				6			14		12		
18	H	Berwick Rangers	375	1-1	1	5	3	2[1]		4	7	8	12	10	11				6			9				
28	A	Montrose	281	0-2	1	2	14	4	5	8	7			9	10	15	12		3	6	11					
Oct 2	H	Dumbarton	397	5-0	1	5	6	2	12		4	9	10[3]	8[1]	14	7[1]			3			11	15			
16	H	Cowdenbeath	399	3-1	1	5	6	2	12		4	9	10[2]	8[1]	14	7			3		15	11				
23	A	Brechin City	502	2-0	1	5	6	2	12	11	4[1]	9	10[1]	8	14	7			3		15					
30	H	East Fife	504	3-2	1	5	6	2	7	11	4[1]	10		8	9[2]				3						12	
Nov 6	A	Berwick Rangers	328	2-2	1	5[1]	6	2	7		4	10[1]	8	9					3			11		14	12	
14	H	Queen's Park	626	2-2	1	5	6		7	14	4[1]	9[1]	10	8	12				3			11			2	
20	A	Albion Rovers	311	1-0	1	2	6	5	7		4	9	10	8					3			11[1]			12	
27	A	Dumbarton	469	3-3	1	2	6[1]	14	5	7	4	9	10[1]	8					3		15	11[1]			12	
Dec 7	H	Montrose	379	1-2	1	5	6	2	7		4	9[1]	10	8		15			3			11				
Jan 15	A	East Fife	577	1-1	1	2	6			8	4		12	9	10				3[1]			11		7	14	5
22	A	Montrose	588	5-1	1	7	12	2		6	4		8[1]	9[1]	10				3			11[2]		15	14[1]	5
29	A	East Stirlingshire	201	2-0	1	7	12	2		6	14	4		9[1]	10				3			11[1]			8	5
Feb 5	H	Dumbarton	439	4-3	1	7	2[1]			6	14	4		9[1]	10				3[2]			11			8	5
12	H	Albion Rovers	395	3-1	1	7	6	2	12	15[1]	4		9	10		14			3[1]			11			8[1]	5
19	H	Queen's Park	818	2-3	1	7	2[1]	6		14	4	12	9	10					3[1]			11			8	5
26	A	Cowdenbeath	354	1-4	1	7	2	6		14	4	12	9[1]	10					3			11	15		8	5
29	H	Brechin City	516	2-0	1	6	2	15			4	9	10[1]	8	12				3			11[1]		7	14	5
Mar 4	H	East Stirlingshire	399	3-0	1	6	2	15			4	9	10	8	12				3[2]			11		7	14[1]	5
7	H	Berwick Rangers	482	2-0	1	6[1]	7	2[1]			4	15	10	8	9				3			11		14	12	5
11	H	East Fife	582	0-1	1	6	7	2			4	15	12	10	8	9			3			11		14		5
18	A	Berwick Rangers	614	0-2	1	6	3	2			4	10	9	7							15	11			8	5
25	A	Albion Rovers	307	1-0	1		3	2	4	14	8	9	7	10					6[1]			11				5
Apr 1	H	Queen's Park	570	4-0	1		3	2			8[1]	9	7	10[2]					6			11[1]	14	12	4	5
8	H	Montrose	516	1-2	1	15	3	2			8	9	7	10					6			11[1]		12	4	5
15	A	Dumbarton	474	0-0	1	4	3	2		6	8	9	15	7	11	10								14		5
22	A	Brechin City	548	0-1	1	2	3				8	7	9	10	15				6			11		12	5	4
29	H	Cowdenbeath	556	2-2	1	2				7	4	9	8	10					3		12	11[1]	15		5[1]	6
May 6	A	East Stirlingshire	409	1-0	1	6	2	7			8	9[1]		10					3			11		14	5	4
TOTAL FULL APPEARANCES				36	31	26	31	13	22	11	30	17	35	31	9	6	3	31	1	3	25	3	7	19	6
TOTAL SUB APPEARANCES					(1)	(3)		(2)	(7)	(8)	(1)	(6)			(11)	(7)			(4)	(4)		(5)	(15)	(2)	
TOTAL GOALS SCORED					2	1	4		1	2	4	6	16	2	4	1		8			9			3	1

Small bold figures denote goalscorers. † *denotes opponent's own goal.*

Station Park

CARSEVIEW ROAD

CAPACITY: 4,602; Seated 711, Standing 3,891
PITCH DIMENSIONS: 115 yds x 69 yds
FACILITIES FOR DISABLED SUPPORTERS:
Ramp entrance via Main Stand.

Team playing kits

How to get there

Station Park can be reached by the following routes:

BUSES: There is a regular service of buses departing from Forfar. The bus station in the town is about half a mile from the ground. There is also a local service.

TRAINS: The nearest railway station is Dundee (14 miles away) and fans who travel to here should then board a bus for Forfar from the city centre. Arbroath station is also about 14 miles away.

CARS: There are car parking facilities in adjacent streets to the ground and also in the Market Muir car park.

The Loons

email: info@sfl.scottishfootball.com • website: www.scottishfootball.com

Partick Thistle

Firhill Stadium, 80 Firhill Road, Glasgow, G20 7AL

CHAIRMAN
T. Brown McMaster

VICE-CHAIRMAN
Thomas Hughes

DIRECTORS
Allan Cowan, James Oliver, Edward Prentice, Norman Springford & Margaret W.G. Forsyth

PRESIDENT
James R. Aitken

HON. VICE-PRESIDENT/ ASSOCIATE DIRECTOR
Robert W. Reid

ASSOCIATE DIRECTORS
Les Hope & Ronnie Gilfillan

CHIEF EXECUTIVE/SECRETARY
Alan C. Dick

MANAGER
John Lambie

ASSISTANT MANAGER
Gerry Collins

COACH
Tommy Callaghan

YOUTH TEAM COACHES
Tommy Callaghan (U18)
John Macdonald (U16)
Alan Harris (U14)

HONORARY MEDICAL OFFICER
Dr Alan W. Robertson

PHYSIOTHERAPIST
Walter Cannon

STADIUM MANAGER & CHIEF OF SECURITY
Alan C. Dick

FOOTBALL SAFETY OFFICERS' ASSOCIATION REPRESENTATIVE
Alan C. Dick (0141) 579 1971

GROUNDSMAN
George Furze

COMMERCIAL MANAGER
Amanda Stark (0141) 579 1971

LOTTERY MANAGER
Bobby Briggs

MEDIA LIAISON OFFICER
Alan C. Dick (0141) 579 1971

MATCHDAY PROGRAMME EDITOR
Tom Hosie

TELEPHONES
Ground/Ticket Office/Commercial
(0141) 579 1971
Fax (0141) 945 1525
Jagsline (09068) 666474

E-MAIL ADDRESS
mail@ptfc.co.uk

CLUB SHOP
80 Firhill Road, Glasgow, G20 7AL
Tel (0141) 579 1971.
Open each matchday and every
Tuesday from 12.30p.m. - 4.30p.m.

OFFICIAL SUPPORTERS CLUB
Ms. Morag McHaffie,
c/o Firhill Stadium, 80 Firhill Road,
Glasgow, G20 7AL

TEAM CAPTAIN
Danny Lennon

SHIRT SPONSOR
D.H. Morris Group

KIT SUPPLIER
SECCA

LIST OF PLAYERS 2000-2001

SURNAME	FIRST NAME	MIDDLE NAME	DATE OF BIRTH	PLACE OF BIRTH	DATE OF SIGNING	HEIGHT FT INS	WEIGHT ST LBS	POS. ON PITCH	PREVIOUS CLUB
Archibald	Alan	Maxwell	13/12/77	Glasgow	19/09/96	6 0.0	11 7	Def	Kilwinning Rangers
Arthur	Kenneth		07/12/78	Bellshill	01/06/97	6 3.0	13 8	Gk	Possilpark Y.M.C.A.
Brand	Andrew	Gerard	17/04/83	Glasgow	06/09/00	5 11.0	10 7	Def	Partick Thistle B.C.
Brown	Michael		07/11/79	Stranraer	03/08/00	6 1.0	12 8	Gk	Motherwell
Cameron	Ian		24/08/66	Glasgow	08/06/00	5 9.0	10 5	Mid	Clydebank
Collins	Nicholas	Charles T.	29/12/83	Glasgow	10/08/00	5 8.0	10 5	Fwd	Maryhill Juniors
Craigan	Stephen	James	29/10/76	Newtonards	12/07/00	6 0.0	12 9	Def	Motherwell
Docherty	Stephen		18/02/76	Glasgow	20/07/99	5 8.0	10 10	Mid/Fwd	Clydebank
Dunn	Robert		28/06/79	Glasgow	27/06/97	5 10.0	10 5	Fwd	Possilpark Y.M.C.A.
Easton	Fraser	John	23/09/82	Larbert	10/08/00	6 0.0	11 2	Def	Linlithgow Bridge B.C.
Gibson	Andrew	Stewart	02/03/82	Glasgow	03/07/00	5 10.0	10 4	Mid	Partick Thistle B.C.
Hardie	Martin		22/04/76	Alexandria	24/03/00	5 11.0	11 0	Mid/Fwd	East Stirlingshire
Howie	William		09/07/82	Rutherglen	21/05/99	5 8.0	10 1	Mid	Partick Thistle B.C.
Kelly	Desmond		14/01/82	Glasgow	12/09/00	5 8.0	10 4	Mid	Partick Thistle B.C.
Lennon	Daniel	Joseph	06/04/70	Whitburn	24/12/99	5 7.0	10 10	Mid	Ross County
Lindau	Peter		09/12/72	Halmstad	04/08/00	6 2.0	12 2	Fwd	Ayr United
Lyle	Derek		13/02/81	Glasgow	14/10/99	5 8.0	10 5	Fwd	Partick Thistle B.C.
McCallum	David	John	07/09/77	Bellshill	03/07/00	5 11.0	10 10	Mid	Stirling Albion
McCann	Garry		26/04/82	Glasgow	31/07/00	5 11.0	12 9	Fwd	Bearsden A.F.C.
McGrillen	Paul	Alexander	19/08/71	Glasgow	12/07/00	5 9.0	11 1	Fwd	Stirling Albion
McKeown	Desmond	Michael	18/01/70	Glasgow	11/06/98	5 11.0	11 0	Def	Queen of the South
McLean	Scott	James	17/06/76	East Kilbride	17/12/99	5 11.5	12 5	Fwd	Inverness Cal. Thistle
McWilliams	Derek		16/01/66	Broxburn	13/07/00	5 10.0	12 4	Mid	Clydebank
Moore	Allan		25/12/64	Glasgow	15/07/00	5 7.0	10 9	Fwd	Airdrieonians
Smith	James		11/07/78	Glasgow	31/05/00	6 3.0	12 7	Def	Stranraer
Stewart	Alexander		14/10/65	Bellshill	08/09/00	5 8.0	11 2	Def	Airdrieonians

Milestones

YEAR OF FORMATION: 1876
MOST CAPPED PLAYER: Alan Rough
NO. OF CAPS: 53 (of which 51 with Partick Thistle)
MOST LEAGUE POINTS IN A SEASON: 57 (First Division - Season 1991/92)
MOST LEAGUE GOALS SCORED BY A PLAYER IN A SEASON: Alec Hair (Season 1926/27)
NO. OF GOALS SCORED: 41
RECORD ATTENDANCE: 49,838 (-v- Rangers – 18.2.1922)
RECORD VICTORY: 16-0 (-v- Royal Albert – Scottish Cup, 17.1.1931)
RECORD DEFEAT: 0-10 (-v- Queen's Park - Scottish Cup, 3.12.1881)

The Jags' ten year league record

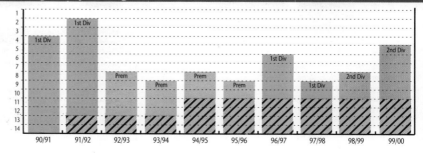

Nationwide

Date	Venue	Opponents	Att.	Res	Budinauskas K.	Duncan G.	McKeown D.	Montgomerie S.R.	Brannigan K.	Archibald A.	Paton E.	Craig A.	Miller S.	Docherty S.	English I.	Dunn R.	McGuinness E.	Dallas S.	Newall R.	Elliot D.	McAllister T.	Jacobs Q.	Walker A.	Ferguson D.	Callaghan T.	Lyle D.	McCann K.	Nesovic A.	McIntyre P.	McKey W.	Martin B.	Arthur K.	Lennon D.	McLean S.	Lindau P.	Blom J.	McWilliams D.	Swan I.	Hardie M.	Rogers D.	Huggon R.	Kelly R.	Howie W.	Rodden P.
Aug 7	H	Stenhousemuir	2,072	0-1	1	2	3	4	5	6	7	8	9	10	11	12		14																										
14	A	Alloa Athletic	1,178	0-1	1	2	3	4	5	6	10		9	7	11	8	12	14	15																									
21	H	Arbroath	1,915	1-3	1	2	3	4	5		8		7	10	11	9							14																					
28	H	Queen of the South	1,959	2-0	1	2	3^1	4	5	6	14	8	9	7	12	10	15		11^1																									
Sep 4	A	Stranraer	1,138	1-1	1	2		4	5	6	7		9		10	11	14	3^1	8	12																								
11	A	Clyde	2,356	0-2	1	2	11	4	5	6	15	8		7	14	10		3		12	9																							
18	H	Hamilton Academical	2,312	0-1	1	2	10	4	5	6	14		7	8	11	12		15	3		9																							
25	H	Ross County	2,171	0-2	1	2	10	4	5	6	8		14		12	15	7		3		11	9																						
Oct 2	A	Stirling Albion	1,333	1-3	1		10	4	5	6		12	7^1	2		9			3		11	8	14	15																				
16	H	Alloa Athletic	1,801	2-2	1		11		5	6		2^1	14	9^1					3		7		4	12	10	15																		
23	A	Stenhousemuir	1,188	1-0	1	14	11	5		6		8		2		9^1			3		7		4	10	15																		
30	H	Clyde	2,617	0-0	1	12	11	5		6		8		2		9			3		7		4	10	14		15																
Nov 6	A	Hamilton Academical	1,828	0-0	1		11	5		6		8		2		12			3		10		4	14	15	9	7	7															
14	A	Stranraer	1,825	2-0	1			3	5		6	8	2			11	9^2				10		4	12	7					15													
20	H	Queen of the South	1,462	2-1	1	14		3	5		6	8	2			11^1					10		4	7^1		12																
27	H	Stirling Albion	2,812	1-0	1	12		3	5		6	8	2^1			14	9				11		15	10		7	4																
Dec 4	A	Ross County	2,392	1-2	1	2		4		3	6	8	12	14	15	9					11^1		10		7	5																	
18	H	Stenhousemuir	1,922	1-0	12			4		3	8		2								11		14		7	5	1	6	9	10^1													
27	A	Arbroath	1,509	0-0	1			3	5		6	8	2		12						11		7			4	9	10															
Jan 3	H	Hamilton Academical	2,755	2-2	1			3	5		6^1	12^1	8		2	10					11		15	14^1		7	4	9															
22	H	Ross County	2,698	4-2	1			3	5		6	7^1	8^1		2						11^1					14	4	9^1	10^2														
Feb 5	A	Stirling Albion	1,704	2-0	1	15		5		3	8		14	2		12					11^1		7^1			6		4	9^1	10^1													
12	H	Queen of the South	2,605	5-4			14	5		3	2	8^1			12						11^1		7^1		15	6	1	4^1	10^1	9^1													
26	A	Alloa Athletic	1,847	1-1	1			3	5		6	7	8^1	12^1	2		9				15					4		10															
29	A	Clyde	2,781	0-1	1	2		3	5		6	7	8				15	9			11		14		12	4																	
Mar 4	H	Arbroath	2,210	2-0	1	2		3	5		6	7^1	8								11		14		15	12		4		10^1													
7	A	Stranraer	628	1-3	1			3^1	5		6	7	8								12		14			2		4	11	10	9												
18	A	Hamilton Academical	2,223	1-0	1	14		3	5		6	2	8	7							11		15					4^1	9		10												
21	H	Clyde	3,012	1-2	1			3	5		6	2	8	9		14					7		11					4			10^1	12											
25	H	Queen of the South	1,813	1-1	1			3	5		6	2	8	9		14					11					15		4			7^1	10											
Apr 1	A	Stranraer	2,351	1-1	1			3	2		15		9										14			6		4			8		10	5	7^1	11							
8	A	Ross County	3,511	3-1	1			3			6		8			9					15		12		14	2		4			11^1		10^2	5	7								
15	A	Stirling Albion	2,160	1-1	1		11				6	8	14^1			9					12		10			2		5			4			15	3	7							
22	A	Stenhousemuir	895	0-2	1		11	14			3	2	8			15					7					5		4			9		10	6	12								
29	A	Alloa Athletic	1,803	0-1	2		11			6		8	9								7					14	5	1	4				10	3			12	15					
May 6	A	Arbroath	889	2-3	12		11	2		3		8	7								14						5	1	4			9	10^1	6		15^1							
TOTAL FULL APPEARANCES					32	12	31	31	10	35	20	28	13	17	7	18	1	1	10	1	22	4	7	3	9	1	7	12	4	19	7	9	2	7	6	6	3	1					
TOTAL SUB APPEARANCES					(8)	(1)	(1)		(6)	(1)	(5)	(1)	(7)	(9)	(4)	(1)	(3)	(1)		(5)			(6)	(13)	(1)	(1)	(6)	(2)	(4)			(2)				(1)	(1)	(1)	(1)			
TOTAL GOALS SCORED							2			1	4	3	1	1	5				2		3				4			2	1	4	1	3		3			1	1			

Small bold figures denote goalscorers. † denotes opponent's own goal.

Firhill Stadium

Jackie Husband (East) Stand

Main (West) Stand — FIRHILL ROAD

CAPACITY: 14,538; Seated 8,397 Standing 6,141

PITCH DIMENSIONS: 110 yds x 75 yds

FACILITIES FOR DISABLED SUPPORTERS:
Covered places are available for 17 disabled supporters in front of the Main Stand (North area). Prior arrangement must be made with the Secretary and a ticket obtained.

Team playing kits

How to get there

The following routes may be used to reach Firhill Stadium:

TRAINS: The nearest railway stations are Glasgow Queen Street and Glasgow Central and buses from the centre of the city pass within 100 yards of the ground.

BUSES: The following buses from the city centre all pass near the ground: No's. 28, 40, 61 and 119 and the frequency of the buses is just under 10 minutes from Hope Street.

UNDERGROUND: The nearest Strathclyde PTE Underground station is St.George's Cross and supporters walking from here should pass through Cromwell Street into Maryhill Road and then walk up this road as far as Firhill Street. The ground is then on the right. The Kelvinbridge Underground Station is also not far from the ground and supporters from here should walk along Great Western Road as far as Napiershill Street and then follow this into Maryhill Road.

CARS: Street parking in the vicinity of the ground is somewhat limited.

The Jags

email: info@sfl.scottishfootball.com • website: www.scottishfootball.com

Queen of the South

Palmerston Park, Terregles Street,
Dumfries, DG2 9BA

CHAIRMAN
Ronald Bradford

VICE-CHAIRMAN
Thomas G. Harkness

DIRECTORS
Keith M. Houliston &
Craig Paterson

COMPANY SECRETARY
Richard Shaw, M.B.E.

MANAGER
John Connolly

FIRST TEAM COACH
Ian Scott

CLUB COACHES
Trevor Wilson, Whiteford Moffat,
Ian Bell, Ian Mundell, Steve Swailes,
George Patterson & Warren Pearson

YOUTH TEAM COACHES
Steve Swailes (U18)
Ian Mundell (U16)
George Patterson (U14)

MATCH ANALYST
Iain McChesney

CLUB DOCTORS
Dr. Phil Clayton & Dr. Steven Morris

ORTHOPAEDIC SURGEON
Mr. Clark Dreghorn

PHYSIOTHERAPIST
Kenneth Crichton

**FOOTBALL SAFETY OFFICERS'
ASSOCIATION REPRESENTATIVE**
George Galbraith (01387) 254853

CHIEF SCOUT
Warren Pearson

GROUNDSMAN
Kevin McCormick

COMMERCIAL MANAGER
Margaret Heuchan (01387) 254853

MATCHDAY PROGRAMME EDITOR
Bruce Wright (01387) 262960

TELEPHONES
Ground/Ticket Office/Information Service
(01387) 254853
Football Office Only (01387) 251666
Restaurant (01387) 252241
Fax (01387) 254853

E-MAIL & INTERNET ADDRESS
mail@qosfc.co.uk
www.qosfc.co.uk

CLUB SHOP
Palmerston Park, Terregles Street,
Dumfries, DG2 9BA (01387) 254853
Open 9.00am – 4.00pm Mon. to Fri.
and 1.30pm – 5.00pm on home
match days.

OFFICIAL SUPPORTERS CLUB
c/o Palmerston Park, Terregles Street,
Dumfries, DG2 9BA

TEAM CAPTAIN
Sandy Hodge

SHIRT SPONSOR
Glass & Glazing (Dumfries)

KIT SUPPLIER
AVEC

LIST OF PLAYERS 2000-2001

SURNAME	FIRST NAME	MIDDLE NAME	DATE OF BIRTH	PLACE OF BIRTH	DATE OF SIGNING	HEIGHT FT INS	WEIGHT ST LBS	POS. ON PITCH	PREVIOUS CLUB
Aitken	Andrew	Robert	02/02/78	Dumfries	10/07/96	6 0.0	12 7	Def	Annan Athletic
Armstrong	Graeme		28/06/83	Hexham	31/07/00	6 0.0	12 8	Mid	Haltwhistle United
Atkinson	Patrick		22/05/70	Singapore	31/07/00	5 10.0	11 10	Def	Blyth Spartans
Atkinson	Ross		27/06/79	Newcastle-U-Tyne	25/07/00	5 11.0	12 6	Mid	Ashington
Boyle	Denis	Patrick	24/04/81	Letterkenny	30/09/97	5 7.0	10 1	Mid	Keadue Youths
Caldwell	Bryan	Robert A. J.	20/03/81	Glasgow	27/07/98	5 7.0	9 0	Fwd	Queen of the South B.C.
Gray	David	Lewis McKenzie	23/09/82	Lanark	15/08/00	6 0.0	12 0	Mid	S Form
Hawke	Warren	Robert	20/09/70	Durham	17/12/99	5 10.5	11 4	Fwd	Morton
Heppell	Stuart		28/02/80	Ashington	27/07/00	6 2.0	14 7	Mid	Ashington
Hodge	Sandy	George	04/10/80	Lanark	01/10/99	6 3.0	13 0	Def	Motherwell
Martin	Andrew	Laurence	08/08/72	Newcastle	27/07/00	6 2.0	14 10	Def	Blyth Spartans
Mathieson	David	James	18/01/78	Dumfries	02/08/96	5 11.0	12 0	Gk	St. Johnstone
McCaig	John	George	19/11/82	Ayr	13/05/99	6 1.0	12 6	Fwd	S Form
McColm	Robert	James	25/08/74	Dumfries	27/07/00	5 10.0	12 3	Gk	Dalbeattie Star
McDonald	Raymond		15/02/81	Irvine	27/07/00	5 7.0	12 4	Fwd	Bonnyton Thistle
Moffat	Adam	James	31/01/81	Lanark	10/09/98	5 10.0	11 0	Def	S Form
Muir	Dean		21/02/81	Bellshill	27/07/00	5 8.0	10 7	Mid	Hamilton Academical
Muirhead	Thomas		03/10/81	Dumfries	10/09/98	5 10.0	11 8	Gk	S Form
Nelson	Anthony		06/02/69	Alston	25/07/00	5 6.0	11 7	Mid	Tow Law
Nixon	Philip		19/11/77	Newcastle-U-Tyne	28/07/00	6 2.0	12 10	Def	Ashington
Paterson	Geoffrey	Samson	10/03/82	Dumfries	28/07/99	5 8.0	10 5	Mid	S Form
Patterson	Daniel		06/03/81	North Shields	28/07/00	5 10.0	11 0	Def	Ashington
Pickering	Steven		25/09/76	Sunderland	27/07/00	5 10.0	10 2	Mid	Tow Law
Preen	Steven		28/09/74	Newcastle	22/08/00	6 2.0	13 0	Fwd	Gateshead
Robison	Kevin	Richard	26/10/80	Dumfries	28/07/99	5 11.0	11 0	Def	Rangers
Strain	Christopher	Robert	25/03/80	Irvine	01/07/99	5 10.0	10 7	Fwd	Kilmarnock
Suddick	Jarrod	Alan	06/07/69	Blackpool	27/07/00	5 10.0	12 10	Mid	Tow Law
Sunderland	Jonathan		02/11/75	Newcastle-U-Tyne	25/07/00	6 0.0	12 0	Mid	Ashington
Weatherson	Peter		29/05/80	North Shields	04/08/00	6 0.0	12 3	Fwd	Newcastle Blue Star
Weir	Mark	John	30/03/80	Lanark	10/07/97	5 8.0	10 10	Mid	Forth Wanderers
Young	Kane		07/06/76	Newcastle	14/08/00	5 9.0	11 0	Mid	Ashington

Milestones

YEAR OF FORMATION: 1919
MOST CAPPED PLAYER: William Houliston
NO. OF CAPS: 3
MOST LEAGUE POINTS IN A SEASON: 55 (Division 2 – Season 1985/86)
MOST LEAGUE GOALS SCORED BY A PLAYER IN A SEASON: Jimmy Gray (Season 1927/28)
NO. OF GOALS SCORED: 37
RECORD ATTENDANCE: 24,500 (-v- Heart of Midlothian – Scottish Cup, 23.2.1952)
RECORD VICTORY: 11-1 (-v- Stranraer – Scottish Cup, 16.1.1932)
RECORD DEFEAT: 2-10 (-v- Dundee – Division 1, 1.12.1962)

The Doonhamers' ten year league record

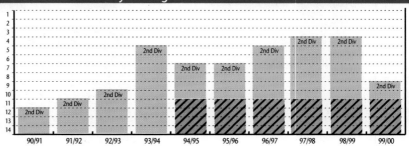

THE DOONHAMERS' CLUB FACTFILE 1999/2000
RESULTS... APPEARANCES... SCORERS... ATTENDANCES...

Date	Venue	Opponents	Att	Res	Hillcoat J.	Lilley D.	Kerr A.	Stewart P.	Aitken A.	Cleeland M.	Harvey P.	Leslie S.	Bailey L.	Mallan S.	Weir M.	Adams C.	Findlay W.	Robison K.	Caldwell B.	Rowe J.G.	Hodge S.	Boyle D.	Strain C.	Dickson J.	Gallacher I.	McMillan A.	McLean S.	Paterson G.	Hawke W.	Preston A.	Eadie K.	Davidson S.	Mathieson D.	Duncan G.	Gallagher J.
Aug 7	H	Arbroath	1,118	2-3	1	2	3	4	5	6	7	8		9	10¹	11¹	12	14																	
14	A	Hamilton Academical	630	3-0	1		3	2	5	6	7	8	12	10¹	15	9		14¹	4	11¹															
21	H	Alloa Athletic	1,204	1-1	1	2	3		5	6	7	8	12	10				14	15	11¹	4	9													
28	A	Partick Thistle	1,959	0-2	1		2		5	6	7	8	12	10				14	15	11	4	3	9												
Sep 4	H	Clyde	1,186	1-1	1		2	3	5	6	7			9¹	10	12				8	11	4													
11	H	Stenhousemuir	928	0-3	1		3	2	5	6	7	14		9	12	10				8	11	4													
18	A	Stranraer	621	0-1	1		3	2	5	6		8		9	10	12				7	11	4													
25	H	Stirling Albion	1,038	3-3	1		3	2	5	6	7¹	8		10¹						9	11	4¹		14	15										
Oct 2	A	Ross County	2,293	1-1	1		2		5	6	7	8		10	9						4	3		11¹		15									
16	H	Hamilton Academical	1,027	3-2	1	15	2		5	6	7¹			10¹	11	9¹	12				4	3		8											
23	A	Arbroath	851	2-5	1	15	2		5	6		8		10	11	9	12¹				4¹	3		14		7									
30	A	Stenhousemuir	447	1-2	1		3	2	5	6		8		10	11	9					4			12		7¹									
Nov 6	H	Stranraer	1,052	0-5	1		2		5	6		8		10		12		14	11	9	4	3				7									
9	A	Clyde	640	0-3	1		3		5	6		8		10		12			11	9	4			14		7				2					
20	H	Partick Thistle	1,462	1-2	1		14		5¹	6				10					11		4	3		8		12				2	9				
27	A	Ross County	862	0-2	1				5	6				12		10				4	3	8		7		11				2	9				
Dec 11	A	Stirling Albion	534	0-3	1		8	15	5	14				12	11					4	3			10		6				2	9				
18	H	Arbroath	837	1-0	1		8		5	6				10¹		14				4	3			7		15			9	2	11				
Jan 3	A	Stranraer	928	2-1	1				5	6				10		14			15	4	3			7		8			9¹	2	11¹				
15	H	Stenhousemuir	1,017	†3-1	1				5	6		8		10¹		12				4	3			7		11		15	9¹	2	14				
22	H	Stirling Albion	1,104	2-3	1				5	6		8		10¹		12				4	3			7		14			9	2	11¹				
Feb 5	A	Ross County	2,018	0-2	1				5	6				10		14			11	4	3	8		7		12			9	2					
12	A	Partick Thistle	2,605	4-5					5					10¹		7				4	3	8¹		2					9	11¹			1	6¹	
26	A	Hamilton Academical	553	1-1					5					10	9¹	14				4	3	8		7		11				2			1	6	
Mar 4	H	Alloa Athletic	1,018	2-1				2	5					10²	11	15	12			4		8		7					9	3			1	6	
11	A	Stenhousemuir	541	0-2				2	5					10	11	15			14	4		8		7					9	3			1	6	
14	H	Clyde	830	3-0			15	2	5					10¹	11	12				4	3¹	8		7					9¹				1	6	
18	H	Stranraer	1,165	0-0			12	2	5					10	11				14	4	3	8		7					9				1	6	
25	H	Partick Thistle	1,813	1-1				2	5					10¹	15					4	3	8		7					9				1	6	11
Apr 1	A	Clyde	1,101	1-3			14¹	2	5					10		12				4	3	8		7					9				1	6	11
8	A	Stirling Albion	520	2-2				2	5					10	12	11²				4	3	8		7			14		9				1	6	15
11	A	Alloa Athletic	620	1-3					5					10¹	11	7				4	3			12					9	2			1	6	8
15	H	Ross County	1,010	0-3					5					10	11	12		14		4	3	8		7					9	2			1	6	
22	A	Arbroath	589	2-1			14	2	5						11	12				4	3			7					9¹	10¹			1	6	15
29	H	Hamilton Academical	2,084	1-1					5						11	7				4¹	3	8		2		12			9	10			1	6	
May 6	A	Alloa Athletic	714	1-6				2	5					10	11	9				4	3	6		7		8				14¹			1		15
TOTAL FULL APPEARANCES					22	2	13	19	33	21	9	13	4	29	10	18	3	14	12	27	26	17	1	23	1	15	3	2	17	6	5	1	14	13	3
TOTAL SUB APPEARANCES						(8)		(1)		(1)	(1)	(1)	(3)	(3)	(4)	(12)	(4)	(6)	(5)	(1)	(1)	(7)	(2)	(1)					(2)	(4)	(1)			(3)
TOTAL GOALS SCORED							1		1		2		1	13	1	4	1			3	3	1		2		1			4	1	4			1	

Small bold figures denote goalscorers.   † denotes opponent's own goal.

Palmerston Park

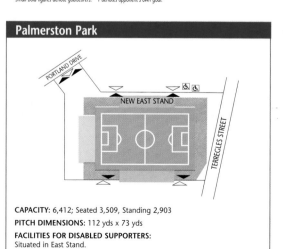

CAPACITY: 6,412; Seated 3,509, Standing 2,903
PITCH DIMENSIONS: 112 yds x 73 yds
FACILITIES FOR DISABLED SUPPORTERS: Situated in East Stand.

Team playing kits

How to get there

Palmerston Park can be reached by the following routes:

TRAINS: There is a reasonable service to Dumfries Station from Glasgow on Saturdays, but the service is more limited in midweek. The station is about ¾ mile from the ground.

BUSES: Buses from Glasgow, Edinburgh, Ayr and Stranraer all pass within a short distance of the park.

CARS: The car park may be reached from Portland Drive or King Street and has a capacity for approximately 174 cars.

LIST OF PLAYERS 2000-2001

SURNAME	FIRST NAME	MIDDLE NAME	DATE OF BIRTH	PLACE OF BIRTH	DATE OF SIGNING	HEIGHT FT INS	WEIGHT ST LBS	POS. ON PITCH	PREVIOUS CLUB
Ajetunmobi	Adewale		27/10/77	Glasgow	11/08/00	5 11.0	11 9	Fwd	Chester City
Borland	Paul	Joseph	28/06/79	Rutherglen	27/08/99	5 9.0	9 8	Def	Celtic
Brown	James	Paul	24/09/77	Greenock	26/11/98	5 11.0	12 7	Mid	Gourock Y.A.C.
Bruce	Gordon		10/07/75	Edinburgh	22/08/00	6 2.0	14 0	Gk	Stranraer
Carmichael	Derek		03/01/79	Rutherglen	18/09/98	5 10.0	11 6	Fwd	Queen's Park B.C.
Carroll	Frank	Andrew	30/01/81	Glasgow	13/07/99	5 8.0	11 7	Fwd	Benburb Juveniles
Caven	Ross		04/08/65	Glasgow	12/08/82	6 0.0	12 0	Def/Mid	Possil Y.M.C.A.
Christie	Francis	James	20/08/80	Glasgow	25/07/00	5 10.0	11 7	Fwd	Chryston U'21s
Connaghan	Denis		09/01/76	Glasgow	05/07/99	5 11.0	11 10	Def	Clydebank
Connell	Graham		31/10/74	Glasgow	21/07/99	5 11.0	11 10	Mid	Partick Thistle
Cunningham	John		28/10/79	Glasgow	19/07/00	6 2.0	13 0	Def	Knightswood U'21s
Duncan	Graham		02/02/69	Glasgow	26/07/00	6 2.0	14 0	Mid	Queen of the South
Ferry	Daniel		31/01/77	Glasgow	23/06/95	5 7.0	11 4	Mid/Fwd	Queen's Park U'18s
Finlayson	Kevin		07/12/79	Glasgow	28/06/00	5 9.0	10 0	Fwd	Ross County
Flannigan	Craig	Alexander	11/02/73	Dumfries	19/07/00	5 7.0	10 4	Fwd	Albion Rovers
Forbes	John	Paul	04/01/82	Rutherglen	15/08/00	5 3.0	9.6	Fwd	Queen's Park Youth
Gallagher	Mark	Andrew	06/12/74	Irvine	23/06/99	6 2.0	11 6	Fwd	Knockentiber A.F.C.
Graham	David	Neil Ramsay	27/01/71	Bellshill	25/07/91	5 10.0	10 8	Def/Mid	Queen's Park Youth
Johnston	Alan		16/04/82	Irvine	15/08/00	6 0.0	12 7	Fwd	Queen's Park Youth
MacNiven	Alistair		05/12/83	Paisley	15/08/00	6 0.0	12.5	Def	Rangers
Magennis	Terence		05/01/82	Glasgow	08/08/00	5 8.0	12.0	Gk	S Form
Marshall	Stephen		30/04/80	Glasgow	25/05/00	5 10.0	10 8	Mid	Clyde
Martin	Paul	John	08/03/65	Bellshill	28/07/98	6 2.0	13 0	Mid/Fwd	Albion Rovers
Martin	William	McLean	21/08/81	Glasgow	25/05/00	6 1.0	13 0	Mid/Fwd	Kilmarnock
McAuley	Mark		01/10/83	Glasgow	15/08/00	5 9.0	12 0	Def	Queen's Park Youth
McColl	Barry		04/08/79	Glasgow	20/06/98	5 5.0	10 11	Mid	Queen's Park B.C.
McDonald	Andrew		24/03/82	Paisley	15/08/00	5 10.0	11 9	Def	S Form
Miller	Greg		23/02/77	Glasgow	26/07/00	5 11.0	12 0	Fwd	Neilston Juniors
O'Brien	Stephen		21/01/73	Glasgow	03/07/00	6 2.0	11 6	Mid	Glasgow University AFC
Orr	Stewart	John	05/11/80	Glasgow	05/06/99	5 11.5	11 7	Mid	St. Johnstone
Parker	Andrew		04/04/83	Paisley	15/08/00	5 7.0	11 0	Mid	Queen's Park Youth
Ridley	Craig		16/07/82	Glasgow	15/08/00	5 10.0	11 10	Mid/Fwd	Queen's Park Youth
Scobie	Ryan		26/07/81	Glasgow	24/09/99	5 8.0	11 2	Fwd	Clyde
Sinclair	Richard		20/05/82	Glasgow	25/05/00	5 10.0	12 0	Def	S Form
Smith	Allan	John	04/08/81	Glasgow	05/06/99	6 0.0	11 8	Gk	Giffnock North A.F.C.
Sweeney	Christopher	Joseph	12/10/81	Glasgow	26/07/00	5 11.0	12 4	Mid/Fwd	Langwarrin S.C.
Travers	Mark		07/02/77	Glasgow	23/06/99	5 7.0	9 0	Def	Possil Y.M.

Milestones

YEAR OF FORMATION: 1867
MOST CAPPED PLAYER: Walter Arnott
NO. OF CAPS: 14
MOST LEAGUE POINTS IN A SEASON: 57 (Division 2 – Season 1922/23) (2 points for a win)
  69 (Third Division – Season 1999/2000) (3 points for a win)
MOST LEAGUE GOALS SCORED BY A PLAYER IN A SEASON: William Martin (Season 1937/38)
NO. OF GOALS SCORED: 30
RECORD ATTENDANCE: 149,547 (Scotland v England – 17.4.1937)
RECORD VICTORY: 16-0 (-v- St. Peters – Scottish Cup, 29.8.1885)
RECORD DEFEAT: 0-9 (-v- Motherwell – Division 1, 29.4.1930)

The Spiders' ten year league record

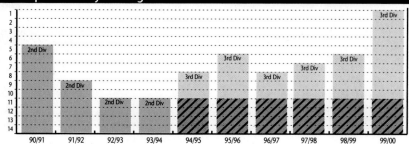

THE SPIDERS' CLUB FACTFILE 1999/2000
RESULTS... APPEARANCES... SCORERS... ATTENDANCES...

Date	Venue	Opponents	Att.	Res	Inglis N.	Sinclair R.	Connaghan D.	Caven R.	Martin P.	MacFarlane N.	Connell G.	Orr S.	Gallagher M.	Brown J.	McGoldrick K.	Edgar S.	Whelan J.	Little T.	Ferry D.	Carroll F.	Borland P.	Tyrrell P.	Scobie R.	Geoghegan J.	Travers M.	Elder G.	Carmichael D.	McKee C.	Reid A.	Finlayson K.	Walker P.
Aug 7	H	East Stirlingshire	450	2-1	1	2	3	4	5	6	7	8^1	9^1	10	11	12	14	15													
14	A	Brechin City	311	2-1	1		3^1	4	5	6	7	8	9	10	11	12	14^1														
21	H	Cowdenbeath	578	1-0	1		3	4	5	6	7	8	9	10	11		14^1	15	2	12											
28	A	Berwick Rangers	710	2-1	1	2	3	4	5^1	6	7		9^1		11	14	8		15	10	12										
Sep 4	H	Forfar Athletic	764	1-1	1	2	3	4	5	6	10	7				12	8^1		11	15	9	14									
11	A	Dumbarton	539	1-0	1	2	3	4		6	7		9	10			8		12	14	11^1	5									
18	H	Albion Rovers	642	2-0	1		3	4		6	7	14	9	10^1		15	8		12	2	11^1	5									
25	A	East Fife	568	0-0	1		3	4		6	7	9	10			12	8		2	11	5	14	15								
Oct 2	H	Montrose	688	2-1	1		3	4	5	6	7	9^2	10	14			8		2	12	11										
16	H	Brechin City	483	5-3	1		3	4	5	6	7	9	10^2	14			8^1		2	11^2			12	15							
23	A	East Stirlingshire	354	1-1	1	15	3	4^1	5	6	7		10	14		12	8		2	11				9							
30	H	Dumbarton	713	3-2	1	15	3^1	4	5	6	7		9^1	10	14	12	8		2	11^1	5			11							
Nov 6	A	Albion Rovers	513	4-2	1	7	3	4^2	5	6		15	9	10	11^1	12	8^1		2				14								
14	A	Forfar Athletic	626	2-2	1	15	3	4^1	5	6			9	10	11^1	12	8		2	7			14								
20	H	Berwick Rangers	678	1-4	1		3	4^1	5	6	14		9	10	11		8		2	7	15		12								
27	A	Montrose	424	1-2	1		3	4	5	6			9^1	10	11	12	8		2	7			14	15							
Dec 4	H	East Fife	742	0-1	1	2	3	4	5	6	7	8	9	10		12			11	15					14						
18	H	East Stirlingshire	413	0-1	1	2	3	4	5	6	7		9		10	15	12		11	8			14								
22	A	Cowdenbeath	221	2-0	1	2	3	4	5	6	7		9^2	10		14			11	8	15										
Jan 3	H	Albion Rovers	742	0-1	1	2	3	4	5	6	7	14	9	10		12	8						11	15							
22	A	East Fife	631	0-0	1	12		4	5	6	7		9	10	15	14			2	11	3							8			
29	A	Dumbarton	492	1-1	1			4	5	6	7		9	8	15	14			2	11^1	3							10			
Feb 5	H	Montrose	505	1-1	1	2	3	4	5	6	7		9^1	8	14					11		12						10	15		
12	A	Berwick Rangers	525	1-1	1	2	3	4	5	6	7		9	10	12		8^1		2	11			14								
19	A	Forfar Athletic	818	3-2	1		3	4	5	6	7^1		9^1	10	14		8^1		2	11			15	12							
26	A	Brechin City	287	0-0	1	4	3			6	7		9	10	14		8		2	11			5	12							
Mar 4	A	Cowdenbeath	625	3-1	1		3			6	7	15	9^1	10^2	8		4		2	5									14	11	
11	H	Dumbarton	788	2-0	1		3			6	7		9	10	8^1		4^1		2	12	5								14	11	
18	A	Albion Rovers	531	3-0	1		3	15		6	7		9^1	10^2	8		4		2	5									14	11	12
25	A	Berwick Rangers	964	0-1	1		3		15	6	7		9	10	8		4		2	5									14	11	12
Apr 1	A	Forfar Athletic	570	0-4	1		3			6	7		9		8		4		2	10	5								14	15	11
11	H	East Fife	788	1-0	1	2		4	5	6	7		9				8		12	10	3									15	11^1
15	A	Montrose	393	2-0	1		4^1		5	6	7		9				8		2		3								10^1		11
22	A	East Stirlingshire	497	1-0	1	12		4	5	6	7		9^1		14		8		2	15	3								10		11
29	H	Brechin City	943	1-0	1	15		4	5	6	7		9		14		8		2	12	3								10		11^1
May 6	A	Cowdenbeath	813	3-2	1			4	5	6	7		9		14		8		2^1	12^2	3								10		11
TOTAL FULL APPEARANCES					36	12	30	29	27	36	30	5	35	28	13	1	27	1	26	21	19	2	1	1	2				8		6
TOTAL SUB APPEARANCES						(3)	(3)	(1)	(1)			(5)		(3)	(7)	(16)	(7)		(4)	(6)	(5)	(1)	(12)	(1)	(2)	(1)		(5)	(1)	(2)	(2)
TOTAL GOALS SCORED							2	6	1	1	1		13	7	3		8		1		8									1	2

Small bold figures denote goalscorers. † denotes opponent's own goal.

The National Stadium, Hampden Park

SOMERVILLE DRIVE

NORTH STAND — C — D
B — F
WEST STAND / Lesser Hampden — EAST STAND
CARMUNNOCK ROAD — AIKENHEAD ROAD
A — G
BT SCOTLAND STAND
P — O — I — J
Letherby Drive — Q — N — M — L — K — H
Exit 46 (West Roadway) — MAIN ENTRANCE — Exit 33 (East Roadway)
Kinghorn Drive
MOUNT ANNAN DRIVE

CAPACITY: 52,046 (All Seated)
PITCH DIMENSIONS: 115 yds x 75 yds
FACILITIES FOR DISABLED SUPPORTERS:
Disabled facilities are situated in the BT Scotland Stand as follows:
West Front (44 places & 44 helpers), West Section A (21 places & 21 helpers)
Ambulant/Blind (55 places), East Front (44 places & 44 helpers)
East Section G (21 places & 21 helpers), Ambulant/Blind (55 places)

Team playing kits

How to get there

The following routes may be used to reach The National Stadium, Hampden Park:

TRAINS: There are two stations within five minutes walk of the ground. Mount Florida Station, on the Cathcart Circle, and King's Park Station. A 15 minute service runs from Glasgow Central.

BUSES: Services to approach Mount Florida end of Stadium: From City Centre: 5, 5A, 5B, M5, M14, 31, 37, 66, 66A, 66B, 66C; From Govan Cross; 34; From Drumchapel: 96, 97, Circular Service: 89, 90; G.C.T. Service: 1; Services to approach King's Park end of Stadium; From City Centre: 12, 12A, 74; Circular Service: 89, 90; G.C.T. Service: 19.

CARS: Car and Coach parking facilities are available in the car park in Letherby Drive, which is capable of holding 200 vehicles. Side streets can also be used.

email: info@sfl.scottishfootball.com • website: www.scottishfootball.com

Stenhousemuir

LIST OF PLAYERS 2000-2001

SURNAME	FIRST NAME	MIDDLE NAME	DATE OF BIRTH	PLACE OF BIRTH	DATE OF SIGNING	HEIGHT FT INS	WEIGHT ST LBS	POS. ON PITCH	PREVIOUS CLUB
Alexander	Andrew		01/08/83	Edinburgh	14/08/00	6 3.0	13 7	Gk	Crammond B.C.
Archer	Steven	Louis	22/01/83	Perth	27/06/00	5 7.0	10 2	Mid	Clyde U'16s
Banner	Alan	William	22/06/64	Manchester	14/07/00	6 0.0	12 0	Gk	Camelon Juniors
Black	Gregor		07/10/83	Falkirk	14/08/00	5 10.0	10 7	Fwd	Stenhousemuir B.C. U'16s
Carlow	Ross		14/09/80	Falkirk	26/07/00	6 0.0	11 3	Def	Fauldhouse United
Chicarella	Riccardo		23/01/82	Lanark	14/08/00	5 7.0	10 0	Fwd	Falkirk
Cormack	Peter	Robert	08/06/74	Liverpool	14/07/00	6 1.0	12 2	Def	Ross County
Croly	Stewart		10/03/82	Glasgow	08/07/99	5 11.0	11 7	Def	Preston North End B.C.
Davidson	Graeme		18/01/68	Edinburgh	21/08/98	5 10.0	11 4	Def	Livingston
Donald	Barry		24/12/78	Glasgow	08/08/00	6 1.0	12 0	Mid	Campsie Black Watch
Duncan	Gavin		07/08/73	Glasgow	24/07/00	5 10.0	11 7	Mid	Partick Thistle
Eeles	Simon	Mervin	09/09/82	Paisley	27/06/00	5 10.5	11 2	Fwd	Stirling Albion
English	Isaac		12/11/71	Paisley	06/07/00	5 9.5	11 7	Mid/Fwd	Partick Thistle
Ferguson	Paul		12/03/75	Bangour	06/07/00	5 8.0	11 0	Mid	Bathgate Juniors
Fisher	James		14/10/67	Bridge of Allan	18/01/92	5 10.0	10 11	Mid	Bo'ness United
Forrest	Fraser	Wilson	14/09/83	Galashiels	14/08/00	6 1.5	12 0	Def	Berwick Rangers
Forrester	Paul		03/11/72	Edinburgh	15/10/99	5 9.0	12 8	Fwd	Berwick Rangers
Gibson	John		20/04/67	Blantyre	22/06/98	5 10.0	11 3	Mid	Stirling Albion
Gibson	Lorn		06/07/76	Paisley	24/07/00	6 0.0	12 7	Mid	Glenafton Juniors
Gow	Garry	Paul	24/06/77	Glasgow	06/07/00	6 1.0	13 10	Gk	Stirling Albion
Graham	Steven		03/08/83	Falkirk	01/08/00	5 11.0	11 4	Def	Heart of Midlothian
Graham	Thomas		12/05/68	Edinburgh	22/06/98	6 0.0	13 0	Def	Livingston
Johnston	Steven		27/01/83	Livingston	14/08/00	5 8.0	9 5	Def	Albion Rovers
Kerr	Paul		17/09/81	Glasgow	08/07/99	6 1.0	12 0	Mid	Preston North End B.C.
Lorimer	David	James	26/01/74	Bellshill	26/06/99	5 9.0	11 5	Mid/Fwd	Albion Rovers
Manson	Robert		16/01/83	Edinburgh	27/06/00	5 9.0	10 0	Mid	Crammond B.C.
McAneny	Paul	James	11/11/73	Glasgow	24/07/00	5 11.0	12 10	Def	Alloa Athletic
McColl	Dean	Aron W.	12/07/83	Falkirk	14/08/00	5 8.0	12 0	Mid	Rangers
McGurk	Ryan		06/06/81	Edinburgh	28/08/99	6 3.0	12 0	Gk	Falkirk
McKinnon	Colin	Graham	29/08/69	Glasgow	13/03/99	6 0.0	11 7	Mid/Fwd	Dumbarton
McLauchlan	Martin	James	02/01/70	Bellshill	21/03/00	6 0.0	12 7	Fwd	Clyde
Menelaws	David		14/04/78	Chorley	31/05/00	5 8.0	10 4	Fwd	Alloa Athletic
Miller	Paul		14/05/83	Falkirk	26/06/99	5 9.0	10 4	Fwd	Gairdoch United
Miller	Scott	Kerr	04/05/75	Glasgow	15/09/00	5 9.0	11 0	Fwd	Partick Thistle
Mooney	Martin	James	25/09/70	Alexandria	31/07/99	5 7.5	11 0	Fwd	Dumbarton
Murphy	Scott		01/12/83	Bellshill	20/08/00	5 8.0	10 4	Mid	Cumbernauld United
O'Rourke	Ryan		01/06/83	Glasgow	14/08/00	5 11.0	10 7	Mid	Cumbernauld United
Perriss	Richard	Elliott	26/03/82	Glasgow	08/07/99	5 6.0	9 0	Fwd	Preston North End B.C.
Pittman	Stephen	Lee	18/07/67	North Carolina	08/08/00	5 10.0	12 4	Def	Linlithgow Juniors
Stacey	Steve		21/04/83	Edinburgh	27/06/00	6 1.0	11 7	Fwd	Crammond B.C.
Storrar	Andrew	David	06/10/77	Stirling	11/08/00	5 6.0	11 4	Def	East Stirlingshire
Stronach	Grant	William	25/10/81	Falkirk	08/07/99	6 1.0	11 0	Fwd	Riverside B.C.
Wood	David	Wilson	30/12/75	Broxburn	04/03/99	5 9.5	11 2	Fwd	Whitburn Juniors

Milestones

YEAR OF FORMATION: 1884
MOST LEAGUE POINTS IN A SEASON: 50 (Division 2 – Season 1960/61) (2 Points for a Win)
64 (Third Division – Season 1998/99) (3 Points for a Win)
MOST LEAGUE GOALS SCORED BY A PLAYER IN A SEASON: Evelyn Morrison (Season 1927/28) and Robert Murray (Season 1936/37)
NO. OF GOALS SCORED: 31
RECORD ATTENDANCE: 12,500 (-v- East Fife – 11.3.1950)
RECORD VICTORY: 9-2 (-v- Dundee United – Division 2, 16.4.1937)
RECORD DEFEAT: 2-11 (-v- Dunfermline Athletic – Division 2, 27.9.1930)

The Warriors' ten year league record

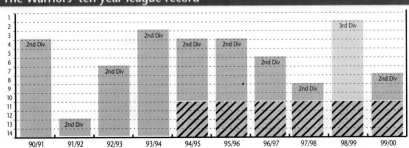

46

Date	V	Opponents	Att.	Res	Hamilton L.	Lawrence A.	Gibson J.	Armstrong C.	Graham T.	Davidson G.	Lorimer D.	Fisher J.	Hamilton R.	McKinnon C.	Wood D.	Watters W.	Banks A.	Cummings A.	McGurk R.	Mooney M.	Roseburgh D.	Watson C.	Forrester P.	Hall M.	Fraser G.	Bradford J.	Welsh B.	McLauchlan M.	Connolly J.	Murphy S.	Wright K.
Aug 7	A	Partick Thistle	2,072	1-0	1	2	3	4	5	6	7^1	8	9	10	11	12															
14	H	Stirling Albion	703	2-1	1	2	10	4	5	6			11	7^1	8	14	9^1	3	15													
21	A	Ross County	2,612	0-0	1	2	11	4	5	6			10	7	8	15	9	3	14													
28	H	Stranraer	427	1-1		2	11	4	5	6			10	7	8^1	9	12	3		1		14										
Sep 5	A	Hamilton Academical	445	1-1	1	2	7	4	5	6			10	9	8^1	11	14	3	15	12												
11	A	Queen of the South	928	3-0	1	2		4	5^2	6			11	7^1	8	12	9	3	10	14	15											
18	H	Arbroath	596	1-3	1	2	11	4	5	6			10	7	8	12	9	3		14^1	15											
25	A	Alloa Athletic	675	†4-1	1	2	8	4		6		10^1	9^1	5	11	12	14	15		7^1			3									
Oct 2	H	Clyde	715	1-3	1	2	3	4	5^1	6			10	9	8	15	12	14	15	7												
16	A	Stirling Albion	649	1-5	1	2	3	4	5	6			11^1	9	8	15	12			7			11	14								
23	H	Partick Thistle	1,188	0-1	1	2	10	15	5	6			11	7	8	12				14		4	9	3								
30	H	Queen of the South	447	2-1	1	2	10	6	5				11	7^1	8^1	12				14		4	9	3								
Nov 6	A	Arbroath	866	3-0	1	2		6	5				11	10	8	12				7^3		4	9	3	14							
10	H	Hamilton Academical	510	0-0	1	2		6	5				11	10	8	15	12			7		4	9	3	14							
20	A	Stranraer	398	0-2	1	2		6	5		15		10	8	14	12				7		4	9	3	11							
27	A	Clyde	882	0-1	1	2		6					10	9	5	7	14	12				4	8	3	11							
Dec 4	H	Alloa Athletic	574	1-3	1	2		6	5^1		10		11	7	8	15	14					4	9		3							
18	A	Partick Thistle	1,922	0-1	1	2		6	5				11	7	8	14		3		9		4			10							
Jan 3	H	Arbroath	381	3-0	1	15		6	5				11	7^1	8	14	12	3		10^1		4^1			2	9						
15	A	Queen of the South	1,017	1-3	1	2		15	5		10		11	7	8^1			3		9		4	12		6	14						
Feb 5	H	Clyde	690	†3-4	1	2		14	5			6	11^1	7	8			3^1		15		4			10	9						
12	H	Stranraer	306	1-1	1	2		6	5		12	10^1	7	8			3			11		4			9							
26	H	Stirling Albion	629	1-2	1	2		6	5	14	12	11	7	8			3			15		4			10^1	9						
Mar 7	A	Alloa Athletic	492	1-3	12			15	5	2	14	11^1	7^1	8			3		1	10		4			6	9						
11	H	Queen of the South	541	2-0	1	2		14	5	4	10	11^1	7^1	8			12								3	9	6					
14	H	Hamilton Academical	347	1-2	1	2			5		10	11	7	8						9^1		4			3	12	6					
18	A	Arbroath	730	2-2	1	2		6	5		12		7^1	8^1	14		3			10		4	15	11	9							
21	H	Ross County	358	0-2	1	2			5		11		7	8			3			15		4			10		6	9				
25	A	Stranraer	409	2-2	1	2		4	5				7	8^2			3			11		10			14	12	6	9				
28	A	Ross County	1,771	0-2	1	2		14	5		10		7	8		12				11		4		3		6	9	1	15			
Apr 8	H	Alloa Athletic	495	2-1	1	2					12	10			11		3			14		4	8		6	7	5^1	9^1				
15	A	Clyde	1,033	0-7	1	2		15	5				10	7	8					14		4			3	12	6	9				11
18	H	Hamilton Academical	309	0-1	1		2		5		12	3	10	8						7		4				14	6	9				11
22	H	Partick Thistle	895	2-0	1	2	3		5			6	11	7	8	14^1				12		4			15			9				10^1
29	A	Stirling Albion	564	0-1	1	15	3		5	2			10	7	8	11				14		4			6			12				9
May 6	H	Ross County	600	2-2	1				5	2			12	8	11^1	15	3			7^1		4	10	6				9				14
TOTAL FULL APPEARANCES					33	31	14	22	33	15	9	30	34	35	9	4	18	1	2	17		27	9	9	15	8	8	8	1		4
TOTAL SUB APPEARANCES							(3)	(7)		(1)	(7)				(1)		(12)	(15)	(4)	(5)		(14)	(2)		(3)	(4)	(5)	(1)		(1)	(1)
TOTAL GOALS SCORED									4		1	5	8	7	2	1	1			8		1			1		1			1

Small bold figures denote goalscorers. † *denotes opponent's own goal.*

Ochilview Park

TRYST ROAD

GLADSTONE ROAD

CAPACITY: 2,376; Seated 626, Standing 1,750
PITCH DIMENSIONS: 110 yds x 72 yds
FACILITIES FOR DISABLED SUPPORTERS:
Accommodation for disabled in new Stand. Toilet facilities also provided.

Team playing kits

How to get there

Ochilview Park can be reached by the following routes:

TRAINS: The nearest station is Larbert, which is about half a mile away from the ground.

BUSES: There are regular bus services from Falkirk.

CARS: There is a large car park on the north side of the ground.

The Warriors

Stirling Albion

LIST OF PLAYERS 2000/2001

SURNAME	FIRST NAME	MIDDLE NAME	DATE OF BIRTH	PLACE OF BIRTH	DATE OF SIGNING	HEIGHT FT INS	WEIGHT ST LBS	POS. ON PITCH	PREVIOUS CLUB
Aitken	Alan	Alexander	04/09/82	Stirling	26/02/99	5 7.0	11 0	Fwd	Sauchie B.C.
Bennett	John	Neil	22/08/71	Falkirk	03/06/00	5 9.0	11 2	Def	Montrose
Brown	Alastair		05/02/82	Irvine	08/08/00	5 10.0	10 7	Mid	Queen of the South
Brown	Paul		22/10/83	Glasgow	15/08/00	5 10.0	11 0	Mid	Queen's Park
Buchanan	Andrew		25/03/83	Stirling	23/08/00	6 1.0	12 7	Gk	Stirling Albion Youth
Butler	David	R.	04/04/83	Glasgow	15/07/00	5 6.0	9 6	Mid	Stirling Albion Youth
Devine	Stewart		11/04/84	Edinburgh	13/07/00	5 10.0	9 11	Mid	Stirling Albion Youth
Donald	Graeme	Still	14/04/74	Stirling	15/07/98	6 0.0	12 4	Def	Hibernian
Feroz	Craig		24/10/77	Aberdeen	19/07/00	5 10.0	12 0	Fwd	Livingston
Gardner	James		27/09/67	Dunfermline	28/07/99	5 11.0	11 10	Mid	Exeter City
Graham	Alastair	Slowey	11/08/66	Glasgow	29/10/98	6 3.0	12 7	Fwd	T.P.V. Tampere
Hunter	Gordon		03/05/67	Wallyford	29/06/00	6 0.0	13 0	Def	Hamilton Academical
Jack	Paul	Dunn	15/05/65	Malaya	04/08/00	5 10.0	12 7	Def	Airdrieonians
Joy	Ian	Paul	14/07/81	San Diego	15/08/00	5 8.0	11 0	Def	Tranmere Rovers
Kelly	Gary	Patrick	01/09/81	Falkirk	25/08/00	5 11.0	10 7	Mid	Sauchie Juniors
Love	Graeme	James	07/12/73	Bathgate	25/08/00	5 10.0	13 5	Def	East Fife
McAulay	Ian	Mackay	06/06/74	Glasgow	15/07/00	5 6.0	11 4	Mid	Hamilton Academical
McCallion	Kevin		23/07/82	Bellshill	31/07/98	5 8.0	9 10	Mid	Mill United B.C.
McGraw	Mark	Robertson	05/01/71	Rutherglen	04/08/00	5 11.5	12 10	Fwd	Clyde
McLellan	Kenneth	John	08/09/83	Stirling	15/07/00	5 10.0	10 7	Def	Falkirk Youth
Millar	John		08/12/66	Bellshill	13/07/00	5 10.0	12 8	Mid	Livingston
Milne	Kevin		27/04/81	Edinburgh	04/08/00	5 11.0	12 5	Def	Aberdeen
Munro	Gareth	Ross	13/10/82	Stirling	05/07/00	5 9.0	10 8	Mid	Cumbernauld Hearts B.C.
Nairn	David		04/02/83	Glasgow	15/08/00	5 11.0	12 7	Fwd	Stirling Albion Youth
Ramage	Michael	George	04/11/83	Stirling	15/08/00	6 1.0	12 0	Fwd	Stirling Albion Youth
Reid	Christopher	Thomas	04/11/71	Edinburgh	03/06/00	6 2.0	13 2	Gk	Hamilton Academical
Ross	Crawford	Peter R.	14/02/83	Melbourne	19/08/00	5 11.0	11 7	Gk	Stirling Albion Youth
Scott	David		25/11/82	Stirling	15/08/00	5 9.0	10 9	Def	Stirling Albion Youth
Scott	Greig		21/07/83	Stirling	13/07/00	6 0.0	12 0	Mid	St. Johnstone Youth
Sinclair	Scott	Ralph	08/05/83	Stirling	05/07/99	5 11.0	11 4	Def	Riverside B.C.
Stuart	William	Gibb	28/01/83	Paisley	05/07/99	5 6.0	8 13	Def	West Park United
Whiteford	Andrew		22/08/77	Bellshill	03/02/00	5 11.0	12 0	Def	St. Johnstone
Williams	Alexander	Boyd	15/01/83	Glasgow	27/08/99	5 10.5	10 7	Fwd	West Park U'15s

Milestones

YEAR OF FORMATION: 1945
MOST LEAGUE POINTS IN A SEASON: 59 (Division 2 – Season 1964/65)(2 Points for a Win)
81 (Second Division – Season 1995/96)(3 Points for a Win)
MOST LEAGUE GOALS SCORED BY A PLAYER IN A SEASON: Joe Hughes (Season 1969/70)
NO. OF GOALS SCORED: 26
RECORD ATTENDANCE: 26,400 (-v- Celtic – Scottish Cup, 11.3.1959)
RECORD VICTORY: 20-0 (-v- Selkirk – Scottish Cup, 8.12.1984)
RECORD DEFEAT: 0-9 (-v- Dundee United – Division 1, 30.12.1967)

The Albion's ten year league record

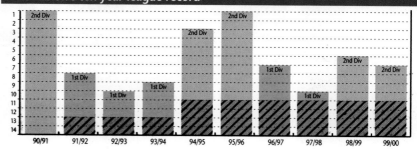

THE ALBION' CLUB FACTFILE 1999/2000
RESULTS... APPEARANCES... SCORERS... ATTENDANCES...

Date	Venue	Opponents	Att.	Res	Gow G.	Paterson A.	Tortolano J.	Donald G.	Martin B.	Wood C.	McQuade J.	Aitken A.	Graham A.	Taggart C.	Gardner J.	Mortimer P.	Gardner I.	Philliben J.	Bell D.	McGillen P.	McCallion K.	McCallum D.	Whiteford A.	Clark P.	Bone A.	Williams A.	McAlpine J.	Gardner G.
Aug 7	H	Stranraer	525	1-1	1	2	3	4	5	6	7	8	9^1	10	11	12												
14	A	Stenhousemuir	703	1-2		2	3	4	5	6	7	8^1	9	10	11	12	1	14		15								
21	H	Hamilton Academical	656	2-0		2	3	4	5	6^1	7^1	8	9	10	11		1	14		15								
28	A	Clyde	1,003	0-3		2	3	4	5	6	7	8	9	10	11	12	1			15								
Sep 4	H	Ross County	1,015	2-1		2	3	4	5	6	7^1	15	9^1	10	11		1	14		8								
11	A	Arbroath	805	1-2		2	3	4	5	6	7		9	10	11	12	1			8^1								
18	H	Alloa Athletic	1,196	0-1			3	4		6	7		9	10		2	1	5	12	8	14							
25	A	Queen of the South	1,038	3-3		2	3	4	5	12	7		9^2	10	11	6	1			8^1								
Oct 2	H	Partick Thistle	1,333	3-1		2	3	4	5		7	15	9	10	11	8	1			12^1	6^1							
16	H	Stenhousemuir	649	5-1		2	3	4	5		7^2	15	9^1	10^1	11	8	1			12	6							
23	A	Stranraer	446	1-2		2	3	4	5		7	15	9	10^1	11	8	1	14		12	6							
30	H	Arbroath	856	3-4		2	3	4	5	6	7		9^1	10	11	8^1	1			12^1	14							
Nov 6	A	Alloa Athletic	909	4-4		2	3	4		12^1	7^1		9^1	10^1	11	6	1	5		8	15							
12	A	Ross County	2,693	3-1		2	3	4		6	7^2	12	9	10	11	5	1	14		8^1								
20	H	Clyde	949	1-2		2	4	3		7	12	9^1	10	11	5	1	14		8	6								
27	A	Partick Thistle	2,812	0-1		2	4	3		7			9	11	5	1	5	15	8	10								
Dec 11	H	Queen of the South	534	3-0		2	4^1	3		7^1			9	10	11	6	1		8	12	5^1							
18	H	Stranraer	571	2-5		2	14	4	3	7^1			9	10	11	6	1	8^1	15	12	5							
27	A	Hamilton Academical	431	2-0	1	2	3	4		6	7^1		9	10	11	15			8^1	14	5	12						
Jan 3	H	Alloa Athletic	1,398	1-1	1	2	3	4		12	7		9	10	11	14			8^1	6	5							
22	A	Queen of the South	1,104	3-2	1	2	3	4			7^1		9^1	10	11				8^1	6	5							
Feb 5	H	Partick Thistle	1,704	0-2	1	2	3	4		12	7		9	10	11				8	6	5	14	15					
12	A	Clyde	1,027	1-4	1	14	4			10	7^1		9	15	11	6		3	8	5	2	12					
19	H	Ross County	661	3-1	1	2	4				7^2		9	10	11	6	1	14	12	5	3	8^1	15				
26	A	Stenhousemuir	629	2-1		2	3	4			7		9^1	10		1			12	5	6	8^1	11				
29	A	Arbroath	580	2-3		2	3	4			7^1		9	10		1			12	5	6	8^1	11				
Mar 4	H	Hamilton Academical	692	1-4		2	3	4			7		9	10	15		1	14^1	12	5	6	8	11				
11	H	Arbroath	681	1-1		2	3	4			7		9	10	14		1	12	11	5	15	8^1				6	
18	A	Alloa Athletic	939	0-1	1	2	3	4			7		9	10					11	15	5	6	8				
25	H	Clyde	1,102	3-6	1	2^1	3	4			7		9^1					6	11^1	12	5	10	8				
Apr 1	A	Ross County	2,148	1-5			3	4			7	12^1	9		8	1	6		11	14	10	5	2	15			
8	H	Queen of the South	520	2-2		2	3	4		6	7	12	9^2		11		1		8	14	10	5		15			
15	A	Partick Thistle	2,160	1-1		2		4			7		9^1		11	3	1	6	8	12	10	5		15			
22	A	Stranraer	447	1-3		2		1			14		9^1		11	6		4	7	3	10	5	8				
29	H	Stenhousemuir	564	1-0				1		6	7	14	9^1		11	4		3	8	12	10	5	2				
May 6	A	Hamilton Academical	498	0-1		2		1			8	14	9		11	4		3	7	12	10	5	6	15			
TOTAL FULL APPEARANCES					8	32	26	36	11	18	34	4	36	27	29	19	25	10		23	4	12	20	11	7		3	1
TOTAL SUB APPEARANCES						(1)	(1)			(5)			(10)		(1)			(8)		(7)	(6)	(6)	(9)	(8)	(3)	(2)	(5)	
TOTAL GOALS SCORED							1	1		2	15	2	17	3	1	1				11				1	1	4		

Small bold figures denote goalscorers.   † denotes opponent's own goal.

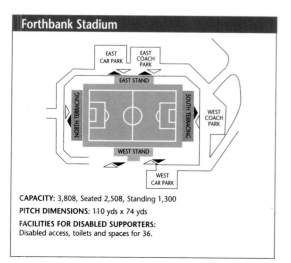

Forthbank Stadium

(Stadium plan: EAST CAR PARK, EAST COACH PARK, EAST STAND, NORTH TERRACING, SOUTH TERRACING, WEST STAND, WEST COACH PARK, WEST CAR PARK)

CAPACITY: 3,808, Seated 2,508, Standing 1,300
PITCH DIMENSIONS: 110 yds x 74 yds
FACILITIES FOR DISABLED SUPPORTERS:
Disabled access, toilets and spaces for 36.

Team playing kits

How to get there

Forthbank Stadium can be reached by the following routes:

TRAINS: The nearest station is Stirling Railway Station, which is approximately 2 miles from the ground. A bus service from Goosecroft Road travels to the stadium (buses run every 25 minutes from 1.50pm – 2.40pm and returns to town at 4.50pm).

BUSES: To Goosecroft Bus Station, Stirling, and bus to stadium from Goosecroft Road (outside Bus Station) Service No 101 operates every 25 minutes from 1.50pm – 2.40pm and returns to town at 4.50pm.

CARS: Follow signs for A91 St. Andrews/Alloa. Car Parking is available in the club car park. Home support in West Car Park and visiting support in East Car Park.

The Albion

email: info@sfl.scottishfootball.com • website: www.scottishfootball.com

Stranraer

LIST OF PLAYERS 2000-2001

SURNAME	FIRST NAME	MIDDLE NAME	DATE OF BIRTH	PLACE OF BIRTH	DATE OF SIGNING	HEIGHT FT INS	WEIGHT ST LBS	POS. ON PITCH	PREVIOUS CLUB
Abbott	Steven	James	04/04/81	Bellshill	28/03/00	5 9.0	10 0	Def	Maybole Juniors
Blaikie	Alan		25/08/72	Greenock	31/03/99	6 1.0	12 0	Fwd	Morton
Blair	Paul		05/07/76	Greenock	12/02/00	5 9.0	11 8	Mid/Fwd	Morton
Edgar	Scott		10/06/76	Glasgow	20/03/00	6 4.0	13 0	Fwd	Queen's Park
George	Duncan	Henry	04/12/67	Paisley	01/08/97	5 10.0	10 7	Mid	Ayr United
Geraghty	Michael	John	30/10/70	Glasgow	28/07/00	5 11.0	11 7	Fwd	Ross County
Harty	Ian	McGuinness	08/04/78	Bellshill	02/07/98	5 8.0	10 7	Fwd	Albion Rovers
Hughes	Martin		09/05/80	Glasgow	03/08/00	5 9.0	11 0	Mid	Hibernian
Jenkins	Allan	David	07/10/81	Stranraer	03/09/98	6 1.0	12 4	Mid	Ayr Boswell
Johnstone	Douglas	Iain	12/03/69	Irvine	30/01/98	6 2.0	12 8	Def	Morton
Knox	Keith		06/08/64	Stranraer	10/07/97	5 10.0	12 2	Def	Clyde
Macdonald	William	James	17/09/76	Irvine	26/11/99	5 8.0	11 0	Mid	Clydebank
McDonald	Greig		05/02/77	Glasgow	28/07/00	6 2.0	13 12	Def	Cambuslang Rangers
McGeown	Mark		10/05/70	Paisley	30/07/99	5 10.5	11 6	Gk	Stirling Albion
McMillan	Allister	Scott	08/08/75	Glasgow	11/09/00	6 0.0	12 2	Def	Queen of the South
O'Neill	Stephen		30/06/75	Paisley	30/07/99	6 0.0	13 0	Gk	Renfrew Juniors
Paterson	Andrew		05/05/72	Glasgow	10/07/00	5 9.5	11 12	Def	Stirling Albion
Rae	Derek	Parlane	02/08/74	Glasgow	03/08/00	6 0.0	11 10	Mid	Lugar Boswell
Walker	Paul		20/08/77	Kilwinning	17/03/99	5 5.5	9 13	Fwd	St. Mirren
Wright	Fraser		23/12/79	East Kilbride	03/09/98	5 10.0	11 10	Def	St. Mirren B.C.

Milestones

YEAR OF FORMATION: 1870
MOST LEAGUE POINTS IN A SEASON: 56 (Second Division – 1993/94)(2 Points for a Win)
61 (Second Division – 1997/98)(3 Points for a Win)
MOST LEAGUE GOALS SCORED BY A PLAYER IN A SEASON: Derrick Frye (Season 1977/78)
NO. OF GOALS SCORED: 27
RECORD ATTENDANCE: 6,500 (-v- Rangers – 24.1.1948)
RECORD VICTORY: 7-0 (-v- Brechin City – Division 2, 6.2.1965)
RECORD DEFEAT: 1-11 (-v- Queen of the South – Scottish Cup, 16.1.1932)

The Blues' ten year league record

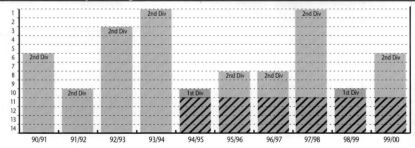

THE BLUES' CLUB FACTFILE 1999/2000
RESULTS... APPEARANCES... SCORERS... ATTENDANCES...

Date	Venue	Opponents	Att.	Res	McGeown M.	Knox K.	Black T.	Furphy W.	Smith J.	Cahoon D.	Bell R.	George D.	Harty I.	Blaikie A.	McMartin G.	Walker P.	Johnstone D.	Jenkins A.	Wright F.	Young J.	Watson P.	Duthie M.	Roddie A.	Ronald P.	Macdonald W.	Ramsay D.	Abbott S.	Feroz C.	Blair P.	Mitchell A.	Edgar S.	Smith D.
Aug 7	A	Stirling Albion	525	1-1	1	2	3	4	5	6¹	7	8	9	10	11	12	14	15														
14	H	Ross County	475	0-0	1	5	3	4	2	6		8	9	10	7	12	14	15	11													
21	A	Clyde	722	0-0	1	6	3	4	2	14		8	9	10	11	12	5	15		7												
28	A	Stenhousemuir	427	1-1	1	4	3		2¹	8		6	11	9	7	12	5	15			10	14											
Sep 4	H	Partick Thistle	1,138	1-1	1	7	3	4	2	6		8	9	11¹	10		14	15	12	5													
11	A	Hamilton Academical	503	1-2	1	2			5		6	8	7	10	11¹	9	3			12	4												
18	H	Queen of the South	621	1-0	1	7		4	2¹	8			9	10	11	12		6	5	14	3												
25	A	Arbroath	811	2-1	1	6		4	2	10		7	12	11¹	5	14		8	15¹	9	3												
Oct 2	H	Alloa Athletic	463	0-0	1	5		4	2	7		6	10	9	11	12		8		14	3												
16	A	Ross County	2,168	1-1	1	5		4	2			6	10	12	7	11	15	14¹			3		9										
23	H	Stirling Albion	446	2-1	1	2		4	5			6		11	3		12	8		9			7¹	10¹	14								
30	H	Hamilton Academical	454	0-2	1	3		4	2	5		7	15	11		9	12	6		8				10	14								
Nov 6	A	Queen of the South	1,052	5-0	1	4	3		2	15		8	9			12	5	6	14				11²	10³	7								
14	A	Partick Thistle	1,825	0-2	1	4	3		2	14		8	9			5	6	12	15			11	10	7									
20	A	Stenhousemuir	398	2-0	1	4			2	15	5¹	8	11		12	3¹		9	14	6			10	7									
27	H	Alloa Athletic	569	1-1	1	4			2	5		9	11			3¹	15	6				8	10	7									
Dec 4	H	Arbroath	384	2-2	1	4			2		7	9	11		12		8¹	6	14	5			10¹	3									
18	A	Stirling Albion	571	5-2	1		4		2¹				9³	11		7		6	3					10¹	8	5	14						
27	H	Clyde	649	2-2	1		4		2¹				9	6	10	8	3				12		11		7¹	5							
Jan 3	H	Queen of the South	928	1-2	1		3		5				9¹	14	11	7	2				12		6	10	8	4							
15	A	Hamilton Academical	576	0-2	1	8			2				9	14	7	12	5				4		11	10	6	3	15						
22	A	Arbroath	720	1-1	1	5			2	3			9	11				6	15		4			10¹	8			7					
Feb 12	A	Stenhousemuir	306	1-1	1	2			12			15	6	10	14	5	3	4						11¹	8			9	7				
26	H	Ross County	472	0-2	1	6	5					11	9		12̣	2	8	3	14	4				10	7						15		
Mar 7	H	Partick Thistle	628	3-1	1	2		4	5¹			8	9¹	11	15			3						10¹	6			7					
11	H	Hamilton Academical	405	2-2	1	2		4	5			8	9¹	11	15		14	12						10	6			7¹					
18	A	Queen of the South	1,165	0-0	1		3	4	2			6	9	7	12		8		15	5								10	11				
21	H	Alloa Athletic	388	2-2	1	2		4	12	14		5	9¹	11¹	8		3	6	15									7	10				
25	H	Stenhousemuir	409	2-2	1	3	15		2¹		14		9¹	10	5			6	11	8	4							7	12				
28	A	Clyde	785	1-1	1	2¹	4				7		9	11	8	5	6						10	3				12	14				
Apr 1	A	Partick Thistle	2,351	1-1	1	2¹	4					8	9	11		5	6	15	10	3								12	14				7
8	H	Arbroath	412	0-1	1	2	4			15	7	6	9	11		5	8	14	10	3								12				
15	H	Alloa Athletic	605	0-4	1	5		4	2	15			9	7		3	8	6	12					10					14	11		
22	H	Stirling Albion	447	3-1	1	6		4	2			8	9			3			11					10³					14			7
29	A	Ross County	2,812	1-3	1	8	4		2¹		11		9				5	6					10					7		12	14
May 6	H	Clyde	471	2-1	1	8	3		2		6		9	14		5		4						7¹					11	10¹	
TOTAL FULL APPEARANCES					36	33	16	16	30	9	9	22	30	28	14	8	17	17	19	9	19	4	9	17	14	4		2	8		3	3
TOTAL SUB APPEARANCES						(1)		(2)	(4)	(5)		(2)	(4)	(3)	(12)	(5)	(8)	(5)	(14)	(5)				(2)				(2)	(3)	(1)	(6)	(1)
TOTAL GOALS SCORED						2			7	1		1	8	2	2		2	1	1	1			1	3	12	1			1		1	

Small bold figures denote goalscorers.   † denotes opponent's own goal.

Stair Park

LONDON ROAD — ENTRY FOR VISITING SUPPORTERS

NORTH STAND

SOUTH STAND

ENTRY TO SOUTH STAND FOR VISITING SUPPORTERS

CAPACITY: 5,600; Seated 1,830, Standing 3,770
PITCH DIMENSIONS: 110 yds x 70 yds
FACILITIES FOR DISABLED SUPPORTERS:
By prior arrangement with Club Secretary.

Team playing kits

How to get there

Stair Park can be reached by the following routes:
TRAINS: There is a regular service of trains from Ayr and the station is only 1 mile from the ground.
BUSES: Two services pass the park. These are the buses from Glenluce to Portroadie and the Dumfries-Stranraer service.
CARS: Car parking is available in the Public Park at the ground, where there is space for approximately 50 vehicles and also in the side streets around the park. Signs for away supporters will be displayed and parking situated at Stranraer Academy, McMasters Road.

The Blues

email: info@sfl.scottishfootball.com • website: www.scottishfootball.com

ARBROATH
SEASON TICKET INFORMATION

SEATED	ADULT	£150
	JUVENILE/OAP	£75
STANDING	ADULT	£130
	JUVENILE/OAP	£75
	JUVENILES UNDER 12 YEARS	£25

LEAGUE ADMISSION PRICES

SEATED	ADULT	£9
	JUVENILE/OAP	£5
STANDING	ADULT	£8
	JUVENILE/OAP/	
	UNEMPLOYED (WITH UB40)	£4

Arbroath's Gayfield Park

CLYDEBANK
SEASON TICKET INFORMATION
SEATED

ADULT	£220
JUVENILE/OAP	£150

STANDING

ADULT	£180
OAP	£75
JUVENILES 15 to U18	£85
JUVENILES 14 & UNDER	£20

LEAGUE ADMISSION PRICES
SEATED

ADULT	£10
JUVENILE/OAP	£5
PARENT & JUVENILE	£15

FORFAR ATHLETIC
SEASON TICKET INFORMATION

SEATED	ADULT	£110
	JUVENILE/OAP	£55
STANDING	ADULT	£105
	JUVENILE/OAP	£48

LEAGUE ADMISSION PRICES

SEATED	ADULT	£7.50
	JUVENILE/OAP	£3.50
STANDING	ADULT	£7
	JUVENILE/OAP	£3

BERWICK RANGERS
SEASON TICKET INFORMATION

	BELL'S FIRST DIV GAMES ONLY	ALL GAMES EXCEPT TENNENTS SCOTTISH CUP
SEATED AND STANDING		
ADULT	£110	£125
CONCESSIONS	£55	£65
(Includes Juvenile/OAP/Unemployed with UB40/Registered Disabled)		
JUVENILE (U-16)	£30	£40
FAMILY TICKET (1 ADULT/1 JUVENILE)	£130	£150
PLUS £10 FOR EACH ADDITIONAL JUVENILE		
OR £30 EACH ADDITIONAL ADULT		

LEAGUE ADMISSION PRICES

SEATED AND STANDING	
ADULT	£8
CONCESSIONS	£4
PRESIDENT'S BOX	
PRICES ON APPLICATION	

N.B. All fans for Stand enter via either Ground 'A' or 'B' and transfer to Stand.

Forfar Athletic's Station Park

PARTICK THISTLE
SEASON TICKET INFORMATION
SEATED

ADULT	£165
OAP/UNDER 16/STUDENT	£80
UNDER 12	£35

LEAGUE ADMISSION PRICES

SEATED

ADULT	£10
OAP/UNDER 16/STUDENT	£5
UNDER 12	£3

STANDING (Overspill only)

ADULT	£9
OAP/UNDER 16/STUDENT	£4
UNDER 12	£3

STENHOUSEMUIR
SEASON TICKET INFORMATION
SEATED

ADULT	£130
JUVENILE/OAP/STUDENT	£65
FAMILY FLEXI - ADD £30 FOR EACH ADDITIONAL FAMILY MEMBER (UNLIMITED) TO A FULL PRICE SEASON TICKET	

STANDING

ADULT	£100
JUVENILE/OAP/STUDENT	£50

LEAGUE ADMISSION PRICES
SEATED

ADULT	£9
JUVENILE/OAP	£5

STANDING

ADULT	£8
JUVENILE/OAP	£4

QUEEN OF THE SOUTH
SEASON TICKET INFORMATION

SEATED	ADULT	£140
	JUVENILE (EAST STAND)	£30
	JUVENILE (WEST STAND)	£70
	OAP	£90
STANDING	ADULT	£140
	OAP	£90
	SCHOOL CHILDREN	£30

LEAGUE ADMISSION PRICES

SEATED	ADULT	£9
	SCHOOL CHILDREN/OAP	£6
STANDING	ADULT	£9
	UNEMPLOYED/OAP/UB40'S/ FAMILY SUPPLEMENT	£6
	SCHOOL CHILDREN	£3

STIRLING ALBION
SEASON TICKET INFORMATION

SEATED

ADULT	£160
JUVENILE/OAP	£85

LEAGUE ADMISSION PRICES
SEATED

ADULT	£9
JUVENILE	£5

STANDING

ADULT	£8
JUVENILE/OAP	£4

QUEEN'S PARK
SEASON TICKET INFORMATION - SEATED

BT SCOTLAND STAND	ADULT	£100
	JUVENILE (OVER 12 AND UNDER 16)/ SENIOR CITIZEN	£40
	PARENT & JUVENILE	£110
	FOR EACH ADDITIONAL JUVENILE	£10
	JUVENILE (UNDER 12)	£25

LEAGUE ADMISSION PRICES - SEATED

BT SCOTLAND STAND	ADULT	£7
	JUVENILE/SENIOR CITIZEN	£2
	PARENT & JUVENILE	£8
	FOR EACH ADDITIONAL JUVENILE	£1

STRANRAER
SEASON TICKET INFORMATION
SEATED

ADULT	£120
JUVENILE/OAP	£60
FAMILY	£40

STANDING

ADULT	£100
JUVENILE/OAP	£50

LEAGUE ADMISSION PRICES

SEATED

ADULT	£8
JUVENILE/OAP	£4

STANDING

ADULT	£6
JUVENILE/OAP	£3

An Investment in the Future

There appears to be a general misconception that life outwith the top flight of Scottish football is hardly worth living and that those clubs who exist in the three divisions of The Scottish Football League survive by means of a hand to mouth existence with no really meaningful purpose. Not so, it would seem, judging by the exciting developments that have taken place and which, in some instances, are about to happen in the foreseeable future.

I refer, in particular, to the emergence of various youth development programmes and the growth of the Under-18 Youth Division (which is competitive) and the Youth Development Initiative at Under-13, 14, 15 and 16 age levels (which is non-competitive). Many of the stars of the future will emerge from these programmes which are being actively pursued by a goodly number of First, Second and Third Division clubs.

The Scottish Football League introduced the Youth Development Initiative in season 1995/96 with the emphasis on the development of young players rather than - thankfully - on a win at all costs mentality. Those responsible for drawing up the Youth Development Initiative displayed common sense and foresight by decreeing that the non-competitive set-up would not require the recording of results, league tables, trophies and medals of any kind, matches to be played for the duration of 90 minutes or for teams to be eleven-a-side.

Flexibility of fixtures and "time-outs" were other interesting innovations, allowing coaches to offer advice, tuition and encouragement during the course of a match. Other aspects, such as an understanding of the Laws of the

Game, fitness, diet and nutrition and media training, are also incorporated in the Initiative which is aimed at establishing a properly co-ordinated structure to unearth the best young players in Scotland.

At the time of writing, a total of 19 First, Second and Third Division clubs were participating in the Under-18 Youth Division, while 15 were enrolled at Under-16 level, nine at Under-15 level, seven at Under-14 level and eight at Under-13 level of the Youth Development Initiative. Of the First Division clubs, Falkirk were participants at every level, while East Stirlingshire, of the Third Division, could make a similar proud boast.

The plain truth is that there has been a realisation these past few

years that many of the lower League clubs - and, indeed, some at a higher level - cannot exist on transfer fees as they once did. Bosman saw to that. Funds, once earmarked for the day-to-day running of a club, disappeared overnight and, suddenly, a fresh strategy had to be found to ensure the future development of our finest young talent.

The Scottish Football League's groundbreaking scheme has been largely instrumental in ensuring the continued development of that talent and removed the dominant competitive edge which often did more harm than good in nurturing youngsters' skills. The clubs, too, have been offered a greater degree of protection with the introduction

Jamie McAllister

*Craig Brown and
Colin Hendry
coach the kids*

of the 'D' Form, a registration document tying each youngster to a single club for the entire season.

Queen of the South are a typical example of a club endeavouring to serve the community at all levels, incorporating in their structure an opportunity for women footballers to advance their skills. Club Secretary Dick Shaw has the onerous task of overseeing a set-up which involves Queens in organising games at Under-16s, 15s and 14s levels as well as running both women's and girls teams, something they have actively encouraged for the past five years.

Shaw admitted that he and many others were somewhat sceptical about the idea of females playing organised football but added: "As the years have gone on, their skill level and commitment has been first class."

All of this, of course, costs money and the club is grateful for the support it receives from both The Scottish Football League and The Scottish Football Association in the shape of monetary and grant awards.

"We employ two coaches at each age level and being based in the

south of the country adds significantly to our overall costs," says Shaw.

"But we see ourselves as a community club and we feel that it's important to give people a platform to play on. The main aim for us is to give as many locals as possible an opportunity to play football at a reasonable level."

Queen of the South can currently count among their successes, Chris Doig, now a first team player with Nottingham Forest and the Aberdeen pair of Jamie McAllister and David Lilley, while Ross Kerr is a member of the Scotland Under-16 squad.

Craig Levein, the current Cowdenbeath manager and former Heart of Midlothian and Scotland

Craig Levein, manager of Cowdenbeath

defender, is a staunch believer in youth football, insisting that it is the only way ahead for the vast majority of senior clubs. Levein, who began his own, highly successful career with the club that he now manages, has already seen several promising youngsters come through the ranks at Central Park. Graeme Brown, a 19-year-old forward, has been attracting a lot of attention since breaking into the first team and Craig McMillan was another notable success before he, unfortunately, suffered a broken leg playing against St.Johnstone, while Levein also has high hopes for teenager James Lakie.

Finance is thin on the ground, but Levein says: "We launched our Youth Development Initiative programme last season after always having run an Under-18 team in past years.

"Really, we have had to start from scratch and we have 80 local kids playing seven-a-side games. The first group of those have now progressed to eleven-a-side football at local level and they will form the basis of an Under-12 team next season.

"Eventually, we will have teams playing at

Tommy Wilson

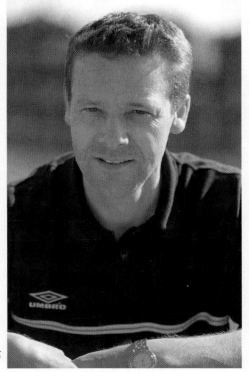

Chris Doig, Nottingham Forest and Scotland Under 21 International

every youth level because that is the only way ahead for clubs like ourselves."

Livingston is another SFL club to have invested heavily in youth development and the club's Youth Co–ordinator, Duncan Bennett, explained that Livingston run various centres in Glasgow, Lanarkshire and Fife as well as locally where youngsters, spotted by the scouting network, are brought for specialised coaching.

"Local businesses also sponsor schools in the area through the auspices of Livingston Football Club and we award in the region of 3,000 free tickets to these schools for home games," said Bennett.

Queen's Park have effectively blanketed Glasgow in their quest to snap up the most promising youth players available after setting up various training camps throughout the city. The scheme is extensive and expensive but it's a measure of the club's success that they won an S.F.A. Gold Award last season for their efforts in developing youngsters' skills.

John McCormack, the Queen's Park Coach, revealed : "We start at Under-12 level and have teams operating at Under-13, 14, 15, 16 and 18 levels as well as the reserves and first team,

and three coaches are allocated at each level.

"We also have a Youth Director, Tommy Wilson, and a Youth Development Officer, Frank Reilly, with me overseeing the entire operation. I am a great believer in youth football and I have to be, given the club's amateur status.

"Last season we had three players who were eligible to play for the Under-18 team winning Third Division Championship medals and that speaks for the success we have had at youth level.

"It's certainly not just about bringing ex-professionals back into the senior game. You have to look to create the right blend of youth and experience.

"Each year, I need to look to sign three or four lads from our Under-18 squad who have come through the ranks and when this season, there were only two who I thought were good enough, it created something of a problem.

"But, hopefully, next year I will get five or six and then we'll have a scenario similar to Dundee United a while back when they brought players like Paul Sturrock, Ralph Milne and David Narey through the system and achieved so much success."

McCormack would like to go even further with the help of the Skill Seekers set-up, explaining that it would bridge the gap between Under-16 and Under-18 age levels.

"Basically, we are foster parents in as much that we have to say bye-bye to boys at the age of 16 when we don't want to lose them and they don't want to leave an environment which they feel comfortable in.

"Neither the club nor our fans are enjoying the benefits

John McCormack, coach of Queen's Park

Scotland coach, Craig Brown

and that will continue to be the case unless we bridge the age gap."

Self help is also a key element and Clyde are one of those growing band of clubs who have pieced together a long-term strategy which they believe will secure their future well-being by attracting the best young talent from within their catchment area.

Manager Allan Maitland explained : "The soccer academy at Broadwood is the key to encouraging youngsters to develop their skills to benefit Clyde.

"We want to get them at a young age and to see the lads in the Cumbernauld and Kirkintilloch areas wearing Clyde strips instead of Celtic and Rangers ones.

"We accept that it will take five to 10 years for that to start paying off, but it will be well worth the effort that has been put in by people like our Chief Executive Ronnie MacDonald."

It would appear, judging by the efforts being made by the majority of Scottish Football League clubs, that Scottish football is not, after all, solely about the aims and aspirations of a few. Let us all hope for the sake of Scottish football that the work currently being undertaken by a number of clubs will bear fruit in the not too distant future.

JIM BLACK
(Jim Black Sport)

Albion Rovers

LIST OF PLAYERS 2000-2001

SURNAME	FIRST NAME	MIDDLE NAME	DATE OF BIRTH	PLACE OF BIRTH	DATE OF SIGNING	HEIGHT FT INS	WEIGHT ST LBS	POS. ON PITCH	PREVIOUS CLUB
Baird	Kevin		12/02/83	Glasgow	01/09/00	6 0.0	11 7	Def	Dumbarton
Begue	Yanis		02/01/82	Saint Pierre	22/04/00	5 11.0	11 0	Fwd	Raith Rovers
Booth	Mark		07/03/80	Coatbridge	06/07/00	5 9.5	12 0	Mid	Cumbernauld United
Carr	David		23/09/83	Bellshill	17/05/00	5 6.0	9 10	Mid	S Form
Clark	Sean	Patrick	10/12/80	Coatbridge	14/07/00	6 2.0	12 10	Def	Livingston
Clyde	Bobby		18/10/79	Edinburgh	01/06/00	6 1.0	11 10	Def	Heart of Midlothian
Cusack	Ryan		15/07/84	Bellshill	07/07/00	5 8.0	9 8	Def	Motherwell B.C.
Diack	Ian	Gordon	17/02/81	Glasgow	21/10/98	5 11.0	10 8	Fwd	Celtic B.C.
Dobbins	Ian	Alexander	24/08/83	Bellshill	17/05/00	6 0.0	10 5	Mid	S Form
Fahey	Christopher		28/06/78	Coatbridge	06/07/00	6 1.0	11 12	Gk	Larkhall Juniors
Fulton	Michael		25/04/84	Greenock	17/05/00	5 8.0	10 8	Mid	Gourock Y.A.C.
Hanlon	Thomas		29/12/81	Glasgow	07/08/00	5 9.0	10 5	Mid	Albion Rovers B.C.
Harty	Martin	John	11/07/82	Bellshill	21/10/98	5 11.0	10 8	Fwd	Albion Rovers B.C.
Hughes	John	Ronald	15/09/83	Glasgow	17/05/00	5 8.0	10 6	Mid	Heart of Midlothian
Hutcheson	Ceiran		24/03/83	Bellshill	17/05/00	5 6.0	11 0	Def	Heart of Midlothian
Kelly	Kieran	Gerard	23/09/82	Bellshill	07/07/00	5 10.0	10 10	Mid	Celtic
Kilpatrick	Andrew		17/03/82	Dumbarton	03/08/00	5 9.0	10 9	Def	Dumbarton
Lumsden	Todd		06/02/78	Consett	10/08/99	6 0.0	12 8	Def	Stirling Albion
Martin	Alexander	William	18/08/79	Glasgow	06/07/00	6 2.0	12 0	Fwd	Cumbernauld United
McBride	Kevin		12/04/80	Glasgow	15/04/99	5 9.0	10 6	Def	Tower Hearts Juveniles
McGuinness	Mark	Alexander	06/11/83	Glasgow	07/07/00	5 6.0	10 9	Fwd	Heart of Midlothian
McIntyre	John		03/08/83	Rutherglen	17/05/00	5 8.0	9 8	Mid	Rangers
McKenzie	James		29/11/80	Bellshill	31/03/00	5 7.5	11 0	Mid	Raith Rovers
McKenzie	James		25/02/84	Glasgow	08/09/00	5 10.0	11 0	Gk	Motherwell
McLees	James	Edward	30/08/80	Coatbridge	21/10/98	5 7.0	10 2	Mid	Lenzie Youth Club
McMillan	James		24/01/84	Bellshill	07/07/00	5 6.0	10 2	Mid	S Form
McMullan	Ryan		26/11/81	Bellshill	14/04/00	5 7.0	9 0	Mid/Fwd	Dundee United
McMullen	Stephen		30/04/82	Bellshill	17/05/00	5 7.0	9 0	Fwd	Dundee United
McNab	William		21/01/84	Bellshill	20/05/00	5 9.0	10 10	Def	Albion Rovers B.C.
Milligan	Christopher		24/10/83	Glasgow	07/07/00	5 5.0	10 2	Fwd	Celtic
Prior	Daniel	James	14/05/82	Glasgow	07/08/00	5 10.0	10 6	Def	Dumbarton
Rankin	Ian		05/09/79	Bellshill	06/07/00	5 5.5	10 0	Fwd	Airdrieonians
Shearer	Scott		15/02/81	Glasgow	06/07/00	6 2.5	11 8	Gk	Tower Hearts
Silvestro	Christopher		16/03/79	Bellshill	15/04/99	5 7.0	10 4	Mid	Glenboig
Smith	Jordan		02/02/82	Bellshill	29/07/99	6 2.0	12 0	Def	S Form
Sutherland	David		21/08/82	Glasgow	02/02/00	6 0.0	10 5	Def	X Form
Tait	Thomas		08/09/67	Ayr	29/07/99	5 11.0	12 7	Def	Hamilton Academical
Waldie	Colin		06/02/81	Lanark	06/07/00	5 8.0	11 0	Mid	Raith Rovers

Milestones

YEAR OF FORMATION: 1882
MOST CAPPED PLAYER: John White
NO. OF CAPS: 1
MOST LEAGUE POINTS IN A SEASON: 54 (Division 2 – Season 1929/30)
MOST LEAGUE GOALS SCORED BY A PLAYER IN A SEASON: John Renwick (Season 1932/33)
NO. OF GOALS SCORED: 41
RECORD ATTENDANCE: 27,381 (-v- Rangers 8.2.1936)
RECORD VICTORY: 12-0 (-v- Airdriehill – Scottish Cup, 3.9.1887)
RECORD DEFEAT: 1-11 (-v- Partick Thistle – League Cup, 11.8.1993)

The Wee Rovers' ten year league record

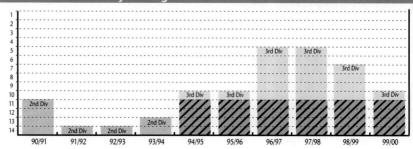

THE WEE ROVERS' CLUB FACTFILE 1999/2000
RESULTS... APPEARANCES... SCORERS... ATTENDANCES...

Nationwide

Date	Venue	Opponents	Att.	Res	McLean M.	Greenock R.	McGowan N.	McStay J.	Duncan G.	McLees J.	Russell G.	Tait T.	Flannigan C.	Nesovic A.	Rae D.	Coulter J.	Silvestro C.	McBride K.	Robertson G.	Lumsden T.	Dick I.	Smith J.	Harty M.	McMillan R.	Hamilton J.	McCondichie A.	Fotheringham G.	McMullen S.	Bonar S.	McCarroll J.	Prentice A.	Sutherland D.	Lyon M.	Vennard D.	McIntyre J.	Clyde B.	Best R.	Hughes M.	Friels G.	McArthur S.	Dobbins I.	Martin C.	Deegan C.	Young F.	McKenzie J.
Aug 7	H	Dumbarton	308	1-3	1	2	3	4	5¹	6	7	8	9	10	11	12	14	15																											
14	A	Berwick Rangers	366	1-1	1		3	4	5	15	7	8	9¹		11		6			2	10	12																							
21	H	Brechin City	273	0-0	1			4	5	6	7	8	9		11			14	3	2	10	12																							
28	A	Forfar Athletic	421	0-2	1			4	2	7	12	8			9	11	5	3		6	10						14																			
Sep 4	H	East Fife	366	1-3	1	2		4¹	5	6	7	8		10	11		9			3	12	14		15																					
11	H	Montrose	243	1-3	1	2			6		7		8	12¹	10		11			3	5		9	4																					
18	A	Queen's Park	642	0-2		4		2	5				8	9	10		11			3	6		14		7	1																			
25	H	East Stirlingshire	280	1-1				2		6			8	9¹	10		11			3	5	12			4	1	7																			
Oct 2	A	Cowdenbeath	382	0-0	1	2			6		12		8	9	10			11	14	3	5				4		7																			
16	H	Berwick Rangers	360	0-3	1				6		7	12	8	9			2	11	3	5	10			4			15	14																		
23	H	Dumbarton	590	1-1	1				4		14		8¹	9			12	7	3	5	10	6	15		11				2																	
30	A	Montrose	261	1-2	1				4				8	9			12	7	3	5	14¹	6	10		11				2																	
Nov 6	H	Queen's Park	513	2-4	1				4		14		8	9			11	7		6	10¹		5¹	15					2	3																
14	A	East Fife	464	4-1	1				4¹	10¹	7		8¹	9			11			6	15¹		5		14				2	3																
20	H	Forfar Athletic	311	0-1	1				4	10	7		8	9			11				15	5							2	3	6															
27	H	Cowdenbeath	276	1-4	1				4¹	10	7		8				12			9	5	14		11				2	3	6																
Dec 11	A	Brechin City	256	1-8	1						7		8				6	15		4¹	9	5	10		3				2	14	11	12													
18	H	Dumbarton	257	3-0	1				2¹	9¹	8¹						12		3	6	15	5		14	4				7		11		10													
Jan 3	A	Queen's Park	742	1-0	1				2¹	9	8		14				12		3	6	15	5			4				7	11			10													
22	H	East Stirlingshire	260	0-1	1				2	9	8			4	10		3	14	11	6	12	5		15				7																		
Feb 5	A	Cowdenbeath	303	0-5	1				4	9	8			7	10		3	11		5	12	6		14				2																		
12	A	Forfar Athletic	395	1-3	1				14	8				10			5¹	15		6	9	4		7				2	3	11																
19	A	East Fife	368	3-1	1				4	8			7	10				9²		6	15							2	3	11¹	12			1	14											
26	A	Berwick Rangers	756	1-2	1				4		6		7	10¹			5	12		9	8							2	3	11																
29	A	East Stirlingshire	191	3-4	1				4¹				8¹	7	10¹		2	6	15	9	5	14							3	11	12															
Mar 4	H	Brechin City	241	0-2	1								8		7	10	2	11	12	6	9	4						14	3						5										
7	H	Montrose	159	0-2	1								8		11		2		3	6	9	4							15							5	1	7	10						
11	A	Montrose	329	2-1	1								8			10	2		11	6	9¹	4						14		3	15					5		7¹	12						
18	A	Queen's Park	531	0-3	1								10				2	7	11	3	9	4						12			14					6	8	5	15						
25	H	Forfar Athletic	307	0-1	1				3					5	12		15	8		14	9	7						6									11	2			4	10			
Apr 1	A	East Fife	512	1-2	1				4	8				12			6	3		9	7										11						14	2			5	10			
8	A	East Stirlingshire	206	1-3	1					6				5¹	7			8	3	9	15	12						14	11									2			4	10¹			
15	H	Cowdenbeath	257	0-3	1				3				5				6			12	2	9						14	11			8									4	10	1	7	
22	A	Dumbarton	415	0-0	1					6		4			11				3	10	2	14																				5	9			8
29	A	Berwick Rangers	443	0-0	1					6		5			11	15			3	10	2	14	7																			4	9			8
May 6	A	Brechin City	257	2-3					6		4				12	8	11		3	10¹		2	14	7					15¹													5	9	1		
TOTAL FULL APPEARANCES					30	5	2	26	13	27	4	30	20	9	5	14	23	14	6	26	20	23	5	5	11	2	2	1	14	13	9		2	1	1	4	1	4	1	4	7	7	2	3
TOTAL SUB APPEARANCES						(1)			(4)	(2)	(1)	(3)					(7)	(6)	(6)			(1)(12)	(2)	(9)	(5)	(2)		(1)	(5)	(1)	(3)		(5)				(1)			(1)		(1)	(1)
TOTAL GOALS SCORED								6	3	2			3	4	1		1				1	7	1						1	1										1			

Small bold figures denote goalscorers.   † denotes opponent's own goal.

Cliftonhill Stadium

[Stadium layout: Car Park, HILLCREST AVENUE, EAST STEWART STREET, MAIN STREET, pitch areas marked "Not in use" and "To B.R."]

CAPACITY: 2,496; Seated 538, Standing 1,958
PITCH DIMENSIONS: 110 yds x 72 yds
FACILITIES FOR DISABLED SUPPORTERS:
Access from East Stewart Street with toilet facilities and space for wheelchairs, cars etc. Advanced contact with club advised – this area is uncovered.

Team playing kits

How to get there

The following routes can be used to reach Cliftonhill Stadium:

BUSES: The ground is conveniently situated on the main Glasgow-Airdrie bus route and there is a stop near the ground. Local buses serving most areas of Coatbridge and Airdrie pass by the stadium every few minutes.

TRAINS: The nearest railway station is Coatdyke on the Glasgow-Airdrie line and the ground is a ten minute walk from there. The frequency of service is 15 minutes.

CARS: Vehicles may park in Hillcrest Avenue, Albion Street and East Stewart Street, which are all adjacent to the ground.

The Wee Rovers

email: info@sfl.scottishfootball.com • website: www.scottishfootball.com

Brechin City

Glebe Park, Trinity Road,
Brechin, Angus, DD9 6BJ

CHAIRMAN
David H. Birse

VICE-CHAIRMAN
Hugh A. Campbell Adamson

HON. LIFE PRESIDENT
David H. Will

HON. LIFE MEMBERS
David K. Lindsay &
George C. Johnston

DIRECTORS
Martin Smith (Treasurer),
I. Michael Holland
(Assistant Treasurer),
Calum I. McK. Brown,
Kenneth W. Ferguson
James Dean & Steven Mitchell

SECRETARY
Kenneth W. Ferguson

MANAGER
Richard M. Campbell

YOUTH TEAM COACH
George Shields (U18)

CLUB DOCTOR
Dr. Archie McInnes

SPORTS THERAPIST
Tom Gilmartin

**FOOTBALL SAFETY OFFICERS'
ASSOCIATION REPRESENTATIVE**
Calum Brown (01307) 461222

GROUNDSMAN
Alex Laing

COMMERCIAL MANAGER
Steve Mitchell (01356) 622767

MEDIA LIAISON OFFICER
Ken Ferguson (07803) 089060

MATCHDAY PROGRAMME EDITOR
Martin Smith

TELEPHONES
Ground (Matchdays Only) (01356) 622856
Fax (01356) 625667
Sec. Home (01356) 625691
Sec. Bus. (01356) 625285/
(01674) 678910
Sec. Bus. Fax (01356) 625667/
(01674) 678345

E-MAIL ADDRESS
kenny@glebepk.demon.co.uk.

CLUB SHOP
Glebe Park, Brechin, Angus, DD9 6BJ
Open during home match days.

OFFICIAL SUPPORTERS CLUB
c/o Glebe Park, Brechin,
Angus, DD9 6BJ

TEAM CAPTAIN
Harry Cairney

SHIRT SPONSOR
A.P. Jess Food Group Ltd.

KIT SUPPLIER
SPALL

LIST OF PLAYERS 2000-2001

SURNAME	FIRST NAME	MIDDLE NAME	DATE OF BIRTH	PLACE OF BIRTH	DATE OF SIGNING	HEIGHT FT INS	WEIGHT ST LBS	POS. ON PITCH	PREVIOUS CLUB
Archibald	Paul		21/12/82	Dundee	18/08/00	5 8.0	10 8	Fwd	Monifieth B.C.
Bailey	Lee		10/07/72	Edinburgh	23/10/99	5 6.0	10 0	Fwd	Queen of the South
Bain	Kevin		19/09/72	Kirkcaldy	29/07/98	6 0.0	11 9	Def	Stirling Albion
Black	Roddy		22/02/78	Dundee	10/09/95	5 9.0	11 0	Mid	Carnoustie Panmure
Boylan	Paul		04/12/80	Dundee	05/03/99	5 10.0	10 2	Def	Dundee United
Cairney	Henry		01/09/61	Holytown	12/02/92	5 7.0	10 8	Def	Stenhousemuir
Campbell	Paul	Richard	18/03/80	Kirkcaldy	23/08/00	5 7.0	11 2	Fwd	Victoria Rovers
Christie	Graeme		01/01/71	Dundee	04/08/93	6 1.0	11 0	Def	Carnoustie Panmure
Coulston	Douglas		12/08/71	Glasgow	30/06/99	5 10.0	11 0	Mid/Fwd	Montrose
Donachie	Barry		21/12/79	Dundee	04/11/99	5 8.0	11 5	Def/Mid	Arbroath
Grant	Roderick	John	16/09/66	Gloucester	04/08/00	5 11.0	12 7	Fwd	Ayr United
Hirons	Kevin	Barry	25/08/82	Dundee	10/09/99	5 6.0	9 8	Def	Forfar Albion
Honeyman	Ben		14/02/77	Adelaide	29/10/99	5 9.0	10 3	Fwd	East Fife
Hood	Gavin		06/05/82	Dundee	10/09/99	5 7.0	9 4	Def	Forfar Albion
Hutcheon	Andrew	John	16/05/79	Aberdeen	19/06/97	5 8.0	9 7	Fwd	Stonehaven U'18s
Leask	Moray	Stuart	02/10/79	Edinburgh	04/08/00	5 9.0	10 12	Fwd	Berwick Rangers
Millar	Bradley	James	03/09/82	Dundee	18/08/00	5 7.0	10 6	Fwd	Dundee United Social Club
Nairn	James		25/08/72	Kirkcaldy	29/10/99	5 10.0	10 10	Mid	Forfar Athletic
Parkyn	Martin		05/05/81	Lisburn	18/08/00	6 2.0	11 2	Gk	Alloa Athletic
Raynes	Steven		04/09/71	Edinburgh	25/11/99	5 9.0	11 0	Mid	Forfar Athletic
Riley	Paul	John	07/08/75	Edinburgh	31/03/99	5 7.0	10 6	Mid	Hibernian
Smith	Daryn	Andrew M.	09/10/80	Dundonald	18/08/00	5 7.0	9 7	Mid	St. Johnstone
Smith	Greig	Robert	26/03/76	Aberdeen	21/12/94	5 9.0	10 12	Def	Culter Juniors
Williamson	Karl		09/11/79	Aberdeen	29/07/98	5 7.5	10 9	Def	Aberdeen

Milestones

YEAR OF FORMATION: 1906
MOST LEAGUE POINTS IN A SEASON: 55 (Second Division – Season 1982/83)(2 Points for a Win)
63 (Third Division – Season 1995/96)(3 Points for a Win)
MOST LEAGUE GOALS SCORED BY A PLAYER IN A SEASON: Ronald McIntosh (Season 1959/60)
NO. OF GOALS SCORED: 26
RECORD ATTENDANCE: 8,122 (-v- Aberdeen – 3.2.1973)
RECORD VICTORY: 12-1 (-v- Thornhill – Scottish Cup, 28.1.1926)
RECORD DEFEAT: 0-10 (-v- Airdrieonians, Albion Rovers and Cowdenbeath – Division 2, 1937/38)

The City's ten year league record

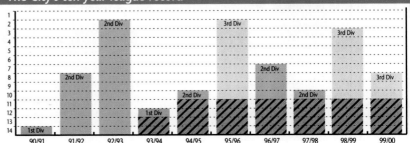

THE CITY'S CLUB FACTFILE 1999/2000
RESULTS... APPEARANCES... SCORERS... ATTENDANCES...

Date	Venue	Opponents	Att.	Res	Geddes A.R.	Smith G.	Christie G.	Cairney H.	Bain K.	Riley P.	Dickson J.	Dailly M.	Sorbie S.	Price G.	Campbell S.	Hutcheon A.	Kerrigan S.	Coulston D.	Durie J.	Buick G.	McKellar J.	Black R.	Armstrong G.	Brown R.	Boyle S.	Williamson K.	Bailey L.	Donnachie B.	Nairn J.	Honeyman B.	Raynes S.	Harris P.
Aug 7	A	Forfar Athletic	620	0-0	1	2	3	4	5	6	7	8	9	10	11	12	14	16														
14	H	Queen's Park	311	1-2	1	2		4	5	6	11	12	9	8		7¹								3	10	16						
21	A	Albion Rovers	273	0-0	1	2	12	4	5	6		14	9	8		10					16			3	7	11						
28	H	Dumbarton	357	0-2	1	2		4	5	6		14	9	16	10	11								3	8	7	12					
Sep 4	A	Cowdenbeath	254	1-6	1		6	4	5		10	7¹	9	12	3			16	2					14		11	8					
11	H	East Stirlingshire	284	1-2	1	2			5	6			8	9	14	11	10¹				7			3	12	4						
18	A	Montrose	512	1-0	1	2			5				8	9	3		10							7	6¹		4	11				
25	A	Berwick Rangers	407	0-2	1	2			5	8			9		3	14	10							7	6	12	4	11				
Oct 2	H	East Fife	365	1-3	1	2			5	8			9		3	12	10¹					14			6	4	11	7				
16	A	Queen's Park	483	3-5	1		3	4	5	8	14				11	12	9	7				6³				10	2					
23	A	Forfar Athletic	502	0-2	1	2	6	4	5	7					3	12	9	11				10				8						
30	A	East Stirlingshire	210	0-0	1		6	4	5						3		9	14				10				16	8	2	7	11		
Nov 6	H	Montrose	366	1-0	1		6	4	5							9						10					8¹	2	7	11	3	
14	A	Cowdenbeath	275	2-0	1		6	4	5¹							7¹	14					10					9	2	8	11	3	16
20	A	Dumbarton	447	3-1	1		6	4	5							9¹	14					10¹					8	2	7	11¹	3	
27	A	East Fife	463	0-1	1		6	4	5							9	14	12				10					8	2	7	11	3	
Dec 7	H	Berwick Rangers	356	0-3	1	5	6	4							12	9						10				14	8	2	7	11	3	
11	H	Albion Rovers	256	8-1	1		6	4	5						16²	14¹	11¹					10¹				12	8¹	2	7	9²	3	
Jan 3	H	Montrose	798	1-0	1	2	6	4	5						12	11						10					8		7	9	3	
22	A	Berwick Rangers	344	1-3	1		6	4	5	11			12		14	7						10					8	2		9¹	3	
Feb 5	H	East Fife	337	†3-1	1		6	4	5	7			16	8¹		14	12					10				11		2		9¹	3	
12	A	Dumbarton	278	1-2	1	6		4	5	7			8			14	16					10¹				11		2		9	3	
19	A	Cowdenbeath	222	1-1	1			4	5				8¹			14						10				11		2		9	3	
26	H	Queen's Park	287	0-0	1	6		4	5				8		14	9	11					10						2			3	
29	A	Forfar Athletic	516	0-2	1	6		4	5	7			8		14	9	12					10				11		2			3	
Mar 4	H	Albion Rovers	241	2-0	1	6		4	5	7			8			11¹	9					10¹						2		12	3	
7	H	East Stirlingshire	207	1-1	1	6		4	5	7			8		16	12	9					10				14		2		11¹	3	
11	H	East Stirlingshire	259	3-0	1	5		4		7			6			12	11¹					10				8		2		9²	3	
18	H	Montrose	360	0-0	1	2		4	5	7			6				11	14				10				8				9	3	16
25	A	Dumbarton	365	1-2	1	5		4	2				8		11		7	12				6¹				10				9	3	
Apr 1	H	Cowdenbeath	244	1-2	1	5		4	7				8		11		9¹					6				10				14	3	
8	H	Berwick Rangers	267	1-2	1	5		4	7				6		16	9¹	8					11				10		2		12	3	
15	H	East Fife	452	†1-1	1	6		4	5	7			10		16	9						11				8		2			3	
22	H	Forfar Athletic	548	1-0	1			4	5	7			8		9			12				11						2	6	10¹	3	
29	A	Queen's Park	943	0-1	1			4	5	7			8		9	16	14					11						2	6	10	3	
May 6	A	Albion Rovers	257	3-2	1	5		4		7			8		9¹	10	14					6						2		11²	3	
TOTAL FULL APPEARANCES					36	25	15	31	29	28	3	1	24	4	13	9	16	12	4	3	5	32	1	4	4	2	20	23	9	19	24	
TOTAL SUB APPEARANCES						(1)					(3)	(2)	(1)	(2)	(4)	(9)	(14)	(9)			(3)	(3)		(1)	(2)		(3)	(1)		(3)		(2)
TOTAL GOALS SCORED							1		1				2			6	6					9							2	11	

Small bold figures denote goalscorers.   † *denotes opponent's own goal.*

Glebe Park

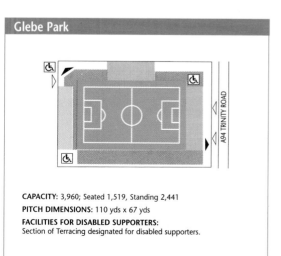

A94 TRINITY ROAD

CAPACITY: 3,960; Seated 1,519, Standing 2,441

PITCH DIMENSIONS: 110 yds x 67 yds

FACILITIES FOR DISABLED SUPPORTERS:
Section of Terracing designated for disabled supporters.

Team playing kits

How to get there

The following routes may be used to reach Glebe Park:

TRAINS: The nearest railway station is Montrose, which is eight miles away. There is a regular Inter-City service from all parts of the country and fans alighting at Montrose can then catch a connecting bus service to Brechin.

BUSES: Brechin bus station is only a few hundred yards from the ground and buses on the Aberdeen-Dundee and Montrose-Edzell routes stop here.

CARS: Car parking is available in the Brechin City car park, which is capable of holding 50 vehicles. There are also a number of side streets which may be used for this purpose.

email: info@sfl.scottishfootball.com • website: www.scottishfootball.com

Central Park, High Street, Cowdenbeath, KY4 9QQ

CHAIRMAN
Gordon McDougall

VICE-CHAIRMAN
Albert Tait

DIRECTORS
James M. Stevenson,
Ian Fraser, Brian Watson,
Dr. Robert Brownlie,
Edward Baigan, Morris Kaplan
& J. Derrick Brown

GENERAL/COMMERCIAL MANAGER
Joe Macnamara

SECRETARY
Thomas Ogilvie

MANAGER
Craig Levein

ASSISTANT MANAGER
Gary Kirk

YOUTH TEAM COACHES
David Liddle, Alan Lawrence (U18)
Ross Hamilton & Andrew Heggie (U15)

SPRINT COACH
Tom Ritchie

CLUB DOCTOR
Dr. Robert Brownlie

PHYSIOTHERAPISTS
Wendy MacDonald & Gordon Clark

FOOTBALL SAFETY OFFICERS' ASSOCIATION REPRESENTATIVE
David Jones
Home (01383) 872074

CHIEF SCOUT
David Dair

GROUNDSMAN
Gordon McDougall Jnr.

MATCHDAY PROGRAMME EDITOR
Andrew Mullen (01383) 611644

TELEPHONES
Ground/Ticket Office/
Information Service
(01383) 610166
Sec. Home (01383) 513013
Sec. Bus (01383) 313400
Fax (01383) 512132

E-MAIL & INTERNET ADDRESS
bluebrazil@cowdenbeathfc.com
www.cowdenbeathfc.com

CLUB SHOP
Situated at Stadium.
Open 10.00 a.m. – 3.00 p.m.
and on Home Match Days

OFFICIAL SUPPORTERS CLUB
Central Park, Cowdenbeath, KY4 9QQ

TEAM CAPTAIN
Craig Winter

SHIRT SPONSOR
Fife Gas Services

KIT SUPPLIER
Paulas Benara

LIST OF PLAYERS 2000-2001

SURNAME	FIRST NAME	MIDDLE NAME	DATE OF BIRTH	PLACE OF BIRTH	DATE OF SIGNING	HEIGHT FT INS	WEIGHT ST LBS	POS. ON PITCH	PREVIOUS CLUB
Allan	James		21/09/79	Glasgow	21/02/00	5 9.0	10 12	Mid	Dunipace Juniors
Banks	Alan		25/02/70	Edinburgh	19/06/00	5 11.0	11 4	Def	Stenhousemuir
Bannatyne	Peter		13/08/82	Edinburgh	16/11/99	5 8.0	10 10	Fwd	Dundonald Bluebell
Boyle	James	Thomson	19/02/67	Glasgow	31/07/00	5 6.0	11 2	Def	Alloa Athletic
Bradley	Mark		10/08/76	Glasgow	18/12/98	5 6.0	9 7	Mid	Stirling Albion
Brown	Graeme	Robert	08/11/80	Johannesburg	19/08/97	5 11.0	11 0	Fwd	Broomhall Saints B.C.
Burns	John	Paul	11/03/78	Kirkcaldy	02/08/98	5 6.0	10 9	Fwd	Heart of Midlothian
Courts	Thomas		10/08/81	Kirkcaldy	25/08/00	6 0.0	11 4	Def	Livingston
Godfrey	Ross		21/01/77	Edinburgh	07/10/98	5 11.0	10 12	Gk	Thornton Hibs
Hutt	Kevin	Peter C.	02/10/80	Kirkcaldy	21/04/00	5 10.0	11 10	Mid	Glenrothes Strollers
Juskowiak	Reon		02/05/81	Kirkcaldy	07/07/00	6 0.0	12 2	Fwd	Auchtermuchty Bellvue
King	Shaun		03/09/81	Kirkcaldy	29/03/99	5 4.0	8 0	Mid/Fwd	Benarty Juniors
Kirkcaldy	Christopher		08/01/82	Edinburgh	26/06/99	5 11.0	11 0	Fwd	Musselburgh Windsor U'16s
Lakie	James		28/04/82	Perth	06/06/00	6 2.0	13 5	Def	S Form
Lawrence	Alan		19/08/62	Edinburgh	06/06/00	5 7.0	10 0	Fwd	Stenhousemuir
Martin	John	Galloway K.	27/10/58	Edinburgh	06/06/00	6 1.0	11 7	Gk	Preston Athletic
McBride	Ross		28/08/84	Kirkcaldy	01/08/00	5 10.0	10 2	Mid	S Form
McCulloch	Keith	George	27/05/67	Edinburgh	08/06/99	5 10.0	12 0	Def	Alloa Athletic
McDonald	Ian		07/03/78	Newcastle	11/03/00	6 0.5	13 3	Mid	Clyde
McDowell	Murray	John L.	17/02/78	Dundee	26/06/99	5 11.0	11 9	Fwd	Carnoustie Panmure
McLean	Kenneth		14/04/83	Edinburgh	08/09/00	5 9.0	11 7	Def	Hibernian
McMillan	Craig		04/12/81	Dunfermline	03/07/98	5 10.0	11 0	Mid	Hill of Beath Swifts
Mitchell	Wesley	Dean	03/03/82	Edinburgh	28/11/98	6 2.0	12 0	Def	Heart of Midlothian B.C.
Ramsay	Steven		13/04/67	Germiston	22/08/00	5 9.0	11 2	Mid	Berwick Rangers
Reilly	Scott	Peter	12/04/82	Kirkcaldy	06/01/00	5 8.0	10 12	Def	Hill of Beath Swifts
Waugh	Colin		04/06/82	Dunfermline	16/11/99	6 1.0	11 7	Def /Mid	Dundonald Bluebell
White	Brian		25/04/83	Edinburgh	14/03/00	6 2.0	12 0	Def	Hutchison Vale B.C.
White	David	William	09/08/79	Edinburgh	09/07/99	6 1.5	11 12	Def	Motherwell
Whyte	Kenneth	Hugh	28/11/82	Kirkcaldy	24/07/00	6 0.0	11 7	Gk	S Form
Winter	Craig	John	30/06/76	Dunfermline	19/07/94	5 9.0	10 0	Mid/Fwd	Raith Rovers
Wright	Keith	Arthur	17/05/65	Edinburgh	24/06/00	6 0.0	12 8	Fwd	Stenhousemuir

Milestones

YEAR OF FORMATION: 1881
MOST CAPPED PLAYER: Jim Paterson
NO. OF CAPS: 3
MOST LEAGUE POINTS IN A SEASON: 60 (Division 2 – Season 1938/39)
MOST LEAGUE GOALS SCORED BY A PLAYER IN A SEASON: Rab Walls (Season 1938/39)
NO. OF GOALS SCORED: 54
RECORD ATTENDANCE: 25,586 (-v- Rangers – 21.9.1949)
RECORD VICTORY: 12-0 (-v- Johnstone – Scottish Cup, 21.1.1928)
RECORD DEFEAT: 1-11 (-v- Clyde – Division 2, 6.10.1951)

The Blue Brazil's ten year league record

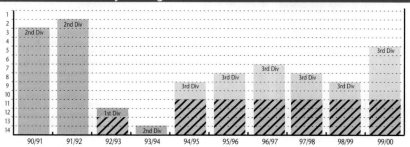

THE BLUE BRAZIL'S CLUB FACTFILE 1999/2000
RESULTS... APPEARANCES... SCORERS... ATTENDANCES...

Date	Venue	Opponents	Att	Res	Godfrey R.	White D.	Berry N.	Snedden S.	Thomson R.	Wilson W.	Winter C.	Bradley M.	Stewart W.	Simpson P.	Burns J.P.	Brown G.	McDowell M.	McMillan C.	Clark R.	McCulloch K.	Johnston D.	King S.	Hutchison S.	Sharp R.	Jackson C.	Carnie G.	Young C.	Mitchell W.	Neilson R.	McDonald I.	Gray D.	Cunning J.	Vaugh B.	Nicol G.	Porteous A.	Laikie J.
Aug 7	A	Montrose	275	1-0	1	2	3	4	5	6	7	8^1	9	10	11	12	15																			
14	H	Forfar Athletic	256	0-3	1	2		4	5	6	7	8		11	10		9	3	14																	
21	A	Queen's Park	578	0-1	1	6	4	12		2	7	8	11	9	15	10		3		5																
28	A	East Stirlingshire	205	1-0	1	2		5		6	7	8	10^1	11	14	9	3			4	15															
Sep 4	H	Brechin City	254	6-1	1	2		4		6^1	7	8		10^2	11^2	14	9^1	3	5																	
11	A	Berwick Rangers	457	2-0	1	2		4		6	7	8	12	10^1	11^1	14	9	3	5																	
18	H	East Fife	670	4-0	1	2		4		6	7	8		10^1	11^1	12	9^2		5				3													
25	A	Dumbarton	424	†1-1	1	2		4		6	7	8		10	11	12	9	15	5				3													
Oct 2	H	Albion Rovers	382	0-0	1	2		4		6	7	8		10	11	12	9		5				3	1												
16	A	Forfar Athletic	399	1-3	1	2		5		6	7	8	14	10	11	15	9^1	3		4																
23	H	Montrose	254	1-1	1			4		15	7	8^1		10	11	9			5		14		3		6	12										
30	H	Berwick Rangers	313	1-1	1	4				6		2	7	10	9		11		14		5		3^1	8		15										
Nov 6	A	East Fife	569	3-2		4				2	7	8	9		11	10^3	12		5			1	3	6		15										
14	A	Brechin City	275	0-2		4				2	7	8	10		11	9	12	14	5			1	3	6		15										
20	H	East Stirlingshire	248	1-2		4				2	7^1	6		9	10	8			5			3	11	12												
27	A	Albion Rovers	276	4-1	1	2		5	3	6	7^1	8^1	15		11^1	9	10^1	14	4																	
Dec 8	H	Dumbarton	262	0-2	1				3	8	7	6	12		11	9	10	2	5								14	4								
18	A	Montrose	318	3-1	1			4	3	2	7	6^1	9		11		10^1		5								8^1									
22	H	Queen's Park	221	0-2	1	2		5	3	12	7	8	9		11	14	10		4		15							6								
Jan 3	H	East Fife	639	1-0		4		3		11	7	8	14	6	10^1	9			5			1				2										
15	A	Berwick Rangers	413	0-0		4		3		6	7			12	15	14	9		5			1				2	11									
22	A	Dumbarton	469	0-2		4		3		6	7			12	15	14	9		5			1		8		2	11									
Feb 5	H	Albion Rovers	303	5-0		4^1		5	3	8	7^1	14	15		10^2	9^1						1		12		2	11	6								
12	A	East Stirlingshire	224	4-0		4		5	3	11	7	12		14	10^1	9^2						1				2	8	6^1								
19	H	Brechin City	222	1-1		4		5	3	11	7	8		15	10	9^1						1				2		6	14							
26	H	Forfar Athletic	354	4-1		4		5	3	11	7^1	6		15	10^1	9^1						1				2	8^1	6								
Mar 4	A	Queen's Park	625	1-3		2		5	3	11	7	14	12		10^1		4		1								8	6	15							
11	H	Berwick Rangers	402	1-3		4				2	7	8	12	9	10^1				5			1				3	14	11	15	6						
18	A	East Fife	702	1-1	1	4		5		7		6		12	11	10	9					8				3	2				14	15^1				
25	H	East Stirlingshire	243	0-0	1	2		5		7			14	11	10	9		4				6				3	15			12						
Apr 1	A	Brechin City	244	2-1	1	4		5		2		6		11	10^1	9						14				3	8^1	15		7						
8	H	Dumbarton	284	1-2	1	4		5		2		6		10	11		9		15			12	14			3	8^1			7						
15	A	Albion Rovers	257	3-0	1	2^1			4		6	7	8^1		11	10	9^1					15				3	14									5
22	H	Montrose	252	2-1	1	4			2	6	7^1	8	15		11	10	9					14				3^1	12									5
29	A	Forfar Athletic	556	2-2	1	2		5^1	3	6	7	8^1	9		11	10	15										12									4
May 6	H	Queen's Park	813	2-3	1	2		5		6	7	8	9		12	10^2	15					14				3	11									4
TOTAL FULL APPEARANCES					24	34	3	29	12	34	32	31	10	13	23	23	27	9	23	3	12	5	5	4	1	8	12	8	4	1	2	4	1	2	4	
TOTAL SUB APPEARANCES						(1)		(2)		(4)	(13)	(6)	(4)	(9)	(2)	(7)	(1)	(1)	(1)	(2)						(8)	(5)		(2)	(5)	(2)	(1)	(2)		
TOTAL GOALS SCORED						2		1		1	5	6		4	6	12	13						1		1				1	4				1	

Small bold figures denote goalscorers. † denotes opponent's own goal.

Central Park

MAIN STREET

CAPACITY: 4,370; Seated 1,431, Standing 2,939
PITCH DIMENSIONS: 107 yds x 64 yds
FACILITIES FOR DISABLED SUPPORTERS:
Direct access from car park into designated area within ground. Toilet and catering facilities also provided.

Team playing kits

How to get there

You can get to Central Park by the following routes:

TRAINS: There is a regular service of trains from Edinburgh and Glasgow (via Edinburgh) which call at Cowdenbeath and the station is only 400 yards from the ground.

BUSES: A limited Edinburgh-Cowdenbeath service stops just outside the ground on matchdays and a frequent service of Dunfermline-Ballingry buses also stop outside the ground, as does the Edinburgh-Glenrothes service.

CARS: Car parking facilities are available in the public car park adjacent to the ground for 190 cars. There are also another 300 spaces at the Stenhouse Street car park, which is 200 yards from the ground.

email: info@sfl.scottishfootball.com • website: www.scottishfootball.com

OFFICE ADDRESS
c/o Neil Rankine,
62 Round Riding Road,
Dumbarton, G82 2JB

CHAIRMAN
Douglas S. Dalgleish, M.A., LL.B.

MANAGING DIRECTOR
Neil Rankine

DIRECTORS
David Wright,
G. James Innes
David O. Stark
& John G. MacFarlane

HON. PRESIDENTS
Ian A. Bell, J.P. &
R. Campbell Ward, C.A.

CLUB SECRETARY
Colin J. Hosie

ASSISTANT CLUB SECRETARY
J. David Prophet

ADMINISTRATION MANAGER
Karen E. Mitchell

MANAGER
Jimmy Brown

ASSISTANT MANAGER
Tom Carson

COACH
John MacCormack

YOUTH COACHES
Iain Lee & Peter McLean

CLUB DOCTORS
James Goldie &
Neil MacKay, MBC, HB

PHYSIOTHERAPISTS
David Steele & Linda McIlwraith

CHIEF SCOUT
Willie Hughes

GROUNDSMAN
Eddie McCreadie

KIT MAN
Jim Cunningham

**PUBLIC RELATIONS EXECUTIVE/
COMMERCIAL MANAGER**
Ian MacFarlane

**FOOTBALL SAFETY OFFICER'S
ASSOCIATION REPRESENTATIVE**
David Douglas

MEDIA LIAISON OFFICER
Ian MacFarlane (01389) 762569

MATCHDAY PROGRAMME EDITOR
Graeme Robertson (0131) 441 5451

TELEPHONES
Ground (01389) 762569/767864
Sec. Bus. (0141) 309 2288
Sec. Home (01389) 841996
Sec. Mobile (0370) 831490
Fax (01389) 762629

CLUB SHOP
Situated in ground –
open on home matchdays and
10.00 a.m. – 4.00 p.m. Mon-Fri

OFFICIAL SUPPORTERS CLUB
c/o Dumbarton FC,
Dumbarton G82 2JB

TEAM CAPTAIN
Toby King

SHIRT SPONSOR
Methode Electronics Europe

KIT SUPPLIER
XARA

64

LIST OF PLAYERS 2000-2001

SURNAME	FIRST NAME	MIDDLE NAME	DATE OF BIRTH	PLACE OF BIRTH	DATE OF SIGNING	HEIGHT FT INS	WEIGHT ST LBS	POS. ON PITCH	PREVIOUS CLUB
Bonar	Steven	Andrew	20/05/79	Glasgow	30/03/00	5 9.5	10 6	Mid	Albion Rovers
Brittain	Craig		10/01/74	Glasgow	14/06/97	5 5.0	9 7	Def	Ashfield Juniors
Brown	Alan		26/06/82	Alexandria	01/09/00	5 9.0	11 12	Mid	Vale of Leven Juniors
Brown	Andrew		11/10/76	Edinburgh	21/07/99	6 4.0	14 0	Fwd	Clydebank
Bruce	Jamie	Ross	29/08/76	East Kilbride	01/02/99	6 0.0	11 4	Def	East Kilbride Thistle
Dickie	Michael	John	05/05/79	Vale of Leven	11/06/99	5 8.0	10 0	Def	Dundee
Dillon	John	Peter	16/12/78	Vale of Leven	30/07/99	5 7.0	10 0	Mid	Clyde
Flannery	Patrick	Martin F.	23/07/76	Glasgow	27/12/97	6 1.0	11 9	Fwd	Morton
Gentile	Christopher		09/09/81	Glasgow	25/02/00	5 10.5	11 0	Mid	Dundee United
Grace	Alexander		20/03/74	Vale of Leven	25/07/97	5 6.0	10 4	Mid	Vale of Leven Juniors
Hillcoat	John	George	16/12/70	Paisley	15/07/00	5 11.5	12 6	Gk	Queen of the South
Jack	Stephen	John	27/03/71	Bellshill	25/02/98	5 11.0	10 0	Mid	Cowdenbeath
King	Thomas	David	23/01/70	Dumbarton	10/08/98	5 9.0	11 3	Mid	Clyde
McCann	Kevin		17/12/80	Bellshill	02/06/00	6 1.0	11 8	Def	Partick Thistle
Meechan	David		23/11/81	Vale of Leven	22/01/00	5 10.0	11 0	Fwd	Vale of Leven Juniors
Melvin	Martin		12/06/77	Glasgow	31/03/00	5 7.0	10 7	Mid/Fwd	Beith Juniors
Robertson	Joseph		12/04/77	Glasgow	14/08/98	5 8.0	11 5	Fwd	Clydebank
Smith	Christopher James		20/12/76	Glasgow	19/01/99	5 11.0	11 7	Fwd	Rutherglen Glencairn
Stewart	David		14/08/78	Irvine	01/12/99	6 1.0	12 4	Def	Clydebank
Wight	John	Campbell	11/12/73	Alexandria	04/08/00	6 0.0	13 0	Gk	Beith Juniors
Wilson	William	Stewart	19/08/72	Glasgow	04/08/00	5 8.0	10 0	Mid	Cowdenbeath

Milestones

YEAR OF FORMATION: 1872
MOST CAPPED PLAYERS: J. Lindsay and J. McAulay
NO. OF CAPS: 8 each
MOST LEAGUE POINTS IN A SEASON: 53 (First Division – Season 1986/87) (2 Points for a Win)
                                     60 (Second Division – Season 1994/95) (3 Points for a Win)
MOST LEAGUE GOALS SCORED BY A PLAYER IN A SEASON: Kenneth Wilson (Season 1971/72)
NO. OF GOALS SCORED: 38
RECORD ATTENDANCE: 18,001 (-v- Raith Rovers – 2.3.1957)
RECORD VICTORY: 13-2 (-v- Kirkintilloch – Scottish Cup)
RECORD DEFEAT: 1-11 (-v- Ayr United/Albion Rovers)

The Sons' ten year league record

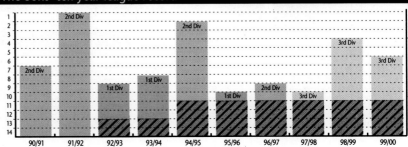

THE SONS' CLUB FACTFILE 1999/2000
RESULTS... APPEARANCES... SCORERS... ATTENDANCES...

Date	V	Opponents	Att.	Res	Meechan K.	Dickie M.	Brittain C.	Bruce J.	Jack S.	King T.	Melvin W.	Grace A.	Flannery P.	Brown Andrew	Robertson J.	Ward H.	McHarg S.	Dillon J.	Smith C.	McCormack J.	Templeman C.	Barnes D.	Melvin M.	Bradford J.	Stewart D.	Finnegan P.	McCann K.	Hingsson H.	Brown Alan	Watters W.	Bonar S.	Gentile C.
Aug 7	A	Albion Rovers	308	3-1	1	2	3	4	5	6¹	7²	8	9	10	11	12		14	15													
14	H	Montrose	436	3-4	1	2	3	4	5	6	7	8	9²	10¹	11																	
21	A	East Fife	591	0-1	1	2	3	4	5		7	8	9	10	6	12		15	11													
28	A	Brechin City	357	2-0	1	2	3	4	5	6¹	7	8	9¹	10	11			14	12	15												
Sep 4	H	Berwick Rangers	324	2-1	1	2	3		5	6	7	8	9¹	10	11¹			15	14	4	12											
11	H	Queen's Park	539	0-1	1	2	3		5	6	7	8	9	10	11			14	15	4	12											
18	A	East Stirlingshire	284	3-1	1	2	3		5	6		8		14	11	7	10	12	15	4	9³											
25	H	Cowdenbeath	424	1-1	1	2	3		5	6		8	9		11¹	7	12		4	10												
Oct 2	A	Forfar Athletic	397	0-5	1	2	3		5	8	7		9	12	11		15	6	14	4	10											
16	H	Montrose	274	4-1		3			5	6		8¹	9¹	10	11			14	4	7²	2	1		12								
23	H	Albion Rovers	590	1-1		3			5	6		8	9	12	11			14	4	7¹	2	1		10								
30	A	Queen's Park	713	2-3		3			5	6	15	8	9	12	11	14¹			4	7	2	1		10¹								
Nov 6	H	East Stirlingshire	415	1-0		2	3		5	6		8	9	12	11	7		14	15			1		10¹	4							
14	A	Berwick Rangers	415	1-0		2	3		5	6		8	9	12	11	15		14				1		10¹	4	7						
20	H	Brechin City	447	1-3		2	3		5	6	7	8	9¹	12	11		3		15			1		10	4							
27	A	Forfar Athletic	469	3-3	1	2	3		8	6		7	9¹		11¹								14	10	4¹		5					
Dec 8	A	Cowdenbeath	262	2-0	1	2	3		8	6			9	10¹	11¹	14			12	15					4		5	7				
18	A	Albion Rovers	257	0-3	1	2	3		5		15		9	10	11			6	12	4			8					7	14			
Jan 3	A	East Stirlingshire	308	1-2		2	3		5	6		8	9¹	7	11	14			10	2		1			4				15			
22	H	Cowdenbeath	469	2-0		2	3		5	6		8	9	10¹	11				12	14		1		15	4	7						
29	A	Queen's Park	492	1-1		2	3		5	6		7	9¹	10	11							1		15	4							
Feb 5	A	Forfar Athletic	439	3-4		2	3	4	8	6		7	9¹	10	11¹						12¹	1		5								
12	A	Brechin City	278	2-1		2	3	8	5				9¹	10¹	11			15	7	12		1		14	4							
26	H	Montrose	482	3-2		2	3	8	5	6¹			10	11¹				14	7	12		1			4			15¹	9			
Mar 4	A	East Fife	436	1-2		2	3	8	5	6			10	11						7		1			4			15	9¹			
11	A	Queen's Park	788	0-2		2	3	8		6	5		9	10	11				14			1			4					7		
14	A	Berwick Rangers	330	0-2		2	3	8	5	6			9	10	7				11			1			4			15				
18	H	East Stirlingshire	367	3-0		2	3	8	5	6		7		10	15				11¹	12		1			4			14¹	9¹			
25	H	Brechin City	365	2-1		2	3¹	8	5	6		7¹	15	10	14				11			1			4			12	9			
28	H	East Fife	394	1-1		2	3	8	5	6		7	15	10	12				11	9		1			4			14¹				
Apr 1	H	Berwick Rangers	560	0-0		2	3	4	5	8			9	10	11				6			1						14	15	7		
8	A	Cowdenbeath	284	2-1		2	3		5	8	6		9²	10	11				7			1			4			14	12			
15	H	Forfar Athletic	474	0-0			3	4	8	6		2	9	10	11				7			1		5				14				
22	H	Albion Rovers	415	0-0		2	3	4	8	6		12		10	11				7			1		5				14	9			
29	A	Montrose	267	1-2		2	3	4		6¹		8		10	11	12		14				1		5				9		7		15
May 6	H	East Fife	3,031	2-1		2	3	4		6¹		8		10	11¹	12		9	15			1		5						7		14
TOTAL FULL APPEARANCES					12	31	35	21	34	32	8	26	27	27	33	3	1	17	9	8	3	24	1	6	21	2	3	3	6	3	
TOTAL SUB APPEARANCES											(2)	(1)	(2)	(7)	(3)	(10)	(6)	(8)	(11)	(10)	(5)							(10)	(3)	(1)	(2)
TOTAL GOALS SCORED							1			5	2	2	14	4	7	1		1		4				3	3		1	3	2		

Small bold figures denote goalscorers.   † denotes opponent's own goal.

Dumbarton F.C.'s new stadium

CAR PARK · CAR PARK · CAR PARK · COACH PARK · CASTLE ROAD

CAPACITY: 2,000 (All Seated)

PITCH DIMENSIONS: 115 yds x 75 yds

FACILITIES FOR DISABLED SUPPORTERS:
20 Wheelchair spaces are accommodated at the front of the stand. Contact the Club Secretary in advance regarding availability.

Team playing kits

How to get there

The New Stadium can be reached by the following routes:

TRAINS: The train service from Glasgow Queen Street and Glasgow Central Low Level both pass through Dumbarton East Station (fans best choice) situated just under a ten minute walk from the ground.

BUSES: There are two main services which pass close to the ground. These are bound for Helensburgh and Balloch from Glasgow.

CARS: Follow A82 then A814 Helensburgh/Dumbarton sign post. Follow Road for about 1 mile. Pass under Dumbarton East Railway Bridge and take second right – Victoria Street (also signposted Dumbarton castle). The car park at the new stadium holds 500 cars and 10 coaches.

The Sons

email: info@sfl.scottishfootball.com • website: www.scottishfootball.com

East Fife

LIST OF PLAYERS 2000-2001

SURNAME	FIRST NAME	MIDDLE NAME	DATE OF BIRTH	PLACE OF BIRTH	DATE OF SIGNING	HEIGHT FT INS	WEIGHT ST LBS	POS. ON PITCH	PREVIOUS CLUB
Agostini	Damiano	Pietro	22/11/78	Irvine	28/07/99	5 11.0	13 6	Def	Queen's Park
Allison	John		05/06/70	Dunfermline	03/08/00	5 8.0	11 4	Mid	Kelty Hearts
Brown	Thomas		11/12/82	Kirkcaldy	26/06/00	5 9.0	11 2	Fwd	Bayview Y.C. U'18s
Burt	Christopher		23/02/82	Kirkcaldy	26/06/00	5 11.0	11 11	Def	Argos Thistle U'18s
Courts	Conrad		13/07/83	Kirkcaldy	26/06/00	5 8.0	10 4	Mid	Bluebell Colts U'16s
Devine	Christopher		21/02/79	Bellshill	15/09/00	5 6.0	11 1	Fwd	Arbroath
Ferguson	Steven		01/04/82	Dunfermline	26/07/00	6 0.0	12 0	Fwd	Musselburgh Windsor U'18s
Gallagher	John		02/06/69	Glasgow	30/05/00	5 9.0	10 10	Def/Mid	Queen of the South
Gibb	Richard		22/04/65	Bangour	17/09/93	5 7.0	11 0	Def	Armadale Thistle
Hunter	Murray	Russell	08/01/71	Edinburgh	26/07/00	6 1.0	13 0	Mid/Fwd	Clydebank
Kerrigan	Steven	Paul	29/09/70	Wolverhampton	26/07/00	5 10.0	11 0	Fwd	Brechin City
Mackay	Stuart	John	03/03/75	Inverness	02/07/99	5 10.0	12 0	Mid	Alloa Athletic
McCloy	Brian		06/08/79	Pontefract	27/01/00	5 10.5	10 11	Def/Mid	Airdrieonians
McCulloch	William		02/04/73	Baillieston	07/08/97	6 6.0	14 2	Gk	Ayr United
McManus	Paul		26/12/82	Kirkcaldy	26/06/00	5 8.0	10 8	Mid	West Park United U'18s
Moffat	Barrie		27/12/72	Bangour	31/12/96	5 8.0	12 2	Fwd	Alloa Athletic
Mortimer	Paul		14/02/80	Falkirk	03/08/00	6 2.0	12 0	Mid	Stirling Albion
Munro	Kenneth	Neil	08/08/77	Edinburgh	20/09/97	5 11.0	12 4	Def/Mid	Cowdenbeath
O'Neill	Martin		17/06/75	Glasgow	25/08/00	5 8.0	11 0	Mid	Stirling Albion
Ovenstone	John	William	07/10/82	Kirkcaldy	26/06/00	6 0.0	12 2	Def	Bayview Y.C. U'18s
Shannon	Robert		20/04/66	Bellshill	15/09/00	5 11.0	12 0	Def	Newcastle Breakers
Sharp	Raymond		16/11/69	Stirling	08/02/00	5 11.0	13 9	Def	Alloa Athletic
Simpson	Paul		09/08/68	St. Andrews	26/07/00	6 6.0	14 7	Fwd	Cowdenbeath
Stewart	Andrew	Thomas	02/01/78	Dumfries	21/03/00	6 2.0	12 13	Gk	St. Andrews
Thomson	Derek		05/12/82	Kirkcaldy	26/06/00	5 11.0	10 2	Def	Dunfermline Colts U'18s
Tinley	Gavin		22/02/79	Dundee	28/03/00	5 9.0	10 13	Mid	Downfield Juniors
Wright	Darren	James	22/09/78	Edinburgh	28/07/99	5 10.0	10 7	Fwd	Rosyth Recreation
Wright	Garry		28/06/82	Kirkcaldy	26/06/00	5 11.0	10 7	Mid	Lochgelly Albert U'18s

Milestones

YEAR OF FORMATION: 1903
MOST CAPPED PLAYER: George Aitken
NO. OF CAPS: 5
MOST LEAGUE POINTS IN A SEASON: 57 (Division 2 – Season 1929/30)(2 Points for a Win)
           67 (Second Division – Season 1995/96)(3 Points for a Win)
MOST LEAGUE GOALS SCORED BY A PLAYER IN A SEASON: Henry Morris (Season 1947/48)
NO. OF GOALS SCORED: 41
RECORD ATTENDANCE: 22,515 (-v- Raith Rovers – 2.1.1950 at Bayview Park – old Stadium)
           1,462 (-v- Forfar Athletic – 14.11.1998 at Bayview Stadium – new Stadium)
RECORD VICTORY: 13-2 (-v- Edinburgh City – Division 2, 11.12.1937)
RECORD DEFEAT: 0-9 (-v- Heart of Midlothian – Division 1, 5.10.1957)

The Fifers' ten year league record

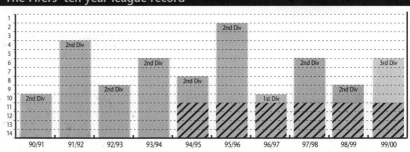

THE FIFERS' CLUB FACTFILE 1999/2000
RESULTS... APPEARANCES... SCORERS... ATTENDANCES...

Date	Venue	Opponents	Att.	Res	McCulloch W.	Munro K.	Gibb R.	Ramsay S.	Agostini D.	Herd W.	Robertson C.	Mackay S.	Wright D.	Kirk S.	Logan R.	Cusick J.	Martin J.	Porteous A.	Shannon R.	Love G.	Honeyman B.	McGrillen P.	Moffat B.	Mooney R.	Forrest G.	Clark P.	Tinley G.	O'Hara G.	McInally D.	Sharp R.	McCloy B.	Jackson C.	McCormick S.	McManus T.
Aug 7	H	Berwick Rangers	549	†1-2	1	2	3	4	5	6	7	8	9	10	11	12	14	15																
14	A	East Stirlingshire	300	2-0	1	15		4		6	11	8[1]	14		7	5			2	3	9	10	12[1]											
21	H	Dumbarton	591	1-0	1	4			14	6	7	8	12		11	5			2	3	15	9[1]	10											
28	H	Montrose	512	0-0	1			4	5	6	7	8	14	15	11	12			2	3		9	10											
Sep 4	H	Albion Rovers	366	3-1	1		3	14	4	5	6	7[1]	8[1]	12	9	11			2			15[1]	10											
11	H	Forfar Athletic	586	2-0	1		3		4	5	6[1]	9	8	12	15[1]	7	11		2		14	10												
18	A	Cowdenbeath	670	0-4	1		3		11	5	6	9	8	15	7	4			2		12		10	14										
25	A	Queen's Park	568	0-0	1	2			12	5		11	8	9	7	4				3	14		10		6									
Oct 2	A	Brechin City	365	3-1	1		3			5	6	8	11[1]		15	12			2	9			10[2]		7									
16	A	East Stirlingshire	446	1-0	1	12				5	6	9	11	15	7[1]	14	4		2	3			10		8									
23	H	Berwick Rangers	506	1-0	1				14	5	6	9	11	15	7	4[1]			2	3			10		8									
30	A	Forfar Athletic	504	2-3	1		14			5	6	9	11[1]	15	7				2				10[1]		8	12								
Nov 6	H	Cowdenbeath	569	2-3	1		3			5	6	7	12	15	9		4		2				10[2]		8	11								
14	H	Albion Rovers	464	†1-4	1	12	3			5	6	9	8	11	14		4		2				10		15	7								
20	A	Montrose	440	2-1	1	2				5	11[1]	7	9[1]		8					6	3		10		15	4								
27	H	Brechin City	463	1-0	1	2			5[1]		9	11	15		7	8				6	3		10		12	4								
Dec 4	H	Queen's Park	742	1-0	1	2[1]				5	11	9			7					6	3		10		8	4								
Jan 3	A	Cowdenbeath	639	0-1	1	2				5	11	9	15		7	14				6	3		10		8	4								
15	H	Forfar Athletic	577	1-1	1	2				5	6	9[1]	11		7								10		8	4		3						
22	H	Queen's Park	631	0-0	1	2				5	6	9	14		12				8		3		10		7			4	11					
Feb 5	A	Brechin City	337	1-3	1	2	3		15	6	11[1]	10	9		7	8			4				12		14	5								
15	H	Montrose	390	2-0	1	2				5	11	10	15	14					6						7[1]					3[1]	4	8	9	
19	A	Albion Rovers	368	1-3	1	2				5	11	10			15[1]				6						7			14		3	4	8	9	
26	A	East Stirlingshire	328	0-1	1	2				5	12	6											10		7			14	4	3	8	11	9	
Mar 4	H	Dumbarton	436	2-1	1	2					12									6			10[1]	11	5					3	4	8	9	7[1]
11	A	Forfar Athletic	582	1-0	1	2				5	12	15		8[1]						6			10							3	4	11	9	7
18	H	Cowdenbeath	702	1-1	1	2				5	7	8		6[1]					14				10							3	4	11		9
21	H	Berwick Rangers	551	3-1	1		3			5	11[1]	14	12	15	6[1]				2				10[1]		7			4				8		9
25	H	Montrose	442	1-1	1					5	11	15							2				10		6					3	4	8		9[1]
28	A	Dumbarton	394	1-1	1					5						4			2				10		6					3	8	7	9[1]	11
Apr 1	H	Albion Rovers	512	2-1	1					5	15	14				4							10[1]		7					3	2	8	9	11[1]
11	A	Queen's Park	788	0-1	1					5					15	7			2				10		14			6		3	4	8	9	11
15	H	Brechin City	452	1-1	1	2				5	15									8	6		10		7					3	4		9[1]	11
22	H	Berwick Rangers	942	1-0	1	2	12			5	14	7	15	8		6							10[1]	11						3	4		9	
29	H	East Stirlingshire	590	3-1	1	2	12			5		8	15	6[1]	14								10[1]		7					3	4		9[1]	11
May 6	A	Dumbarton	3,031	1-2	1	2	5				15	11	12		8[1]	6					14		10		7					3	4			9
TOTAL FULL APPEARANCES					36	24	6	6	31	16	26	26	4	5	21	23			24	13	2	3	28		23	1	1	14	2	14	14	11	11	11
TOTAL SUB APPEARANCES						(3)	(4)	(3)	(1)		(7)	(5)	(14)	(6)	(10)	(3)	(1)	(1)	(1)	(3)	(3)		(2)	(1)	(3)	(3)	(2)						
TOTAL GOALS SCORED						1			1	1	5	4	1	2	3	4				1	1		11		1					1			3	3

Small bold figures denote goalscorers.   † denotes opponent's own goal.

Bayview Stadium

TO LEVEN — SOUTH STREET — TO BUCKHAVEN — TO METHIL DOCKS — HARBOUR VIEW — RIVER FORTH — CAR PARK — CAR PARK — AWAY SUPPORTERS — HOME SUPPORTERS

CAPACITY: 2,000 (All Seated)
PITCH DIMENSIONS: 115 yds x 75 yds
FACILITIES FOR DISABLED SUPPORTERS:
Area available at both Home & Away Sections of the Stand.
CATERING FACILITIES:
Restaurant facilities are available at the stadium on matchdays and visiting supporters are also welcome.

Team playing kits

How to get there

Bayview Stadium can be reached by the following routes:

TRAINS: The nearest railway station is Kirkcaldy (8 miles away), and fans will have to catch an inter-linking bus service from just outside the station to the ground.

BUSES: A regular service from Kirkcaldy to Leven passes close to the ground, as does the Leven to Dunfermline service. The Leven bus terminus is approximately 2/3 mile from the ground (5 minutes walk).

CARS: There are Car Parking facilities available for both Home and Away fans at the ground.

The Fifers

email: info@sfl.scottishfootball.com • website: www.scottishfootball.com

EST. 1881

Firs Park, Firs Street,
Falkirk, FK2 7AY

CHAIRMAN
Alan J. Mackin

VICE-CHAIRMAN
Alexander Miller

DIRECTORS
Alexander S. H. Forsyth,
Alexander M. McCabe
& John M. D. Morton

HON. PRESIDENT
James Middlemass

CHIEF EXECUTIVE/SECRETARY
Leslie G. Thomson

MANAGER
George Fairley

ASSISTANT MANAGER
Brian Ross

COACHES
James Butter (Goalkeeping)
Tom Beattie (U18),
John Anderson (U16 & U14),
Archie Morrison (U15),
Jack Martin (U13),

YOUTH DEVELOPMENT COACH
Ian Brown (01324) 679796

PHYSIOTHERAPIST
Laura Gillogley

**FOOTBALL SAFETY OFFICERS'
ASSOCIATION REPRESENTATIVE**
Alan Connor (01324) 875091

CHIEF SCOUT
Sandy Craig

STADIUM DIRECTOR
John Morton

GROUNDSMAN
James Wilson

KITMAN
James Wilson

COMMERCIAL DIRECTOR
Alex Miller (01324) 626278

MEDIA LIAISON OFFICER
Leslie G. Thomson (01324) 623583

MATCHDAY PROGRAMME EDITOR
Alan Connor (01324) 875091

TELEPHONES
Ground (01324) 623583
Fax (01324) 637862
Manager (at Ground) (01324) 679796
(Sec. Home) (01324) 551099
(Sec. Bus) (01324) 623583

INTERNET ADDRESS
www.eaststirlingshire.co.uk

CLUB SHOP
Situated at ground. Open Mon-Fri
10.00 a.m. till 3.00 p.m. (except
Wednesday) and on all home
matchdays

CLUB CAPTAIN
Gordon Russell

SHIRT SPONSOR
Finewood Joinery Products Ltd

KIT SUPPLIER
SECCA

East Stirlingshire

LIST OF PLAYERS 2000-2001

SURNAME	FIRST NAME	MIDDLE NAME	DATE OF BIRTH	PLACE OF BIRTH	DATE OF SIGNING	HEIGHT FT INS	WEIGHT ST LBS	POS. ON PITCH	PREVIOUS CLUB
Butter	James	Ross	14/12/66	Dundee	07/07/00	6 1.0	13 0	Gk	Brechin City
Campbell	Derek		10/11/83	Dechmont	02/08/00	5 11.0	11 6	Mid	East Stirlingshire Under 16s
Clarke	John		23/11/70	Glasgow	06/07/00	5 11.0	12 0	Def	Camelon Juniors
Comrie	Stuart		06/05/82	Falkirk	02/08/00	5 8.0	11 3	Fwd	Zeneca Under 18s
Connelly	David		22/03/83	Bangour	02/08/00	5 7.0	10 10	Mid	East Stirlingshire Under 16s
Craig	Sandy		04/03/83	Falkirk	02/09/00	5 10.0	10 0	Mid	Stenhousemuir U'16s
Docherty	Ryan		18/10/83	Bangour	02/08/00	5 10.0	11 6	Fwd	East Stirlingshire Under 16s
Donnelly	Patrick		26/11/82	Falkirk	02/08/00	5 7.0	9 0	Def	Bonnybridge U'16s
Fairley	Kenneth		21/10/83	Falkirk	02/08/00	5 8.0	10 6	Def	Stenhousemuir
Ferguson	Brown	Alexander	04/06/81	Falkirk	26/07/99	5 10.0	11 8	Def	S Form
Foster	Stuart		06/08/82	Falkirk	02/08/00	5 9.0	11 9	Mid	Bonnybridge Juniors
Gordon	Kevin	Mervyn	01/05/77	Tranent	14/07/99	5 8.0	10 7	Mid	Easthouses U'21s
Hall	Michael		11/12/74	Edinburgh	01/06/00	6 2.0	12 6	Def	Stenhousemuir
Higgins	Gary		15/09/72	Stirling	02/06/99	5 11.0	12 0	Mid/Fwd	Ross County
Hislop	Steven		14/06/78	Edinburgh	22/06/00	6 2.0	12 7	Fwd	Easthouses U'21s
Irvine	Gordon	James	30/01/83	Edinburgh	02/09/00	6 1.0	12 0	Gk	S Form
Lynes	Craig		07/02/81	Edinburgh	24/03/00	6 3.0	12 3	Mid/Fwd	Hutchison Vale U'21s
MacKenzie	James		22/10/82	Falkirk	02/09/00	5 10.0	12 0	Fwd	Linlithgow Bridge
McDonald	Allan	John	18/03/83	Glasgow	02/08/00	5 7.0	11 8	Def	East Stirlingshire Under 16s
McKechnie	Gregor	Alistair	04/06/74	Stirling	10/06/00	5 11.0	12 7	Fwd	Alloa Athletic
McKenzie	Christopher		02/01/68	Bridge of Allan	06/07/00	5 6.0	11 0	Fwd	Camelon Juniors
McPherson	Dean		07/06/78	Aberdeen	29/07/00	6 0.0	11 0	Mid	Berwick Rangers
Meikle	David		13/02/83	Bangour	02/08/00	5 10.0	11 6	Def	East Stirlingshire Under 16s
Miller	Neil		16/02/82	Falkirk	02/08/00	5 11.0	11.8	Mid	Zeneca Under 18s
Quinn	Ciaran		06/10/77	Dublin	03/08/00	6 0.0	13 0	Def	Clyde
Reid	Craig	Andrew	08/09/83	Falkirk	14/08/00	5 10.0	11 9	Def	Falkirk
Ross	Brian		15/08/67	Stirling	31/03/91	5 11.0	13 0	Def	Ayr United
Russell	Gordon	Alan	03/03/68	Falkirk	23/09/95	5 9.5	10 0	Def	Stenhousemuir
Scott	Andrew	McKean	11/03/81	Glasgow	14/07/99	5 9.0	10 0	Fwd	S Form
Spence	James		31/03/78	Edinburgh	06/07/00	5 7.0	10 4	Mid	Easthouses Under 21s
Stewart	Steven		15/12/72	Dundee	06/07/00	5 11.0	12 5	Mid	Tayport Juniors
Stuart	Marc		28/01/83	Falkirk	02/08/00	5 10.0	11 4	Def	Dunfermline Athletic U16s
Sutherland	Michael		30/12/81	Edinburgh	24/03/00	5 11.5	11 7	Fwd	Links United
Todd	Christopher	James	01/07/82	Stirling	02/08/00	5 11.0	12 0	Gk	Kilsyth B.C.
Todd	Douglas		07/07/70	Stirling	06/07/00	5 9.0	12 0	Mid	Bo'ness United Juniors
Tortolano	Joseph		06/04/66	Stirling	29/07/00	5 9.5	11 10	Def	Stirling Albion
Wilson	John	Kerr T.	29/04/83	Bangour	19/08/00	5 6.0	10 5	Mid	East Stirlingshire B.C.

Milestones

YEAR OF FORMATION: 1881
MOST CAPPED PLAYER: Humphrey Jones
NO. OF CAPS: 5 (for Wales)
MOST LEAGUE POINTS IN A SEASON: 55 (Division 2 – Season 1931/32) (2 Points for a Win)
 59 (Third Division – Season 1994/95) (3 Points for a Win)
MOST LEAGUE GOALS SCORED BY A PLAYER IN A SEASON: Malcolm Morrison (Season 1938/39)
NO. OF GOALS SCORED: 36
RECORD ATTENDANCE: 11,500 (-v- Hibernian – 10.2.1969)
RECORD VICTORY: 10-1 (-v- Stenhousemuir – Scottish Cup, 1.9.1888)
RECORD DEFEAT: 1-12 (-v- Dundee United – Division 2, 13.4.1936)

The Shire's ten year league record

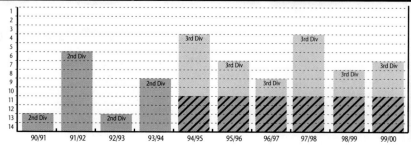

THE SHIRES' CLUB FACTFILE 1999/2000
RESULTS... APPEARANCES... SCORERS... ATTENDANCES...

Nationwide

Date	Venue	Opponents	Att.	Res	Butter J.	Storrar A.	Brown M.	Ross B.	Bowsher C.	Muirhead D.	Ferguson B.	Barr A.	Laidlaw S.	Higgins C.	Elliott A.	Gordon K.	Lynes C.	Russell C.	Hardie M.	McNeill W.	Donnelly S.	McDonald G.	O'Hara C.	McMillan G.	Menmuir S.	Hay D.	Campbell M.	Allan G.	Morrison S.	Crawford G.	Scott A.	McPherson D.	McCann K.	Sutherland M.	Abdulrahman K.
Aug 7	A	Queen's Park	450	1-2	1	2	3	4	5	6	7	8¹	9	10	11	12	14	15																	
14	H	East Fife	300	0-2	1	2	15	4	5	6	8	7	9	10	11	12		3																	
21	A	Forfar Athletic	416	1-1	1	2	4		5	6¹	7		9		11	12		3	8	10	14	15													
28	H	Cowdenbeath	205	0-1	1	2	4			6	12	7	9		11	14	15	3	8	10				5											
Sep 4	A	Montrose	278	2-1	1	2	4			6	8	7	9	10¹	15	14		3	11	12				5											
11	A	Brechin City	284	2-1	1	2	4			6		7	9¹	10	11	14		3	8¹	12	15		5												
18	H	Dumbarton	284	1-3	1	2	4			6	12	7	9¹	10	11			3	8		15		5												
25	A	Albion Rovers	280	1-1	1	2	4	15		6	11	7	9¹	10		12		3	8		14				5										
Oct 2	H	Berwick Rangers	266	0-3	1	2	4		5	6	12	7	9	10	11			3	8		14														
16	A	East Fife	446	0-1	1	3	4		5	6	12	2	9	10	11				8		14					7									
23	H	Queen's Park	354	1-1	1	3	4		5	6		2	9¹	10	11				8		14					7									
30	H	Brechin City	210	0-0	1	3	4		5	6	12	2	9	15	11				8	10						7									
Nov 6	A	Dumbarton	415	0-1	1	3	6	4		8	14	2	9	10	11	7					15					5									
14	H	Montrose	241	2-0	1	2¹	4			8	14	7	9	10¹	11	12		3			15	6				5									
20	A	Cowdenbeath	248	2-1	1	2	4			8	14	7	9²	10	11	12		3			15	6				5									
27	H	Berwick Rangers	318	0-1	1	2	4			6		7	9	10	11	12		3	8							5									
Dec 18	A	Queen's Park	413	1-0	1	2	4			8	12	7	9	10¹	11	14	6	3								5									
Jan 3	H	Dumbarton	308	2-1	1	2	4			8	12	7	9²			14	6	3								5	10	11							
22	A	Albion Rovers	260	1-0	1	2	4			6	14	7	9	10	11	12		3								5¹		8							
29	H	Forfar Athletic	201	0-2	1	2	5			6	12	7	9	10	11			3								4	14	8	15						
Feb 5	H	Berwick Rangers	255	0-1	1	2	4			8						12		3	10							5			6	9	11				
12	A	Cowdenbeath	224	0-4	1	2	4			8	14					12	10	3			15		6			5			9	7	11				
19	A	Montrose	327	0-0	1	2	4		5	6			9	10	11			3	8										15	7	12				
26	H	East Fife	328	1-0	1	2	5			4			9¹	10	11			3	8										6	14	7		15		
29	H	Albion Rovers	191	4-3	1	2	5			4			9²	10	11			3	8								12		6	14	7¹		15¹		
Mar 4	A	Forfar Athletic	399	0-3	1	2	5			4			9	10	11			3	8								12		6	14	7		15		
7	H	Brechin City	207	1-1	1	2	5			4			9¹	10	11			3	8										6	14	7		15		
11	H	Brechin City	259	0-3	1	2	5			4			9	10	11			3	8								12		6	14	7		15		
18	A	Dumbarton	367	0-3	1	2	6			4	7							3	8	10						5				9	11	12			
25	A	Cowdenbeath	243	0-0	1	2	6			4			9	14	11			3										8			7		10	5	
Apr 1	H	Montrose	205	1-0	1	2	6			4			9	12	11			3										8¹			7		10	5	
8	H	Albion Rovers	206	3-1	1	2¹	6			4	12		9¹	10	11			3										8¹			7		15	5	
15	A	Berwick Rangers	486	0-3	1	2	6			4	12		9	10	11			3										8			7		15	5	
22	H	Queen's Park	497	0-1	1	2	6			4			9	10	11			3									15			14	7			5	8
29	A	East Fife	590	1-3	1	7	3			8		2	10¹	9	11				6										5	14	12			4	
May 6	H	Forfar Athletic	409	0-1	1	2	6			8		4	10	9	11			3											7	14			5	12	
TOTAL FULL APPEARANCES					36	36	35	7	3	36	16	10	19	22	19	22	21	31	21	3	2		2	2	1	12	1	3	3	7	15	1	7	2	1
TOTAL SUB APPEARANCES							(1)	(1)			(7)	(7)	(4)	(3)	(13)	(5)	(1)			(6)	(3)	(2)				(3)	(1)		(3)	(6)	(1)	(10)		(2)
TOTAL GOALS SCORED						2				1		1	9	9					1							1				2	1	1		

Small bold figures denote goalscorers.   † denotes opponent's own goal.

Firs Park

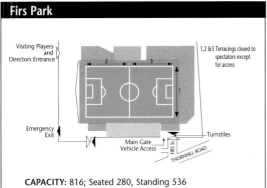

Visiting Players and Directors Entrance

1, 2 & 3 Terracings closed to spectators except for access

Emergency Exit

Main Gate Vehicle Access

FIRS ST.

THORNHILL ROAD

Turnstiles

CAPACITY: 816; Seated 280, Standing 536
PITCH DIMENSIONS: 108 yds x 71 yds
FACILITIES FOR DISABLED SUPPORTERS:
By prior arrangement with Secretary.

Team playing kits

How to get there

The following routes may be used to reach Firs Park:

TRAINS: Passengers should alight at Grahamston Station and the ground is then five minutes walk.

BUSES: All buses running from the town centre pass close by the ground. The Grangemouth via Burnbank Road and Tamfourhill via Kennard Street services both stop almost outside the ground.

CARS: Car parking is available in the adjacent side streets. There are also spaces available in the car park adjacent to the major stores around the ground.

The Shire

email: info@sfl.scottishfootball.com • website: www.scottishfootball.com

Borough Briggs, Borough Briggs Road, Elgin, IV30 1AP

CHAIRMAN
Denis Miller

DIRECTORS
Norman Green, Martyn Hunter,
Alan McGregor, Ronald McHardy,
Ewen Menzies, John Meichan
& John A. Milton

SECRETARY
John A. Milton

GENERAL MANAGER
Harry McFadden

MANAGER
Alexander Caldwell

COACH
Neil McLennan

HEAD YOUTH COACH
Graeme Porter

CLUB DOCTOR
Dr. Alan Rodger, MB, ChB

PHYSIOTHERAPIST
Maurice O'Donnell

**FOOTBALL SAFETY OFFICERS'
ASSOCIATION REPRESENTATIVE**
Steven Hamilton

HEAD GROUNDSMAN
Steven Dunn

KIT MAN
Ricky Graham

COMMERCIAL DEPARTMENT
Audrey Fanning, Kaye Sutherland
& James Falconer

MATCHDAY PROGRAMME EDITOR
Craig Christie

TELEPHONES
Ground (01343) 551114
Ground Fax (01343) 547921
Sec. Bus. (01343) 822541
Sec. Home (01343) 546312

CLUB SHOP
Situated at Stadium (01343) 551114.
Mon – Fri 9.30a.m.-12.30p.m.
& 1.30p.m.-3.30p.m.
Sat – 10.00a.m.-12Noon
Matchday – 2.00p.m.-5.00p.m.

OFFICIAL SUPPORTERS CLUB
Borough Briggs, Borough Briggs Road,
Elgin, IV30 1AP
President: Cecil Jack;
Secretary: Mrs. June Jack

ECFC SOCIAL CLUB
Situated within the Main Stand
Steward: Edith Lewis (01343) 542710

CLUB CAPTAIN
Colin Milne

SHIRT SPONSOR
J. Gordon Williamson

KIT SUPPLIER
ERREA

LIST OF PLAYERS 2000-2001

SURNAME	FIRST NAME	MIDDLE NAME	DATE OF BIRTH	PLACE OF BIRTH	DATE OF SIGNING	HEIGHT FT INS	WEIGHT ST LBS	POS. ON PITCH	PREVIOUS CLUB
Blackhall	David	Richard	13/07/83	Aberdeen	21/08/00	5 9.0	11 5	Fwd	Elgin City
Cameron	Stuart		18/11/74	Aberdeen	26/07/00	5 7.0	10 0	Mid	Deveronvale
Campbell	Connor		26/01/80	Inverness	25/08/00	5 6.0	10 0	Mid/Fwd	Ross County
Clinton	Stephen		02/11/72	Glasgow	26/07/00	5 9.0	11 11	Fwd	Lossiemouth
Ellis	Steven	Robert	23/10/82	Aberdeen	27/07/00	5 10.0	10 5	Mid	Unattached
Green	Michael		02/01/76	Elgin	31/07/00	5 7.0	11 0	Mid	Unattached
Green	Ryan	Donald	14/06/76	Aberdeen	27/07/00	6 3.0	14 3	Fwd	Buckie Thistle
MacDonald	Jordan		07/09/82	Inverness	26/07/00	5 11.0	11 6	Def	Inverness Cal. Thistle
Maguire	Peter	Jason	11/09/69	Huddersfield	26/07/00	5 8.0	13 0	Mid	Unattached
McMullan	Martin		31/07/82	Glasgow	21/08/00	6 0.0	10 0	Fwd	Unattached
Milne	Colin	Richard	23/10/74	Aberdeen	27/07/00	6 2.0	13 10	Fwd	Peterhead
Milne	Craig	David	01/04/81	Perth	26/07/00	5 10.0	12 0	Def	Forfar Athletic
Morris	Alan	James	27/02/70	Bellshill	06/08/00	5 10.0	11 10	Def	Unattached
Morrison	Michael	Ian	21/10/79	Elgin	26/07/00	6 2.0	14 0	Def	Unattached
Noble	Shaun		08/12/78	Aberdeen	26/07/00	5 9.0	10 0	Mid	Unattached
O'Brien	Lee		05/04/72	Renfrew	26/07/00	5 10.0	11 9	Def	Unattached
Rae	Michael	Allan	19/08/81	Inverness	06/08/00	6 1.0	12 0	Gk	Fort William
Russell	George	Raymond	20/07/74	Kirkcaldy	26/07/00	5 7.0	10 10	Mid	Unattached
Slythe	Mark	Alan	25/05/73	Falkirk	31/07/00	5 7.0	10 0	Fwd	Benburb
Whyte	Marc		14/01/82	Aberdeen	21/08/00	5 11.0	11 0	Mid	Unattached
Whyte	Neil	Gordon	07/03/75	Elgin	26/07/00	6 0.0	10 0	Fwd	Unattached
Youngson	Gary	Mark	23/02/81	Elgin	12/08/00	5 11.0	11 0	Def	Elgin City

Milestones

YEAR OF FORMATION: 1893
MOST CAPPED PLAYER: – None
MOST LEAGUE POINTS IN A SEASON: 55 (Highland League - Season 1967/68 (2 Points for a Win)
81 (Highland League - Season 1989/90 (3 Points for a Win)
MOST LEAGUE GOALS SCORED BY A PLAYER IN A SEASON: Matt Armstrong (Season 1947/48)
NO. OF GOALS SCORED: 52
RECORD ATTENDANCE: 12,608 (-v- Arbroath – 17.2.1968)
RECORD VICTORY: – 18-1 (-v- Brora Rangers – North of Scotland Cup – 6.2.1960)
RECORD DEFEAT: – 1-14 (-v- Heart of Midlothian – Scottish Cup – 4.2.1939)

ELGIN CITY F.C. – A BRIEF HISTORY
FORMED 1893

HONOURS
Scottish Cup: Quarter Finalists 1967/68
Highland League Champions: 1931/32, 1934/35, 1952/53, 1955/56, 1959/60, 1960/61, 1962/63, 1964/65, 1965/66, 1967/68, 1968/69, 1969/70, 1973/74, 1989/90
Highland League Cup Winners: 1959/60, 1966/67, 1982/83, 1990/91, 1997/98
Scottish Qualifying Cup (North) Winners: 1935/36, 1937/38, 1959/60, 1964/65, 1967/68, 1970/71, 1989/90
North of Scotland Cup Winners: 1898/99, 1923/24, 1936/37, 1954/55, 1955/56, 1960/61, 1961/62, 1967/68, 1968/69, 1970/71, 1972/73, 1975/76, 1982/83, 1988/89, 1989/90, 1997/98, 1998/99

The present club was formed on the 10th August, 1893 by the amalgamation of Elgin Rovers and Vale of Lossie. They were admitted to the Highland League in 1895, but resigned at the end of the season, only to rejoin in 1897. However, once more in 1900 City quit the competition, only to return in 1902, and up to May, 2000 were continuous members.

Over the 107 years of the club's existence, they have been Highland League Champions on 14 occasions, the first of which was in season 1931/32, under the guidance of former Aberdeen player, Bert MacLachlan, and the title was won again shortly thereafter in season 1934/35. In 1947/48 former Don, Matt Armstrong, netted 52 goals. The next flag to fly over Borough Briggs was in season 1952/53 when former St. Mirren, Aberdeen and Dundee centre-half Willie Roy led the side. In August, 1955 former Hamilton Accies centre-forward Ian Rae was appointed Elgin City's first Manager and led the club to the title in 1955/56 after a 3-2 play-off win over Buckie Thistle. During the halcyon days from 1959 to 1974, the club produced two great sides who captured nine Highland League Championships, coached firstly by former player Stewart McLachlan between 1959 to 1963 and Innes MacDonald (Trainer/Coach) from 1965 to 1973. Star players of the time included Alex Jenkins, Dave Lawrie, Jim Gerrard, Gordon Laing, George "Bunny" McCall, Douglas Grant (captain 1964-71 and capped by Scotland at amateur International level), Sandy MacKenzie, Willie Grant (who hit 348 goals in 255 games, and during the 1960/61 season hit a club record 66 goals in all competitions), Gerry

Graham with 371 goals in 376 games, Rod Clyne and George Gilbert. After a 15 year wait, the club achieved its last success in the League when Steve Paterson was at the helm. Elgin were Champions for six days in their Centenary year 1993, but were sensationally stripped of the title for alleged fixture rigging!

In Cup football, Elgin have been Scottish Qualifying Cup (North) winners on seven occasions, the first in season 1935/36, when Blairgowrie were beaten 4-2 with the last being in season 1989/90, when Cove Rangers were defeated 1-0. For the record, City were also Cup Finalists on eight other occasions.

In the Scottish Cup, Elgin were Quarter Finalists in season 1967/68, and had runs to the Fourth Round (or the last 16 equivalent) in seasons 1959/60, 1966/67, 1971/72 and 1976/77 which included wins over Scottish Football League clubs Albion Rovers (twice), Arbroath (twice), Ayr United, Berwick Rangers, Forfar Athletic (three times), Meadowbank Thistle, Stenhousemuir (twice) & Stirling Albion. The Black and Whites have also enjoyed big games with Aberdeen and Celtic home and away, Rangers three times at Ibrox, one of which was attended by a crowd of 36,500.

Returning to North competitions, City have been winners of the Highland League Cup five times, the first of which was in season 1959/60 when Clachnacuddin were defeated 3-2, with the last being in September, 1997, when Cove Rangers were beaten 1-0. In the North of Scotland Cup, Elgin have played in 26 Cup Finals, 17 of which have been won. The club's first success came in December, 1898, when they became the first club from outside Inverness to win the trophy, beating Clachnacuddin 2-1 with the last being in September, 1998, beating Rothes 2-0.

Elgin have produced a number of excellent players to make their mark including R.C. (Bob) Hamilton, later a Rangers and Scotland captain, capped 15 times by his country, Billy Farqhuar (Sunderland), Jimmy Low (Heart of Midlothian and Newcastle United), Sandy MacLennan (Partick Thistle), Iain MacDonald (St. Johnstone, Carlisle United & Dundee), Ian Wilson (Leicester City, Everton, Derby County & Scotland), Nicky Walker (Leicester City, Motherwell, Rangers, Heart of Midlothian, Partick Thistle, Ross County & Scotland), Alan Main (Dundee United & St. Johnstone), John McGinlay (Bolton Wanderers & Scotland) and Mike Teasdale (Dundee & Inverness Caledonian Thistle).

ROBERT WEIR
(Club Historian)

Borough Briggs Stadium

CAPACITY: 6,000; Seated 475, Standing 5,525
PITCH DIMENSIONS: 111 yds x 76 yds
FACILITIES FOR DISABLED SUPPORTERS:
An area is designated in the south east enclosure.

Team playing kits

How to get there
Borough Briggs Stadium can be reached by the following routes:
TRAINS: – Elgin Railway Station is situated approximately one mile south of the stadium.
BUSES: – Elgin bus station is situated in the town centre, which is only half a mile from Borough Briggs.
CARS: – Elgin is situated on the A96, 38 miles east of Inverness and 67 miles west of Aberdeen. From the south, leave A9 at Aviemore and take the A95 as far as Craigellachie then take A941 to Elgin.

Hamilton Academical

Firhill Stadium, 80 Firhill Road,
Glasgow, G20 7AL

OFFICE ADDRESS
Enable Building, Prospect House,
New Park Street, Hamilton, ML3 0BN

CHAIRMAN
Jan W. Stepek

VICE-CHAIRMAN
George McLachlan

DIRECTORS
William A. Donnelly & William Sherry

SECRETARY
Scott A. Struthers, B.A. (Hons)

HON. LIFE PRESIDENT
Dr. Alexander A. Wilson

MANAGER
Alistair Dawson

ASSISTANT MANAGER
Robert Prytz

YOUTH DEVELOPMENT MANAGER
Bobby Jenks

HON. MEDICAL OFFICER
Dr. Brian Lynas

PHYSIOTHERAPIST/COACH
Jim Fallon

**FOOTBALL SAFETY OFFICERS'
ASSOCIATION REPRESENTATIVE**
Scott A. Struthers, B.A. (Hons)
(01698) 286103

COMMERCIAL DEPARTMENT
Contact Club

MATCHDAY PROGRAMME EDITOR
Scott A. Struthers, B.A. (Hons)
(01698) 286103

TELEPHONES
Office/Commercial 01698 286103
Ground 0141 579 1971
(Matchdays Only)
Fax-Office 01698 285422
Information Service
(09068) 666492

CLUB SHOP
"The Acciesshop",
Hamilton Academical F.C.,
Enable Building, Prospect House,
New Park Street, Hamilton, ML3 0BN

OFFICIAL SUPPORTERS CLUB
The Stand Club,
c/o Hamilton Academical F.C.,
Enable Building, Prospect House,
New Park Street, Hamilton, ML3 0BN

TEAM CAPTAIN
Chris Hillcoat

SHIRT SPONSOR
M.J. Gleeson Group plc.

KIT SUPPLIER
Russell Athletic

LIST OF PLAYERS 2000-2001

SURNAME	FIRST NAME	MIDDLE NAME	DATE OF BIRTH	PLACE OF BIRTH	DATE OF SIGNING	HEIGHT FT INS	WEIGHT ST LBS	POS. ON PITCH	PREVIOUS CLUB
Bonnar	Martin	Michael	12/01/79	Bellshill	02/07/97	5 7.0	9 4	Mid	X Form
Boyle	Gerard		17/04/82	Bellshill	17/05/00	5 8.0	9 0	Fwd	Morriston Y.M.C.A.
Clark	Gary		13/09/64	Glasgow	31/07/00	5 10.0	11 10	Mid	Alloa Athletic
Cowan	Brian		03/07/82	Motherwell	08/09/00	5 10.0	11 7	Mid	S Form
Davidson	Scott	Joseph	20/08/83	Bellshill	22/08/00	5 6.0	9 0	Fwd	Albion Rovers Youth
Davidson	William	Andrew	01/12/77	Bellshill	08/08/96	5 10.0	11 0	Fwd	X Form
Downs	Robert		22/04/79	Glasgow	08/07/00	5 10.0	11 0	Fwd	Pollok Juniors
Eadie	Alexander	Broadley	07/11/67	Glasgow	08/07/00	6 1.0	11 8	Fwd	Pollok Juniors
Frame	Alan	James	20/04/83	Lanark	12/08/00	6 3.0	13 6	Gk	Dundee United
Gaughan	Paul		27/09/80	Glasgow	04/09/97	6 2.0	12 5	Def	West Park United B.C.
Grant	David		03/07/82	Bellshill	12/08/00	5 10.5	10 8	Def	X Form
Hillcoat	Christopher	Patrick	03/10/69	Glasgow	19/05/87	5 10.0	12 0	Def	St. Bridget's B.G.
Hogg	Keith		23/01/80	Lanark	05/07/00	6 0.0	12 0	Def	Ayr United
Johnstone	Richard	Gary	29/01/82	Bellshill	12/08/00	5 5.0	10 2	Mid	Queen's Park
Kelly	Ryan	William	07/08/80	Rutherglen	05/07/99	5 10.0	11 3	Def/Mid	Rutherglen Thistle
Lurinsky	Alexander		22/07/82	Bangour	12/08/00	5 6.0	9 7	Fwd	Ayr United
Lynn	Gary		16/12/80	Glasgow	30/03/99	5 11.0	11 6	Def	Scarborough
Macfarlane	Ian	John P.	05/12/68	Bellshill	06/03/99	6 2.0	13 3	Gk	Glenafton Athletic
Maclaren	Ross	Stewart	09/07/81	Bellshill	25/08/97	6 1.0	11 10	Def	S Form
Martin	Michael	Benjamin	23/05/81	Glasgow	22/10/98	5 8.0	10 7	Def	Preston North End B.C.
McCreadie	Iain	Hugh	20/01/82	Kilmarnock	04/09/99	5 8.5	10 0	Mid	Kello Rovers
McFarlane	Andrew		06/07/82	Glasgow	12/08/00	5 11.0	10 4	Def	S Form
McFarlane	David	Thomas M.	10/04/79	Glasgow	06/08/96	5 11.0	12 2	Fwd	S Form
McGeachie	Scott		12/06/82	Lanark	24/08/00	6 3.0	10 7	Mid	Carluke Milton Rovers
McShane	John		27/01/83	Bellshill	12/08/00	5 8.0	9 10	Mid	Queen's Park
Moore	Michael	Jordan	24/03/81	Paisley	16/12/98	6 0.0	11 9	Mid/Fwd	Unattached
Nelson	Mark	John	09/08/69	Bellshill	06/07/00	5 11.0	12 7	Def	Alloa Athletic
Peutherer	Stewart		14/01/82	Bellshill	05/09/00	5 11.0	11 0	Fwd	S Form
Potter	Derek	Robert	01/06/82	Rutherglen	12/08/00	5 8.0	9 7	Fwd	S Form
Potter	Graham	Joseph	04/06/79	Rutherglen	14/07/00	6 0.0	12 7	Gk	Annan Athletic
Prytz	Robert		12/01/60	Malmo	08/07/00	5 6.0	11 13	Mid	Pollok Juniors
Renicks	Steven	John	28/11/75	Bellshill	01/06/94	5 8.5	10 8	Def	Hamilton Academical B.C.
Russell	Allan	John	13/12/80	Glasgow	02/07/99	6 0.0	12 1	Mid	Hibernian
Steele	Colin	William	20/12/82	Bellshill	12/08/00	5 11.0	10 7	Fwd	S Form
Sullivan	Nicholas		21/10/83	Lanark	24/08/00	5 8.0	9 7	Mid	Wishaw B.C.
Thomson	Stewart		24/12/82	Motherwell	07/09/00	5 11.0	11 10	Gk	Netherdale Community A.F.C.
Vaugh	Brian	James	22/08/78	Belfast	25/07/00	6 0.0	12 0	Fwd	Cowdenbeath

Milestones

YEAR OF FORMATION: 1874
MOST CAPPED PLAYER: Colin Miller (Canada)
NO. OF CAPS: 29
MOST LEAGUE POINTS IN A SEASON: 57 (First Division – Season 1991/92)(2 Points for a Win)
74 (Second Division – Season 1996/97)(3 Points for a Win)
MOST LEAGUE GOALS SCORED BY A PLAYER IN A SEASON: David Wilson (Season 1936/37)
NO. OF GOALS SCORED: 35
RECORD ATTENDANCE: 28,690 (-v- Heart of Midlothian – Scottish Cup 3.3.1937)
RECORD VICTORY: 10-2 (-v- Cowdenbeath – Division 1, 15.10.1932)
RECORD DEFEAT: 1-11 (-v- Hibernian – Division 1, 6.11.1965)

The Accies' ten year league record

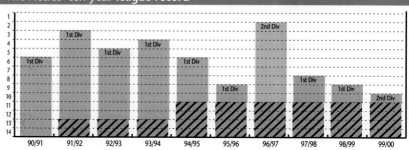

THE ACCIES' CLUB FACTFILE 1999/2000
RESULTS... APPEARANCES... SCORERS... ATTENDANCES...

Date	Venue	Opponents	Att.	Res	Reid C.	Martin M.	Cunnington E.	Miller C.	Maclaren R.	Thomson S.	Muir D.	Davidson W.	McFarlane D.	Moore M.	Henderson N.	McCormick S.	Russell A.	Gaughan P.	Lynn G.	Renicks S.	McAulay I.	Kelly R.	Bonnar M.	Henderson D.	Hunter G.	Crossley G.	Ferguson I.	MacFarlane I.	Hillcoat C.	Quitongo J.	Coubrough J.
Aug 7	A	Ross County	2,312	1-2	1	2	3	4	5	6	7	8	9	10	11	12[1]	14	15													
14	H	Queen of the South	630	0-3	1	14	3		2	6	7	8		9	4	10	12	5	11												
21	A	Stirling Albion	656	0-2	1	2	3		5	6		4		11	10	9	15				7	8	12								
28	A	Alloa Athletic	689	1-1	1		3		5	6		4		9	8[1]	10	14			2		11	7								
Sep 5	H	Stenhousemuir	445	1-1	1	14	3		5	6		4		9	7	10				2		8	11[1]								
11	H	Stranraer	503	2-1	1	12	3		5	8		4			10	9[1]				2		7	11[1]	6							
18	A	Partick Thistle	2,312	1-0	1	2	3		5	8		4	12		10	9	15				14	7	11	6[1]							
25	A	Clyde	865	1-2	1	2	3		5	8		4	12		10[1]	9	14					8	7	11							
Oct 2	A	Arbroath	489	2-2	1	2	3[1]		5	8		4			10[1]	9					14		7	11	6	12					
9	H	Ross County	392	1-0	1	2	3		5	6		4	12[1]		8	10				14			7	11			9				
16	H	Queen of the South	1,027	2-3	1	2	3		5	6		4			8[1]	10				12			7	11	14		9[1]				
30	A	Stranraer	454	2-0		2	3		5	6				14	10	9[1]	15						7	11	4		8[1]		1		
Nov 6	H	Partick Thistle	1,828	0-0		2	3		5	6				14	10	9				12			7	11	4		8		1		
10	A	Stenhousemuir	510	0-0		2	3		5	6				14	10	9				12			7	11	4		8		1		
16	H	Alloa Athletic	401	1-2		2	3		5	6			9[1]	15	10			4		12	14		7	11			8		1		
27	H	Arbroath	764	1-1			3		5	6			9[1]		10			4		2	14		7	11			8		1		
Dec 4	H	Clyde	731	2-3			3		5[1]	6		4	9[1]		10	14	15			2	12		7	11			8				
27	A	Stirling Albion	431	0-2	1	2	3			6		8		9	10		5				12	15	7	11	4						
Jan 3	A	Partick Thistle	2,755	2-2		2	3		14	6				15	9		5				10	7	8[1]	11[1]	4			1		12	
15	H	Stranraer	576	2-0	1		3		2	6							5[1]				8	15	7[1]	11	4	9	14		12	10	
22	A	Clyde	975	0-1	1				2	6							5				8		7	11	4	12	9			3	10
29	A	Ross County	1,860	1-0	1				2	6							5				8		7[1]	11	4	12	9			3	10
Feb 5	A	Arbroath	407	2-2	1				12	6[1]					9		5				8		7[1]	11	4		14			3	10
26	H	Queen of the South	553	1-1	1				3	6		2			14	12	5				8		7	11[1]	4		9				10
Mar 4	A	Stirling Albion	692	4-1	1				10	6					15[1]	14	5				8		12	11[1]	4		9[2]		3	7	
11	A	Stranraer	405	2-2	1				10	6		15			7	14	5				8			11[1]	4		9[1]		3		
14	H	Stenhousemuir	347	2-1	1				10[1]	6		3			7[1]	12	5				8		4	11			14	9			
18	H	Partick Thistle	2,223	0-1	1				10	6		3				9	5				8		4	11			12			7	
25	A	Alloa Athletic	508	0-0	1				3	6						8	5			10	14		4	11	4	12				7	9
Apr 4	A	Alloa Athletic	482	0-2					10	2		6	3	14			5					8		11	4			1		7	9
8	H	Clyde	851	1-1					10[1]	2		6	3	12			5					8	11	4	14			1		7	9
15	A	Arbroath	604	1-1					11	2		6	3	10		12	5					8		4				1		7	9[1]
18	A	Stenhousemuir	309	1-0					11[1]	2		6	3	10		4	5				15	8						1		7	9
22	H	Ross County	693	0-3					11	2		6	4				5	3				8		10			1		7	9	
29	A	Queen of the South	2,084	1-1					11			6	2	10	14		12	5	3			8		4			1		7[1]	9	
May 6	H	Stirling Albion	498	1-0			2			6			10[1]	14	11		5	3				15	8		4	12		1		7	9
TOTAL FULL APPEARANCES					23	15	31	1	30	36	2	22	8	6	19	20	22	4	6	12	4	30	27	21	8	8	13	5	15	15	8
TOTAL SUB APPEARANCES						(3)	(1)		(1)		(1)		(1)	(5)	(8)	(2)	(8)	(6)	(3)	(1)	(5)	(3)	(8)	(1)		(1)	(9)	(2)		(2)
TOTAL GOALS SCORED							4	1	1			5		6	3	1							4	6	1	1	4			1	1

Small bold figures denote goalscorers. † denotes opponent's own goal.

The Accies

email: info@sfl.scottishfootball.com • website: www.scottishfootball.com

Links Park Stadium,
Wellington Street,
Montrose, DD10 8QD

**ALL CORRESPONDENCE
SHOULD BE ADDRESSED TO:**
Malcolm J. Watters Esq.,
133 Murray Street, Montrose, DD10 8JQ

CHAIRMAN
John F. Paton

VICE-CHAIRMAN
Malcolm J. Watters

DIRECTORS
John D. Crawford & David I. Tait

HON. PRESIDENT
William Johnston, M.B.E., J.P.

SECRETARY
Malcolm J. Watters

ASSISTANT SECRETARY
Andrew Stephen

MATCHDAY SECRETARY
Iain Gordon

MANAGER
Kevin Drinkell

ASSISTANT MANAGER
John Sheran

YOUTH COACHES
Andy Milne (U16) & Nom Douglas

YOUTH CO-ORDINATOR
Graham Anderson

COMMERCIAL EXECUTIVE
Glynis Crawford (01674) 673758

CLUB DOCTOR
Dr. Matthew Howe

PHYSIOTHERAPIST
Allan Borthwick

KIT MANAGER
Brian Leiper

**FOOTBALL SAFETY OFFICERS'
ASSOCIATION REPRESENTATIVE**
Wilson Patrick (01674) 673200

GROUNDSMAN
Ron Marquis

MATCHDAY PROGRAMME EDITOR
Andrew Stephen
Bus (01356) 626766
Home (01674) 672314

TELEPHONES
Ground/Commercial (01674) 673200
Sec. Home (01674) 674838
Sec. Bus. (01674) 674941
Sec. Fax (01674) 677830
Ground Fax (01674) 677311

CLUB SHOP
Situated at Stadium (01674) 674941.
Open 10.30 a.m. – 5.00 p.m. Fri.
and on home matchdays

OFFICIAL SUPPORTERS CLUB
c/o Links Park, Wellington Street,
Montrose, DD10 8QD

TEAM CAPTAIN
Mark Craib

SHIRT SPONSOR
The Bervie Chipper

KIT SUPPLIER
SPALL

LIST OF PLAYERS 2000-2001

SURNAME	FIRST NAME	MIDDLE NAME	DATE OF BIRTH	PLACE OF BIRTH	DATE OF SIGNING	HEIGHT FT INS	WEIGHT ST LBS	POS. ON PITCH	PREVIOUS CLUB
Black	Martin	William	29/01/77	Forfar	19/11/99	6 0.0	11 6	Def	Forfar West End
Craib	Mark		08/02/70	St. Andrews	17/07/92	5 10.0	11 12	Def	Dundee
Dailly	Gareth	James	26/10/79	Dundee	31/03/00	5 11.0	11 0	Mid	Bankfoot Juniors
Ferguson	Stuart		09/11/80	Bangour	03/08/00	5 10.0	10 5	Def/Mid	Forfar Athletic
Harrison	Thomas	Edward	22/01/74	Edinburgh	03/09/99	5 9.0	11 8	Mid	East Fife
Lowe	Bradley		16/07/81	Dundee	24/05/00	6 0.0	11 2	Mid	Forfar Athletic
Mailer	Craig	James	27/09/67	Perth	20/02/95	5 11.0	11 7	Def	Kinnoull Juniors
Marwick	Steven	Gordon	11/09/81	Aberdeen	03/08/00	5 7.0	10 10	Mid	Aberdeen
McGlynn	Gary	Dominic	24/11/77	Falkirk	30/07/99	5 11.0	12 5	Gk	Dundee
McHattie	Keith		23/12/80	Aberdeen	15/03/99	5 10.0	10 8	Mid	Parkvale Juniors
McIlravey	Paul	James	11/04/79	Dundee	24/05/00	5 11.0	12 0	Fwd	Forfar Athletic
McKellar	James	Robert	29/12/76	Bellshill	24/05/00	5 8.0	11 0	Fwd	Forfar Athletic
McKenzie	Michael	Stancey	22/06/79	Aberdeen	03/08/00	6 1.0	13 7	Fwd	Lossiemouth
McWilliam	Ross	John	13/03/81	Aberdeen	29/08/98	5 10.0	11 7	Mid	Parkvale Juniors
Mitchell	Brian	Charles	29/02/68	Arbroath	05/02/00	5 9.0	12 2	Def	Arbroath
Mitchell	Jonathan	Andrew	22/06/81	Dundee	24/05/00	5 10.0	10 4	Fwd	Forfar Athletic
Muirhead	David		16/02/78	Stirling	24/05/00	6 0.0	13 0	Mid	East Stirlingshire
Niddrie	Kristopher		22/01/80	Aberdeen	29/08/98	6 0.0	11 12	Def	Glentanner Juniors
O'Driscoll	Jerry	William	04/04/78	Aberdeen	07/07/99	6 0.0	11 9	Fwd	Dundee
Ogboke	Christopher		18/02/82	Aberdeen	05/02/00	5 11.0	12 0	Fwd	Parkvale/Stoneywood U'18s
Robertson	Stuart	James	09/03/78	Aberdeen	30/07/99	5 7.0	9 11	Mid	Stonehaven Juniors
Scott	Walter	Douglas	01/01/64	Dundee	17/07/99	5 9.0	10 7	Mid	Arbroath
Shand	Martin	Graham	27/06/80	Aberdeen	19/11/98	5 11.0	11 10	Fwd	Stonehaven Juniors
Snedden	Scott		07/12/71	Dechmont	15/08/00	6 4.0	14 0	Def	Cowdenbeath
Thompson	Barry	Crawford	12/07/75	Glasgow	28/07/00	6 2.0	13 0	Gk	Ross County
Young	John		11/03/81	Aberdeen	16/05/00	6 1.0	12 5	Def	Parkvale/Stoneywood U'18s

Milestones

YEAR OF FORMATION: 1879
MOST CAPPED PLAYER: Sandy Keiller
NO. OF CAPS: 6 (2 whilst with Montrose)
MOST LEAGUE POINTS IN A SEASON: 53 (Division 2 – 1974/75 and Second Division 1984/85) (2 Points for a Win)
67 (Third Division – Season 1994/95) (3 Points for a Win)
RECORD ATTENDANCE: 8,983 (-v- Dundee – 17.3.1973)
RECORD VICTORY: 12-0 (-v- Vale of Leithen – Scottish Cup, 4.1.1975)
RECORD DEFEAT: 0-13 (-v- Aberdeen, 17.3.1951)

The Gable Endies' ten year league record

	90/91	91/92	92/93	93/94	94/95	95/96	96/97	97/98	98/99	99/00
	2nd Div	1st Div	2nd Div	2nd Div	3rd Div	2nd Div	3rd Div	3rd Div	3rd Div	3rd Div

THE GABLE ENDIES' CLUB FACTFILE 1999/2000
RESULTS... APPEARANCES... SCORERS... ATTENDANCES...

Date	Venue	Opponents	Att	Res	McClymn G.	Mailer C.	Scott W.D.	Farnan C.	Paterson G.	Craib M.	Shand M.	Duffy K.	Taylor S.	McWilliam R.	Meldrum G.	Niddrie K.	Stevenson C.	Dorward R.	Clark S.	Bennett J.N.	O'Driscoll J.	Robertson S.	Harrison T.	Craig M.	Craib S.	Craig D.	Black M.	Ogboke C.	Mitchell B.	Jackson C.	Young J.	Fitzpatrick F.	Daily G.
Aug 7	H	Cowdenbeath	275	0-1	1		2	3	4	5	6	7	8	9	10	11	12	14	15														
14	A	Dumbarton	436	4-3	1		3	4¹	5	6		7		9	14	11				2	8	10³											
21	H	Berwick Rangers	313	1-2	1		3	4	5	6	14	7¹	9	12	11				2		10	8											
28	A	East Fife	512	0-0	1		3	4	5	6	7	8	9	12	11	14	15		2		10												
Sep 4	H	East Stirlingshire	278	1-2	1		3	8	5¹	6	14	7	10	2	12	15								4	9	11							
11	A	Albion Rovers	243	3-1	1	8	3	4		6		7	10¹	12	15¹	5			2			14		9	11¹								
18	H	Brechin City	512	0-1	1	8	3	11	4	6		7	9	14	15	5			2			12		10								
28	H	Forfar Athletic	281	2-0	1	8¹	3	4	5	6	12	14	9¹	10	11				2			7										
Oct 2	A	Queen's Park	688	1-2	1	8	3	4	5	6	12	14	9¹	10	11				2							7						
16	H	Dumbarton	274	1-4	1	7¹	3	8		6	14	9	10	11	5				2		15				12	4						
23	A	Cowdenbeath	254	1-1	1	8	3	4		6	14	10	9¹		12	5				15	7			11	2							
30	H	Albion Rovers	261	2-1	1	8	3	4		6	7¹	14	9	12	15	5				10¹				11	2							
Nov 6	A	Brechin City	366	0-1	1	4	3			6	7	8	9	12	5					10				11	2							
14	A	East Stirlingshire	241	0-2	1	4	3			6		7	9	14	11					10	8					2	5					
20	H	East Fife	440	†1-2	1	8	4		5	6		14	9	11						10	7					2	3	14				
27	H	Queen's Park	424	2-1	1	8	11¹		5	6			9¹	7						10	4		12			2	3					
Dec 7	A	Forfar Athletic	379	2-1	1	7			5	6¹			11	8						10	4		9	15¹		2	3					
18	H	Cowdenbeath	318	1-3	1	8			5	6	14		11	7						10	4		9¹	12		2	3					
27	A	Berwick Rangers	472	0-0	1	8			5	6	12		11	7	14					10	4		9			2	3					
Jan 3	H	Brechin City	798	1-0	1	7	8		5				11	4	6					10	12		9		2¹	3						
22	A	Forfar Athletic	588	1-5	1	4	8		5	6		15	11¹	2	12					10	7		9				3	14				
Feb 5	A	Queen's Park	505	1-1	1				5	6			7	11¹		4	10	15		9				3	14	2	8				
15	A	East Fife	390	0-2	1				5	6		8	7	11	12	4	10	15		14				3	9	2					
19	H	East Stirlingshire	327	0-0	1		4		5	6	7		10	11		8				9				3	12	2					
26	A	Dumbarton	482	2-3	1		4		5	6	7¹	15	10¹	11	14	8				2			9			3					
Mar 4	H	Berwick Rangers	302	2-3	1		4¹		5	6	7		9	11		8	10¹						3	12	2					2		
7	A	Albion Rovers	159	2-0	1		4	7¹	5¹	6			9	11		8	10	15					3	14	2					2		
11	H	Albion Rovers	329	1-2	1		4	7		6	15		9¹	11	3	8	10	2			14				5	12						
18	A	Brechin City	360	0-0			7		6	14			11		5	8	10	4		9				3	12	2						
25	H	East Fife	442	1-1	1		4	11		6	15		10¹	7	5	8		12		9				3	14	2						
Apr 1	A	East Stirlingshire	205	0-1	1		4	7		6			10	11	5	8	9			14				3	15	2						
8	A	Forfar Athletic	516	2-1	1		4	10		6¹			11	7	5	8¹	9							3			2					
15	H	Queen's Park	393	0-2	1		4	10		6	14	15	11	7	5	8	9							3	12	2						
22	A	Cowdenbeath	252	1-2			7		4	6		15	11¹	10	5	8	14		9				3			2	1					
29	H	Dumbarton	267	2-1	1		7			6	14		10¹	11	5	8	12						3	9¹		2						4
May 6	A	Berwick Rangers	1,224	1-2	1		7			4		14	10¹	11	5	8	12	15		3				9	2						6	
TOTAL FULL APPEARANCES					35	29	25	12	24	33	7	11	35	27	11	13			8	16	20	13	1	15	6	12	23	3	6	1	7	1	2
TOTAL SUB APPEARANCES											(11)	(11)			(8)	(9)	(3)	(2)	(1)		(4)	(9)		(4)	(3)				(11)			
TOTAL GOALS SCORED						3	2	1	2	2	2	1	12	1	1				1	5				1	2	1				1			

Small bold figures denote goalscorers. † denotes opponent's own goal.

Links Park Stadium

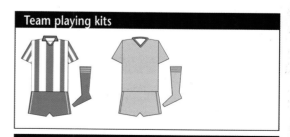

WELLINGTON PARK

UNION ROW

WELLINGTON STREET

CAPACITY: 4,338; Seated 1,338, Standing 3,000
PITCH DIMENSIONS: 110 yds x 70 yds
FACILITIES FOR DISABLED SUPPORTERS:
Area set aside for wheelchairs and designated area in new stand.

Team playing kits

How to get there

Links Park can be reached by the following routes:

TRAINS: Montrose is on the Inter-City 125 route from London to Aberdeen and also on the Glasgow-Aberdeen route. There is a regular service and the station is about 15 minutes walk from the ground.

BUSES: An hourly service of buses from Aberdeen and Dundee stop in the town centre and it is a 15 minute walk from here to the ground.

CARS: Car parking is available in the car park at the ground and there are numerous side streets all round the park which can be used if necessary.

email: info@sfl.scottishfootball.com • website: www.scottishfootball.com

Peterhead

Balmoor Stadium, Lord Catto Park, Balmoor Terrace, Peterhead, AB42 1EU

CHAIRMAN
Rodger Taylor

VICE-CHAIRMAN
Rodger Morrison

DIRECTORS
Colin Grant, George Watson,
Gerry Gaffney, Gordon MacGregor

MANAGEMENT COMMITTEE
Dave Watson, Arthur Duncan,
George Moore

SECRETARY
George Moore

GENERAL MANAGER
Dave Watson

MANAGER
Ian Wilson

ASSISTANT MANAGER
Alan Lyons

YOUTH DEVELOPMENT OFFICER
John Sievewright

YOUTH COACHES
Nat Porter & Walter Innes

CLUB DOCTOR
Dr. Ian Small

PHYSIOTHERAPIST
Jennifer Johnson

ACCOUNTS
Shona Aird

**FOOTBALL SAFETY OFFICERS'
ASSOCIATION REPRESENTATIVE**
Arthur Duncan (01779) 873171

STADIUM & GROUND MAINTENANCE
Jack Wilson

COMMERCIAL MANAGER
Colin Grant (01358) 724270

KIT MAN
William Spence

MEDIA LIAISON OFFICERS
Dave Watson (01224) 771100 &
George Watson (01224) 820851

MATCHDAY PROGRAMME EDITOR
Colin Grant (01358) 724270

TELEPHONES
Ground (01779) 478256
Fax (01779) 490682
Sec. Bus. (01224) 820851
Sec. Home (01779) 476870

OFFICIAL SUPPORTERS CLUB
c/o Balmoor Stadium,
Peterhead, AB42 1EU

TEAM CAPTAIN
Steve King

SHIRT SPONSOR
ASCO UK

KIT SUPPLIER
RIVA

LIST OF PLAYERS 2000-2001

SURNAME	FIRST NAME	MIDDLE NAME	DATE OF BIRTH	PLACE OF BIRTH	DATE OF SIGNING	HEIGHT FT INS	WEIGHT ST LBS	POS. ON PITCH	PREVIOUS CLUB
Brown	Scott	Edward A.	19/02/68	Aberdeen	03/08/00	5 6.0	11 0	Mid	Unattached
Buchanan	Ross	Alexander	20/10/80	Aberdeen	01/08/00	6 1.0	15 0	Gk	Buchanhaven Hearts Juniors
Clark	Gary		01/11/71	Aberdeen	03/08/00	5 10.0	12 3	Fwd	Unattached
Clark	Scott	Norman	24/04/72	Aberdeen	01/08/00	5 8.0	11 2	Def	Unattached
Cooper	Craig		17/01/73	Arbroath	14/09/00	5 10.0	10 13	Mid	Arbroath
Craig	David	Charles	23/06/77	Dundee	03/08/00	5 10.0	11 0	Mid	Hong Kong Rangers
Davidson	Neil	Iain	22/03/83	Aberdeen	08/09/00	5 7.0	10 3	Mid	Westhill B.C.
De-Barros	Marco		18/08/71	London	14/08/00	5 10.0	11 0	Fwd	Huntly
Gibson	Andrew	Mitchell	02/02/69	Broxburn	01/08/00	5 9.0	11 12	Mid	Forfar Athletic
Gilbert	Scott		26/08/83	Aberdeen	08/09/00	5 10.0	10 6	Mid	Westhill B.C.
Herd	William	David	03/09/65	Buckhaven	03/08/00	5 11.0	13 0	Def	East Fife
Johnston	Martin		24/06/78	Aberdeen	03/08/00	6 2.0	12 0	Mid	Cove Rangers
Keddie	Joel		04/05/83	Aberdeen	03/08/00	6 0.0	14 10	Fwd	Westhill B.C.
King	Steven	Charles	06/04/67	Aberdeen	03/08/00	5 11.0	12 7	Def	Unattached
Leyden	Craig		16/03/83	Inverness	06/09/00	6 1.0	11 8	Def	Westhill B.C.
Livingstone	Richard		10/04/74	Aberdeen	01/08/00	5 11.0	12 4	Fwd	Unattached
Mars	Vince		21/06/83	Essex	06/09/00	5 10.0	10 8	Fwd	Westhill B.C.
Morrison	Bruce	Schaedel	27/09/64	Aberdeen	01/08/00	5 10.0	11 10	Def	Montrose
Ness	Christopher		09/01/83	Glasgow	06/09/00	5 5.0	9 1	Def	Westhill B.C.
Paterson	Scott	Thomas	13/05/72	Aberdeen	04/08/00	6 2.0	12 12	Mid	Plymouth Argyle
Pirie	Ivor	Douglas L.	30/06/64	Inverurie	01/08/00	6 0.0	13 0	Gk	Unattached
Simpson	Mark		04/11/75	Aberdeen	01/08/00	5 11.0	12 6	Def	Unattached
Smith	Derek		15/02/75	Falkirk	03/08/00	6 1.0	12 0	Fwd	Unattached
Tindall	Kevin	Douglas	11/04/71	Arbroath	14/09/00	5 8.0	12 4	Mid	Arbroath
Warman	Steven		18/08/83	Aberdeen	06/09/00	5 11.0	11 2	Def	Westhill B.C.
Watson	Craig	John R.	02/05/71	Aberdeen	01/08/00	5 11.0	11 7	Def	Unattached
Yeats	Craig		28/09/69	Aberdeen	18/08/00	5 9.0	12 9	Mid	Unattached

Milestones

YEAR OF FORMATION: 1891

MOST CAPPED PLAYER: – None

MOST LEAGUE POINTS IN A SEASON: 89 (Highland League – Season 1989/90)

MOST LEAGUE GOALS SCORED BY A PLAYER IN A SEASON: J. Patterson

NO. OF GOALS SCORED: 42

RECORD ATTENDANCE: 6,310 (-v- Celtic – 1948)

RECORD VICTORY: 17-0 (-v- Fort William – Season 1998/99)

RECORD DEFEAT: 0-13 (-v- Aberdeen, Scottish Cup, Season 1923/24)

S·F·L

PETERHEAD F.C. – A Brief History
FORMED 1891

HONOURS

Highland League Champions:
1946/47, 1948/49, 1949/50, 1988/89, 1998/99

Highland League Cup Winners: 1962/63, 1965/66, 1967/68, 1980/81, 1988/89

Scottish Qualifying Cup (North) Winners: 1946/47, 1975/76, 1977/78, 1978/79, 1985/86, 1997/98

Aberdeenshire Cup Winners: 1905/06, 1934/35, 1935/36, 1946/47, 1948/49, 1949/50, 1958/59, 1962/63, 1964/65, 1967/68, 1968/69, 1969/70, 1970/71, 1974/75, 1976/77, 1978/79, 1984/85, 1987/88, 1988/89, 1998/99

Within the annals of the town history, organised football is first recorded as taking place at Peterhead Links in the 1870's. It was in 1890 though that a body of enthusiasts formed a committee to oversee the promotion of football within the accorded rules and regulations of the governing Scottish Football Association. Peterhead Football Club was born. Similarly at this time, moves were accelerated to secure an enclosed playing area with the provision of changing facilities for all playing participants.

With the assistance of the town's Feuars Managers, an area of ground was made available from the 14 acres of Raemoss Park. This new enclosed facility was named Recreation Park and was opened by Dunfermline born philanthropist Andrew Carnegie in August, 1891.

Nine years later, Peterhead became members of the Aberdeenshire Football Association, and by so doing became affiliated members of the S.F.A. The season then was extremely short, only six teams taking part in the Aberdeenshire League and Aberdeen Football Club joining them for the Aberdeenshire County Cup.

Peterhead were to have their first trophy success in season 1905/06 winning the County Cup. There were no further successes for the club until the 1930's and again it was the same Cup. The following year Peterhead gained admission to the Highland League. This move was to make a large difference to the duration of the playing season, the team now competing in the Highland Football League, Qualifying Cup and Aberdeenshire Cup, with the second eleven taking part in the old Aberdeenshire League.

This era of North football was to see the advent of the "Player/Coach". Peterhead were fortunate to secure the services of former Falkirk, Leeds United and Scotland centre-half Tom Townsley. The football world was, of course, then about to be interrupted from 1939 until 1946 by World War Two. Percy Dickie, formerly of Aberdeen and Blackburn Rovers, was then to take over as coach. A great favourite with the fans, Percy's tenure was to coincide with great success for the club with the Blue Toon winning seven trophies in four years, including Highland League Championship titles in seasons 1946/47, 1948/49 and 1949/50. The club at this time was privately owned, having been reformed after the war by 14 directors with a cash injection of £250 each. This administration was to continue until 1954, when the club was then reformed to being run by a Management Committee elected by supporters, who by payment of a membership fee (2/6d) became club members. This administration was to continue until 1993 when the club was to change to the present status of a Private Limited Company.

The Seventies saw Highland League clubs take a more professional outlook to improving standards with all clubs seeing the benefits of employing team managers and fully qualified coaching staff. The club's first manager was the former Hibernian player from the late sixties, Colin Grant, now a Director and also Commercial Manager at the club. Colin had early success as team boss winning the Scottish Qualifying Cup three times in four years with victories in back to back Cup Finals against Inverness Caledonian (1977/78) and Inverness Thistle (1978/79). Peterhead since that time have been fortunate to have a number of former international players at the helm with Joe Harper (ex Aberdeen, Everton & Hibernian), Dave Smith (ex Rangers) both having spells at the club with Ian Wilson (ex Leicester City, Everton, Derby County) currently in charge at Balmoor Stadium. Another top player to have managed the club was Jim Hamilton (ex Aberdeen) who also had great success as team manager. More recent achievements under former Highland League players Dave Watson and Ronnie Brown have also brought glory to the club.

COLIN GRANT
(Director and Comercial Secretary)

Balmoor Stadium

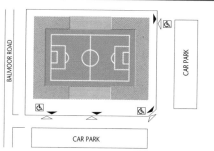

CAPACITY: 3,250; Seated 1,000, Standing 2,250

PITCH DIMENSIONS: 105 yds x 70 yds

FACILITIES FOR DISABLED SUPPORTERS:
Designated area in new stand

Team playing kits

How to get there

Balmoor Stadium can be reached by the following routes:
TRAINS: The nearest Train Station is Aberdeen. From Aberdeen you would have to travel by bus to Peterhead. Travel time 1 hour.
BUSES: Buses leave Aberdeen City every hour for Peterhead. Travel time 1 hour.
CARS: From Aberdeen City: Take A90 to Peterhead, at first roundabout approaching Peterhead take a left at McDonalds to St Fergus (still on A90). Continue on this road to next roundabout - go straight on to the next T-junction. Take right A980 back into Peterhead - continue on A980 through next roundabout and Balmoor Stadium is about ½ mile past the roundabout on the right hand side.

ALBION ROVERS
SEASON TICKET INFORMATION

SEATED	ADULT	£80
	OAP/UNEMPLOYED	£40
	12-16 YEARS	£20
	UNDER 12'S (FREE ADMISSION TO FIRST 250)	
STANDING	ADULT	£80

LEAGUE ADMISSION PRICES

SEATED	ADULT	£7
	JUVENILE/OAP	£4
STANDING	ADULT	£6
	JUVENILE/OAP	£3

DUMBARTON
SEASON TICKET INFORMATION

SEATED		
BUSINESS CLUB	ADULT/JUVENILE/OAP	£150+VAT
STAND	ADULT	£75
	JUVENILE/OAP	£35
	PARENT & JUVENILE	£100
	FAMILY OF FOUR	£160

LEAGUE ADMISSION PRICES

SEATED	ADULT	£7
	JUVENILE/OAP	£3.50

PRICES FOR SEASON TICKETS AND ADMISSION WILL BE AS ABOVE FOR ALL MATCHES AT CLIFTONHILL STADIUM AND THE NEW STADIUM. PLEASE NOTE HOWEVER, THERE IS NO GUARANTEE OF A SEAT WHILE THE CLUB IS PLAYING ITS HOME MATCHES AT CLIFTONHILL.

BRECHIN CITY
SEASON TICKET INFORMATION

SEATED	ADULT	£110
	PARENT & JUVENILE (UNDER 12)	£130
	OAP	£65
	JUVENILE	£40

LEAGUE ADMISSION PRICES

SEATED	ADULT	£7
	JUVENILE/OAP	£3
ENCLOSURE	ADULT	£7
	JUVENILE/OAP	£3
STANDING	ADULT	£7
	JUVENILE/OAP	£3
	PARENT & JUVENILE	£8

EAST FIFE
SEASON TICKET INFORMATION

SEATED	ADULT	£140
	JUVENILE/OAP	£70
	PARENT & JUVENILE	£200

LEAGUE ADMISSION PRICES

SEATED	ADULT	£8.50
	JUVENILE/OAP	£4

COWDENBEATH
SEASON TICKET INFORMATION

SEATED	ADULT	£100
	JUVENILE/OAP	£50
STANDING	ADULT	£100
	JUVENILE/OAP	£50

LEAGUE ADMISSION PRICES

SEATED	ADULT	£8
	JUVENILE/OAP	£3.50
STANDING	ADULT	£7
	JUVENILE/OAP	£3

EAST STIRLINGSHIRE
SEASON TICKET INFORMATION

SEATED	ADULT	£110
OR STANDING	CONCESSIONS*	£60
	FAMILY TICKET	£140

LEAGUE ADMISSION PRICES

SEATED	ADULT	£9
	JUVENILE/OAP	£5.50
STANDING	ADULT	£7
	CONCESSIONS*	£3.50

* Concessionary tickets allow OAPs, Juveniles, UB40 holders, Students and people with long term illness to be admitted to ground at the stated concessionary price. Production of DSS Benefit book or similar documentary proof required.

ELGIN CITY
SEASON TICKET INFORMATION
SEATED
ADULT	£120
JUVENILE /OAP	£55

STANDING
ADULT	£100
JUVENILE /OAP	£35

LEAGUE ADMISSION PRICES
SEATED
ADULT	£7
JUVENILE /OAP	£3

STANDING
ADULT	£6
JUVENILE /OAP	£2

MONTROSE
SEASON TICKET INFORMATION
SEATED OR STANDING	ADULT	£105
	JUVENILE/OAP	£55
	FAMILY- (1 ADULT & 1 JUVENILE)	£125

LEAGUE ADMISSION PRICES
STANDING	ADULT	£7
	JUVENILE/OAP	£3.50
	STAND TRANSFER	50p

HAMILTON ACADEMICAL
SEASON TICKET INFORMATION
SEATED
ADULT	£140
JUVENILE /OAP	£70
JUVENILE (U-14)	£35

LEAGUE ADMISSION PRICES
SEATED
ADULT	£10
U-16/SENIOR CITIZEN	£5

Elgin City's Borough Briggs Stadium

Peterhead's Balmoor Stadium

PETERHEAD
SEASON TICKET INFORMATION
SEATED
ADULT	£120
ADULT & JUVENILE	£180
OAP	£60

STANDING
ADULT	£100
JUVENILE /OAP	£50

LEAGUE ADMISSION PRICES
SEATED
ADULT	£7.50
JUVENILE /OAP	£4

STANDING
ADULT	£6
JUVENILE /OAP	£3

Playing the Supporting Role

The Scottish Federation of Football Supporters' Clubs was established to represent members of supporters clubs and to raise matters of concern with football clubs and the relevant governing bodies. In addition, it represents members of supporters clubs to local and national government. The Federation is recognised for consultative purposes by The Scottish Football Association, The Scottish Football League and The Scottish Premier League. Until 1992 when it became a purely Scottish organisation, it had been a member of the United Kingdom National Federation of Football Supporters' Clubs.

Its current membership includes Supporters' Clubs or Associations from Aberdeen, Airdrieonians, Arbroath, Ayr United, Celtic, Dumbarton, Dunfermline Athletic, Dundee United, Heart of Midlothian, Hibernian, Inverness Caledonian Thistle, Kilmarnock, Livingston, Lossiemouth, Motherwell, Partick Thistle, Queen of the South and St. Mirren. Members meet every two months at locations throughout the country. Through an arrangement with the National Federation of Football Supporters' Clubs in England and Wales, it offers Personal Accident Insurance cover for its members and cover for supporters' teams.

As part of its advocacy and campaigning role, the Federation has in the past made submissions to The Scottish Football League and The Scottish Premier League on various League reconstruction proposals; on safety matters by providing evidence to the Commissions of Inquiry chaired by Lord Justice Taylor (Hillsborough) and Justice Popplewell (Bradford); and on a range of other matters such as policies and practices in relation to the late cancellation of matches, the timing of matches particularly in relation to televised matches and ticketing arrangements for major matches. Although there has been some success in relation to certain of these matters, the Federation will continue to lobby the relevant bodies as necessary.

As well as formal contacts, the Federation also maintains dialogue with the game's governing bodies by welcoming guest speakers to its meetings. Recent guests have included Willie McDougall, The Scottish Football Association's Security Adviser, Iain Blair of The Scottish Premier League, George Cumming, the Association's former Referee Development Director, who is now in charge of refereeing matters at FIFA, and Calum Grant, Ross County's Director of Coaching. The Federation, through the involvement of one of its office bearers, participated in the Independent Review Commission established by The Scottish Football Association under the chairmanship of Ernie Walker C.B.E. and the current Secretary is a member of The Scottish Football Association's Arbitration Panel.

There is no doubt that the football map both nationally and internationally is likely to change significantly in the near future. Issues such as the abolition of transfer fees as they are currently structured; the possible establishment of new pan-European Leagues; the financial stability and long-term viability of some of our clubs; the control and management of clubs and the continuing impact that television will have on the game as it operates currently. These and other issues are of great concern to supporters particularly those who, as members of supporters clubs, travel to watch their teams both home and away. It is the Federation's objective to ensure when matters affecting football fans are considered that the views and opinions of supporters are taken into account. In this connection, the Federation will work with other supporters' groups who seek to influence the game's governing bodies and central and local government.

MARTIN H. ROSE
(Secretary of The Scottish Federation of Football Supporters' Clubs)

For further information on The Scottish Federation of Football Supporters' Clubs, please write to Martin H. Rose, Secretary, 4 Bowling Green Road, Strathaven, ML10 6DP.

S.F.L. and S.P.L. – Final Tables 1999/2000

BELL'S S.F.L. FIRST DIVISION

	P	W	L	D	F	A	PTS
ST. MIRREN	36	23	6	7	75	39	76
DUNFERMLINE ATHLETIC	36	20	5	11	66	33	71
FALKIRK	36	20	8	8	67	40	68
LIVINGSTON	36	19	10	7	60	45	64
RAITH ROVERS	36	17	11	8	55	40	59
INVERNESS CAL. THISTLE	36	13	13	10	60	55	49
AYR UNITED	36	10	18	8	42	52	38
MORTON	36	10	20	6	45	61	36
AIRDRIEONIANS	36	7	21	8	29	69	29
CLYDEBANK	36	1	28	7	17	82	10

BELL'S S.F.L. SECOND DIVISION

	P	W	L	D	F	A	PTS
CLYDE	36	18	7	11	65	37	65
ALLOA ATHLETIC	36	17	6	13	58	38	64
ROSS COUNTY	36	18	10	8	57	39	62
ARBROATH	36	11	11	14	52	55	47
PARTICK THISTLE	36	12	14	10	42	44	46
STRANRAER	36	9	9	18	47	46	45
STIRLING ALBION	36	11	18	7	60	72	40
STENHOUSEMUIR	36	10	18	8	44	59	38
QUEEN OF THE SOUTH	36	8	19	9	45	75	33
HAMILTON ACADEMICAL ***	36	10	12	14	39	44	29

*** 15 POINTS DEDUCTED FOR HAMILTON ACADEMICAL F.C. FAILING TO FULFIL ITS FIXTURE AGAINST STENHOUSEMUIR F.C. ON SATURDAY, 1ST APRIL, 2000

BELL'S S.F.L. THIRD DIVISION

	P	W	L	D	F	A	PTS
QUEEN'S PARK	36	20	7	9	54	37	69
BERWICK RANGERS	36	19	8	9	53	30	66
FORFAR ATHLETIC	36	17	9	10	64	40	61
EAST FIFE	36	17	11	8	45	39	59
COWDENBEATH	36	15	12	9	59	43	54
DUMBARTON	36	15	13	8	53	51	53
EAST STIRLINGSHIRE	36	11	18	7	28	50	40
BRECHIN CITY	36	10	18	8	42	51	38
MONTROSE	36	10	19	7	39	54	37
ALBION ROVERS	36	5	24	7	33	75	22

BANK OF SCOTLAND SCOTTISH PREMIER LEAGUE

	P	W	L	D	F	A	PTS
RANGERS	36	28	2	6	96	26	90
CELTIC	36	21	9	6	90	38	69
HEART OF MIDLOTHIAN	36	15	12	9	47	40	54
MOTHERWELL	36	14	12	10	49	63	52
ST. JOHNSTONE	36	10	14	12	36	44	42
HIBERNIAN	36	10	15	11	49	61	41
DUNDEE	36	12	19	5	45	64	41
DUNDEE UNITED	36	11	19	6	34	57	39
KILMARNOCK	36	8	15	13	38	52	37
ABERDEEN	36	9	21	6	44	83	33

RESERVE LEAGUE EAST

	P	W	L	D	F	A	PTS
DUNFERMLINE ATHLETIC	21	17	4	0	68	16	51
INVERNESS CAL. THISTLE	21	11	7	3	49	38	36
ARBROATH	21	10	7	4	35	25	34
RAITH ROVERS	21	9	6	6	31	24	33
FORFAR ATHLETIC	21	8	8	5	33	30	29
MONTROSE	21	7	11	3	34	54	24
BRECHIN CITY	21	5	12	4	32	59	19
EAST FIFE	21	3	15	3	18	54	12

RESERVE LEAGUE WEST

	P	W	L	D	F	A	PTS
AYR UNITED	18	12	2	4	53	20	40
LIVINGSTON	18	8	3	7	43	19	31
STRANRAER	18	9	6	3	27	31	30
MORTON	18	4	4	10	29	28	22
CLYDE	18	5	10	3	24	41	18
ST. MIRREN	18	3	8	7	21	34	16
QUEEN'S PARK	18	3	11	4	22	46	13

YOUTH DIVISION "A"

	P	W	L	D	F	A	PTS
CELTIC	18	14	3	1	47	20	43
DUNDEE UNITED	18	9	3	6	31	20	33
HEART OF MIDLOTHIAN	18	8	6	4	28	27	28
ABERDEEN	18	6	5	7	25	32	25
ST. JOHNSTONE	18	7	8	3	29	30	24
DUNDEE	18	6	8	4	26	24	22
RANGERS	18	5	6	7	22	21	22
KILMARNOCK	18	7	11	0	26	36	21
HIBERNIAN	18	5	10	3	27	41	18
MOTHERWELL	18	3	10	5	20	30	14

YOUTH DIVISION "B"

	P	W	L	D	F	A	PTS
AIRDRIEONIANS	27	21	1	5	78	26	68
PARTICK THISTLE	27	18	6	3	65	39	57
MORTON	27	15	6	6	77	42	51
* ROSS COUNTY	26	13	7	6	47	32	45
QUEEN OF THE SOUTH	27	14	12	1	49	55	43
ST. MIRREN	27	7	15	5	44	54	26
CLYDE	27	6	14	7	46	54	25
ALBION ROVERS	27	6	16	5	40	67	23
* DUMBARTON	26	6	16	4	32	75	22
STIRLING ALBION	27	6	19	2	38	72	20

*DUMBARTON F.C AND ROSS COUNTY F.C. WERE UNABLE TO FULFIL THEIR FINAL FIXTURE

YOUTH DIVISION "C"

	P	W	L	D	F	A	PTS
FALKIRK	27	21	3	3	67	29	66
ARBROATH	27	16	5	6	65	45	54
RAITH ROVERS	27	13	8	6	58	39	45
FORFAR ATHLETIC	27	12	8	7	42	37	43
STENHOUSEMUIR	27	10	11	6	38	40	36
BERWICK RANGERS	27	9	13	5	46	43	32
DUNFERMLINE ATHLETIC	27	9	13	5	50	54	32
EAST STIRLINGSHIRE	27	9	13	5	34	50	32
COWDENBEATH	27	5	12	10	34	39	25
ALLOA ATHLETIC	27	3	21	3	26	84	12

Scottish League

SEASON	DIVISION ONE	POINTS	DIVISION TWO	POINTS
1890/91	Dumbarton/Rangers	29	(No Competition)	
1891/92	Dumbarton	37	(No Competition)	
1892/93	Celtic	29	(No Competition)	
1893/94	Celtic	29	Hibernian	29
1894/95	Heart of Midlothian	31	Hibernian	30
1895/96	Celtic	30	Abercorn	27
1896/97	Heart of Midlothian	28	Partick Thistle	31
1897/98	Celtic	33	Kilmarnock	29
1898/99	Rangers	36	Kilmarnock	32
1899-1900	Rangers	32	Partick Thistle	29
1900/01	Rangers	35	St. Bernards	25
1901/02	Rangers	28	Port Glasgow	32
1902/03	Hibernian	37	Airdrieonians	35
1903/04	Third Lanark	43	Hamilton Academical	37
1904/05	Celtic (after play-off)	41	Clyde	32
1905/06	Celtic	49	Leith Athletic	34
1906/07	Celtic	55	St. Bernards	32
1907/08	Celtic	55	Raith Rovers	30
1908/09	Celtic	51	Abercorn	31
1909/10	Celtic	54	Leith Athletic	33
1910/11	Rangers	52	Dumbarton	31
1911/12	Rangers	51	Ayr United	35
1912/13	Rangers	53	Ayr United	34
1913/14	Celtic	65	Cowdenbeath	31
1914/15	Celtic	65	Cowdenbeath	37
1915/16	Celtic	67	(No Competition)	
1916/17	Celtic	64	(No Competition)	
1917/18	Rangers	56	(No Competition)	
1918/19	Celtic	58	(No Competition)	
1919/20	Rangers	71	(No Competition)	
1920/21	Rangers	76	(No Competition)	
1921/22	Celtic	67	Alloa	60
1922/23	Rangers	55	Queen's Park	57
1923/24	Rangers	59	St. Johnstone	56
1924/25	Rangers	60	Dundee United	50
1925/26	Celtic	58	Dunfermline Athletic	59
1926/27	Rangers	56	Bo'ness	56
1927/28	Rangers	60	Ayr United	54
1928/29	Rangers	67	Dundee United	51
1929/30	Rangers	60	Leith Athletic*	57
1930/31	Rangers	60	Third Lanark	61
1931/32	Motherwell	66	East Stirlingshire*	55
1932/33	Rangers	62	Hibernian	54
1933/34	Rangers	66	Albion Rovers	45
1934/35	Rangers	55	Third Lanark	52
1935/36	Celtic	66	Falkirk	59
1936/37	Rangers	61	Ayr United	54
1937/38	Celtic	61	Raith Rovers	59
1938/39	Rangers	59	Cowdenbeath	60
Seasons 1939/40 to 1945/46 - (No Competition)				
1946/47	Rangers	46	Dundee	45
1947/48	Hibernian	48	East Fife	53
1948/49	Rangers	46	Raith Rovers*	42
1949/50	Rangers	50	Morton	47
1950/51	Hibernian	48	Queen of the South*	45
1951/52	Hibernian	45	Clyde	44

Champions since 1890

SEASON	DIVISION ONE	POINTS	DIVISION TWO	POINTS
1952/53	Rangers*	43	Stirling Albion	44
1953/54	Celtic	43	Motherwell	45
1954/55	Aberdeen	49	Airdrieonians	46
1955/56	Rangers	52	Queen's Park	54
1956/57	Rangers	55	Clyde	64
1957/58	Heart of Midlothian	62	Stirling Albion	55
1958/59	Rangers	50	Ayr United	60
1959/60	Heart of Midlothian	54	St. Johnstone	53
1960/61	Rangers	51	Stirling Albion	55
1961/62	Dundee	54	Clyde	54
1962/63	Rangers	57	St. Johnstone	55
1963/64	Rangers	55	Morton	67
1964/65	Kilmarnock*	50	Stirling Albion	59
1965/66	Celtic	57	Ayr United	53
1966/67	Celtic	58	Morton	69
1967/68	Celtic	63	St. Mirren	62
1968/69	Celtic	54	Motherwell	64
1969/70	Celtic	57	Falkirk	56
1970/71	Celtic	56	Partick Thistle	56
1971/72	Celtic	60	Dumbarton¥	52
1972/73	Celtic	57	Clyde	56
1973/74	Celtic	53	Airdrieonians	60
1974/75	Rangers	56	Falkirk	54

SEASON	PREMIER DIVISION	POINTS	FIRST DIVISION	POINTS	SECOND DIVISION	POINTS	THIRD DIVISION	POINTS
1975/76	Rangers	54	Partick Thistle	41	Clydebank¥	40		
1976/77	Celtic	55	St. Mirren	62	Stirling Albion	55		
1977/78	Rangers	55	Morton¥	58	Clyde¥	53		
1978/79	Celtic	48	Dundee	55	Berwick Rangers	54		
1979/80	Aberdeen	48	Heart of Midlothian	53	Falkirk	50		
1980/81	Celtic	56	Hibernian	57	Queen's Park	50		
1981/82	Celtic	55	Motherwell	61	Clyde	59		
1982/83	Dundee United	56	St. Johnstone	55	Brechin City	55		
1983/84	Aberdeen	57	Morton	54	Forfar Athletic	63		
1984/85	Aberdeen	59	Motherwell	50	Montrose	53		
1985/86•	Celtic¥	50	Hamilton Academical	56	Dunfermline Athletic	57		
1986/87•	Rangers	69	Morton	57	Meadowbank Thistle	55		
1987/88•	Celtic	72	Hamilton Academical	56	Ayr United	61		
1988/89§	Rangers	56	Dunfermline Athletic	54	Albion Rovers	50		
1989/90§	Rangers	51	St. Johnstone	58	Brechin City	49		
1990/91§	Rangers	55	Falkirk	54	Stirling Albion	54		
1991/92§	Rangers	72	Dundee	58	Dumbarton	52		
1992/93	Rangers	73	Raith Rovers	65	Clyde	54		
1993/94	Rangers	58	Falkirk	66	Stranraer	56		
1994/95†	Rangers	69	Raith Rovers	69	Greenock Morton	64	Forfar Athletic	80
1995/96†	Rangers	87	Dunfermline Athletic	71	Stirling Albion	81	Livingston	72
1996/97†	Rangers	80	St. Johnstone	80	Ayr United	77	Inverness Caledonian Thistle	76
1997/98†	Celtic	74	Dundee	70	Stranraer	61	Alloa Athletic	76

SEASON	SCOTTISH PREMIER LEAGUE	POINTS	S.F.L. FIRST DIVISION	POINTS	S.F.L. SECOND DIVISION	POINTS	S.F.L. THIRD DIVISION	POINTS
1998/99	Rangers	77	Hibernian	89	Livingston	77	Ross County	77
1999/2000	Rangers	90	St. Mirren >	76	Clyde >	65	Queen's Park >	69

* Champions on goal average.
¥ Champions on goal difference.
• Competition known as Fine Fare League.
§ Competition known as B&Q League.
† Competition known as Bell's League Championship.
> Competition known as Bell's Scottish Football League Championship.

FIRST ROUND
Saturday, 31st July, 1999

EAST FIFE 2   STIRLING ALBION 2
(AET - 1-1 After 90 Minutes)

D. Agostini,	C. Wood,
S. Kirk	A. Graham

East Fife won 8-7 on Kicks from the Penalty Mark

East Fife: W. McCulloch, K. Munro, S. Ramsay, (S. Kirk), S. Mackay, D. Agostini, W. Herd, G. Robertson, J. Martin, (G. Tinley), D. Wright, R. Logan, K. Grattan
Substitute not used: D. Hay
Stirling Albion: G. Gow, A. Paterson, J. Tortolano, G. Donald, B. Martin, C. Wood, J. McQuade, (P. Mortimer), A. Aitken, (D. Bell), A. Graham, C. Taggart, J. Gardner
Substitute not used: J. Philliben
Referee: John Fleming
Attendance: 631

PARTICK THISTLE 0   ALLOA ATHLETIC 2
G. McKechnie (2)

Partick Thistle: K. Arthur, G. Duncan, D. McKeown, S.R. Montgomerie, K. Brannigan, A. Archibald, E. Paton, (R. Newall), A. Craig, S. Miller, S. Docherty, I. English, (S. Dallas)
Substitute not used: T. McAllister
Alloa Athletic: M. Cairns, J. Boyle, D. Clark, P. McAneny, D. Beaton, C. Valentine, M. Wilson, D. Menelaws, (G. McKechnie), M. Cameron, W. Irvine, M. Donaghy, (M. Nelson)
Substitute not used: R. Sharp
Referee: Brian McGarry
Attendance: 2,143

BRECHIN CITY 0   DUMBARTON 2
P. Flannery (2)

Brechin City: A.R. Geddes, P. Boylan, (J. Durie), G. Smith, H. Cairney, K. Bain, R. Brown, D. Coulston, (J. Dickson), P. Riley, S. Sorbie, S. Kerrigan, (M. Dailly), S. Campbell
Dumbarton: K. Meechan, M. Dickie, C. Brittain, S. Jack, J. Bruce, T. King, W. Melvin, (S. McHarg), A. Grace, P. Flannery, A. Brown, J. Robertson, (H. Ward)
Substitute not used: C. Smith
Referee: Alan Gemmill
Attendance: 346

ROSS COUNTY 2   FORFAR ATHLETIC 1
(AET - 1-1 After 90 Minutes)

B. Irvine,	I. MacDonald
G. Shaw	

Ross County: J.N. Walker, C. Tully, R. McBain, I. Maxwell, B. Irvine, K. Gilbert, F. Escalon, (M. Geraghty), J. McGlashan, G. Shaw, S. Ferguson, (K. Finlayson), P. Kinnaird, (J. Fraser)
Forfar Athletic: J. Moffat, G. McCheyne, E. Donaldson, R. Morris, (J. Nairn), A. Rattray, G. McPhee, B. McLean, A. Taylor, R. Brand, A. Cargill, I. MacDonald, (P. McIlravey)
Substitute not used: R. Kiddie
Referee: Kevin Bisset
Attendance: 1,115

STRANRAER 0   RAITH ROVERS 1 (AET)
K. Black

Stranraer: M. McGeown, K. Knox, T. Black, W. Furphy, J. Smith, D. George, G. McMartin, R. Bell, I. Harty, A. Blaikie, (P. Walker), F. Wright, (A. Jenkins)
Substitute not used: D. Johnstone
Raith Rovers: G. Van De Kamp, S. Hamilton, G. McCulloch, M. Andrews, (P. Browne), K. Gaughan, K. Black, C. McEwan, P. Agnew, P. Tosh, (P. Shields), (D. Kirkwood), A. Burns, J. Stein
Referee: Kevin Toner
Attendance: 622

QUEEN OF THE SOUTH 1   ARBROATH 0
L. Bailey

Queen of the South: J. Hillcoat, D. Lilley, A. Kerr, J.G. Rowe, A. Aitken, M. Cleeland, (W. Findlay), P. Harvey, S. Leslie, L. Bailey, (K. Robison), S. Mallan, D. Boyle, (C. Adams)
Arbroath: C. Hinchcliffe, J. McAulay, S. Florence, D. Arbuckle, J. Thomson, (S. Peters), J. Crawford, J. Mercer, T. Bryce, (C. Devine), C. McGlashan, P. Brownlie, (C. Cooper), J. Gallagher
Referee: Bobby Orr
Attendance: 986

ALBION ROVERS 0   CLYDE 3 (AET)
B. Carrigan, D. Murray, T. Farrell

Albion Rovers: M. McLean, R. Greenock, (K. McBride), N. McGowan, J. McStay, G. Duncan, J. McLees, (I. Diack), G. Russell, T. Tait, A. Nesovic, C. Flannigan, D. Rae
Substitute not used: J. Smith
Clyde: D. Wylie, J. Mitchell, C. Cranmer, J.I. Spittal, B. Smith, P. Keogh, (T. Farrell), S. Convery, (D. Murray), A. McClay, M. McLauchlan, (B. Carrigan), R. McCusker, J. Barrett
Referee: George Clyde
Attendance: 576

CLYDEBANK 1   EAST STIRLINGSHIRE 2
D. Stewart   D. Muirhead, G. Higgins

Clydebank: C. Scott, F. Wishart, D. Stewart, S. Murdoch, (M. O'Neill), J. McLaughlin, N. Oliver, J. McKinstrey, P. McIntyre, (C. Ewing), D. McKelvie, (I. McCall), R.L. Gardner, D. McWilliams
East Stirlingshire: J. Butter, A. Storrar, (K. Gordon), M. Brown, B. Ross, C. Bowsher, D. Muirhead, A. Barr, M. Hardie, (B. Ferguson), S. Laidlaw, G. Higgins, A. Elliott, (G. Russell)
Referee: Michael McCurry
Attendance: 69

COWDENBEATH 0   LIVINGSTON 2
G. Britton (2)

Cowdenbeath: R. Godfrey, W. Wilson, C. McMillan, (R. Thomson), N. Berry, (D. White), K. McCulloch, S. Snedden, C. Winter, M. Bradley, W. Stewart, P. Simpson, J.P. Burns, (G. Brown)
Livingston: I. McCaldon, P. Kelly, P. Deas, (W. Macdonald), G. Watson, G. Coughlan, J. Millar, M. McCormick, (C. King), M. Millar, G. Britton, (M. Keith), D. Bingham, I. Little
Referee: John Underhill
Attendance: 655

STENHOUSEMUIR 1   INVERNESS CAL. THISTLE 3
M. Mooney   B. Wilson, S. McLean (2)

Stenhousemuir: L. Hamilton, A. Lawrence, J. Gibson, G. Armstrong, (A. Banks), T. Graham, G. Davidson, D. Lorimer, J. Fisher, W. Watters, (M. Mooney), A. Cummings, (C. McKinnon), D. Wood
Inverness Caledonian Thistle: L. Fridge, R. Tokely, S. Golabek, M. Teasdale, R. Mann, M. McCulloch, B. Wilson, I. Stewart, (M. Glancy), S. McLean, P. Sheerin, (B. Robson), R. Hastings, (C. Christie)
Referee: George Simpson
Attendance: 528

QUEEN'S PARK 2   BERWICK RANGERS 1
K. McGoldrick,   P. Patterson
J. Brown

Queen's Park: N. Inglis, D. Ferry, J. Geoghegan, R. Caven, P. Martin, N. MacFarlane, G. Connell, S. Orr, (J.Whelan), S. Edgar, J. Brown, K. McGoldrick
Substitutes not used: R. Sinclair, A. Smith
Berwick Rangers: G. O'Connor, G. McNicoll, (M. Leask), L. Haddow, I. Ritchie, A. Neill, M. Neil, M. Hunter, M. Anthony, P. Forrester, (C. Campbell), P. Patterson, (D. Watt), K. Magee
Referee: Dougie Smith
Attendance: 390

MONTROSE 1   HAMILTON ACADEMICAL 2
J. O'Driscoll   D. Henderson (2)

Montrose: G. McGlynn, C. Mailer, W.D. Scott, C. Farnan, G. Paterson, M. Craib, K. Duffy, (M. Shand), S. Robertson, (C. Stevenson), S. Taylor, J. O'Driscoll, G. Meldrum
Substitute not used: K. Niddrie
Hamilton Academical: C. Reid, M. Martin, E. Cunnington, C. Miller, R. Maclaren, S. Thomson, D. Muir, (N. Henderson), W. Davidson, M. Moore, (S. McCormick), D. McFarlane, D. Henderson
Substitute not used: P. Gaughan
Referee: Ian Fyfe
Attendance: 327

SECOND ROUND
Tuesday, 17th August, 1999

DUNDEE 4   DUMBARTON 0
S. Boyack (2), W. Falconer (2)

Dundee: R. Douglas, B. Smith, L. Sharp, W. Miller, (F. Van Eijs), S. Tweed, H. Robertson, (S. McSkimming), S. Boyack, G. Rae, E. Annand, M. Yates, (R. Raeside), W. Falconer
Dumbarton: K. Meechan, M. Dickie, C. Brittain, J. Bruce, S. Jack, T. King, W. Melvin, (M. Melvin), A. Grace, (J. Dillon), P. Flannery, A. Brown, J. Robertson, (S. McHarg)
Referee: Tom Brown
Attendance: 2,675

INVERNESS CAL. THISTLE 2   **ST. MIRREN 0 (AET)**
P. Sheerin, K. Byers
Inverness Caledonian Thistle: L. Fridge, R. Tokely, (K. Byers), S. Golabek, R. Hastings, R. Mann, M. McCulloch, M. Teasdale, (B. Robson), M. Bavidge, S. McLean, (I. Stewart), C. Christie, P. Sheerin
St. Mirren: L. Roy, I. Nicolson, C. Kerr, T. Turner, (S. Baltacha), B. McLaughlin, S. Walker, H. Murray, (T. Brown), I. Ross, B. Lavety, J. Mendes, (S. McGarry), M. Yardley
Referee: Kevin Bisset
Attendance: 1,238

AYR UNITED 2   **HAMILTON ACADEMICAL 1**
M. Reynolds,   D. Henderson
A. Bone
Ayr United: T. Gill, B. Prenderville, D. Rogers, C. Duffy, M. Wilson, (J. Robertson), D. Craig, M. Reynolds, J. Davies, A. Bone, G. Teale, A. Lyons, (P. Lindau)
Substitute not used: G. Bowman
Hamilton Academical: C. Reid, M. Martin, E. Cunnington, N. Henderson, R. Maclaren, S. Thomson, S. Renicks, (M. Moore), W. Davidson, S. McCormick, I. McAulay, (R. Kelly), D. Henderson
Substitute not used: P. Gaughan
Referee: Bobby Orr
Attendance: 1,789

EAST FIFE 2   **AIRDRIEONIANS 2**
(AET - 2-2 After 90 Minutes)
R. Logan,   S. McCormick (2)
G. Robertson
East Fife won 5-4 on Kicks from the Penalty Mark
East Fife: W. McCulloch, K. Munro, G. Love, S. Ramsay, (R. Gibb), J. Cusick, W. Herd, G. Robertson, S. Mackay, P. McGrillen, B. Moffat, (D. Wright), R. Logan, (B. Honeyman)
Airdrieonians: S. Thomson, G. Farrell, P. Jack, E. Forrest, D. Farrell, A. Stewart, (F. Conway), A. Moore, (S. Ingram), J. Dick, G. Evans, (D. McGuire), S. McCormick, F. Johnston
Referee: Kevin Toner
Attendance: 741

ABERDEEN 1   **LIVINGSTON 0**
R. Gillies
Aberdeen: D. Preece, G. Smith, R. Anderson, D. Whyte, A. Dow, R. Gillies, (I. Kiriakov), N. Pepper, A. Mayer, (M. Hart), D. Mackie, R. Winters, D. Young, (E. Jess)
Livingston: I. McCaldon, P. Kelly, P. Deas, A. McManus, G. Coughlan, J. Millar, (D. Fleming), G. King, (J. Robertson), M. Millar, G. Britton, D. Bingham, M. Keith, (B. McPhee)
Referee: John Rowbotham
Attendance: 6,756

CLYDE 2   **HIBERNIAN 2**
(AET - 2-2 After 90 Minutes)
T. Woods, B. Carrigan   P. McGinlay, P. Hartley
Hibernian won 5-4 on Kicks from the Penalty Mark
Clyde: D. Wylie, D. Murray, C. Cranmer, J.I. Spittal, B. Smith, P. Keogh, S. Convery, M. McLaughlin, (M. McLauchlan), T. Woods, (J. Ross), R. McCusker, (S. Craib), B. Carrigan
Hibernian: N. Colgan, T. Smith, J. Hughes, A. Marenkov, (M. Jack), P. Lovering, P. Hartley, (K. Miller) S. Lovell, S. Crawford, D. Lehmann, (R. Latapy), J. Skinner, P. McGinlay
Referee: Douglas McDonald
Attendance: 2,008

MORTON 1   **ALLOA ATHLETIC 3**
H. Curran   M. Cameron, W. Irvine (2)
Morton: A. Maxwell, D. Murie, (P. McDonald), O. Archdeacon, A. Millen, D. Anderson, J. Anderson, H. Curran, R. Matheson, I. Ferguson, (W. Hawke), K. Thomas, C. McPherson
Substitute not used: S. Aitken
Alloa Athletic: M. Cairns, J. Boyle, D. Clark, M. Nelson, D. Beaton, C. Valentine, R. Sharp, D. Menelaws, (G. Clark), M. Cameron, W. Irvine, M. Donaghy
Substitutes not used: G. McKechnie, S. Bovill
Referee: Michael McCurry
Attendance: 747

Wednesday, 18th August, 1999
RAITH ROVERS 2   **MOTHERWELL 2**
(AET - 2-2 After 90 Minutes)
A. Burns,   P. Browne (o.g.),
C. Dargo   S. Halliday
Motherwell won 5-4 on Kicks from the Penalty Mark

Raith Rovers: G. Van De Kamp, C. McEwan, L. Ellis, M. Andrews, P. Browne, K. Black, (S. Hamilton), P. Tosh, S. Tosh, (P. Agnew), A. Clark, (C. Dargo), A. Burns, J. Stein
Motherwell: A. Goram, M. Doesburg, S. McMillan, J. McGowan, G. Brannan, (S. Craigan), J. Spencer, D. Goodman, P. Nevin, (S. Nicholas), A. Thomas, D. Townsley, (S. Halliday), D. Adams
Referee: Ian Fyfe
Attendance: 2,393

DUNDEE UNITED 3   **ROSS COUNTY 1**
(AET - 1-1 After 90 Minutes)
J. Ferraz,   F. Escalon, S. Thompson (2)
Dundee United: A. Combe, B. Pascual, D. Hannah, J. De Vos, M. Skoldmark, J. Ferraz, (S. Thompson), W. Dodds, J. Paterson, D. Worrell, (C. Easton), D. Partridge, H. Davidson, (A. Mathie)
Ross County: J.N. Walker, C. Tully, R. McBain, I. Maxwell, B. Irvine, K. Gilbert, G. Shaw, J. McGlashan, K. Finlayson, (M. Geraghty), F. Escalon, (J. Fraser), S. Ferguson, (G. Wood)
Referee: Kenny Clark
Attendance: 4,673

QUEEN OF THE SOUTH 1   **HEART OF MIDLOTHIAN 3**
S. Leslie   S. Severin, D. Jackson (2)
Queen of the South: J. Hillcoat, D. Lilley, A. Kerr, J.G. Rowe, A. Aitken, M. Cleeland, P. Harvey, (W. Findlay), S. Leslie, C. Adams, (L. Bailey), S. Mallan, B. Caldwell
Substitute not used: K. Robison
Heart of Midlothian: G. Rousset, S. Pressley, G. Naysmith, G. Locke, K. James, P. Ritchie, G. McSwegan, (J. Quitongo), L. Makel, (S. Fulton), J. Perez, (D. Jackson), C. Cameron, S. Severin
Referee: Hugh Dallas
Attendance: 4,633

DUNFERMLINE ATHLETIC 4   **QUEEN'S PARK 0**
O. Coyle (2), S. Petrie, A. Smith
Dunfermline Athletic: I. Westwater, G. Shields, J. Dair, A. Tod, B. Reid, (C. Ireland), J. Dolan, H. French, (C. McGroarty), (C. Nish), E. May, A. Smith, O. Coyle, S. Petrie
Queen's Park: N. Inglis, D. Ferry, D. Connaghan, R. Caven, P. Martin, N. MacFarlane, J. Whelan, (J. Geoghegan), S. Orr, (S. Edgar), M. Gallagher, (D. Carmichael), J. Brown, K. McGoldrick
Referee: George Clyde
Attendance: 2,596

EAST STIRLINGSHIRE 0   **FALKIRK 2 (AET)**
     S. Crabbe, C. Bowsher (o.g.)
East Stirlingshire: J. Butter, A. Storrar, G. Russell, M. Brown, C. Bowsher, D. Muirhead, B. Ferguson, (K. Gordon), M. Hardie, S. Laidlaw, G. Higgins, S. Donnelly, (A. Barr)
Substitute not used: G. McDonald
Falkirk: M. Hogarth, S. Rennie, J. McQuilken, A. Lawrie, D. Sinclair, S. McKenzie, C. McDonald, (A. Seaton), T. Coyne, (D. Nicholls), S. Crabbe, D. Moss, G. Hutchison. (D. Hagen)
Referee: John Fleming
Attendance: 1,201

THIRD ROUND
Tuesday, 12th October, 1999

ST. JOHNSTONE 1   **DUNDEE UNITED 2**
D. Griffin   J. Telesnikov, H. Davidson
St. Johnstone: A. Main, J. McQuillan, N. Dasovic, A. Kernaghan, M. Simao, (G. McMahon), J. O'Neil, P. Kane, N. Lowndes, G. Bollan, D. Griffin, K. O'Halloran
Substitutes not used: K. McAnespie, G. O'Boyle
Dundee United: A. Combe, B. Pascual, D. Hannah, J. De Vos, W. Dodds, J. Telesnikov, J. Paterson, (M. Malpas), S. Thompson, (J. Ferraz), D. Partridge, A. Venetis, R. Bove, (H. Davidson)
Referee: Jim McCluskey
Attendance: 4,806

INVERNESS CAL. THISTLE 0   **MOTHERWELL 1**
     L. McCulloch
Inverness Caledonian Thistle: L. Fridge, R. Tokely, R. Hastings, M. Teasdale, M. McCulloch, P. Sheerin, B. Wilson, M. Glancy, D. Wyness, C. Christie, S. Golabek, (K. Byers)
Substitutes not used: S. McLean, M. Bavidge
Motherwell: A. Goram, M. Doesburg, S. McMillan, T. Thomas, G. Brannan, S. Teale, J. Spencer, (S. Halliday), S. Valakari, L. McCulloch, D. Townsley, (D. Goodman), P. Nevin
Substitute not used: S. Craigan
Referee: Stuart Dougal
Attendance: 2,195

ABERDEEN 1 **FALKIRK 1**
(AET - 1-1 After 90 Minutes)
A. Lawrie (o.g.) S. Crabbe
Aberdeen won 5-3 on Kicks from the Penalty Mark
Aberdeen: D. Preece, M. Perry, R. Anderson, T. Solberg,
A. Dow, R. Gillies, (J. McAllister), M.J. Buchan, A. Mayer,
(D. Young), R. Winters, J. Hamilton, (M. Hart), E. Jess
Falkirk: M. Hogarth, S. McKenzie, J. McQuilken, A. Lawrie,
D. Sinclair, D. Nicholls, K. McAllister, (C. McDonald), T. Coyne, S. Crabbe,
G. Hutchison, D. Hagen, (A. Seaton)
Substitute not used: S. Rennie
Referee: Hugh Dallas
Attendance: 8,166

ALLOA ATHLETIC 1 **DUNDEE 3**
M. Cameron J. Grady, W. Falconer (2)
Alloa Athletic: M. Cairns, J. Boyle, D. Clark, G. Clark, (R. Sharp), D. Beaton,
C. Valentine, S. Bannerman, (D. Menelaws), M. Wilson, (M. Donaghy),
M. Cameron, W. Irvine, M. Christie
Dundee: R. Douglas, B. Smith, L. Maddison, W. Miller, S. Tweed,
S. McSkimming, S. Boyack, G. Rae, (H. Robertson), E. Annand, J. Grady,
W. Falconer
Substitutes not used: M. Slater, R. Puras
Referee: John Underhill
Attendance: 1,344

KILMARNOCK 3 **HIBERNIAN 2**
J. Vareille, A. McCoist (2) K. Miller, P. McGinlay
Kilmarnock: C. Meldrum, (A. Mahood), A. MacPherson, M. Baker,
F. Dindeleux, K. McGowne, J. Vareille, (C. Cocard), M. Reilly, G. Holt,
A. McCoist, (M. Jeffrey), I. Durrant, A. Mitchell
Hibernian: N. Colgan, M. Renwick, (P. Hartley), P. Lovering, F. Sauzee,
M. Jack, (M. Dempsie), S. Dennis, K. Miller, (D. Lehmann), G. Brebner,
M-M. Paatelainen, R. Latapy, P. McGinlay
Referee: Bobby Orr
Attendance: 6,837

RANGERS 1 **DUNFERMLINE ATHLETIC 0**
R. Wallace
Rangers: M. Brown, D. Adamczuk, C. Moore, L. Amoruso, A. Vidmar,
A. Kanchelskis, D. McInnes, J. Albertz, J. Johansson, (M. Mols), R. Wallace,
G. Amato, (S. Porrini)
Substitute not used: S. Wilson
Dunfermline Athletic: I. Westwater, S. Thomson, J. Dair, J. Potter, B. Reid,
J. Dolan, (C. McGroarty), D. Graham, H. French, A. Smith, (E. May),
O. Coyle, S. Petrie
Substitute not used: C. Ireland
Referee: Michael McCurry
Attendance: 30,024

EAST FIFE 0 **HEART OF MIDLOTHIAN 2**
C. Cameron, D. Holmes
Match Played at Stark's Park, Kirkcaldy
East Fife: W. McCulloch, R. Shannon, G. Love, J. Cusick, (S. Ramsay),
D. Agostini, W. Herd, R. Logan, (B. Honeyman), G. Forrest, G. Robertson,
B. Moffat, (S. Kirk), S. Mackay
Heart of Midlothian: G. Rousset, S. Pressley, R. McKinnon, S. Severin,
F. Leclercq, P. Ritchie, T. Flögel, S. Fulton, (D. Holmes), G. McSwegan,
(G. Wales), C. Cameron, D. Jackson
Substitute not used: L. Makel
Referee: Kenny Clark
Attendance: 3,337

Wednesday, 13th October, 1999
AYR UNITED 0 **CELTIC 4**
J. Mjallby, R. Blinker,
M. Viduka, B. Petta
Ayr United: C. Nelson, J. Robertson, D. Rogers, C. Duffy, M. Campbell,
D. Craig, (G. Teale), G. Hurst, J. Davies, P. Shepherd, N. Jemson,
(M. Reynolds), M. Wilson
Substitute not used: G. Bowman
Celtic: J. Gould, V. Riseth, J. Mjallby, A. Stubbs, J. McNamara, O. Tebily,
C. Burley, (M. Wieghorst), R. Blinker, L. Moravcik, (B. Petta), M. Burchill,
M. Viduka
Substitute not used: D. Kharine
Referee: John Rowbotham
Attendance: 8,421

FOURTH ROUND
Wednesday, 1st December, 1999
DUNDEE UNITED 3 **MOTHERWELL 2**
C. Easton, W. Dodds, S. Teale, D. Townsley
S. Thompson
Dundee United: A. Combe, B. Pascual, D. Hannah, J. De Vos, C. Easton,
W. Dodds, J. Telesnikov, S. Thompson, (M. Malpas), D. Worrell, D. Partridge,
H. Davidson, (J. Ferraz)
Substitute not used: A. Smith
Motherwell: S. Woods, M. Doesburg, S. McMillan, G. Brannan, S. Teale,
S. Valakari, D. Goodman, S. Halliday, (J. Spencer), D. Townsley, K. Twaddle,
(P. Nevin), B. Kemble
Substitute not used: T. Thomas
Referee: Douglas McDonald
Attendance: 5,086

ABERDEEN 1 **RANGERS 0 (AET)**
A. Dow
Aberdeen: J. Leighton, J. Cobian, (M. Perry), C. Guntveit, (R. Belabed),
J. McAllister, A. Dow, D. Whyte, E. Jess, (K. Rutkiewicz), R. Anderson,
R. Winters, A. Stavrum, P. Bernard
Rangers: T. Myhre, L. Amoruso, A. Numan, B. Ferguson, A. Kanchelskis,
G. Van Bronckhorst, N. McCann, S. Wilson, J. Johansson, (S. Carson),
B. Nicholson, (T. Pentila), G. Durie, (I. Ferguson)
Referee: Stuart Dougal
Attendance: 11,380

CELTIC 1 **DUNDEE 0**
M. Wieghorst
Celtic: J. Gould, V. Riseth, (M. Burchill), S. Mahe, J. McNamara, O. Tebily,
A. Stubbs, J. Mjallby, M. Wieghorst, L. Moravcik, I. Wright, (S. Petrov),
M. Viduka
Substitute not used: S. Kerr
Dundee: R. Douglas, B. Smith, L. Sharp, (H. Robertson), P. Billio, (J. Grady),
S. Tweed, F. Van Eijs, S. Boyack, G. Rae, E. Annand, (N. Banger), L. Wilkie,
W. Falconer
Referee: Hugh Dallas
Attendance: 38,922

Wednesday, 2nd February, 2000
KILMARNOCK 1 **HEART OF MIDLOTHIAN 0**
M. Jeffrey
Kilmarnock: C. Meldrum, A. MacPherson, M. Jeffrey, M. Reilly, G. Holt,
I. Durrant, A. Mahood, (D. Bagan), J. Vareille, (A. Burke), M. Baker,
F. Dindeleux, J. Lauchlan
Substitute not used: S. Hessey
Heart of Midlothian: A. Niemi, S. Pressley, G. Naysmith, F. Leclercq,
(F. Simpson), G. Petric, G. Murray, G. McSwegan, S. Fulton,
G. Wales, C. Cameron, D. Jackson, (J. Perez)
Substitute not used: R. Tomaschek
Referee: Willie Young
Attendance: 6,648

SEMI-FINALS
Sunday, 13th February, 2000
Dens Park Stadium, Dundee
ABERDEEN 1 **DUNDEE UNITED 0**
A. Stavrum
Aberdeen: J. Leighton, R. Anderson, D. Whyte, P. Bernard, T. Solberg,
J. McAllister, C. Guntveit, A. Dow, R. Winters, (K. Rutkiewicz), A. Stavrum,
H. Zerouali, (R. Belabed)
Substitute not used: M. Perry
Dundee United: A. Combe, B. Pascual, M. Malpas, D. Hannah, C. Easton,
J. Ferraz, (A. Mathie), J. Telesnikov, (A Venetis), D. Patterson, S. Thompson,
D. Partridge, A. Preget, (S. McConalogue)
Referee: John Rowbotham
Attendance: 10,169

Wednesday, 16th February, 2000
The National Stadium, Hampden Park, Glasgow
CELTIC 1 **KILMARNOCK 0**
L. Moravcik
Celtic: D. Kharine, J. McNamara, S. Mahe, J. Mjallby, A. Stubbs, V. Riseth,
T. Boyd, L. Moravcik, M. Viduka, M. Burchill, (C. Healy), O. Tebily
Substitutes not used: S. Kerr, T. Johnson
Kilmarnock: C. Meldrum, A. MacPherson, C. Cocard, M. Reilly, G. Holt,
I. Durrant, (M. Jeffrey), A. Mitchell, (D. Bagan), F. Dindeleux, J. Lauchlan,
G. McCutcheon, (A. Burke), T. McKinlay
Referee: Jim McCluskey
Attendance: 22,926

FINAL

The National Stadium, Hampden Park, Glasgow

ABERDEEN 0   **CELTIC 2**

Aberdeen: J. Leighton, M. Perry, J. McAllister, P. Bernard, T. Solberg, R. Anderson, H. Zerouali, (R. Winters), E. Jess, (A. Mayer), A. Stavrum, C. Guntviet, (R. Belabed), A. Dow

Celtic: J. Gould, V. Riseth, J. Mjallby, T. Boyd, S. Mahe, J. McNamara, S. Petrov, M. Wieghorst, L. Moravcik, (A. Stubbs), M. Viduka, T. Johnson, (E. Berkovic)
Substitute not used: S. Kerr

Scorers: Celtic: V. Riseth, T. Johnson

Referee: Kenny Clark

Attendance: 50,073

THE CIS INSURANCE CUP
SEASON 1999/2000

ROUND BY ROUND
GOALS ANALYSIS

	No. of Goals Scored	Ties Played	Average Per Game
First Round	31	12	2.6
Second Round	40	12	3.3
Third Round	22	8	2.75
Fourth Round	8	4	2
Semi-Finals	2	2	1
Final	2	1	2
Total No. of Goals Scored:	**105**		
Total No. of Ties Played:	**39**		
Average Goals per Game:	**2.7**		

Vidar Riseth celebrates scoring Celtic's first goal

Tommy Johnson scores Celtic's second goal

SEASON 1946/47

5th April, 1947 at Hampden Park;
Attendance 82,584; Referee: Mr R. Calder (Rutherglen)

RANGERS 4   **ABERDEEN 0**
Gillick, Williamson,
Duncanson (2)

SEASON 1947/48

25th October, 1947 at Hampden Park;
Attendance 52,781; Referee: Mr P. Craigmyle (Aberdeen)

EAST FIFE 0   **FALKIRK 0**
After Extra Time

REPLAY
1st November, 1947 at Hampden Park;
Attendance 30,664; Referee: Mr. P. Craigmyle (Aberdeen)

EAST FIFE 4   **FALKIRK 1**
Duncan (3), Adams   Aikman

SEASON 1948/49

12th March, 1949 at Hampden Park; Attendance 53,359;
Referee: Mr W. G. Livingstone (Glasgow)

RANGERS 2   **RAITH ROVERS 0**
Gillick, Paton

SEASON 1949/50

29th October, 1949 at Hampden Park;
Attendance 38,897; Referee: Mr W. Webb (Glasgow)

EAST FIFE 3   **DUNFERMLINE ATHLETIC 0**
Fleming, Duncan, Morris

SEASON 1950/51

28th October, 1950 at Hampden Park;
Attendance 63,074; Referee: Mr J. A. Mowat (Glasgow)

MOTHERWELL 3   **HIBERNIAN 0**
Kelly, Forrest, Watters

SEASON 1951/52

27th October, 1951 at Hampden Park;
Attendance 91,075; Referee: Mr J. A. Mowat (Glasgow)

DUNDEE 3   **RANGERS 2**
Flavell, Pattillo, Boyd   Findlay, Thornton

SEASON 1952/53

25th October, 1952 at Hampden Park;
Attendance 51,830; Referee: Mr J. A. Mowat (Glasgow)

DUNDEE 2   **KILMARNOCK 0**
Flavell (2)

SEASON 1953/54

24th October, 1953 at Hampden Park;
Attendance 88,529; Referee: Mr J. S. Cox (Rutherglen)

EAST FIFE 3   **PARTICK THISTLE 2**
Gardiner, Fleming, Christie   Walker, McKenzie

SEASON 1954/55

23rd October, 1954 at Hampden Park;
Attendance 55,640; Referee: Mr J. A. Mowat (Glasgow)

HEART OF MIDLOTHIAN 4   **MOTHERWELL 2**
Bauld (3), Wardhaugh   Redpath (pen), Bain

SEASON 1955/56

22nd October, 1955 at Hampden Park;
Attendance 44,103; Referee: Mr H. Phillips (Wishaw)

ABERDEEN 2   **ST. MIRREN 1**
Mallan (og), Leggat   Holmes

SEASON 1956/57

27th October, 1956 at Hampden Park;
Attendance 58,973; Referee: Mr J. A. Mowat (Glasgow)

CELTIC 0   **PARTICK THISTLE 0**

REPLAY
31st October, 1956 at Hampden Park;
Attendance 31,126; Referee: Mr J. A. Mowat (Glasgow)

CELTIC 3   **PARTICK THISTLE 0**
McPhail (2), Collins

SEASON 1957/58

19th October, 1957 at Hampden Park;
Attendance 82,293; Referee: Mr J. A. Mowat (Glasgow)

CELTIC 7   **RANGERS 1**
Mochan (2), McPhail (3),   Simpson
Wilson, Fernie (pen)

SEASON 1958/59

25th October, 1958 at Hampden Park;
Attendance 59,960; Referee: Mr R. H. Davidson (Airdrie)

HEART OF MIDLOTHIAN 5   **PARTICK THISTLE 1**
Murray (2), Bauld (2), Hamilton   Smith

SEASON 1959/60

24th October, 1959 at Hampden Park;
Attendance 57,974; Referee: Mr R. H. Davidson (Airdrie)

HEART OF MIDLOTHIAN 2   **THIRD LANARK 1**
Hamilton, Young   Gray

SEASON 1960/61

29th October, 1960 at Hampden Park;
Attendance 82,063; Referee: Mr T. Wharton (Glasgow)

RANGERS 2   **KILMARNOCK 0**
Brand, Scott

SEASON 1961/62

28th October, 1961 at Hampden Park;
Attendance 88,635; Referee: Mr R. H. Davidson (Airdrie)

RANGERS 1   **HEART OF MIDLOTHIAN 1**
Millar   Cumming (pen)

REPLAY
18th December, 1961 at Hampden Park;
Attendance 47,552; Referee: Mr R. H. Davidson (Airdrie)

RANGERS 3   **HEART OF MIDLOTHIAN 1**
Millar, Brand, McMillan   Davidson

SEASON 1962/63

27th October, 1962 at Hampden Park;
Attendance 51,280; Referee: Mr T. Wharton (Glasgow)

HEART OF MIDLOTHIAN 1   **KILMARNOCK 0**
Davidson

SEASON 1963/64

26th October, 1963 at Hampden Park;
Attendance 105,907; Referee: Mr H. Phillips (Wishaw)

RANGERS 5   **MORTON 0**
Forrest (4), Willoughby

SEASON 1964/65

24th October, 1964 at Hampden Park;
Attendance 91,000; Referee: Mr H. Phillips (Wishaw)

RANGERS 2   **CELTIC 1**
Forrest (2)   Johnstone

SEASON 1965/66

23rd October, 1965 at Hampden Park;
Attendance 107,609; Referee: Mr H. Phillips (Wishaw)

CELTIC 2   **RANGERS 1**
Hughes (2 (2 pen))   Young (o.g.)

SEASON 1966/67

29th October, 1966 at Hampden Park;
Attendance 94,532; Referee: Mr T. Wharton (Glasgow)

CELTIC 1   **RANGERS 0**
Lennox

SEASON 1967/68

28th October, 1967 at Hampden Park;
Attendance 66,660; Referee: Mr R. H. Davidson (Airdrie)

CELTIC 5
Chalmers (2), Hughes,
Wallace, Lennox

DUNDEE 3
G. McLean (2), J. McLean

SEASON 1968/69

5th April, 1969 at Hampden Park;
Attendance 74,000; Referee: Mr W. M. M. Syme (Airdrie)

CELTIC 6
Lennox (3), Wallace, Auld, Craig

HIBERNIAN 2
O'Rourke, Stevenson

SEASON 1969/70

25th October, 1969 at Hampden Park;
Attendance 73,067; Referee: Mr J. W. Paterson (Bothwell)

CELTIC 1
Auld

ST. JOHNSTONE 0

SEASON 1970/71

24th October, 1970 at Hampden Park;
Attendance 106,263; Referee: Mr T. Wharton (Glasgow)

RANGERS 1
Johnstone

CELTIC 0

SEASON 1971/72

23rd October, 1971 at Hampden Park;
Attendance 62,740; Referee: Mr W. J. Mullan (Dalkeith)

PARTICK THISTLE 4
Rae, Lawrie, McQuade, Bone

CELTIC 1
Dalglish

SEASON 1972/73

9th December, 1972 at Hampden Park;
Attendance 71,696; Referee: Mr A. MacKenzie (Larbert)

HIBERNIAN 2
Stanton, O'Rourke

CELTIC 1
Dalglish

SEASON 1973/74

15th December, 1973 at Hampden Park;
Attendance 27,974; Referee: Mr R. H. Davidson (Airdrie)

DUNDEE 1
Wallace

CELTIC 0

SEASON 1974/75

26th October, 1974 at Hampden Park;
Attendance 53,848;
Referee: Mr J. R. P. Gordon (Newport on Tay)

CELTIC 6
Johnstone, Deans (3), Wilson, Murray

HIBERNIAN 3
Harper (3)

SEASON 1975/76

25th October, 1975 at Hampden Park;
Attendance 58,806; Referee: Mr W. Anderson (East Kilbride)

RANGERS 1
MacDonald

CELTIC 0

SEASON 1976/77

6th November, 1976 at Hampden Park;
Attendance 69,268; Referee: Mr J. W. Paterson (Bothwell)

ABERDEEN 2
Jarvie, Robb

CELTIC 1
Dalglish (pen.)

After extra-time – 1-1 After 90 Minutes

SEASON 1977/78

18th March, 1978 at Hampden Park;
Attendance 60,168; Referee: Mr D. F. T. Syme (Rutherglen)

RANGERS 2
Cooper, Smith

CELTIC 1
Edvaldsson

After extra-time – 1-1 After 90 Minutes

SEASON 1978/79

31st March, 1979 at Hampden Park;
Attendance 54,000; Referee: Mr I. M. D. Foote (Glasgow)

RANGERS 2
McMaster (o.g.), Jackson

ABERDEEN 1
Davidson

SEASON 1979/80 – BELL'S LEAGUE CUP

8th December, 1979 at Hampden Park;
Attendance 27,299; Referee: Mr B. R. McGinlay (Balfron)

DUNDEE UNITED 0
After extra-time

ABERDEEN 0

REPLAY

12th December, 1979 at Dens Park;
Attendance 28,984; Referee: Mr B. R. McGinlay (Balfron)

DUNDEE UNITED 3
Pettigrew (2), Sturrock

ABERDEEN 0

SEASON 1980/81 – BELL'S LEAGUE CUP

6th December, 1980 at Dens Park;
Attendance 24,466; Referee: Mr R. B. Valentine (Dundee)

DUNDEE UNITED 3
Dodds, Sturrock (2)

DUNDEE 0

SEASON 1981/82

28th November, 1981 at Hampden Park;
Attendance 53,795;
Referee: Mr E. H. Pringle (Edinburgh)

RANGERS 2
Cooper, Redford

DUNDEE UNITED 1
Milne

SEASON 1982/83

4th December, 1982 at Hampden Park;
Attendance 55,372; Referee: Mr K. J. Hope (Clarkston)

CELTIC 2
Nicholas, MacLeod

RANGERS 1
Bett

SEASON 1983/84

25th March, 1984 at Hampden Park;
Attendance 66,369; Referee: Mr R. B. Valentine (Dundee)

RANGERS 3
McCoist 3 (1 pen)

CELTIC 2
McClair, Reid (pen)

After extra-time – 2-2 After 90 Minutes

SEASON 1984/85 – SKOL CUP

28th October, 1984 at Hampden Park;
Attendance 44,698; Referee: Mr B. R. McGinlay (Balfron)

RANGERS 1
Ferguson

DUNDEE UNITED 0

SEASON 1985/86 – SKOL CUP

27th October, 1985 at Hampden Park;
Attendance 40,065; Referee: Mr R. B. Valentine (Dundee)

ABERDEEN 3
Black (2), Stark

HIBERNIAN 0

SEASON 1986/87 – SKOL CUP

26th October, 1986 at Hampden Park;
Attendance 74,219; Referee: Mr D. F. T. Syme (Rutherglen)

RANGERS 2
Durrant, Cooper (pen)

CELTIC 1
McClair

SEASON 1987/88 – SKOL CUP

25th October, 1987 at Hampden Park;
Attendance 71,961; Referee: Mr R. B. Valentine (Dundee)

RANGERS 3   **ABERDEEN 3**
Cooper, Durrant, Fleck   Bett, Falconer, Hewitt
After extra-time – 3-3 After 90 Minutes
Rangers won 5-3 on Kicks from the Penalty Mark

SEASON 1988/89 – SKOL CUP

23rd October, 1988 at Hampden Park;
Attendance 72,122; Referee: Mr G. B. Smith (Edinburgh)

RANGERS 3   **ABERDEEN 2**
McCoist (2), I. Ferguson   Dodds (2)

SEASON 1989/90 – SKOL CUP

22nd October, 1989 at Hampden Park;
Attendance 61,190; Referee: Mr G. B. Smith (Edinburgh)

ABERDEEN 2   **RANGERS 1**
Mason (2)   Walters (pen)
After extra-time – 1-1 after 90 minutes

SEASON 1990/91 – SKOL CUP

28th October, 1990 at Hampden Park;
Attendance 62,817; Referee: Mr J. McCluskey (Stewarton)

RANGERS 2   **CELTIC 1**
Walters, Gough   Elliott

SEASON 1991/92 – SKOL CUP

27th October, 1991 at Hampden Park;
Attendance 40,377; Referee: Mr B. R. McGinlay (Balfron)

HIBERNIAN 2   **DUNFERMLINE ATHLETIC 0**
McIntyre (pen), Wright

SEASON 1992/93 – SKOL CUP

25th October, 1992 at Hampden Park;
Attendance 45,298; Referee: Mr D. D. Hope (Erskine)

RANGERS 2   **ABERDEEN 1**
McCall, Smith (o.g.)   Shearer
After extra-time – 1-1 after 90 minutes

SEASON 1993/94

24th October, 1993 at Celtic Park;
Attendance 47,632; Referee: Mr J. McCluskey (Stewarton)

RANGERS 2   **HIBERNIAN 1**
Durrant, McCoist   McPherson (o.g.)

SEASON 1994/95 – COCA-COLA CUP

27th November, 1994 at Ibrox Stadium;
Attendance 45,384; Referee: Mr J. McCluskey (Stewarton)

RAITH ROVERS 2   **CELTIC 2**
S. Crawford, G. Dalziel C. Nicholas, A. Walker
After extra-time – 2-2 after 90 minutes
Raith Rovers won 6-5 on Kicks from the Penalty Mark

SEASON 1995/96 – COCA-COLA CUP

26th November, 1995 at Hampden Park;
Attendance 33,099; Referee: Mr L.W. Mottram (Forth)

ABERDEEN 2   **DUNDEE 0**
D. Shearer, W. Dodds

SEASON 1996/97 – COCA-COLA CUP

24th November, 1996 at Celtic Park;
Attendance 48,559; Referee: Mr H. Dallas (Motherwell)

RANGERS 4   **HEART OF MIDLOTHIAN 3**
P. Gascoigne (2),A. McCoist (2)   D. Weir, S. Fulton, J. Robertson

SEASON 1997/98 – COCA-COLA CUP

30th November, 1997 at Ibrox Stadium, Glasgow;
Attendance 49,305; Referee: Mr J. McCluskey (Stewarton)

CELTIC 3   **DUNDEE UNITED 0**
M. Rieper, H. Larsson, C. Burley

SEASON 1998/99

29th November, 1998 at Celtic Park, Glasgow;
Attendance 45,533; Referee: Mr H. Dallas (Motherwell)

RANGERS 2   **ST. JOHNSTONE 1**
S. Guivarc'h, J. Albertz N. Dasovic

SEASON 1999/2000 – CIS INSURANCE CUP

19th March, 2000 at The National Stadium, Hampden Park,
Glasgow; Attendance 50,073; Referee: Mr K. Clark (Paisley)

ABERDEEN 0   **CELTIC 2**
                        V. Riseth, T. Johnson

WINNERS AT A GLANCE

RANGERS	21
CELTIC	11
ABERDEEN	5
HEART OF MIDLOTHIAN	4
DUNDEE	3
EAST FIFE	3
DUNDEE UNITED	2
HIBERNIAN	2
MOTHERWELL	1
PARTICK THISTLE	1
RAITH ROVERS	1

APPEARANCES IN FINALS
(Figures do not include replays)

RANGERS	27
CELTIC	23
ABERDEEN	12
HIBERNIAN	7
DUNDEE	6
HEART OF MIDLOTHIAN	6
DUNDEE UNITED	5
PARTICK THISTLE	4
EAST FIFE	3
KILMARNOCK	3
DUNFERMLINE ATHLETIC	2
MOTHERWELL	2
RAITH ROVERS	2
ST. JOHNSTONE	2
FALKIRK	1
MORTON	1
ST. MIRREN	1
THIRD LANARK	1

FIRST ROUND

Saturday, 11th December, 1999

HUNTLY 0   EAST STIRLINGSHIRE 1
                Higgins

Huntly: Morgan, Smith, Allan, Guild, Paterson, Black, Addicoat, (Farmer), MacRonald, Stewart, Whyte, De Barros
Substitutes not used: N. Grant, Will
East Stirlingshire: Butter, Storrar, Russell, Brown, Hay, Lynes, (Elliott), Ferguson, (Gordon), Muirhead, Laidlaw, Higgins, (McMillan), Hardie
Referee: John Underhill
Attendance: 467

ROSS COUNTY 2   FORFAR ATHLETIC 2
Shaw, Irvine   Donaldson, Robson

Ross County: Walker, Duthie, McBain, Maxwell, D. Mackay, Gilbert, Shaw, Geraghty, (Irvine), Wood, Fraser, (Finlayson), Kinnaird
Substitute not used: Ross
Forfar Athletic: Garden, McCheyne, Craig, Rattray, Johnston, Donaldson, Morris, Farnan, Milne, Cargill, Robson
Substitutes not used: Brand, McPhee, MacDonald
Referee: John Fleming
Attendance: 749

HAMILTON ACADEMICAL 1   CLYDE 2
D. Henderson   Carrigan, Grant

Hamilton Academical: Reid, Maclaren, Cunnington, Davidson, Gaughan, Thomson, Renicks, N. Henderson, (Crossley), (McAulay), McFarlane, Bonnar, (McCormick), D. Henderson
Clyde: Wylie, Murray, McLaughlin, Keogh, Cranmer, Ross, Carrigan, McClay, Barrett, (Woods), Mitchell, Grant
Substitutes not used: Hay, Dunn
Referee: Ian Fyfe
Attendance: 777

Monday, 27th December, 1999

THREAVE ROVERS 1   STENHOUSEMUIR 7
Smith   Fisher (2), Graham (2),
         Mooney, Forrester, Fraser (o.g.)

Threave Rovers: McWilliam, Smith, Tuchewicz, (Livingstone), Wilson, (Adams), Fraser, McGinley, Kirkpatrick, McCulloch, Possee, (Little), Hudson, Cook
Stenhousemuir: L. Hamilton, Lawrence, Banks, Davidson, (Armstrong), Graham, Watson, R. Hamilton, McKinnon, Mooney, (Forrester), Fisher, Lorimer, (Watters)
Referee: Colin Hardie
Attendance: 526

FIRST ROUND REPLAY

Monday, 3rd January, 2000

FORFAR ATHLETIC 0   ROSS COUNTY 0 (AET)
Forfar Athletic won 4-2 on Kicks from the Penalty Mark
Forfar Athletic: Garden, McCheyne, Craig, Rattray, Johnston, Donaldson, Morris, (McPhee), McLean, (Brand), Milne, Cargill, Robson
Substitute not used: McKellar
Ross County: Walker, Duthie, Mackay, Maxwell, Irvine, Gilbert, Shaw, Geraghty, Holmes, (Wood), Ferguson, Kinnaird, (McBain)
Substitute not used: Tully
Referee: John Fleming
Attendance: 1,057

SECOND ROUND

Saturday, 8th January, 2000

ALBION ROVERS 0   DALBEATTIE STAR 0
Albion Rovers: McLean, McStay, McBride, Hamilton, Smith, Lumsden, Bonar, (Tait), McLees, Duncan, Lyon, (Diack), Prentice, (Coulter)
Dalbeattie Star: Fitzpatrick, McMinn, D. Campbell, Skachill, Dingwall, McGinley, Pearson, Parker, Johnston, Black, (Telfer), Rodgerson, (Glendinning)
Substitute not used: Paisley
Referee: Craig Mackay
Attendance: 422

ARBROATH 0   FRASERBURGH 0
Arbroath: Wight, Florence, Gallagher, McAulay, J. Thomson, Crawford, Cooper, Bryce, (Brownlie), McGlashan, Arbuckle, Mercer, (Sellars)
Substitute not used: Steel

Fraserburgh: Gordon, Milne, McBride, Murray, Fleming, Geddes, Norris, Thomson, Wemyss, (Young), Hunter, M. Stephen
Substitutes not used: Mackie, Martin
Referee: Ian Frickleton
Attendance: 1,235

STIRLING ALBION 2   EAST FIFE 1
Whiteford, Graham   O'Hara

Stirling Albion: Gow, Paterson, Tortolano, Donald, (Clark), Whiteford, McCallum, (Mortimer), McQuade, McGrillen, (Wood), Graham, Taggart, Gardner
East Fife: McCulloch, Munro, Gibb, (Forrest), O'Hara, (Herd), Agostini, Shannon, Logan, Cusick, (Wright), Robertson, Moffat, Mackay
Referee: Mike Ritchie
Attendance: 728

DUMBARTON 0   STENHOUSEMUIR 2
         Fisher, R. Hamilton

Dumbarton: Barnes, Dickie, Brittain, Stewart, Bruce, King, Grace, (Hringsson), Jack, Flannery, Andrew Brown, Robertson
Substitutes not used: Smith, Alan Brown
Stenhousemuir: L. Hamilton, Lawrence, Banks, Watson, Graham, Lorimer, R. Hamilton, McKinnon, Mooney, (Wood), Fisher, Fraser
Substitutes not used: Forrester, Watters
Referee: Dougie Smith
Attendance: 302

MONTROSE 1   QUEEN OF THE SOUTH 3
O'Driscoll   Eadie, Hawke, Adams

Montrose: McGlynn, D. Craig, Black, McWilliam, (Ogboke), Paterson, M. Craib, Mailer, Scott, M. Craig, O'Driscoll, Taylor
Substitutes not used: Robertson, Meldrum
Queen of the South: Hillcoat, McMillan, Hodge, Rowe, Robison, Cleeland, Dickson, Kerr, (Leslie), Hawke, Mallan, (Weir), Eadie, (Adams)
Referee: Brian McGarry
Attendance: 380

STRANRAER 1   CLACHNACUDDIN 0
Blaikie

Stranraer: McGeown, J. Smith, Wright, Watson, Jenkins, Macdonald, Walker, (Blaikie), Ramsay, Harty, Ronald, (Young), Roddie
Substitute not used: Cahoon
Clachnacuddin: Rae, MacCuish, MacLeod, Bennett, Sinclair, Douglas, (McCraw), Williamson, Munro, Stewart, (Holmes), Brennan, Richardson
Substitute not used: Mitchell
Referee: Kevin Toner
Attendance: 351

BRECHIN CITY 2   ANNAN ATHLETIC 2
Bailey, Smith   McGuffie, Sloan

Brechin City: Geddes, Smith, Raynes, Cairney, Bain, Christie, Nairn, Bailey, Honeyman, Black, Coulston, (Kerrigan)
Substitutes not used: Sorbie, Donachie
Annan Athletic: Potter, Hannay, Leslie, (Sloan), Proudfoot, Laurie, Irons, Nicoll, Jardine, Docherty, (Thomson), McMenimin, McGuffie
Substitute not used: Little
Referee: Alan Gemmill
Attendance: 396

QUEEN'S PARK 1   BERWICK RANGERS 2
Carroll   Haddow, Findlay

Queen's Park: Inglis, Ferry, Connaghan, Caven, Martin, MacFarlane, Connell, Borland, (Whelan), Gallagher, Carmichael, (Brown), Carroll
Substitute not used: Sinclair
Berwick Rangers: O'Connor, McNicoll, Haddow, Campbell, A. Neill, M. Neil, Patterson, Watt, Findlay, Anthony, (Leask), D. Smith, (Magee)
Substitute not used: Porteous
Referee: Steven Kaney
Attendance: 630

PETERHEAD 2   FORFAR ATHLETIC 1
G. Clark, Cheyne   Milne

Peterhead: Pirie, S. Clark, Morrison, King, Simpson, Gibson, Yeats, (Copeland), G. Clark, Milne, (Yule), Brown, Cheyne
Substitute not used: Bray
Forfar Athletic: Garden, McCheyne, Craig, McPhee, (Brand), Farnan, Donaldson, Morris, (Taylor), McLean, Milne, Cargill, Robson, (McKellar)
Referee: David Somers
Attendance: 1,130

PARTICK THISTLE 2   **EAST STIRLINGSHIRE 1**
Lennon, Brown (o.g.)   Hay
Partick Thistle: Budinauckis, Duncan, McKeown, Lennon, McCann, (Martin), Archibald, Paton, Docherty, McLean, Lyle, Jacobs, (Miller)
Substitute not used: T. Callaghan
East Stirlingshire: Butter, Storrar, Russell, Brown, Hay, Muirhead, Ferguson, Hardie, Laidlaw, Higgins, (Gordon), Elliott
Substitutes not used: Barr, Lynes
Referee: Ian Elmslie
Attendance: 2,262

COWDENBEATH 2   **CLYDE 3**
Brown (2)   Carrigan (2), McLaughlin
Cowdenbeath: Hutchison, White, King, Snedden, McCulloch, Carnie, (Stewart), Winter, Bradley, McDowell, (Simpson), Brown, Wilson
Substitute not used: McMillan
Clyde: McIntyre, Murray, McLaughlin, Smith, Cranmer, Ross, (Mitchell), Carrigan, McClay, Woods, (Convery), Keogh, Grant, (McLauchlan)
Referee: George Clyde
Attendance: 622

WHITEHILL WELFARE 2   **ALLOA ATHLETIC 2**
Bird, Samuel   Irvine, McKechnie
Whitehill Welfare: Cantley, McLaren, Gowrie, Malcolm, Steel, Bennett, Jardine, Samuel, Tulloch, (McGovern), Bird, (Hope), Manson, (Smith)
Alloa Athletic: Cairns, Wilson, D. Clark, Conway, Beaton, Valentine, G. Clark, (Christie), Walker, (McKechnie), Cameron, Irvine, Donaghy, (Boyle)
Referee: Cammy Melville
Attendance: 813

SECOND ROUND REPLAYS

Saturday, 15th January, 2000

FRASERBURGH 1   **ARBROATH 3**
Florence (o.g.)   McGlashan, Mercer, Devine
Fraserburgh: Gordon, Milne, McBride, Fleming, A. Stephen, (McLaren), Murray, Norris, Thomson, Wemyss, (Young), (Martin), Mackie, M. Stephen
Arbroath: Wight, Arbuckle, Florence, McAulay, J. Thomson, Crawford, Cooper, (Gallagher), Bryce, (Devine), McGlashan, Sellars, Mercer
Substitute not used: Peters
Referee: Ian Frickleton
Attendance: 1,967

ANNAN ATHLETIC 2   **BRECHIN CITY 3**
Docherty, Thomson   Christie, Nairn, Black
Annan Athletic: Potter, Hannay, Leslie, (Sloan), Proudfoot, Laurie, Irons, Nicol, (Elliott), Jardine, Docherty, (Thomson), McMenamin, McGuffie
Brechin City: Geddes, Smith, (Coulston), Raynes, Cairney, Bain, Christie, Nairn, Bailey, (Kerrigan), Honeyman, (Sorbie), Black, Donachie
Referee: Alan Gemmill
Attendance: 1,039

Wednesday, 19th January, 2000

DALBEATTIE STAR 1   **ALBION ROVERS 5**
Parker   McLees, McStay, Flannigan (3)
Dalbeattie Star: Fitzpatrick, McMinn, Campbell, Skachill, Dingwall, McGinley, Pearson, (Telfer), Parker, Johnston, Black, (True), Rogerson, (Harkness)
Albion Rovers: McLean, McStay, Coulter, Tait, (McMillan), Smith, Lumsden, Hamilton, (Diack), McLees, Duncan, (Silvestro), Flannigan, Prentice
Referee: Dougie Smith
Attendance: 483

Saturday, 29th January, 2000

ALLOA ATHLETIC 2   **WHITEHILL WELFARE 0**
Donaghy, Cameron
Alloa Athletic: Cairns, Wilson, D. Clark, Conway, Beaton, (Boyle), Valentine, G. Clark, Walker, (McKechnie), Cameron, Irvine, Donaghy, (Christie)
Whitehill Welfare: Cantley, McLaren, Gowrie, Malcolm, Steel, (McGovern), Bennett, Jardine, Samuel, Hope, Bird, (Tulloch), Manson, (Smith)
Referee: Cammy Melville
Attendance: 640

THIRD ROUND

Saturday, 29th January, 2000

HEART OF MIDLOTHIAN 3   **STENHOUSEMUIR 2**
Cameron, McSwegan (2)   Hamilton, Mooney

Heart of Midlothian: Niemi, Pressley, Naysmith, Petric, Murray, (McSwegan), Locke, Tomaschek, (Perez), Cameron, Fulton, Wales, Jackson
Substitute not used: Simpson
Stenhousemuir: L. Hamilton, Lawrence, Banks, (Lorimer), Watson, Graham, (Wood), Armstrong, R. Hamilton, McKinnon, Mooney, (Forrester), Fraser, Fisher
Referee: Bobby Orr
Attendance: 11,439

ST. MIRREN 1   **ABERDEEN 1**
McGarry   Zerouali
St. Mirren: Roy, Nicolson, Ross, Baltacha, (Bowman), McLaughlin, Walker, Murray, (Rudden), Brown, McGarry, (Lavety), Mendes, Yardley
Aberdeen: Leighton, Solberg, McAllister, Whyte, Anderson, Dow, (Belabed), Bernard, Jess, (Winters), Guntveit, Stavrum, Zerouali
Substitute not used: Perry
Referee: Willie Young
Attendance: 7,139

ALBION ROVERS 1   **PARTICK THISTLE 2**
Duncan   Dunn, Lennon
Albion Rovers: McLean, Bonar, Smith, Tait, Lumsden, McStay, Silvestro, McLees, Duncan, Flannigan, Prentice, (Diack)
Substitutes not used: Hamilton, McMullen
Partick Thistle: Budinauckas, Docherty, McKeown, Lennon, Montgomerie, Archibald, Paton, (Miller), Craig, McLean, Dunn, (Lyle), Jacobs, (Martin)
Referee: Tom Brown
Attendance: 1,679

FALKIRK 3   **PETERHEAD 1**
Nicholls, Crabbe,   Gibson
Hagen
Falkirk: Hogarth, Lawrie, McQuilken, (Seaton), Den Bieman, Christie, Nicholls, McKenzie, Donald, (Hutchison), Crabbe, Henry, Hagen
Substitute not used: Sinclair
Peterhead: Pirie, S. Clark, (Watson), Morrison, King, Simpson, Cheyne, Yeats, (G. Clark), Yule, Milne, (Copeland), Brown, Gibson
Referee: Eric Martindale
Attendance: 3,165

ARBROATH 0   **MOTHERWELL 1**
    D. Townsley
(Match Abandoned at Half-Time)
Arbroath: Wight, Florence, Peters, Scott, McAulay, J. Thomson, Arbuckle, Cooper, Bryce, McGlashan, Tindal, Mercer
Substitutes not used: Devine, Crawford, Gallagher
Motherwell: Goram, Doesburg, McMillan, Brannan, Valakari, McCulloch, Goodman, Nicholas, Craigan, Denham, Townsley
Substitutes not used: Adams, Nevin, J. Davies
Referee: Michael McCurry
Attendance: 2,665

QUEEN OF THE SOUTH 0   **LIVINGSTON 7**
    McKinnon (2), Keith (3), Kerr (o.g.), McPhee
Queen of the South: Hillcoat, McMillan, (Kerr), Hodge, (Adams), Rowe, Aitken, Cleeland, Dickson, Leslie, Hawke, Mallan, Eadie, (Caldwell)
Livingston: McCaldon, Kelly, Deas, (Bennett), McManus, Coughlan, McKinnon, King, (McCormick), M. Millar, (Sweeney), Keith, Bingham, McPhee
Referee: Hugh Dallas
Attendance: 1,530

CLYDE 3   **RAITH ROVERS 1**
Carrigan (2), Woods   Dargo
Clyde: Wylie, Keogh, McLaughlin, Smith, Cranmer, (McLauchlan), Ross, Convery, (Woods), McClay, Carrigan, Mitchell, Grant
Substitute not used: McCusker
Raith Rovers: Van De Kamp, McEwan, Andrews, Browne, Opinel, Black, Agathe, S. Tosh, Dargo, Burns, Stein, (Hetherston)
Substitutes not used: McCulloch, Clark
Referee: George Simpson
Attendance: 1,831

STRANRAER 1   **BERWICK RANGERS 2**
Ronald   Haddow, Findlay
Stranraer: McGeown, J. Smith, Wright, Watson, Kerr, Macdonald, J. Young, Jenkins, (Cahoon), Harty, (Johnstone), Ronald, Blaikie, (Walker)
Berwick Rangers: O'Connor, McNicoll, Haddow, Campbell, A. Neill, Watt, Patterson, Anthony, (Ritchie), Findlay, (Carr-Lawton), D. Smith, Magee

Substitute not used: Weir
Referee: Brian Cassidy
Attendance: 406

CLYDEBANK 1   **STIRLING ALBION 0**
Wishart
Clydebank: Scott, Murray, (Jackson), McLaughlin, McKinstrey, Murdoch, Miller, (O'Neil), Brannigan, Gardner, Wishart, Cameron, McKelvie, (Oliver)
Stirling Albion: Gow, Paterson, Tortolano, Donald, Whiteford, McCallum, McQuade, McGrillen, (Wood), Graham, Taggart, Gardner
Substitutes not used: Mortimer, Clark
Referee: Kevin Bisset
Attendance: 355

HIBERNIAN 4   **DUNFERMLINE ATHLETIC 1**
Miller, Brebner,   Graham
Murray, Collins
Hibernian: Colgan, Collins, Smith, Hughes, Jack, Sauzee, Brebner, (Hartley), Latapy, Lovell, (Murray), Paatelainen, (Lehmann), Miller
Dunfermline Athletic: Mampaey, McGroarty, Dair, Tod, Reid, (Coyle), Dolan, (Moss), Thomson, Ferguson, Graham, Hampshire, Petrie
Substitute not used: Potter
Referee: Stuart Dougal
Attendance: 11,537

DUNDEE 0   **AYR UNITED 0**
Dundee: Douglas, Smith, Wilkie, Tweed, Ireland, McSkimming, Boyack, (Bayne), Rae, Banger, Annand, Falconer, (Robertson)
Substitute not used: Billio
Ayr United: Nelson, Robertson, Rogers, Scally, Craig, Duffy, Teale, Wilson, Hurst, Tarrant, Reynolds, (Shepherd)
Substitutes not used: McMillan, Hansen
Referee: Jim Herald
Attendance: 3,925

Sunday, 30th January, 2000

ST. JOHNSTONE 0   **RANGERS 2**
         Numan, Van Bronckhorst
St. Johnstone: Main, Griffin, Bollan, Weir, Dods, O'Halloran, McBride, (McAnespie), Kane, O'Neil, Lowndes, (Simao), Jones
Substitute not used: McCluskey
Rangers: Klos, Vidmar, Moore, Amoruso, Numan, Kanchelskis, (Reyna), B. Ferguson, Van Bronckhorst, Albertz, (Kerimoglu), Durie, Wallace, (McCann)
Referee: John Rowbotham
Attendance: 9,111

MORTON 1   **BRECHIN CITY 1**
J. Anderson   Black
Morton: Maxwell, Murie, (Reid), D. Anderson, Millen, Morrison, Fenwick, Matheson, J. Anderson, Whalen, Curran, (Tweedie), McDonald, (McPherson)
Brechin City: Geddes, Donachie, Raynes, Cairney, Bain, Christie, Riley, Sorbie, Honeyman, (Coulston), Black, Bailey, (Kerrigan)
Substitute not used: Durie
Referee: Jim McCluskey
Attendance: 990

DUNDEE UNITED 4   **AIRDRIEONIANS 1**
Hannah (2), Mathie,   McCann
Ferraz
Dundee United: Combe, Pascual, Partridge, De Vos, Jonsson, Davidson, Telesnikov, (Skoldmark), Hannah, Preget, Mathie, (Ferraz), Thompson
Substitute not used: Malpas
Airdrieonians: Thomson, Johnston, McCann, Jack, Forrest, Stewart, Moore, Dick, Thompson, (McCormick), Evans, (Neil), Easton, (Taylor)
Referee: Alan Freeland
Attendance: 5,172

Tuesday, 1st February, 2000

ARBROATH 1   **MOTHERWELL 1**
Bryce   Goodman
Arbroath: Wight, Florence, Peters, McAulay, J. Thomson, Arbuckle, Cooper, Bryce, (Devine), McGlashan, Tindal, Mercer
Substitutes not used: Crawford, Gallagher
Motherwell: Goram, Doesburg, McMillan, Denham, Craigan, Townsley, (Nevin), Brannan, Valakari, Twaddle, McCulloch, Goodman
Substitutes not used: Nicholas, J. Davies
Referee: Michael McCurry
Attendance: 2,665

Saturday, 5th February, 2000

KILMARNOCK 0   **ALLOA ATHLETIC 0**
Kilmarnock: Meldrum, MacPherson, Baker, Lauchlan, Dindeleux, Reilly, Holt, Durrant, (Bagan), Burke, Vareille, Jeffrey, (Smith) Substitute not used: Hessey
Alloa Athletic: Cairns, Wilson, D. Clark, Conway, Valentine, (G. Clark), Beaton, Christie, Walker, (McKechnie), Cameron, Irvine, Donaghy
Substitute not used: Boyle
Referee: Garry Mitchell
Attendance: 5,584

Tuesday, 8th February, 2000

CELTIC 1   **INVERNESS CALEDONIAN THISTLE 3**
Burchill   Wilson, Moravcik (o.g.), Sheerin
Celtic: Gould, Boyd, Riseth, Tebily, Mahe, Blinker, Healy, Berkovic, Moravcik, Viduka, (Wright), Burchill
Substitutes not used: Kerr, Petta
Inverness Caledonian Thistle: Calder, Teasdale, Golabek, Mann, Hastings, Sheerin, Tokely, (Byers), McCulloch, Wilson, (Glancy), Christie, Wyness, (Bavidge)
Referee: Douglas McDonald
Attendance: 40,018

THIRD ROUND REPLAYS

Tuesday, 8th February, 2000

ABERDEEN 2   **ST. MIRREN 0**
Zerouali, Bernard
Aberdeen: Leighton, Solberg, McAllister, Whyte, Anderson, Dow, (Belabed), Bernard, Guntveit, Winters, Stavrum, (Rutkiewicz), Zerouali
Substitute not used: Perry
St. Mirren: Roy, Nicolson, Ross, Rudden, McLaughlin, Walker, Murray, (McGarry), Bowman, Lavety, (Turner), Mendes, Yardley, (Baltacha)
Referee: Willie Young
Attendance: 12,947

BRECHIN CITY 0   **MORTON 0 (AET)**
Morton won 4-2 on Kicks from the Penalty Mark
Brechin City: Geddes, Donachie, Raynes, Cairney, Bain, Smith, Riley, Sorbie, Honeyman, (Kerrigan), Black, Bailey. Substitutes not used: Coulston, Dailly
Morton: Maxwell, Murie, (Tweedie), D. Anderson, Millen, Morrison, Slavin (Aitken), Whalen, (Hart), J. Anderson, Matheson, Curran, McDonald
Referee: Jim McCluskey
Attendance: 756

Wednesday, 9th February, 2000

ALLOA ATHLETIC 1   **KILMARNOCK 0**
Cameron
Alloa Athletic: Cairns, Wilson, D. Clark, Conway, Beaton, Valentine, Christie, Walker, (McKechnie), Cameron, Irvine, Donaghy, (G. Clark)
Substitute not used: Boyle
Kilmarnock: Meldrum, MacPherson, Baker, Lauchlan, Dindeleux, Reilly, (Durrant), Holt, Burke, Mitchell, (Bagan), Smith, Cocard
Substitute not used: Jeffrey
Referee: Garry Mitchell
Attendance: 1,894

Tuesday, 15th February, 2000

AYR UNITED 1   **DUNDEE 1 (AET)**
Duffy   Rae
Ayr United won 7-6 on Kicks from the Penalty Mark
Ayr United: Nelson, McMillan, (Grant), Robertson, Scally, (Crilly), Craig, Duffy, Teale, Wilson, Hurst, Tarrant, (Reynolds), Shepherd
Dundee: Langfield, Smith, Raeside, Tweed, Wilkie, Robertson, Boyack, (Banger), Rae, McSkimming, (Sharp), Bayne, (Grady), Falconer
Referee: Jim Herald
Attendance: 3,029

Saturday, 19th February, 2000

MOTHERWELL 2   **ARBROATH 0**
Goodman, McCulloch
Motherwell: Goram, Doesburg, McMillan, McGowan, Denham, J. Davies, (Townsley), Brannan, Valakari, Goodman, (Twaddle), Spencer, (Nicholas), McCulloch
Arbroath: Wight, Peters, Gallagher, McAulay, J. Thomson, Webster, Cooper, (Brownlie), Bryce, (Devine), McGlashan, Sellars, Mercer
Substitute not used: Crawford
Referee: Michael McCurry **Attendance:** 5,311

FOURTH ROUND
Saturday, 19th February, 2000

MORTON 0　　　**RANGERS 1**
　　　　　　　　Moore
Match Played at St. Mirren Park, Paisley
Morton: Maxwell, Murie, D. Anderson, Millen, Morrison, Pluck, Earnshaw, (Slavin), J. Anderson, (Aitken), Matheson, Curran, McDonald, (Wright)
Rangers: Klos, Vidmar, Moore, Van Bronckhorst, Numan, Kanchelskis, B. Ferguson, Kerimoglu, McCann, (Albertz), Durie, (Negri), Wallace
Substitute not used: Wilson
Referee: Willie Young
Attendance: 7,984

HIBERNIAN 1　　　**CLYDEBANK 1**
Hartley　　　　　　　Gardner
Hibernian: Colgan, Collins, Smith, Hughes, Jack, Murray, Brebner, Sauzee, Hartley, (Lovell), Paatelainen, (Lehmann), Miller
Substitute not used: Lovering
Clydebank: Scott, Murray, Sutherland, Murdoch, (McKinstrey), (O'Neil), Brannigan, Wishart, Miller, Gardner, McKelvie, (Hunter), McWilliams, Cameron
Referee: John Rowbotham
Attendance: 10,822

CLYDE 0　　　**HEART OF MIDLOTHIAN 2**
　　　　　　　　Jackson, Wales
Clyde: Wylie, Ross, McLaughlin, Smith, Murray, Mitchell, (McLauchlan), Carrigan, McClay, (McCusker), Woods, (Barrett), Keogh, Grant
Heart of Midlothian: Niemi, Pressley, Naysmith, Petric, Murray, Tomaschek, Simpson, Cameron, Adam, (Severin), Jackson, (McSwegan), Wales
Substitute not used: Makel
Referee: Stuart Dougal
Attendance: 6,427

BERWICK RANGERS 0　　　**FALKIRK 0**
Berwick Rangers: O'Connor, McNicoll, Haddow, Ritchie, A. Neill, Watt, Rafferty, Anthony, Findlay, (Carr-Lawton), D. Smith, Magee
Substitutes not used: Patterson, Ramsay
Falkirk: Hogarth, Lawrie, McQuilken, Den Bieman, Christie, Nicholls, McKenzie, McDonald, Crabbe, Henry, (Hutchison), Hagen
Substitutes not used: Seaton, Sinclair
Referee: Jim McCluskey
Attendance: 2,035

ALLOA ATHLETIC 2　　　**DUNDEE UNITED 2**
Beaton, Cameron　　　　Hamilton (2)
Alloa Athletic: Cairns, (McKechnie), Wilson, D. Clark, Conway, Beaton, Valentine, Christie, Little Cameron, Irvine, Donaghy, (G. Clark)
Substitute not used: Boyle
Dundee United: Combe, Skoldmark, (Mathie), Partridge, Malpas, D. Patterson, Jenkins, Telesnikov, (Smith), Hannah, Easton, Hamilton, Thompson, (Ferraz)
Referee: Hugh Dallas
Attendance: 2,570

PARTICK THISTLE 2　　　**LIVINGSTON 1**
Craig, McLean　　　　　Bingham
Partick Thistle: Budinauckas, Docherty, McKeown, Lennon, Montgomerie, Archibald, Lyle, Craig, Dunn, Miller, (McLean), Jacobs
Substitutes not used: Martin, Callaghan
Livingston: McCaldon, Kelly, Deas, McManus, Coughlan, McKinnon, (Fleming), McCormick, (King), M. Millar, Keith, (McPhee), Bingham, Richardson
Referee: George Simpson
Attendance: 4,850

Sunday, 20th February, 2000

INVERNESS CALEDONIAN THISTLE 1　　　**ABERDEEN 1**
Mann　　　　　　　　　　　　　　　　　Guntveit
Inverness Caledonian Thistle: Calder, Tokely, Golabek, Teasdale, Mann, Sheerin, Bavidge, (Byers), McCulloch, Wilson, Christie, Wyness, (Glancy)
Substitute not used: Hind
Aberdeen: Leighton, Solberg, McAllister, (Clark), Whyte, Anderson, Dow, Bernard, Rutkiewicz, (Belabed), Guntveit, Stavrum, Winters, (Perry)
Referee: Kenny Clark
Attendance: 6,290

MOTHERWELL 3　　　**AYR UNITED 4**
McCulloch, Goodman,　Teale (2), Tarrant (2)
Brannan
Motherwell: Goram, Doesburg, McMillan, McGowan, Denham, (J. Davies), Townsley, (Nevin), Brannan, Valakari, Twaddle, (Nicholas), McCulloch, Goodman
Ayr United: Nelson, McMillan, Robertson, Shepherd, Craig, Duffy, Teale, Wilson, Hurst, Tarrant, (Crilly), Reynolds
Substitutes not used: Grant, Campbell
Referee: Martin Clark
Attendance: 5,470

FOURTH ROUND REPLAYS
Tuesday, 22nd February, 2000

DUNDEE UNITED 4　　　**ALLOA ATHLETIC 0**
Preget, Hamilton, Thompson (2)
Dundee United: Combe, Pascual, Partridge, Jenkins, Malpas, Davidson, Preget, (Smith), Hannah, Easton, Hamilton, (Ferraz), McConalogue, (Thompson)
Alloa Athletic: Parkyn, Boyle, (McKechnie), D. Clark, Conway, Beaton, (McAneny), Valentine, Little, Walker, (Donaghy), Cameron, Irvine, G. Clark
Referee: Hugh Dallas
Attendance: 4,913

Tuesday, 29th February, 2000

CLYDEBANK 0　　　**HIBERNIAN 3**
　　　　　　　　　Lovell, Lehmann, Sauzee
Clydebank: Morrison, Murray, Oliver, Murdoch, Brannigan, Wishart, Miller, (Hunter), Gardner, (O'Neil), McKelvie, Cameron, McWilliams
Substitute not used: McKinstrey
Hibernian: Colgan, Collins, Smith, Hughes, Sauzee, Lovell, Brebner, Latapy, McGinlay, Lehmann, Miller. Substitutes not used: Dennis, Paatelainen, Hartley
Referee: John Rowbotham
Attendance: 2,225

ABERDEEN 1　　　**INVERNESS CALEDONIAN THISTLE 0**
Stavrum
Aberdeen: Leighton, Perry, McAllister, Solberg, Anderson, Dow, Bernard, Mayer, (Darren Young), Belabed, (Rutkiewicz), Stavrum, Zerouali
Substitute not used: Preece
Inverness Caledonian Thistle: Calder, Teasdale, Golabek, Mann, Hastings, Sheerin, Tokely, McCulloch, (Byers), Wilson, (Bavidge), Christie, Xausa, (Wyness)
Referee: Kenny Clark
Attendance: 18,451

FALKIRK 3　　　**BERWICK RANGERS 0**
Crabbe, Hagen, McQuilken
Falkirk: Hogarth, Lawrie, McQuilken, Den Bieman, Christie, Nicholls, (Sinclair), McKenzie, Henry, Crabbe, (McDonald), Hutchison, Hagen, (Seaton)
Berwick Rangers: O'Connor, McNicoll, Haddow, Ritchie, A. Neill, Watt, (Carr–Lawton), Patterson, D. Smith, (Campbell), Findlay, (Rafferty) Anthony, Magee
Referee: Jim McCluskey
Attendance: 3,708

FIFTH ROUND
Saturday, 11th March, 2000

AYR UNITED 2　　　**PARTICK THISTLE 0**
Campbell, Tarrant
Ayr United: Nelson, McMillan, Craig, Scally, Campbell, Duffy, Teale, (Grant), Shepherd, Hurst, Tarrant, Hansen, (Robertson). Substitute not used: Dodds
Partick Thistle: Budinauckas, Martin, McKeown, Lennon, Montgomerie, Archibald, Paton, Craig, McLean, Dunn, (English), Jacobs
Substitutes not used: Duncan, Callaghan
Referee: Kenny Clark
Attendance: 8,365

HIBERNIAN 3　　　**FALKIRK 1**
Latapy (2), McGinlay　Lawrie
Hibernian: Colgan, Collins, Smith, Hughes, McIntosh, Sauzee, Lovell, (Brebner), Latapy, McGinlay, Paatelainen, (Lehmann), Miller
Substitute not used: Dennis
Falkirk: Hogarth, Lawrie, McQuilken, Den Bieman, Christie, Nicholls, McKenzie, Henry, (McDonald), Crabbe, Hutchison, (McAllister), Hagen
Substitute not used: Seaton
Referee: Willie Young
Attendance: 14,041

Sunday, 12th March, 2000

RANGERS 4
Ferguson, Numan,
Amoruso, Dodds

HEART OF MIDLOTHIAN 1
Cameron

Rangers: Klos, Reyna, (Wilson), Moore, Amoruso, Numan, (Kanchelskis), B. Ferguson, Albertz, Van Bronckhorst, McCann, Wallace, Rozental, (Dodds)
Heart of Midlothian: Niemi, Pressley, Naysmith, Murray, (McSwegan), Leclercq, Tomaschek, (Severin), Simpson, (Adam), Cameron, Flögel, Wales, Jackson
Referee: Hugh Dallas
Attendance: 31,471

DUNDEE UNITED 0

ABERDEEN 1
Jess

Dundee United: Combe, Pascual, Partridge, De Vos, McQuillan, Jonsson, McCulloch, (Davidson), Hannah, Easton, Hamilton, (Ferraz), Mathie
Substitute not used: Malpas
Aberdeen: Leighton, Lilley, (Perry), McAllister, Solberg, Anderson, Dow, Bernard, Jess, Mayer, (Belabed), Guntveit, Stavrum
Substitute not used: Preece
Referee: Michael McCurry
Attendance: 6,738

SEMI-FINALS

Saturday, 8th April, 2000
The National Stadium, Hampden Park, Glasgow

AYR UNITED 0

RANGERS 7
Rozental (2), Kanchelskis,
Wallace, Dodds (3)

Ayr United: Rovde, McMillan, Robertson, Shepherd, (Scally), Campbell, (Craig), Duffy, Teale, Wilson, Hurst, Tarrant, Reynolds, (Lyons)
Rangers: Klos, Reyna, Wilson, Amoruso, Numan, Kanchelskis, B. Ferguson, Van Bronckhorst, (Kerimoglu), Albertz, (McCann), Wallace, (Dodds), Rozental
Referee: John Rowbotham
Attendance: 38,357

Sunday, 9th April, 2000
The National Stadium, Hampden Park, Glasgow

HIBERNIAN 1
Latapy

ABERDEEN 2
Stavrum, Dow

Hibernian: Colgan, Collins, (Hartley), Smith, Hughes, McIntosh, Sauzee, Lovell, Latapy, McGinlay, Paatelainen, (Lehmann), Miller
Substitute not used: Dennis
Aberdeen: Leighton, Solberg, McAllister, Whyte, Anderson, Dow, (Lilley), Bernard, Jess, Mayer, Guntveit, Stavrum, (Belabed)
Substitute not used: Winters
Referee: Stuart Dougal
Attendance: 22,193

FINAL

Saturday, 27th May, 2000

The National Stadium,
Hampden Park, Glasgow

ABERDEEN 0   **RANGERS 4**

Aberdeen: Leighton, (Winters), Whyte, Solberg, Anderson, (Belabed), McAllister, Bernard, Jess, Rowson, Guntveit, Stavrum, (Zerouali), Dow

Rangers: Klos, Reyna, Moore, (Porrini), Vidmar, Numan, Kanchelskis, B. Ferguson, Albertz, Van Bronckhorst, (Kerimoglu), Wallace, (McCann), Dodds

Scorers: Rangers: Van Bronckhorst, Vidmar, Dodds, Albertz
Referee: Jim McCluskey
Attendance: 50,685

Billy Dodds scores for Rangers

SEASON 1919/20

17th April, 1920 at Hampden Park; Attendance 95,000;
Referee: Mr W. Bell (Hamilton)

KILMARNOCK 3	ALBION ROVERS 2
Culley, Shortt, J. Smith	Watson, Hillhouse

SEASON 1920/21

16th April, 1921 at Celtic Park; Attendance 28,294;
Referee: Mr H. Humphreys (Greenock)

PARTICK THISTLE 1	RANGERS 0
Blair	

SEASON 1921/22

15th April, 1922 at Hampden Park; Attendance 75,000
Referee: Mr T. Dougray (Bellshill)

MORTON 1	RANGERS 0
Gourlay	

SEASON 1922/23

31th March, 1923 at Hampden Park;
Attendance 80,100; Referee: Mr T. Dougray (Bellshill)

CELTIC 1	HIBERNIAN 0
Cassidy	

SEASON 1923/24

19th April, 1924 at Ibrox Stadium; Attendance 59,218;
Referee: Mr T. Dougray (Bellshill)

AIRDRIEONIANS 2	HIBERNIAN 0
Russell (2)	

SEASON 1924/25

11th April, 1925 at Hampden Park;
Attendance 75,137; Referee: Mr T. Dougray (Bellshill)

CELTIC 2	DUNDEE 1
Gallacher, McGrory	McLean

SEASON 1925/26

10th April, 1926 at Hampden Park; Attendance 98,620;
Referee: Mr P. Craigmyle (Aberdeen)

ST. MIRREN 2	CELTIC 0
McCrae, Howieson	

SEASON 1926/27

16th April, 1927 at Hampden Park; Attendance 80,070;
Referee: Mr T. Dougray (Bellshill)

CELTIC 3	EAST FIFE 1
Robertson (o.g.), McLean, Connolly	Wood

SEASON 1927/28

14th April, 1928 at Hampden Park; Attendance 118,115;
Referee: Mr W. Bell (Motherwell)

RANGERS 4	CELTIC 0
Meiklejohn (pen), McPhail, Archibald (2)	

SEASON 1928/29

6th April, 1929 at Hampden Park; Attendance 114,708;
Referee: Mr T. Dougray (Bellshill)

KILMARNOCK 2	RANGERS 0
Aitken, Williamson	

SEASON 1929/30

12th April, 1930 at Hampden Park; Attendance 107,475;
Referee: Mr W. Bell (Motherwell)

RANGERS 0	PARTICK THISTLE 0

REPLAY
16th April, 1930 at Hampden Park; Attendance 103,686;
Referee: Mr W. Bell (Motherwell)

RANGERS 2	PARTICK THISTLE 1
Marshall, Craig	Torbet

SEASON 1930/31

11th April, 1931 at Hampden Park; Attendance 104,803;
Referee: Mr P. Craigmyle (Aberdeen)

CELTIC 2	MOTHERWELL 2
McGrory, Craig (o.g.)	Stevenson, McMenemy

REPLAY
15th April, 1931 at Hampden Park; Attendance 98,579;
Referee: Mr P. Craigmyle (Aberdeen)

CELTIC 4	MOTHERWELL 2
R. Thomson (2), McGrory (2)	Murdoch, Stevenson

SEASON 1931/32

16th April, 1932 at Hampden Park; Attendance 111,982;
Referee: Mr P. Craigmyle (Aberdeen)

RANGERS 1	KILMARNOCK 1
McPhail	Maxwell

REPLAY
20th April, 1932 at Hampden Park; Attendance 110,695;
Referee: Mr P. Craigmyle (Aberdeen)

RANGERS 3	KILMARNOCK 0
Fleming, McPhail, English	

SEASON 1932/33

15th April, 1933 at Hampden Park; Attendance 102,339;
Referee: Mr T. Dougray (Bellshill)

CELTIC 1	MOTHERWELL 0
McGrory	

SEASON 1933/34

21st April, 1934 at Hampden Park; Attendance 113,430;
Referee: Mr M. C. Hutton (Glasgow)

RANGERS 5	ST. MIRREN 0
Nicholson (2), McPhail, Main, Smith	

SEASON 1934/35

20th April, 1935 at Hampden Park; Attendance 87,286;
Referee: Mr H. Watson (Glasgow)

RANGERS 2	HAMILTON ACADEMICAL 1
Smith (2)	Harrison

SEASON 1935/36

18th April 1936 at Hampden Park; Attendance 88,859;
Referee: Mr J. M. Martin (Ladybank)

RANGERS 1	THIRD LANARK 0
McPhail	

SEASON 1936/37

24th April, 1937 at Hampden Park; Attendance 147,365;
Referee: Mr M. C. Hutton (Glasgow)

CELTIC 2	ABERDEEN 1
Crum, Buchan	Armstrong

SEASON 1937/38

23rd April, 1938 at Hampden Park; Attendance 80,091;
Referee: Mr H. Watson (Glasgow)

EAST FIFE 1	KILMARNOCK 1
McLeod	McAvoy

REPLAY
27th April, 1938 at Hampden Park; Attendance 92,716;
Referee: Mr H. Watson (Glasgow)

EAST FIFE 4	KILMARNOCK 2
McKerrell (2), McLeod, Miller	Thomson (pen), McGrogan
After extra–time	

SEASON 1938/39

22nd April, 1939 at Hampden Park; Attendance 94,799;
Referee: Mr W. Webb (Glasgow)

CLYDE 4	MOTHERWELL 0
Wallace, Martin (2), Noble	

SEASON 1946/47

19th April, 1947 at Hampden Park; Attendance 82,140;
Referee: Mr R. Calder (Glasgow)

ABERDEEN 2
Hamilton, Williams

HIBERNIAN 1
Cuthbertson

SEASON 1947/48

17th April, 1948 at Hampden Park; Attendance 129,176;
Referee: Mr J. M. Martin (Blairgowrie)

RANGERS 1
Gillick
After extra–time

MORTON 1
Whyte

REPLAY
21st April, 1948 at Hampden Park; Attendance 131,975;
Referee: Mr J. M. Martin (Blairgowrie)

RANGERS 1
Williamson
After extra–time

MORTON 0

SEASON 1948/49

23rd April, 1949 at Hampden Park; Attendance 108,435;
Referee: Mr R. G. Benzie (Irvine)

RANGERS 4
Young (2 (2 pens)),
Williamson, Duncanson

CLYDE 1
Galletly

SEASON 1949/50

22nd April, 1950 at Hampden Park; Attendance 118,262
Referee: Mr J. A. Mowat (Burnside)

RANGERS 3
Findlay, Thornton (2)

EAST FIFE 0

SEASON 1950/51

21st April, 1951 at Hampden Park; Attendance 131,943
Referee: Mr J. A. Mowat (Burnside)

CELTIC 1
McPhail

MOTHERWELL 0

SEASON 1951/52

19th April, 1952 at Hampden Park; Attendance 136,304;
Referee: Mr J. A. Mowat (Burnside)

MOTHERWELL 4
Watson, Redpath, Humphries, Kelly

DUNDEE 0

SEASON 1952/53

25th April, 1953 at Hampden Park; Attendance 129,861;
Referee: Mr J. A. Mowat (Burnside)

RANGERS 1
Prentice

ABERDEEN 1
Yorston

REPLAY
29th April, 1953 at Hampden Park; Attendance 112,619;
Referee: Mr J. A. Mowat (Burnside)

RANGERS 1
Simpson

ABERDEEN 0

SEASON 1953/54

24th April, 1954 at Hampden Park; Attendance 129,926;
Referee: Mr C. E. Faultless (Giffnock)

CELTIC 2
Young (o.g.), Fallon

ABERDEEN 1
Buckley

SEASON 1954/55

23rd April, 1955 at Hampden Park; Attendance 106,111;
Referee: Mr C. E. Faultless (Giffnock)

CLYDE 1
Robertson

CELTIC 1
Walsh

REPLAY
27th April, 1955 at Hampden Park; Attendance 68,735;
Referee: Mr C. E. Faultless (Giffnock)

CLYDE 1
Ring

CELTIC 0

SEASON 1955/56

21st April, 1956 at Hampden Park; Attendance 133,399;
Referee: Mr R. H. Davidson (Airdrie)

HEART OF MIDLOTHIAN 3
Crawford (2), Conn

CELTIC 1
Haughney

SEASON 1956/57

20th April, 1957 at Hampden Park; Attendance 81,057;
Referee: Mr J. A. Mowat (Burnside)

FALKIRK 1
Prentice (pen)

KILMARNOCK 1
Curlett

REPLAY
24th April, 1957 at Hampden Park; Attendance 79,785;
Referee: Mr J. A. Mowat (Burnside)

FALKIRK 2
Merchant, Moran
After extra–time

KILMARNOCK 1
Curlett

SEASON 1957/58

26th April, 1958 at Hampden Park; Attendance 95,123;
Referee: Mr J. A. Mowat (Burnside)

CLYDE 1
Coyle

HIBERNIAN 0

SEASON 1958/59

25th April 1959 at Hampden Park; Attendance 108,951;
Referee: Mr J. A. Mowat (Burnside)

ST. MIRREN 3
Bryceland, Miller, Baker

ABERDEEN 1
Baird

SEASON 1959/60

23rd April, 1960 at Hampden Park; Attendance 108,017;
Referee: Mr R. H. Davidson (Airdrie)

RANGERS 2
Millar (2)

KILMARNOCK 0

SEASON 1960/61

22nd April, 1961 at Hampden Park; Attendance 113,618;
Referee: Mr H. Phillips (Wishaw)

DUNFERMLINE ATHLETIC 0

CELTIC 0

REPLAY
26th April, 1961 at Hampden Park; Attendance 87,866;
Referee: Mr H. Phillips (Wishaw)

DUNFERMLINE ATHLETIC 2
Thomson, Dickson

CELTIC 0

SEASON 1961/62

21st April, 1962 at Hampden Park; Attendance 126,930;
Referee: Mr T. Wharton (Clarkston)

RANGERS 2
Brand, Wilson

ST. MIRREN 0

SEASON 1962/63

4th May, 1963 at Hampden Park; Attendance 129,527;
Referee: Mr T. Wharton (Clarkston)

RANGERS 1
Brand

CELTIC 1
Murdoch

REPLAY
15th May, 1963 at Hampden Park; Attendance 120,263;
Referee: Mr T. Wharton (Clarkston)

RANGERS 3
Brand (2), Wilson

CELTIC 0

SEASON 1963/64

25th April, 1964 at Hampden Park; Attendance 120,982
Referee: Mr H. Phillips (Wishaw)

RANGERS 3
Millar (2), Brand

DUNDEE 1
Cameron

SEASON 1964/65

24th April, 1965 at Hampden Park; Attendance 108,800;
Referee: Mr H. Phillips (Wishaw)

CELTIC 3   **DUNFERMLINE ATHLETIC 2**
Auld (2), McNeill   Melrose, McLaughlin

SEASON 1965/66

23rd April, 1966 at Hampden Park; Attendance 126,559;
Referee: Mr T. Wharton (Clarkston)

RANGERS 0   **CELTIC 0**

REPLAY
27th April, 1966 at Hampden Park; Attendance 96,862;
Referee: Mr T. Wharton (Clarkston)

RANGERS 1   **CELTIC 0**
Johansen

SEASON 1966/67

29th April, 1967 at Hampden Park; Attendance 127,117;
Referee: Mr W. M. M. Syme (Glasgow)

CELTIC 2   **ABERDEEN 0**
Wallace (2)

SEASON 1967/68

27th April, 1968 at Hampden Park; Attendance 56,365;
Referee: Mr W. Anderson (East Kilbride)

DUNFERMLINE ATHLETIC 3   **HEART OF MIDLOTHIAN 1**
Gardner (2), Lister (pen)   Lunn (o.g.)

SEASON 1968/69

26th April, 1969 at Hampden Park; Attendance 132,870;
Referee: Mr J. Callaghan (Glasgow)

CELTIC 4   **RANGERS 0**
McNeill, Lennox, Connelly, Chalmers

SEASON 1969/70

11th April, 1970 at Hampden Park; Attendance 108,434;
Referee: Mr R. H. Davidson (Airdrie)

ABERDEEN 3   **CELTIC 1**
Harper (pen), McKay (2)   Lennox

SEASON 1970/71

8th May, 1971 at Hampden Park; Attendance 120,092;
Referee: Mr T. Wharton (Glasgow)

CELTIC 1   **RANGERS 1**
Lennox   D. Johnstone

REPLAY
12th May, 1971 at Hampden Park; Attendance 103,332;
Referee: Mr T. Wharton (Glasgow)

CELTIC 2   **RANGERS 1**
Macari, Hood (pen)   Callaghan (o.g.)

SEASON 1971/72

6th May, 1972 at Hampden Park; Attendance 106,102;
Referee: Mr A. MacKenzie (Larbert)

CELTIC 6   **HIBERNIAN 1**
McNeill, Deans (3), Macari (2)   Gordon

SEASON 1972/73

5th May, 1973 at Hampden Park; Attendance 122,714;
Referee: Mr J. R. P. Gordon (Newport–on–Tay)

RANGERS 3   **CELTIC 2**
Parlane, Conn, Forsyth   Dalglish, Connelly (pen)

SEASON 1973/74

4th May, 1974 at Hampden Park; Attendance 75,959;
Referee: Mr W. S. Black (Glasgow)

CELTIC 3   **DUNDEE UNITED 0**
Hood, Murray, Deans

SEASON 1974/75

3rd May, 1975 at Hampden Park; Attendance 75,457;
Referee: Mr I. M. D. Foote (Glasgow)

CELTIC 3   **AIRDRIEONIANS 1**
Wilson (2), McCluskey (pen)   McCann

SEASON 1975/76

1st May 1976 at Hampden Park; Attendance 85,354;
Referee: Mr R. H. Davidson (Airdrie)

RANGERS 3   **HEART OF MIDLOTHIAN 1**
Johnstone (2), MacDonald   Shaw

SEASON 1976/77

7th May, 1977 at Hampden Park; Attendance 54,252;
Referee: Mr R. B. Valentine (Dundee)

CELTIC 1   **RANGERS 0**
Lynch (pen)

SEASON 1977/78

6th May, 1978 at Hampden Park; Attendance 61,563;
Referee: Mr B. R. McGinlay (Glasgow)

RANGERS 2   **ABERDEEN 1**
MacDonald, Johnstone   Ritchie

SEASON 1978/79

12th May, 1979 at Hampden Park; Attendance 50,610;
Referee: Mr B. R. McGinlay (Glasgow)

RANGERS 0   **HIBERNIAN 0**

REPLAY
16th May, 1979 at Hampden Park; Attendance 33,504;
Referee: Mr B. R. McGinlay (Glasgow)

RANGERS 0   **HIBERNIAN 0**
After extra–time

SECOND REPLAY
28th May, 1979 at Hampden Park; Attendance 30,602;
Referee: Mr I. M. D. Foote (Glasgow)

RANGERS 3   **HIBERNIAN 2**
Johnstone (2), Duncan (o.g.)   Higgins, MacLeod (pen)
After extra–time – 2-2 After 90 Minutes

SEASON 1979/80

10th May, 1980 at Hampden Park; Attendance 70,303;
Referee: Mr G. B. Smith (Edinburgh)

CELTIC 1   **RANGERS 0**
McCluskey
After extra–time

SEASON 1980/81

9th May, 1981 at Hampden Park; Attendance 53,000;
Referee: Mr I. M. D. Foote (Glasgow)

RANGERS 0   **DUNDEE UNITED 0**
After extra–time

REPLAY
12th May, 1981 at Hampden Park; Attendance 43,099;
Referee: Mr I. M. D. Foote (Glasgow)

RANGERS 4   **DUNDEE UNITED 1**
Cooper, Russell, MacDonald (2)   Dodds

SEASON 1981/82

22nd May, 1982 at Hampden Park; Attendance 53,788;
Referee: Mr B. R. McGinlay (Balfron)

ABERDEEN 4   **RANGERS 1**
McLeish, McGhee, Strachan, Cooper   MacDonald
After extra–time – 1-1 after 90 minutes

SEASON 1982/83

21st May, 1983 at Hampden Park; Attendance 62,979;
Referee: Mr D. F. T. Syme (Rutherglen)

ABERDEEN 1   **RANGERS 0**
Black
After extra–time

SEASON 1983/84

19th May 1984 at Hampden Park; Attendance 58,900;
Referee: Mr R. B. Valentine (Dundee)

ABERDEEN 2   **CELTIC 1**
Black, McGhee   P. McStay
After extra–time – 1-1 after 90 minutes

SEASON 1984/85

18th May, 1985 at Hampden Park; Attendance 60,346;
Referee: Mr B. R. McGinlay (Balfron)

CELTIC 2   **DUNDEE UNITED 1**
Provan, McGarvey   Beedie

SEASON 1985/86

10th May, 1986 at Hampden Park; Attendance 62,841;
Referee: Mr H. Alexander (Irvine)

ABERDEEN 3   **HEART OF MIDLOTHIAN 0**
Hewitt (2), Stark

SEASON 1986/87

16th May, 1987 at Hampden Park; Attendance 51,782;
Referee: Mr K. J. Hope (Clarkston)

ST. MIRREN 1   **DUNDEE UNITED 0**
Ferguson
After extra–time

SEASON 1987/88

14th May, 1988 at Hampden Park; Attendance 74,000;
Referee: Mr G. B. Smith (Edinburgh)

CELTIC 2   **DUNDEE UNITED 1**
McAvennie (2)   Gallacher

SEASON 1988/89

20th May, 1989 at Hampden Park; Attendance 72,069;
Referee: Mr R. B. Valentine (Dundee)

CELTIC 1   **RANGERS 0**
Miller

SEASON 1989/90

12th May, 1990 at Hampden Park; Attendance 60,493;
Referee: Mr G. B. Smith (Edinburgh)

ABERDEEN 0   **CELTIC 0**
After extra–time. Aberdeen won 9–8 on Kicks from the Penalty Mark

SEASON 1990/91

18th May, 1991 at Hampden Park; Attendance 57,319;
Referee: Mr D. F. T. Syme (Rutherglen)

MOTHERWELL 4   **DUNDEE UNITED 3**
Ferguson, O'Donnell, Angus, Kirk Bowman, O'Neil, Jackson
After extra–time - 3-3 after 90 minutes

SEASON 1991/92

9th May 1992 at Hampden Park; Attendance 44,045;
Referee: Mr D. D. Hope (Erskine)

RANGERS 2   **AIRDRIEONIANS 1**
Hateley, McCoist   Smith

SEASON 1992/93

29th May, 1993 at Celtic Park; Attendance 50,715;
Referee: Mr J. McCluskey (Stewarton)

RANGERS 2   **ABERDEEN 1**
Murray, Hateley   Richardson

SEASON 1993/94

21st May, 1994 at Hampden Park; Attendance 37,709;
Referee: Mr D. D. Hope (Erskine)

DUNDEE UNITED 1   **RANGERS 0**
Brewster

SEASON 1994/95

27th May, 1995 at Hampden Park; Attendance 38,672;
Referee: Mr L. W. Mottram (Forth)

CELTIC 1   **AIRDRIEONIANS 0**
Van Hooijdonk

SEASON 1995/96

18th May, 1996 at Hampden Park; Attendance 37,760;
Referee: Mr H. Dallas (Motherwell)

RANGERS 5   **HEART OF MIDLOTHIAN 1**
Laudrup (2), Durie (3)   Colquhoun

SEASON 1996/97

24th May, 1997 at Ibrox Stadium; Attendance 48,953;
Referee: Mr H. Dallas (Motherwell)

KILMARNOCK 1   **FALKIRK 0**
Wright

SEASON 1997/98

16th May, 1998 at Celtic Park; Attendance 48,946;
Referee: Mr W. Young (Clarkston)

HEART OF MIDLOTHIAN 2   **RANGERS 1**
Cameron, Adam   McCoist

SEASON 1998/99

29th May, 1999 at The National Stadium, Hampden Park;
Attendance 51,746;
Referee: Mr H. Dallas (Motherwell)

RANGERS 1   **CELTIC 0**
Wallace

SEASON 1999/2000

27th May, 2000 at The National Stadium, Hampden Park;
Attendance 50,685;
Referee: Mr J. McCluskey

ABERDEEN 0   **RANGERS 4**
                                  Van Bronckhorst, Vidmar,
                                  Dodds, Albertz

S·F·L

FIRST ROUND

Tuesday, 10th August, 1999

BERWICK RANGERS 4   **QUEEN OF THE SOUTH 1**
A. Neill, P. Patterson,   C. Adams
M. Neil, M. Leask

Berwick Rangers: G. O'Connor, G. McNicoll, (M. Humphreys), L. Haddow,
K. Rafferty, A. Neill, I. Ritchie, M. Anthony, P. Patterson, (B. Quinn), M. Neil,
(M. Hunter), D. Smith, M. Leask
Queen of the South: J. Hillcoat, D. Lilley, A. Kerr, J.G. Rowe, A. Aitken, W.
Findlay, (M. Cleeland), P. Harvey, S. Leslie, L. Bailey, (C. Adams), S. Mallan,
D. Boyle, (C. Strain)
Referee: Tom Brown
Attendance: 336

AIRDRIEONIANS 2   **DUMBARTON 1**
A. Moore (2)   J. Dillon
Airdrieonians: S. Thomson, G. Farrell, A. Stewart, D. Farrell, F. Conway,
F. Johnston, A. Moore, (D. McGuire), J. Dick, G. Evans, S. McCormick,
H.A. McCann
Substitutes not used: S. Taylor, J. McClelland
Dumbarton: D. Barnes, M. Dickie, C. Brittain, J. Bruce, S. Jack, (J. Dillon),
T. King, S. McHarg, A. Grace, P. Flannery, A. Brown, (C. Smith), H. Ward,
(M. Melvin)
Referee: John Fleming
Attendance: 826

CLYDE 0   **ROSS COUNTY 4**
     B. Irvine, J. Fraser,
     G. Shaw, M. Geraghty
Clyde: D. Wylie, P. Keogh, M. McLaughlin, J.I. Spittal, B. Smith, J. Mitchell,
(J. Barrett), S. Convery, A. McClay, B. Carrigan, J. Ross, M. McLauchlan,
(S. Craib).
Substitute not used: C. Cranmer
Ross County: J.N. Walker, C. Tully, R. McBain, I. Maxwell, B. Irvine,
J. Fraser, G. Shaw, J. McGlashan, M. Geraghty, (K. Finlayson), F. Escalon,
P. Kinnaird, (K. Gilbert)
Substitute not used: G. Wood
Referee: Ian Fyfe
Attendance: 586

MONTROSE 1   **HAMILTON ACADEMICAL 3**
S. Taylor   N. Henderson, M. Moore,
     S. McCormick
Montrose: G. McGlynn, S. Clark, W.D. Scott, C. Farnan, (R. McWilliam),
G. Paterson, M. Craib, K. Duffy, N. Bennett, S. Taylor, J. O'Driscoll,
G. Meldrum, (C. Stevenson) **Substitute not used:** K. Niddrie
Hamilton Academical: C. Reid, R. Maclaren, E. Cunnington, N. Henderson,
P. Gaughan, S. Thomson, D. Muir, (A. Russell), W. Davidson, (M. Bonnar),
M. Moore, S. McCormick, D. Henderson, (G. Lynn)
Referee: Alan Gemmill
Attendance: 224

AYR UNITED 0   **RAITH ROVERS 1**
     A. Clark
Ayr United: C. Nelson, J. Robertson, D. Rogers, C. Duffy, J. Traynor,
(N. Scally), M. Wilson, G. Hurst, J. Davies, P. Lindau, (J. Bradford), G. Teale,
(A. Bone), D. Lennon
Raith Rovers: G. Van De Kamp, C. McEwan, L. Ellis, M. Andrews,
P. Browne, S. Tosh, D. Kirkwood, P. Agnew, P. Shields, (D. Shields),
A. Clark, (G. McCulloch), B. Hetherston
Substitute not used: D. McInally
Referee: Jim McCluskey
Attendance: 1,881

ARBROATH 3   **EAST FIFE 2**
J. Mercer, C. McGlashan,   G. Robertson,
P. Brownlie   D. Wright
Arbroath: C. Hinchcliffe, S. Florence, J. Gallagher, J. McAulay, D. Arbuckle,
J. Crawford, B. Sellars, T. Bryce, (S. Peters), C. McGlashan, C. Devine,
(P. Brownlie), J. Mercer, (N. Thomson)
East Fife: W. McCulloch, R. Shannon, R. Gibb, S. Ramsay, J. Cusick,
W. Herd, G. Robertson, R. Logan, B. Honeyman, (D. Wright), P. McGrillen,
S. Mackay
Substitutes not used: G. Tinley, K. Munro
Referee: Kevin Bisset
Attendance: 553

BRECHIN CITY 0   **QUEEN'S PARK 1**
     J. Brown
Brechin City: A.R. Geddes, G. Christie, R. Smith,
H. Cairney, K. Bain, M. Dailly, J. Dickson, (S. Kerrigan),
G. Price, S. Sorbie, A. Hutcheon, D. Coulston, (J. Durie).
Substitute not used: K. Williamson
Queen's Park: N. Inglis, R. Sinclair, D. Connaghan, R. Caven, P. Martin,
N. MacFarlane, G. Connell, S. Orr, (J. Whelan), M. Gallagher, (S. Edgar),
J. Brown, K. McGoldrick
Substitute not used: J. Geoghegan
Referee: Ian Elmslie
Attendance: 224

COWDENBEATH 0   **ALLOA ATHLETIC 4**
     M. Cameron, D. Beaton,
     G. McKechnie, S. Snedden (o.g.),
Cowdenbeath: R. Godfrey, W. Wilson, R. Thomson, S. Snedden,
K. McCulloch, D. White, M. Perry, (M. McDowell), M. Bradley,
W. Stewart, G. Brown, (C. McMillan), J.P. Burns
Substitute not used: D. Johnston
Alloa Athletic: M. Cairns, J. Boyle, D. Clark, P. McAneny, D. Beaton,
C. Valentine, M. Nelson, (S. Bovill), G. McKechnie, M. Cameron,
(R. Sharp), W. Irvine, M. Donaghy, (G. Clark)
Referee: Colin Hardie
Attendance: 206

DUNFERMLINE ATHLETIC 2   **MORTON 2**
(AET - 2-2 After 90 Minutes)
O. Coyle (2)   K. Thomas, W. Hawke
Morton won 5-4 on Kicks from the Penalty Mark
Dunfermline Athletic: I. Westwater, G. Shields, S. McGroarty, A. Tod,
B.Reid, J. Dolan, S. Thomson, E. May, (H. French), A. Smith, O. Coyle,
S. Petrie, (D. Graham)
Substitute not used: C. Ireland
Morton: A. Maxwell, D. Murie, P. McDonald, (C. McPherson), A. Millen,
D. Anderson, P. Fenwick, (R. Matheson), H. Curran, J. Anderson,
I. Ferguson, K. Thomas, W. Hawke, (S. Aitken)
Referee: George Simpson
Attendance: 2,892

EAST STIRLINGSHIRE 1   **CLYDEBANK 2**
(AET - 1-1 After 90 Minutes)
M. Hardie   J. McLaughlin, P. Cormack
East Stirlingshire: J. Butter, A. Storrar, G. Russell, B. Ross, C. Bowsher,
D. Muirhead, A. Barr, (M. Brown), (G. McDonald), M. Hardie, S. Laidlaw,
G. Higgins, A. Elliott, (B. Ferguson)
Clydebank: C. Scott, F. Wishart, D. Stewart, (P. Cormack), S. Murdoch,
J. McLaughlin, N. Oliver, J. McKinstrey, P. McIntyre, (S. Morrison),
G. Miller, R.L. Gardner, D. McKelvie, (C. Ewing)
Referee: Douglas McDonald
Attendance: 227

INVERNESS CALEDONIAN THISTLE 1   **ST. MIRREN 0**
M. Teasdale
Inverness Caledonian Thistle: L. Fridge, R. Tokely, S. Golabek,
R. Hastings, R. Mann, M. McCulloch, M. Teasdale, I. Stewart,
(M. Glancy), S. McLean, C. Christie, P. Sheerin, (B. Robson)
Substitute not used: D. Shearer
St. Mirren: L. Roy, I. Nicolson, C. Kerr, T. Turner, S. Baltacha,
B. McLaughlin, H. Murray, C. Drew, (J. Mendes), S. McGarry, (B. Lavety),
T. Brown, M. Yardley
Substitute not used: I. Ross
Referee: Garry Mitchell
Attendance: 1,343

STRANRAER 2   **FALKIRK 2**
(AET - 2-2 After 90 Minutes)
A. Blaikie (2)   A. Lawrie, C. McDonald
Stranraer won 5-4 on Kicks from the Penalty Mark
Stranraer: M. McGeown, J. Smith, K. Knox, W. Furphy, D. Johnstone,
T. Black, (P. Walker), G. McMartin, D. Cahoon, (A. Jenkins), I. Harty,
A. Blaikie, D. George
Substitute not used: R. Bell
Falkirk: M. Hogarth, S. Rennie, J. McQuilken, A. Lawrie, D. Sinclair,
S. McKenzie, G. McStay, (K. Deuchar), C. McDonald, S. Crabbe,
G. Hutchison, D. Hagen. **Substitutes not used:** G. O'Hara, R. Waddell
Referee: Brian McGarry
Attendance: 362

BELL'S CHALLENGE CUP

STIRLING ALBION 2   **STENHOUSEMUIR 2**
(AET - 1-1 After 90 Minutes)
A. Paterson, J. Gardner   R. Hamilton, W. Watters
Stirling Albion won 6-5 on Kicks from the Penalty Mark
Stirling Albion: J. Gardiner, A. Paterson, J. Tortolano, G. Donald, B. Martin,
C. Wood, J. McQuade, P. Mortimer, (D. Bell), A. Aitken, (K. McCallion),
C. Taggart, J. Gardner, (J. Philliben)
Stenhousemuir: L. Hamilton, A. Lawrence, A. Banks, G. Davidson,
(J. Gibson), T. Graham, J. Fisher, (D. Lorimer), (A. Cummings), M. Mooney,
R. Hamilton, W. Watters, C. McKinnon, D. Wood
Referee: Dougie Smith
Attendance: 412

PARTICK THISTLE 0   **ALBION ROVERS 2**
                             T. Tait, D. Rae
Partick Thistle: K. Budinauckas, G. Duncan, D. McKeown, (I. English),
S.R. Montgomerie, K. Brannigan, A. Archibald, E. Paton, (S. Dallas), A. Craig,
S. Miller, (E. McGuiness), T. McAllister, R. Dunn
Albion Rovers: M. McLean, R. Greenock, (J. McLees), N. McGowan,
J. McStay, G. Duncan, C. Silvestro, G. Russell, T. Tait, A. Nesovic, (I. Diack),
T. Lumsden, D. Rae. Substitute not used: J. Smith
Referee: Eric Martindale
Attendance: 1,231

SECOND ROUND
Tuesday, 24th August, 1999

QUEEN'S PARK 3   **ALBION ROVERS 1**
J. Whelan,   T. Tait
M. Gallagher (2)
Queen's Park: N. Inglis, D. Ferry, D. Connaghan, R. Caven, (R. Sinclair),
P. Martin, N. MacFarlane, G. Connell, J. Whelan, M. Gallagher, (S. Orr),
F. Carroll, (T. Little), K. McGoldrick
Albion Rovers: M. McLean, G. Robertson, (D. Rae), K. McBride, (M. Harty),
J. McStay, G. Duncan, J. Coulter, (C. Silvestro), J. McLees, T. Tait, A. Nesovic,
T. Lumsden, I. Diack
Referee: Bobby Orr
Attendance: 480

ROSS COUNTY 3   **MORTON 0**
B. Irvine, G. Shaw, G. Wood
Ross County: J.N. Walker, M. Canning, R. McBain, I. Maxwell, B. Irvine,
K. Gilbert, G. Shaw, J. Fraser, (M. Geraghty), G. Wood, S. Ferguson, D. Ross.
Substitutes not used: K. Finlayson, S. Mackay
Morton: A. Carlin, D. Murie, O. Archdeacon, (C. McPherson), A. Millen,
D. Anderson, J. Anderson, H. Curran, S. Aitken, I. Ferguson, (K. Wright),
W. Hawke, R. Matheson
Substitute not used: B. Slavin
Referee: Kevin Bisset
Attendance: 1,030

AIRDRIEONIANS 1   **ALLOA ATHLETIC 2**
F. Johnston   M. Nelson, I. Little
Airdrieonians: S. Thomson, J. McClelland, (F. Johnston), G. Farrell, P. Jack,
E. Forrest, A. Stewart, A. Moore, (S. McKeown), J. Dick, (S. Taylor), S. Ingram,
S. McCormick, H.A. McCann
Alloa Athletic: M. Cairns, J. Boyle, R. Sharp, M. Nelson, D. Beaton,
C. Valentine, I. Little, G. McKechnie, (D. Clark), M. Cameron,
W. Irvine, M. Donaghy
Substitutes not used: S. Bovill, G. Clark
Referee: John Underhill
Attendance: 765

LIVINGSTON 2   **BERWICK RANGERS 1**
(AET - 1-1 After 90 Minutes)
D. Bingham (2)   P. Patterson
Livingston: I. McCaldon, P. Kelly, P. Deas, A. McManus, S. Sweeney, J. Millar,
(C. King), B. McPhee, W. Macdonald, G. Britton, (M. McCormick),
D. Bingham, D. Fleming, (J. Robertson)
Berwick Rangers: G. O'Connor, K. Rafferty, L. Haddow, M. Hunter,
(M. Leask), A. Neill, I. Ritchie, P. Patterson, M. Anthony, (M. Humphreys),
D. Smith, (D. Watt), M. Neil, K. Magee
Referee: Jim McCluskey
Attendance: 1,384

CLYDEBANK 4   **FORFAR ATHLETIC 3**
D. McWilliams, C. Ewing (3)   S. Christie, S. Milne (2)
Clydebank: C. Scott, F. Wishart, P. Cormack, (D. Stewart), D. McWilliams,
(S. Murdoch), J. McLaughlin, N. Oliver, J. McKinstrey, C. Ewing, (D. McKelvie),
G. Miller, R.L. Gardner, I. Cameron
Forfar Athletic: S. Garden, A. Rattray, E. Donaldson, G. Ferguson,
(G. McCheyne), G. Johnston, (R. Brand), D. Craig, I. MacDonald,
(G. McPhee), A. Taylor, S. Milne, J. Nairn, S. Christie
Referee: Hugh Dallas
Attendance: 179

STRANRAER 1   **RAITH ROVERS 2**
K. Knox   M. Andrews, C. Dargo
Stranraer: M. McGeown, J. Smith, T. Black, W. Furphy, (A. Jenkins),
D. Johnstone, K. Knox, G. McMartin, D. George, J. Young, D. Cahoon,
I. Harty, (P. Walker)
Substitute not used: A. Blaikie
Raith Rovers: C. Coyle, G. McCulloch, (S. Hamilton), D. Kirkwood,
M. Andrews, P. Browne, K. Black, (S. Tosh), P. Tosh, P. Agnew, C. Dargo,
A. Clark, B. Hetherston, (J. Stein)
Referee: Eric Martindale
Attendance: 351

HAMILTON ACADEMICAL 0   **INVERNESS CALEDONIAN THISTLE 3**
                                  S. McLean, I. Stewart (2)
Hamilton Academical: C. Reid, M. Martin, (D. Muir), E. Cunnington, R. Kelly,
P. Gaughan, S. Thomson, S. Renicks, W. Davidson, (M. Moore), S. McCormick,
N. Henderson, D. Henderson
Substitute not used: A. Russell
Inverness Caledonian Thistle: L. Fridge, M. McCulloch, R. Hastings,
M. Teasdale, R. Mann, P. Sheerin, K. Byers, (B. Wilson), S. McLean, I. Stewart,
C. Christie, S. Golabek
Substitutes not used: M. Bavidge, M. Glancy
Referee: John Fleming
Attendance: 298

STIRLING ALBION 1   **ARBROATH 1**
(AET - 1-1 after 90 Minutes)
A. Graham   C. McGlashan
Stirling Albion won 4-3 on Kicks from the Penalty Mark
Stirling Albion: J. Gardiner, A. Paterson, J. Tortolano, G. Donald, B. Martin,
C. Wood, J. McQuade, (J. Philliben), A. Aitken, (D. Bell), (K. McCallion),
A. Graham, C. Taggart, P. Mortimer
Arbroath: C. Hinchcliffe, S. Florence, J. Gallagher, J. McAulay, A. Webster,
J. Crawford, C. Cooper, T. Bryce, (N. Thomson), C. McGlashan, C. Devine,
(D. Evans), B. Sellars
Substitute not used: F. Deswarte
Referee: Martin Clark
Attendance: 427

THIRD ROUND
Tuesday, 14th September, 1999

LIVINGSTON 3   **RAITH ROVERS 1**
M. Millar,   A. McManus (o.g.)
G. Britton, B. McPhee
Livingston: I. McCaldon, P. Kelly, P. Deas, A. McManus, S. Sweeney, J. Millar,
C. King, (D. Bingham), M. Millar, G. Britton, (M. McCormick), B. McPhee,
G. McCann, (D. Fleming)
Raith Rovers: G. Van De Kamp, C. McEwan, D. Kirkwood, (P. Shields),
M. Andrews, P. Browne, S. Hamilton, P. Tosh, (D. Agathe), S. Tosh, C. Dargo,
A. Burns, J. Stein
Substitute not used: G. McCulloch
Referee: Jim McCluskey
Attendance: 2,233

ROSS COUNTY 1   ALLOA ATHLETIC 2
(AET - 1-1 After 90 Minutes)
G. Shaw   M. Donaghy, W. Irvine
Ross County: J.N. Walker, M. Canning, J. Fraser,
I. Maxwell, B. Irvine, K. Gilbert, G. Shaw, F. Escalon,
G. Wood, (D. Ross), S. Ferguson, (K. Finlayson),
P. Kinnaird, (R. McBain)
Alloa Athletic: M. Cairns, R. Sharp, (J. Boyle), D. Clark,
M. Nelson, D. Beaton, C. Valentine, D. Menelaws, M. Christie, (G. Clark),
M. Cameron, G. McKechnie, (W. Irvine), M. Donaghy
Referee: George Simpson **Attendance:** 948

INVERNESS CALEDONIAN THISTLE 2   CLYDEBANK 0
M. Glancy, B. Robson
Inverness Caledonian Thistle: L. Fridge, R. Tokely, R. Hastings,
M. Teasdale, R. Mann, M. McCulloch, B. Wilson, (K. Byers), M. Glancy,
(C. Christie), M. Bavidge, (D. Shearer), B. Robson, P. Sheerin
Clydebank: C. Scott, F. Wishart, D. Stewart, (P. Cormack),
S. Murdoch, (I. Cameron), J. McLaughlin, N. Oliver, J. McKinstrey,
P. McIntyre, G. Miller, R.L. Gardner, A. Roddie, (C. Ewing)
Referee: Alan Freeland **Attendance:** 635

STIRLING ALBION 4   QUEEN'S PARK 0
C. Wood, A. Aitken,
A. Graham, J. Gardner
Stirling Albion: J. Gardiner, A. Paterson, K. McCallion, G. Donald,
(J. Philliben), B. Martin, C. Wood, J. McQuade, (P. Mortimer),
A. Aitken, (D. Bell), A. Graham, C. Taggart, J. Gardner
Queen's Park: N. Inglis, R. Sinclair, (D. Ferry), D. Connaghan,
R. Caven, P. Borland, N. MacFarlane, G. Connell, J. Whelan,
(S. Orr), M. Gallagher, J. Brown, F. Carroll, (T. Little)
Referee: John Underhill **Attendance:** 535

SEMI-FINALS

Tuesday, 28th September, 1999

INVERNESS CALEDONIAN THISTLE 1   LIVINGSTON 0
P. Sheerin
Inverness Caledonian Thistle: L. Fridge, R. Tokely, R. Hastings,
M. Teasdale, M. McCulloch, K. Byers, B. Wilson, (M. Bavidge),
S. McLean, D. Wyness, C. Christie, (S. Golabek), P. Sheerin
Substitute not used: M. Glancy
Livingston: I. McCaldon, P. Kelly, P. Deas, A. McManus,
G. Coughlan, S. Sweeney, C. King, (G. Britton), M. Millar, C. Feroz,
(M. McCormick), B. McPhee, D. Fleming, (R. McKinnon)
Referee: Michael McCurry **Attendance:** 1,025

STIRLING ALBION 1   ALLOA ATHLETIC 2
J. McQuade   S. Bannerman, W. Irvine
Stirling Albion: J. Gardiner, A. Paterson, J. Tortolano, G. Donald,
B. Martin, C. Wood, J. McQuade, P. Mortimer, (A. Aitken),
A. Graham, C. Taggart, J. Gardner, (K. McCallion)
Substitute not used: J. Philliben
Alloa Athletic: M. Cairns, J. Boyle, R. Sharp, M. Nelson, D. Beaton,
C. Valentine, S. Bannerman, M. Wilson, M. Cameron, W. Irvine,
M. Christie, (G. Allan)
Substitutes not used: G. McKechnie, G. Clark
Referee: Kenny Clark **Attendance:** 877

FINAL

Sunday, 21st November, 1999

**INVERNESS
CALEDONIAN THISTLE 4   ALLOA ATHLETIC 4**
(AET - 3-3 After 90 Minutes)
P. Sheerin (3), B. Wilson   G. Clark, M. Cameron (2),
                            M. Wilson

Alloa Athletic won 5-4 on Kicks from the Penalty Mark

Inverness Caledonian Thistle: L. Fridge, R. Tokely, R. Hastings,
M. Teasdale, M. McCulloch, P. Sheerin, B. Wilson, D. Xausa,
(M. Bavidge), D. Wyness, (M. Glancy), C. Christie, S. Golabek, (K. Byers)
Alloa Athletic: M. Cairns, J. Boyle, D. Clark, P. McAneny, D. Beaton,
C. Valentine, I. Little, G. Clark, (M. Christie), M. Cameron, W. Irvine,
M. Wilson, (G. McKechnie)
Substitute not used: M. Donaghy

Referee: Jim McCluskey
Attendance: 4,043

ROUND BY ROUND GOALS ANALYSIS

	No. of Goals Scored	Ties Played	Average Per Game
First Round	45	14	3.2
Second Round	28	8	3.5
Third Round	13	4	3
Semi-Finals	4	2	2
Final	8	1	8
Total No. of Goals Scored	98		
Total No. of Ties Played	29		
Average Goals per Game	3.4		

League Challenge Cup Final
Results Since 1990/91

(In Season 1990/91 known as The B&Q Centenary Cup; In Seasons 1991/92 to 1994/95 known as The B&Q Cup;
In Season 1995/96 to 1997/98 known as the League Challenge Cup; In Season 1999/2000 known as Bell's Challenge Cup)

SEASON 1990/91
Sunday, 11th November, 1990 at Fir Park, Motherwell;
Attendance 11,506, Referee: K. J. Hope (Clarkston)
AYR UNITED 2   DUNDEE 3
(AET - 2-2 After 90 Minutes)
D. Smyth, I. McAllister   W. Dodds (3)

SEASON 1991/92
Sunday, 8th December, 1991 at Fir Park, Motherwell;
Attendance 9,663, Referee: L.W. Mottram (Forth)
HAMILTON ACADEMICAL 1   AYR UNITED 0
C. Harris

SEASON 1992/93
Sunday, 13th December, 1992 at St. Mirren Park, Paisley;
Attendance 7,391, Referee: J.J. Timmons (Kilwinning)
MORTON 2   HAMILTON ACADEMICAL 3
R. Alexander (2)   C. Hillcoat, G. Clark (2)

SEASON 1993/94
Sunday, 12th December, 1993 at Fir Park, Motherwell;
Attendance 13,763, Referee: D.D. Hope (Erskine)
FALKIRK 3   ST. MIRREN 0
C. Duffy, J. Hughes, R. Cadette

SEASON 1994/95
Sunday, 6th November, 1994 at McDiarmid Park, Perth;
Attendance 8,844, Referee: H.F. Williamson (Renfrew)
DUNDEE 2   AIRDRIEONIANS 3
(AET - 2-2 After 90 Minutes)
G. Britton, G. Hay (o.g.)   P. Harvey, J. Boyle, Andrew Smith

SEASON 1995/96
Sunday, 5th November, 1995 at McDiarmid Park, Perth;
Attendance 7,856, Referee: J. Rowbotham (Kirkcaldy)
STENHOUSEMUIR 0   DUNDEE UNITED 0 (A.E.T.)
Stenhousemuir won 5-4 on Kicks from the Penalty Mark

SEASON 1996/97
Sunday, 3rd November, 1996 at Broadwood Stadium, Cumbernauld;
Attendance 5,522, Referee: K.W. Clark (Paisley)
STRANRAER 1   ST. JOHNSTONE 0
T. Sloan

SEASON 1997/98
Sunday, 2nd November, 1997 at Fir Park, Motherwell;
Attendance 9,735, Referee: R.T. Tait (East Kilbride)
FALKIRK 1   QUEEN OF THE SOUTH 0
D. Hagen

SEASON 1998/99
No Competition

SEASON 1999/2000
Sunday, 21st November, 1999 at Excelsior Stadium, Airdrie;
Attendance 4,043, Referee: Jim McCluskey
(AET – 3-3 after 90 minutes)
INVERNESS CAL. THISTLE 4   ALLOA ATHLETIC 4
P. Sheerin (3), B. Wilson   G. Clark, M. Cameron (2), M. Wilson
Alloa Athletic won 5-4 on Kicks from the Penalty Mark.

Reserve League Cup – Season 1999/2000

FIRST ROUND
13th September, 1999
RAITH ROVERS 4   STENHOUSEMUIR 0
14th September, 1999
COWDENBEATH 2   PARTICK THISTLE 4
21st September, 1999
ARBROATH 2   MONTROSE 1
27th September, 1999
BRECHIN CITY 1   QUEEN'S PARK 2
(AET – 1-1 after 90 minutes)
28th September, 1999
BERWICK RANGERS 1   MORTON 2
FALKIRK 4   CLYDE 1
2nd October, 1999
INVERNESS CAL. TH. 12   ALBION ROVERS 2
7th October, 1999
QUEEN OF THE SOUTH 1   LIVINGSTON 2
11th October, 1999
STRANRAER 4   HAMILTON ACADEMICAL 6
(AET – 3-3 after 90 minutes)

SECOND ROUND
12th October, 1999
QUEEN'S PARK 0   ROSS COUNTY 2
1st November, 1999
LIVINGSTON 7   ST. MIRREN 0
2nd November, 1999
PARTICK THISTLE 4   ARBROATH 0
16th November, 1999
EAST FIFE 3   INVERNESS CAL.TH. 1
17th November, 1999
AYR UNITED 1   DUNFERMLINE ATHLETIC 1
(AET – 1-1 after 90 minutes)
Dunfermline Athletic won 3–1 on Kicks from the Penalty Mark

2nd February, 2000
AIRDRIEONIANS 1   RAITH ROVERS 2
FALKIRK 3   FORFAR ATHLETIC 1
28th March, 2000
HAMILTON ACADEMICAL 3   MORTON 5
(AET – 3-3 after 90 minutes)

THIRD ROUND
27th January, 2000
DUNFERMLINE ATHLETIC 3   EAST FIFE 2
8th February, 2000
FALKIRK 2   LIVINGSTON 3
23rd March, 2000
PARTICK THISTLE 0   RAITH ROVERS 1
5th April, 2000
ROSS COUNTY 0   MORTON 1

SEMI-FINALS
11th April, 2000
LIVINGSTON 0   RAITH ROVERS 2
25th April, 2000
DUNFERMLINE ATHLETIC 2   MORTON 0

FINAL
Wednesday, 10th May, 2000, Stark's Park, Kirkcaldy
RAITH ROVERS 1   DUNFERMLINE ATHLETIC 2
Raith Rovers: C. Coyle, R. Maughan, L. Ellis, (P. Hampshire),
D. Kirkwood, S. Hamilton, K. Black, G. Fotheringham,
(J. Rushford), S. Tosh, D. Shields, S. Craig, J. Stein
Substitute not used: K. Nicol
Dunfermline Athletic: D. Hay, M. McCarty, (K. Nicol),
C. McCroarty, (K. McLeish), H. French, J. Potter, B. Reid,
D. Graham, S. Hampshire, C. Nish, C. Templeman, J. Dair
Substitute not used: D. Fleming
Scorers: Raith Rovers: D. Shields
Dunfermline Athletic: C. Nish, C. Templeman
Referee: Eddie Mack   Attendance: 347

Scottish Football's Annual Report

JULY

- **Alex McLeish signs a new three-year contract as manager of Hibernian as they prepare for their return to The Scottish Premier League.**

Alex McLeish

- Dundee United sign Tony Smith from Airdrieonians and hand Joe Miller a free transfer.

- Celtic break the Scottish transfer record when they sign Israeli international midfielder Eyal Berkovic from West Ham United for £5.75 million. New Celtic Head Coach John Barnes also recruits Dutch winger Bobby Petta from Ipswich Town under freedom of contract, Ivory Coast defender Olivier Tebily from Sheffield United for £1.2 million and Russian goalkeeper Dmitri Kharine from Chelsea.

- Rangers sign Dutch striker Michael Mols from Utrecht for £4 million and Polish defender Dariusz Adamczuk under freedom of contract from Dundee.

- Motherwell name former Scotland goalkeeper Andy Goram as their new captain.

- Ally McCoist signs a new one-year contract with Kilmarnock.

- Members of The Scottish Premier League endorse a new 12-team set up for the 2000-01 season.

- Rangers launch their bid to reach the group stages of the Champions League with a Second Qualifying Round, First Leg 4-1 win over Haka in Finland.

- Scotland Under-21 international winger Iain Anderson leaves Dundee to sign for French club Toulouse.

- Other transfers this month include: Matthias Jack (Fortuna Dusseldorf to Hibernian), Dirk Lehmann (Fulham to Hibernian), Nick Colgan (Bournemouth to Hibernian), Ian Ross (Motherwell to St. Mirren), Gary Wales (Hamilton Academical to Heart of Midlothian), David Preece (Darlington to Aberdeen), Michael Yates (Burscough to Dundee), Fabrice Henry (Basel to Hibernian), Ian Murray (Dundee United to Hibernian), Frank Van Eijs (Vinkenslag to Dundee), Mike Jeffrey (Fortuna

Ally McCoist in European action for Kilmarnock

Sittard to Kilmarnock), Colin Stewart (Ipswich Town to Kilmarnock), Frederic Dindeleux (Lille to Kilmarnock), Michael Brown (Manchester City to Motherwell), Alex Burns (Southend United to Raith Rovers), Jim Dick (Ayr United to Airdrieonians), Walter Scott (Arbroath to Montrose), Euan Donaldson (Albion Rovers to Forfar Athletic), Thomas Gill (FC Copenhagen to Ayr United)

AUGUST

- Dundee United sign Israeli international Jan Telesnikov from Beitar Jerusalem.

- Celtic sign Bulgarian international Stilian Petrov from CSKA Sofia for £2.2 million and release Italian defender Enrico Annoni.

- Alan Main and Nick Dasovic sign new long term contracts with St. Johnstone.

- Rangers reach the Third Qualifying Round of the Champions League when they beat Haka 3-0 at Ibrox to complete a 7-1 aggregate victory.

- Celtic are fined £45,000 by the SPL Commission of Enquiry into the unruly scenes at the controversial Old Firm fixture at Parkhead on 2nd May, 1999.

- Rangers defeat Parma 2-0 at Ibrox in the First Leg of their Champions League Third Qualifying Round Tie. In the UEFA Cup Qualifying Round First Leg, Celtic beat Cwmbran 6-0 in Cardiff, Kilmarnock lose 1-0 to KR Reykjavik in Iceland and St. Johnstone draw 1-1 with Vaasa in Finland.

- Celtic recruit Terry Gennoe as their new goalkeeping coach.

- Hibernian sign Scotland Under-21 international midfielder Grant Brebner from Reading for £400,000.

- Rangers reach the first group stages of the Champions League when they lose 1-0 to Parma in Italy to secure a 2-1 aggregate win. All three Scottish participants reach the First Round proper of the UEFA Cup; Celtic beat Cwmbran 4-0 at Parkhead for a 10-0 aggregate win, Kilmarnock defeat KR Reykjavik 2-0 at Rugby Park for a 2-1 success and St. Johnstone's 2-0 McDiarmid Park win over Vaasa earns a 3-1 aggregate scoreline.

- Other transfers this month include: Greg Shields (Dunfermline Athletic to Charlton Athletic), Neil McGowan (Albion Rovers to Oxford United), Kevin Thomas (Morton to St. Johnstone), David Lilley (Queen of the South to Aberdeen), David Byrne (Shelbourne to Dundee United), Thomas Solberg (Viking Stavanger to Aberdeen), Jean Pierre Delauney (Le Havre to Dundee United), Tassos Venetis (Larissa to Dundee United), Michael Watt (Norwich City to Kilmarnock), Darren Beesley (Rotherham United to Kilmarnock), Sean Hessey (Huddersfield Town to Kilmarnock).

SEPTEMBER

- Rangers are cleared by the SPL Commission of Enquiry of provocative celebrations by their players following the infamous Old Firm fixture at Parkhead on 2nd May, 1999.

- Scotland secure a crucial 2-1 win over Bosnia in Sarajevo to maintain their hopes of Euro 2000 qualification. Don Hutchison and Billy Dodds are the scorers.

- Mark Burchill claims a hat-trick as Scotland's Under-21 side defeat their Bosnian counterparts 5-2.

- Heart of Midlothian announce a £5 million cash injection from the Scottish Media Group.

- Scotland's Euro 2000 hopes take a dent when they draw 0-0 with Estonia in Tallinn.

- Celtic are reported to have held talks with Ajax and PSV Eindhoven over the formation of an Atlantic League.

- Rangers lose their opening Champions League Group fixture 2-0 to Valencia in Spain. They subsequently revive their qualification hopes with a 1-1 draw against Bayern Munich at Ibrox and a 1-0 win over PSV Eindhoven in Holland.

- Celtic reach the Second Round of the UEFA Cup with a 2-1 aggregate win over Israeli side Hapoel Tel Aviv.

- Kilmarnock are knocked out of the UEFA Cup 5-0 on aggregate by powerful German side Kaiserslautern. St. Johnstone also make their exit from the competition but take some credit from a 6-3 aggregate loss to Monaco.

- Former Hibernian chairman Lex Gold is named the new chairman of The Scottish Premier League following the resignation of Robert Wilson.

- Motherwell's SPL clash with Heart of Midlothian at Fir Park is the subject of controversy when it is abandoned at half-time because of rain with the home side leading 1-0.

- Ross County briefly sign former Rangers and England striker Mark Hateley before releasing him after just three weeks with the club.

- Rangers sell former Scotland Under–21 midfielder Charlie Miller to Watford for £400,000.

Don Hutchison celebrates scoring for Scotland

- Kilmarnock sign French striker Christophe Cocard from Auxerre under freedom of contract.
- Celtic striker Tommy Johnson signs a three-month loan deal with Everton.
- Other transfers this month include: Rachid Belabed (Molenbeek to Aberdeen), Stephen Craib (Clyde to Montrose), Justin Skinner (Hibernian to Dunfermline Athletic), John Henry (Kilmarnock to Falkirk), David Moss (Falkirk to Dunfermline Athletic), Lee Butler (Dunfermline Athletic to Halifax Town)

Neil McCann scores for Rangers against PSV Eindhoven

- Scotland clinch a place in the Play-Offs for Euro 2000 when a penalty kick from John Collins gives them a 1–0 win over Bosnia at Ibrox.
- Scotland complete their group fixtures with a comfortable 3-0 win over Lithuania at Hampden.
- Paul Lambert signs a new four year contract with Celtic.
- The draw for the Euro 2000 Play-Offs in Aachen creates massive headlines as it pairs Scotland with England.
- Rangers record an impressive 4-1 Champions League win over PSV Eindhoven at Ibrox but their hopes of further progress are left in the balance when they then lose 2-1 at home to Valencia.
- Aberdeen record their first SPL win of the season in remarkable fashion as they defeat Motherwell 6-5 at Fir Park.
- Celtic suffer a dreadful blow when Swedish striker and reigning Scottish Player of the Year Henrik Larsson breaks a leg during their 1-0 UEFA Cup Second Round, First Leg defeat against Lyon in France.
- Dundee sign striker Nicky Banger from Oxford United.

- Celtic sign former England striker Ian Wright on a free transfer from West Ham United as cover for the injured Larsson.
- Other transfers this month include: Paul Harvey (Queen of the South to Motherwell), Pat Onstad (Rochester Raging Rhinos to Dundee United), John Davies (Ayr United to Motherwell), Benito Kemble (SVV Eindhoven to Motherwell), Patrizio Billio (Ancona to Dundee), Ian Ferguson (Morton to Hamilton Academical), Paul Forrester (Berwick Rangers to Stenhousemuir), Derek Holmes (Heart of Midlothian to Ross County), Lee Bailey (Queen of the South to Brechin City), John Dickson (Brechin City to Queen of the South), Barry Lavety (Hibernian to St. Mirren), Mark Duthie (Ayr United to Ross County), Ben Honeyman (East Fife to Brechin City), James Nairn (Forfar Athletic to Brechin City), Jim McKellar (Brechin City to Forfar Athletic).

- Rangers are knocked out of the Champions League when they lose their final phase one group fixture 1-0 to Bayern Munich in Germany. To compound their misery, Dutch striker Michael Mols suffers a serious knee injury which will rule him out for the rest of the season.
- Aberdeen sign Norwegian midfielder Cato Guntveit from Brann.

- Miodrag Krivokapic replaces Jim Griffin as the Assistant Manager of Motherwell.
- Celtic are knocked out of the UEFA Cup when they lose 1-0 to Lyon at Parkhead, completing a 2-0 aggregate Second Round loss.
- Rangers beat Celtic 4-2 at Ibrox in the first Old Firm clash of the season. Paul Lambert is carried off with an injury which rules him out of Scotland's Euro 2000 Play-Off games against England.
- Paul Scholes breaks Scottish hearts at Hampden when he scores both goals in England's 2-0 Play-Off, First Leg win.
- Steve Kirk is dismissed as Player-Manager of East Fife. He is replaced by Rab Shannon.
- Rangers sign Finnish international defender Tero Penttila from Haka for £300,000 and recruit Danish goalkeeper Thomas Myhre on a three-month loan from Everton.
- Dick Campbell resigns as manager of Dunfermline Athletic. His replacement is Jimmy Calderwood.
- Scotland beat England 1-0 at Wembley with a goal from Don Hutchison but lose the Euro 2000 Play-Off 2-1 on aggregate.
- Rangers defeat Borussia Dortmund 2-0 at Ibrox in the First Leg of their UEFA Cup Third Round tie.
- Alloa Athletic defeat Inverness Caledonian Thistle in a dramatic penalty shoot-out to win the

Alloa Athletic, winners of the Bell's Challenge Cup

Bell's Challenge Cup after the teams had shared eight goals at the Excelsior Stadium.

- Other transfers this month include: Graeme Jones (Wigan Athletic to St. Johnstone), Arild Stavrum (Helsingborgs to Aberdeen), Nicky Banger (Oxford United to Dundee), Craig Farnan (Montrose to Forfar Athletic).

DECEMBER

- Celtic sell Scotland midfielder Craig Burley to Derby County for £3 million.
- Rangers buy Scotland striker Billy Dodds from Dundee United for £1.3 million.

Billy Dodds playing for Scotland

- The 2002 World Cup qualifying draw is made in Tokyo and places Scotland in a group with Belgium, Croatia, Latvia and San Marino.
- Scotland's participation in the European club competitions ends for the season when Rangers lose 2-0 in Germany to Borussia Dortmund in the Second Leg of their UEFA Cup Third Round tie. It finishes 2-2 on aggregate with Rangers losing out 3–1 in a penalty shoot-out.
- Heart of Midlothian sign Finnish international goalkeeper Antti Niemi from Rangers for £400,000.
- Celtic sign Brazilian international defender Rafael Scheidt from Gremio for £5 million.
- John McVeigh is sacked as manager of Raith Rovers and is replaced by his assistant Peter Hetherston.
- Falkirk re-sign Dutch defender Ivo Den Bieman who had returned to Holland for six months.
- Aberdeen sign Moroccan midfielder Hicham Zerouali from Rabat.
- Hugh McCann leaves East Stirlingshire and is replaced as manager by George Fairley.
- The final Old Firm match of the century is a 1-1 draw at Parkhead with Mark Viduka's opening goal for Celtic cancelled out by a Billy Dodds strike for Rangers.
- Other transfers this month include: Fitzroy Simpson (Portsmouth to Heart of Midlothian), Craig Ireland (Dunfermline Athletic to Dundee), Martin Wood (Rothes to Motherwell), Warren Hawke (Morton to Queen of the South), Scott McLean (Inverness Caledonian Thistle to Partick Thistle).

JANUARY

- Rangers sign Turkish international midfielder Tugay Kerimoglu from Galatasaray for £1.3 million.
- Celtic sell Norwegian striker Harald Brattbakk to FC Copenhagen for £600,000.
- Kilmarnock sign former Scotland full-back Tosh McKinlay under freedom of contract.
- Morton dismiss Billy Stark as manager. He is replaced by Clydebank boss Ian McCall.
- Ian Ferguson leaves Rangers after 12 years at Ibrox to sign for Dunfermline Athletic.
- Steve Morrison is named the new Clydebank manager following the departure of Ian McCall.
- Dundee United sign Jim Hamilton from Aberdeen for £300,000.
- Heart of Midlothian sign Slovakian international midfielder Robert Tomaschek from Slovan Bratislava for £400,000.
- Motherwell sign former Falkirk full-back Martyn Corrigan under freedom of contract.
- Other transfers this month include: Andy Smith (Dunfermline Athletic to Kilmarnock), Steven Hampshire (Chelsea to Dunfermline Athletic), Kris Mampaey (Willem II to Dunfermline Athletic), Dennis Wyness (Aberdeen to Inverness Caledonian Thistle), Garry Wood (Ross County to Berwick Rangers), Robert Brown (Brechin City to Deveronvale).

- Rangers sell Argentinian striker Gabriel Amato to Gremio for £3.5 million.

- Inverness Caledonian Thistle produce one of the biggest upsets in Scottish Cup history when they defeat Celtic 3-1 at Parkhead in the Fourth Round. Another shock result sees Alloa Athletic defeat Kilmarnock 1-0 in a replay.

- John Barnes is sacked as Head Coach of Celtic in the wake of the Inverness defeat. Director of Football Kenny Dalglish takes over on a temporary basis for the rest of the season.

- Aberdeen defeat Dundee United 1-0 at Dens Park in the first of the CIS Insurance Cup Semi-Finals with a goal from Arild Stavrum. Celtic join them in the Final when a Lubomir Moravcik goal earns them a 1-0 win over Kilmarnock at Hampden.

- Ian Wright leaves Celtic to sign for Burnley.

- Tommy Burns rejoins Celtic as first team coach to assist Dalglish.

Celtic celebrate winning last season's CIS Insurance Cup

- Rangers sell Scotland captain Colin Hendry to Coventry City for £1 million.

- Former Scotland Under-21 winger Andy McLaren is charged with misconduct by the FA in England after failing a random drugs test while with Reading.

- Other transfers this month include: Stephen Frail (Tranmere Rovers to St. Johnstone), Martin McIntosh (Stockport County to Hibernian), John McQuillan (St. Johnstone to Dundee United), Miguel Simao (St. Johnstone to Sanfrecce Hiroshima), Sean O'Connor (Hednesford Town to Dundee United), Stephen Crawford (Hibernian to Dunfermline Athletic), Steve Laidlaw (East Stirlingshire to Berwick Rangers), Ian Little (Livingston to Alloa Athletic), Andy Whiteford (St. Johnstone to Stirling Albion), Brian Mitchell (Arbroath to Montrose), Raymond Sharp (Alloa Athletic to East Fife), Graham Duncan (Albion Rovers to Queen of the South), Dean McPherson (Berwick Rangers to East Stirlingshire), Gerry O'Hara (Falkirk to East Fife), Roddy Grant (St. Johnstone to Ayr United).

- Motherwell midfielder Ged Brannan upsets his club when he agrees to play for the Cayman Islands in their World Cup qualifying campaign.

- A late Rod Wallace goal earns Rangers a crucial 1-0 win over Celtic at Parkhead to move 12 points clear at the top of the SPL table.

- Mark Shanks resigns as manager of Albion Rovers. He is subsequently replaced by John McVeigh.

John McVeigh

- Scotland winger Allan Johnston signs a pre-contract agreement to join Rangers from Sunderland in the summer.

- Ray Stewart is dismissed as Head Coach of Livingston and is replaced by former Celtic boss Davie Hay.

- Celtic win the CIS Insurance Cup as they defeat Aberdeen in the Final at Hampden with goals from Vidar Riseth and Tommy Johnson.

- Rangers defeat Celtic 4-0 at Ibrox in the final Old Firm fixture of the season to move 15 points clear at the top of the SPL.

Nationwide

- Scotland's Under-21 side lose 2-0 to their French counterparts in a friendly international at Rugby Park.

- Goals from Sylvain Wiltord and Thierry Henry give World Champions France a 2-0 win over Scotland in a friendly international at Hampden.

- Other transfers this month include: Javier Artero (San Lorenzo to Dundee), Paul Ritchie (Heart of Midlothian to Bolton Wanderers), Paul Shields (Raith Rovers to Celtic), Marc Millar (Livingston to St. Johnstone), Chris Coyne (West Ham United to Dundee), Barry Elliot (Celtic to Dundee), Leigh Jenkinson (Heart of Midlothian to Dundee United), Michel Doesburg (Motherwell to Dunfermline Athletic), Gerry Farrell (Airdrieonians to Alloa Athletic), Nicky Henderson (Hamilton Academical to Clyde), Martin McLauchlan (Clyde to Stenhousemuir),Craig Taggart (Stirling Albion to Ross County), John Gallagher (Arbroath to Queen of the South), Martin Hardie (East Stirlingshire to Partick Thistle), Robbie Horn (Heart of Midlothian to Forfar Athletic), Stephen McCormick (Airdrieonians to East Fife), Paul McKnight (Rangers to St. Mirren), Keith Wright (Morton to Stenhousemuir).

Clyde are Second Division Champions

- Graeme Armstrong is dismissed as manager of Stenhousemuir. He is replaced by Brian Fairley.
- Hamilton Academical are deducted 15 points by The Scottish Football League for their failure to fulfil their fixture at Stenhousemuir.
- Celtic's 1-1 draw with Hibernian at Parkhead means Rangers are Scottish Premier League Champions for the second successive season. The Ibrox club celebrate by beating St. Johnstone 2-0 at McDiarmid Park the following day.

St. Mirren clinch the First Division title

- St. Mirren clinch promotion to the SPL with a 2-1 win over Ayr United at Somerset Park. Dunfermline Athletic will join them in the top flight.
- Scotland's Under-21 side lose 2-0 to Holland in a friendly international.
- The Scotland senior side record a creditable 0-0 draw with Holland in Arnhem in a friendly.
- Clyde become Second Division Champions with a 4-1 home win over Arbroath.
- St. Mirren clinch the First Division title with a 3-0 home win over Raith Rovers.

APRIL

- Hamilton Academical are unable to fulfil their Second Division fixture at Stenhousemuir when their players go on strike over unpaid wages.
- Rangers crush Ayr United 7-0 in the first Tennents Scottish Cup Semi-Final at Hampden. Aberdeen defeat Hibernian 2-1 at the same venue the following day to join them in the Final.
- Celtic open negotiations with former Holland coach Guus Hiddink over the vacant managerial position at Parkhead.

- Finnish international midfielder Simo Valakari signs a pre-contract agreement to join Derby County from Motherwell.

- Hamilton Academical fail in their appeal to The Scottish Football Association against the 15-point deduction which has seen them relegated to the Third Division.

- Queen's Park clinch the Third Division title with a 3-2 win over Cowdenbeath at Central Park. Berwick Rangers and Forfar Athletic are also promoted with East Fife missing out on the final day of the season.

Queen's Park - Bell's Third Division Champions

- Dundee announce that Jocky Scott will not be retained as manager when his contract expires at the end of the season. He will be replaced at Dens Park by Italian Ivano Bonetti who will be player-manager.

- Tommy Moller-Nielsen quits his post as assistant manager of Aberdeen.

- Rangers midfielder Barry Ferguson is named as Scotland's Player of the Year by the Scottish Football Writers Association.

- Ian McCall is sacked as manager of Morton after just 15 games in charge of the Cappielow club.

- John Philliben is dismissed as manager of Stirling Albion and replaced by the club's former coach Ray Stewart.

- Ken Eadie and George Rowe resign as

co-managers of Queen of the South. John Connolly is named as the club's new manager.

- Heart of Midlothian clinch a UEFA Cup place when they beat Hibernian 2-1 at Tynecastle on the final day of the SPL season.

- Rangers defeat Aberdeen 4-0 in the Tennents Scottish Cup Final at Hampden to complete the domestic double.

- A goal from Manchester United striker Alex Notman earns Scotland's Under-21's a 1-1 draw away to Northern Ireland in the President's Cup.

- Scotland defeat the Republic of Ireland 2-1 in a friendly international in Dublin with goals from Don Hutchison and Barry Ferguson.

Kenny Miller scores for Scotland's Under 21s against Wales

- Rangers sign Dutch international defender Bert Konterman from Feyenoord for £4 million.

- Kilmarnock sign Andy McLaren on a short-term contract as the winger bids to get his career back on track. Scotland Under-21 striker Craig Dargo also moves to Rugby Park in a £100,000 switch from Raith Rovers.

- Rangers continue their summer recruitment drive as they sign Paul Ritchie from Bolton Wanderers, Peter Lovenkrands from AB Copenhagen and Kenny Miller from Hibernian.

- Mark Viduka agrees to join Leeds United in a £7 million move from Celtic.

- Kenny Dalglish's contract as Director of Football at Celtic is terminated by the Parkhead club.

Rangers' Captain Arthur Numan lifts the Tennents Scottish Cup

- Kenny Miller scores the goal as Scotland's Under-21's complete a successful President's Cup with a 1-0 win over Wales in Northern Ireland.

- Other transfers this month: Scott Taylor (Montrose to Forfar Athletic), Barry Wilson (Inverness Caledonian Thistle to Livingston), Paul Lovering (Hibernian to Ayr United), Paul McIlravey (Forfar Athletic to Montrose), Jim McKellar (Forfar Athletic to Montrose), Aidan McVeigh (Glenavon to Ayr United), Jim Smith (Stranraer to Partick Thistle).

JUNE

- Martin O'Neill signs a three-year contract to become the new manager of Celtic.

Martin O'Neill, Celtic's new manager

Nationwide · THE SCOTTISH FOOTBALL LEAGUE

FIRST DIVISION

AIRDRIEONIANS
League Champions:
Division II: 1902/03, 1954/55,1973/74
Scottish Cup Winners: 1924
B&Q Cup Winners: 1994/95
Scottish Spring Cup Winners: 1976

ALLOA ATHLETIC
League Champions:
Division II: 1921/22
Third Division: 1997/98
Bell's Challenge Cup Winners:
1999/2000

AYR UNITED
League Champions:
Division II: 1911/12, 1912/13,
1927/28, 1936/37, 1958/59, 1965/66
Second Division: 1987/88, 1996/97

CLYDE
League Champions:
Division II: 1904/05, 1951/52,
1956/57, 1961/62, 1972/73,
Second Division:
1977/78, 1981/82, 1992/93,
1999/2000
Scottish Cup Winners:
1939, 1955, 1958

FALKIRK
League Champions:
First Division: 1990/91, 1993/94
Division II: 1935/36, 1969/70,1974/75
Second Division: 1979/80
Scottish Cup Winners: 1913, 1957
SFL Challenge Cup Winners:
1993/94 (known as B&Q Cup),
1997/98

INVERNESS CALEDONIAN THISTLE
League Champions:
Third Division: 1996/97

LIVINGSTON
(Formerly Meadowbank Thistle)
League Champions:
Second Division: 1986/87, 1998/99
Third Division: 1995/96

MORTON
League Champions:
Division II: 1949/50, 1963/64,1966/67
First Division: 1977/78, 1983/84,
1986/87
Second Division: 1994/95
Scottish Cup Winners: 1922

RAITH ROVERS
League Champions:
First Division: 1992/93, 1994/95
Division II: 1907/08, 1909/10 (shared)
1937/38, 1948/49
League Cup Winners: 1994/95

ROSS COUNTY
League Champions:
Third Division: 1998/99

SECOND DIVISION

ARBROATH
League Runners-up:
Division II: 1934/35, 1958/59,
1967/68, 1971/72,
Third Division: 1997/98

BERWICK RANGERS
League Champions:
Second Division: 1978/79
Runners-up: 1993/94
Third Division Runners-up:
1999/2000

CLYDEBANK
League Champions:
Second Division: 1975/76

FORFAR ATHLETIC
League Champions:
'C' Division: 1948/49
Second Division: 1983/84
Third Division: 1994/95

PARTICK THISTLE
League Champions:
First Division: 1975/76 Runners-up: 1999/92
Division II: 1896/97, 1899/1900,
1970/71 Runners-up: 1901/02
League Cup Winners: 1971/72
Runners-up: 1953/54, 1956/57, 1958/59
Scottish Cup Winners: 1921
Runners-up: 1930
Glasgow Cup Winners: 1935, 1951,
1952, 1954, 1960, 1981, 1989

QUEEN OF THE SOUTH
League Champions:
Division II: 1950/51

QUEEN'S PARK
League Champions:
Division II: 1922/23
'B' Division 1955/56
Second Division: 1980/81
Third Division: 1999/2000
Scottish Cup Winners:
1874, 1875, 1876, 1880, 1881,
1882, 1884, 1886, 1890, 1893
FA Cup: Runners-up: 1884, 1889
FA Charity Shield: 1899 (Shared
with Aston Villa)

STENHOUSEMUIR
SFL Challenge Cup Winners: 1995/96

STIRLING ALBION
League Champions:
Division II: 1952/53, 1957/58,
1960/61, 1964/65,
Second Division: 1976/77, 1990/91,
1995/96

STRANRAER
League Champions:
Second Division: 1993/94, 1997/98
SFL Challenge Cup Winners: 1996/97

THIRD DIVISION

ALBION ROVERS
League Champions:
Division II: 1933/34
Second Division: 1988/89
Scottish Qualifying Cup Winners: 1913/14

BRECHIN CITY
League Champions:
'C' Division: 1953/54
Second Division: 1982/83, 1989/90

COWDENBEATH
League Champions:
Division II: 1913/14, 1914/15, 1938/39

DUMBARTON
League Champions:
Division I: 1890/91 (shared with
Rangers), 1891/92
Division II: 1910/11, 1971/72
Second Division: 1991/92
Scottish Cup Winners: 1883

EAST FIFE
League Champions:
Division II: 1947/48
League Cup Winners:
1947/48, 1949/50, 1953/54
Scottish Cup Winners: 1938

EAST STIRLINGSHIRE
League Champions:
Division II: 1931/32

HAMILTON ACADEMICAL
League Champions:
Division II: 1903/04
First Division: 1985/86, 1987/88
B&Q Cup Winners: 1991/92, 1992/93
Scottish Cup Runners-up:
1910/11, 1934/35
Second Division Runners-up:
1952/53, 1964/65, 1996/97
Lanarkshire Cup Winners: 10 Times

MONTROSE
League Champions:
Second Division: 1984/85

THE SCOTTISH PREMIER LEAGUE

ABERDEEN

League Champions:
Division I: 1954/55
Premier Division: 1979/80, 1983/84, 1984/85
League Cup Winners:
1955/56, 1976/77, 1985/86, 1989/90, 1995/96
Scottish Cup Winners: 1947, 1970, 1982, 1983, 1984, 1986, 1990
European Cup Winners' Cup: 1982/83
European Super Cup: 1983
Drybrough Cup Winners: 1970/71, 1980/81

CELTIC

League Champions:
Division I: 1892/93, 1893/94, 1895/96, 1897/98, 1904/05, 1905/06, 1906/07, 1907/08, 1908/09, 1909/10, 1913/14, 1914/15, 1915/16, 1916/17, 1918/19, 1921/22, 1925/26, 1935/36, 1937/38, 1953/54, 1965/66, 1966/67, 1967/68, 1968/69, 1969/70, 1970/71, 1971/72, 1972/73, 1973/74
Premier Division: 1976/77, 1978/79, 1980/81, 1981/82, 1985/86, 1987/88, 1997/98
League Cup Winners:
1956/57, 1957/58, 1965/66, 1966/67, 1967/68, 1968/69, 1969/70, 1974/75, 1982/83, 1997/98, 1999/2000
Scottish Cup Winners:
1892, 1899, 1900, 1904, 1907, 1908, 1911, 1912, 1914, 1923, 1925, 1927, 1931, 1933, 1937, 1951, 1954, 1965, 1967, 1969, 1971, 1972, 1974, 1975, 1977, 1980, 1985, 1988, 1989, 1995
European Cup Winners: 1966/67
Runners-up: 1969/70
Empire Exhibition Cup Winners: 1938
Coronation Cup Winners: 1953
Drybrough Cup Winners: 1974/75

DUNDEE

League Champions:
Division I: 1961/62
Division II: 1946/47
First Division: 1978/79, 1991/92, 1997/98
League Cup Winners:
1951/52, 1952/53, 1973/74
Scottish Cup Winners: 1910
B&Q Centenary Cup: 1990/91

DUNDEE UNITED

League Champions:
Division II: 1924/25, 1928/29
Premier Division: 1982/83
League Cup Winners:
1979/80, 1980/81
Scottish Cup Winners: 1993/94
UEFA Cup Runners-up: 1986/87

DUNFERMLINE ATHLETIC

League Champions:
Division II: 1925/26
First Division: 1988/89, 1995/96
Second Division: 1985/86
Scottish Cup Winners: 1961, 1968
Scottish Qualifying Cup: 1911/12

HEART OF MIDLOTHIAN

League Champions:
Division I: 1894/95, 1896/97, 1957/58, 1959/60
First Division: 1979/80
League Cup Winners: 1954/55, 1958/59, 1959/60, 1962/63
Scottish Cup Winners: 1891, 1896, 1901, 1906, 1956, 1998

HIBERNIAN

League Champions:
Division I: 1902/03, 1947/48, 1950/51, 1951/52
Division II: 1893/94, 1894/95, 1932/33
First Division: 1980/81, 1998/99
League Cup Winners: 1972/73, 1991/92
Scottish Cup Winners: 1887, 1902
Drybrough Cup Winners: 1972/73, 1973/74

KILMARNOCK

League Champions:
Division I: 1964/65
Division II: 1897/98, 1898/99
Scottish Cup Winners:
1920, 1929, 1997
Scottish Qualifying Cup Winners: 1896/97

MOTHERWELL

League Champions:
Division I: 1931/32
First Division: 1981/82, 1984/85
Division II: 1953/54, 1968/69
League Cup Winners: 1950/51
Scottish Cup Winners: 1952, 1991

RANGERS

League Champions:
Division I: 1890/91 (shared), 1898/99, 1899/1900, 1900/01, 1901/02, 1910/11, 1911/12, 1912/13, 1917/18, 1919/20, 1920/21, 1922/23, 1923/24, 1924/25, 1926/27, 1927/28, 1928/29, 1929/30, 1930/31, 1932/33, 1933/34, 1934/35, 1936/37, 1938/39, 1946/47, 1948/49, 1949/50, 1952/53, 1955/56, 1956/57, 1958/59, 1960/61, 1962/63, 1963/64, 1974/75
Premier Division: 1975/76, 1977/78, 1986/87, 1988/89, 1989/90, 1990/91, 1991/92, 1992/93, 1993/94, 1994/95, 1995/96, 1996/97
SPL: 1998/99, 1999/2000
League Cup Winners:
1946/47, 1948/49, 1960/61, 1961/62, 1963/64, 1964/65, 1970/71, 1975/76, 1977/78, 1978/79, 1981/82, 1983/84, 1984/85, 1986/87, 1987/88, 1988/89, 1990/91, 1992/93, 1993/94, 1996/97, 1998/99
Scottish Cup Winners:
1894, 1897, 1898, 1903, 1928, 1930, 1932, 1934, 1935, 1936, 1948, 1949, 1950, 1953, 1960, 1962, 1963, 1964, 1966, 1973, 1976, 1978, 1979, 1981, 1992, 1993, 1996, 1999, 2000
European Cup Winners' Cup: 1971/72
Runners-up: 1960/61, 1966/67
Drybrough Cup Winners: 1979/80

ST. JOHNSTONE

League Champions:
First Division: 1982/83, 1989/90, 1996/97
Division II: 1923/24, 1959/60, 1962/63

ST. MIRREN

League Champions:
First Division: 1976/77, 1999/2000
Division II: 1967/68
Scottish Cup Winners: 1926, 1959, 1987
Victory Cup: 1919
Anglo Scottish Cup Winners: 1979/80
Summer Cup: 1943

S.P.L. Club Honours

Player of the Year Awards

Scottish Professional Footballers' Association

1992/93
Premier Division — Andy Goram *(Rangers)*
First Division — Gordon Dalziel *(Raith Rovers)*
Second Division — Alexander Ross *(Brechin City)*
Young Player of the Year — Eoin Jess *(Aberdeen)*

1993/94
Premier Division — Mark Hateley *(Rangers)*
First Division — Richard Cadette *(Falkirk)*
Second Division — Andrew Thomson *(Queen of the South)*
Young Player of the Year — Philip O'Donnell *(Motherwell)*

1994/95
Premier Division — Brian Laudrup *(Rangers)*
First Division — Stephen Crawford *(Raith Rovers)*
Second Division — Derek McInnes *(Greenock Morton)*
Third Division — David Bingham *(Forfar Athletic)*
Young Player of the Year — Charlie Miller *(Rangers)*

1995/96
Premier Division — Paul Gascoigne *(Rangers)*
First Division — George O'Boyle *(St. Johnstone)*
Second Division — Stephen McCormick *(Stirling Albion)*
Third Division — Jason Young *(Livingston)*
Young Player of the Year — Jackie McNamara *(Celtic)*

1996/97
Premier Division — Paolo Di Canio *(Celtic)*
First Division — Roddy Grant *(St. Johnstone)*
Second Division — Paul Ritchie *(Hamilton Academical)*
Third Division — Iain Stewart *(Inverness Cal. Thistle)*
Young Player of the Year — Robbie Winters *(Dundee United)*

1997/98
Premier Division — Jackie McNamara *(Celtic)*
First Division — James Grady *(Dundee)*
Second Division — Paul Lovering *(Clydebank)*
Third Division — Willie Irvine *(Alloa Athletic)*
Young Player of the Year — Gary Naysmith *(Heart of Midlothian)*

1998/99
Scottish Premier League — Henrik Larsson *(Celtic)*
First Division — Russell Latapy *(Hibernian)*
Second Division — David Bingham *(Livingston)*
Third Division — Neil Tarrant *(Ross County)*
Young Player of the Year — Barry Ferguson *(Rangers)*

1999/2000
Scottish Premier League — Mark Viduka *(Celtic)*
First Division — Stevie Crawford *(Dunfermline Athletic)*
Second Division — Brian Carrigan *(Clyde)*
Third Division — Steven Milne *(Forfar Athletic)*
Young Player of the Year — Kenny Miller *(Hibernian)*

Scottish Football Writers' Association

1965 — Billy McNeill *(Celtic)*
1966 — John Greig *(Rangers)*
1967 — Ronnie Simpson *(Celtic)*
1968 — Gordon Wallace *(Raith Rovers)*
1969 — Bobby Murdoch *(Celtic)*
1970 — Pat Stanton *(Hibernian)*
1971 — Martin Buchan *(Aberdeen)*
1972 — Dave Smith *(Rangers)*
1973 — George Connelly *(Celtic)*
1974 — World Cup Squad
1975 — Sandy Jardine *(Rangers)*
1976 — John Greig *(Rangers)*
1977 — Danny McGrain *(Celtic)*
1978 — Derek Johnstone *(Rangers)*
1979 — Andy Ritchie *(Morton)*
1980 — Gordon Strachan *(Aberdeen)*
1981 — Alan Rough *(Partick Thistle)*
1982 — Paul Sturrock *(Dundee United)*
1983 — Charlie Nicholas *(Celtic)*
1984 — Willie Miller *(Aberdeen)*
1985 — Hamish McAlpine *(Dundee United)*
1986 — Sandy Jardine *(Heart of Midlothian)*
1987 — Brian McClair *(Celtic)*
1988 — Paul McStay *(Celtic)*
1989 — Richard Gough *(Rangers)*
1990 — Alex McLeish *(Aberdeen)*
1991 — Maurice Malpas *(Dundee United)*
1992 — Alistair McCoist *(Rangers)*
1993 — Andy Goram *(Rangers)*
1994 — Mark Hateley *(Rangers)*
1995 — Brian Laudrup *(Rangers)*
1996 — Paul Gascoigne *(Rangers)*
1997 — Brian Laudrup *(Rangers)*
1998 — Craig Burley *(Celtic)*
1999 — Henrik Larsson *(Celtic)*
2000 — Barry Ferguson *(Rangers)*

Mark Viduka

Barry Ferguson

Bell's Award Winners 1999/2000

MONTHLY AWARD WINNERS

AUGUST, 1999

Player	Owen Coyle *(Dunfermline Athletic)*
Young Player	Martin Cameron *(Alloa Athletic)*
First Division Manager	Tom Hendrie *(St. Mirren)*
Second Division Manager	Dave Baikie *(Arbroath)*
Third Division Manager	John McCormack *(Queen's Park)*

SEPTEMBER, 1999

Player	Didier Agathe *(Raith Rovers)*
Young Player	Hugh Murray *(St. Mirren)*
First Division Manager	Stevie Paterson *(Inverness Cal. Thistle)*
Second Division Manager	Terry Christie *(Alloa Athletic)*
Third Division Manager	Craig Levein *(Cowdenbeath)*

OCTOBER, 1999

Player	Barry Lavety *(St. Mirren)*
Young Player	Steven Milne *(Forfar Athletic)*
First Division Manager	Tom Hendrie *(St. Mirren)*
Second Division Manager	Dave Baikie *(Arbroath)*
Third Division Manager	Ian McPhee *(Forfar Athletic)*

NOVEMBER, 1999

Player	Mark Yardley *(St. Mirren)*
Young Player	Martin Cameron *(Alloa Athletic)*
First Division Manager	Tom Hendrie *(St. Mirren)*
Second Division Manager	Allan Maitland *(Clyde)*
Third Division Manager	John Young *(Brechin City)*

DECEMBER, 1999

Player	Stevie Crawford *(Dunfermline Athletic)*
Young Player	Ian Harty *(Stranraer)*
First Division Manager	Ray Stewart *(Livingston)*
Second Division Manager	Billy McLaren *(Stranraer)*
Third Division Manager	Rab Shannon *(East Fife)*

JANUARY, 2000

Player	Ivo Den Bieman *(Falkirk)*
Young Player	Brian Carrigan *(Clyde)*
First Division Manager	Alex Totten *(Falkirk)*
Second Division Manager	Allan Maitland *(Clyde)*
Third Division Manager	Paul Smith *(Berwick Rangers)*

FEBRUARY, 2000

Player	Scott Crabbe *(Falkirk)*
Young Player	Martin Cameron *(Alloa Athletic)*
First Division Manager	Alex Totten *(Falkirk)*
Second Division Manager	John Lambie *(Partick Thistle)*
Third Division Manager	Craig Levein *(Cowdenbeath)*

MARCH, 2000

Player	Brian Carrigan *(Clyde)*
Young Player	John Potter *(Dunfermline Athletic)*
First Division Manager	Alex Totten *(Falkirk)*
Second Division Manager	Allan Maitland *(Clyde)*
Third Division Manager	Paul Smith *(Berwick Rangers)*

Mark Yardley

Brian Carrigan

Tom Hendrie

Allan Maitland

John McCormack

SEASON AWARD WINNERS

Player of the Year
Mark Yardley *(St. Mirren)*

Young Player of the Year
Brian Carrigan *(Clyde)*

First Division Manager of the Year
Tom Hendrie *(St. Mirren)*

Second Division Manager of the Year
Allan Maitland *(Clyde)*

Third Division Manager of the Year
John McCormack *(Queen's Park)*

SCOTTISH PROGRAMME AWARDS

SCOTTISH PROGRAMME OF THE YEAR AWARDS 1999/2000

SCOTTISH PREMIER LEAGUE

99/00	(98/99)	CLUB
1.	(1)	Dundee United
2.	(2)	Rangers
3.	(10)	Dundee
4.	(6)	Heart of Midlothian
5.	(9)	Aberdeen
6.	(1(FD))	Hibernian
7.	(3)	Kilmarnock
8.	(5)	Celtic
9.	(6)	St. Johnstone
10.	(8)	Motherwell

SFL FIRST DIVISION

99/00	(98/99)	CLUB
1.	(4 (SPL))	Dunfermline Athletic
2.	(5)	Falkirk
3.	(2)	St. Mirren
4.	(3)	Morton
5.	(4 (SD))	Livingston
6.	(4)	Ayr United
7.	(6)	Raith Rovers
8.	(5 (SD))	Inverness Cal. Thistle
9.	(7)	Airdrieonians
10.	(10)	Clydebank

SFL SECOND DIVISION

99/00	(98/99)	CLUB
1.	(1)	Clyde
2.	(2)	Partick Thistle
3.	(3)	Stirling Albion
4.	(6)	Queen of the South
5.	(7)	Alloa Athletic
6.	(9 (FD))	Stranraer
7.	(4 (TD))	Ross County
8.	(8 (FD))	Hamilton Academical
9.	(8 (TD))	Stenhousemuir
10.	(10)	Arbroath

SFL THIRD DIVISION

99/00	(98/99)	CLUB
1.	(1)	Queen's Park
2.	(2)	Montrose
3.	(7)	Cowdenbeath
4.	(8 (SD))	Forfar Athletic
5.	(6)	Brechin City
6.	(5)	Berwick Rangers
7.	(3)	Albion Rovers
8.	(9 (SD))	East Fife
9.	(9)	Dumbarton
10.	(10)	East Stirlingshire

SCOTTISH PROGRAMMES OF THE YEAR - PREVIOUS WINNERS

1973/74	Ayr United
1974/75	Hamilton Academical
1975/76	Heart of Midlothian
1976/77	Motherwell
1977/78	Hamilton Academical
1978/79	Hamilton Academical
1979/80	Berwick Rangers
1980/81	Aberdeen
1981/82	Hamilton Academical
1982/83	Dundee
1983/84	Dundee United
1984/85	Aberdeen
1985/86	Celtic
1986/87	Rangers
1987/88	Rangers
1988/89	Rangers
1989/90	Aberdeen
1990/91	Celtic
1991/92	Aberdeen
1992/93	Rangers
1993/94	Rangers
1994/95	Rangers
1995/96	Clyde
1996/97	Clyde
1997/98	Clyde
1998/99	Clyde
1999/2000	Clyde

PREMIER LEAGUE PROGRAMME OF THE YEAR

as above, except for ...)

1974/75	Motherwell (old Div.One)
1975/76	Heart of Midlothian
1976/77	Motherwell
1977/78	Rangers
1978/79	Morton
1979/80	Morton
1995/96	Kilmarnock
1996/97	Dundee United
1997/98	Dundee United
1998/99	Dundee United
1999/2000	Dundee United

FIRST DIVISION PROGRAMME OF THE YEAR

1975/76	Hamilton Academical
1976/77	Hamilton Academical
1977/78	Hamilton Academical
1978/79	Hamilton Academical
1979/80	Berwick Rangers
1980/81	Hamilton Academical
1981/82	Hamilton Academical
1982/83	Queen's Park
1983/84	Hamilton Academical
1984/85	Clyde
1985/86	Clyde
1986/87	Clyde

1987/88	Hamilton Academical & Clydebank
1988/89	Dunfermline Athletic
1989/90	Airdrieonians
1990/91	Dundee
1991/92	Partick Thistle
1992/93	Kilmarnock
1993/94	Dunfermline Athletic
1994/95	Dunfermline Athletic
1995/96	Dundee United
1996/97	Partick Thistle
1997/98	St. Mirren
1998/99	Hibernian
1999/2000	Dunfermline Athletic

SECOND DIVISION PROGRAMME OF THE YEAR

1973/74	Hamilton Academical
1974/75	Hamilton Academical
1975/76	Berwick Rangers
1976/77	Albion Rovers
1977/78	Meadowbank Thistle
1978/79	Berwick Rangers
1979/80	Albion Rovers
1980/81	Clyde
1981/82	Clyde
1982/83	Stirling Albion
1983/84	Stirling Albion
1984/85	Stirling Abion
1985/86	Stirling Albion
1986/87	Raith Rovers
1987/88	Stirling Albion
1988/89	Stirling Albion
1989/90	Kilmarnock
1990/91	Stirling Albion
1991/92	Clyde
1992/93	Clyde
1993/94	Forfar Athletic
1994/95	Clyde
1995/96	Clyde
1996/97	Clyde
1997/98	Clyde
1998/99	Clyde
1999/2000	Clyde

THIRD DIVISION PROGRAMME OF THE YEAR

1994/95	Forfar Athletic
1995/96	Livingston
1996/97	Inverness Cal. Thistle
1997/98	Montrose
1998/99	Queen's Park
1999/2000	Queen's Park

Information supplied by John Litster (Editor of "Programme Monthly & Football Collectable" Magazine)

Leading Goalscorers Since 1996/97

1996/97

Premier Division
25 J. Cadete (Celtic)
16 B. Laudrup (Rangers)
15 W. Dodds (Aberdeen)
P. Wright (Kilmarnock)
14 J. Robertson (Heart of Midlothian)
P. Van Hooijdonk (Celtic)
13 G. Britton (Dunfermline Athletic)
P. Gascoigne (Rangers)
12 P. Di Canio (Celtic)
K. Olofsson (Dundee United)
11 T. Coyne (Motherwell)
D. Jackson (Hibernian)
10 J. Albertz (Rangers)
A. McCoist (Rangers)
A. Smith (Dunfermline Athletic)
D. Windass (Aberdeen)

First Division
19 R. Grant (St. Johnstone)
15 D. Lilley (Greenock Morton)
M. Yardley (St. Mirren)
12 G. O'Boyle (St. Johnstone)
P. Scott (St. Johnstone)
11 D. Moss (Partick Thistle)
10 J. O'Driscoll (Dundee)
9 A. Bone (Stirling Albion)
G. Evans (Partick Thistle)
8 C. Adams (Partick Thistle)
P. Connolly (Airdrieonians)
S. Cooper (Airdrieonians)
J. Grady (Clydebank)
S. McCormick (Stirling Albion)
M. McGraw (Falkirk)
B. McPhee (Airdrieonians)

Second Division
31 P. Ritchie (Hamilton Academical)
21 E. Annand (Clyde)
15 G. Harvey (Livingston)
14 S. Kerrigan (Ayr United)
I. Little (Stenhousemuir)
13 S. Mallan (Queen of the South)
12 T. Bryce (Queen of the South)
11 C. Flannigan (Queen of the South)
10 L. Haddow (Stenhousemuir)
9 P. Smith (Ayr United)

Third Division
27 I. Stewart (Inverness Caledonian Thistle)
22 D. Adams (Ross County)
17 B. Honeyman (Forfar Athletic)
15 A. Morgan (Forfar Athletic)
W. Watters (Albion Rovers (4 for Arbroath)
12 W. Irvine (Alloa)
11 P. Dwyer (Alloa)
C. McGlashan (Montrose)
10 B. Thomson (Inverness Caledonian Thistle)
9 G. Inglis (East Stirlingshire)
A. Ross (Ross County)
S. Taylor (Montrose)

1997/98

Premier Division
32 M. Negri (Rangers)
18 K. Olofsson (Dundee United)
16 H. Larsson (Celtic)
A. Smith (Dunfermline Athletic)
15 T. Coyne (Motherwell)
14 J. Hamilton (Heart of Midlothian)
10 J. Albertz (Rangers)
C. Burley (Celtic)
O. Coyle (Motherwell)
W. Dodds (Aberdeen)
S. Donnelly (Celtic)
N. McCann (Heart of Midlothian)
G. O'Boyle (St. Johnstone)
P. Wright (Kilmarnock)

First Division
15 J. Grady (Dundee)
13 A. Bone (Stirling Albion)
12 E. Annand (Dundee)
B. McPhee (Airdrieonians)
D. Moss (Falkirk)
11 S. Cooper (Airdrieonians)
10 L. D'Jaffo (Ayr United)
P. Hartley (Raith Rovers)
W. Hawke (Greenock Morton)
M. Keith (Falkirk)
K. Wright (Raith Rovers)

Second Division
16 I. Stewart (Inverness Caledonian Thistle)
15 G. Harvey (Livingston)
I. Little (Stenhousemuir)
14 M. McLauchlan (Forfar Athletic)
13 C. McDonald (Clydebank)
B. Thomson (Inverness Caledonian Thistle)
12 B. Honeyman (Forfar Athletic)
11 T. Bryce (Queen of the South)
M. Dyer (East Fife)
G. Young (Stranraer)

Third Division
20 C. McGlashan (Montrose)
18 W. Irvine (Alloa Athletic)
16 D. Adams (Ross County)
W. Spence (Arbroath)
13 D. Watt (East Stirlingshire)
W. Watters (Albion Rovers)
10 P. Forrester (Berwick Rangers)
R.L. Gardner (Albion Rovers)
B. Grant (Arbroath)
C. McKinnon (Dumbarton)

1998/99

Scottish Premier League
29 H. Larsson (Celtic)
18 R. Wallace (Rangers)
17 W. Dodds (Dundee United)
14 E. Jess (Aberdeen)
13 R. Winters (12 for Aberdeen, 1 for Dundee United)
11 J. Albertz (Rangers)
10 S. Adam (Heart of Midlothian)
9 E. Annand (Dundee)
M. Burchill (Celtic)
C. Burley (Celtic)

First Division
18 G. Hurst (Ayr United)
17 M. Keith (Falkirk)
15 A. Walker (Ayr United)
14 S. Crawford (Hibernian)
12 P. McGinlay (Hibernian)
M-M. Paatelainen (Hibernian)
11 S. Lovell (Hibernian)
G. Wales (Hamilton Academical)
M. Yardley (St. Mirren)
10 S. Crabbe (Falkirk)

Second Division
21 A. Bone (Stirling Albion)
19 S. McLean (Inverness Caledonian Thistle)
15 M. Cameron (Alloa Athletic)
W. Irvine (Alloa Athletic)
S. Mallan (Queen of the South)
14 B. Wilson (Inverness Caledonian Thistle)
13 B. Moffat (East Fife)
12 S. Convery (Clyde)
C. McGlashan (Arbroath)
J. Robertson (Livingston)
D. Shearer (Inverness Caledonian Thistle)

Third Division
17 S. Ferguson (Ross County)
P. Flannery (Dumbarton)
N. Tarrant (Ross County)
15 J. Dickson (Brechin City)
12 M. Leask (Berwick Rangers)
S. Sorbie (Brechin City)
G. Wood (Ross County)
11 R. Hamilton (Stenhousemuir)
10 D. Lorimer (Albion Rovers)
9 P. Forrester (Berwick Rangers)
W. Watters (Stenhousemuir)

1999/2000

Scottish Premier League
25 M. Viduka (Celtic)
19 W. Dodds (10 for Rangers, 9 for Dundee United)
17 J. Albertz (Rangers)
16 R. Wallace (Rangers)
13 W. Falconer (Dundee)
G. McSwegan (Heart of Midlothian)
11 M. Burchill (Celtic)
K. Miller (Hibernian)
J. Spencer (Motherwell)
10 N. Lowndes (St. Johnstone)

First Division
19 M. Yardley (St. Mirren)
16 S. Crawford (Dunfermline Athletic)
B. Lavety (St. Mirren)
15 D. Bingham (Livingston)
14 S. Crabbe (Falkirk)
G. Hurst (Ayr United)
B. McPhee (Livingston)
13 B. Wilson (Inverness Caledonian Thistle)
12 C. Dargo (Raith Rovers)
D. Nicholls (Falkirk)

Second Division
18 B. Carrigan (Clyde)
17 A. Graham (Stirling Albion)
16 C. McGlashan (Arbroath)
15 M. Cameron (Alloa Athletic)
J. McQuade (Stirling Albion)
13 W. Irvine (Alloa Athletic)
S. Mallan (Queen of the South)
G. Shaw (Ross County)
12 P. Ronald (Stranraer)
11 P. Keogh (Clyde)
P. McGrillen (Stirling Albion)

Third Division
16 S. Milne (Forfar Athletic)
14 P. Flannery (Dumbarton)
13 M. Gallagher (Queen's Park)
M. McDowell (Cowdenbeath)
12 G. Brown (Cowdenbeath)
B. Honeyman (11 for Brechin City, 1 for East Fife)
S. Laidlaw (3 Berwick Rangers, 9 for East Stirlingshire)
S. Taylor (Montrose)
11 B. Moffat (East Fife)
9 M. Anthony (Berwick Rangers)
R. Black (Brechin City)
G. Higgins (East Stirlingshire)
B. Robson (Forfar Athletic)

Leading Goalscorers Club By Club Since 1984/85

ABERDEEN

Season	Div	No. of Goals	Player
1984-85	P	22	F. McDougall
1985-86	P	14	F. McDougall
1986-87	P	12	W. Stark
1987-88	P	10	J. Bett
1988-89	P	16	C. Nicholas
1989-90	P	11	C. Nicholas
1990-91	P	14	H. Gillhaus
1991-92	P	12	E. Jess
1992-93	P	22	D. Shearer
1993-94	P	17	D. Shearer
1994-95	P	15	W. Dodds
1995-96	P	9	S. Booth
			J. Miller
1996-97	P	15	W. Dodds
1997-98	P	10	W.Dodds
1998-99	P	14	E. Jess
1999-00	P	9	A. Stavrum

AIRDRIEONIANS

Season	Div	No. of Goals	Player
1984-85	F	21	D. MacCabe
1985-86	F	11	J. Flood
1986-87	F	13	D. MacCabe
1987-88	F	20	D. MacCabe
1988-89	F	22	K. Macdonald
1989-90	F	10	O. Coyle
1990-91	F	20	O. Coyle
1991-92	P	11	O. Coyle
1992-93	P	9	O. Coyle
1993-94	F	10	D. Kirkwood
1994-95	F	12	Andrew Smith
1995-96	F	9	J. McIntyre
1996-97	F	8	P. Connolly
			S. Cooper
			B. McPhee
1997-98	F	12	B. McPhee
1998-99	F	8	S. Cooper
1999-00	F	5	A. Neil
			N. Thompson

ALBION ROVERS

Season	Div	No. of Goals	Player
1984-85	S	27	B. Slaven
1985-86	S	6	S. Conn
			V. Kasule
			A. Rodgers
1986-87	S	11	C. Wilson
1987-88	S	10	A. Graham
1988-89	S	15	J. Chapman
			A. Graham
1989-90	F	10	M. McAnenay
1990-91	S	12	M. McAnenay
1991-92	S	11	G. McCoy
1992-93	S	16	M. Scott
1993-94	S	17	M. Scott
1994-95	T	7	M. Scott
1995-96	T	12	G. Young
1996-97	T	11	W. Watters
1997-98	T	13	W. Watters
1998-99	T	10	D. Lorimer
1999-00	T	7	I. Diack

ALLOA ATHLETIC

Season	Div	No. of Goals	Player
1984-85	S	16	D. Lloyd
1985-86	F	11	M. Jamieson
			S. Sorbie
1986-87	S	14	S. Sorbie
1987-88	S	14	P. Rutherford
1988-89	S	23	C. Lytwyn
1989-90	F	9	P. Lamont
1990-91	S	11	J. Irvine
1991-92	S	12	M. Hendry
1992-93	S	19	B. Moffat
1993-94	S	7	W. Newbigging
1994-95	T	13	B. Moffat
1995-96	T	5	B. Moffat
			S. Rixon
1996-97	T	12	W. Irvine
1997-98	T	18	W. Irvine
1998-99	S	15	M. Cameron
			W. Irvine
1999-00	S	15	M. Cameron

ARBROATH

Season	Div	No. of Goals	Player
1984-85	S	6	R. Brown
1985-86	S	14	M. McWalter
1986-87	S	14	J. Fotheringham
1987-88	S	13	A. McKenna
1988-89	S	11	J. Fotheringham
1989-90	S	12	J. Marshall
1990-91	S	10	M. Bennett
			S. Sorbie
1991-92	S	12	S. Sorbie
1992-93	S	19	S. Sorbie
1993-94	S	10	D. Diver
1994-95	T	11	S. Tosh
1995-96	T	8	S. McCormick
			D. Pew
1996-97	T	5	B. Grant
1997-98	T	16	W. Spence
1998-99	S	12	C. McGlashan
1999-00	S	16	C. McGlashan

AYR UNITED

Season	Div	No. of Goals	Player
1984-85	F	8	G. Collins
			J. McNiven
1985-86	F	6	D. Irons
1986-87	S	26	J. Sludden
1987-88	S	31	J. Sludden
1988-89	F	17	H. Templeton
1989-90	F	10	T. Bryce
1990-91	F	11	T. Bryce
1991-92	F	14	A. Graham
1992-93	F	9	A. Graham
1993-94	F	12	S. McGivern
1994-95	F	4	J. Jackson
1995-96	S	5	B. Bilsland
			I. English
1996-97	S	14	S. Kerrigan
1997-98	F	10	L. D'Jaffo
1998-99	F	18	G. Hurst
1999-00	F	14	G. Hurst

BERWICK RANGERS

Season	Div	No. of Goals	Player
1984-85	S	9	P. Davidson
1985-86	S	12	J. Sokoluk
1986-87	S	8	E. Tait
1987-88	S	3	M. Cameron
			H. Douglas
			T. Graham
			G. Leitch
			C. Lytwyn
			M. Thompson
1988-89	S	10	J. Hughes
1989-90	S	16	S. Sloan
1990-91	S	14	K. Todd
1991-92	S	12	S. Bickmore
1992-93	S	11	D. Scott
1993-94	S	15	W. Irvine
1994-95	S	16	W. Hawke
1995-96	S	13	W. Irvine
1996-97	S	6	P. Forrester
1997-98	T	10	P. Forrester
1998-99	T	12	M. Leask
1999-00	T	9	M. Anthony

BRECHIN CITY

Season	Div	No. of Goals	Player
1984-85	F	17	K. Eadie
1985-86	F	22	K. Eadie
1986-87	F	12	C. Adam
1987-88	S	15	G. Buckley
1988-89	S	15	C. Adam
1989-90	S	12	G. Lees
1990-91	F	14	P. Ritchie
1991-92	S	12	P. Ritchie
1992-93	S	23	A. Ross
1993-94	F	10	M. Miller
1994-95	S	6	G. Price
			R. Smith
1995-96	T	8	A. Ross
1996-97	S	7	S. Kerrigan
1997-98	S	7	C. Feroz
1998-99	T	15	J. Dickson
1999-00	T	11	B. Honeyman

CELTIC

Season	Div	No. of Goals	Player
1984-85	P	19	B. McClair
1985-86	P	22	B. McClair
1986-87	P	35	B. McClair
1987-88	P	26	A. Walker
1988-89	P	16	M. McGhee
1989-90	P	8	D. Dziekanowski
1990-91	P	18	T. Coyne
1991-92	P	21	C. Nicholas
1992-93	P	13	A. Payton
1993-94	P	10	P. McGinlay
1994-95	P	8	J. Collins
1995-96	P	26	P. Van Hooijdonk
1996-97	P	25	J. Cadete
1997-98	P	16	H. Larsson
1998-99	P	29	H. Larsson
1999-00	P	25	M. Viduka

CLYDE

Season	Div	No. of Goals	Player
1984-85	F	19	J. F. Frye
1985-86	F	12	J. F. Frye
1986-87	F	12	J. Murphy
1987-88	F	16	C. McGlashan
			D. Walker
1988-89	F	16	C. McGlashan
1989-90	F	11	C. McGlashan
1990-91	F	8	S. Mallan
1991-92	S	16	D. Thompson
1992-93	S	16	F. McGarvey
1993-94	F	5	I. McConnell
			G. Parks
1994-95	S	10	J. Dickson
1995-96	S	21	E. Annand
1996-97	S	21	E. Annand
1997-98	S	8	P. Brownlie
1998-99	S	12	S. Convery
1999-00	S	18	B. Carrigan

CLYDEBANK

Season	Div	No. of Goals	Player
1984-85	F	11	M. Conroy
1985-86	P	7	M. Conroy
			D. Lloyd
1986-87	P	9	M. Conroy
			S. Gordon
1987-88	F	11	M. Conroy
1988-89	F	21	K. Eadie
1989-90	F	21	K. Eadie
1990-91	F	29	K. Eadie
1991-92	F	22	K. Eadie
1992-93	F	21	C. Flannigan
1993-94	F	11	K. Eadie
			C. Flannigan
1994-95	F	9	K. Eadie
1995-96	F	11	J. Grady
1996-97	F	8	J. Grady
1997-98	S	13	C. McDonald
1998-99	F	9	C. McDonald
1999-00	F	5	I. Cameron

COWDENBEATH

Season	Div	No. of Goals	Player
1984-85	S	16	K. Ward
1985-86	S	15	C. McGlashan
1986-87	S	14	W. Blackie
			R. Grant
1987-88	S	11	R. Grant
1988-89	S	8	A. McGonigal
1989-90	S	16	A. Ross
1990-91	S	15	A. MacKenzie
1991-92	S	26	G. Buckley
1992-93	F	9	W. Callaghan
1993-94	S	11	W. Callaghan
1994-95	T	23	M. Yardley
1995-96	T	11	D. Scott
1996-97	T	6	G. Wood
1997-98	T	6	W. Stewart
1998-99	T	7	W. Stewart
1999-00	T	13	M. McDowell

DUMBARTON

Season	Div	No. of Goals	Player
1984-85	P	7	J. Coyle
1985-86	F	13	G. McCoy
1986-87	F	21	G. McCoy
1987-88	F	14	O. Coyle
1988-89	S	13	S. MacIver
1989-90	S	20	C. Gibson
1990-91	S	14	J. McQuade
1991-92	S	19	J. Gilmour
1992-93	F	15	J. McQuade
1993-94	F	13	C. Gibson
1994-95	S	17	M. Mooney
1995-96	F	5	M. Mooney
1996-97	S	7	H. Ward
1997-98	T	10	C. McKinnon
1998-99	T	17	P. Flannery
1999-00	T	14	P. Flannery

DUNDEE

Season	Div	No. of Goals	Player
1984-85	P	8	R. Stephen
1985-86	P	14	R. Stephen
1986-87	P	12	G. Harvey
1987-88	P	33	T. Coyne
1988-89	P	9	T. Coyne
1989-90	P	13	W. Dodds
1990-91	F	18	K. Wright
1991-92	F	19	W. Dodds
1992-93	P	16	W. Dodds
1993-94	P	6	D. Ristic
1994-95	F	16	G. Shaw
1995-96	F	14	J. Hamilton
1996-97	F	10	J. O'Driscoll
1997-98	F	15	J. Grady
1998-99	P	9	E. Annand
1999-00	P	13	W. Falconer

DUNDEE UNITED

Season	Div	No. of Goals	Player
1984-85	P	14	P. Sturrock
1985-86	P	12	D. Dodds
1986-87	P	12	I. Ferguson
1987-88	P	11	I. Ferguson
1988-89	P	10	M-M. Paatelainen
1989-90	P	7	D. Jackson
			M-M. Paatelainen
1990-91	P	12	D. Jackson
1991-92	P	17	D. Ferguson
1992-93	P	16	P. Connolly
1993-94	P	16	C. Brewster
1994-95	P	7	C. Brewster
1995-96	F	17	C. Brewster
			G. McSwegan
1996-97	P	12	K. Olofsson
1997-98	P	18	K. Olofsson
1998-99	P	17	W. Dodds
1999-00	P	9	W. Dodds

DUNFERMLINE ATHLETIC

Season	Div	No. of Goals	Player
1984-85	S	15	J. Watson
1985-86	S	24	J. Watson
1986-87	F	13	J. Watson
1987-88	P	13	C. Robertson
1988-89	F	18	R. Jack
1989-90	P	16	R. Jack
1990-91	P	8	R. Jack
1991-92	P	6	D. Moyes
1992-93	F	12	H. French
1993-94	F	17	G. O'Boyle
1994-95	F	14	S. Petrie
1995-96	F	13	S. Petrie
1996-97	P	13	G. Britton
1997-98	P	16	A. Smith
1998-99	P	8	A. Smith
1999-00	F	16	S. Crawford

EAST FIFE

Season	Div	No. of Goals	Player
1984-85	F	12	G. Murray
1985-86	S	14	S. Kirk
1986-87	F	15	B. McNaughton
1987-88	F	17	P. Hunter
1988-89	S	9	P. Hunter
1989-90	S	14	P. Hunter
1990-91	S	10	W. Brown
			R. Scott
1991-92	S	21	J. Sludden
1992-93	S	16	R. Scott
1993-94	S	10	R. Scott
1994-95	S	14	R. Scott
1995-96	S	11	R. Scott
1996-97	F	4	M. Dyer
			P. Ronald
1997-98	S	11	M. Dyer
1998-99	S	13	B. Moffat
1999-00	T	11	B. Moffat

EAST STIRLINGSHIRE

Season	Div	No. of Goals	Player
1984-85	S	12	S. Maskrey
1985-86	S	12	S. Maskrey
1986-87	S	5	A. McGonigal
			J. Paisley
			D. Strange
1987-88	S	9	G. Murray
1988-89	S	16	W. McNeill
1989-90	S	4	W. McNeill
			D. Wilcox
			C. Wilson
1990-91	S	10	C. Lytwyn
			Dk. Walker
1991-92	S	18	D. Diver
1992-93	S	9	P. Roberts
1993-94	S	12	M. McCallum
1994-95	T	16	M. Geraghty
1995-96	T	21	P. Dwyer
1996-97	T	9	G. Inglis
1997-98	T	13	D. Watt
1998-99	T	8	W. McNeill
1999-00	T	9	G. Higgins
			S. Laidlaw

FALKIRK

Season	Div	No. of Goals	Player
1984-85	F	22	G. McCoy
1985-86	F	15	J. Gilmour
1986-87	P	6	K. Eadie
1987-88	P	9	C. Baptie
1988-89	F	12	A. Rae
1989-90	P	17	D. McWilliams
1990-91	F	16	S. Stainrod
1991-92	P	9	K. McAllister
			E. May
1992-93	P	8	R. Cadette
1993-94	F	18	R. Cadette
1994-95	P	9	C. McDonald
1995-96	P	6	P. McGrillen
1996-97	F	8	M. McGraw
1997-98	F	12	D. Moss
1998-99	F	17	M. Keith
1999-00	F	14	S. Crabbe

FORFAR ATHLETIC

Season	Div	No. of Goals	Player
1984-85	F	14	K. Macdonald
1985-86	F	10	J. Clark
1986-87	F	17	K. Macdonald
1987-88	F	20	K. Macdonald
1988-89	F	12	K. Ward
1989-90	F	8	C. Brewster
1990-91	F	12	G. Whyte
1991-92	F	8	G. Winter
1992-93	S	21	S. Petrie
1993-94	S	13	D. Bingham
1994-95	T	22	D. Bingham
1995-96	S	12	G. Higgins
1996-97	T	17	B. Honeyman
1997-98	S	14	M. McLauchlan
1998-99	S	10	R. Brand
1999-00	T	16	S. Milne

HAMILTON ACADEMICAL

Season	Div	No. of Goals	Player
1984-85	F	8	J. Brogan
			J. McGachie
1985-86	F	23	J. Brogan
1986-87	P	6	J. Brogan
1987-88	F	10	M. Caughey
1988-89	P	5	S. Gordon
			C. Harris
1989-90	F	9	C. Harris
1990-91	F	14	G. McCluskey
1991-92	F	14	G. Clark
1992-93	F	11	P. McDonald
1993-94	F	19	P. Duffield
1994-95	F	20	P. Duffield
1995-96	F	11	P. Hartley
1996-97	S	31	P. Ritchie
1997-98	F	7	P. Ritchie
1998-99	F	11	G. Wales
1999-00	S	6	D. Henderson
			N. Henderson

HEART OF MIDLOTHIAN

Season	Div	No. of Goals	Player
1984-85	P	8	A. Clark
			J. Robertson
1985-86	P	20	J. Robertson
1986-87	P	16	J. Robertson
1987-88	P	26	J. Robertson
1988-89	P	5	J. Colquhoun
			I. Ferguson
1989-90	P	17	J. Robertson
1990-91	P	12	J. Robertson
1991-92	P	15	S. Crabbe
1992-93	P	11	J. Robertson
1993-94	P	10	J. Robertson
1994-95	P	10	J. Robertson
1995-96	P	11	J. Robertson
1996-97	P	14	J. Robertson
1997-98	P	14	J. Hamilton
1998-99	P	10	S. Adam
1999-00	P	13	G. McSwegan

HIBERNIAN

Season	Div	No. of Goals	Player
1984-85	P	8	G. Durie
			P. Kane
1985-86	P	19	S. Cowan
1986-87	P	9	G. McCluskey
1987-88	P	10	P. Kane
1988-89	P	13	S. Archibald
1989-90	P	8	K. Houchen
1990-91	P	6	P. Wright
1991-92	P	11	M. Weir
1992-93	P	13	D. Jackson
1993-94	P	16	K. Wright
1994-95	P	10	D. Jackson
			M. O'Neill
			K. Wright
1995-96	P	9	D. Jackson
			K. Wright
1996-97	P	11	D. Jackson
1997-98	P	9	S. Crawford
1998-99	F	14	S. Crawford
1999-00	P	11	K. Miller

INVERNESS CALEDONIAN THISTLE

Season	Div	No. of Goals	Player
1994-95	T	6	C. Christie
			A. Hercher
1995-96	T	23	I. Stewart
1996-97	T	27	I. Stewart
1997-98	S	16	I. Stewart
1998-99	S	20	S. McLean
1999-00	F	13	B. Wilson

KILMARNOCK

Season	Div	No. of Goals	Player
1984-85	F	12	B. Millar
1985-86	F	14	I. Bryson
1986-87	F	10	I. Bryson
1987-88	F	16	C. Harkness
1988-89	F	12	W. Watters
1989-90	S	23	W. Watters
1990-91	F	14	R. Williamson
1991-92	F	10	C. Campbell
			A. Mitchell
1992-93	F	11	G. McCluskey
1993-94	P	7	R. Williamson
1994-95	P	6	C. McKee
1995-96	P	13	P. Wright
1996-97	P	15	P. Wright
1997-98	P	10	P. Wright
1998-99	P	7	A. McCoist
1999-00	P	8	C. Cocard

LIVINGSTON
FORMERLY MEADOWBANK THISTLE

Season	Div	No. of Goals	Player
1984-85	F	14	A. Sprott
1985-86	S	17	D. Jackson
			A. Lawrence
1986-87	S	21	J. McGachie
1987-88	F	14	J. McGachie
1988-89	F	6	D. Roseburgh
1989-90	F	8	B. McNaughton
1990-91	F	15	D. Roseburgh
1991-92	F	8	D. Roseburgh
1992-93	F	9	P. Rutherford
1993-94	S	12	I. Little
1994-95	S	6	L. Bailey
1995-96	S	18	J. Young
1996-97	S	15	G. Harvey
1997-98	S	15	G. Harvey
1998-99	S	12	J. Robertson
1999-00	F	15	D. Bingham

MONTROSE

Season	Div	No. of Goals	Player
1984-85	S	12	D. Somner
1985-86	F	6	M. Allan
1986-87	F	10	I. Paterson
1987-88	S	11	H. Mackay
1988-89	S	21	G. S. Murray
1989-90	S	11	D. Powell
1990-91	S	11	G. Murray
1991-92	F	9	J. McGachie
1992-93	S	10	D. Grant
1993-94	S	12	D. Grant
1994-95	T	19	C. McGlashan
1995-96	S	16	C. McGlashan
1996-97	T	11	C. McGlashan
1997-98	T	20	C. McGlashan
1998-99	T	7	S. Taylor
1999-00	T	12	S. Taylor

MORTON

Season	Div	No. of Goals	Player
1984-85	P	5	J. Gillespie
1985-86	F	14	J. McNeil
1986-87	F	23	R. Alexander
1987-88	P	8	Jim Boag
1988-89	F	11	R. Alexander
1989-90	F	11	R. Alexander
1990-91	F	21	D. MacCabe
1991-92	F	18	A. Mathie
1992-93	F	13	A. Mathie
1993-94	F	11	R. Alexander
1994-95	S	16	D. Lilley
1995-96	F	14	D. Lilley
1996-97	F	15	D. Lilley
1997-98	F	10	W. Hawke
1998-99	F	9	K. Thomas
1999-00	F	9	H. Curran

MOTHERWELL

Season	Div	No. of Goals	Player
1984-85	F	9	A. Harrow
			R. Stewart
1985-86	P	9	J. Reilly
1986-87	P	10	S. Kirk
			A. Walker
1987-88	P	9	S. Cowan
1988-89	P	14	S. Kirk
1989-90	P	11	N. Cusack
1990-91	P	14	D. Arnott
1991-92	P	8	D. Arnott
1992-93	P	10	S. Kirk
1993-94	P	12	T. Coyne
1994-95	P	16	T. Coyne
1995-96	P	5	W. Falconer
1996-97	P	11	T. Coyne
1997-98	P	15	T. Coyne
1998-99	P	7	O. Coyle
			J. Spencer
1999-00	P	11	J. Spencer

PARTICK THISTLE

Season	Div	No. of Goals	Player
1984-85	F	12	A. Logan
1985-86	F	11	G. Smith
1986-87	F	10	C. West
1987-88	F	13	E. Gallagher
1988-89	F	19	G. McCoy
1989-90	F	18	C. Campbell
1990-91	F	13	D. Elliot
1991-92	F	18	C. McGlashan
1992-93	P	12	G. Britton
1993-94	P	14	A. Craig
1994-95	P	7	W. Foster
1995-96	P	5	A. Lyons
			R. McDonald
1996-97	F	11	D. Moss
1997-98	F	6	J. Stirling
1998-99	S	10	R. Dunn
1999-00	S	5	R. Dunn

QUEEN OF THE SOUTH

Season	Div	No. of Goals	Player
1984-85	S	9	G. Cloy
1985-86	S	15	T. Bryce
			S. Cochrane
1986-87	F	20	T. Bryce
1987-88	F	17	J. Hughes
1988-89	F	7	G. Fraser
1989-90	S	8	S. Gordon
1990-91	S	11	A. Thomson
1991-92	S	26	A. Thomson
1992-93	S	21	A. Thomson
1993-94	S	29	A. Thomson
1994-95	S	9	D. Campbell
			S. Mallan
1995-96	S	12	S. Mallan
1996-97	S	13	S. Mallan
1997-98	S	11	T. Bryce
1998-99	S	15	S. Mallan
1999-00	S	13	S. Mallan

QUEEN'S PARK

Season	Div	No. of Goals	Player
1984-85	S	18	J. Nicholson
1985-86	S	11	G. Fraser
1986-87	S	13	R. Caven
1987-88	S	17	P. O'Brien
1988-89	S	9	M. Hendry
1989-90	S	10	M. Hendry
1990-91	S	17	M. Hendry
1991-92	S	17	S. McCormick
1992-93	S	11	R. Caven
1993-94	S	18	J. O'Neill
1994-95	T	8	S. McCormick
1995-96	T	6	S. Edgar
			K. McGoldrick
1996-97	T	7	D. Ferry
1997-98	T	8	S. Edgar
			J. Mercer
1998-99	T	7	S. Edgar
1999-00	T	13	M. Gallagher

RAITH ROVERS

Season	Div	No. of Goals	Player
1984-85	S	22	K. Wright
1985-86	S	21	P. Smith
			K. Wright
1986-87	S	22	C. Harris
1987-88	F	25	G. Dalziel
1988-89	F	11	G. Dalziel
1989-90	F	20	G. Dalziel
1990-91	F	25	G. Dalziel
1991-92	F	26	G. Dalziel
1992-93	F	32	G. Dalziel
1993-94	P	8	G. Dalziel
1994-95	F	15	G. Dalziel
1995-96	P	9	C. Cameron
1996-97	P	5	P. Duffield
			D. Lennon
1997-98	F	10	P. Hartley
			K. Wright
1998-99	F	8	C. Dargo
1999-00	F	12	C. Dargo

RANGERS

Season	Div	No. of Goals	Player
1984-85	P	12	A. McCoist
1985-86	P	24	A. McCoist
1986-87	P	33	A. McCoist
1987-88	P	31	A. McCoist
1988-89	P	12	K. Drinkell
1989-90	P	15	M. Johnston
1990-91	P	12	M. Walters
1991-92	P	34	A. McCoist
1992-93	P	34	A. McCoist
1993-94	P	22	M. Hateley
1994-95	P	13	M. Hateley
1995-96	P	17	G. Durie
1996-97	P	16	B. Laudrup
1997-98	P	32	M. Negri
1998-99	P	18	R. Wallace
1999-00	P	17	J. Albertz

ROSS COUNTY

Season	Div	No. of Goals	Player
1994-95	T	12	B. Grant
1995-96	T	15	C. Milne
1996-97	T	22	D. Adams
1997-98	T	16	D. Adams
1998-99	T	17	S. Ferguson
			N. Tarrant
1999-00	S	13	G. Shaw

ST. JOHNSTONE

Season	Div	No. of Goals	Player
1984-85	F	9	J. Reid
1985-86	S	11	W. Brown
1986-87	S	25	W. Brown
1987-88	S	16	W. Watters
1988-89	F	12	S. Maskrey
1989-90	F	19	R. Grant
1990-91	P	9	H. Curran
1991-92	P	18	P. Wright
1992-93	P	14	P. Wright
1993-94	P	7	P. Wright
1994-95	F	19	G. O'Boyle
1995-96	F	21	G. O'Boyle
1996-97	F	19	R. Grant
1997-98	P	10	G. O'Boyle
1998-99	P	4	G. Bollan
			R. Grant
			M. Simao
1999-00	P	10	N. Lowndes

ST. MIRREN

Season	Div	No. of Goals	Player
1984-85	P	16	F. McAvennie
1985-86	P	7	G. Speirs
1986-87	P	10	F. McGarvey
1987-88	P	10	P. Chalmers
1988-89	P	11	P. Chalmers
1989-90	P	12	G. Torfason
1990-91	P	4	P. Kinnaird
			K. McDowall
			G. Torfason
1991-92	P	8	G. Torfason
1992-93	F	18	B. Lavety
1993-94	F	10	B. Lavety
1994-95	F	7	B. Lavety
1995-96	F	11	B. Lavety
1996-97	F	15	M. Yardley
1997-98	F	9	J. Mendes
1998-99	F	11	M. Yardley
1999-00	F	19	M. Yardley

STENHOUSEMUIR

Season	Div	No. of Goals	Player
1984-85	S	6	H. Erwin
			A. McNaughton
1985-86	S	11	J. Sinnet
1986-87	S	5	A. Bateman
			P. Russell
1987-88	S	10	T. Condie
1988-89	S	9	C. Walker
1989-90	S	15	S. McCormick
1990-91	S	17	A. Speirs
1991-92	S	6	M. Mathieson
1992-93	S	26	M. Mathieson
1993-94	S	14	M. Mathieson
1994-95	S	10	G. Hutchison
1995-96	S	10	M. Mathieson
1996-97	S	14	I. Little
1997-98	S	15	I. Little
1998-99	F	11	R. Hamilton
1999-00	S	8	M. Mooney

STIRLING ALBION

Season	Div	No. of Goals	Player
1984-85	S	21	W. Irvine
1985-86	S	17	W. Irvine
1986-87	S	7	S. Gavin
			C. Gibson
1987-88	S	23	J. Brogan
1988-89	S	18	C. Gibson
1989-90	S	16	J. Reid
1990-91	S	14	D. Lloyd
1991-92	F	17	W. Watters
1992-93	F	11	W. Watters
1993-94	F	13	W. Watters
1994-95	S	15	W. Watters
1995-96	S	25	S. McCormick
1996-97	F	9	A. Bone
1997-98	F	13	A. Bone
1998-99	S	20	A. Bone
1999-00	S	17	A. Graham

STRANRAER

Season	Div	No. of Goals	Player
1984-85	S	10	J. Sweeney
1985-86	S	8	J. McGuire
			S. Mauchlen
1986-87	S	13	B. Cleland
1987-88	S	8	B. Cleland
1988-89	S	11	D. Lloyd
1989-90	S	13	C. Harkness
1990-91	S	14	C. Harkness
1991-92	S	14	T. Sloan
1992-93	S	19	T. Sloan
1993-94	S	16	T. Sloan
1994-95	F	4	D. Henderson
			T. Sloan
1995-96	S	6	A. Grant
1996-97	S	7	P. McIntyre
1997-98	S	11	G. Young
1998-99	S	5	P. Ronald
			G. Young
1999-00	S	12	P. Ronald

THE SCOTTISH FOOTBALL LEAGUE

FIRST DIVISION

AIRDRIEONIANS:

ALLOA ATHLETIC
TERRY CHRISTIE
Player: Dundee, Raith Rovers, Stirling Albion
Manager: Meadowbank Thistle, Stenhousemuir, Alloa Athletic

AYR UNITED
GORDON DALZIEL
Player: Rangers, Manchester City, Partick Thistle, East Stirlingshire, Raith Rovers, Ayr United
Manager: Ayr United

CLYDE
ALLAN MAITLAND
Player: Did Not Play at Senior Level
Manager: Clyde

FALKIRK
ALEX TOTTEN
Player: Liverpool, Dundee, Dunfermline Athletic, Falkirk, Queen of the South, Alloa Athletic
Manager: Alloa Athletic, Falkirk, Dumbarton, St. Johnstone, East Fife, Kilmarnock, Falkirk

INVERNESS CALEDONIAN THISTLE
STEVE PATERSON
Player: Manchester United, Sheffield United, Hong Kong Rangers, Sydney Olympic, Yorniuri Tokyo
Manager: Inverness Caledonian Thistle

LIVINGSTON
JAMES LEISHMAN
Player: Dunfermline Athletic, Cowdenbeath
Manager: Dunfermline Athletic, Montrose, Livingston (Formerly Meadowbank Thistle), Livingston

MORTON
ALLAN EVANS
Player: Dunfermline Athletic, Aston Villa
Manager: Morton

RAITH ROVERS
PETER HETHERSTON
Player: Falkirk (twice), Sheffield United, Watford, Raith Rovers, Aberdeen, Airdrieonians, Partick Thistle
Manager: Raith Rovers

ROSS COUNTY
NEALE COOPER
Player: Aberdeen, Aston Villa, Rangers, Reading, Dunfermline Athletic, Ross County
Manager: Ross County

SECOND DIVISION

ARBROATH

BERWICK RANGERS
PAUL SMITH
Player: Dundee, Dundee United, Raith Rovers, Motherwell, Dunfermline Athletic, Falkirk, Dunfermline Athletic, Heart of Midlothian, Ayr United, Berwick Rangers
Manager: Berwick Rangers

CLYDEBANK
TOMMY COYNE
Player: Clydebank, Dundee United, Dundee, Celtic, Tranmere Rovers, Motherwell, Dundee, Falkirk (loan), Clydebank
Manager: Clydebank

FORFAR ATHLETIC
IAN McPHEE
Player: Forfar Athletic, Dundee United, Airdrieonians, Forfar Athletic
Manager: Forfar Athletic

PARTICK THISTLE
JOHN LAMBIE
Player: Falkirk, St. Johnstone
Manager: Hamilton Academical, Partick Thistle, Hamilton Academical, Partick Thistle, Falkirk, Partick Thistle

QUEEN OF THE SOUTH
JOHN CONNOLLY
Player: St. Johnstone, Everton, Birmingham City, Newcastle United, Hibernian, Scotland
Manager: Queen of the South

QUEEN'S PARK
JOHN McCORMACK
Player: Clydebank, St. Mirren, Dundee, Airdrieonians, Partick Thistle
Coach: Dundee (Manager), Queen's Park

STENHOUSEMUIR
BRIAN FAIRLEY
Player: Hibernian, Cowdenbeath
Manager: Stenhousemuir

STIRLING ALBION
RAY STEWART
Player: Dundee United, West Ham United, St. Johnstone, Stirling Albion, Scotland
Manager: Livingston, Stirling Albion

STRANRAER
BILLY McLAREN
Player: Queen of the South (twice), Morton (twice), East Fife, Cowdenbeath, Dunfermline Athletic, Hibernian, Partick Thistle
Manager: Queen of the South, Hamilton Academical, Albion Rovers, Queen of the South, Albion Rovers, Stranraer

THIRD DIVISION

ALBION ROVERS
JOHN McVEIGH
Player: Airdrieonians, Clyde, Hamilton Academical, Kilmarnock, Falkirk
Manager: Partick Thistle, Raith Rovers, Albion Rovers

BRECHIN CITY
DICK CAMPBELL
Player: Brechin City, East Stirlingshire
Manager: Dunfermline Athletic, Brechin City

COWDENBEATH
CRAIG LEVEIN
Player: Cowdenbeath, Heart of Midlothian, Scotland
Manager: Cowdenbeath

DUMBARTON
JIMMY BROWN
Player: Partick Thistle, Dumbarton, Oxford United
Manager: Dumbarton

EAST FIFE
ROBERT SHANNON
Player: Dundee, Middlesbrough (loan), Dunfermline Athletic, Motherwell, Dundee United, Hibernian, East Fife
Manager: East Fife

EAST STIRLINGSHIRE
GEORGE FAIRLEY
Player: Did Not Play at Senior Level.
Manager: East Stirlingshire

ELGIN CITY
ALEXANDER CALDWELL
Player: St. Johnstone, Dundee
Manager: Elgin City

HAMILTON ACADEMICAL
ALLY DAWSON
Player: Rangers, Blackburn Rovers, Airdrieonians, St. Andrews (Malta)
Manager: St. Andrews (Malta), Hamilton Academical

MONTROSE
KEVIN DRINKELL
Player: Grimsby Town, Norwich City, Rangers, Coventry City, Falkirk, Stirling Albion
Manager: Stirling Albion, Montrose

PETERHEAD
IAN WILSON
Player: Aberdeen, Dundee, Leicester City, Everton, Derby County, Wigan Athletic, Bury, Besiktas, Scotland
Manager: Peterhead

THE SCOTTISH PREMIER LEAGUE

ABERDEEN
EBBE SKOVDAHL
Player: Van Loes, Brondby, Hvalsoe
Manager: Hvalsoe, Glostrop BC, Bronshoi, Brondby IF, Benfica, Brondby IF, Vejle, Brondby IF, Aberdeen

CELTIC
MARTIN O'NEILL
Player: Distillery, Derry City, Nottingham Forest, Norwich City, Manchester City, Norwich City, Notts County, Northern Ireland
Manager: Wycombe Wanderers, Leicester City, Celtic

DUNDEE
IVANO BONETTI
Player: Torino, Brescia, Bologna, Sampdoria, Atalanta, Genoa, Tranmere Rovers, Grimsby Town
Manager: Dundee

DUNDEE UNITED
ALEX SMITH
Player: Stirling Albion, East Stirlingshire, Albion Rovers, Stenhousemuir
Manager: Stenhousemuir, Stirling Albion, St. Mirren, Aberdeen, Clyde, Dundee United

DUNFERMLINE ATHLETIC
JAMES CALDERWOOD
Player: Birmingham City, Cambridge United (loan), Sparta Rotterdam, Willem II, Roda JC, SC Heracles

Manager: Rietvogels, FC Zwolle, SC Cambuur Leeuwarden, Willem II, NEC Nijmegen, Dunfermline Athletic

HEART OF MIDLOTHIAN
JIM JEFFERIES
Player: Heart of Midlothian, Berwick Rangers
Manager: Berwick Rangers, Falkirk, Heart of Midlothian

HIBERNIAN
ALEX McLEISH
Player: Aberdeen, Motherwell, Scotland
Manager: Motherwell, Hibernian

KILMARNOCK
BOBBY WILLIAMSON
Player: Clydebank, Rangers, West Bromwich Albion, Rotherham United, Kilmarnock
Manager: Kilmarnock

MOTHERWELL
BILLY DAVIES
Player: Rangers, St. Mirren, Leicester City, IF Elfsborg, Dunfermline Athletic, Motherwell
Manager: Motherwell

RANGERS
DICK ADVOCAAT
Player: Den Haag, Breda Kerkrod, Berlow, Chicago Sting
Manager: Haarlem, Dordrecht, Holland, PSV Eindhoven, Rangers

ST. JOHNSTONE
SANDY CLARK
Player: Airdrieonians, West Ham United, Rangers, Heart of Midlothian, Partick Thistle, Dunfermline Athletic, Heart of Midlothian
Manager: Partick Thistle, Heart of Midlothian, Hamilton Academical, St. Johnstone

ST. MIRREN
TOM HENDRIE
Player: Meadowbank Thistle, Berwick Rangers
Manager: Berwick Rangers, Alloa Athletic, St. Mirren

INFORMATION COMPILED BY JIM JEFFREY

UEFA CHAMPIONS LEAGUE
Qualifying Round 2 - First Leg
Wednesday, 28th July, 1999

FC HAKA 1
Niemi

RANGERS 4
Amoruso, Mols (2),
Johansson

FC Haka: Vilnrotter, Penttila, Karjalainen, Rasanen, Ivanov, (Torkelli), Hyokyvarra, (Okkenen), Reynders, Popovitch, Savolienan, Wilson, Niemi, (Nyssonen)
Substitutes not used: Toivonen, Rantala, Pasanen
Rangers: Klos, Adamczuk, Moore, Amoruso, Numan, Ferguson, Reyna, (Nicholson), Van Bronckhorst, (Albertz), Mols, Wallace, (Johansson), McCann
Substitutes not used: Niemi, Amato, Vidmar, Wilson
Referee: V. Hrinak, Slovakia
Attendance: 3,341

Qualifying Round 2 - Second Leg
Wednesday, 4th August, 1999

RANGERS 3
Wallace, Johansson, Amato

FC HAKA 0

Rangers: Klos, Adamczuk, Numan, (Vidmar), Moore, Amoruso, B. Ferguson, (Nicholson), Wallace, Mols, (Amato), Johansson, Van Bronckhorst, Albertz
Substitutes not used: Niemi, Wilson
FC Haka: Vilnrotter, Penttila, Karjalainen, Rasanen, (Savolainen), Ivanov, (Nyssonen), Reynders, Popovitch, Rantala, Wilson, Okkonen, Niemi, (Torkkeli)
Substitutes not used: Toivonen, Salli, Pasanten
Referee: L. Pucek (Poland)
Attendance: 46,443
(Rangers won 7-1 on Aggregate)

Qualifying Round 3 - First Leg
Wednesday, 11th August, 1999

RANGERS 2
Vidmar, Reyna

PARMA 0

Rangers: Klos, Porrini, Moore, Amoruso, Vidmar, (Albertz), B. Ferguson, Van Bronckhorst, Mols, Wallace, Reyna, McCann
Substitutes not used: Niemi, Amato, Adamczuk, Wilson, Johansson, McInnes
Parma: Buffon, Sartor, Baggio, (Fuser), Ortega, (Bredam), Boghossian, Cannavaro, Di Vaio, (Stanic), Thuram, Serena, Vanoli, Walem
Substitutes not used: Micillo, Benarrivo, Torrisi, Montano
Referee: J. Encinar (Spain)
Attendance: 49,263

Qualifying Round 3 - Second Leg
Wednesday, 25th August, 1999

PARMA 1
Walem

RANGERS 0

Parma: Buffon, Lassissi, Torrisi, Thuram, Fuser, Baggio, Boghossian, (Stanic), Vanoli, (Serena), Ortega, Crespo, Di Vaio, (Walem)
Substitutes not used: Micillo, Benarrivo, Breda, Maini
Rangers: Charbonnier, Porrini, Moore, Amoruso, Vidmar, Reyna, B. Ferguson, (Albertz), Van Bronckhorst, Adamczuk, (Hendry), Wallace, (McCann), Mols
Substitutes not used: Niemi, I. Ferguson, Johansson, Amato
Referee: K. Nilsson (Sweden)
Attendance: 28,500
(Rangers won 2-1 on Aggregate)

FIRST GROUP MATCH STAGE
Wednesday, 15th September, 1999

VALENCIA 2
Moore (o.g.),
Kily Gonzalez

RANGERS 0

Valencia: Canizares, Pellegrino, Bjorklund, Mendieta, Lopez, (Llie), Gerard, Carboni, Sanchez, (Angulo), Kily Gonzalez, Angloma, Albelda
Substitutes not used: Palop, Camarasa, Djukic, Oscar, Serban
Rangers: Charbonnier, Porrini, (Kanchelskis), Moore, Amoruso, Vidmar, Reyna, B. Ferguson, Van Bronckhorst, (Johansson), Mols, Amato, McCann, (Albertz)
Substitutes not used: Niemi, Numan, Hendry, Adamczuk
Referee: L. Michel (Slovakia)
Attendance: 54,971

Tuesday, 21st September, 1999

RANGERS 1
Albertz

BAYERN MUNICH 1
Tarnat

Rangers: Charbonnier, Numan, Moore, Amoruso, Porrini, Albertz, B. Ferguson, Van Bronckhorst, Reyna, Mols, (Hendry), Johansson, (McCann)
Substitutes not used: Niemi, Kanchelskis, Wallace, Vidmar, Adamczuk
Bayern Munich: Wessels, Kuffour, Matthaus, (Zickler), Linke, Lizarazu, (Jancker), Effenberg, Tarnat, Jeremies, Scholl, Elber, (Santa Cruz), Salinmidzic
Substitutes not used: Schlosser, Andersson, Strunz, Fink
Referee: R. Wojcik (Poland)
Attendance: 49,960

Tuesday, 28th September, 1999

PSV EINDHOVEN 0

RANGERS 1
Albertz

PSV Eindhoven: Waterreus, Dirkx, Heintze, Khokhlov, Van Nistelrooy, Nilis, Van Der Doelen, (Bruggink), Rommedahl, (Kolkka), Nikiforov, Stinga, (Bourna), Wielaert
Substitutes not used: Lodewijks, Fuchs, Iwan, Skerla
Rangers: Charbonnier, Porrini, Moore, Amoruso, Numan, B. Ferguson, Van Bronckhorst, Reyna, (Albertz), McCann, Mols, Wallace
Substitutes not used: Niemi, Kanchelskis, Vidmar, Amato, Hendry, Adamczuk
Referee: A. Frisk (Sweden)
Attendance: 30,000

Wednesday, 20th October, 1999

RANGERS 4
Amoruso, Mols (2),
McCann

PSV EINDHOVEN 1
Van Nistelrooy

Rangers: Klos, Porrini, Moore, Amoruso, B. Ferguson, Van Bronckhorst, Mols, (Johansson), Wallace, (Kanchelskis), Vidmar, McCann, (Albertz), McInnes
Substitutes not used: Charbonnier, Amato, Adamczuk, Wilson
PSV Eindhoven: Kralj, Faber, Heintze, Van Brommel, Khokhlov, Van Nistelrooy, Nilis, (Bruggink), Vogel, Nikiforov, Stinga, (Rommedahl), Wielaert, (Kolkka)
Substitutes not used: Lodewijks, Dirkx, Van Der Doelen, Addo
Referee: R. Temmink (Holland)
Attendance: 50,083

Tuesday, 26th October, 1999

RANGERS 1   **VALENCIA 2**
Moore   Mendieta, Lopez
Rangers: Klos, Porrini, Amoruso, Moore, Vidmar, (Albertz), McInnes, (Kanchelskis), B. Ferguson, Van Bronckhorst, McCann, Mols, Wallace, (Johansson)
Substitutes not used: Charbonnier, Numan, Amato, Adamczuk
Valencia: Palop, Angulo, Pellegrino, Djukic, Carboni, Mendieta, (Soria Lopez), Albeda, Kily Gonzalez, (Farinos), Llie, Gerard, Lopez
Substitutes not used: Bartual Molina, Oscar, Sanchez, Milla, Fagiani
Referee: G. Benko (Austria)
Attendance: 50,063

Wednesday, 3rd November, 1999

BAYERN MUNICH 1   **RANGERS 0**
Strunz
Bayern Munich: Kahn, Matthaus, Linke, Babbel, Strunz, Fink, Effenberg, (Tarnat), Lizarazu, Scholl, (Salihamidzic), Elber, Santa Cruz, (Sergio)
Substitutes not used: Wessels, Andersson, Jancker, Zickler
Rangers: Klos, Porrini, Moore, Amoruso, Numan, (McCann), Reyna, B. Ferguson, Albertz, Van Bronckhorst, Mols, (Johansson), Wallace, (Amato)
Substitutes not used: Charbonnier, Kanchelskis, Vidmar, Adamczuk
Referee: V. Pereira (Portugal)
Attendance: 54,000

FINAL GROUP TABLE

	P	W	D	L	F	A	Pts
VALENCIA	6	3	3	0	8	4	12
BAYERN MUNICH	6	2	3	1	7	6	9
RANGERS	6	2	1	3	7	7	7
PSV EINDHOVEN	6	1	1	4	5	10	4

UEFA CUP

UEFA CUP

Qualifying Round - First Leg

Thursday, 12th August, 1999

VPS VAASA 1   **ST. JOHNSTONE 1**
Pohja   Lowndes
VPS Vaasa: Toiiuoonem, Kaultonem, Swoste, Koko, Jallonen, Priha, Kangaskorpi, Enquist, Jaakkola, Pohja, Sykora
Substitutes: Stringham, Nygard, Sidonen, Essandoh, Tarkkio, Kaijasitta, Sund
St. Johnstone: Main, McQuillan, Bollan, Dasovic, Weir, Dods, Simao, (Grant), O'Neil, McAnespie, McMahon, Kane
Substitutes not used: Griffin, O'Halloran, McCluskey, Lauchlan, Lowndes, Ferguson
Referee: S. Basakov (Russia)
Attendance: 8,500

KR REYKJAVIK 1   **KILMARNOCK 0**
Hinriksson
KR Reykjavik: Finnbogason, Portsteinsson, Gislason, Egilsson, Winnie, S. Jonnson, Juliusson, (Birgison), Danielsson, Hinriksson, Gunnlugsson, Benediktsson
Substitutes not used: Gunnleifsson, Sigurgeirsson, P. Jonnson, Petersson, Porhallson
Kilmarnock: Meldrum, MacPherson, Jeffrey, (Wright), McGowne, Reilly, Holt, Mitchell, Dindeleux, Roberts, (Vareille), Innes, Hay
Substitutes not used: Henry, Durrant, McCoist, Mahood, Watt
Referee: W. Stark (Germany)
Attendance: 5,500

CWMBRAN 0   **CELTIC 6**
     Berkovic, Tebily, Larsson (2), Viduka, Brattbakk
Cwmbran: O'Hagan, Wills, John, Blackie, O'Brien, Dyson, Wigley, (Aizlewood), Moore, Evans, (Thomas), Graham, Summers, (Hughes)
Substitutes not used: Pattimore, Goodridge, Sterch, Morris
Celtic: Gould, Stubbs, Larsson, (Johnson), Burley, Berkovic, Lambert, Petta, (Blinker), Tebily, Riseth, Viduka, (Brattbakk), Mahe
Substitutes not used: Wieghorst, Kerr, Healy
Referee: M. Ross (Northern Ireland)
Attendance: 8,920

Qualifying Round - Second Leg

Thursday, 26th August, 1999

ST. JOHNSTONE 2   **VPS VAASA 0**
Simao (2)
St. Johnstone: Main, McQuillan, Bollan, Dasovic, Weir, Dods, McAnespie, (Grant), O'Neil, Lowndes, (Simao), McMahon, Kane
Substitutes not used: Griffin, McCluskey, McBride, O'Halloran, Ferguson
VPS Vaasa: Stringhim, (Sillanpaa), Kaultonen, Koko, Jallonen, Kangaskorpi, Sihvonen, Enqvist, Essandoh, Jaakkola, (Nygard), Pohja, Kaiijassitta
Substitutes not used: Sueste, Huhtamaki, Sund, Sykora
Referee: J. Arceo (Spain)
Attendance: 8,392
(St. Johnstone won 3-1 on aggregate)

KILMARNOCK 2   **KR REYKJAVIK 0**
Wright, Bagan
Kilmarnock: Meldrum, MacPherson, Henry, (Bagan), Holt, Wright, Durrant, McCoist, (Jeffrey), Mahood, (Vareille), Baker, Dindeleux, Lauchlan
Substitutes not used: Stewart, Reilly, Mitchell, Burke
KR Rekjavik: Finnbogason, Porsteinsson, Gislason, Egilsson, Winnie, S. Jonsson, Juliiusson, (P. Jonsson), Danielsson, Hinriksson, Gunnlugsson, (Sigurdsson), Benediktsson, (Birgisson)
Substitutes not used: Gunnleifsson, Sidurgeirsson, Porhallsson
Referee: L. Bazzoli (Italy)
Attendance: 11,760
(Kilmarnock won 2-1 on aggregate)

CELTIC 4   **CWMBRAN 0**
Brattbakk, Smith,
Mjallby, Johnson
Celtic: Kharine, Stubbs, Brattbakk, Wieghorst, (Smith), Petta, (Johnson), McKinlay, Blinker, Healy, Riseth, Mjallby, Burchill
Substitutes not used: Mahe, Bonnes, Elliot, Convery, Corr
Cwmbran: Morris, Willis, John, Blackie, O'Brien, (B. Graham), Summers, (Goodridge), Moore, D. Graham, Wigley, (Pattimore), Aizlewood, Futcher
Substitutes not used: O'Hagan, Thomas, Powell, Evans
Referee: P. McKeon (Ireland)
Attendance: 46,975
(Celtic won 10-0 on aggregate)

First Round - First Leg

Thursday, 16th September, 1999

CELTIC 2   **HAPOEL TEL-AVIV 0**
Larsson (2)
Celtic: Gould, McNamara, Mahe, Tebily, Stubbs, Burley, Lambert, Moravcik, Petta, (Blinker), Larsson, Burchill
Substitutes not used: Kharine, Petrov, Mjallby, Riseth, Brattbakk, Johnson
Hapoel Tel-Aviv: Elimelech, Antebi, Bakhar, Ohaion, Pisont, Rupnik, Udi, Toema, (Gohen), Cimirotic, Harazi, (Tikva), Gershon
Substitutes not used: Hillel, Racunica, Balali, Afek, Rahmin
Referee: F. De Bleecker (Belgium)
Attendance: 45,171

KAISERSLAUTERN 3   **KILMARNOCK 0**

Koch, Djorkaeff, Marschall

Kaiserslautern: Reinke, Ramzy, Hristov, (Strasser), Wagner, (Reich), Petterson, Sforza, Marschall, Djorkaeff, Ratinho, (Sobotzik), Buck, Koch

Substitutes not used: Gospodarek, Komljenovic, Rische, Tare

Kilmarnock: Meldrum, MacPherson, McGowne, Holt, Durrant, (Reilly), Mitchell, (Burke), Mahood, Vareille, (Jeffrey), Baker, Lauchlan, Bagan

Substitutes not used: Watt, Wright, McCoist, Hessey

Referee: J. Coroado (Portugal)

Attendance: 21,000

MONACO 3   **ST. JOHNSTONE 0**

Simone (2), Trezeguet

Monaco: Barthez, Marquez, Christanval, Lamouchi, (Riise), Giuly, (N'Diaye), Trezeguet, Gallardo, Simone, Leonard, (Legwinski), Da Costa, Sagnoi

Substitutes not used: Eloi, Samerud, Iries, Sylva

St. Johnstone: Main, McQuillan, Bollan, McAnespie, Weir, Griffin, Simao, (McCluskey) O'Neill, Thomas, (Lowndes), O'Halloran, Kane

Substitutes not used: McBride, O'Boyle, Grant, Lauchlan, Ferguson

Referee: E. Steinborn (Germany)

Attendance: 7,000

First Round - Second Leg

Thursday, 30th September, 1999

HAPOEL TEL AVIV 0   **CELTIC 1**

Larsson

Hapoel Tel Aviv: Elimelech, Cohen, (Balali), Gershon, Ohaion, Antebi, Rupnik, Racunica, Bakhar, (Balali), Pisont, Toema, (Harazi), Cimirotic

Substitutes not used: Rahmin, Elksyam, Hillel, Afek, Kbada

Celtic: Gould, Stubbs, Tebily, Riseth, Petrov, (Wieghorst), McNamara, Burley, Lambert, Viduka, (Berkovic), Moravcik, (Blinker), Larsson

Substitutes not used: Kharine, Petta, Burchill, Mjallby

Referee: J. Arceo (Spain)

Attendance: 6,400

(Celtic won 3-0 on Aggregate)

KILMARNOCK 0   **KAISERSLAUTERN 2**

Djorkaeff, Ramzy

Kilmarnock: Meldrum, MacPherson, Baker, McGowne, Dindeleux, Innes, Durrant, Reilly, Holt, McCoist, (Mitchell), Vareille, (Jeffrey)

Substitutes not used: Watt, Mahood, Bagan, Burke, Roberts

Kaiserslautern: Reinke, Schjonberg, Ramzy, Wagner, Sforza, (Sobotzik), Marschall, (Petterson), Komljenovic, Djorkaeff, Ratinho, (Buck), Strasser, Koch

Substitutes not used: Gospodarek, Reich, Rische, Tare

Referee: C. Kapitanis (Cyprus)

Attendance: 8,074

(Kaiserslautern won 5-0 on Aggregate)

ST. JOHNSTONE 3   **MONACO 3**

Leonard (o.g),   Prso, Rilse,

Dasovic, O'Neil   Legwinski

St. Johnstone: Main, McQuillan, Bollan, Dasovic, Kernaghan, Griffin, Simao, O'Neil, Lowndes, (O'Boyle), O'Halloran, (Grant), Kane, (McAnespie)

Substitutes not used: Thomas, McCluskey, McBride, Ferguson

Monaco: Barthez, Marquez, Lamouchi, (Gallardo), Simone, (Trezeguet), Legwinski, Leonard, Sagnoi, Prso, N'Diaye, (Giuly), Irles, Rilse

Substitutes not used: Contreras, Sarnerud, Rodriguez, Sylva

Referee: V. Torres (Spain)

Attendance: 7,706

(Monaco won 6-3 on Aggregate)

Second Round - First Leg

Thursday, 21st October, 1999

LYON 1   **CELTIC 0**

Blanc

Lyon: Coupet, Carteron, Laigle, Bak, (Malbranque), Violeau, Anderson, Dhorasoo, Vairelles, (Caveglia), Blanc, Delmotte, Brechet

Substitutes not used: Devaux, Govou, Linares, Uras, Hugues

Celtic: Gould, McNamara, Stubbs, Tebily, Riseth, Burley, Lambert, Mjallby, Larsson, (Burchill), Moravcik, (Petta), Viduka

Substitutes not used: Kharine, Blinker, Wieghorst, Brattbakk, Petrov

Referee: R. Temmink (Holland)

Attendance: 37,500

Second Round - Second Leg

Thursday, 4th November, 1999

CELTIC 0   **LYON 1**

Vairelles

Celtic: Gould, Stubbs, Tebily, McNamara, Burley, Lambert, Riseth, Berkovic, Moravcik, (Blinker), Viduka, Burchill

Substitutes not used: Kharine, Petta, Mjallby, Wieghorst, Petrov, Brattbakk

Lyon: Coupet, Carteron, Laville, Bak, Violeau, Anderson, (Uras), Dhorasoo, (Malbranque), Vairelles, Blanc, (Devaux), Delmotte, Linares

Substitutes not used: Govou, Caveglia, Querdi, Hugues

Referee: G. Vardenne (Germany)

Attendance: 54,291

(Lyon won 2-0 on Aggregate)

Third Round - First Leg

Thursday, 25th November, 1999

RANGERS 2   **BORUSSIA DORTMUND 0**

Kohler (o.g.), Wallace

Rangers: Myhre, Adamczuk, Moore, Vidmar, Numan, Reyna, (Kanchelskis), Van Bronckhorst, B. Ferguson, Albertz, Wallace, (McCann), Amato, (Johansson)

Substitutes not used: Wilson, Nicholson, Durie, Brown

Borussia Dortmund: Lehmann, Worns, Feiersinger, Kohler, Evanilson, Addo (Reina), Stevic, Ricken, (But), Barbarez, Bobic, (Herrich), Moller

Substitutes not used: De Beer, Baumann, Nijhuis, Ikpeba

Referee: U. Meier (Switzerland)

Attendance: 49,268

Third Round - Second Leg

Tuesday, 7th December, 1999

BORUSSIA DORTMUND 2   **RANGERS 0**

Ikpeba, Bobic

Borussia Dortmund: Lehmann, Nijhuis, Worns, Reuter, Nerlinger, Stevic, (Tanko), But, Addo, Ikpeba, Ricken, (Barbarez), Herrlich, (Bobic)

Substitutes not used: De Beer, Baumann

Rangers: Myhre, Adamczuk, (Kanchelskis), Moore, Amoruso, Numan, Reyna, Van Bronckhorst, B. Ferguson, Albertz, (Durie), Wallace, (Reyna), McCann

Substitutes not used: Brown, Vidmar, Wilson, Carson, I. Ferguson

Referee: S. Oguz (Turkey)

Attendance: 30,000

(Aggregate 2-2. Borussia Dortmund won 3-1 on Kicks from the Penalty Mark)

A Record of European Championship and International Friendly Matches played by Scotland during Season 1999/2000

EUROPEAN CHAMPIONSHIP

Saturday, 4th September, 1999 - Olympic Stadium, Sarajevo

BOSNIA HERZEGOVINA 1   **SCOTLAND 2**
Bolic   D. Hutchison, W. Dodds

Bosnia Herzegovina: Dedic, Joldic, (Repuh), Mujdza, (Demirovic), Konjic, Hibic, Besirevic, Bolic, Halilovic, (Mujcin), Kodro, Barbarez, Topic
Substitutes not used: Becirevic, Ihtijarevic, Skoro, Memic
Scotland: N. Sullivan, D. Weir, C. Hendry, C. Calderwood, (C. Dailly), D Hopkin, C. Burley, B. Ferguson, (I. Durrant), J. Collins, N. McCann, (K. Gallacher), D. Hutchison, W. Dodds
Substitutes not used: J. Gould, P. Ritchie, S. Gemmill, A. Johnston
Referee: N. Levnikov (Russia)
Attendance: 26,000

Wednesday, 8th September, 1999 - Kadrioru Stadium, Tallinn

ESTONIA 0   **SCOTLAND 0**

Estonia: Poom, Piiroga, Kirs, Hohlov-Simson, Savinuk, Anniste, Terennov, Oper, Kristal, Reim, O'Konnel-Bronin, (Zelinski), (Viikmae)
Substitutes not used: Tohver, Haavista, Lemsalu, Zelinski, Reiska, Meet, Ustritski
Scotland: N. Sullivan, D. Weir, C. Dailly, C. Hendry, C. Burley, J. Collins, I. Durrant, (B. Ferguson), C. Davidson, A. Johnston, (N. McCann), D. Hutchison, W. Dodds. Substitutes not used: J. Gould, P. Ritchie, C. Calderwood, K. Gallacher, S. Gemmill
Referee: F. Stuchlick (Austria)
Attendance: 4,500

Tuesday, 5th October, 1999 - Ibrox Stadium, Glasgow

SCOTLAND 1   **BOSNIA HERZEGOVINA 0**
J. Collins

Scotland: N. Sullivan, D. Weir, C. Davidson, P. Lambert, C. Hendry, (C. Calderwood), C. Dailly, W. Dodds, (G. McSwegan), C. Burley, K. Gallacher, (M. Burchill), D. Hopkin, J. Collins
Substitutes not used: J. Gould, P. Ritchie, C. Cameron, I. Durrant
Bosnia Herzegovina: Guso, Kapetanovic, Besirevic, Hujdorovic, Varesanovic, Barbarez, Ihtijarevic, (Topic), Sabic, Bolic, Mujcin, (Avdic), Baljic
Substitutes not used: Joldic, Cahtarevic, Becirevic
Referee: L. Sundell (Sweden)
Attendance: 30,574

Saturday, 9th October, 1999

The National Stadium, Hampden Park, Glasgow

SCOTLAND 3   **LITHUANIA 0**
D. Hutchison, G. McSwegan, C. Cameron

Scotland: J. Gould, C. Davidson, P. Ritchie, B. O'Neil, C. Dailly, D. Weir, P. Lambert, C. Burley, (C. Cameron), D. Hutchison, M. Burchill, (W. Dodds), G. McSwegan, (K. Gallacher)
Substitutes not used: N. Sullivan, C. Calderwood, I. Durrant, S. Gemmill
Lithuania: Leus, Skerla, Skinderis, Tereskinas, Zutautas, Zvirgzdauskas, Stumbrys, Mikalajunas, Razanauskas, Mikulenas, Dancenko
Substitutes not used: Padimanskas, Maciulevicius, Vencevicius, Fornenko, Ksanavicius, Dziaukstas, Grudzinskas
Referee: S. Bre (France)
Attendance: 22,059

GROUP NINE TABLE

	P	W	D	L	F	A	PTS
CZECH REPUBLIC	10	10	0	0	26	5	30
SCOTLAND	10	5	3	2	15	10	18
ESTONIA	10	3	2	5	15	17	11
BOSNIA HERZEGOVINA	10	3	2	5	14	17	11
LITHUANIA	10	3	2	5	8	16	11
FAROE ISLANDS	10	0	3	7	4	17	3

Championship Play-Off Match - First Leg

Saturday, 13th November, 1999

The National Stadium, Hampden Park, Glasgow

SCOTLAND 0   **ENGLAND 2**
    Scholes (2)

Scotland: N. Sullivan, D. Weir, C. Hendry, P. Ritchie, C. Burley, B. Ferguson, D. Hutchison, J. Collins, C. Dailly, W. Dodds, K. Gallacher, (M Burchill)
Substitutes not used: J. Gould, C. Calderwood, C. Cameron, C. Davidson, I. Durrant, N. McCann
England: Seaman, Campbell, Neville, Ince, Adams, Keown, Beckham, Scholes, Shearer, Owen, (Cole), Redknapp
Substitutes not used: Southgate, Froggatt, Wise, Sinclair, Philips, Martyn
Referee: Manuel Diaz-Vega (Spain)
Attendance: 50,132

Wednesday, 17th November, 1999 - Wembley Stadium, London

ENGLAND 0   **SCOTLAND 1**
    D. Hutchison

England: Seaman, Campbell, Neville, Ince, Adams, Southgate, Beckham, Scholes, (Parlour), Shearer, Owen, (Heskey), Redknapp
Substitutes not used: Ferdinand, Wise, Guppy, Cole, Martyn
Scotland: N. Sullivan, D. Weir, C. Hendry, C. Dailly, C. Burley, B. Ferguson, J. Collins, C. Davidson, W. Dodds, D. Hutchison, N. McCann, (M. Burchill)
Substitutes not used: J. Gould, P. Ritchie, C. Calderwood, I. Durrant, C. Cameron, G. McSwegan
Referee: P. Collina (Italy)
Attendance: 75,848
(Aggregate: England won 2-1)

Craig Burley playing for Scotland against England at Hampden Park

FULL INTERNATIONAL FRIENDLY MATCHES

Wednesday, 29th March, 2000

The National Stadium, Hampden Park, Glasgow

SCOTLAND 0   **FRANCE 2**
    Wiltord, Henry

Scotland: N. Sullivan, P. Telfer, (A. Johnston), C. Davidson, C. Dailly, C. Hendry, P. Ritchie, (S. Pressley), W. Dodds, B. Ferguson, K. Gallacher, (M. Burchill), D. Hutchison, C. Cameron, (N. McCann)
Substitutes not used: J. Gould, R. Anderson, G. Naysmith
France: Ramé, Lizarazu, Blanc, Djorkaeff, (Wiltord), Deschamps, (Vieira), Desailly, Henry, Thuram, Petit, Giuly, (Micoud), Dugarry, (Pires)
Substitute not used: Trezeguet, Djetou, Letizi, Leboeuf
Referee: R. Pedersen (Norway)
Attendance: 48,157

Wednesday, 26th April, 2000 - Geledome, Arnhem

HOLLAND 0 **SCOTLAND 0**

Holland: Van der Sar, Ooijer, Konterman, F. De Boer, Numan, Bosvelt, Makaay, (Talan), Davids, Hasselbaink, (Van Hooijdonk), Bergkamp, (Kluivert), Overmars, (Zenden)
Substitutes not used: Reiziger, Cocu, Bogarde, Seedorf, Westerveid, Van Bronckhorst
Scotland: N. Sullivan, C. Dailly, (B. O'Neil), P. Ritchie, D. Weir, M. Elliott, P. Lambert, W. Dodds, C. Burley, (I. Durrant), J. McNamara, (M. Burchill), D. Hutchison, N. McCann
Substitutes not used: J. Gould, G. Holt, A. Johnston, C. Cameron
Referee: H. Strampe (Germany)   **Attendance:** 25,000

Tuesday, 30th May, 2000 - Lansdowne Road, Dublin

REPUBLIC OF IRELAND 1 **SCOTLAND 2**
C. Burley (o.g.) D. Hutchison, B. Ferguson

Republic of Ireland: A. Kelly, Carr, Kilbane, Babb, Breen, (Dunne), McPhail, (Phelan), McAteer, Finnan, Quinn, (Foley), Robbie Keane, Kennedy, (Duff)
Substitutes not used: Mahon, Kiely, Farrelly
Scotland: N. Sullivan, C. Dailly, G. Naysmith, (I. Durrant), P. Lambert, (A. Johnston), M. Elliott, B. Ferguson, (C. Cameron), W. Dodds, (K. Gallacher), B. O'Neil, N. McCann, (S. Pressley), D. Hutchison, C. Burley
Substitutes not used: J. Gould, G. Holt, M. Burchill
Referee: V. Pereira (Portugal)   **Attendance:** 30,213

EUROPEAN 'UNDER 21' CHAMPIONSHIP

Saturday, 4th September, 1999 - Josik Stadium, Lukavac

BOSNIA HERZEGOVINA 2 **SCOTLAND 5**
Avdic, Dujmovic M. Burchill (3), S. Thompson, J. Paterson

Bosnia Herzegovina: Kruzik, Mulaosmanovic, Ferhatovic, Duro, Jugo, Lagumdzija, Dujmovic, Bistrivoda, Zeric, Avdic, Beslija
Substitutes: Mitrovic, Simic, Halilovic, Zubanovic, Aritovic, Kajtaz, Berberovic
Scotland: P. Gallacher, R. Anderson, G. Naysmith, G. Rae, J. Lauchlan, R. Hughes, (H. Davidson), B. Nicholson, S. Severin, S. Thompson, (N. Tarrant), M. Burchill, (P. Dalglish), J. Paterson
Substitutes not used: J. Langfield, A. Jordan, K. McAnespie, G. Strachan
Referee: A. Micallef (Malta)   **Attendance:** 3,000

Tuesday, 7th September, 1999 - Kadriorg Stadium, Tallinn

ESTONIA 0 **SCOTLAND 4**
G. Rae, M. Burchill, S. Thompson, P. Dalglish

Estonia: Kutt, Rahn, Anis, Nommik, (Sova), Leetma, Samarov, Rooba, Allas, (Jurisson), Tkatsuk, Kulikov, Murumets, (Korju)
Substitutes not used: Kaalma, Kosemets, Parnpuu, Kahr
Scotland: P. Gallacher, R. Anderson, G. Naysmith, G. Rae, J. Lauchlan, L. Wilkie, B. Nicholson, S. Severin, (G. Strachan), S. Thompson, (P. Dalglish), M. Burchill, K. McAnespie, (N. Tarrant)
Substitutes not used: R. Esson, A. Jordan, R. Hughes, H. Davidson
Referee: K. Nalbandyan (Armenia)   **Attendance:** 350

Tuesday 5th October, 1999 - St. Mirren Park, Paisley

SCOTLAND 2 **BOSNIA HERZEGOVINA 0**
J. Lauchlan, P. Dalglish

Scotland: P. Gallacher, S. Baltacha, G. Naysmith, G. Rae, (H. Murray), J. Lauchlan, L. Wilkie, (A. Jordan), B. Nicholson, S. Severin, S. Thompson, (N. Tarrant), P. Dalglish, J. Paterson
Bosnia Herzegovina: Kruzik, Gredic, Basic, Jahic, Duro, Lagumdzija, Simic, (Masic), Zubanovic, Dujmovic, (Zeric), Ferhatovic, (Mesic), Halilovic
Substitutes not used: Mitrovic, Tomic, Bogojevic, Kajtaz
Referee: R. Lajuks (Latvia)   **Attendance:** 1,518

Friday, 8th October, 1999 - Firhill Stadium, Glasgow

SCOTLAND 1 **LITHUANIA 2**
C. Easton Ksanavicius, Laurisas

Scotland: R. Esson, B. Nicholson, G. Naysmith, C. Easton, J. Lauchlan, A. Jordan, H. Davidson, (S. Severin), G. Strachan, (S. Baltacha), A. Notman, N. Tarrant, (P. Dalglish), J. Paterson
Substitutes not used: J. Langfield, M. Dempsie, H. Murray, K. McAnespie
Lithuania: Valius, Kauspadas, Samusiovas, Dedura, Dziaukstas, Graziunas, Ksanavicius, Gardzijauskas, Laurisas, (Trakys), Fomenka, Danilevicius, (Vasiliauskas)
Substitutes not used: Maksvytis, Veikutis
Referee: B. Pregja (Albania)
Attendance: 1,805

GROUP NINE TABLE

	P	W	D	L	F	A	PTS
BELGIUM	10	8	1	1	31	9	25
CZECH REPUBLIC	10	8	1	1	17	5	25
LITHUANIA	10	5	1	4	14	10	16
SCOTLAND	10	4	2	4	18	12	14
BOSNIA HERZEGOVINA	10	2	1	7	11	24	7
ESTONIA	10	0	0	10	4	35	0

'UNDER-21' INTERNATIONAL FRIENDLIES

Tuesday, 28th March, 2000 - Rugby Park, Kilmarnock

SCOTLAND 0 **FRANCE 2**
Sorlin, Reveillere

Scotland: P. Gallacher, P. Canero, (S. Baltacha), W. Cummings, (S. Crainey), L. Wilkie, (K. Milne), S. Caldwell, A. Jordan, H. Davidson, (H. Murray), C. Easton, K. Miller, S. Severin, G. Wales, (A. Notman)
Substitutes not used: J. Langfield, N. Tarrant
France: Landreau, Ehret, (Sable), Escude, (Reveillere), Camara, Matingou, Luccin, Sorlin, (Meriem), Dalmat, Brechet, Luyundula, (Maoulida), Johansen
Substitutes not used: Devineau, Riou, Malbranque
Referee: T. Henning Ovrebo (Norway)   **Attendance:** 4,537

Tuesday, 25th April, 2000 - Stadion de Adelaarshorst, Deventer

HOLLAND 2 **SCOTLAND 0**
Van Steenveldt, Kromkamp

Holland: Van Der Ban, (Graafland), Shuurman, Wolters, Broerse, Mathijssen, Heye, Van Der Meyde, (Van Der Woude), Van Steenveldt, Kuyt, Kromkamp, Van Dinteren, (Ax)
Substitutes not used: Linssen, Zuidam, Pique
Scotland: P. Gallacher, R. Neilson, W. Cummings, (S. Fraser), L. Wilkie, S. Caldwell, A. Jordan, (C. Doig), G. Wales, (N. Tarrant), S. Severin, A. Notman, (B. Carrigan), C. Easton, K. McAnespie, (H. Davidson)
Substitutes not used: R. Esson, H. Murray, C. Stewart
Referee: W. Stark (Germany)
Attendance: 1,200

'UNDER 21' - TRIANGULAR TOURNAMENT

Monday, 29th May, 2000 - The Showgrounds, Newry

NORTHERN IRELAND 1 **SCOTLAND 1**
Kirk A. Notman

Northern Ireland: Miskelly, McReavey, (McCann), Graham, Convery, Dolan, Holmes, Clarke, (Toner), Whitley, Kirk, Hamilton, (Harkin), Friars
Substitutes not used: Ingham, Kelly, McFlynn, Morrow
Scotland: R. Esson, R. Neilson, W. Cummings, (S. Fraser), L. Wilkie, S. Caldwell, C. Doig, A. Notman, S. Severin, K. Miller, M. Stewart, (I. Murray), K. McAnespie, (N. Tarrant)
Substitutes not used: P. Gallacher, P. Canero, A. Jordan, D. Young
Referee: A. Snoddy (Northern Ireland)
Attendance: 300

Wednesday, 31st May, 2000 - Lakeview Park, Loughgall

SCOTLAND 1 **WALES 0**
K. Miller

Scotland: J. Langfield, S. Fraser, K. McAnespie, L. Wilkie, S. Caldwell, C. Doig, A. Notman, (N. Tarrant), S. Severin, (P. Canero), K. Miller, I. Murray, D. Young, (M. Stewart)
Wales: Walsh, Green, Gabbidon, Roberts, (Gibson), Jenkins, Slatter, Williams, Davies, (Day), Maxwell, Jeanne, (Earnshaw), Llewellyn
Referee: K. Guerguinov (Bulgaria)
Attendance: 50

FINAL TABLE

	P	W	D	L	F	A	PTS
SCOTLAND	2	1	1	0	2	1	4
NORTHERN IRELAND	2	0	2	0	3	3	2
WALES	2	0	1	1	2	3	1

125

Official List of Referees 2000/2001

CLASS 1
Kevin Bisset
Iain Brines
Tom Brown
Brian Cassidy
Kenny Clark
George Clyde
Steve Conroy
Hugh Dallas
Stuart Dougal
John Fleming
Alan Freeland
Ian Frickleton
Ian Fyfe
Alan Gemmill
John Gilmour
Colin Hardie
Steve Kaney
Michael McCurry
Douglas McDonald
Brian McGarry
Craig MacKay
Eddie Mack
Eric Martindale
Cammy Melville
Garry Mitchell
Calum Murray
Bobby Orr
Charlie Richmond
Mike Ritchie
John Rowbotham
Dougie Smith
David Somers
Craig Thomson
George Thomson
Kevin Toner
John Underhill
Willie Young

Hugh Dallas

126

CLASS 1 SPECIALIST ASSISTANT REFEREES
Graeme Alison
Neil Brand
Roddy Cobb
Peter Crilley
Frank Cole
Alan Cunningham
Graeme Curr
Andy Davis
Willie Dishington
David Doig
Martin Doran
Jim Dunne

Kenny Clark

Keith Hadden
Gordon Hunter
Wilson Irvine
Robert Johnston
Stuart Logan
Derek Lowe
Jim Lyon
Stuart Macaulay
Gordon McBride
Jim McBride
Ross McCluskie
Joe McDowall
Brian McDuffie
John McElhinney
Robert McKendry
Derek Mason
Gordon Middleton
Ricky Mooney
Tom Murphy
Peter Peace
Andrew Seymour
Stewart Shearer
Ricky Smith
Allen Thurston

Stuart Dougal

CLASS 1 ASSISTANT REFEREES (SELECTED)
Crawford Allan
James Bee
John Bicknell
Alan Boyd
Jim Boyd
Chris Boyle
John Brady
Kevin Carter
Derek Clark
Martin Cryans
Jamie Downie
George Drummond
Steven Duff
Stephen Finnie
Joe Heggie
Willie Hornby
Andrew Hunter
Raymond King
Mike MacGregor
Alan Muir
Willie Murray
Martin Sproule
Mike Tumilty
Brian Winter

CLASS 1 ASSISTANT REFEREES
Francis Andrews
Jeff Banks
Stuart Bennett

Colin Brown
Scott Brown
John Campbell
Gary Cheyne
Paul Cheyne
William Collum
Steven Craven
Hugh Dalgetty
David Davidson
Mark Doyle
Ian Elmslie
Andrew Gault
William Gilfillan
Jason Hasson
David Hodgson
Robert Hunter
Tommy Johnston
Steve Jolly
Lawrence Kerrigan
Gary Kirkwood
Scott MacDonald
Steve McGeouch
Gordon MacKay
Cameron McKay
John McKendrick
Willie McKnight
Jim McNeil
Craig Marshall
Brian Martin
Michael Monaghan
Steven Nicholls
Euan Norris
Stevie O'Reilly
Steve Pullar
Eric Robertson
Scott Robertson
Thomas Robertson
Charlie Smith
Eddie Smith
Gary Sweeney
Keith Sorbie
Steve Todd
Jim Walker
Paul Watson
Willie Weir
Rod Williamson
Chris Young
Ewan Young

COMPLETE FIXTURE LISTS FOR
THE SCOTTISH FOOTBALL LEAGUE
SEASON 2000/01

Saturday, August 5th, 2000
BELL'S SCOTTISH LEAGUE FIRST DIVISION
Ayr United v. Ross County
Clyde v. Falkirk
Inverness Cal. Th. v. Airdrieonians
Morton v. Livingston
Raith Rovers v. Alloa Athletic
BELL'S SCOTTISH LEAGUE SECOND DIVISION
Arbroath v. Partick Thistle
Queen's Park v. Berwick Rangers
Stenhousemuir v. Queen of the South
Stirling Albion v. Clydebank
Stranraer v. Forfar Athletic
BELL'S SCOTTISH LEAGUE THIRD DIVISION
Albion Rovers v. East Fife
Brechin City v. Elgin City
East Stirlingshire v. Cowdenbeath
Hamilton Academical v. Dumbarton
Peterhead v. Montrose

Saturday, August 12th, 2000
BELL'S SCOTTISH LEAGUE FIRST DIVISION
Airdrieonians v. Raith Rovers
Alloa Athletic v. Ayr United
Falkirk v. Morton
Livingston v. Inverness Cal. Th.
Ross County v. Clyde
BELL'S SCOTTISH LEAGUE SECOND DIVISION
Berwick Rangers v. Arbroath
Clydebank v. Stenhousemuir
Forfar Athletic v. Queen's Park
Partick Thistle v. Stranraer
Queen of the South v. Stirling Albion
BELL'S SCOTTISH LEAGUE THIRD DIVISION
Cowdenbeath v. Albion Rovers
Dumbarton v. Brechin City
East Fife v. Peterhead
Elgin City v. Hamilton Academical
Montrose v. East Stirlingshire

Saturday, August 19th, 2000
BELL'S SCOTTISH LEAGUE FIRST DIVISION
Ayr United v. Airdrieonians
Clyde v. Livingston
Inverness Cal. Th. v. Falkirk
Morton v. Alloa Athletic
Raith Rovers v. Ross County
BELL'S SCOTTISH LEAGUE SECOND DIVISION
Arbroath v. Clydebank
Queen's Park v. Queen of the South
Stenhousemuir v. Partick Thistle
Stirling Albion v. Forfar Athletic
Stranraer v. Berwick Rangers
BELL'S SCOTTISH LEAGUE THIRD DIVISION
Albion Rovers v. Elgin City
Brechin City v. Cowdenbeath
East Stirlingshire v. East Fife
Hamilton Academical v. Montrose
Peterhead v. Dumbarton

Saturday, August 26th, 2000
BELL'S SCOTTISH LEAGUE FIRST DIVISION
Alloa Athletic v. Livingston
Ayr United v. Falkirk
Clyde v. Morton
Raith Rovers v. Inverness Cal. Th.
Ross County v. Airdrieonians
BELL'S SCOTTISH LEAGUE SECOND DIVISION
Clydebank v. Queen of the South
Forfar Athletic v. Stenhousemuir
Partick Thistle v. Berwick Rangers
Stirling Albion v. Queen's Park
Stranraer v. Arbroath

BELL'S SCOTTISH LEAGUE THIRD DIVISION
Albion Rovers v. Dumbarton
Cowdenbeath v. Elgin City
East Stirlingshire v. Hamilton Academical
Montrose v. East Fife
Peterhead v. Brechin City

Saturday, September 9th, 2000
BELL'S SCOTTISH LEAGUE FIRST DIVISION
Airdrieonians v. Alloa Athletic
Falkirk v. Raith Rovers
Inverness Cal. Th. v. Clyde
Livingston v. Ayr United
Morton v. Ross County
BELL'S SCOTTISH LEAGUE SECOND DIVISION
Arbroath v. Forfar Athletic
Berwick Rangers v. Clydebank
Queen of the South v. Stranraer
Queen's Park v. Partick Thistle
Stenhousemuir v. Stirling Albion
BELL'S SCOTTISH LEAGUE THIRD DIVISION
Brechin City v. Montrose
Dumbarton v. East Stirlingshire
East Fife v. Cowdenbeath
Elgin City v. Peterhead
Hamilton Academical v. Albion Rovers

Saturday, September 16th, 2000
BELL'S SCOTTISH LEAGUE FIRST DIVISION
Clyde v. Airdrieonians
Falkirk v. Alloa Athletic
Inverness Cal. Th. v. Ross County
Livingston v. Raith Rovers
Morton v. Ayr United
BELL'S SCOTTISH LEAGUE SECOND DIVISION
Arbroath v. Stenhousemuir
Berwick Rangers v. Queen of the South
Forfar Athletic v. Clydebank
Partick Thistle v. Stirling Albion
Stranraer v. Queen's Park
BELL'S SCOTTISH LEAGUE THIRD DIVISION
Albion Rovers v. Brechin City
Cowdenbeath v. Hamilton Academical
East Fife v. Elgin City
Montrose v. Dumbarton
Peterhead v. East Stirlingshire

Saturday, September 23rd, 2000
BELL'S SCOTTISH LEAGUE FIRST DIVISION
Airdrieonians v. Livingston
Alloa Athletic v. Inverness Cal. Th.
Ayr United v. Clyde
Raith Rovers v. Morton
Ross County v. Falkirk
BELL'S SCOTTISH LEAGUE SECOND DIVISION
Clydebank v. Partick Thistle
Queen of the South v. Forfar Athletic
Queen's Park v. Arbroath
Stenhousemuir v. Berwick Rangers
Stirling Albion v. Stranraer
BELL'S SCOTTISH LEAGUE THIRD DIVISION
Brechin City v. East Fife
Dumbarton v. Cowdenbeath
East Stirlingshire v. Albion Rovers
Elgin City v. Montrose
Hamilton Academical v. Peterhead

Saturday, September 30th, 2000
BELL'S SCOTTISH LEAGUE FIRST DIVISION
Ayr United v. Inverness Cal. Th.
Clyde v. Raith Rovers
Falkirk v. Livingston

Morton v. Airdrieonians
Ross County v. Alloa Athletic
BELL'S SCOTTISH LEAGUE SECOND DIVISION
Arbroath v. Queen of the South
Berwick Rangers v. Stirling Albion
Partick Thistle v. Forfar Athletic
Queen's Park v. Stenhousemuir
Stranraer v. Clydebank
BELL'S SCOTTISH LEAGUE THIRD DIVISION
Albion Rovers v. Peterhead
Brechin City v. East Stirlingshire
Cowdenbeath v. Montrose
East Fife v. Hamilton Academical
Elgin City v. Dumbarton

Saturday, October 7th, 2000
BELL'S SCOTTISH LEAGUE FIRST DIVISION
Airdrieonians v. Falkirk
Alloa Athletic v. Clyde
Inverness Cal. Th. v. Morton
Livingston v. Ross County
Raith Rovers v. Ayr United
BELL'S SCOTTISH LEAGUE SECOND DIVISION
Clydebank v. Queen's Park
Forfar Athletic v. Berwick Rangers
Queen of the South v. Partick Thistle
Stenhousemuir v. Stranraer
Stirling Albion v. Arbroath
BELL'S SCOTTISH LEAGUE THIRD DIVISION
Dumbarton v. East Fife
East Stirlingshire v. Elgin City
Hamilton Academical v. Brechin City
Montrose v. Albion Rovers
Peterhead v. Cowdenbeath

Saturday, October 14th, 2000
BELL'S SCOTTISH LEAGUE FIRST DIVISION
Airdrieonians v. Inverness Cal. Th.
Alloa Athletic v. Raith Rovers
Falkirk v. Clyde
Livingston v. Morton
Ross County v. Ayr United
BELL'S SCOTTISH LEAGUE SECOND DIVISION
Berwick Rangers v. Queen's Park
Clydebank v. Stirling Albion
Forfar Athletic v. Stranraer
Partick Thistle v. Arbroath
Queen of the South v. Stenhousemuir
BELL'S SCOTTISH LEAGUE THIRD DIVISION
Cowdenbeath v. East Stirlingshire
Dumbarton v. Hamilton Academical
East Fife v. Albion Rovers
Elgin City v. Brechin City
Montrose v. Peterhead

Saturday, October 21st, 2000
BELL'S SCOTTISH LEAGUE FIRST DIVISION
Ayr United v. Alloa Athletic
Clyde v. Ross County
Inverness Cal. Th. v. Livingston
Morton v. Falkirk
Raith Rovers v. Airdrieonians
BELL'S SCOTTISH LEAGUE SECOND DIVISION
Arbroath v. Berwick Rangers
Queen's Park v. Forfar Athletic
Stenhousemuir v. Clydebank
Stirling Albion v. Queen of the South
Stranraer v. Partick Thistle
BELL'S SCOTTISH LEAGUE THIRD DIVISION
Albion Rovers v. Cowdenbeath
Brechin City v. Dumbarton

East Stirlingshire v. Montrose
Hamilton Academical v. Elgin City
Peterhead v. East Fife

Tuesday, October 24th, 2000
BELL'S SCOTTISH LEAGUE THIRD DIVISION
Hamilton Academical v. East Stirlingshire

Saturday, October 28th, 2000
BELL'S SCOTTISH LEAGUE FIRST DIVISION
Airdrieonians v. Ross County
Falkirk v. Ayr United
Inverness Cal. Th. v. Raith Rovers
Livingston v. Alloa Athletic
Morton v. Clyde
BELL'S SCOTTISH LEAGUE SECOND DIVISION
Arbroath v. Stranraer
Berwick Rangers v. Partick Thistle
Queen of the South v. Clydebank
Queen's Park v. Stirling Albion
Stenhousemuir v. Forfar Athletic
BELL'S SCOTTISH LEAGUE THIRD DIVISION
Brechin City v. Peterhead
Dumbarton v. Albion Rovers
East Fife v. Montrose
Elgin City v. Cowdenbeath

Saturday, November 4th, 2000
BELL'S SCOTTISH LEAGUE FIRST DIVISION
Alloa Athletic v. Airdrieonians
Ayr United v. Livingston
Clyde v. Inverness Cal. Th.
Raith Rovers v. Falkirk
Ross County v. Morton
BELL'S SCOTTISH LEAGUE SECOND DIVISION
Clydebank v. Berwick Rangers
Forfar Athletic v. Arbroath
Partick Thistle v. Queen's Park
Stirling Albion v. Stenhousemuir
Stranraer v. Queen of the South
BELL'S SCOTTISH LEAGUE THIRD DIVISION
Albion Rovers v. Hamilton Academical
Cowdenbeath v. East Fife
East Stirlingshire v. Dumbarton
Montrose v. Brechin City
Peterhead v. Elgin City

Saturday, November 11th, 2000
BELL'S SCOTTISH LEAGUE FIRST DIVISION
Clyde v. Ayr United
Falkirk v. Ross County
Inverness Cal. Th. v. Alloa Athletic
Livingston v. Airdrieonians
Morton v. Raith Rovers
BELL'S SCOTTISH LEAGUE SECOND DIVISION
Arbroath v. Queen's Park
Berwick Rangers v. Stenhousemuir
Forfar Athletic v. Queen of the South
Partick Thistle v. Clydebank
Stranraer v. Stirling Albion
BELL'S SCOTTISH LEAGUE THIRD DIVISION
Albion Rovers v. East Stirlingshire
Cowdenbeath v. Dumbarton
East Fife v. Brechin City
Montrose v. Elgin City
Peterhead v. Hamilton Academical

Saturday, November 18th, 2000
BELL'S SCOTTISH LEAGUE FIRST DIVISION
Airdrieonians v. Clyde
Alloa Athletic v. Falkirk
Ayr United v. Morton
Raith Rovers v. Livingston
Ross County v. Inverness Cal. Th.

BELL'S SCOTTISH LEAGUE SECOND DIVISION
Clydebank v. Forfar Athletic
Queen of the South v. Berwick Rangers
Queen's Park v. Stranraer
Stenhousemuir v. Arbroath
Stirling Albion v. Partick Thistle
BELL'S SCOTTISH LEAGUE THIRD DIVISION
Brechin City v. Albion Rovers
Dumbarton v. Montrose
East Stirlingshire v. Peterhead
Elgin City v. East Fife
Hamilton Academical v. Cowdenbeath

Saturday, November 25th, 2000
BELL'S SCOTTISH LEAGUE FIRST DIVISION
Ayr United v. Raith Rovers
Clyde v. Alloa Athletic
Falkirk v. Airdrieonians
Morton v. Inverness Cal. Th.
Ross County v. Livingston
BELL'S SCOTTISH LEAGUE SECOND DIVISION
Arbroath v. Stirling Albion
Berwick Rangers v. Forfar Athletic
Partick Thistle v. Queen of the South
Queen's Park v. Clydebank
Stranraer v. Stenhousemuir
BELL'S SCOTTISH LEAGUE THIRD DIVISION
Albion Rovers v. Montrose
Brechin City v. Hamilton Academical
Cowdenbeath v. Peterhead
East Fife v. Dumbarton
Elgin City v. East Stirlingshire

Saturday, December 2nd, 2000
BELL'S SCOTTISH LEAGUE FIRST DIVISION
Airdrieonians v. Morton
Alloa Athletic v. Ross County
Inverness Cal. Th. v. Ayr United
Livingston v. Falkirk
Raith Rovers v. Clyde
BELL'S SCOTTISH LEAGUE SECOND DIVISION
Clydebank v. Stranraer
Forfar Athletic v. Partick Thistle
Queen of the South v. Arbroath
Stenhousemuir v. Queen's Park
Stirling Albion v. Berwick Rangers
BELL'S SCOTTISH LEAGUE THIRD DIVISION
Dumbarton v. Elgin City
East Stirlingshire v. Brechin City
Hamilton Academical v. East Fife
Montrose v. Cowdenbeath
Peterhead v. Albion Rovers

Saturday, December 9th, 2000
BELL'S SCOTTISH LEAGUE FIRST DIVISION
Airdrieonians v. Ayr United
Alloa Athletic v. Morton
Falkirk v. Inverness Cal. Th.
Livingston v. Clyde
Ross County v. Raith Rovers

Saturday, December 16th, 2000
BELL'S SCOTTISH LEAGUE FIRST DIVISION
Ayr United v. Ross County
Clyde v. Falkirk
Inverness Cal. Th. v. Airdrieonians
Morton v. Livingston
Raith Rovers v. Alloa Athletic
BELL'S SCOTTISH LEAGUE SECOND DIVISION
Arbroath v. Partick Thistle
Queen's Park v. Berwick Rangers
Stenhousemuir v. Queen of the South

Stirling Albion v. Clydebank
Stranraer v. Forfar Athletic
BELL'S SCOTTISH LEAGUE THIRD DIVISION
Albion Rovers v. East Fife
Brechin City v. Elgin City
East Stirlingshire v. Cowdenbeath
Hamilton Academical v. Dumbarton
Peterhead v. Montrose

Tuesday, December 26th, 2000
BELL'S SCOTTISH LEAGUE FIRST DIVISION
Airdrieonians v. Alloa Athletic
Falkirk v. Raith Rovers
Inverness Cal. Th. v. Clyde
Livingston v. Ayr United
Morton v. Ross County
BELL'S SCOTTISH LEAGUE SECOND DIVISION
Berwick Rangers v. Stranraer
Clydebank v. Arbroath
Forfar Athletic v. Stirling Albion
Partick Thistle v. Stenhousemuir
Queen of the South v. Queen's Park
BELL'S SCOTTISH LEAGUE THIRD DIVISION
Cowdenbeath v. Brechin City
Dumbarton v. Peterhead
East Fife v. East Stirlingshire
Elgin City v. Albion Rovers
Montrose v. Hamilton Academical

Saturday, December 30th, 2000
BELL'S SCOTTISH LEAGUE FIRST DIVISION
Alloa Athletic v. Livingston
Ayr United v. Falkirk
Clyde v. Morton
Raith Rovers v. Inverness Cal. Th.
Ross County v. Airdrieonians
BELL'S SCOTTISH LEAGUE SECOND DIVISION
Clydebank v. Queen of the South
Forfar Athletic v. Stenhousemuir
Partick Thistle v. Berwick Rangers
Stirling Albion v. Queen's Park
Stranraer v. Arbroath
BELL'S SCOTTISH LEAGUE THIRD DIVISION
Albion Rovers v. Dumbarton
Cowdenbeath v. Elgin City
East Stirlingshire v. Hamilton Academical
Montrose v. East Fife
Peterhead v. Brechin City

Tuesday, January 2nd, 2001
BELL'S SCOTTISH LEAGUE FIRST DIVISION
Clyde v. Airdrieonians
Falkirk v. Alloa Athletic
Inverness Cal. Th. v. Ross County
Livingston v. Raith Rovers
Morton v. Ayr United
BELL'S SCOTTISH LEAGUE SECOND DIVISION
Arbroath v. Forfar Athletic
Berwick Rangers v. Clydebank
Queen of the South v. Stranraer
Queen's Park v. Partick Thistle
Stenhousemuir v. Stirling Albion
BELL'S SCOTTISH LEAGUE THIRD DIVISION
Brechin City v. Montrose
Dumbarton v. East Stirlingshire
East Fife v. Cowdenbeath
Elgin City v. Peterhead
Hamilton Academical v. Albion Rovers

Saturday, January 6th, 2001
BELL'S SCOTTISH LEAGUE FIRST DIVISION
Airdrieonians v. Livingston
Alloa Athletic v. Inverness Cal. Th.

BELL'S SCOTTISH FOOTBALL LEAGUE

yr United v. Clyde
aith Rovers v. Morton
oss County v. Falkirk

urday, January 13th, 2001
'S SCOTTISH LEAGUE FIRST DIVISION
yr United v. Inverness Cal. Th.
lyde v. Raith Rovers
alkirk v. Livingston
orton v. Airdrieonians
oss County v. Alloa Athletic
'S SCOTTISH LEAGUE SECOND DIVISION
rbroath v. Stenhousemuir
erwick Rangers v. Queen of the South
orfar Athletic v. Clydebank
artick Thistle v. Stirling Albion
ranraer v. Queen's Park
'S SCOTTISH LEAGUE THIRD DIVISION
lbion Rovers v. Brechin City
owdenbeath v. Hamilton Academical
ast Fife v. Elgin City
ontrose v. Dumbarton
eterhead v. East Stirlingshire

urday, January 20th, 2001
'S SCOTTISH LEAGUE FIRST DIVISION
irdrieonians v. Falkirk
lloa Athletic v. Clyde
verness Cal. Th. v. Morton
vingston v. Ross County
aith Rovers v. Ayr United
'S SCOTTISH LEAGUE SECOND DIVISION
lydebank v. Partick Thistle
ueen of the South v. Forfar Athletic
ueen's Park v. Arbroath
enhousemuir v. Berwick Rangers
irling Albion v. Stranraer
'S SCOTTISH LEAGUE THIRD DIVISION
rechin City v. East Fife
umbarton v. Cowdenbeath
ast Stirlingshire v. Albion Rovers
gin City v. Montrose
amilton Academical v. Peterhead

urday, February 3rd, 2001
'S SCOTTISH LEAGUE FIRST DIVISION
yr United v. Airdrieonians
lyde v. Livingston
verness Cal. Th. v. Falkirk
orton v. Alloa Athletic
aith Rovers v. Ross County
'S SCOTTISH LEAGUE SECOND DIVISION
lydebank v. Queen's Park
orfar Athletic v. Berwick Rangers
ueen of the South v. Partick Thistle
enhousemuir v. Stranraer
irling Albion v. Arbroath
'S SCOTTISH LEAGUE THIRD DIVISION
umbarton v. East Fife
ast Stirlingshire v. Elgin City
amilton Academical v. Brechin City
ontrose v. Albion Rovers
eterhead v. Cowdenbeath

urday, February 10th, 2001
'S SCOTTISH LEAGUE FIRST DIVISION
irdrieonians v. Raith Rovers
lloa Athletic v. Ayr United
alkirk v. Morton
vingston v. Inverness Cal. Th.
oss County v. Clyde

Arbroath v. Queen of the South
Berwick Rangers v. Stirling Albion
Partick Thistle v. Forfar Athletic
Queen's Park v. Stenhousemuir
Stranraer v. Clydebank
BELL'S SCOTTISH LEAGUE THIRD DIVISION
Albion Rovers v. Peterhead
Brechin City v. East Stirlingshire
Cowdenbeath v. Montrose
East Fife v. Hamilton Academical
Elgin City v. Dumbarton

Saturday, February 17th, 2001
BELL'S SCOTTISH LEAGUE SECOND DIVISION
Arbroath v. Clydebank
Queen's Park v. Queen of the South
Stenhousemuir v. Partick Thistle
Stirling Albion v. Forfar Athletic
Stranraer v. Berwick Rangers
BELL'S SCOTTISH LEAGUE THIRD DIVISION
Albion Rovers v. Elgin City
Brechin City v. Cowdenbeath
East Stirlingshire v. East Fife
Hamilton Academical v. Montrose
Peterhead v. Dumbarton

Saturday, February 24th, 2001
BELL'S SCOTTISH LEAGUE FIRST DIVISION
Airdrieonians v. Ross County
Falkirk v. Ayr United
Inverness Cal. Th. v. Raith Rovers
Livingston v. Alloa Athletic
Morton v. Clyde
BELL'S SCOTTISH LEAGUE SECOND DIVISION
Berwick Rangers v. Arbroath
Clydebank v. Stenhousemuir
Forfar Athletic v. Queen's Park
Partick Thistle v. Stranraer
Queen of the South v. Stirling Albion
BELL'S SCOTTISH LEAGUE THIRD DIVISION
Cowdenbeath v. Albion Rovers
Dumbarton v. Brechin City
East Fife v. Peterhead
Elgin City v. Hamilton Academical
Montrose v. East Stirlingshire

Saturday, March 3rd, 2001
BELL'S SCOTTISH LEAGUE FIRST DIVISION
Alloa Athletic v. Airdrieonians
Ayr United v. Livingston
Clyde v. Inverness Cal. Th.
Raith Rovers v. Falkirk
Ross County v. Morton
BELL'S SCOTTISH LEAGUE SECOND DIVISION
Clydebank v. Berwick Rangers
Forfar Athletic v. Arbroath
Partick Thistle v. Queen's Park
Stirling Albion v. Stenhousemuir
Stranraer v. Queen of the South
BELL'S SCOTTISH LEAGUE THIRD DIVISION
Albion Rovers v. Hamilton Academical
Cowdenbeath v. East Fife
East Stirlingshire v. Dumbarton
Montrose v. Brechin City
Peterhead v. Elgin City

Saturday, March 10th, 2001
BELL'S SCOTTISH LEAGUE SECOND DIVISION
Arbroath v. Stranraer
Berwick Rangers v. Partick Thistle
Queen of the South v. Clydebank
Queen's Park v. Stirling Albion
Stenhousemuir v. Forfar Athletic
BELL'S SCOTTISH LEAGUE THIRD DIVISION
Brechin City v. Peterhead
Dumbarton v. Albion Rovers
East Fife v. Montrose
Elgin City v. Cowdenbeath
Hamilton Academical v. East Stirlingshire

Saturday, March 17th, 2001
BELL'S SCOTTISH LEAGUE FIRST DIVISION
Clyde v. Ayr United
Falkirk v. Ross County
Inverness Cal. Th. v. Alloa Athletic
Livingston v. Airdrieonians
Morton v. Raith Rovers
BELL'S SCOTTISH LEAGUE SECOND DIVISION
Arbroath v. Queen's Park
Berwick Rangers v. Stenhousemuir
Forfar Athletic v. Queen of the South
Partick Thistle v. Clydebank
Stranraer v. Stirling Albion
BELL'S SCOTTISH LEAGUE THIRD DIVISION
Albion Rovers v. East Stirlingshire
Cowdenbeath v. Dumbarton
East Fife v. Brechin City
Montrose v. Elgin City
Peterhead v. Hamilton Academical

Saturday, March 31st, 2001
BELL'S SCOTTISH LEAGUE FIRST DIVISION
Airdrieonians v. Clyde
Alloa Athletic v. Falkirk
Ayr United v. Morton
Raith Rovers v. Livingston
Ross County v. Inverness Cal. Th.
BELL'S SCOTTISH LEAGUE SECOND DIVISION
Clydebank v. Forfar Athletic
Queen of the South v. Berwick Rangers
Queen's Park v. Stranraer
Stenhousemuir v. Arbroath
Stirling Albion v. Partick Thistle
BELL'S SCOTTISH LEAGUE THIRD DIVISION
Brechin City v. Albion Rovers
Dumbarton v. Montrose
East Stirlingshire v. Peterhead
Elgin City v. East Fife
Hamilton Academical v. Cowdenbeath

Saturday, April 7th, 2001
BELL'S SCOTTISH LEAGUE FIRST DIVISION
Ayr United v. Raith Rovers
Clyde v. Alloa Athletic
Falkirk v. Airdrieonians
Morton v. Inverness Cal. Th.
Ross County v. Livingston
BELL'S SCOTTISH LEAGUE SECOND DIVISION
Arbroath v. Stirling Albion
Berwick Rangers v. Forfar Athletic
Partick Thistle v. Queen of the South
Queen's Park v. Clydebank
Stranraer v. Stenhousemuir
BELL'S SCOTTISH LEAGUE THIRD DIVISION
Albion Rovers v. Montrose
Brechin City v. Hamilton Academical
Cowdenbeath v. Peterhead
East Fife v. Dumbarton
Elgin City v. East Stirlingshire

Saturday, April 14th, 2001
BELL'S SCOTTISH LEAGUE FIRST DIVISION
Airdrieonians v. Morton
Alloa Athletic v. Ross County
Inverness Cal. Th. v. Ayr United
Livingston v. Falkirk
Raith Rovers v. Clyde
BELL'S SCOTTISH LEAGUE SECOND DIVISION
Clydebank v. Stranraer
Forfar Athletic v. Partick Thistle
Queen of the South v. Arbroath
Stenhousemuir v. Queen's Park
Stirling Albion v. Berwick Rangers
BELL'S SCOTTISH LEAGUE THIRD DIVISION
Dumbarton v. Elgin City
East Stirlingshire v. Brechin City
Hamilton Academical v. East Fife
Montrose v. Cowdenbeath
Peterhead v. Albion Rovers

Nationwide

Saturday, April 21st, 2001
BELL'S SCOTTISH LEAGUE FIRST DIVISION
Airdrieonians v. Inverness Cal. Th.
Alloa Athletic v. Raith Rovers
Falkirk v. Clyde
Livingston v. Morton
Ross County v. Ayr United
BELL'S SCOTTISH LEAGUE SECOND DIVISION
Berwick Rangers v. Queen's Park
Clydebank v. Stirling Albion
Forfar Athletic v. Stranraer
Partick Thistle v. Arbroath
Queen of the South v. Stenhousemuir
BELL'S SCOTTISH LEAGUE THIRD DIVISION
Cowdenbeath v. East Stirlingshire
Dumbarton v. Hamilton Academical
East Fife v. Albion Rovers
Elgin City v. Brechin City
Montrose v. Peterhead

Saturday, April 28th, 2001
BELL'S SCOTTISH LEAGUE FIRST DIVISION
Ayr United v. Alloa Athletic
Clyde v. Ross County
Inverness Cal. Th. v. Livingston
Morton v. Falkirk
Raith Rovers v. Airdrieonians
BELL'S SCOTTISH LEAGUE SECOND DIVISION
Arbroath v. Berwick Rangers
Queen's Park v. Forfar Athletic
Stenhousemuir v. Clydebank
Stirling Albion v. Queen of the South
Stranraer v. Partick Thistle
BELL'S SCOTTISH LEAGUE THIRD DIVISION
Albion Rovers v. Cowdenbeath
Brechin City v. Dumbarton
East Stirlingshire v. Montrose
Hamilton Academical v. Elgin City
Peterhead v. East Fife

Saturday, May 5th, 2001
BELL'S SCOTTISH LEAGUE FIRST DIVISION
Airdrieonians v. Ayr United
Alloa Athletic v. Morton
Falkirk v. Inverness Cal. Th.
Livingston v. Clyde
Ross County v. Raith Rovers
BELL'S SCOTTISH LEAGUE SECOND DIVISION
Berwick Rangers v. Stranraer
Clydebank v. Arbroath
Forfar Athletic v. Stirling Albion
Partick Thistle v. Stenhousemuir
Queen of the South v. Queen's Park
BELL'S SCOTTISH LEAGUE THIRD DIVISION
Cowdenbeath v. Brechin City
Dumbarton v. Peterhead
East Fife v. East Stirlingshire
Elgin City v. Albion Rovers
Montrose v. Hamilton Academical

The CIS Insurance
Cup Draw Season 2000/2001

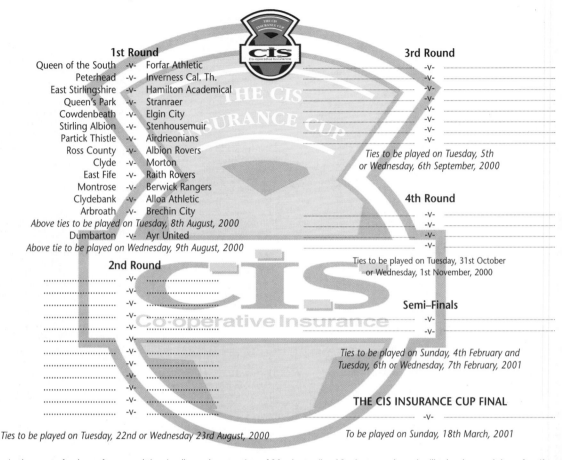

1st Round

Queen of the South	-v-	Forfar Athletic
Peterhead	-v-	Inverness Cal. Th.
East Stirlingshire	-v-	Hamilton Academical
Queen's Park	-v-	Stranraer
Cowdenbeath	-v-	Elgin City
Stirling Albion	-v-	Stenhousemuir
Partick Thistle	-v-	Airdrieonians
Ross County	-v-	Albion Rovers
Clyde	-v-	Morton
East Fife	-v-	Raith Rovers
Montrose	-v-	Berwick Rangers
Clydebank	-v-	Alloa Athletic
Arbroath	-v-	Brechin City

Above ties to be played on Tuesday, 8th August, 2000

Dumbarton	-v-	Ayr United

Above tie to be played on Wednesday, 9th August, 2000

2nd Round

....	-v-	....
....	-v-	....
....	-v-	....
....	-v-	....
....	-v-	....
....	-v-	....
....	-v-	....
....	-v-	....
....	-v-	....
....	-v-	....

Ties to be played on Tuesday, 22nd or Wednesday 23rd August, 2000

3rd Round

-v-	....
-v-	....
-v-	....
-v-	....
-v-	....
-v-	....
-v-	....

*Ties to be played on Tuesday, 5th
or Wednesday, 6th September, 2000*

4th Round

-v-	....
-v-	....
-v-	....
-v-	....

Ties to be played on Tuesday, 31st October
or Wednesday, 1st November, 2000

Semi–Finals

-v-	....
-v-	....

*Ties to be played on Sunday, 4th February and
Tuesday, 6th or Wednesday, 7th February, 2001*

THE CIS INSURANCE CUP FINAL

-v-

To be played on Sunday, 18th March, 2001

In the event of a draw after normal time in all rounds, extra time of 30 minutes (i.e. 15 minutes each way) will take place and thereafter, if necessary, Kicks from the Penalty Mark in accordance with the Rules laid down by The International Football Association Board will be taken.

Tommy Boyd, Jackie McNamara and Tommy Johnson celebrate Celtic's CIS Insurance Cup Final triumph

Tom Boyd of Celtic receives his Man of the Match award

The Bell's Challenge Cup Draw
Season 2000/2001

1st Round

Cowdenbeath	-v-	Falkirk
Airdrieonians	-v-	Queen of the South
Raith Rovers	-v-	Morton
Forfar Athletic	-v-	Peterhead
Stranraer	-v-	Berwick Rangers
Brechin City	-v-	Ayr United
Albion Rovers	-v-	Clydebank
Ross County	-v-	Clyde
East Stirlingshire	-v-	East Fife
Queen's Park	-v-	Montrose
Stirling Albion	-v-	Arbroath
Partick Thistle	-v-	Livingston
Elgin City	-v-	Dumbarton
Alloa Athletic	-v-	Inverness Caledonian Thistle

Byes: Stenhousemuir and Hamilton Academical

Above ties to be played on Tuesday, 15th August, 2000

2nd Round

....	-v-	....
....	-v-	....
....	-v-	....
....	-v-	....
....	-v-	....
....	-v-	....
....	-v-	....
....	-v-	....

Ties to be played on Wednesday, 29th August, 2000

3rd Round

....	-v-	....
....	-v-	....
....	-v-	....
....	-v-	....

Ties to be played on Tuesday, 12th September, 2000

Semi-Finals

....	-v-	....
....	-v-	....

Ties to be played on Tuesday, 26th September, 2000

THE BELL'S CHALLENGE CUP FINAL

.... -v- ....

To be played on Sunday, 19th November, 2000

In the event of a draw after normal time in all rounds, extra time of 30 minutes (i.e. 15 minutes each way) will take place and thereafter, if necessary, Kicks from the Penalty Mark in accordance with the Rules laid down by The International Football Association Board will be taken.

BREAKDOWN OF HOW ALL THE SCOTTISH FOOTBALL LEAGUE SPONSORSHIP MONIES WILL BE ALLOCATED DURING SEASON 2000/2001

DISTRIBUTION OF BELL'S SCOTTISH FOOTBALL LEAGUE CHAMPIONSHIP MONIES

First Division	£17,000 per club
Second Division	£10,000 per club
Third Division	£8,500 per club

DISTRIBUTION OF CIS INSURANCE CUP MONIES

1st Round Losers	12 x £6,000
2nd Round Losers	12 x £8,500
3rd Round Losers	8 x £15,000
4th Round Losers	4 x £20,000
Semi-Final Losers	2 x £30,000
Runner-up	£60,000
Winner	£80,000

DISTRIBUTION OF BELL'S CHALLENGE CUP MONIES

1st Round Losers	14 x £3,000
2nd Round Losers	8 x £4,000
3rd Round Losers	4 x £5,000
Semi-Final Losers	2 x £6,000
Runner-up	£12,000
Winner	£16,000

We have five Scots in the side today – great!

On the last Saturday in August of the year 2000, St. Johnstone met Kilmarnock at McDiarmid Park in a Scottish Premier League match. There were fewer than 4,000 people at the match which was played on a pleasant summer afternoon at a stage in the season when neither side had as yet done anything to antagonise its supporters.

On the same day, Dunfermline Athletic played Dundee United in the same competition while Motherwell and Aberdeen met the following day. The gate at each of these two matches barely exceeded 5,000 spectators. I mention these crowds because they are far more symptomatic of the present state of Scottish football than the sixty odd

Robert Douglas

thousand who were in attendance for an Old Firm game during the same weekend. Remember that the purpose of The Scottish Premier League is avowedly to bring about increased attendances. It is as yet in its green years and merits being given some time, although not too much, to shake down. The many empty seats which I witnessed at first hand sent me searching for reasons why it should be so. The Perth game was perfectly passable as was the one the following day

Derek Ferguson playing for Clydebank

between Dundee and Heart of Midlothian. Yet the people stayed away in droves. Why?

One of the reasons may be that the supporters no longer feel involved emotionally at many clubs. I do not think that this is entirely or perhaps even mainly due to the fact that increasingly, it becomes more difficult to spot a Scot on the field. To my mind, it has more to do with the curse of the new century - the impermanence of players. Little is to be gained from condemning the foreign player out of hand. Many of them are extremely skilful. One had only to

Mark Burchill in action for Scotland U21s

watch Billio and Caballero of Dundee and Calderon of Airdrieonians to realise that these were no ordinary talents. It is logical too that Ivan Bonetti and Steve Archibald should play to their manifest strengths, which are an encyclopedic knowledge of Italian and Spanish football respectively.

Worth remembering too, before we rush to judgement what the alternatives might have been had not these two gentlemen come forward. Yet the heart sinks when contemplating the probability that both clubs will import clever players, respray them as it were, and send the cleaned and polished article back to the continent for further and more meaningful campaigns.

Robert Douglas is a fine goalkeeper, not only holding down the Dundee post but in the Scotland squad and presumably not a hundred miles from a Scottish cap. Yet he is quoted in early September, 2000 to the effect that he fully expects to lose his place to a Continental goalkeeper before the season is much older. This time last year, I did a brief survey of the

options open to Craig Brown in that position in The Scottish Premier League. Of the ten goalkeepers, only five were even eligible - we have not begun to consider ability - and of the five who were eligible, Jonathan Gould and Andy Goram would not have been under the old stricter nationality regulations.

Nothing is more depressing in Scottish football than to see the number of young Old Firm players who appear in the first team, seem to have made it and yet fail to establish themselves. The names of Pressley, McSwegan, McInnes and Derek Ferguson spring to life in a Rangers connection and those of McLaughlin, Kerr and perhaps Burchill on the other side of the city.

Perhaps there is something even more depressing and that will be the fate of the traditional nursery clubs if Part Two of Bosman is implemented in all its severity. The

fine Raith Rovers side which won the League Cup in the early 1990's had among its members, Jason Dair, Stephen McAnespie, Colin Cameron and Stevie Crawford. It is no exaggeration to say that the Stark's Park side probably had more good young players than any other club in Scotland. Of course, it could not retain them indefinitely but the money from transfer fees got some enthusiastic if less gifted replacements and allowed much needed refurbishment and extension to be done at the ground.

We have uprooted the branches by which we did ascend. In the traditional pattern of Scottish football, a promising lad played schools football, went on to a well doing juvenile club, thence to the juniors, to a small but senior club and finally if good enough, to a leading light in either the Scottish League or Football League.

Horizons were no broader in those days. Chances were taken, people like Willie Henderson of Rangers, his club mate Sandy Jardine, Jimmy Johnstone of Celtic and Alec Young of Heart of Midlothian had all first team experience by the time they were twenty.

As ever, we thought that our way of doing was the norm for the civilised world. It was not. I well remember going to do a Schools International match for Scottish Television about 1960. The venue was Ibrox Park and the opposition was West Germany. I asked my German colleague why no schools were given for the German boys and he answered: "Why should they be?" I told him that this seemed logical since it was a Schools International. He aced me with the reply that it was not, it was an international between 15-year-olds wherein the Scots played for their schools and all the young Germans were attached to professional clubs.

It was precisely because this was the direction that our football had taken that the school strikes of the late 1970's were so disastrous. Almost 30 years have passed and no real replacement machinery has been put in place until recently and it is even yet in its formative stage. Nor can the schools be replaced by the brave talk of new Academies. The big clubs may build them, although future developments which whittle away at the transfer system may make them less appealing if you may simply be rearing young players for someone else's benefit.

In any event, the reality is that the pressure on the Old Firm is such that in any playing crisis - that is, the loss of two consecutive matches - there will be an irresistible temptation to use

Raith Rovers' Stevie Crawford, Scott Thomson and Gordon Dalziel with the 1994/95 Coca-Cola Cup

shorthand and reach for the cheque book.

Increasingly wise parents and canny agents will steer their children and clients away from the Old Firm in the short-term. The home Scot is unlikely to make it with them as things stand and then risk playing out the rest of his career as a perceived failure. If he goes somewhere else first, the big two will still come looking for him and, as matters stand at present, are marginally more likely to play him having given a transfer fee for him.

I would stress that this is not to be seen as an anti-foreign player piece. They have an honorable place in Scotland's football history and as long as 35 years ago, they were to be found in numbers in the colours of Morton and Dundee United. In Greenock, the names of Sorensen, Bertelsen and Bartram are still revered as are those of Berg, Dossing, Wing and Seeman on Tayside. In matters dietary as in dress and comportment, our young players have much to learn from today's crop of European visitors.

The first priority must be to restore a line of promotion which is suitable for today. The mythical schoolboy who spent all his life playing in the streets is perhaps not all that mythical but he would be a stiffened corpse inside an hour if he tried it today. The cure comes with the realisation that we have lost the habit of playing football as an automatic reflex action. Forget the street footballer and look at our open spaces such as the cradle of the game, Queen's Park Recreation Ground. Night after night in the height of summer, its pitches lie idle and empty. Twenty years ago even, there would have been a

Jimmy Johnstone

game on every pitch and for every pitch a game waiting to come on.

The links between fan and game are fraying. You cannot develop a fan-player link when players are in and out almost by the week. It is a great error to think that for every business problem in sport there is a business solution. To believe so is to forget that the essence of spectator sport is uncertainty and that uncertainty involves at least the occasional defeat of the powerful.

Small clubs such as Forfar Athletic, Arbroath, East Stirlingshire and Stranraer are player producing and community clubs. To attempt to merge them will not work, to close them down is possible but it will not bring a single soul through the turnstiles fired with the thought of seeing Lanarkshire United or Tayside Athletic. All that will happen is that 500 or so supporters will walk away from the game permanently.

The game cannot exist in a cocoon. It must always evolve but the shape and speed of that evolution needs the sharpest of scrutiny. Were I Chairman of any club in The Scottish Premier League other than the Old Firm, I might be putting the following propositions to myself:-

"We were sold The Scottish Premier League, indeed the old Premier Division of The Scottish Football League, on the argument that clubs such as ours needed the four games at home per season against the Old Firm. But I cannot remember the last time our ground was full for a visit by Rangers or Celtic because they now take active steps to dissuade their supporters from going to away matches in order to utilise to the full their Beam Back facilities."

This is the kind of reflection that might lead a Chairman to compose

Willie Henderson

a draft of a preliminary letter to apply to rejoin The Scottish Football League. As it is, defeatism stalks the land, large clubs such as Aberdeen and the two Edinburgh ones, proclaim almost as a badge of pride that of course they cannot be expected to compete with the Old Firm. Up to a point one sympathises, and with the likes of Kenny Miller and Didier Agathe both moving on to Rangers and Celtic from Hibernian, it seems to indicate that by defensive signings, the Old Firm can eliminate off-field anything that seems likely to be a threat on the pitch. This does not answer the vital question, "Why

should I be a Hibernian or Aberdeen supporter this season?"

Schools football had room for the indifferent player. Such encouraged a football climate because although they were not gifted as players, they became the committee-men, the referees, the fans, and – you're already saying it – the writers and commentators. It is very important that the Old Firm does well and it is a great showcase for Scottish football when it does, but on the logical road down which we are cheerfully going, Celtic will play Rangers every week in a one match League programme.

BOB CRAMPSEY 135

Useful Football Addresses

FIFA:

General Secretary: M. Zen-Ruffinen,
P.O. Box 85, 8030 Zurich, Switzerland.
Tel: 00 411 384 9595 Fax: 00 411 384 9696
Website: www.fifa.com

UEFA:

Chief Executive: G. Aigner, Route de Genève 46, CH-1260,
Nyon 2, Switzerland.
Tel: 00 41 22 994 4444 Fax: 00 41 22 994 4488
Website: www.uefa.com

LEAGUES IN MEMBERSHIP OF THE INTERNATIONAL FOOTBALL LEAGUE BOARD

THE SCOTTISH FOOTBALL LEAGUE:

Secretary: P. Donald, 188 West Regent Street, Glasgow, G2 4RY.
Tel: 0141 248 3844 Fax: 0141 221 7450
e-mail: info@sfl.scottishfootball.com
Website: www.scottishfootball.com

THE SCOTTISH PREMIER LEAGUE:

Chief Executive: R. Mitchell, Hampden Park, Somerville Drive,
Glasgow, G42 9BA.
Tel: 0141 649 6962 Fax: 0141 649 6963
Website: www.scotprem.co.uk

THE F.A. PREMIER LEAGUE:

Secretary: M. Foster, 11 Connaught Place, London, W2 2ET.
Tel: 0207 298 1600 Fax: 0207 298 1601
Website: www.fa-carling.com

THE FOOTBALL LEAGUE:

Secretary: J.D. Dent, Edward VII Quay, Navigation Way, Preston, PR2 2YF.
Tel: 01772 325800 Fax: 01772 325801
e-mail: fl@football-league.co.uk
Website: www.football-league.co.uk

THE IRISH FOOTBALL LEAGUE:

Secretary: H. Wallace, 96 University Street, Belfast, BT7 1HE.
Tel: 02890 242888 Fax: 02890 330773

NATIONAL ASSOCIATIONS WITHIN THE UNITED KINGDOM

THE SCOTTISH FOOTBALL ASSOCIATION:

Chief Executive: D. Taylor, 6 Park Gardens, Glasgow, G3 7YF.
Tel: 0141 332 6372 Fax: 0141 332 7559
e-mail: info@scottishfa.co.uk
           coaching@scottishfa.co.uk
           referee@scottishfa.co.uk
           travel@scottishfa.co.uk
           media@scottishfa.co.uk
           womensfootball@scottishfa.co.uk
Website: www.scottishfa.co.uk

THE FOOTBALL ASSOCIATION:

Chief Executive: A. Crozier, 16 Lancaster Gate, London, W2 2LW.
Tel: 0207 262 4542 Fax: 0207 402 0486
Website: www.the-FA.org

THE IRISH FOOTBALL ASSOCIATION:

Secretary: D.I. Bowen, 20 Windsor Avenue, Belfast, BT9 6EG.
Tel: 02890 669458 Fax: 02890 667620
Website: www.irishfa.com

THE FOOTBALL ASSOCIATION OF WALES:

Secretary: D.G. Collins, 3 Westgate Street, Cardiff, CF10 1DP.
Tel: 02920 372325 Fax: 02920 343961

OTHER LEAGUES IN SCOTLAND

THE HIGHLAND FOOTBALL LEAGUE:

Secretary: J.H. Grant, 35 Hamilton Drive, Elgin, IV30 4NN.
Tel/Fax: 01343 544995
e-mail: hfleague@globalnet.co.uk

EAST OF SCOTLAND LEAGUE:

Secretary: J.M. Greenhorn, 2 Babberton Mains Court,
Edinburgh, EH14 3ER
Tel: 0131 442 1402
e-mail: John.Greenhorn@tesco.net

SOUTH OF SCOTLAND LEAGUE:

Secretary: R. Shaw M.B.E., 8 Kirkland Road, Heathhall,
Dumfries, DG1 3RN.
Tel: 01387 261736

AFFILIATED NATIONAL ASSOCIATIONS OF THE SCOTTISH FOOTBALL ASSOCIATION

THE SCOTTISH JUNIOR FOOTBALL ASSOCIATION:

Secretary: T. Johnston, 46 St. Vincent Crescent, Glasgow, G3 8NG.
Tel: 0141 248 1095 Fax: 0141 248 1130

THE SCOTTISH AMATEUR FOOTBALL ASSOCIATION:

Secretary: H. Knapp, 6 Park Gardens, Glasgow, G3 7YF.
Tel: 0141 333 0839

THE SCOTTISH YOUTH FOOTBALL ASSOCIATION:

Secretary: D. Little, 4 Park Gardens, Glasgow, G3 7YE.
Tel: 0141 332 7106 Fax: 0141 332 5865

THE SCOTTISH WELFARE FOOTBALL ASSOCIATION:

Secretary: D. McNair, 14 Yair Drive, Glasgow, G52 2JX.
Tel: 0141 883 5008

THE SCOTTISH SCHOOLS FOOTBALL ASSOCIATION:

Secretary: J.C. Watson, 6 Park Gardens, Glasgow, G3 7YF.
Tel: 0141 353 3215

THE SCOTTISH WOMEN'S FOOTBALL ASSOCIATION:

Executive Administrator: Mrs. M. McGonigle, 4 Park Gardens,
Glasgow, G3 7YE.
Tel: 0141 353 1162 Fax: 0141 353 1823
e-mail: swfa@supanet.com

PLAYER'S UNION

THE SCOTTISH PROFESSIONAL FOOTBALLERS ASSOCIATION:

Secretary: T. Higgins, Fountain House, 1/3 Woodside Crescent,
Charing Cross, Glasgow, G3 7UJ.
Tel: 0141 332 8641 Fax: 0141 332 4491
e-mail: SPFA@gmb.org.uk

THE HIGHLAND FOOTBALL LEAGUE DIRECTORY OF CLUBS

BRORA RANGERS F.C.

Secretary:	Kevin MacKay
Manager:	Andrew MacLeod
Club Address:	Dudgeon Park, Dudgeon Drive, Brora, KW9 6QA.
Ground Tel/Fax No:	01408 621231
Sec Bus:	01408 623005
Sec Home:	01408 621114
Playing Kits:	**1st Choice**

Shirt:	Red
Shorts:	White
Stockings:	Red
2nd Choice	
Shirt:	White
Shorts:	Red
Stockings:	White
3rd Choice	
Shirt:	Scarlet & Royal Blue
Shorts:	Royal Blue
Stockings:	Scarlet

BUCKIE THISTLE F.C.

Secretary:	Easton Thain
Manager:	Alan Scott
Club Address:	Victoria Park, Midmar Street, Buckie, AB56 1BT.
Ground Tel No:	01542 836468 (Matchdays Only)
Sec Home:	01542 886141
Playing Kits:	**1st Choice**

Shirt:	Green & White Hoops
Shorts:	White
Stockings:	Green
2nd Choice	
Shirt:	White with Green/Black Facings
Shorts:	White
Stockings:	White

CLACHNACUDDIN F.C. (1990) LTD.

Secretary:	Gilbert Skinner
Manager:	Brian Black
Club Address:	Grant Street Park, Wyvis Place, Inverness, IV3 6DR.
Ground Tel No:	01463 710707
Sec Home:	01463 235339
Fax No:	01463 718261
Playing Kits:	**1st Choice**

Shirt:	White
Shorts:	Black
Stockings:	White
2nd Choice	
Shirt:	Red
Shorts:	Red
Stockings:	White

COVE RANGERS F.C.

Secretary:	Duncan Little
Manager:	Robert Summers
Club Address:	Allan Park, Loirston Road, Cove, Aberdeen, AB12 3NR.
Ground Tel No:	01224 890433
Sec Bus:	01224 854990
Sec Home:	01224 896282
Fax No:	01224 895199
Playing Kits:	**1st Choice**

Shirt:	Blue & White
Shorts:	Blue & White
Stockings:	White & Blue
2nd Choice	
Shirt:	Yellow & Blue
Shorts:	Yellow & Blue
Stockings:	Yellow & Blue

DEVERONVALE F.C.

Secretary:	Stewart McPherson
Manager:	Gregg Carrol
Club Address:	Princess Royal Park, Airlie Gardens, Banff, AB45 1HB.
Ground Tel No:	01261 818489/818303
Sec Bus:	01261 835015
Fax No:	01261 833736
Website:	www.deveronvale.freeserve.co.uk
Playing Kits:	**1st Choice**

Shirt:	Red with White Trim
Shorts:	White with Red Trim
Stockings:	Black with Red Tops
2nd Choice	
Shirt:	Sky Blue
Shorts:	Navy Blue
Stockings:	Sky Blue

FORRES MECHANICS F.C.

Secretary:	Campbell C. Fraser
Manager:	Fraser Kellas
Club Address:	Mosset Park, Lea Road, Forres, Moray, IV36 0AU.
Ground Tel No:	01309 675096
Sec Home:	01309 672349
Playing Kits:	**1st Choice**

Shirt:	Yellow & Maroon Stripes
Shorts:	Maroon
Stockings:	Yellow
2nd Choice	
Shirt:	White
Shorts:	White
Stockings:	White

FORT WILLIAM F.C.

Secretary:	James Campbell
Manager:	Dave Milroy
Club Address:	Claggan Park, Fort William
Sec Home/Fax:	01397 772298
Playing Kits:	**1st Choice**

Shirt:	Gold
Shorts:	Black
Stockings:	Gold
2nd Choice	
Shirt:	White
Shorts:	Black
Stockings:	Black

FRASERBURGH F.C.

Secretary:	Finlay M. Noble
Manager:	Charles Duncan
Club Address:	Bellslea Park, Seaforth Street, Fraserburgh, AB43 9BD.
Ground Tel No:	01346 518444
Sec Bus:	07747 003806
Sec Home:	01346 513474
Website:	www.burghfc.demon.co.uk
E-Mail:	ffc@burghfc.demon.co.uk
Playing Kits:	**1st Choice**
Shirt:	Black and White Stripes
Shorts:	Black
Stockings:	Red
	2nd Choice
Shirt:	Red
Shorts:	White
Stockings:	White

HUNTLY F.C.

Secretary:	Peter Morrison
Co-Managers:	William Lawson & Kevin Will
Club Address:	Christie Park, East Park Street, Huntly, AB54 8JE.
Ground Tel No:	01466 793548
Sec Bus:	01467 626528
Sec Home:	01466 793269
Fax No:	01467 626559
Playing Kits:	**1st Choice**
Shirt:	Black & Gold
Shorts:	Black
Stockings:	Black & Gold
	2nd Choice
Shirt:	White
Shorts:	White
Stockings:	White

KEITH F.C.

Secretary:	Norman Brown
Manager:	Martin Allan
Club Address:	Kynoch Park, Balloch Road, Keith, AB55 5EN.
Ground Tel No:	01542 887407 (Matchdays Only)
Sec Bus/Fax:	01542 882629
Sec Home:	07779 550343
Playing Kits:	**1st Choice**
Shirt:	Maroon with Sky Blue Facings
Shorts:	Maroon and Sky Blue
Stockings:	Maroon
	2nd Choice
Shirt:	White, Yellow and Navy Blue
Shorts:	Navy Blue
Stockings:	Navy Blue

LOSSIEMOUTH F.C.

Secretary:	Alan McIntosh
Manager:	Jim George
Club Address:	Grant Park, Kellas Avenue, Lossiemouth, IV31 6JG.
Ground Tel No:	01343 813717
Sec Home:	01343 813328
Fax No:	01343 815440
Playing Kits:	**1st Choice**
Shirt:	Red
Shorts:	Red
Stockings:	Red
	2nd Choice
Shirt:	Yellow
Shorts:	Blue
Stockings:	Blue

NAIRN COUNTY F.C.

Secretary:	John McNeill
Manager:	Ron Sharp
Club Address:	Station Park, Balblair Road, Nairn, IV12 5LT.
Ground Tel No:	01667 454298
Sec Bus:	01463 795157/792424
Sec Home/Fax:	01667 462510
Playing Kits:	**1st Choice**
Shirt:	Yellow
Shorts:	Yellow
Stockings:	Yellow
	2nd Choice
Shirt:	Red
Shorts:	Black
Stockings:	White

ROTHES F.C.

Secretary:	Neil McKenzie
Manager:	Graham McBeath
Club Address:	Mackessack Park, Station Street, Rothes, Aberlour
Ground Tel No:	01340 831972
Sec Home:	01340 831344
Playing Kits:	**1st Choice**
Shirt:	Tangerine
Shorts:	Black
Stockings:	Tangerine
	2nd Choice
Shirt:	Black
Shorts:	Black
Stockings:	Black

WICK ACADEMY F.C.

Secretary:	Andrew Carter
Manager:	Peter Budge
Club Address:	Harmsworth Park, South Road, Wick, KW1 5NH.
Ground Tel No:	01955 602446
Sec Bus/Fax:	01847 802277
Sec Home:	01955 604275
Playing Kits:	**1st Choice**
Shirt:	Black & White Stripes
Shorts:	Black
Stockings:	Black
	2nd Choice
Shirt:	Sky Blue and White Stripes
Shorts:	Navy Blue
Stockings:	Sky Blue

PRESS & JOURNAL LEAGUE

FINAL TABLE – SEASON 1999/2000

	P	W	D	L	F	A	Pts
Keith	30	21	3	6	76	38	66
Fraserburgh	30	17	10	3	75	32	61
Buckie Thistle	30	18	7	5	58	31	61
Peterhead	30	18	4	8	66	39	58
Huntly	30	15	7	8	69	46	52
Forres Mechanics	30	15	7	8	60	42	52
Clachnacuddin	30	14	6	10	55	37	48
Cove Rangers	30	12	6	12	81	54	42
Elgin City	30	12	6	12	45	44	42
Lossiemouth	30	12	6	12	51	54	42
Deveronvale	30	11	5	14	51	63	38
Brora Rangers	30	9	6	15	53	61	33
Rothes	30	8	5	17	41	52	29
Wick Academy	30	6	5	19	36	84	23
Nairn County	30	3	8	19	24	91	17
Fort William	30	1	5	24	34	107	8

THE EAST OF SCOTLAND LEAGUE DIRECTORY OF CLUBS

ANNAN ATHLETIC F.C.

Secretary:	Alan T. Irving
Manager:	David Irons
Club Address:	Galabank, North Street, Annan, Dumfries & Galloway.
Ground Tel/Fax No:	01461 204108
Sec Bus:	01461 207218
Sec Home:	01461 203702
Website:	www.members.synup.com
E-Mail:	annanathletic@synup.net
Playing Kits:	**1st Choice**
Shirt:	Black and Gold Broad Vertical Stripes
Shorts:	Black
Stockings:	Black with Two Gold Rings
	2nd Choice
Shirt:	Blue
Shorts:	White
Stockings:	White with Blue Tops

CIVIL SERVICE STROLLERS F.C.

Secretary:	E.S. Turnbull
Manager:	S. Torrance
Club Address:	Muirhouse Civil Service Sports Ground, Marine Drive, Edinburgh.
Ground Tel No:	0131 332 1175 (Matchdays Only)
Sec Bus:	0131 314 4220
Sec Home:	0131 539 0171
Fax No:	0131 314 4344
Website:	www.strollers.org.uk
E-Mail:	eddie.turnbull@gro-scotland.gov.uk
Playing Kits:	**1st Choice**
Shirt:	White
Shorts:	Black
Stockings:	Red
	2nd Choice
Shirt:	Red
Shorts:	Black
Stockings:	Red

COLDSTREAM F.C.

Secretary:	Mrs. R.B. Purvis
Manager:	J. McLean
Club Address:	Home Park, Coldstream, Berwickshire.
Ground Tel/Fax No:	01890 883085
Sec Home:	01890 882912
Playing Kits:	**1st Choice**
Shirt:	Royal Blue with Black Trim
Shorts:	Black
Stockings:	Royal Blue
	2nd Choice
Shirt:	Red
Shorts:	Red
Stockings:	Red

CRAIGROYSTON F.C.

Secretary:	K. Richardson
Club Address:	St. Mark's Park, Warriston, Edinburgh
Playing Kits:	**1st Choice**
Shirt:	Yellow
Shorts:	Blue

EASTHOUSES LILY MINERS WELFARE F.C.

Secretary:	R. Paul
Club Address:	Newbattle Complex, Easthouses, Dalkeith.
Ground Tel No:	0131 6639768
Playing Kits:	**1st Choice**
Shirt:	Red
Shorts:	White

EDINBURGH ATHLETIC F.C.

Secretary:	I. Gracie
Club Address:	Muirhouse Sports Ground, Marine Drive, Edinburgh.
Ground Tel No:	0131 332 0650
Sec Home:	01875 340938
Playing Kits:	**1st Choice**
Shirt:	Navy Blue
Shorts:	Navy Blue

EDINBURGH CITY F.C.

Secretary:	K. Hogg
Manager:	G. Wilson
Club Address:	Meadowbank Stadium, London Road, Edinburgh, EH7 6AE.
Ground Tel No:	0131 661 5351
Sec Bus:	0131 245 6882
Sec Home:	0131 228 1882
Playing Kits:	**1st Choice**
Shirt:	White with Black Trim
Shorts:	Black
Stockings:	White with Black Trim
	2nd Choice
Shirt:	Yellow with Black Trim
Shorts:	Black
Stockings:	Yellow with Black Trim

EDINBURGH UNIVERSITY ASSOCIATION F.C.

Secretary:	J. Busher
Manager:	N. Orr
Club Address:	Peffermill Playing Fields, Peffermill Road, Edinburgh.
Ground Tel No:	0131 667 7541
Sec Bus:	0131 650 2346
Sec Home:	0131 229 3356
Fax No:	0131 557 4172
E-Mail:	sports.union@ed.ac.uk
Playing Kits:	**1st Choice**
Shirt:	Forest Green with Navy Blue Sleeves
Shorts:	Navy Blue
Stockings:	Navy Blue
	2nd Choice
Shirt:	Black and White Stripes
Shorts:	Black
Stockings:	Black
	3rd Choice
Shirt:	Red
Shorts:	Red
Stockings:	Red

EYEMOUTH UNITED F.C.

Secretary:	I. Thomson
Club Address:	Gunsgreen Park, Johns Road, Eyemouth
Sec Home:	01890 751301
Playing Kits:	1st Choice
Shirt:	Maroon
Shorts:	White

GALA FAIRYDEAN F.C.

Secretary:	G. McGill
Manager:	D. Smith
Club Address:	Netherdale, Galashiels.
Ground Tel No:	01896 753554
Sec Home/Fax:	01896 754500
E-Mail:	gmcgill@cwcom.net
Playing Kits:	1st Choice
Shirt:	Black and White
Shorts:	Black
Stockings:	Black with White Tops
	2nd Choice
Shirt:	White
Shorts:	White
Stockings:	White
	3rd Choice
Shirt:	Yellow
Shorts:	Black
Stockings:	Black with White Tops

HAWICK ROYAL ALBERT F.C.

Secretary:	D.J. Purves
Club Address:	Albert Park, Mansfield Road, Hawick.
Ground Tel No:	01450 374231
Sec Bus:	0131 537 9233
Sec Home:	0131 440 3417
Playing Kits:	1st Choice
Shirt:	Royal Blue with Red and White Stripe
Shorts:	Royal Blue
Stockings:	Royal Blue
	2nd Choice
Shirt:	Red with Black Detail
Shorts:	Black
Stockings:	Black with Red and White Detail

HERIOT-WATT UNIVERSITY F.C.

Secretary:	M. McConnell
Club Address:	Heriot-Watt University Riccarton Campus, Edinburgh
Sec Home:	01592 754286
Playing Kits:	1st Choice
Shirt:	Blue and Yellow
Shorts:	Blue

KELSO UNITED F.C.

Secretary:	A. Douglas
Club Address:	Woodside Park, Kelso.
Ground Tel No:	01573 223780
Sec Home:	01573 225314
Playing Kits:	1st Choice
Shirt:	Black and White Stripes
Shorts:	Black

LOTHIAN THISTLE F.C.

Secretary:	T. Allison
Club Address:	Saughton Sports Complex, Edinburgh.
Ground Tel No:	0131 444 0422 (Matchdays Only)
Sec Home:	0131 336 1751
Playing Kits:	1st Choice
Shirt:	Maroon
Shorts:	Sky Blue

PEEBLES ROVERS F.C.

Secretary:	C. Morrish
Club Address:	Whitestone Park, Peebles.
Sec Home:	01721 720543
Playing Kits:	1st Choice
Shirt:	Red and White
Shorts:	Red and White

PENCAITLAND & ORMISTON F.C.

Secretary:	J.M. Greenhorn
Club Address:	Recreation Park, Ormiston.
Sec Home:	0131 442 1402
Playing Kits:	1st Choice
Shirt:	Maroon and White
Shorts:	Maroon

PRESTON ATHLETIC F.C.

Secretary:	R. McNeil
Manager:	W. Aitchison
Club Address:	Pennypitt Park, Rope Walk, Prestonpans, East Lothian.
Ground Tel No:	01875 815221
Sec Bus:	01698 413216
Sec Home:	01875 611830
E-Mail:	preston.athletic@ondigital.com
Playing Kits:	1st Choice
Shirt:	Blue
Shorts:	White with Blue Stripe
Stockings:	Black with Red Top
	2nd Choice
Shirt:	Red with White Stripe
Shorts:	White with Red Stripe
Stockings:	Red with White Top

SELKIRK F.C.

Secretary/Manager: D. Kerr
Club Address: Ettrick Park, Riverside Road, Selkirk
Ground Tel No: 01750 20478
Sec Bus: 01896 758871
Sec Home: 01750 23060
Playing Kits: **1st Choice**
    Shirt: Half Blue and Half White
    Shorts: Blue
    Stockings: Blue
    2nd Choice
    Shirt: White
    Shorts: Blue
    Stockings: Blue
    3rd Choice
    Shirt: White with Blue vertical stripe
    Shorts: Blue
    Stockings: Blue

SPARTANS F.C.

Secretary: J. Murray
Co-Managers: S. Lynch & D. Rodier
Club Address: City Park, Ferry Road, Edinburgh.
Sec Bus/Fax: 0131 667 9923
Sec Home: 0131 668 2188
Playing Kits: **1st Choice**
    Shirt: White with Red Trim
    Shorts: Red
    Stockings: White with Red Tops
    2nd Choice
    Shirt: Blue
    Shorts: Blue
    Stockings: Blue

THREAVE ROVERS F.C.

Secretary: Robert McCleary
Manager: William C. Sim
Club Address: Meadow Park, Castle Douglas, Dumfries & Galloway.
Ground Tel No: 01556 504536
Sec Home: 01556 503512
Fax No: 01556 503185
Playing Kits: **1st Choice**
    Shirt: Black and White Vertical Stripes
    Shorts: Black
    Stockings: White with Black Tops
    2nd Choice
    Shirt: Blue
    Shorts: White
    Stockings: Blue
    3rd Choice
    Shirt: White
    Shorts: White
    Stockings: White

TOLLCROSS UNITED F.C.

Secretary: A. Wilkie
Club Address: Fernieside Recreation Park, Fernieside Avenue, Edinburgh.
Sec Bus: 0131 467 5555
Sec Home: 0131 622 1148
Playing Kits: **1st Choice**
    Shirt: Red and White Sleeves
    Shorts: White

VALE OF LEITHEN F.C.

Secretary: I. Haggarty
Manager: S.A. Robertson
Club Address: Victoria Park, Innerleithen.
Sec Bus: 0131 244 2524
Sec Home/Fax: 01896 830995
Fax No: 0131 244 2326
Playing Kits: **1st Choice**
    Shirt: Navy with White Sleeves
    Shorts: Navy
    Stockings: White
    2nd Choice
    Shirt: Red with White Sleeves
    Shorts: Red
    Stockings: Red

WHITEHILL WELFARE F.C.

Secretary: P. McGauley
Manager: M. Lawson
Club Address: Ferguson Park, Carnethie Street, Rosewell, Midlothian.
Ground Tel No: 0131 440 0115
Sec Home: 0131 440 3417
Website: www.members.aol.com/wwelfare
E-Mail: w.welfarew@aol.com
Playing Kits: **1st Choice**
    Shirt: Claret Body with Sky Blue Sleeves
    Shorts: White
    Stockings: White with Two Claret Bands
    2nd Choice
    Shirt: Sky Blue with White Flash on Shoulder
    Shorts: Sky Blue with Claret Panel on Side of Leg
    Stockings: Sky Blue with Two Claret Hoops on Top

EAST OF SCOTLAND LEAGUE

FINAL TABLES – SEASON 1999/2000

PREMIER DIVISION

	P	W	D	L	F	A	Pts
Annan Athletic	22	15	6	1	62	21	51
Whitehill Welfare	22	15	5	2	59	13	50
Spartans	22	14	5	3	62	31	47
Lothian Thistle	22	11	4	7	45	32	37
Vale of Leithen	22	11	3	8	50	42	36
Edinburgh City	22	9	5	8	42	39	32
Civil Service Strollers	22	9	3	10	42	47	30
Coldstream	22	7	4	11	34	40	25
Craigroyston	22	8	1	13	29	53	25
Easthouses Lily	22	6	2	14	27	50	20
Peebles Rovers	22	6	1	15	29	56	19
Tollcross United	22	1	1	20	19	76	4

FIRST DIVISION

	P	W	D	L	F	A	Pts
Threave Rovers	20	15	3	2	55	26	48
Gala Fairydean	20	13	3	4	41	21	42
Kelso United	20	10	3	7	30	31	33
*Preston Athletic	20	12	2	6	58	29	32
†Edinburgh Univ.	20	11	2	7	39	22	32
Eyemouth United	20	8	3	9	27	44	27
Pencait. & Ormiston	20	7	4	9	24	29	25
Hawick Royal Albert	20	6	4	10	32	38	22
Heriot-Watt Univ.	20	4	4	12	26	42	16
Edinburgh Athletic	20	5	1	14	20	44	16
Selkirk	20	3	3	14	29	55	12

* Preston Athletic had 6 Points Deducted
† Edinburgh University had 3 Points Deducted

THE SOUTH OF SCOTLAND LEAGUE DIRECTORY OF CLUBS

ANNAN ATHLETIC F.C.

Secretary:	Alan T. Irving
Manager:	David Irons
Club Address:	Galabank, North Street, Annan, Dumfries & Galloway.
Ground Tel/Fax No:	01461 204108
Sec Bus:	01461 207218
Sec Home:	01461 203702
Website:	www.members.synup.com
E-Mail:	annanathletic@synup.net
Playing Kits:	**1st Choice**
Shirt:	Black and Gold Broad Vertical Stripes
Shorts:	Black
Stockings:	Black with Two Gold Rings
	2nd Choice
Shirt:	Blue
Shorts:	White
Stockings:	White with Blue Tops

CREETOWN F.C.

Secretary:	Andrew Ward
Manager:	Kenneth Maxwell
Club Address:	Cassencarrie Park, Creetown.
Sec Home:	01671 820251
Playing Kits:	Black & Orange

CRICHTON F.C.

Secretary:	Kenny Cameron
Manager:	Keith Brown
Club Address:	Crichton Park, Dumfries
Sec Home:	01387 265939
Playing Kits:	Blue & White

DALBEATTIE STAR F.C.

Secretary:	Robert Geddes
Manager:	Brian Aitchison
Club Address:	Islecroft Stadium, Dalbeattie.
Sec Bus/Home:	01556 610563
Fax No:	01556 611747
Playing Kits:	**1st Choice**
Shirt:	Red and Black Stripes
Shorts:	Black
Stockings:	Red
	2nd Choice
Shirt:	Blue
Shorts:	Blue
Stockings:	Blue

DUMFRIES F.C.

Secretary:	Tommy Parker
Manager:	Colin Lennox
Club Address:	Norfolk Park, Glencaple
Sec Home:	01387 263258
Playing Kits:	Yellow & Green

GIRVAN F.C.

Secretary:	John M. Irvine
Manager:	Robert McLeish
Club Address:	Hamilton Park, Girvan.
Sec Bus:	01465 714440
Sec Home:	01465 712702
Playing Kits:	**1st Choice**
Shirt:	Azure Blue with Black Vertical Stripe
Shorts:	Azure Blue
Stockings:	Black
	2nd Choice
Shirt:	Purple with White Pinstripe
Shorts:	Purple
Stockings:	Purple with White Flash

NEWTON STEWART F.C.

Secretary:	John R. McNaught
Manager:	Alan Groves
Club Address:	Blairmount Park, Newton Stewart
Sec Bus:	01671 402776
Sec Home:	01671 403066
Playing Kits:	**1st Choice**
Shirt:	Black and White Vertical Stripes
Shorts:	Black
Stockings:	Black with White Tops
	2nd Choice
Shirt:	Yellow and Black
Shorts:	Black and Yellow
Stockings:	Black and Yellow

STRANRAER ATHLETIC F.C.

Secretary:	Yvonne Lees
Manager:	Sandy Sutherland
Club Address:	Stranraer Academy, Stranraer.
Sec Home:	01776 707279
Playing Kits:	Blue & White

ST. CUTHBERT WANDERERS F.C.

Secretary: William J. McKenzie
Manager: James Thompson
Club Address: St. Mary's Park, Kirkcudbright.
Sec Bus/Home/Fax: 01557 330680
Playing Kits:
    1st Choice
    Shirt: Blue with White Hoops
    Shorts: Blue with White Narrow Band
    Stockings: Blue with White Band on Tops
    2nd Choice
    Shirt: Yellow
    Shorts: Blue
    Stockings: Blue with White Band on Tops

TARFF ROVERS F.C.

Secretary: Gavin McCleary
Manager: Derek Frye
Club Address: Ballgreen Park, Kirkcowan
Sec Bus: 01671 403603
Sec Home: 01671 830340
Playing Kits:
    1st Choice
    Shirt: Jade with Black Trim
    Shorts: Black
    Stockings: Jade and Black
    2nd Choice
    Shirt: Azure Blue and Black
    Shorts: Black
    Stockings: Black and Blue

THREAVE ROVERS F.C.

Secretary: Robert McCleary
Manager: William C. Sim
Club Address: Meadow Park, Castle Douglas, Dumfries & Galloway.
Ground Tel No: 01556 504536
Sec Home: 01556 503512
Fax No: 01556 503185
Playing Kits:
    1st Choice
    Shirt: Black and White Vertical Stripes
    Shorts: Black
    Stockings: White with Black Tops
    2nd Choice
    Shirt: Blue
    Shorts: White
    Stockings: Blue
    3rd Choice
    Shirt: White
    Shorts: White
    Stockings: White

WIGTOWN AND BLADNOCH F.C.

Secretary: Roger Docherty
Manager: Andrew Kiltie
Club Address: Trammondford Park, Wigtown.
Sec Bus: 01988 402322
Sec Home: 01988 402352
Playing Kits:
    1st Choice
    Shirt: Red with White Trim
    Shorts: Red
    Stockings: Red
    2nd Choice
    Shirt: Blue with Yellow Trim
    Shorts: Blue and Yellow
    Stockings: Blue and Yellow

SOUTH OF SCOTLAND LEAGUE

FINAL TABLE – SEASON 1999/2000

	P	W	D	L	F	A	Pts
*Tarff Rovers	24	22	1	1	118	27	64
Dalbeattie Star	24	19	2	3	98	18	59
Newton Stewart	24	14	2	8	80	42	44
St. Cuthbert Wand.	24	13	5	6	69	46	44
Annan Athletic	24	12	5	7	57	42	41
Stranraer Athletic	24	11	5	8	53	43	38
Crichton	24	11	4	9	61	59	37
Creetown	24	10	3	11	60	68	33
†Threave Rovers	24	6	3	15	35	65	21
Maxwelltown High School F.P.	24	5	5	14	49	95	20
Girvan	24	5	3	16	47	88	18
Wigtown & Bladnoch	24	4	3	17	33	85	15
Dumfries High School F.P.	24	3	1	20	26	108	10

* Tarff Rovers had 3 Points and 3 Goals Deducted

† Threave Rovers had 1 Goal Deducted

Aberdeen

Pittodrie Stadium, Pittodrie Street,
Aberdeen, AB24 5QH

CHAIRMAN
Stewart Milne

VICE-CHAIRMAN
Ian R. Donald

DIRECTORS
Gordon A. Buchan,
Martin J. Gilbert,
Keith H. Burkinshaw &
William Gilmore

**FOOTBALL GENERAL
MANAGER/SECRETARY**
David Johnston (01224) 650433

MANAGER
Ebbe Skovdahl

ASSISTANT MANAGER
Gardner Spiers

YOUTH DEVELOPMENT MANAGER
Drew Jarvie

FITNESS COACH
Stuart Hogg

KIT MANAGERS
Teddy Scott & Jim Warrender

CLUB DOCTORS
Dr. Derek Gray &
Dr. Stephen Wedderburn

PHYSIOTHERAPISTS
David Wylie & John Sharp

COMMUNITY OFFICERS
Bill Gordon & Sandy Finnie

CHIEF SCOUT
John Kelman

**FOOTBALL SAFETY OFFICERS'
ASSOCIATION REPRESENTATIVE**
John Morgan (01224) 650400

GROUNDSMAN
Moray Galbraith

MARKETING & SALES MANAGER
Harvey Smith (01224) 650426

HOSPITALITY MANAGER
Paul Quick

CORPORATE SALES MANAGER
Alan Dinnett

PROMOTIONS MANAGER
Jim Whyte

TICKET SERVICES MANAGER
Andy Ward

PUBLIC RELATIONS MANAGER
Dave Mcdermid

MATCHDAY PROGRAMME EDITOR
Paul Third (01224) 650442

TELEPHONES
Ground/General Enquiries
(01224) 650400
Ticket Office (01224) 631903
Fax (01224) 644173
Dons Clubcall (09068) 121551

E-MAIL & INTERNET ADDRESS
feedback@afc.co.uk
http://www.afc.co.uk
http://www.thedons.co.uk

CLUB SHOPS
AFC Direct, 19 Bridge Street,
Aberdeen, Tel (01224) 405305
and **Ticket Office**, c/o Aberdeen F.C.,
Pittodrie Stadium, Aberdeen

OFFICIAL SUPPORTERS CLUB
Association Secretary:
Mrs. Susan Scott, 'Aldon',
Wellington Road,
Aberdeen, AB12 4BJ
susan.scottone@virgin.net

TEAM CAPTAIN
Derek Whyte

SHIRT SPONSOR
Atlantic Telecom Group plc

KIT SUPPLIER
Puma

LIST OF PLAYERS 2000-2001

Squad No.	Name	Place & date of birth	Previous Club	Lge Career Apps	Gls
2	Russell Anderson	Aberdeen 25.10.78	Dyce Juniors	81 (9)	1
16	Rachid Belabed	Brussels 30.10.80	RWD Molenbbek	6 (15)	1
14	Paul Bernard	Edinburgh 30.12.72	Oldham Athletic	87 (9)	6
18	Chris Clark	Aberdeen 15.9.80	Hermes	- (2)	-
12	Andy Dow	Dundee 7.2.73	Hibernian	57 (3)	5
23	Ryan Esson	Aberdeen 19.3.80	Parkvale	1	-
4	Cato Guntveit	Drammen, Norway 6.8.75	Brann Bergen	20	3
8	Eoin Jess	Aberdeen 13.12.70	Coventry City	263(35)	78
15	David Lilley	Bellshill 31.10.77	Queen of the South	14 (2)	-
6	Jamie McAllister	Glasgow 26.4.78	Queen of the South	29 (5)	-
24	Philip McGuire	Glasgow 3.3.80	Dyce Juniors	- (3)	-
31	Kevin McNaughton	Dundee 28.8.82	'S' Form	-	-
25	Darren Mackie	Inverurie 5.1.82	'S' Form	2 (2)	-
7	Andreas Mayer	Burgau, Germany 13.9.72	Rosenborg BK	33 (1)	2
26	Mark Perry	Aberdeen 7.2.71	Dundee United	42 (7)	4
30	David Preece	Sunderland 26.8.76	Darlington	9 (1)	-
17	David Rowson	Aberdeen 14.9.76	FC Stoneywood	81(19)	8
20	Kevin Rutkiewcz	Glasgow 10.5.80	Larkhall Thistle	1 (9)	-
5	Thomas Solberg	Moss, Norway 25.1..70	Viking Satvanger	26	4
10	Arild Stavrum	Kristiansuno, Norway 16.4.72	Viking Satvanger	22	9
3	Derek Whyte	Glasgow 31.8.68	Middlesbrough	73 (1)	-
9	Robbie Winters	East Kilbride 4.11.74	Dundee United	51(10)	19
19	Darren Young	Glasgow 13.10.78	Crombie Sports	36 (8)	1
21	Derek Young	Glasgow 27.5.80	Lewis United	9 (9)	-
0	Hicham Zerouali	Morocco 17.1.77	Fus Rabat	6 (8)	3

NEW SIGNINGS

None

Milestones

YEAR OF FORMATION: 1903
MOST CAPPED PLAYER: Alex McLeish
NO. OF CAPS: 77
MOST LEAGUE POINTS IN A SEASON: 64 (Premier Division - Season 1992/93) (44 games)(2 Points for a Win)
MOST LEAGUE GOALS SCORED BY A PLAYER IN A SEASON: Benny Yorston (Season 1929/30)
NO. OF GOALS SCORED: 38
RECORD ATTENDANCE: 45,061 (-v- Heart of Midlothian – 13.3.1954)
RECORD VICTORY: 13-0 (-v- Peterhead – Scottish Cup, 9.2.1923)
RECORD DEFEAT: 0-8 (-v- Celtic - Division 1, 30.1.65)

The Dons' ten year league record

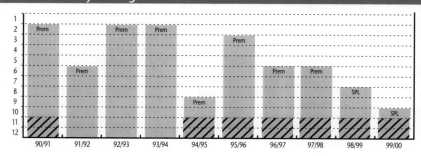

THE DONS' CLUB FACTFILE 1999/2000
RESULTS... APPEARANCES... SCORERS... ATTENDANCES...

Small bold figures denote goalscorers. † denotes opponent's own goal.

Date	Venue	Opponents	Att	Res	Preece D.	Smith G.	Anderson R.	Whyte D.	Pepper C.	Dow A.	Bernard P.	Jess E.	Young Derek	Wyness D.	Winters R.	Hamilton I.	Kiriakov I.	McAllister J.	Gillies R.	Hart M.	Mackie D.	Mayer A.	Solberg T.	Buchan I.	Perry M.	Lilley D.	Bett B.	Leighton J.	Guntveit C.	Cobian J.	Stavrum A.	Rutkiewicz K.	Belabed R.	Zerouali H.	McGuire P.	Clark C.	Young Darren	Rowson D.	Esson R.
Aug 1	H	Celtic	16,080	0-5	1	2	3	4	5	6	7	8	9	10	11	12	13	14																					
7	A	Kilmarnock	8,378	0-2	1	2	3	4	5	6		8	9	13	11	10		7	14	12																			
14	H	Dundee	9,041	0-2	1	2	3	4	5	6		8	11	14	13		7		12	9	10																		
22	A	Heart of Midlothian	12,803	0-3	1	2	3	4	5	6		8	9		11	13	14	10		12	7																		
29	H	St. Johnstone	9,600	0-3	1	2	5			6	14	8			12		3	10		11	9	4	7	13															
Sep 11	A	Rangers	49,226	0-3	1	2	5			6	7	8			11	12		13		10	14	9	4	3															
18	H	Dundee United	11,814	1-2	1		5			6^1		8	13		11	10		3	12		9	4	7	2															
Oct 2	H	Hibernian	11,876	2-2	1		5			6		8^1	11		13	10		3	14^1		9	4	7	2	12														
16	A	Celtic	59,931	0-7	1		5			6		8	9		11	14		12	10		7	4	3	2	13														
20	A	Motherwell	5,009	6-5			5			6^1	10^1	8^1			11^3		9	3	12		7	4	14	13	2		1												
23	H	Kilmarnock	10,552	2-2			5			6	10^2	8			11		9	3	13		7	4		12	2		1												
30	H	Rangers	16,846	1-5			5			6	10	8			11		9	3	12	14	7	4^1		13	2		1												
Nov 6	A	Dundee United	8,170	1-3			5			6		8			11	14	9	3			7	4^1	12		2		1	10	13										
21	A	St. Johnstone	6,279	1-1			5	12		6^1					11			3			8	4	13		2		1	9	7	10									
27	A	Hibernian	11,627	0-2			5	4		6	7				11			3			8		12				1	9		2	10	13	14						
Dec 8	H	Heart of Midlothian	10,274	3-1			5	4		6	7	8^1			11			3				2					1	9^1		10^1	14	13	12						
11	H	Celtic	16,532	0-6			5	4		6	7	8			11			3				2					1	9		10		13	12	14					
27	H	Dundee United	16,586	3-1			5	4		6	7	8			13			3				2					1	9		10^1	14	12^1	11^1						
Jan 22	A	Rangers	50,023	0-5			5	4		6	7	8			12			3			9	2					1			10	14	13	11						
26	H	Motherwell	10,314	1-1			5	4		6	7	8			11			3				2					1	9		10	14	13	12^1						
Feb 5	H	St. Johnstone	17,568	2-1			5			6	7				9^1			3				4					1	8		10^1	13	14	11	12					
23	A	Dundee	5,784	3-1			5	4		6^1	7^1				11			3			14	2					1	9		10^1	8	13		12					
26	H	Hibernian	12,630	4-0	15		5^1	4		6	7				11			3				2					1	9^1		10^2	12	8							
Mar 4	A	Motherwell	7,528	0-1			5			6	7				9			3				4	2					1	8		10		12	11	14	13				
22	A	Heart of Midlothian	13,249	0-3			5			6	8	12			11			3			7	4				2		1		10	14	13				9			
25	A	Dundee United	6,723	1-1			5			6	9	8			12			3			7	4				2		1	10		11^1					13			
Apr 1	H	Rangers	16,521	1-1			5			6	9	8			12			3			7	4				2		1^1	10		11		13			14			
12	A	Kilmarnock	11,525	0-1			5	4		6	9	8	14		13			3			.7					2		1	10		11	12							
15	H	Heart of Midlothian	12,626	1-2			5	4		6	9	8						3			7	2				14		1	10		11^1		12	13					
18	H	Dundee	12,403	0-1			5	4		6		8	13					3			7		14	2				1	10		11^1		9	12					
22	H	Motherwell	9,348	2-1			5			6^1		13		10				3			7	4^1	12	2				1	9		11	14	8						
29	H	Hibernian	9,659	0-1			5	4		6		8						3			7	2				14		1	10		9	12					13		
May 2	A	St. Johnstone	3,991	1-2			5	4			7		8		10^1						3	13	2				1		9	12							6		
6	A	Celtic	56,235	1-5				4		6	7	12		11^1			3				5	2					1	9		10	14	13					8		
14	H	Kilmarnock	9,275	5-1				4		6	7	8^1	10	13^1			3				5^1		2						9	11^1							12^1		1
21	A	Dundee	6,449	2-0			5			6	7	8^1			12			3				4	2				1	9		10^1	14	11					13		
TOTAL FULL APPEARANCES					9	6	34	19		4	35	24	25	9	1	23	3	6	29	3	2	2	20	26	5	10	14		26	20	2	22	1	6	6		1	2	1
TOTAL SUB APPEARANCES						(1)				(1)		(1)	(1)	(5)	(2)	(10)	(4)	(2)	(5)	(7)	(1)	(2)	(1)						(3)	(8)	(3)	(1)			(1)		(9)	(15)	(8)	(3)	(2)	(2)	(3)
TOTAL GOALS SCORED							1			5	4	5			7					1			4						3	9	1	3				1

Pittodrie Stadium

CAPACITY: 21,662 (All Seated)

PITCH DIMENSIONS: 109 yds x 72 yds

FACILITIES FOR DISABLED SUPPORTERS:
Wheelchair section in front of Merkland Stand and in front row of Richard Donald Stand and also front row of Main Stand Section F.
(Please telephone Ticket Office and reserve place(s) in advance).

Team playing kits

FIRST CHOICE
Shirt: Red with White Band across Shoulder and down Sides.
Shorts: Red with White Stripe on Sides.
Stockings: Red and White Hoops.

SECOND CHOICE
Shirt: Black with Gold Panel on centre of Sleeve. Collar Gold with two Black Stripes.
Shorts: Black with Gold Stripe on Sides.
Stockings: Black with Two Gold Calf Hoops and Gold Tops.

How to get there

You can reach Pittodrie Stadium by these routes:

BUSES: The following buses all depart from the city centre to within a hundred yards of the ground: Nos. 1, 2, 3 and 11.

TRAINS: The main Aberdeen station is in the centre of the city and the above buses will then take fans to the ground.

CARS: Motor vehicles coming from the city centre should travel along Union Street, then turn into King Street and the park will be on your right, about half a mile further on.
Parking on Beach Boulevard and Beach Esplanade.

Aberdeen F.C. is a member of The Scottish Premier League

Celtic

Celtic Park, Glasgow, G40 3RE

CELTIC PLC DIRECTORS
Brian Quinn, C.B.E. (Chairman),
Allan MacDonald O.B.E. (Chief Executive),
Eric J. Riley, Dermot F. Desmond,
Sir Patrick Sheehy & Kevin Sweeney

CELTIC F.C. DIRECTORS
Allan MacDonald O.B.E. (Chairman),
Eric J. Riley, John S. Keane,
Michael A. McDonald,
James Hone & Kevin Sweeney

COMPANY SECRETARY
Kevin Sweeney

MANAGER
Martin O'Neill

ASSISTANT MANAGER
John Robertson

COACHES
Steve Walford & Tommy Burns

HEAD YOUTH COACH
Willie McStay

DEVELOPMENT COACHES
Kenny McDowall & Tom O'Neill

CLUB DOCTOR
Roddy MacDonald

PHYSIOTHERAPIST
Brian Scott

**FOOTBALL SAFETY OFFICERS'
ASSOCIATION REPRESENTATIVE**
George E. Douglas
(0141) 556 2611/551 4256

GROUNDSMAN
John Hayes

KIT CONTROLLER
John Clark

CORPORATE SERVICES MANAGER
Frank McNally
(0141) 551 4278

MANAGING DIRECTOR CELTIC POOLS
John Maguire
(0141) 551 9922

MATCHDAY PROGRAMME EDITOR
Joe Sullivan

TELEPHONES
Ground (0141) 556 2611
Fax (0141) 551 8106
Ticket Services (0141) 551 4223
Credit Card Hotline (0141) 551 8653/4
Celtic Hotline (0891) 1967 21
Celtic View (0141) 551 8103
Walfrid Restaurant (0141) 551 9955
Mail Order Hotline (0141) 550 1888

CELTIC WORLD WIDE WEBSITE
http://www.celticfc.co.uk

CLUB SHOPS
Superstore, Celtic Park, Glasgow, G40 3RE
Tel (0141) 554 4231
(9.00 a.m. to 6.00 p.m. Mon-Sat,
10.00a.m. to 5.00p.m. Sunday),
40 Dundas Street, Glasgow G1 2AQ
Tel (0141) 332 2727
(9.00 a.m. to 5.00 p.m Mon-Sat) and
21 High Street, Glasgow, G1 1LX
Tel (0141) 552 7630
(9.30 a.m. to 5.30 p.m. Mon-Sat,
11.30 a.m. to 4.30 p.m. Sunday)

OFFICIAL SUPPORTERS CLUB
Celtic Supporters Association,
1524 London Road, Glasgow G40 3RJ
Tel (0141) 556 1882/554 6250/554 6342

TEAM CAPTAIN
Tom Boyd

SHIRT SPONSOR
NTL

KIT SUPPLIER
Umbro

LIST OF PLAYERS 2000-2001

Squad No.	Name	Place & date of birth	Previous Club	Lge Career Apps	Gls
10	Eyal Berkovic	Haifa, Isreal 2.4.72	West Ham United	27(1)	9
22	Stephane Bonnes	France 26.2.78	FC Mulhouse	-	-
2	Tom Boyd	Glasgow 24.11.65	Chelsea	266 (1)	2
27	Mark Burchill	Broxburn 18.8.80	Celtic BC	13 (32)	17
40	Stephen Crainey	Glasgow 22.6.81	Celtic BC	5 (4)	-
34	Mark Fotheringham	Dundee 22.10.83	Celtic BC	1 (1)	-
42	James Goodwin	Waterford 20.11.81	Tramore	1	-
1	Jonathan Gould	Paddington 18.7.68	Bradford City	91 (1)	-
24	Colin Healy	Cork 14.3.80	Wilton United	10 (3)	1
12	Tommy Johnson	Newcastle 15.1.71	Aston Villa	14 (5)	13
41	John Kennedy	Bellshill 18.8.83	'S' Form	1 (4)	-
21	Stewart Kerr	Bellshill 13.11.74	Celtic BC	33 (1)	-
23	Dimitre Kharine	Moscow, Russia 16.8.68	Chelsea	4	-
14	Paul Lambert	Glasgow 7.8.69	Borussia Dortmund	83 (1)	4
7	Henrik Larsson	Helsingborg, Sweden 20.9.71	Feyenoord	77 (2)	52
32	Simon Lynch	Montreal 19.5.82	Celtic Youth Initiative	1 (1)	1
28	Ryan McCann	Bellshill 21.9.81	Celtic BC	1	-
45	Brian McColligan	Glasgow 31.10.80	Celtic BC	1	-
4	Jackie McNamara	Glasgow 24.10.73	Dunfermline Athletic	123 (4)	4
3	Stephane Mahe	Puteaux, France 23.9.68	Stade Rennais	66	4
35	Johan Mjallby	Sweden 9.2.71	AIK Stockholm	43 (4)	3
25	Lubomir Moravcik	Slovakia 22.6.65	MSV Duisburg	43 (1)	14
15	Bobby Petta	Rotterdam, Holland 6.8.74	Ipswich Town	2 (10)	-
19	Stilian Petrov	Bulgaria 5.7.79	CSKA Sofia	20 (6)	1
31	Rafael Scheidt	Brazil 10.2.76	Gremio Porto Alegrens	1 (2)	-
30	Vidmar Riseth	Levanger, Norway 21.4.72	LASK Linz	52 (1)	3
26	Paul Shields	Dunfermline 15.8.81	Raith Rovers	- (1)	-
39	James Smith	Alexandria 20.11.80	Celtic BC	-	-
6	Alan Stubbs	Kirkby 6.10.71	Bolton Wanderers	94 (1)	2
16	Olivier Tebily	Abidjan, Ivory Coast 19.2.75	Sheffield United	19 (4)	-
11	Morten Wieghorst	Glostrup, Denmark 25.2.71	Dundee	58(25)	10

NEW SIGNINGS

17	Didier Agathe	Saint Pierre, France 16.8.75	Hibernian
9	Chris Sutton	Nottingham 10.3.73	Chelsea
8	Alan Thompson	Newcastle 22.12.73	Aston Villa
5	Joos Valgaeran	Louvain, Belgium 3.3.76	Roda JC

Milestones

YEAR OF FORMATION: 1888
MOST CAPPED PLAYER: Paul McStay
NO. OF CAPS: 76
MOST LEAGUE POINTS IN A SEASON: 72 (Premier Division – Season 1987/88) (2 points for a Win)
83 (Premier Division – Season 1995/96) (3 points for a Win)
MOST LEAGUE GOALS SCORED BY A PLAYER IN A SEASON: Jimmy McGrory (Season 1935/36)
NO. OF GOALS SCORED: 50
RECORD ATTENDANCE: 92,000 (-v- Rangers – 1.1.1938)
RECORD VICTORY: 11-0 (-v- Dundee – Division 1, 26.10.1895)
RECORD DEFEAT: 0-8 (-v- Motherwell – Division 1, 30.4.1937)

The Bhoys' ten year league record

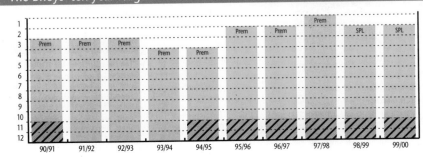

RESULTS... APPEARANCES... SCORERS... ATTENDANCES...

Date	Venue	Opponents	Att	Res	Gould J.	Boyd T.	Riseth V.	Mjallby J.	Tebily O.	Berkovic E.	Wieghorst M.	Lambert P.	Moravcik L.	Larsson H.	Viduka M.	Burchill M.	Burley C.	Petta B.	Mahe S.	Petrov S.	Stubbs A.	McNamara J.	Blinker R.	Khairine D.	Brattbakk H.	Wright I.	Healy C.	Johnson T.	Scheidt R.	Crainey S.	Kennedy J.	De Omelas F.	Kerr S.	Lynch S.	Shields P.	Fotheringham M.	Goodwin J.	McColligan B.	McCann R.	Convery J.	Miller L.
Aug 1	A	Aberdeen	16,080	5-0	1		2	3		4	5	6		7	8		9	10²	11²	12¹																					
7	H	St. Johnstone	60,282	3-0	1		2	3	4¹	5		6	7¹		8	9	10	11¹			12	13																			
15	A	Dundee United	12,375	1-2	1			2		4	3	6¹		7	8	9	10	11			5	12																			
21	A	Dundee	10,531	2-1	1			3	14	4	6			8	9	10¹	11			12	13	5¹	7	2																	
29	H	Heart of Midlothian	60,107	4-0	1			3	2	8²				9	10¹	11¹	12	7	13	5			4	6	14																
Sep 12	A	Kilmarnock	14,318	1-0	1			3	5	2				8	9	10		11¹	7	12		13	4	6																	
25	A	Hibernian	14,747	2-0				3		2				8	9	10 11²					6	4	5	7	1																
Oct 16	A	Aberdeen	59,931	7-0	1			3	12	2	6¹			8	9	10³ 11³	14	7				4	5	13																	
24	A	St. Johnstone	9,066	2-1	1			3	12	2		7¹		8		11	10¹		5		6	4		9																	
27	H	Motherwell	57,898	0-1	1			3	2	12		13	8	9		11	10	7	5		6	4					14														
30	H	Kilmarnock	59,791	5-1	1			3		2		14	8	9		11³	13	7¹			12	4	5	6		10¹															
Nov 7	A	Rangers	50,026	2-4	1			3	12	2	9²		8			11	14	7			6	4	5	13		10															
20	A	Heart of Midlothian	17,184	2-1	1			3	2		8		9¹			11			5	7	4	6			12	10¹															
28	H	Motherwell	10,730	2-1	1			3	2	9¹	10	12		10	11		5	8	4	6			13																		
Dec 4	H	Hibernian	60,092	4-0	1			3	5	2	9	7¹	8	10²		11¹ 13¹	14	12	4	6																					
11	A	Aberdeen	16,532	6-0	1			3	2	9	7	8¹	10¹	11¹			5¹	12	4	6 14¹		13¹																			
18	H	Dundee United	58,181	4-1	1			3	2	9	7	8	10¹	11¹ 13¹			14	12	4	5	6¹																				
27	H	Rangers	59,619	1-1	1			3	5	2	9		8	10		11¹			7	4	6	12				13															
Jan 23	A	Kilmarnock	14,126	1-1	1	2	3		4		9			10		11¹			6		5	7				12	8	13													
Feb 5	H	Heart of Midlothian	59,735	2-3	1	2	3		7			9		10¹		11¹	12		5	6	4		14				8	13													
12	A	Dundee	10,044	3-0		2	3		4¹	13		7		9		11¹	12		5		8	6		1			10 14¹														
Mar 1	H	Dundee	55,628	6-2		2			3		12	7		9		11²	14		5	8¹	4	6		1			10³	13													
5	A	Hibernian	12,239	1-2	15	2			3		9	7		10		11¹	12		5	8	4	6		1																	
8	H	Rangers	59,220	0-1	1	2	3		7			8		10		11	12		5	9	4	6																			
11	H	St. Johnstone	59,331	4-1	1	2	3			12	9	7				11² 10²			5	8		6	13				4	14													
26	A	Rangers	50,039	0-4	1	2	3		4			8	9			11	12		5	7	6					10															
Apr 2	H	Kilmarnock	55,194	4-2	1		2		3	4	9¹		8	10			13¹	14	6			7¹				5	11¹		12												
5	H	Motherwell	55,689	4-0	1				3		9¹	7	8	12		11	13		5		4	6¹				10²		2	14												
8	A	Heart of Midlothian	16,046	0-1	1				2	3		9	7	8	10		12		5		4	6				13	11	14													
15	H	Dundee	56,403	2-2	1				2	3	4	9				11	10¹		5¹	7		6	8					12	13												
22	H	Hibernian	56,843	1-1	1				2	3	9		8	10		11			5¹	6		7				4		12	13												
29	A	Motherwell	7,405	1-1					2		4	9		8		11 10¹			12	5	6					7		3			1	13									
May 2	A	Dundee United	7,449	1-0					2			7		8	9	11 10¹		13	5		4					6	12		3	14		1									
6	H	Aberdeen	56,235	5-1					2			7		8	9²		10		14	5		4				6	11³		3	12		1		13							
13	A	St. Johnstone	6,739	0-0					2		7			8	9		10			5		4				6	11		3	13		1		12							
21	A	Dundee United	56,749	2-0	1					2		9		8		12	10¹											3			11¹		7	2	5		6	13	14		
TOTAL FULL APPEARANCES					28	10	28		26	19	27	14	25	29	8	28	12	6	2	19	21	23	22	10		4			4	8	7	1	5	1		4	1		1	1	1	1
TOTAL SUB APPEARANCES						(1)			(4)	(3)	(1)	(3)		(1)		(16)	(2)	(10)		(6)			(7)			(2)	(4)	(2)	(3)	(2)	(4)	(4)	(2)		(1)	(1)	(1)			(1)	(1)
TOTAL GOALS SCORED									2		9	3	1	8	7	25	11	1		4	1			4			3	1	9							1				

Small bold figures denote goalscorers.   † denotes opponent's own goal.

Celtic Park

NORTH STAND (JANEFIELD STREET)

JOCK STEIN STAND — **EAST STAND**

MAIN SOUTH STAND (KERRYDALE STREET)

CAPACITY: 60,506 (All Seated)

PITCH DIMENSIONS: 120 yds x 74 yds

FACILITIES FOR DISABLED SUPPORTERS:
There is provision for 142 wheelchair positions for disabled supporters and their helpers. These are split into 87 in the North Stand, at the front of the lower terracing, 10 in the East Stand, lower terracing and 37 in the South Stand, lower terracing. Celtic fans should contact the club for availability. There is also a provision for 6 away positions in the lower East Stand.

Team playing kits

FIRST CHOICE		**SECOND CHOICE**	
Shirt:	Green and White Hoops. Collar White with Two Green Stripes.	Shirt:	Gold with Petrol Green Trim.
Shorts:	White.	Shorts:	Petrol Green with Gold Waistband.
Stockings:	White with Green Tops and Two Green Leg Bands.	Stockings:	Petrol Green with Two Gold Hoops on Turnover.

How to get there

The following routes may be used to reach Celtic Park:

BUSES: The following buses all leave from the city centre and pass within 50 yards of the ground. Nos. 61, 62, and 64.

TRAINS: There is a frequent train service from Glasgow Central Low Level station to Bridgeton Cross Station and this is only a ten minute walk from the ground. There is also a train from Queen Street Station (lower level) to Bellgrove Rail Station, approximately 1½ miles from the ground.

CARS: From the city centre, motor vehicles should travel along London Road and this will take you to the ground. Parking spaces are available in various areas close to the ground. On matchdays all car parking is strictly limited and is only available to those in possession of a valid car park pass.

The Bhoys

Celtic F.C. is a member of The Scottish Premier League

Dundee

Dens Park Stadium,
Sandeman Street, Dundee, DD3 7JY

CHAIRMAN
James M. Marr

DIRECTORS
James H. C. Connor, Peter Marr
& A. Ritchie Robertson

CHIEF EXECUTIVE
Peter Marr

COMPANY SECRETARY
A. Ritchie Robertson

FINANCIAL MANAGER
Michael G. Craig

PLAYER/MANAGER
Ivano Bonetti

ASSISTANT MANAGER
Dario Bonetti

ASSISTANT COACH
Enzo Romaro

CLUB CO-ORDINATOR
Dario Magri

YOUTH TEAM COACH
Ray Farningham

GOALKEEPING COACH
Billy Thomson

FITNESS COACH
Harry Hay

MASSEUR
Jack Cashley

CLUB DOCTOR
Dr. Phyllis Windsor, M.D., FRCR

**FOOTBALL SAFETY OFFICERS'
ASSOCIATION REPRESENTATIVE**
John Malone (01382) 889966

**YOUTH DEVELOPMENT
CO-ORDINATOR**
Kenny Cameron

MANAGER'S SECRETARY
Mrs Laura Hayes

STADIUM MANAGER
Jim Thomson

TICKET OFFICE MANAGER
Neil Cosgrove

GROUNDSMAN
Brian Robertson

COMMERCIAL DIRECTOR
Jim Connor Tel (01382) 884450
Fax (01382) 858963

MARKETING MANAGER
Brian Gray

MATCHDAY PROGRAMME EDITOR
Dave Forbes (0467) 214520

TELEPHONES
Football/Manager (01382) 826104
Administration/Accounts/
Youth Development (01382) 889966
Commercial/ Marketing
(01382) 884450
Ticket Office (01382) 204777
Stadium Manager (01382) 815250
Fax (01382) 832284
Commercial Fax (01382) 858963

E-MAIL & INTERNET ADDRESS
www.dundeefc.co.uk
dfc@dundeefc.co.uk

CLUB SHOP
Dundee F.C. Shop, situated between
Main Stand and Bobby Cox Stand

OFFICIAL SUPPORTERS CLUB
Contact: Norrie Price (01224) 818697

TEAM CAPTAIN
Barry Smith

SHIRT SPONSOR
Ceramic Tile Warehouse

KIT SUPPLIER
Xara

LIST OF PLAYERS 2000-2001

Squad No.	Name	Place & date of birth	Previous Club	Lge Career Apps	Gls
18	Javier Artero	Madrid, Spain 16. 4.75	San Lorenzo	6 (3)	1
-	Nicky Banger	Southampton 25.2.71	Oxford United	2 (4)	-
21	Graham Bayne	Kirkcaldy 22.8.79	Cupar Hearts	3 (16)	1
19	Patrizio Billio	Treviso, Italy 19.4.74	Ancona	16 (1)	1
-	Steven Boyack	Edinburgh 4.9.76	Rangers	40 (4)	3
22	Chris Coyne	Brisbane, Australia 20.12.78	West Ham United	- (1)	-
1	Robert Douglas	Lanark 26.4.72	Livingston	106	-
11	Willie Falconer	Aberdeen 5.4.66	Motherwell	62 (2)	16
-	Craig Ireland	Dundee 29.11.75	Dunfermline	14	1
13	Jamie Langfield	Paisley 22.12.79	Glasgow City BC	2 (1)	-
12	Shaun McSkimming	Stranraer 29.5.70	Motherwell	66 (8)	7
-	Lee Maddison	Bristol 5.10.72	Northampton	59 (6)	1
-	Willie Miller	Edinburgh 1.11.69	Hibernian	37 (2)	-
15	Steven Milne	Dundee 5.5.80	Downfield	1 (1)	-
14	Gavin Rae	Aberdeen 28.11.77	Hermes Juniors	73 (20)	7
23	Hugh Robertson	Aberdeen 19.3.75	Aberdeen	39 (9)	3
-	Lee Sharp	Glasgow 25.5.75	Dumbarton	15 (5)	2
-	Mark Slater	Buckie 2.4.79	Buckie Thistle	-	(1)-
2	Barry Smith	Paisley 19.2.74	Celtic	151(4)	1
6	Steven Tweed	Edinburgh 8.8.72	Stoke City	44	3
17	Frank van Eijs	Geleen, Holland 6.11.71	Vinkenslag	14 (2)	-
20	Lee Wilkie	Dundee 20.4.80	Downfield	21 (3)	-
16	Michael Yates	Liverpool 7.11.79	Burscough	2 (3)	1

NEW SIGNINGS

8	Ivano Bonetti	Brescia 1.8.64	
-	Walter Del Rio	Argentina 16.6.76	
4	Marcello Marrocco	Italy 7.6.69	Modena
5	Marco de Marchi	Milan 8.9.66	Vitesse Arnhem
10	Georgi Nemsadze	Georgia 10.5.72	Reggiani
29	Alessandro Romano	Italy	
7	Fabian Caballero	Misiones, Argentina 31.1.78	Sol de America
9	Juan Sara	Argentina 13.10.78	Cerro Portino

Milestones

YEAR OF FORMATION: 1893
MOST CAPPED PLAYER: Alex Hamilton
NO. OF CAPS: 24
MOST LEAGUE POINTS IN A SEASON: 58 (First Division – Season 1991/92) (2 points for a Win)
70 (First Division – Season 1997/98) (3 points for a Win)
MOST LEAGUE GOALS SCORED BY A PLAYER IN A SEASON: Alan Gilzean (Season 1963/64)
NO. OF GOALS SCORED: 32
RECORD ATTENDANCE: 43,024 (-v- Rangers – 1953)
RECORD VICTORY: 10-0 (-v- Fraserburgh, 1931; -v- Alloa, 1947; -v- Dunfermline Athletic, 1947; -v- Queen of the South, 1962)
RECORD DEFEAT: 0-11 (-v- Celtic – Division 1, 26.10.1895)

The Dark Blues' ten year league record

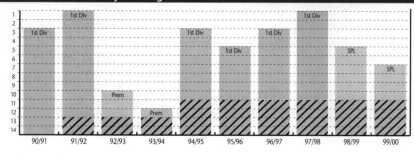

THE DARK BLUES' CLUB FACTFILE 1999/2000
RESULTS... APPEARANCES... SCORERS... ATTENDANCES...

Date	Venue	Opponents	Att.	Res	Douglas R.	Smith B.	Miller W.	Tweed S.	Maddison L.	Sharp L.	Boyack S.	Rae G.	McSkimming S.	Grady J.	Falconer W.	Coyne T.	Robertson H.	Yates M.	Van Eijs F.	Annand E.	Bayne G.	Willie L.	Puras R.	Slater M.	Elliott J.	Ireland C.	Billio P.	Banger N.	Langfield J.	Raeside R.	Lopez J.	Luna
July 31	A	Dundee United	11,693	1-2	1	2	3	4	5	6	7	8	9	10	11[1]	12	13	14														
Aug 8	H	Hibernian	6,050	†3-4	1	2	3	4	5		7	8	9[1]	12	11		13			6	10[1]											
14	A	Aberdeen	9,041	2-0	1	2	3	4	5		7	8	12		11[2]				6	9	10	13										
21	H	Celtic	10,531	1-2	1	2	3	4		6[1]	7	8	11	12				13	9			5										
28	A	Motherwell	6,278	2-0	1	2	3	4	5		7	8	6	9	11[1]			14	12	10[1]	13											
Sep 11	A	Heart of Midlothian	13,378	0-4	1	2	3	4	5		7	8	6	9	11		13			10	12											
19	H	St. Johnstone	5,283	1-2	1	2	3	4	5		7	8	6	10	11			9[1]		13			12	14								
25	A	Kilmarnock	7,433	2-0	1	2		4	5		7[1]	8[1]	9	12	11					6	10	3	13									
Oct 2	H	Rangers	10,494	2-3	1	2		4	5	14	7	8	9[1]	12	11[1]					6	10	3	13									
17	H	Dundee United	9,484	0-2	1			4	2	5	7	8	6	9	11		14	13		10		3	12									
23	A	Hibernian	10,162	2-5	1		3	4		6	7	8			11[2]			9	5	13			2	10	12	14						
30	H	Heart of Midlothian	6,018	1-0	1			4[1]		3	7	8	6	12	11				5	10						2	9					
Nov 6	A	St. Johnstone	4,917	1-0	1	2		4			7	8	6	12	11				5	10[1]						3	9					
20	A	Motherwell	4,340	0-1	1	2		4			7	8	6	13	11				5	10						3	9	12				
28	A	Rangers	47,154	2-1	1	2		4			7	8[1]	6		11	12			5	10	13						3[1]	9				
Dec 12	A	Dundee United	9,185	0-1	1	2		4			7	8	6	14	11		13		5	10		3					9	12				
27	H	St. Johnstone	6,232	1-1	1	2		4		5	7	8		12	11[1]		13			6		3					9	10				
Jan 22	A	Heart of Midlothian	13,112	0-2	1	2		4		5	14	8	7	10	11					6				12		3	9	13				
26	H	Kilmarnock	4,039	0-0	1	2		4			7	8	6		11					10	12	3				5	13	9				
Feb 5	A	Motherwell	5,856	3-0	1	2		4			7	8[1]	9	12[1]	11				6[1]	13	10	3				5						
12	H	Celtic	10,044	0-3	1	2		4		14	7	8	9	12	11				6	13	10	3				5						
23	H	Aberdeen	5,784	1-3	1	2	3	4			7	8	9	10	11					6	14	12[1]			5					13	1		
27	H	Rangers	9,297	1-7	1	2	3	4[1]		6	12	8		10	11		9	7						5									
Mar 1	A	Celtic	55,628	2-6	1			4	13	5	7	8			11[1]		9[1]			6	10			12		3						2	
4	A	Kilmarnock	8,460	2-2	1	2		4		5	7	8		10[1]	11					6						12[1]	9	3				
21	A	Hibernian	10,208	2-1	1	2		4		5	7	8	13	10	11[2]					6						12		3				9
25	A	St. Johnstone	4,655	1-2	1	2		4	5		7	8		9	11[1]					6	10						3					12
Apr 1	H	Heart of Midlothian	6,291	0-0	1	2		4	5		7	8		10	11					6	13			14		3	9				12	
8	H	Motherwell	4,701	4-1	1	2			5		7	8		10[2]						6	13	4				3	9[1]				12	11[1]
15	A	Celtic	56,403	†2-2	1	2	14			5	13	8	6							10	12	4				3	7				9	11[1]
18	A	Aberdeen	12,403	1-0	1	2		4	5		7		9		11					6	13	3					8				12[1]	10
22	A	Kilmarnock	6,208	1-2	1	2		4	5		14	8	7		11					6	10	3				12					7	13[1]
30	A	Rangers	50,032	0-3	1	2		4	5		7	8		12	11											6	3				9	10
May 6	H	Dundee United	8,580	3-0	1	2	13	4	5		7	8		12[1]	11[2]	14						3					9				9	10
14	H	Hibernian	5,060	1-0	1	2		4	5		7	8[1]		10	11	12						3					9				9	13
21	H	Aberdeen	6,449	0-2	1	2		4	5	13	7	8		10	11					6				14	3		9					12
TOTAL FULL APPEARANCES					35	32	10	34	19	11	32	35	20	18	31		15	2	14	18	3	21	1			14	16	2	1	1	6	5
TOTAL SUB APPEARANCES							(2)		(1)	(3)	(4)		(2)	(13)		(2)			(9)	(3)	(2)	(9)	(10)	(3)	(4)	(1)	(1)	(1)	(4)		(3)	(4)
TOTAL GOALS SCORED									2	1	1	4	2	6	13	2	1			4	1						1	1			1	3

Small bold figures denote goalscorers. † denotes opponent's own goal.

Dens Park Stadium

CAPACITY: 11,850 (All Seated)

PITCH DIMENSIONS: 115 yds x 74 yds

FACILITIES FOR DISABLED SUPPORTERS:
There is provision for disabled supporters in both the East and West Stands.

Team playing kits

FIRST CHOICE

Shirt: Navy Blue with White Panel down Raglan Sleeve and Under Arm. Collar White.

Shorts: Navy Blue with Broad White Side Panels and White Piping Leg Band.

Stockings: Navy Blue with Two White Hoops on Tops.

SECOND CHOICE

Shirt: Red with Navy Blue Piping and Navy Blue Collar.

Shorts: White with Red Side Panels.

Stockings: Navy Blue with Red Ankle Band and Red Stripe on Tops.

How to get there

You can reach Dens Park Stadium by the following routes:

BUSES: There is a frequent service of buses from the city centre. Nos. 1A and 1B leave from Albert Square and Nos. 18, 19 and 21 leave from Commercial Street.

TRAINS: Trains from all over the country pass through the mainline Dundee station and fans can then proceed to the ground by the above buses from stops situated close to the station.

CARS: Cars may be parked in the car park (Densfield Park) and local streets adjacent to the ground.

Dundee F.C. is a member of The Scottish Premier League

Dundee United

Tannadice Park, Tannadice Street,
Dundee, DD3 7JW

**CHAIRMAN/MANAGING
DIRECTOR**
James Y. McLean

VICE-CHAIRMAN
Douglas B. Smith

DIRECTORS
Alistair B. Robertson,
William M. Littlejohn &
Donald T. Ridgway

CLUB SECRETARY
Spence Anderson

ASSISTANT CLUB SECRETARY
Mrs. Elisabeth Leslie

MANAGER
Alexander N. Smith

ASSISTANT MANAGER
John Blackley

COACHING STAFF
Maurice Malpas,
Ian Campbell & Graeme Liveston

CLUB DOCTOR
Dr. Derek J. McCormack

PHYSIOTHERAPIST
David Rankine

CHIEF SCOUT
Graeme Liveston

GROUNDSMAN
Peter Fox

**FOOTBALL SAFETY OFFICERS'
ASSOCIATION REPRESENTATIVE**
David Anderson (01382) 833166

**COMMUNITY
DEVELOPMENT OFFICER**
John Holt

COMMERCIAL MANAGER
Bill Campbell (01382) 832202

MATCHDAY PROGRAMME EDITOR
Peter Rundo

TELEPHONES
Ground (01382) 833166
Fax (01382) 889398
Clubcall (0891) 881909

E-MAIL & INTERNET ADDRESS
dundee.united.fc@cableinet.co.uk
www.dundeeunitedfc.co.uk

CLUB SHOP
The United Shop, Unit 2,
5 Victoria Road, Dundee
Tel/Fax (01382) 204066 -
Open 9.00 a.m. to 5.30 p.m.
Mon-Fri, 9.00a.m. to 5.00 p.m. Sat
Souvenir shops are also situated
within the ground in the East and
George Fox Stands and are open
on home match days.

OFFICIAL SUPPORTERS CLUB
Andrew Woodrow, Secretary,
Federation of Dundee United
Supporters Clubs, 3 Stevenson
Avenue, Glenrothes, Fife, KY6 1EE
(01592) 752129

TEAM CAPTAIN
Jason De Vos

SHIRT SPONSOR
Telewest Communications

KIT SUPPLIER
TFG Sports

LIST OF PLAYERS 2000-2001

Squad No.	Name	Place & date of birth	Previous Club	Lge Career Apps	Gls
1	Alan Combe	Edinburgh 3.4.74	St Mirren	45	-
5	Jason de Vos	London, Ontario 2.1.74	Darlington	58 (2)	2
26	Hugh Davidson	Dundee 3.8.80	Dundee United BC	17 (6)	-
7	Craig Easton	Bellshill 26.2.79	Dundee United BC	71(22)	3
13	Paul Gallacher	Glasgow 16.8.79	Lochee United	1	-
17	Jim Hamilton	Aberdeen 9.2.76	Aberdeen	8 (5)	1
4	David Hannah	Coatbridge 4.8.73	Celtic	96(16)	14
25	Stephen McConalogue	Glasgow 16.6.81	Dundee United BC	9(8)	-
32	David McCracken	Glasgow 16.10.81	Dundee United BC	2	-
35	Kevin McDonald	Rutherglen 23.1.81	Dundee United BC	-	-
2	John McQuillan	Stranraer 20.7.70	St Johnstone	11	-
9	Alex Mathie	Bathgate 20.12.68	Ipswich Town	23(11)	5
31	Sean O'Connor	Wolverhampton 7.8.81	Hednesford Town	1	-
22	Pat Onstad	Vancouver 13.1.68	Rochester Raging Rhinos	-	-
21	David Partridge	Westminster 26.11.78	West Ham United	29 (1)	-
18	Jim Paterson	Bellshill 25.9.79	Dundee United BC	16 (7)	1
27	Tony Smith	Bellshill 28.10.73	Airdrie	4 (3)	-
19	Steve Thompson	Paisley 14.10.78	Dundee United BC	24(27)	2
8	Anastasios Venetis	Larissa, Greece 24.3.80	Larissa	12 (5)	-
20	David Worrell	Dublin 12.1.78	Blackburn Rovers	13 (5)	-

NEW SIGNINGS

15	Mvondo Atangana	Yaounde, 10.7.79	Tonnerre Kalara		
14	Hasney Aljofree	Manchester 11.7.78	Bolton Wanderers		
24	Jamie Buchan	Manchester 3.4.77	Aberdeen		
6	Joachim Fernandez	Zijuinchor, Senegal 16.12.72	AC Milan		
16	Danny Griffin	Belfast 10.8.77	St Johnstone		
11	Neil Heaney	Middlesbrough 3.11.71	Darlington		
12	Stephane Leoni	St Mihiel, France 5.3.76	Bristol Rovers		
28	John Licina	Belfort, France 6.8.76	Sochaux		
10	Alphonse Tchami	Kekem, Cameroon 14.2.71	Al Wasl Sports Club		
3	Stephen Wright	Bellshill 27.8.71	Bradford City		

Milestones

YEAR OF FORMATION: 1923 (1909 as Dundee Hibs)
MOST CAPPED PLAYER: Maurice Malpas
NO. OF CAPS: 55
MOST LEAGUE POINTS IN A SEASON: 60 (Premier Division - Season 1986/87) (2 Points for a Win)
67 (First Division - Season 1995/96) (3 Points for a Win)
MOST LEAGUE GOALS SCORED BY A PLAYER IN A SEASON: John Coyle (Season 1955/56)
NO. OF GOALS SCORED: 41
RECORD ATTENDANCE: 28,000 (-v- Barcelona – 16.11.1966)
RECORD VICTORY: 14-0 (-v- Nithsdale Wanderers – Scottish Cup, 17.1.1931)
RECORD DEFEAT: 1-12 (-v- Motherwell – Division 2, 23.1.1954)

The Terrors' ten year league record

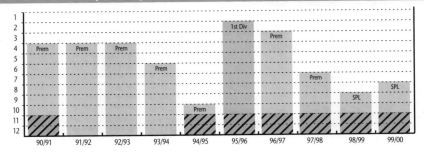

THE TERRORS' CLUB FACTFILE 1999/2000
RESULTS... APPEARANCES... SCORERS... ATTENDANCES...

Date	Venue	Opponents	Att.	Res	Combe A.	Pascual B.	Skoldmark M.	De Vos J.	Worrell D.	Jonsson S.	Davidson H.	Hannah D.	Paterson J.	Dodds W.	Thompson S.	Ferraz J.	Easton C.	Partridge D.	Mathie A.	Smith R.	Telesnikov I.	Delauney J.	Venetis A.	McCulloch S.	Bove R.	McConalogue S.	Malpas M.	Preget A.	Byrne D.	Hamilton J.	Gallacher P.	Jenkins I.	Patterson D.	McQuillan J.	O'Connor S.	Jenkinson L.	McCracken D.
Jul 31	H	Dundee	11,693	2-1	1	2	3^1	4	5	6	7	8	9	10	11	12^1	13																				
Aug 7	A	Motherwell	6,791	2-2	1	2	3	4	5	6	7	8	9	10^1	11	12^1	13																				
15	H	Celtic	12,375	2-1	1	2		5	4	6		12	8	7	10^1	11			9^1	3																	
21	A	Rangers	48,849	1-4	1	12		5	4^1	6		8	7	10	11	12	9	3	13	14																	
29	H	Kilmarnock	6,621	0-0	1	12		5	4	2		8	7	10	13	11	9	3			6																
Sep 11	H	Hibernian	8,167	3-1	1	2	14	4				8^1	7	10^1	12	11	9	3			6^1	5	13														
18	A	Aberdeen	11,814	2-1	1	2		4	5	6		8^1		10^1	12	11	9	3			7																
25	H	Heart of Midlothian	8,510	0-2	1	2		4		5	13	8	7	10		11	9	3			6			12													
Oct 17	A	Dundee	9,484	2-0	1	2	12	4				6	8	10^1	11^1		9	3			7	5															
23	H	Motherwell	6,213	0-2	1	2		4				6	8	10	11	12	9	3			7	13	5	14													
27	A	St. Johnstone	4,236	1-0	1	2		4	5			6	8		11	12	3				7		9														
31	A	Hibernian	11,073	2-3	1	2		4	5			6	8	10^1		11	9	3			7^1		12	13													
Nov 6	H	Aberdeen	8,170	3-1	1	2		4	5			6	8	9^1	10^2		12	3			7		13	11													
20	A	Kilmarnock	7,012	1-1	1	2		4	5			6	8^1		10	11	13	9	3		7		12			14											
27	H	St. Johnstone	6,367	1-0	1	2		4	12			6	8		10	11		9	3		7^1		5														
Dec 5	A	Heart of Midlothian	10,598	0-3	1	2		4	5			13			11	14	9	3	12	7		8	6		10												
12	H	Dundee	9,185	1-0	1	2		4	13			6	8		11	12^1	9	3			5	7		10													
18	A	Celtic	58,181	1-4	1	2	6	4	5						11	10^1	9	3			12		8			13		7	14								
27	A	Aberdeen	16,586	1-3	1	2	12	4	5	6	7	8^1			11	10	9	3						13													
Jan 22	H	Hibernian	7,457	0-0	1	2		4	14	5		8			11	13	9	3	10		6						7		12								
Feb 2	A	Rangers	11,241	0-4	1	2		5	4			6	7	8	11	14		3	10	9				13			12										
26	A	St. Johnstone	4,732	0-2		2						6	8		11	14	9			12				13	3	7			10	1	4	5					
Mar 4	H	Heart of Midlothian	6,928	0-1	1	2		4		6		8			11	13		3		7	14					12	10					5	6				
15	H	Kilmarnock	6,966	2-2	1	2		4		7	12	8^1			13^1		9	3	11			14	6				10					5					
25	H	Aberdeen	6,723	1-1	1	2		4		6					12	11^1	9			7		8			5		10					3			13		
Apr 1	H	Hibernian	10,264	0-1	1	2		4		6		8			11	14			7		13	5				10					3	12				
4	A	Rangers	45,829	0-3	1	2		4	6			8			13	11	10	5		7	9				12					3	14					
8	A	Kilmarnock	6,037	0-1	1	2		4	6			8			10	11	7	5	14		12					13					3	9				
15	H	Rangers	11,419	0-2	1			4				8			13				2	14	12		9	7	11	6		10		5	3					
19	A	Motherwell	4,271	3-1	1	2		4^1				14	8^1			12	3	10^1			9	7	11	6		13		5								
22	H	Heart of Midlothian	12,604	2-1	1	2		4				12	8			13	3	10^2			9	7	11	6		14		5								
29	H	St. Johnstone	5,843	0-1	1	2		4				13	8			14	12	3	10			9	7	11	6				5							
May 2	H	Celtic	7,449	0-1	1			4				6	8		13	11	12	5	10		7		9								3				2	
6	A	Dundee	8,580	0-3	1	12		4				8			13	11	9	3	10		6		7			14					5	2				
13	H	Motherwell	5,908	1-2	1			4				8			13			10	5	6		7		11	12		9^1			2			3				
21	A	Celtic	56,749	0-2	1			4				6	8		12		14	10	3	7			13	11	5		9			2						
TOTAL FULL APPEARANCES					35	30	7	35	10	14	17	33	8	15	16	15	22	29	10	4	22	1	12	10		9	8	3		8	1	1	6	11	1	1	2
TOTAL SUB APPEARANCES						(2)	(3)		(3)		(7)			(10)	(13)	(10)		(2)	(3)	(3)			(5)	(5)	(1)	(7)	(4)	(1)	(1)	(5)						(3)	
TOTAL GOALS SCORED							1	2				6	1	9	1	6	1		3	3													1			

Small bold figures denote goalscorers. † denotes opponent's own goal.

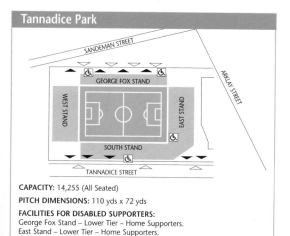

Tannadice Park

SANDEMAN STREET — ARKLAY STREET — TANNADICE STREET — GEORGE FOX STAND — WEST STAND — EAST STAND — SOUTH STAND

CAPACITY: 14,255 (All Seated)

PITCH DIMENSIONS: 110 yds x 72 yds

FACILITIES FOR DISABLED SUPPORTERS:
George Fox Stand – Lower Tier – Home Supporters.
East Stand – Lower Tier – Home Supporters.
West Stand – Away Supporters.

Team playing kits

FIRST CHOICE
Shirt: Tangerine with Black Crew Neck and Black Cuffs.
Shorts: Black with Tangerine Side Stripes.
Stockings: Tangerine with Black Turnover.

SECOND CHOICE
Shirt: Green 'V' Neck with Black Collar and White Trim and Tangerine Piping from Shoulder to Underarm.
Shorts: White with Two Sets of Tangerine Piping down both Sides.
Stockings: White with Tangerine and Green Thin Stripe on Turnover.

THIRD CHOICE
Shirt: Black with Tangerine Panel edged with Green Stripe across Shoulder and Down Sleeve. White and Green Collar.
Shorts: Black with Tangerine Side Panels.
Stockings: Tangerine with Black Leg Hoop and Black Hoop on Tops.

How to get there

Tannadice Park can be reached by the following routes:
BUSES: The following buses leave from the city centre at frequent intervals:- Nos. 1a, 18, 19 and 21 from Meadowside and No. 20 from Littlewoods High Street.
TRAINS: Trains from all over the country pass through the main Dundee station and fans can then proceed to the ground by the above bus services from stops situated within walking distance of the station.
CARS: There is parking in the streets adjacent to the ground.

Dundee United F.C. is a member of The Scottish Premier League

East End Park, Halbeath Road,
Dunfermline, Fife, KY12 7RB

CHAIRMAN
John W. Yorkston

DIRECTORS
C. Roy Woodrow, William M. Rennie,
Gavin G. Masterton, C.B.E., F.I.B. (Scot),
Andrew T. Gillies, John Meiklem,
W. Brian Robertson, W.S.,
Graham A Thomson &
Francis M. McConnell, SSC.

SECRETARY/GENERAL MANAGER
Paul A. M. D'Mello

HEAD COACH
James Calderwood

ASSISTANT HEAD COACH
James Nicholl

PRINCIPAL COACHING STAFF
Hamish French & Joe Nelson

CHIEF SCOUT
Robert Paton

CLUB DOCTOR
Dr. Gerry D. Gillespie

PHYSIOTHERAPIST
Philip Yeates, M.C.S.P.

YOUTH DEVELOPMENT MANAGER
John B. Ritchie

FOOTBALL SAFETY OFFICERS' ASSOCIATION REPRESENTATIVE/ SECURITY ADVISOR
David Dickson
Tel: (01383) 725557

STADIUM MANAGER
Brian Gallagher

HEAD GROUNDMAN
John Wilson

COMMERCIAL MANAGER
Miss Audrey M. Bastianelli

MATCHDAY PROGRAMME EDITOR
Duncan Simpson

TELEPHONES
Ground/Commercial/Ticket Office
(01383) 724295/721749
Fax (01383) 723468
Clubcall (0930) 555060

CLUB SHOP
Situated at Ground
Open 9.00 a.m. – 5.00 p.m.
Mon to Sat. Tel: (01383) 724295

OFFICIAL SUPPORTERS CLUB
c/o Mrs. Joan Malcolm, Secretary,
Dunfermline Athletic
Supporters Club,
13 South Knowe,
Crossgates, KY4 8AW

TEAM CAPTAIN
Ian Ferguson

SHIRT SPONSOR
Auto Windscreens

KIT SUPPLIERS
TFG Sports

LIST OF PLAYERS 2000-2001

Squad No.	Name	Place & date of birth	Previous Club	Lge Career Apps	Gls
10	Lee Bullen	Edinburgh 24-9-71	PAE Kalamata	11 (2)	7
17	Owen Coyle	Paisley 14-7-66	Motherwell	34 (7)	10
9	Stephen Crawford	Dunfermline 9-1-74	Hibernian	25	16
3	Jason Dair	Dunfermline 11-6-74	Raith Rovers	31 (3)	1
2	Michel Doesborg	Beverwyk 10-8-68	Motherwell	5	-
8	Ian Ferguson	Glasgow 15-3-67	Rangers	12	2
22	David Graham	Edinburgh 6-10-78	Rangers	14 (22)	4
12	Steven Hampshire	Edinburgh 17-10-79	Chelsea	11 (8)	3
26	Chris McGroarty	Bellshill 6-12-81	Rosyth Rec U-18	17 (8)	-
27	Craig Martin	Uphall 10-11-78	Links Utd U-18	2 (1)	-
15	Eddie May	Edinburgh 30-8-67	Motherwell	19 (4)	2
14	David Moss	Doncaster 15-11-68	Falkirk	18 (6)	6
28	Colin Nish	Edinburgh 17-3-81	Rosyth Rec U-18	- (4)	-
11	Stewart Petrie	Dundee 20-2-70	Forfar Athletic	186(35)	43
25	John Potter	Dunfermline 15-12-79	Celtic	17 (4)	1
19	Brian Reid	Paisley 15-6-70	Burnley	21 (2)	3
4	Justin Skinner	London 30-1-69	Hibernian	26 (2)	-
29	Chris Templeman	Kirkcaldy 12-1-80	Rosyth Rec U-18	5 (9)	-
6	Scott M Thomson	Aberdeen 29-1-72	Raith Rovers	48 (2)	4
18	Andrew Tod	Dunfermline 4-11-71	Kelty Hearts	206 (12)	34

NEW SIGNINGS

16	Rob Matthei	Amsterdam 20-9-66	Motherwell		
7	Junior Mendes	London 15-0-76	St Mirren		
21	Barry Nicholson	Dumfries 24-8-78	Rangers		
1	Marco Ruitenbeek	Weesp 12-5-68	Go Ahead Eagles		
5	Andrius Skerla	Vilnius 29-4-77	PSV Eindhoven		
20	Scott Y Thomson	Edinburgh 8-11-66	Airdrie		

Milestones

YEAR OF FORMATION: 1885
MOST CAPPED PLAYER: Istvan Kozma
NO. OF CAPS: Hungary 29 (13 whilst with Dunfermline Athletic)
MOST LEAGUE POINTS IN A SEASON: 65 (First Division – Season 1993/94) (2 Points for a Win)
71 (First Division – Seasons 1995/96 and 1999/2000) (3 Points for a Win)
MOST LEAGUE GOALS SCORED BY A PLAYER IN A SEASON: Bobby Skinner (Season 1925/26)
NO. OF GOALS SCORED: 53
RECORD ATTENDANCE: 27,816 (-v- Celtic – 30.4.1968)
RECORD VICTORY: 11-2 (-v- Stenhousemuir – Division 2, 27.9.1930)
RECORD DEFEAT: 0-10 (-v- Dundee – Division 2, 22.3.1947)

The Pars' ten year league record

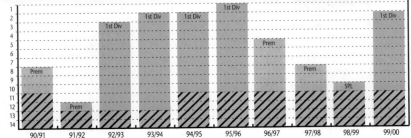

THE PARS' CLUB FACTFILE 1999/2000
RESULTS... APPEARANCES... SCORERS... ATTENDANCES...

Date	Venue	Opponents	Att.	Res	Westwater I.	Shields G.	McGroarty C.	Tod A.	Reid B.	Dolan J.	Thomson S.	May E.	Smith A.	Coyle O.	Petrie S.	Graham D.	Ireland C.	French H.	Nish C.	Dair J.	Huxford R.	Skinner J.	Moss D.	Potter J.	Hampshire S.	Crawford S.	Mampaey K.	Ferguson I.	Bullen L.	Doesburg M.	Templeman C.	McCarty M.
Aug 7	H	Inverness Cal. Th.	4,677	4-0	1	2	3	4	5[1]	6	7[1]	8	9[1]	10	11[1]	12	15															
14	A	Airdrieonians	2,930	2-2	1	2	3	4	5	6	7	8	9	10[2]	11			12	15													
21	H	Morton	4,030	2-1	1	2	3	4	5	6	7	8	9[2]	10	11			14	15													
28	H	Falkirk	6,520	1-1	1		14	4	5	6	2	8	9	10	11	15[1]		7	3													
Sep 4	A	Livingston	5,302	1-0	1			4	5	6		12	9	10[1]	11	15				8		3	2	7								
11	H	St. Mirren	6,128	1-1	1		15	4	5	6			9	10			11	12		3	2[1]	7	8									
18	A	Raith Rovers	6,087	2-2	1		3	4	5[1]	6	7		9[1]	10	11			12		2			8									
25	H	Ayr United	4,044	2-1	1			5	6	12	2	9	10[2]	11	15			3			7	8	4									
Oct 9	A	Clydebank	475	4-1	1			5[1]	6	7	2	9	10[1]	11	14	12[1]		3[1]		8			4									
16	H	Airdrieonians	3,964	0-0	1		14	5	6	11	2	9	10	15				3		8	12	4	7									
23	A	Inverness Cal. Th.	3,006	1-1	1			4	5	6	7	2	11	10	15			3		8	12	14	9[1]									
30	A	St. Mirren	6,130	1-3	1			4	5	6	2	15	11	12			3		7	8[1]	14	10	9									
Nov 6	H	Raith Rovers	6,953	1-1	1		3	4	5	2	10	6	11		8[1]		7	9															
14	H	Livingston	4,163	3-0	1		3	4	5	6	2	12	9	10			7	8[1]				15	11[2]									
20	A	Falkirk	4,263	3-1	1		3	4	5	6	2		10[1]	11			7	8				15	9[2]									
27	H	Clydebank	4,224	2-1	1			4	5	6	3	2	10	11[1]	8		7					12	9[1]									
Dec 4	A	Ayr United	2,113	3-0	1		15	4	5	6	3	2	10	11	8[2]		7	12				14	9[1]									
11	A	Morton	1,289	3-0	1		15	4	5	3	2	10[1]	11	6			7	8[1]		12	14	9[1]										
18	H	Inverness Cal. Th.	3,775	1-0	1		3	4[1]	5	10	11	12	2				7	8	6	9												
Jan 3	A	Raith Rovers	7,464	0-3	1		3	4	5	6	12	10	11	2			7	8		15	9											
8	A	Livingston	3,800	0-1	1		3	4	6	7	11	15	2	12	5	8	10	9														
15	H	Falkirk	7,233	2-2			6	4	2	10	11	15	3	5	12	14	7[1]	9[1]	1	8											
22	H	Ayr United	3,684	2-0			3	4	5	7	11	15	12	2	6	14	10[1]	9	1	8[1]											
Feb 5	A	Clydebank	601	3-1			12	4	2	7	11	15	3	6	5	14	9[2]	1	8	10[1]												
12	H	Morton	4,289	1-1			3	4	2	7	12	11	14	15	6	5	9	1	8	10[1]												
19	H	St. Mirren	7,132	1-1				4	3	12	11[1]	2	6	5	7	9	1	8	10													
26	A	Airdrieonians	2,304	2-1			15	4	3	12	11	2	14	6	5[1]	7	9	1	8	10[1]												
Mar 4	A	St. Mirren	6,938	2-0				4	2	12	11	15	3	14	6	5	7	9[2]	1	8	10											
18	H	Raith Rovers	6,694	0-2				4	2	15	14	11	12	3	8	6	5	7	9	1	10											
25	A	Falkirk	5,242	1-1				4	3	10	11	7	6[1]	5	9	1	8	16	2													
Apr 1	H	Livingston	4,337	4-1			15	6	7[1]	10[1]	11	14	3	4	5	9[1]	1	8	12[1]	2												
11	A	Ayr United	1,798	2-0				6	7	11	3	4	5	9[1]	1	8	10[1]	2														
15	H	Clydebank	4,969	6-0			15	6[1]	7[1]	12	11	14	3	4	5	9[2]	1	8[1]	10[1]	2												
22	A	Inverness Cal. Th.	2,677	2-1			3	6	7	12	11	4	15[1]	5	9	1	8	10[1]	2													
29	A	Airdrieonians	4,378	1-0			14	6	2	10	11	12[1]	8	3	4	5	9	1	7	15											
May 6	A	Morton	1,039	0-2	1		12	6	10	11	8	3	4	5	16	9	7	14	2												
TOTAL FULL APPEARANCES					22	3	13	27	21	19	28	19	11	23	32		1	13		22	2	26	18	17	11	25	14	12	11	5		1
TOTAL SUB APPEARANCES							(7)	(3)	(2)		(1)	(4)	(1)	(7)		(15)	(2)	(8)	(2)		(2)	(2)	(6)	(4)	(8)			(2)		(2)		
TOTAL GOALS SCORED									1	3		2	2	4	9	3		2		3	1	1	6	1	3	16			2		7	

Small bold figures denote goalscorers. † denotes opponent's own goal.

East End Park

NORTH STAND
NORRIE McCATHIE STAND
EAST STAND
SOUTH STAND
HALBEATH ROAD

CAPACITY: 12,565 (All Seated)
PITCH DIMENSIONS: 115 yds x 70 yds
FACILITIES FOR DISABLED SUPPORTERS:
12 spaces in East Stand for Away Supporters. 12 spaces in the Norrie McCathie Stand for Home Supporters. 24 seats for helpers.

Team playing kits

FIRST CHOICE
Shirt: Black and White Vertical Stripes. Black Collar with White Trim. Black 'V' Neck with Red Trim.
Shorts: Black with Red Side Panels Trimmed with White.
Stockings: Black with White Tops.

SECOND CHOICE
Shirt: Red.
Shorts: Red with White Piping on Sides.
Stockings: Red with White Tops.

How to get there

East End Park may be reached by the following routes:
TRAINS: Dunfermline Station is served by trains from both Glasgow and Edinburgh and the ground is a 15 minute walk from here.
BUSES: Buses destined for Kelty, Perth, St. Andrews and Kirkcaldy all pass close to East End Park.
CARS: Car Parking is available in a large car park adjoining the east end of the ground and there are also facilities in various side streets. Multi-storey car parking approximately 10 minutes walk from the ground.

Dunfermline Athletic F.C. is a member of The Scottish Premier League

Heart of Midlothian

Tynecastle Stadium, Gorgie Road,
Edinburgh, EH11 2NL

CHAIRMAN
Douglas A. Smith

DIRECTORS
Christopher P. Robinson,
Fraser S. Jackson, Stewart Fraser,
Brian J. Duffin & Andrew Flanagan

CHIEF EXECUTIVE
Christopher P. Robinson

P.A. to CHIEF EXECUTIVE
Irene McPhee (0131) 200 7245

**FINANCE DIRECTOR/
COMPANY SECRETARY**
Stewart Fraser

MANAGER
James Jefferies

ASSISTANT MANAGER
Billy Brown

COACH
Peter Houston

YOUTH COACH
John McGlynn

CLUB DOCTOR
Dr. Dewar Melvin

PHYSIOTHERAPIST
Alan Rae

KIT CONTROLLER
Norrie Gray

S.F.A. COMMUNITY OFFICER
Alan White (0131) 200 7242

CHIEF SCOUT
John Murray

PITCH MAINTENANCE
Souters of Stirling

RETAIL MANAGER
Clare Sargent (0131) 200 7211

**CORPORATE CONFERENCE/
BANQUETING**
Graeme Pacitti (0131) 200 7240

PUBLIC RELATIONS MANAGER
Douglas Dalgleish (0131) 200 7260

SALES MANAGER
Kenny Wittmann (0131) 200 7205

**FOOTBALL SAFETY OFFICERS'
ASSOCIATION REPRESENTATIVE**
James Johnstone (0370) 578858

STADIUM MANAGER
John Boag

TICKET MANAGER
Neil Hunter (0131) 200 7201

MATCHDAY PROGRAMME EDITOR
Douglas Dalgleish

TELEPHONES
Ground (0131) 200 7200
Fax (0131) 200 7222
Ticket Office (0131) 200 7201
Information Service (0131) 200 7255
Sales & Marketing (0131) 200 7205
Credit Card Bookings (0131) 200 7209
Superstore (0131) 200 7211
Clubcall (0891) 121183

E-MAIL & INTERNET ADDRESS
irene @homplc.co.uk
www.heartsfc.co.uk

CLUB SHOP
Heart of Midlothian Superstore,
Tynecastle Stadium, Gorgie Road,
Edinburgh. Tel (0131) 200 7211
Open 9.30 a.m. – 5.30 p.m.
Mon. to Sat. and match days.

OFFICIAL SUPPORTERS CLUB
Heart of Midlothian Federation,
John N. Borthwick, 21/9 Festival
Gardens, Edinburgh, EH11 1RB

TEAM CAPTAIN
Colin Cameron

SHIRT SPONSOR
Strongbow

KIT SUPPLIER
Errea

LIST OF PLAYERS 2000-2001

Squad No.	Name	Place & date of birth	Previous Club	Lge Career Apps	Gls
10	Lee Bullen	Edinburgh 24-9-71	PAE Kalamata	11 (2)	7
9	Stephane Adam	Lille, France 15.5.69	Metz	74 (10)	21
10	Colin Cameron	Kirkcaldy 23.10.72	Raith Rovers	111 (3)	32
14	Thomas Flogel	Vienna, Austria 7.6.71	Austria Vienna	59 (19)	8
8	Stephen Fulton	Greenock 10.8.70	Falkirk	130 (14)	11
31	Alisdair Graham	Lanark 17.8.80	Musselburgh Ath	- (1)	-
11	Darren Jackson	Edinburgh 25.7.66	Celtic	40 (4)	7
5	Kevin James	Edinburgh 3.12.75	Falkirk	9 (5)	-
20	Juanjo	Barcelona, Spain 4.5.77	Barcelona	3 (24)	3
24	Andrew Kirk	Belfast 3.5.79	Glentoran	1 (9)	-
4	Gary Locke	Keith 7.12.65	Whitehill Welfare	119(22)	5
13	Roddy McKenzie	Bellshill 6.8.75	Stenhousemuir	20 (2)	-
7	Gary McSwegan	Glasgow 24.9.70	Dundee United	40 (10)	21
16	Lee Makel	Sunderland 11.1.73	Huddersfield Town	20 (16)	1
28	Kenny Milne	Stirling 26.8.79	Edinburgh United	- (1)	-
12	Grant Murray	Edinburgh 29.8.75	Bonnyrigg Rose	43 (12)	-
3	Gary Naysmith	Edinburgh 16.11.78	Whitehill Welfare	83 (5)	3
26	Antti Niemi	Oulu, Finland 31.5.72	Rangers	17	-
30	Kris O'Neil	Edinburgh 29.9.80	Musselburgh Ath	- (3)	-
29	Robbie Neilson	Paisley 19.6.80	Rangers BC	-	-
6	Gordan Petric	Belgrade 30.7.69	AEK Athens	17 (1)	-
2	Steven Pressley	Elgin 11.10.73	Dundee United	65 (1)	1
1	Gilles Rousset	Hyeres, France 22.8.63	Rennes	132	-
19	Scott Severin	Stirling 15.2.79	Musselburgh Juniors	23 (7)	2
18	Fitzroy Simpson	Trowbridge 26.2.70	Portsmouth	7 (4)	-
21	Robert Tomaschek	Nitra, Slovakia 1972	Slovan Bratislava	13 (1)	-
15	Gary Wales	East Calder 4/1/79	Hamilton Accies	17 (8)	6

NEW SIGNINGS

17	Gordon Durie	Paisley 6.12.65	Rangers		

Milestones

YEAR OF FORMATION: 1874
MOST CAPPED PLAYER: Bobby Walker
NO. OF CAPS: 29
MOST LEAGUE POINTS IN A SEASON: 63 (Premier Division - Season 1991/92)(2 Points for a Win)
67 (Premier Division - Season 1997/98)(3 Points for a Win)
MOST LEAGUE GOALS SCORED BY A PLAYER IN A SEASON: Barney Battles (Season 1930/31)
NO. OF GOALS SCORED: 44
RECORD ATTENDANCE: 53,396 (-v- Rangers – 13.2.1932)
RECORD VICTORY: 21-0 (-v- Anchor – EFA Cup, 1880)
RECORD DEFEAT: 1-8 (-v- Vale of Leven – Scottish Cup, 1883)

The Jam Tarts' ten year league record

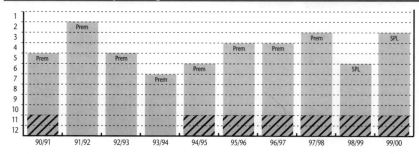

THE JAM TARTS' CLUB FACTFILE 1999/2000
RESULTS… APPEARANCES… SCORERS… ATTENDANCES…

Note: small bold figures after a shirt number denote goalscorers and are shown here as [n]. † denotes opponent's own goal.

Date	Venue	Opponents	Att.	Res	Rousset G.	Presley S.	James K.	Murray G.	Severin S.	Fulton S.	Flögel T.	Cameron C.	Adam S.	McSwegan G.	Jackson D.	Makel L.	Perez J.	Wales G.	Naysmith G.	Locke G.	Ritchie P.	Quitongo J.	McKinnon R.	Leclercq F.	McKenzie R.	Graham A.	Petric G.	Niemi A.	Simpson F.	Milne K.	Tomaschek R.	Kirk A.
Jul 31	A	St. Johnstone	†6,707	4-1	1	2	3	4	5	6	7[1]	8[1]	9	10[1]	11	12	13	14														
Aug 7	H	Rangers	17,893	0-4	1	2	5	4	6	7		9	8	10		11	14	12	3	13												
Aug 14	H	Hibernian	15,858	1-1	1	2	3		5	6	7	8	9	10[1]	11			12		13			4									
Aug 22	H	Aberdeen	12,803	3-0	1			4	6	12	7	8	9	10[3]	11				3				5									
Aug 29	A	Celtic	60,107	0-4	1	2		4	6	14		9	8	12	10	11			3	7	5	13										
Sep 11	H	Dundee	13,378	4-0	1	2		4		6[1]	7	8[1]	9[1]	10	11[1]	12	13		3	14	5											
Sep 25	A	Dundee United	8,510	2-0	1	2		4	12	6	13	7	8	9[2]	10	11			3	14	5											
Oct 16	A	St. Johnstone	12,872	1-1	1	2		4	6	13	7	8		10[1]	11	12		9	3		5											
Oct 27	H	Kilmarnock	12,541	2-2	1	2		4	6	13	7	8[1]	9	10	11	14[1]		12	3		5											
Oct 30	A	Dundee	6,018	0-1	1	2		4		6	7		8	13	10	11	14	12	3	9	5											
Nov 6	H	Motherwell	12,514	1-1	1	2			4	13	7	12	8	9	10[1]	11		14	3	6	5											
Nov 20	H	Celtic	17,184	1-2	1	2			6	9	11	8[1]		10	13				3	7	5	4	12									
Nov 23	A	Motherwell	7,793	1-2	1	2			14		8	9		10[1]	11	13			3	7	5	4	6	12								
Nov 27	A	Kilmarnock	8,326	2-2	1	2			13	6	9	11	8	12	10[1]	14			3	7	5[1]	4	1									
Dec 5	H	Dundee United	10,598	3-0		2	13	4	6	7		9[1]		10	11[1]	8[1]	12		3		5			1	14							
Dec 8	A	Aberdeen	10,274	1-3		2			6[1]	9		8		10	11	13	12		3	7	4			5								
Dec 19	H	Hibernian	17,954	0-3		2	12		6	9		8		10	11	14	13		3				4		5			1	7			
Dec 22	A	Rangers	49,907	0-1		2		4	12			8	11	10					3	7			6		5			1	9	13		
Jan 22	H	Dundee	13,112	2-0		2		4	6	9		8			11[1]				3	7			12		13			1	5			
Feb 5	A	Celtic	59,735	3-2		2		4			9	8[2]	12		11				10	3[1]					5			1	7		6	13
Feb 26	H	Kilmarnock	14,243	0-0	1	2		4			9	8		12	11				10	3			5						7		6	
Mar 1	A	Motherwell	5,588	2-0		2		4	12		9	8	14	13	11[1]				10[1]	3			5						7		6	
Mar 4	A	Dundee United	6,928	1-0		2		4			9	8[1]		12	11				10	3			5		13				7		6	
Mar 15	A	St. Johnstone	4,468	1-0		2		4	7		9	8	14	10[1]	13	12			11	3			5					1			6	
Mar 18	A	Hibernian	15,908	1-3		2		4			8	12	9	11[1]	13				10	3			6		5			1			7	
Mar 22	H	Aberdeen	13,249	3-0		2		14	6[1]		7	8[1]	9	13	11				5	10[1]			3			15	4	1				
Mar 25	H	Motherwell	13,702	0-0		2			6		7	8	9	12	11				5	10			3				4					
Apr 1	A	Dundee	6,291	0-0	1	2			13	6	7	8	9	12	11				5	10			3				4		14			
Apr 8	H	Celtic	16,046	1-0		2			13	7	8	9		10[1]	11				5	12			3				4	1	14		6	
Apr 12	H	Rangers	16,314	1-2		2			8	12	7	9		10[1]	11				5				3				4	1	13		6	
Apr 15	A	Aberdeen	12,626	2-1		2		12	14		8	9		13	11[1]				5	10[1]			3				4	1	7		6	
Apr 22	H	Dundee United	12,604	1-0		2		12			7	8	9		11				5	10[1]			3				4	1			6	13
Apr 29	A	Kilmarnock	8,057	1-0		2		13			12	7	8	9	11				5	10[1]			3				4	1	14		6	
May 6	H	St. Johnstone	12,368	0-0		2				8	7	12	9		11				5	14	10		3		13		4	1			6	
May 13	A	Rangers	49,140	0-1		2		5	14		9	8		12		6	13		10	3			4					1			7	11
May 21	H	Hibernian	17,391	2-1		2		13	6		7	8		10[1]	11				5	9[1]			3				4	1			14	12
TOTAL FULL APPEARANCES					16	36	8	15	18	16	28	31	18	23	31	11	2	17	34	9	14		3	8	3		17	17	7		13	1
TOTAL SUB APPEARANCES						(2)	(6)	(6)	(10)	(1)	(1)	(7)	(7)	(4)	(6)	(13)	(7)	(1)	(4)		(1)	(2)	(2)	(1)	(1)				(4)	(1)	(1)	(3)
TOTAL GOALS SCORED									2	1	1	8	4	13	6			3	6	1	1											

Small bold figures denote goalscorers. † denotes opponent's own goal.

Tynecastle Stadium

Stadium plan: Wheatfield Road / Wheatfield Stand; Gorgie Road / Gorgie Stand; Roseburn Stand / Russell Road; Main Stand / McLeod Street.

CAPACITY: 18,000 (All Seated)

PITCH DIMENSIONS: 107 yds x 74 yds

FACILITIES FOR DISABLED SUPPORTERS:
There are 15 spaces for visiting fans at the Roseburn Stand. Regarding facilities for home supporters, fans should contact the club in advance for availability.

Team playing kits

FIRST CHOICE

Shirt: Maroon with White Round Neck. Cuffs White.
Shorts: White with Maroon Piping on Sides.
Stockings: Maroon with White Ankle Band.

SECOND CHOICE

Shirt: White with Maroon Round Neck. Cuffs Maroon.
Shorts: Maroon with White Piping on Sides.
Stockings: White with Maroon Ankle Band.

How to get there

Tynecastle Stadium can be reached by the following routes:

BUSES: A frequent service of buses leaves from the city centre, Nos. 1, 2, 3, 4, 33, 34, 35 and 44 all pass the ground.

TRAINS: Haymarket Station is about half a mile from the ground.

CARS: Car Parking facilities exist in the adjacent side streets in Robertson Avenue and also the Westfield area.

Heart of Midlothian F.C. is a member of The Scottish Premier League

Hibernian

Easter Road Stadium,
12 Albion Place,
Edinburgh, EH7 5QG

CHAIRMAN
Malcolm H. McPherson

MANAGING DIRECTOR
Rod M. Petrie

DIRECTORS
Stephen W. Dunn, Erick Davidson
& Colin I.M. Deas

SECRETARY
Mrs Gillian Coleman

MANAGER
Alexander McLeish

ASSISTANT MANAGER
Andy Watson

COACH
Donald Park

CLUB DOCTOR
Dr. Tom Schofield

PHYSIOTHERAPIST
Malcolm Colquhoun

S.F.A. COMMUNITY COACH
Malcolm J. Thomson

**YOUTH DEVELOPMENT
OFFICER/CHIEF SCOUT**
John Park

COMMERCIAL DIRECTOR
Colin Deas

CATERING MANAGER
Craig Samson

**BUSINESS DEVELOPMENT
MANAGER**
Beverley Thorpe

STADIUM MANAGER
Garry O'Hagen

**FOOTBALL SAFETY OFFICERS'
ASSOCIATION REPRESENTATIVE**
Gordon Jackson (0131) 313 0507

HEAD GROUNDSMAN
Tom McCourt

MATCHDAY PROGRAMME EDITOR
James Alexander

TELEPHONES
Ground/Commercial (0131) 661 2159
Fax (0131) 659 6488/652 1907
Ticket Office (0131) 661 1875
Information Service (0891) 707070

E-MAIL & INTERNET ADDRESS
club@hibernianfc.co.uk
www.hibernianfc.co.uk

CLUB SHOP
26 Albion Place, Edinburgh
Open Tue.-Sat.: 9.00a.m. - 5.00p.m.,
Home Match Days:
9.30a.m. - 3.00p.m.
Away First Team Match Days:
9.00a.m. - 5.00p.m.
Tel (0131) 656 7078/7079

OFFICIAL SUPPORTERS CLUB
11 Sunnyside Lane, Off Easter Road,
Edinburgh, EH7

TEAM CAPTAIN
Franck Sauzee

SHIRT SPONSOR
Carlsberg

KIT SUPPLIER
Le Coq Sportif

LIST OF PLAYERS 2000-2001

Squad No.	Name	Place & date of birth	Previous Club	Lge Career Apps	Gls
23	Scott Bannerman	Edinburgh 21.3.79	Hutchison Vale BC	2 (12)	-
24	Emilio Bottiglieri	Port Hardy, Canada 13.4.79	Metro Ford	- (1)	-
8	Grant Brebner	Edinburgh 6.12.77	Reading	36(1)	1
1	Nick Colgan	Drogheda 19.9.73	Bournemouth	24	-
2	Derek Collins	Glasgow 15.4.69	Morton	39 (1)	-
22	Mark Dempsie	Bellshill 19.10.80	Hibernian BC	12(4)	-
19	Fabrice Henry	Argenteuil, France 13.2.68	Basle	20 (2)	1
21	Matthais Jack	Leipzig, Germany 15.2.69	Fortuna Dusseldorf	6 (3)	-
10	Russell Latapy	Trinidad & Tobago 2.8.68	Boavista	51	15
16	Dirk Lehmann	Aachen, Germany 16.8.71	Fulham	18 (12)	7
7	Stuart Lovell	Sydney, Australia 9.1.72	Reading	45 (11)	12
3	Paul Lovering	Glasgow 25.11.75	Clydebank	26 (1)	1
5	Martin McIntosh	East Kilbride 19.3.71	Stockport County	9	-
27	Thomas McManus	Glasgow 28.2.81	'S' Form	1 (2)	-
28	Ian Murray	Edinburgh 20.3.81	Dundee United	8 (1)	-
9	Mixu Paatelainen	Helsinki, Finland 3.2.67	Wolverhampton W	50 (7)	21
28	Alan Reid	Paisley 21.10.80	Renfrew Victoria	- (2)	-
4	Frank Sauzee	Aubenas, France 28.10.65	Montpellier	33 (1)	7
17	Tom Smith	Glasgow 12.10.73	Clydebank	24(2)	-

NEW SIGNINGS

Squad No.	Name	Place & date of birth	Previous Club		
15	Lyndon Andrews	Trinidad & Tobago 20.1.76	Joe Public (Trinidad)		
14	Paul Fenwick	London 25.8.69	Raith Rovers		
3	Ulrich Laursen	Denmark 28.2.76	OB Odense		
11	John O'Neil	Bellshill 6.7.71	St Johnstone		
25	Hakim Sar-Temeoury	France 6.3.81	Nantes		
18	Gary Smith	Glasgow 25.3.71	Aberdeen		
13	Ian Westwater	Loughborough 6.11.63	Dunfermline Athletic		
20	David Zitelli	France 3.10.68	Strasbourg		

Milestones

YEAR OF FORMATION: 1875
MOST CAPPED PLAYER: Lawrie Reilly
NO. OF CAPS: 38
MOST LEAGUE POINTS IN A SEASON: 57 (First Division – Season 1980/81)(2 Points for a Win)
89 (First Division – Season 1998/99)(3 Points for a Win)
MOST LEAGUE GOALS SCORED BY A PLAYER IN A SEASON: Joe Baker (Season 1959/60)
NO. OF GOALS SCORED: 42
RECORD ATTENDANCE: 65,860 (-v- Heart of Midlothian – 2.1.1950)
RECORD VICTORY: 22-1 (-v- 42nd Highlanders 3.9.1881)
RECORD DEFEAT: 0-10 (-v- Rangers – 24.12.1898)

The Hibees' ten year league record

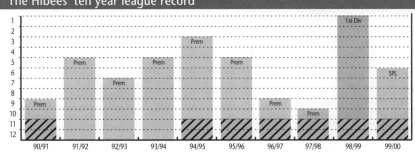

THE HIBEES' CLUB FACTFILE 1999/2000
RESULTS... APPEARANCES... SCORERS... ATTENDANCES...

Player columns (left to right): Gottskalksson O., Lovering P., Renwick M., Dennis S., Jack M., Sauzee F., Henry F., Latapy R., Lovell S., Crawford S., Lehmann D., Hartley P., Skinner J., McGinlay J., Paatelainen M.M., Miller K., Collins D., Brebner G., Hughes J., Dempsie M., Smith T., Colgan N., Bannerman S., Murray I., Jean E., McIntosh M., McManus T., Reid A.

Date	Venue	Opponents	Att.	Res	Got	Lov	Ren	Den	Jac	Sau	Hen	Lat	Lvl	Cra	Leh	Har	Ski	McG	Paa	Mil	Col	Bre	Hug	Dem	Smi	Cog	Ban	Mur	Jea	McI	McM	Rei
Jul 31	H	Motherwell	13,015	2-2	1	2	3	4	5	6	7	8	9	10	11²	12	13															
Aug 8	A	Dundee	6,050	4-3	1	2	3	4	5	6²	7	8			11¹	13		9	10	12¹												
Aug 14	H	Heart of Midlothian	15,858	1-1	1	2	3	4	5	9	6	8	7¹		11	12		6	10	13	14											
Aug 21	A	St. Johnstone	6,165	†1-1	1		3	4	5	9	6	8			11	12			10		2	7										
Aug 28	H	Rangers	15,587	0-1	1		3	4		6	12	8			11	10		9	13	14	2	7	5									
Sep 11	A	Dundee United	8,167	1-3	1	2		4	5	6		8¹	13		11	10		9	12			7	3									
Sep 19	A	Kilmarnock	11,219	0-3	1	2	3	4	5	6		8			11	12		9	13	14		7										
Sep 25	H	Celtic	14,747	0-2	1	2	3	4	5	6		8	9		12	13	11		10			7	14									
Oct 2	A	Aberdeen	11,876	2-2	1		3	4	5¹			8	9	13				14	10¹	12	2	7	6									
Oct 16	A	Motherwell	7,559	2-2	1			4	3	6		8¹			13	12		9	10¹	11		7	5	2									
Oct 23	H	Dundee	10,162	5-2	1			4	3	6¹		8²			13¹	12		9	10	11¹		7	5	2									
Oct 31	H	Dundee United	11,073	†3-2	1			4	3	6	13	8²						9	10	11	12	7	5	2									
Nov 6	A	Kilmarnock	8,735	2-0				4		6		8			13	12		9	10	11²	2	7	5		3	1						
Nov 20	A	Rangers	49,544	0-2				4		6	14	8			13	10		9	12	11	2	7	5		3	1						
Nov 24	H	St. Johnstone	9,454	0-1			13	4	12			8			14	9		6	10	11	2	7	5		3	1						
Nov 27	A	Aberdeen	11,627	2-0				4	12	6		8	14		11			9¹	10¹	13	2	7	5		3	1						
Dec 4	A	Celtic	60,092	0-4				4	6			8	12		13	14		9	10	11	2	7	5		3	1						
Dec 11	H	Motherwell	9,955	2-2				4		6		8	9			13		12¹	10¹	11	2	7	5		3	1						
Dec 19	A	Heart of Midlothian	17,954	3-0				4		6¹		8	9		11¹			13	10	12¹	2	7	5		3	1	14					
Dec 27	H	Kilmarnock	11,900	2-2			3	4		6		8	9		11	12		10¹	13¹		2	7	5			1						
Jan 22	A	Dundee United	7,457	0-0	3			4				8	9		14	12		13	10	11	2	7	5				6					
Feb 6	H	Rangers	13,420	2-2				4	9			8			12			13	10	11²	2	7	5		3	1	6					
Feb 22	A	St. Johnstone	8,236	0-1	3			4				8			12	9			10	11	2	7	5			1	6	13				
Feb 26	A	Aberdeen	12,630	0-4				4	6			12				9			10	11	2	7	5		3	1	8	13				
Mar 5	H	Celtic	12,239	2-1					6			7		9				8¹	10	11¹	2		5		3	1			12	4		
Mar 18	H	Heart of Midlothian	15,908	3-1					6¹		8¹	7						9	10¹	11	2		5		3	1				4		
Mar 21	H	Dundee	10,208	1-2							8	6		9				7	10¹	11	2		5		3	1				4		
Mar 25	A	Kilmarnock	8,068	0-1			4		6		8	7		12	9			13	10	11	2				3	1				5		
Apr 1	A	Dundee United	10,264	1-0			4	12	6			7			11	9¹		8	10		2	13			3	1			14	5		
Apr 15	H	St. Johnstone	9,211	3-3	2						8¹	6			12¹			9	10	11¹		7	5		3	1				4		
Apr 22	A	Celtic	56,843	1-1	2		4	6			8	9¹			10	12		13				7	5		3	1			14			
Apr 29	H	Aberdeen	9,659	1-0			4			3	8	9			10				11¹		2	7	5			1	6					
May 3	A	Rangers	44,359	2-5		3	4				8				10¹	9		12		11¹	2	7	5			1	6					
May 6	A	Motherwell	5,426	0-2	14	12					6				9	8		7	10	11			3		2	1			5	13	4	
May 14	A	Dundee	5,060	0-1	12		4	3			6				10	9		8	13	11		7			2	1				5	14	
May 21	H	Heart of Midlothian	17,391	1-2	3						13							8	10¹	11	2	7	5			1	6		4	9	12	

				TOTAL FULL APPEARANCES	12	9	11	23	20	24	6	28	19	1	18	14	1	22	25	23	23	27	20	7	21	24		8			9	1
				TOTAL SUB APPEARANCES		(1)	(2)	(1)	(2)	(1)	(3)				(7)			(2)	(12)	(10)	(1)	(9)	(6)	(8)	(1)	(1)		(1)		(1)	(1)	(5)	(1)	(1)
				TOTAL GOALS SCORED					1	5		9	1		7	1		3	9	11													

Small bold figures denote goalscorers.   † denotes opponent's own goal.

Easter Road Stadium

CAPACITY: 16,032 (All Seated)

PITCH DIMENSIONS: 112 yds x 74 yds

FACILITIES FOR DISABLED SUPPORTERS:
Area in South Seated Enclosure and North Stand.

Team playing kits

FIRST CHOICE
Shirt: Green with White Sleeves. White Round Neck Collar.
Shorts: White.
Stockings: Green with White Turnover.

SECOND CHOICE
Shirt: White with Green Side Panels and Green Piping on Sleeves. Collar and Cuffs Green.
Shorts: Green with White Side Panels.
Stockings: White with Green Turnover.

How to get there

Easter Road Stadium can be reached by the following routes:

BUSES: The main bus station in the city is served by buses from all over the country and the following local buses departing from Princes Street all stop near the ground:- Nos. 4, 15, 42 and 44.

TRAINS: Edinburgh Waverley Station is served by trains from all parts of the country and the above buses all stop near the ground.

The Hibees

Hibernian F.C. is a member of The Scottish Premier League

Kilmarnock

Rugby Park, Rugby Road,
Kilmarnock, KA1 2DP

CHAIRMAN
William Costley

VICE-CHAIRMAN
John Paton

DIRECTORS
James T. Moffat,
James H. Clark,
Robert Wyper, Thomas Cairns,
Ian Welsh, MA (Hons), MA, DPSE, FRSA
& Brian J. Sage

CHIEF EXECUTIVE
Ian Welsh, MA (Hons), MA, DPSE, FRSA

SECRETARY
Kevin D. Collins

MANAGER
Robert Williamson

ASSISTANT MANAGERS
Jim Clark & Gerry McCabe

GOALKEEPING COACH
Jim Stewart

YOUTH COACHES
Paul Clarke & Stuart McLean

YOUTH DEVELOPMENT COACH
Alan Robertson

HON. MEDICAL OFFICER
Dr. Masood Zaidi

CROWD DOCTOR
Dr. Brian Syme

PHYSIOTHERAPISTS
Alistair Macfie, B.Sc. (Hons),
M.C.S.P., S.R.P. &
Hugh Allan, M.B.E.

S.F.A. COMMUNITY OFFICER
Eric Young

**COMMERCIAL MANAGER/
PRESS OFFICER**
Jim McSherry (01563) 545305

COMMERCIAL ASSISTANT
Anne Clark

STADIUM MANAGER
Angus Hollas

**FOOTBALL SAFETY OFFICERS'
ASSOCIATION REPRESENTATIVE**
Kevin D. Collins (01563) 545306

MATCHDAY PROGRAMME EDITOR
Richard Cairns

TELEPHONES
Ground (01563) 545300
Fax (01563) 522181
Matchday/Ticket Information
(0891) 633249

E-MAIL & INTERNET ADDRESS
kfc@sol.co.uk
www.kilmarnockkfc.co.uk

CLUB SHOP
Situated in the Commercial Centre
at the ground. Tel (01563) 545310.
Open Mon to Fri
9.00 a.m.–5.00 p.m.
Saturday home matchdays
10.00 a.m.–5.30 p.m.
Saturday away matchdays
10.00 a.m.–2.00 p.m.

OFFICIAL SUPPORTERS CLUB
c/o Rugby Park, Kilmarnock, KA1 2DP

TEAM CAPTAIN
Ian Durrant

SHIRT SPONSOR
scotlandonline.com

KIT SUPPLIER
TFG Sports

LIST OF PLAYERS 2000-2001

Squad No.	Name	Place & date of birth	Previous Club	Lge Career Apps	Gls
16	Martin Baker	Govan 8.6.74	St Mirren	46 (1)	-
32	Darren Beasley	Rotherham 16.3.81	Rotherham United	1 (1)	-
25	Alexander Burke	Glasgow 11.11.77	Kilmarnock BC	35(30)	6
31	Peter Canero	Glasgow 18.1.81	Kilmarnock Youth	6 (5)	-
6	Christophe Cocard	Bernay, France 23.11.67	Olympic Lyon	24 (1)	8
28	Stuart Davidson	Glasgow 3.8.79	Glasgow City BC	- (2)	-
30	Paul Di Giacomo	Glasgow 30.6.82	Kilmarnock Youth	-	-
17	Frederick Dindeleux	Lille, France 16.1.74	Lille Olympic SC	28	1
10	Ian Durrant	Glasgow 29.10.66	Rangers	68	8
26	James Fowler	Stirling 26.10.80	Gairdoch BC	1 (4)	-
24	Garry Hay	Irvine 7.9.77	Kilmarnock BC	8 (2)	2
18	Sean Hessey	Liverpool 19.9.78	Huddersfield Town	7 (4)	-
8	Gary Holt	Irvine 4.1.73	Stoke City	120(12)	6
21	Christopher Innes	Broxburn 13.7.76	Stenhousemuir	9	1
22	James Lauchlan	Glasgow 2.2.77	Highbury BC	79 (2)	3
13	Alistair McCoist	Bellshill 24.9.62	Rangers	21 (14)	8
27	Gary McCutcheon	Dumfries 8.10.78	Kilmarnock BC	2 (14)	2
5	Kevin McGowne	Kilmarnock 16.12.69	St Johnstone	92 (6)	4
34	Thomas McKinlay	Glasgow 3.12.64	Celtic	14 (1)	-
2	Angus MacPherson	Glasgow 11.10.68	Rangers	322 (2)	14
14	Alan Mahood	Kilwinning 26.3.73	Morton	22 (23)	3
1	Gordon Marshall	Edinburgh 19.4.64	Celtic	62	-
12	Colin Meldrum	Kilmarnock 26.11.75	Kilwinning Rangers	40	-
11	Alistair Mitchell	Kirkcaldy 3.12.68	East Fife	258 (35)	40
7	Mark Reilly	Bellshill 30.3.69	Reading	235(17)	11
33	Andrew Smith	Aberdeen 27.11.68	Dunfermline Athletic	11 (4)	2
31	Colin Stewart	Middlesbrough 10.1.80	Ipswich Town	-	-
15	Jerome Vareille	Vernoux, France 1.6.74	FC Mulhouse	57 (23)	12
9	Paul Wright	East Kilbride 17.8.67	St Johnstone	134 (17)	50

NEW SIGNINGS

19	Craig Dargo	Edinburgh 3.1.78	Raith Rovers		
3	Neil MacFarlane	Dunoon 10.10.77	Queen's Park		
20	Andy McLaren	Glasgow 5.6.73	Reading		

Milestones

YEAR OF FORMATION: 1869
MOST CAPPED PLAYER: Joe Nibloe
NO. OF CAPS: 11
MOST LEAGUE POINTS IN A SEASON: 58 (Division 2 - Season 1973/74)
MOST LEAGUE GOALS SCORED BY A PLAYER IN A SEASON: Harry "Peerie" Cunningham (Season 1927/28) and Andy Kerr (Season 1960/61)
NO. OF GOALS SCORED: 34
RECORD ATTENDANCE: 34,246 (-v- Rangers – August, 1963)
RECORD VICTORY: 13-2 (-v- Saltcoats – Scottish Cup, 12.9.1896)
RECORD DEFEAT: 0-8 (-v- Rangers and Hibernian - Division 1)

Killie's ten year league record

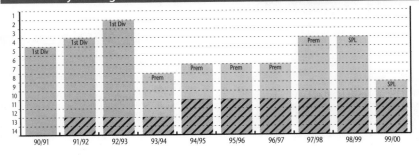

RESULTS... APPEARANCES... SCORERS... ATTENDANCES...

Date	Venue	Opponents	Att.	Res	Meldrum G.	MacPherson A.	Hay C.	McGowne K.	Dindeleux F.	Reilly M.	Holt G.	Innes C.	Mitchell A.	Roberts M.	Jeffrey M.	Vareille J.	Mahood A.	Canero P.	Lauchlan J.	Henry J.	Wright P.	Bagan D.	Baker M.	Durrant I.	McCoist A.	Fowler J.	Davidson S.	Burke A.	Hessey S.	Watt M.	Cocard C.	Smith A.	McKinlay T.	McCutcheon G.	Marshall G.	Abou S.	Beesley D.
Jul 31	A	Rangers	48,074	1-2	1	2	3	4	5	6	7	8	9[1]	10	11	12	13																				
Aug 7	H	Aberdeen	8,378	2-0	1	2	3[2]	4	5	6	7	8	9	10	11	12	13	14																			
15	A	St. Johnstone	4,681	0-2	1	2	3	4		6	7				11	10	8	14	5	9	12	13															
21	H	Motherwell	7,732	0-1	1				5	6	7					12	9	13	4		10		3	8	11	14											
29	A	Dundee United	6,621	0-0	1				5	13	7		9		11				4		10	6	3	8	12												
Sep 12	H	Celtic	14,318	0-1	1	2			5		7		9		11				4		10	6	3	8	13			12	14								
19	A	Hibernian	11,219	3-0	1	2			5		6[1]	7			13[1]	9			4		10		3	8	11[1]			12	14								
25	H	Dundee	7,433	0-2	1	2		4	5	6	7				12	10	13						3	8	11			9	14								
Oct 16	H	Rangers	15,795	1-1		2			5	6	7		9		12[1]	10			4				3	8	11					1	13						
23	A	Aberdeen	10,552	2-2		2			5		7	6[1]			11	9			4				3	8						1	10[1]						
27	A	Heart of Midlothian	12,541	2-2		2[1]			5		7		9		11	13	12		4				3	8						1	10[1]						
30	A	Celtic	59,791	1-5		2	12		5	6			9		11	13	7		4				3	8						1	10[1]						
Nov 6	A	Hibernian	8,735	0-2	1	2	3		5	6	7		9		12	11			4					8							10						
20	H	Dundee United	7,012	1-1	1	2	3	5		6	7		9		11				4					8						12	10[1]						
27	H	Heart of Midlothian	8,326	2-2	1		3		5	6[1]	7		9		11	13[1]	2	4	12					8						14	10						
Dec 11	A	Rangers	47,169	0-1	1		3		5	6	7		9			2	4							8						12	10	11					
18	H	St. Johnstone	6,002	1-2	1		3	5		6	7		13	14	12	2	4	9[1]						8						10	11						
27	A	Hibernian	11,900	2-2	1				5	6	7	3	9	12		2	4	13						8						10[1]	11[1]						
Jan 23	H	Celtic	14,126	1-1	1	2			5	6[1]	7		9	12	13	14	4						3	8						10	11						
26	A	Dundee	4,039	0-0	1	2			5	6	7		13	9					3	8			4						10	11	12						
Feb 12	H	Motherwell	7,057	0-2	1	2			5	6	7		9	11			4							8			13			10		3	12				
22	H	Motherwell	5,813	4-0		2			5	6	7		9	13[2]	14		4							8			12	10[2]	3			1	11				
26	A	Heart of Midlothian	14,243	0-0		2			5	6	7		9	13			4							8			12	10	3			1	11				
Mar 4	H	Dundee	8,460	2-2		2			5[1]	6	7		9	12	13		4							8[1]				10	3			1	11				
15	A	Dundee United	6,966	2-2		2			5	6	7		9			12	4							8[2]				10	13	3		1	11				
18	A	St. Johnstone	4,688	0-0		2			5	6	7		11	9			4							8				10	13	3		1	12				
25	H	Dundee	8,068	1-0		2			5	6	7		13	9[1]			4							8	11				10		3		1	12			
Apr 2	A	Celtic	55,194	2-4		2			5	6	7		9			4[1]	13[1]							8			12			10		3		1	12		
8	H	Dundee United	6,037	†1-0		2			5	6	7		13			4		11						8			3	10	9			1	12				
12	H	Aberdeen	11,525	1-0		2			5	6	7		13			4	11[1]							8			3	10	9			1	12				
16	A	Motherwell	5,429	0-2		2			5	6	7		13			4	11							8				10	9	3	12	1	14				
22	A	Dundee	6,208	2-1		2			5		7		10			9	12	11[2]						8	13		6	4				14	3	1			
29	A	Heart of Midlothian	8,057	0-1		2			7	5	6		9			11								8			4			10	12	3		1			
May 7	H	Rangers	13,284	0-2		2			7	5			9	12			11							8	14	13	6	4		10	3		1				
14	A	Aberdeen	9,275	1-5					8	7		12			9	2	4[1]	11						14	13		5		10	3		1				6	
21	H	St. Johnstone	9,192	†3-2	1		12	5		7			13	9	2	4		8[1]				6		10[1]	11	3			14								
TOTAL FULL APPEARANCES					18	30	8	9	28	28	35	5	22	2	10	13	6	6	29	1	12	2	11	32	5	1		3	7	4	24	11	14		14	5	1
TOTAL SUB APPEARANCES						(2)		(1)			(4)		(8)	(10)	(12)	(5)			(4)	(1)					(4)	(4)	(2)	(6)	(4)		(1)	(4)	(1)	(2)	(5)	(1)
TOTAL GOALS SCORED						1	2		1	3			2		2	3	1		2		5			4	1					8	1					

Small bold figures denote goalscorers. † *denotes opponent's own goal.*

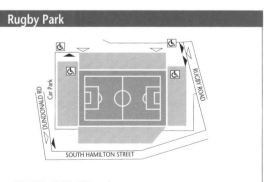

Rugby Park

CAPACITY: 18,128 (All Seated)

PITCH DIMENSIONS: 112 yds x 74 yds

FACILITIES FOR DISABLED SUPPORTERS:
Contact: John Toal, Secretary, Persons with a Disability Association, 71B Mill Street, Ayr KA7 1PH. Tel: (01292) 288905

Team playing kits

	FIRST CHOICE	SECOND CHOICE
Shirt:	Royal Blue and White Broad Vertical Stripes.	Navy Blue Edged with Burgundy Trim.
Shorts:	White with Royal Blue Trim.	Navy Blue with White Trim.
Stockings:	White.	Navy Blue.

How to get there

Rugby Park can be reached by the following routes:

BUSES: The main bus station, which is served by buses from all over the country, is ten minutes walk from the ground, but there are three local services which run from here to within a two minute walk of the park. These are the Kilmarnock-Saltcoats, Kilmarnock-Ardrossan and Kilmarnock-Largs.

TRAINS: Kilmarnock Station is well served by trains from Glasgow and the West Coast, and the station is only 15 minutes walk from the ground.

CARS: Car parking is available in the club car park by permit only. Entry **ONLY** from Dundonald Road. Visiting supporters enter **ONLY** from Rugby Road Entrance.

Kilmarnock F.C. is a member of The Scottish Premier League

Motherwell

Chapman Building, Fir Park
Stadium, Firpark Street,
Motherwell, ML1 2QN

HON. LIFE PRESIDENT
James C. Chapman, O.B.E.

CHAIRMAN
John Boyle

DIRECTORS
William H. Dickie, R.I.B.A., A.R.I.A.S,
Alisdair F. Barron, Fiona Boyle,
Andrew Lapping & John Swinburne

DIRECTOR OF FOOTBALL
Patrick Nevin

SECRETARY
Alisdair F. Barron

MANAGER
William Davies

COACH
Miodrag Krivokapic

YOUTH COACHES
Michael Weir & John Philliben

CLUB DOCTOR
Dr. Robert Liddle

PHYSIOTHERAPIST
John Porteous

S.F.A. COMMUNITY OFFICER
Colin McKinnon

**YOUTH DEVELOPMENT OFFICER/
CHIEF SCOUT**
Dave McParland

**FOOTBALL SAFETY OFFICERS'
ASSOCIATION REPRESENTATIVE**
Kenneth Davies
(0411) 237800 (Mobile)

GROUNDSMAN
Grant Murdoch

COMMERCIAL MANAGER
Mrs Karen Paterson
Tel (01698) 338011

HOSPITALITY CO-ORDINATOR
Elaine Connelly

MATCHDAY PROGRAMME EDITOR
Graeme Barnstaple

KIT CO-ORDINATOR
Alan MacDonald

TELEPHONES
Ground/Commercial
(01698) 333333
Fax (01698) 338003
Ticket Office (01698) 333030
Clubcall (09068) 121553

E-MAIL & INTERNET ADDRESS
online@motherwellfc.
www.motherwellfc.co.uk

CLUB SHOP
Motherwell Football & Athletic Club,
Firpark Street, Motherwell, ML1 2QN.
Tel (01698) 333333. Open Tues,
Thurs & Fri from 10.00 a.m. to
3.00 p.m. Saturday (Home Match
days), 10.00 a.m. to 3.00 p.m. and
Saturday (Away Matches)
10.00 a.m. to 1.00 p.m.

OFFICIAL SUPPORTERS CLUB
c/o Fir Park, Firpark Street,
Motherwell, ML1 2QN.

TEAM CAPTAIN
Andy Goram

SHIRT SPONSOR
Motorola

KIT SUPPLIER
Xara

LIST OF PLAYERS 2000-2001

Squad No.	Name	Place & date of birth	Previous Club	Lge Career Apps	Gls
12	Derek Adams	Glasgow 25.6.75	Ross County	26 (17)	4
5	Ged Brannan	Liverpool 15.1.72	Tranmere Rovers	58	10
2	Martyn Corrigan	Glasgow 14.8.77	Falkirk	18 (1)	-
8	John Davies	Glasgow 25.9.66	Ayr United	7 (1)	-
10	Don Goodman	Leeds 9.5.66	Hiroshima	33 (4)	8
1	Andy Goram	Bury 13.4.64	Sheffield United	35	-
16	Steven Hammell	Rutherglen 18.2.82	'X' Form	3 (1)	-
21	Paul Harvey	Glasgow 28.8.68	Queen of the South	6 (7)	-
4	Benito Kemble	Nieuw Nickerie 27.8.68	PSV Eindhoven	21	1
9	Lee McCulloch	Bellshill 14.5.78	Cumbernauld United	49 (47)	14
3	Stephen McMillan	Edinburgh 19.1.76	Troon Juniors	119 (8)	6
11	Steven Nicholas	Stirling 8.7.81	Stirling Albion	3 (25)	2
20	Douglas Ramsay	Irvine 26.4.79	Bearsden BC	- (6)	1
7	John Spencer	Glasgow 11.9.70	Everton	48 (3)	18
6	Greg Strong	Bolton 5.9.75	Bolton Wanderers	10	-
15	Tony Thomas	Liverpool 12.7.71	Tranmere Rovers	16	-
18	Derek Townsley	Carlisle 21.3.73	Queen of the South	16 (9)	1
14	Kevin Twaddle	Edinburgh 31.10.71	Morton	18 (7)	5
24	Martin Wood	Aberdeen 28.8.82	Rothes	-	-
17	Stephen Woods	Glasgow 23.2.70	Preston North End	95 (1)	-

NEW SIGNINGS

23	Ange Oueifio	Bangui, Cen Africa Rep 29.3.76	Denderleeun		
19	Stuart Elliot	Belfast 23.7.78	Glentoran		
43	Scott Leitch	Motherwell 6.10.69	Swindon Town		

Milestones

YEAR OF FORMATION: 1886
MOST CAPPED PLAYER: Tommy Coyne (Republic of Ireland)
NO. OF CAPS: 13
MOST LEAGUE POINTS IN A SEASON: 66 (Division 1 - Season 1931/32)
MOST LEAGUE GOALS SCORED BY A PLAYER IN A SEASON: William McFadyen (Season 1931/32)
NO. OF GOALS SCORED: 52
RECORD ATTENDANCE: 35,632 (-v- Rangers – Scottish Cup, 12.3.1952)
RECORD VICTORY: 12-1 (-v- Dundee United – Division 2, 23.1.1954)
RECORD DEFEAT: 0-8 (-v- Aberdeen - Premier Division, 26.3.1979)

The Well's ten year league record

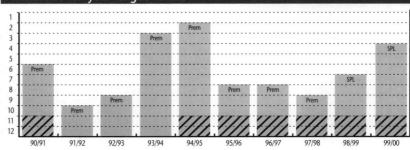

THE WELL'S CLUB FACTFILE 1999/2000
RESULTS... APPEARANCES... SCORERS... ATTENDANCES...

Date	Venue	Opponents	Att.	Res	Goram A.	Craigan S.	McGowan J.	Teale S.	Thomas A.	Townsley D.	Brannan G.	Valakari S.	Adams D.	Goodman D.	McCulloch L.	Nevin P.	Doesburg M.	Nicholas S.	McMillan S.	Matthaei R.	Spencer J.	Halliday S.	Woods S.	Twaddle K.	Kemble B.	Harvey P.	Denham G.	Davies J.	Corrigan M.	Curcic S.	Strong G.	Ramsay D.	Hammell S.
Jul 31	A	Hibernian	13,015	2-2	1	2	3	4	5	6	7	8	9	10	11	12¹		13	14¹														
Aug 7	H	Dundee United	6,791	2-2				4	5	12	7	8	14	9	11²		2	13	3		6	10											
15	A	Rangers	45,264	1-4	1			4	5	13	7	8			11¹	12	2	9	3		6	10											
21	A	Kilmarnock	7,732	1-0	1		6	5				8¹	9		11	14	2		3		12	10	13										
28	H	Dundee	6,278	0-2	1		6	5				7	12	8	9	11	13	2	3			10	14										
Sep 11	A	St. Johnstone	5,468	1-1	1			4	5	6	7	8	9		11	12	2	14	3		10¹	13	1										
Oct 16	H	Hibernian	7,559	2-2	1			4	5	6	7	8		12	11¹	9	2	14	3¹		10			13									
20	A	Aberdeen	5,009	5-6	1	12		4¹	5	6	7	8			11¹		9	2	3		10³	13		14									
23	A	Dundee United	6,213	2-0	1			4¹		13	7	8		12	11	9	2		3		10¹			6	5	14								
27	A	Celtic	57,898	1-0	1		12	4			7	8		9	11	13	2	14	3		10			6¹	5									
30	H	St. Johnstone	6,173	1-0	1		3			13	7	8		9	11	12	2				10	15	6¹	5		4								
Nov 6	A	Heart of Midlothian	12,514	1-1				4		12	7	8			11		2		3		10¹		1	6	5	13								
20	A	Dundee	4,340	1-0				4		12	7	8			11¹	9	2	14	3		10		1	6	5	13								
23	H	Heart of Midlothian	7,793	2-1				4		6	7	8		13	11	12¹	2		3		10		1	9	5									
28	A	Celtic	10,730	3-2				4		6¹	7¹	8		10¹	11	12	2	13	3				1	9	5			14						
Dec 11	A	Hibernian	9,955	2-2				4		6	7	8			9	2	12	3		10²	11	1	5	13									
18	H	Rangers	12,640	1-5	1			4		6	7	8		11¹		12	2	13	3		10		9	5									
Jan 22	A	St. Johnstone	4,158	1-1	1					6		8		11		13	2	14	3¹		10		9	5		4	7	12					
26	A	Aberdeen	10,314	1-1	1						7	8		9	11		13	3			10¹		6	5		4	2						
Feb 5	H	Dundee	5,856	0-3	1					6	7	8		13	11	12		3			10		9	5		4	2						
12	A	Kilmarnock	7,057	2-0	1			5			7	8		9	11		14	13	3¹		10¹		12			4	6	2					
22	H	Kilmarnock	5,813	0-4	1			5		13	7	12			11			3			10		14	6	9	4	8	2					
Mar 1	A	Heart of Midlothian	5,588	0-2	1			4		6		8	9	10	11	12		13	3				5	14		7	2						
4	H	Aberdeen	7,528	1-0	1			4		6		8	9	11¹	13	12		3			10		5	7		2							
18	A	Rangers	49,622	2-6	1			4			7	8	9		11¹	12		3					6	5¹	14	2	10						
25	H	Heart of Midlothian	13,702	0-0						7	8	9	10	11	12		3				1	6	5	13		2		4					
Apr 1	H	St. Johnstone	5,934	2-1			12			7¹	8	6	9	11			13	3			1	14				5	2¹	10	4				
5	A	Celtic	55,689	0-4			12			7		9	11	13		14	3			1	8	5			6	2	10	4					
8	A	Dundee	4,701	1-4		12	4			7		9	10¹	11		14	3			1	8	5			6	2	13						
16	H	Kilmarnock	5,429	2-0						6	7¹	8	14	10	11¹			3			1	12	9	5		2	13	4					
19	H	Dundee United	4,271	1-3						6	7	8		10	11¹			3			1	12	9	5		2	13	4					
22	A	Aberdeen	9,348	1-2						5	7¹	8	6	10	11	14	9			1					2	3	13	4					
29	H	Celtic	7,405	1-1						12	7¹		8	10	11	9		14			1		5	6		2		4				3	
May 6	H	Hibernian	5,426	2-0						6	7		8	10			13	3			11	1	12²	5	9	2			4	14			
13	A	Dundee United	5,908	2-1	1					13	7		8	10²		14		3			11		9	5	6	2			4			12	
21	H	Rangers	12,310	2-0	1						7	8	9	10		13					11¹		12¹	5	6	2			4			3	
TOTAL FULL APPEARANCES					22	3	10	16	6	16	33	28	15	25	28	6	17	2	31	2	25	1	14	18	25	6	6	7	18	3	10		3
TOTAL SUB APPEARANCES						(2)	(3)		(9)		(2)	(2)	(4)	(1)	(22)	(2)	(19)		(1)	(3)	(4)	(1)	(7)		(7)		(1)	(1)	(3)		(2)	(1)	
TOTAL GOALS SCORED								2		1	5		1	7	9	2			1		3			11				5	1			1	

Small bold figures denote goalscorers.   † denotes opponent's own goal.

Fir Park

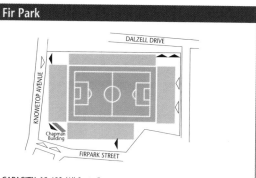

DALZELL DRIVE · KNOWETOP AVENUE · Chapman Building · FIRPARK STREET

CAPACITY: 13,450 (All Seated)

PITCH DIMENSIONS: 110 yds x 75 yds

FACILITIES FOR DISABLED SUPPORTERS:
Area between Main Stand and South Stand. Prior arrangement must be made with the Secretary and a ticket obtained.

Team playing kits

FIRST CHOICE
Shirt: Amber with Claret Collar and Cuffs.
Shorts: Claret and Amber Piping and Bands.
Stockings: Amber.

SECOND CHOICE
Shirt: White with Black and Claret Trim.
Shorts: White with Claret Trim.
Stockings: White.

THIRD CHOICE
Shirt: Black with White Collar and Cuffs.
Shorts: Black with White Trim.
Stockings: White.

How to get there

The following routes can be used to reach Fir Park:
BUSES: Fir Park is less than a quarter of a mile from the main thoroughfare through the town and numerous buses serving Lanarkshire and Glasgow all pass along this road. De-bus at the Civic Centre.
TRAINS: Motherwell Station is a main-line station on the Glasgow–London (Euston) route, and the station is particularly well served by trains running from numerous points throughout the Strathclyde Region. Motherwell Station is a twenty minute walk from Fir Park, while the station at Airbles Road is only ten minutes away. East Coast access is via Motherwell Central Station on the Glasgow-London East Coast line. Travel from West Coast and Glasgow areas is via the low level Glasgow Central line to Airbles and Motherwell Central. This is a regular service on a 30 minute basis (8 mins & 38 mins past).
CARS: Controlled supervised car parking is available in the immediate area of Fir Park. Car park season tickets are available for closest proximity car parks. Away fan car parking is extensive in the grounds of Motherwell College on a day rate basis of £5.00. Access to South Stand is within a maximum of 5 minutes walk.

Motherwell F.C. is a member of The Scottish Premier League

Rangers

Ibrox Stadium,150 Edmiston Drive, Glasgow, G51 2XD
CHAIRMAN
David E. Murray
DIRECTORS
Hugh R. W. Adam, Douglas Odam, Donald Wilson, David King, Daniel P. Levy, James MacDonald, R. Campbell Ogilvie & Ian B. Skelly
ASSOCIATE DIRECTORS
Ian Russell & Bill Thornton
SECRETARY
R. Campbell Ogilvie
MANAGER
Dick Advocaat
ASSISTANT MANAGER
Bert van Lingen
RESERVE COACHES
John McGregor & John Brown
YOUTH DEVELOPMENT COACH
Jan Derks
CHIEF SCOUT
Ewan Chester
CLUB DOCTOR
Dr. Gert Jan Goudswaard
PHYSIOTHERAPIST
Grant Downie
PUBLIC RELATIONS EXECUTIVE
John Greig, M.B.E.
FINANCIAL CONTROLLER
Douglas Odam
RANGERS HOSPITALITY MANAGER
Peter Kingstone
MARKETING & MEDIA MANAGER
Martin Bain
HEAD OF SALES
Alistair Wilson
HOSPITALITY SALES MANAGER
Scot Gardiner
CUSTOMER SERVICES TICKET OPERATIONS MANAGER
Jim Hannah
OPERATIONS EXECUTIVE/ FOOTBALL SAFETY OFFICERS' ASSOCIATION REPRESENTATIVE
Laurence MacIntyre
PITCH SUPERINTENDENT
David Roxburgh
STADIUM FACILITIES MANAGER
Ken Crawford
MATCHDAY PROGRAMME EDITOR
Gavin Berry
TELEPHONES
Main Switch Board (0141) 580 8500
Administration (0141) 580 8609
Fax (0141) 580 8947
Ticket Centre
0870-600 1993 Fax (0141) 580 8504
Customer Services 0870-600 1972
Hospitality 0870-600 1964
Commercial 0870-600 1899
Retail/Mail Order 0990 99 1998
Fax Enquiries 0870-600 1978
E-MAIL & INTERNET ADDRESS
dora_howie@rangers.co.uk
http://www.rangers.co.uk
CLUB SHOPS
1873 Superstore, Ibrox Stadium, Glasgow G51. Open until 10.00p.m. on Matchdays and 9.30a.m.-5.30p.m. Mon to Sat and 11.00a.m. to 5.00p.m. on Sunday.
The Rangers Shop, 84-92 Sauchiehall Street, Glasgow, G2. Open 9.00a.m.-5.30p.m. Mon to Sat and Sun Noon-4.00p.m.
The Rangers Shop, 21 Trongate, Glasgow. Open 10.00a.m.-5.30p.m. Mon to Sat and 11.30a.m. to 4.00p.m. on Sun.
The Rangers Shop, St. Enoch Centre, Glasgow. Open 9.00a.m.-6.00p.m. Mon, Tue, Wed, Fri and Sat., 9.00a.m.-8.00p.m. Thurs and Sun, 11.00a.m.-5.00p.m.
OFFICIAL SUPPORTERS CLUB
Rangers F.C. Supporters' Association, 250 Edmiston Drive, Glasgow, G51 1YU
TEAM CAPTAIN
Lorenzo Amoruso
SHIRT SPONSOR
NTL
KIT SUPPLIER
Nike

LIST OF PLAYERS 2000-2001

Squad No.	Name	Place & date of birth	Previous Club	Lge Career Apps	Gls
28	Dariusz Adamczuk	Stettin, Poland 20.10,69	Dundee	5 (5)	-
11	Jorg Albertz	M'chengladbach, Germany 29.1.71	Hamburg	121 (11)	48
4	Lorenzo Amoruso	Bari, Italy 28.6.71	Fiorentina	67	3
	Mark Brown	Motherwell 28.2,71	'S' Form	1	-
16	Billy Dodds	New Cumnock 5.2.69	Dundee United	16 (2)	10
-	Lee Feeney	Newry 21.3.78	Linfield	- (1)	-
6	Barry Ferguson	Glasgow 2.2.78	Rangers SABC	60 (1)	5
7	Andrei Kanchelskis	Kirovgrad, Ukraine 23.1.69	Fiorentina	55 (4)	11
17	Tugay Kerimoglu	Istanbul, Turkey 24.8.70	Galatasaray	9 (7)	1
1	Stefan Klos	Dortmund, Germany 16.8.71	Borussia Dortmund	42	-
18	Neil McCann	Greenock 11.8.74	Hearts	27 (22)	8
-	Robert Malcolm	Glasgow 12.11.80	'S' Form	1 (2)	-
9	Michael Mols	Amsterdam 17.12.70	FC Utrecht	9	9
3	Craig Moore	Canterbury, Australia 12.12.75	Crystal Palace	90 (6)	6
5	Arthur Numan	Heemskerek, Holland 14.2.69	PSV Eindhoven	37 (3)	1
29	Tero Pentilla	Finland 9.3.75	FC Haka	3	-
21	Sergio Porrini	Milan, Italy 8.11.68	Juventus	72 (1)	6
12	Claudio Reyna	Livingston, USA 20.7.73	VFL Wolfsburg	31 (4)	5
-	Maurice Ross	Dundee 3.2.81	Rangers SABC	- (1)	-
8	Gio Van Bronckhorst	Rotterdam, Holland 5.2.75	Feyenoord	62	11
25	Tony Vidmar	Adelaide, Australia 4.7.70	NAC Breda	55 (12)	6
10	Rod Wallace	Lewisham 2.10.69	Leeds United	50 (3)	35
19	Scott Wilson	Edinburgh 19.3.77	Rangers BC	17 (5)	1

NEW SIGNINGS

Squad No.	Name	Place & date of birth	Previous Club		
14	Ronald de Boer	Hoorn, Holland 15.5.70	Barcelona		
24	Allan Johnston	Glasgow 14.12.73	Sunderland		
15	Bert Konterman	Rouveen, Holland 14.1.71	Feyenoord		
15	Peter Lovenkrands	Horsholm, Denmark 29.1.80	AB Copenhagen		
23	Kenny Miller	Edinburgh 23.12.79	Hibernian		
2	Fernando Ricksen	Heerlen, Holland 20.7.76	AZ Alkmaar		

Milestones

YEAR OF FORMATION: 1873
MOST CAPPED PLAYER: Alistair McCoist
NO. OF CAPS: 58
MOST LEAGUE POINTS IN A SEASON: 76 (Division 1 - Season 1920/21) (2 Points for a Win)
97 (Scottish Premier League - Season 1999/2000) (3 Points for a Win)
MOST LEAGUE GOALS SCORED BY A PLAYER IN A SEASON: Sam English (Season 1931/32)
NO. OF GOALS SCORED: 44
RECORD ATTENDANCE: 118,567 (-v- Celtic – 2.1.1939)
RECORD VICTORY: 14-2 (-v- Blairgowrie – Scottish Cup, 20.1.1934)
RECORD DEFEAT: 2-10 (-v- Airdrieonians – 1886)

The Gers' ten year league record

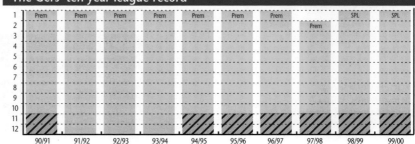

THE GERS' CLUB FACTFILE 1999/2000
RESULTS... APPEARANCES... SCORERS... ATTENDANCES...

Date	Venue	Opponents	Att.	Res	Klos S.	Adamczuk D.	Moore C.	Amoruso L.	Numan A.	Ferguson B.	Reyna C.	Van Bronckhorst G.	Albertz J.	Wallace R.	Amato G.	Porrini S.	Johansson J.	Vidmar A.	Mols M.	Ferguson I.	Niemi A.	McCann N.	Charbonnier L.	Kanchelskis A.	Hendry C.	McInnes D.	Durie G.	Brown M.	Myhre T.	Wilson S.	Dodds W.	Kerimoglu T.	Nicholson B.	Rozental S.	Ross M.	Pentilla T.	Malcolm R.	Gibson J.	Hughes S.
Jul 31	H	Kilmarnock	48,074	2-1	1	2	3	4	5	6	7[1]	8	9	10[1]	11	12	13	14																					
Aug 7	A	Heart of Midlothian	17,893	4-0	1	12	3	4		7	6[2]		8[1]	9	13	2	11	5	10[1]	14																			
15	H	Motherwell	45,264	4-1		13	3	4		7	6	8	12	10		2	14	5	11[4]		1	9																	
21	H	Dundee United	48,849	4-1		12	3	4		7	6[1]	8[1]	13	10[1]		2		5[1]	11		9	1																	
28	A	Hibernian	15,587	1-0		2	3	4		7	9	8	13			12[1]	5	11			10	1	6	14															
Sep 11	H	Aberdeen	49,226	3-0			3	4	13	7	6	8	12[1]		11	2		5	10[2]			9	1	14															
25	H	St. Johnstone	47,475	3-1		2	3		5	7		8	9[2]	13		11		10[1]			12	1	6	4															
Oct 2	A	Dundee	10,494	3-2		14	3	4	5	7		8	6	11[1]	13[1]	2	12	10				1	9[1]																
16	A	Kilmarnock	15,795	1-1			3	4	5	7		8[1]	6	11		2	14	13	10			12	9																
30	A	Aberdeen	16,846	5-1	1	13	3	4	9	7		8			12[1]	2	11[3]	5	10[1]			6		14															
Nov 7	H	Celtic	50,026	4-2	1		3	4[1]	5	7	6	8	9[1]		10[1]	2	11[1]	14			12			13															
20	H	Hibernian	49,544	2-0		2	3	4	5		6	8	9[1]	12	10	11[1]					7				1														
28	H	Dundee	47,154	1-2		2	3	4	5	7	6		9	11[1]		10	12				8	13		14	1														
Dec 11	H	Kilmarnock	47,169	1-0			4	5	7	6		8[1]	11		2		14		9			12		13		1	3	10											
18	H	Motherwell	12,640	5-1		3	4[1]	5	7	12	8	9	11		2				13			6[2]		14		1	10[2]												
22	H	Heart of Midlothian	49,907	1-0		3	4	5	7		8	6[1]	11		2				12		1	9		13			10												
27	A	Celtic	59,619	1-1		3	4	5	7	6	8	9	11	12	2					1						10[1]												
Jan 22	A	Aberdeen	50,023	5-0	1		3[1]	4	5[1]	7[1]	13	8[1]	9	11[1]		2			12		6					10	14												
Feb 2	A	Dundee United	11,241	4-0	1		3	4	5	7	13	8	9	11[1]		2[2]			12[1]		6					10	14												
6	A	Hibernian	13,420	2-2	1		3	4	5	7	13	8	9	11[1]		2			12[1]		6					10													
15	A	St. Johnstone	9,608	1-1	1		3	4	5	7		8	9	11		2[1]			13		6		10							12									
27	A	Dundee	9,297	7-1	1			5		4	7	9[1]	11[3]			2[2]			12		6								3		8	10[1]	13						
Mar 4	A	St. Johnstone	49,907	0-0	1		4	5		3	7	9	11			2			13		6							12	8	10								
8	A	Celtic	59,220	1-0	1		3	4	5	7	6	8	9	11[1]		2			10																			
18	A	Motherwell	49,622	6-2	1		2	4		7		5	9[1]	11[3]					12		6						3	13	8[1]	14	10[1]							
26	H	Celtic	50,039	4-0	1		4	5	7	2	8[1]	9[2]	11						12		6[1]					3	10	13										
Apr 1	A	Aberdeen	16,521	1-1	1		4	5	7[1]	2		8	10		12				11		6					3	9											
4	H	Dundee United	45,829	3-0	1		4	5	7	2		8[1]	10[1]						12		6					3	11[1]	9	13		14							
12	A	Heart of Midlothian	16,314	2-1	1		4	5	7	2	8	12	10[1]								6					3	11[1]	9										
15	A	Dundee United	11,419	2-0	1		4	5	7[1]	2	8	9[1]	10						13		6					3	11	14		12								
23	A	St. Johnstone	10,016	2-0	1		4	5	7	2	8	9	10						13		6					3	11[2]	14		12								
30	H	Dundee	50,032	3-0	1		4	5	7	2	8		12	13					9[1]		6					11[1]	14	10[1]		3								
May 3	H	Hibernian	44,359	†5-2	1			5	7[1]	2	8[2]								14	4	13		6			11[1]	9	10		3	12							
7	A	Kilmarnock	13,284	2-0	1			7[1]		8[1]		2	12	5					11		6					10	9	13		3	4	14						
13	H	Heart of Midlothian	49,140	1-0	1			5	2	8		3	11	4					9		6		12			10[1]	7	13						14				
21	A	Motherwell	12,310	0-2	1			5	7	2	9	8	13						3	11	4		6			12					14	10						
TOTAL FULL APPEARANCES			24		5	22	30	29	31	25	27	30	25	4	11	8	21	9		1	12	7	25	1		1	1	3	9	16	9		6		3	1		
TOTAL SUB APPEARANCES			(5)			(1)		(4)		(5)	(3)	(4)	(1)		(8)	(6)		(2)				(18)		(3)	(1)	(1)	(6)			(2)	(7)	(2)	(5)	(1)		(2)	(1)	(1)
TOTAL GOALS SCORED			1		2	1	4	5	4	17	16	3			6	6	9			3	4							10	1	3							

Small bold figures denote goalscorers.   † denotes opponent's own goal.

Ibrox Stadium

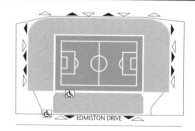

EDMISTON DRIVE

CAPACITY: 50,444 (All Seated)
PITCH DIMENSIONS: 115yds x 75yds
FACILITIES FOR DISABLED SUPPORTERS:
Special area within stadium and also special toilet facilities provided. The club also have a Rangers Disabled Supporters' Club. Contact: David Milne, Secretary, Disabled Supporters' Club, c/o Ibrox Stadium, Glasgow, G51 2XD. This is free of charge.

Team playing kits

FIRST CHOICE
Shirt: Royal Blue with White Band on 'V' Neck, White Trim Running from Sleeve down front to Underarm.
Shorts: White with Royal Blue Trim.
Stockings: Black with Red Tops.

SECOND CHOICE
Shirt: White with Red Band on 'V' Neck with One Red and One Blue Horizontal Band across Chest, Red Trim on Sleeves.

Shorts: White with Red Trim.
Stockings: White with Red Trim.

THIRD CHOICE
Shirt: Red with Black Trim Running from Neck to Sleeve. Black Trim on Sleeve.
Shorts: Red with Black Trim.
Stockings: Red with Black Horizontal Bands.

How to get there

You can reach Ibrox Stadium by these routes:
BUSES: The following buses all pass within 300 yards of the Stadium and can be boarded from Glasgow city centre:- Nos. 4, 9A, 23, 23A, 52, 53, 53A, 54A, 54B, 65, 89 and 91.
UNDERGROUND: GGPTE Underground station is Ibrox, which is two minutes walk from the Stadium.
CARS: Motor Vehicles can head for the Stadium from the city centre by joining the M8 Motorway from Waterloo Street. Take the B768 turn-off for Govan. This will then take you to the ground. A limited number of parking spaces will be available in the Albion Car Park.

Rangers F.C. is a member of The Scottish Premier League

St. Johnstone

McDiarmid Park, Crieff Road, Perth, PH1 2SJ

CHAIRMAN
Geoffrey S. Brown

DIRECTORS
Douglas B. McIntyre & Bob Reid

MANAGING DIRECTOR/ SECRETARY
A. Stewart M. Duff

MANAGER
Alexander Clark

FIRST TEAM COACH
William Kirkwood

YOUTH COACHES
Alastair Stevenson & Henry Hall

CLUB DOCTOR
Alistair McCracken

PHYSIOTHERAPIST
Nick Summersgill

S.F.A. COMMUNITY OFFICER
Atholl Henderson

STADIUM MANAGER
Jimmy Hogg

FOOTBALL SAFETY OFFICERS' ASSOCIATION REPRESENTATIVE
Sandy Drummond (01738) 459090

MARKETING EXECUTIVE
Paul Fraser

COMMERCIAL MANAGER
Diane Knight
(01738) 459090

SALES EXECUTIVE
Margot A. Dempsey
(01738) 459090

LOTTERY MANAGER
Anne Connolly

CATERING MANAGER
Stuart MacColl

MATCHDAY PROGRAMME EDITOR
Alistair Blair

TELEPHONES
Ground (01738) 459090
Ticket Office (01738) 455000
Fax (01738) 625771
Information Service (09068) 121559

E-MAIL & INTERNET ADDRESS
anyone@saints.sol.co.uk
www.stjohnstonefc.co.uk

CLUB SHOP
Mon-Fri at Main Reception
at Ground. A shop is also open on
matchdays and is situated at
Ormond (South) Stand

OFFICIAL SUPPORTERS CLUB
157 Dunkeld Road, Perth
Tel: (01738) 442022

TEAM CAPTAIN
Jim Weir

SHIRT SPONSOR
Scottish Hydro-Electric plc

KIT SUPPLIER
Xara

LIST OF PLAYERS 2000-2001

Squad No.	Name	Place & date of birth	Previous Club	Lge Career Apps	Gls
3	Gary Bollan	Dundee 24.3.73	Rangers	66 (1)	-
14	Paddy Connolly	Glasgow 25.6.70	Airdrieonians	17 (7)	2
39	Chris Conway	Glasgow 17.7.83	'S' Form	- (1)	-
30	Brendan Crozier	Glasgow 7.10.82	Busby BC	-	-
35	Kevin Cuthbert	Perth 8.9.82	St Johnstone BC	-	-
4	Nick Dasovic	Vancouver, Canada 5.12.68	Trelleborg FC	76 (1)	1
2	Darren Dods	Edinburgh 7.6.75	Hibernian	56	4
-	Allan Ferguson	Lanark 21.3.69	Hamilton Academical	5 (1)	-
15	Stephen Frail	Glasgow 10.8.69	Tranmere Rovers	9	-
9	Graeme Jones	Gateshead 13.3.70	Wigan Athletic	15 (4)	3
11	Paul Kane	Edinburgh 20.6.65	Viking Stavanger	90 (5)	5
6	Alan Kernaghan	Otley 25.4.67	Manchester City	54	5
28	Martin Lauchlan	Rutherglen 1.10.80	Partick Thistle	- (5)	-
12	Nathan Lowndes	Salford 2.6.77	Watford	28 (26)	12
20	John Paul McBride	Hamilton 28.11.78	Celtic	20 (2)	1
19	Stuart McCluskey	Bellshill 29.10.77	'S' Form	33 (11)	2
27	Marc McCulloch	Edinburgh 14.3.80	Musselburgh Athletic	-	-
1	Alan Main	Elgin 5.12.67	Dundee United	174	-
26	Stuart Malcolm	Edinburgh 20.8.79	Hutchison Vale BC	-	-
10	George O'Boyle	Belfast 14.12.67	Dunfermline Athletic	135 (11)	64
22	Keigan Parker	Livingston 8.6.62	St Johnstone BC	6 (6)	2
18	Stephen Robertson	Glasgow 16.3.77	Ashfield Juniors	19 (1)	-
8	Craig Russell	Jarrow 4.2.74	Manchester City	1	1
21	Kevin Thomas	Edinburgh 25.4.75	Morton	5 (7)	2
5	Jim Weir	Motherwell 15.6.69	Heart of Midlothian	140 (1)	5

NEW SIGNINGS

17	Paul Hartley	Glasgow 19.10.76	Hibernian		
7	Tommy Lovenkrands	Copenhagen 30.5.74	AB Copenhagen		
16	Mohammed Sylla	Bouakake, Ivory Coast 13.5.77	Le Havre		

Milestones

YEAR OF FORMATION: 1884
MOST CAPPED PLAYER: Sandy McLaren
NO. OF CAPS: 5
MOST LEAGUE POINTS IN A SEASON: 59 (Second Division – Season 1987/88)(2 Points for a Win)
80 (First Division – Season 1996/97)(3 Points for a Win)
MOST LEAGUE GOALS SCORED BY A PLAYER IN A SEASON: Jimmy Benson (Season 1931/32)
NO. OF GOALS SCORED: 38
RECORD ATTENDANCE: 29,972 (-v- Dundee 10.2.1951 at Muirton Park)
10,545 (-v- Dundee – SPL, 23.05.1999 at McDiarmid Park)
RECORD VICTORY: 8-1 (-v- Partick Thistle – League Cup, 16.8.1969)
RECORD DEFEAT: 0-12 (-v- Cowdenbeath – Scottish Cup, 21.1.1928)

The Saints' ten year league record

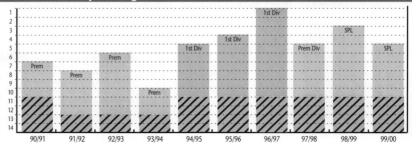

THE SAINTS' CLUB FACTFILE 1999/2000
RESULTS... APPEARANCES... SCORERS... ATTENDANCES...

Date	Venue	Opponents	Att.	Res	Main A.	McQuillan J.	Bollan G.	Dods D.	Weir J.	O'Halloran K.	McBride J.P.	Kane P.	Dasovic N.	Simao M.	Grant R.	O'Neil J.	Griffin D.	McMahon G.	Lowndes N.	Lauchlan M.	McAnespie K.	Thomas K.	Parker K.	O'Boyle G.	McCluskey S.	Jones G.	Frail S.	Connolly P.	Ferguson A.	Robertson S.	Millar M.	Russell C.	Conway C.
Jul 31	H	Heart of Midlothian	6,707	1-4	1	2¹	3	4	5	6	7	8	9	10	11	12	13	14															
Aug 7	A	Celtic	60,282	0-3	1	2	3	4	5	6	7	8	9	10		11	12		13	14													
15	H	Kilmarnock	4,681	2-0	1	2	3¹	4	5			8	6	12		9				7	10¹	11											
21	H	Hibernian	6,165	1-1	1	2	3	4	5			8	6	14		9	12			7	10¹	11	13										
29	A	Aberdeen	9,600	3-0	1	2	3	4	5¹			8	7	9	13	10	6			12¹	14	11¹											
Sep 11	H	Motherwell	5,468	1-1	1	2	3	4	5	12		8	7	9		10	6				11¹	13	14										
19	A	Dundee	5,283	2-1	1	2	3		5	6		8	12			7	4	10²		9	11		13										
25	A	Rangers	47,475	1-3	1	2	3		5	6		8	7	12¹		9	4			10	13	11	14										
Oct 16	A	Heart of Midlothian	12,872	1-1						6		8	7	14		12	4			10¹	9	13		11		5							
24	H	Celtic	9,066	1-2	1	2	3			6		8	7	12			4			10¹	9			11		5							
27	H	Dundee United	4,236	0-1	1	2	3			6		8	7		12		4			10	9	13		11		5							
30	A	Motherwell	6,173	0-1	1	2	3			6		14	8	13			4	7		10	9			11	12	5							
Nov 6	H	Dundee	4,917	0-1	1	2	3		5	6		8	13			9	4	7	10	12				11									
21	H	Aberdeen	6,279	1-1	1	2	3		5	6		8	12			9	4	7	10			13				11¹							
24	H	Hibernian	9,454	1-0	1	2	3		5	6		9	8	10		4		7	12			13				11¹							
27	A	Dundee United	6,367	0-1	1	2	3		5	6		8	13			9	4	7	10			12				11							
Dec 18	H	Kilmarnock	6,002	2-1	1	2	3		5	6	7¹	8				9¹	4	12	10	13						11							
27	A	Dundee	6,232	1-1	1	2	3		5	6	7	8				9	4		10¹	12		13				11							
Jan 22	A	Motherwell	4,158	1-1	1		3		5	6	7	8	12			9	4		10		2					11¹							
Feb 5	A	Aberdeen	17,568	1-2	1		3		5	6	7	8		9		10¹	4	13	12	14				11	2								
15	H	Rangers	9,608	1-1	1		3	4	5	7	9	8				10	2	13¹		14		12		6	11								
22	H	Hibernian	8,236	1-0			3	4	5	6¹	7	8				9		13	12			10		2	11			1					
26	H	Dundee United	4,732	2-0			3	4	5	7	9	8				10	2¹		12¹			13		6	11			1					
Mar 4	H	Rangers	49,907	0-0			3	4	5	7	9	8				10	2	13	14					6	11			1		15			
11	A	Celtic	59,331	1-4			3	4	5	7	9	8				10	2	13	12					6	11¹			1					
15	H	Heart of Midlothian	4,468	0-1			3	4	5	7		8	9			2	12	10	13					6	11			1					
18	H	Kilmarnock	4,688	0-0			3	4	5	6	7	8				9	2	13	10			12			11			1					
25	H	Dundee	4,655	2-1			3¹	4	5	7		8				10	2	9				11		6	12			1		13¹			
Apr 1	A	Motherwell	5,934	1-2				4	5	6	7	8				10	2	12	9						11			1		13	3¹		
15	A	Hibernian	9,211	3-3				4	5	6	7	8				10¹	2	13	9¹		12¹				3	11		1					
23	H	Rangers	10,016	0-2			3	4	5	6		8				7	2	12	10		9				11			1		13			
29	A	Dundee United	5,843	2-1			3	2¹	4	6	5	8				7			10	12	9				11			1		13			
May 2	H	Aberdeen	3,991	2-1			3	2¹	4	6	5	8¹				7			10		9				11			1		12			
6	A	Heart of Midlothian	12,368	0-0			3	2	4	6		8				7	12		10	13	9				11			1		5			
13	H	Celtic	6,739	0-0			3	2	4	6	9	8				7		13		10					11		12	1		5			
21	A	Kilmarnock	9,192	2-3			3	2		6	13	8				7	4	14	9		10¹				11			1		5¹			12
TOTAL FULL APPEARANCES					21	18	34	22	31	31	18	33	13	6	1	31	26	9	16	14	5	6	4	5	15	9	9	3	12	3	1		
TOTAL SUB APPEARANCES								(1)	(1)	(1)		(11)	(2)	(2)	(3)	(10)	(9)	(5)	(6)	(7)	(4)	(4)	(1)	(4)		(2)			(1)	(5)		(1)
TOTAL GOALS SCORED					1	2	2	1	1	1	1	1				3	1							10	1	2	2		3	1		2	1

Small bold figures denote goalscorers. † denotes opponent's own goal.

McDiarmid Park

CAPACITY: 10,723 (All Seated)

PITCH DIMENSIONS: 115 yds x 75 yds

FACILITIES FOR DISABLED SUPPORTERS:
Entrance via south end of West Stand and south end of East Stand. Visiting disabled fans should contact the club in advance. Headphones available in West and North Stands for blind and partially sighted supporters.

Team playing kits

FIRST CHOICE
Shirt: Royal Blue with White Piping on Shoulders and Sides. Collar and Cuffs White.
Shorts: White with Royal Blue Piping down Sides and around Hem.
Stockings: Royal Blue with two White Hoops on Tops.

SECOND CHOICE
Shirt: White with Royal Blue Sleeves with White Panel.
Shorts: White with Royal Blue Side Panels.
Stockings: White with Two Royal Blue Hoops on Tops.

THIRD CHOICE
Shirt: Yellow with Black Side Panel. Sleeves Yellow with Black Stripe. Collar Yellow with One Black Stripe.
Shorts: Yellow with Black Side Panel with Black Leg Band.
Stockings: Yellow with Two Black Hoops on Tops.

How to get there

The following routes can be used to reach McDiarmid Park:
TRAINS: Perth Station is well served by trains from all parts of the country. The station is about 40 minutes walk from the park.
BUSES: Local services nos. 1 and 2 pass near the ground. Both leave from Mill Street in the town centre.
CARS: The car park at the park holds 1,500 cars and 100 coaches. Vehicles should follow signs A9 to Inverness on Perth City by-pass, then follow "Football Stadium" signs at Inveralmond Roundabout South onto slip road adjacent to McDiarmid Park. Vehicle charges are £2.00 for cars and no charge for coaches.

St. Johnstone F.C. is a member of The Scottish Premier League

LIST OF PLAYERS 2000-2001

Squad No.	Name	Place & date of birth	Previous Club	Lge Career Apps	Gls
18	Sergei Baltacha	Kiev, Ukraine 28.7.79	Kinnoull	18 (9)	1
12	Gary Bowman	Glasgow 12.8.74	Ayr United	10(9)	1
8	Tom Brown	Glasgow 1.4.68	Kilmarnock	62(15)	11
27	Colin Drew	Paisley 5.5.79	Giffnock North	20(9)	-
10	Ricky Gillies	Glasgow 24.8.76	Aberdeen	84(36)	15
3	Chris Kerr	Paisley 6.9.78	St Mirren BC	28 (4)	2
9	Steven McGarry	Paisley 28.9.79	Giffnock North	65(40)	19
20	Paul McKnight	Belfast 8.2.77	Rangers	1 (3)	2
5	Barry McLaughlin	Paisley 19.4.73	St Mirren BC	200(8)	7
7	Hugh Murray	Bellshill 8.1.79	Giffnock North	73 (4)	8
2	Iain Nicolson	Glasgow 13.10.76	Partick Thistle	57 (7)	5
25	Jens Paeslack	Hamburg 25.2.74	Karlsruhe	1 (1)	-
16	Ryan Robinson	Paisley 30.8.80	St Mirren BC	- (10)	-
15	Ian Ross	Broxburn 27.8.74	Motherwell	30 (1)	3
17	Ludovic Roy	Tours, France 18.8.77	La Berrichone de Chateauroux	48	-
14	Paul Rudden	Glasgow 10.8.80	St Mirren BC	27(16)	-
1	Derek Scrimgour	Glasgow 29.3.79	Largs Thistle	33	-
4	Tommy Turner	11.10.63 Johnstone	Partick Thistle	85 (2)	8
6	Scott Walker	Glasgow 5.3.75	East Stirlingshire	33	4
11	Mark Yardley	Livingston 14.9.69	Cowdenbeath	131	59

NEW SIGNINGS

24	Jamie McGowan	Morecambe 5.12.70	Motherwell		
19	Scott MacKenzie	Glasgow 7.7.70	Falkirk		
21	Jose Quitongo	Luanda 18.11.74	Heart of Midlothian		

Milestones

YEAR OF FORMATION: 1877
MOST CAPPED PLAYERS: Iain Munro & Billy Thomson
NO. OF CAPS: 7
MOST LEAGUE POINTS IN A SEASON: 62 (Division 2 – Season 1967/68) (2 Points for a Win)
　　　　　　　　　　　　　　　　　　76 (First Division – Season 1999/2000) (3 Points for a Win)
MOST LEAGUE GOALS SCORED BY A PLAYER IN A SEASON: Dunky Walker (Season 1921/22)
NO. OF GOALS SCORED: 45
RECORD ATTENDANCE: 47,438 (-v- Celtic 7.3.1925)
RECORD VICTORY: 15-0 (-v- Glasgow University – Scottish Cup, 30.1.1960)
RECORD DEFEAT: 0-9 (-v- Rangers – Division 1, 4.12.1897)

The Buddies' ten year league record

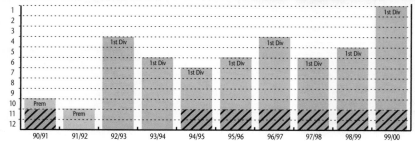

THE BUDDIES' CLUB FACTFILE 1999/2000
RESULTS… APPEARANCES… SCORERS… ATTENDANCES…

Date	V	Opponents	Att.	Res	Roy L.	Nicolson I.	Kerr C.	Turner T.	McLaughlin B.	Walker S.	Murray H.	Ross I.	McGarry S.	Brown T.	Baltacha S.	Drew C.	Yardley M.	Lavety B.	Mendes J.	Rudden P.	Robinson R.	Bowman G.	Scrimgour D.	McLaughlin J.	Paislick J.	McKnight P.	Gillies R.	Donnachie S.
Aug 7	H	Ayr United	3,671	1-1	1	2	3	4	5	6	7	8	9	10¹	11	12	15											
14	A	Raith Rovers	2,787	6-0	1	2	3	4	5	6¹	7	8¹	14¹	12	15		11²	9¹	10									
21	H	Inverness Cal. Th.	3,040	3-2	1	2	3	4	5	6¹	7	8	14¹	12			11¹	9	10									
29	A	Clydebank	1,513	3-2	1	2		4	5	6	7	3		8¹	14	15	11	9²	10									
Sep 4	H	Airdrieonians	3,117	5-0	1	2		4	5	6	7²	3¹	12	8	14		11	9¹	10¹	15								
11	A	Dunfermline Athletic	6,128	1-1	1	2		4	5	6	7	3		8¹	14		11	9	10									
18	H	Morton	6,773	3-2	1	2		4	5¹	6	7	3	12	8		15	11¹	9¹	10									
25	A	Falkirk	4,505	1-3	1	2		4	5	6	7¹	3	12	9	8	15	11		10									
Oct 2	H	Livingston	4,520	1-1	1	2		4	5	6	7	3	9	14	8	15	12	11¹	10									
16	H	Raith Rovers	3,815	3-2	1	2		4¹	5	6	7	3	14	12	8		11¹	9¹	10									
23	A	Ayr United	3,467	3-0	1	2		4	5	6	7	3	12	8		15	11²	9¹	10									
30	H	Dunfermline Athletic	6,130	†3-1	1	2		4	5	6	7	3	12	8			11¹	9¹	10									
Nov 6	A	Morton	3,733	4-1	1	2		4	5	6¹	7	3	12	15	8¹		11¹	9¹	10	14								
12	A	Airdrieonians	3,209	2-0	1	2		4		6	7	3	8		5		11¹	9¹	10		14	15						
20	H	Clydebank	4,434	2-1	1	2		4		6		3	10¹	8	7		11¹	9			14	12	15					
27	A	Livingston	4,239	2-1	1	2		4	5¹	6		3	10¹	8	7		11	9			14	15						
Dec 4	H	Falkirk	4,980	2-1	1	2		4	5	6		3	10	8	7		11¹	9¹				15						
11	A	Inverness Cal. Th.	2,893	1-1		2		4	5	6		3	10	8	7		11¹	9	15			12	1					
18	H	Ayr United	3,607	1-2		2		4	5	6	7	3	10	12	8		11	9¹				14	1					
Jan 3	H	Morton	7,266	1-1		2		4	5	6	7	3	9	8	12		11¹		10			14	1					
8	H	Airdrieonians	3,636	3-1		2		4	5	6	7	3	9¹	8	14		11		10²			15	1					
22	A	Falkirk	4,746	0-2		2		4	5	6		3	9	8	7		11	14	10			12	1					
Feb 5	H	Livingston	5,015	0-2	1	2		4	5	6		3	9	8	7		11	12	10		14	15						
12	H	Inverness Cal. Th.	3,742	2-0	1	2		4	5	6		3¹	8	9	7		11¹	14	10			12						
19	A	Dunfermline Athletic	7,132	1-1	1	2¹		4	5	6	7	3	8	12			11	9	10			15						
26	A	Raith Rovers	4,662	2-1	1	2		4	5	6	7	3	8	12			11¹	9	10¹			15						
Mar 4	H	Dunfermline Athletic	6,938	0-2		2		4	5	6	7	3	8	9			11	12	10		14							
11	H	Clydebank	3,388	8-0		2		4	5	6¹	7²	3¹	9¹	8		15	11	12³	10		14							
18	A	Morton	3,768	2-0		2		4	5	6	7	3	8	9¹			11¹		10		14	12						
25	A	Clydebank	2,244	0-0		2		4	5		7	3	9	8			11	12	10			15					6	
Apr 1	A	Airdrieonians	2,909	1-0	1	2		4	5¹	6	7	3	9	8			11		10			12		14	15			
8	H	Falkirk	6,742	1-0	1	2		4	5	6	7	3	9	8			11	12	10			15				14¹		
15	A	Livingston	4,531	2-1	1	2		4	5	6	7	3	9¹	8			11¹	12	10			15						
22	A	Ayr United	4,678	2-1	1	2		4	5	6	7	3	9	8			11	14	10¹			15					12¹	
29	H	Raith Rovers	8,386	3-0	1	2		4	5¹	6	7	3	9¹				11¹	12	10		15	14					8	
May 6	A	Inverness Cal. Th.	3,218	0-5	1	2		4	5	6	7	3	9	8	12		11		10		14							15
TOTAL FULL APPEARANCES					31	33	3	31	34	33	29	30	22	19	18		33	21	28	9		10	5	3	1	1	2	
TOTAL SUB APPEARANCES						(1)				(1)			(10)	(7)	(9)	(6)		(2)	(8)	(5)	(7)	(9)	(9)	(1)		(3)	(2)	(1)
TOTAL GOALS SCORED						1		1	3	4	5	3	9	3	1		19	16	5			1			1	2	

Small bold figures denote goalscorers. † denotes opponent's own goal.

St. Mirren Park

LOVE STREET

ALBION STREET

CAPACITY: 10,778; (All Seated)
PITCH DIMENSIONS: 112 yds x 74 yds
FACILITIES FOR DISABLED SUPPORTERS:
Full wheelchair facilities available for supporters in the Caledonia Stand.

Team playing kits

	FIRST CHOICE	SECOND CHOICE
Shirt:	Two Inch Black and White Vertical Stripes. Black Collar with Open Neck. White Sleeves with Single Black Stripe.	White Sleeves and Sides with Red Centre Panel. Red Central Panel with Black Trim. White Open Neck Collar.
Shorts:	Black with White Trim.	White with Black and Red Trim.
Stockings:	Black with White Tops.	Red with White Tops.

How to get there

St. Mirren Park can be reached by the following routes:

TRAINS: There is a frequent train service from Glasgow Central Station and all coastal routes pass through Gilmour Street. The ground is about half a mile from the station.

BUSES: All SMT coastal services, plus buses to Johnstone and Kilbarchan, pass within 300 yards of the ground.

CARS: The only facilities for car parking are in the streets surrounding the ground.

St. Mirren F.C. is a member of The Scottish Premier League

Dates for your Diary Season 2000/2001

TENNENTS SCOTTISH CUP 2000/01

First Round ....Saturday, 9th December, 2000
Second Round ....Saturday, 6th January, 2001
Third Round..Saturday, 27th January, 2001
Fourth Round...Saturday, 17th February, 2001
Fifth Round ....Saturday, 10th March, 2001
Semi-Finals...Saturday, 14th April, 2001
Final ....Saturday, 26th May, 2001

WORLD CUP 2002 - QUALIFYING COMPETITION GROUP 6

Latvia -v- Scotland ....Saturday, 2nd September, 2000
San Marino -v- Scotland ....Saturday, 7th October, 2000
Croatia -v- Scotland ....Wednesday, 11th October, 2000
Scotland -v- Belgium...Saturday, 24th March, 2001
Scotland -v- San Marino ....Wednesday, 28th March, 2001

EUROPEAN 'UNDER-21' CHAMPIONSHIP, 2000/02 QUALIFYING MATCHES

Latvia -v- Scotland...Friday, 1st September, 2000
Croatia -v- Scotland...Tuesday, 10th October, 2000
Scotland -v- Belgium ....Friday, 23rd March, 2001

EUROPEAN 'UNDER 18' CHAMPIONSHIP 1999/2000 QUALIFYING GROUP - MINI TOURNAMENT

To be played in Sweden

Sweden -v- Scotland...Friday, 6th October, 2000
Yugoslavia -v- Scotland ....Sunday, 8th October, 2000

THREE NATIONS 'UNDER 17' INTERNATIONAL TOURNAMENT

To be played in Denmark

Denmark -v- Scotland ....Monday, 11th September, 2000
Belgium -v- Scotland ....Wednesday, 13th September, 2000

EUROPEAN 'UNDER 16' CHAMPIONSHIP 2000/01 QUALIFYING MATCHES - MINI TOURNAMENT

To be played in Scotland

Scotland -v- Wales ....Monday, 5th March, 2001
Scotland -v- Norway ....Friday, 9th March, 2001

UEFA CHAMPIONS LEAGUE

Qualifying Round 1

First-Leg matches...Wednesday, 12th July, 2000
Second-Leg matches ....Wednesday, 19th July, 2000

Qualifying Round 2

First-Leg matches...Wednesday, 26th July, 2000
Second-Leg matches ....Wednesday, 2nd August, 2000

Qualifying Round 3

First-Leg matches ....Wednesday, 9th August, 2000
Second-Leg matches ....Wednesday, 23rd August, 2000

First Group Stage:

1st Match Days: ....Tuesday, 12th September and
....Wednesday, 13th September, 2000
2nd Match Days: ....Tuesday, 19th September and
....Wednesday, 20th September, 2000
3rd Match Days:..Tuesday, 26th September and
....Wednesday, 27th September, 2000
4th Match Days: ....Tuesday, 17th October and
....Wednesday, 18th October, 2000
5th Match Days:..Tuesday, 24th October and
....Wednesday, 25th October, 2000
6th Match Days: ....Tuesday, 7th November and
....Wednesday, 8th November, 2000

Second Group Stage:

1st Match Days:..Tuesday, 21st November and
....Wednesday, 22nd November, 2000
2nd Match Days:..Tuesday, 5th December and
....Wednesday, 6th December, 2000
3rd Match Days: ....Tuesday, 13th February and
....Wednesday, 14th February, 2001
4th Match Days: ....Tuesday, 20th February and
....Wednesday, 21st February, 2001
5th Match Days: ....Tuesday, 6th March and
....Wednesday, 7th March, 2001
6th Match Days: ....Tuesday, 13th March and
....Wednesday, 14th March, 2001

Quarter Finals:

First Leg: ....Tuesday, 3rd April and
....Wednesday, 4th April, 2001
Second Leg: ....Tuesday, 17th April and
....Wednesday, 18th April, 2001

Semi-Finals:

First Leg: ....Tuesday, 1st May and
....Wednesday, 2nd May, 2001
Second Leg: ....Tuesday, 8th May and
....Wednesday, 9th May, 2001
Final: ....Wednesday, 23rd May, 2001

U.E.F.A. CUP

Qualifying Round:

First-Leg matches: ....Thursday, 10th August, 2000
Second-Leg matches:....................................Thursday, 24th August, 2000

First Round:

First-Leg matches: ....Thursday, 14th September, 2000
Second-Leg matches:.............................Thursday, 28th September, 2000

Second Round:

First-Leg matches: ....Thursday, 26th October, 2000
Second-Leg matches: ....Thursday, 9th November, 2000

Third Round:

First-Leg matches: ....Thursday, 23rd November, 2000
Second-Leg matches: ....Thursday, 7th December, 2000

Fourth Round:

First-Leg matches: ....Thursday, 15th February, 2001
Second-Leg matches: ....Thursday, 22nd February, 2001

Quarter Finals:

First-Leg matches:..Thursday, 8th March, 2001
Second-Leg matches: ....Thursday, 15th March, 2001

Semi-Finals:

First-Leg matches: ....Thursday, 5th April, 2001
Second-Leg matches: ....Thursday, 19th April, 2001
Final: ....Wednesday, 16th May, 2001